WOTAKOI:
LOVE IS HARD FOR OTAKU

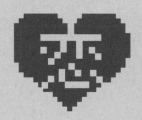

① 1

FUJITA

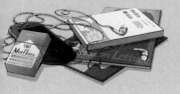

Episode....0

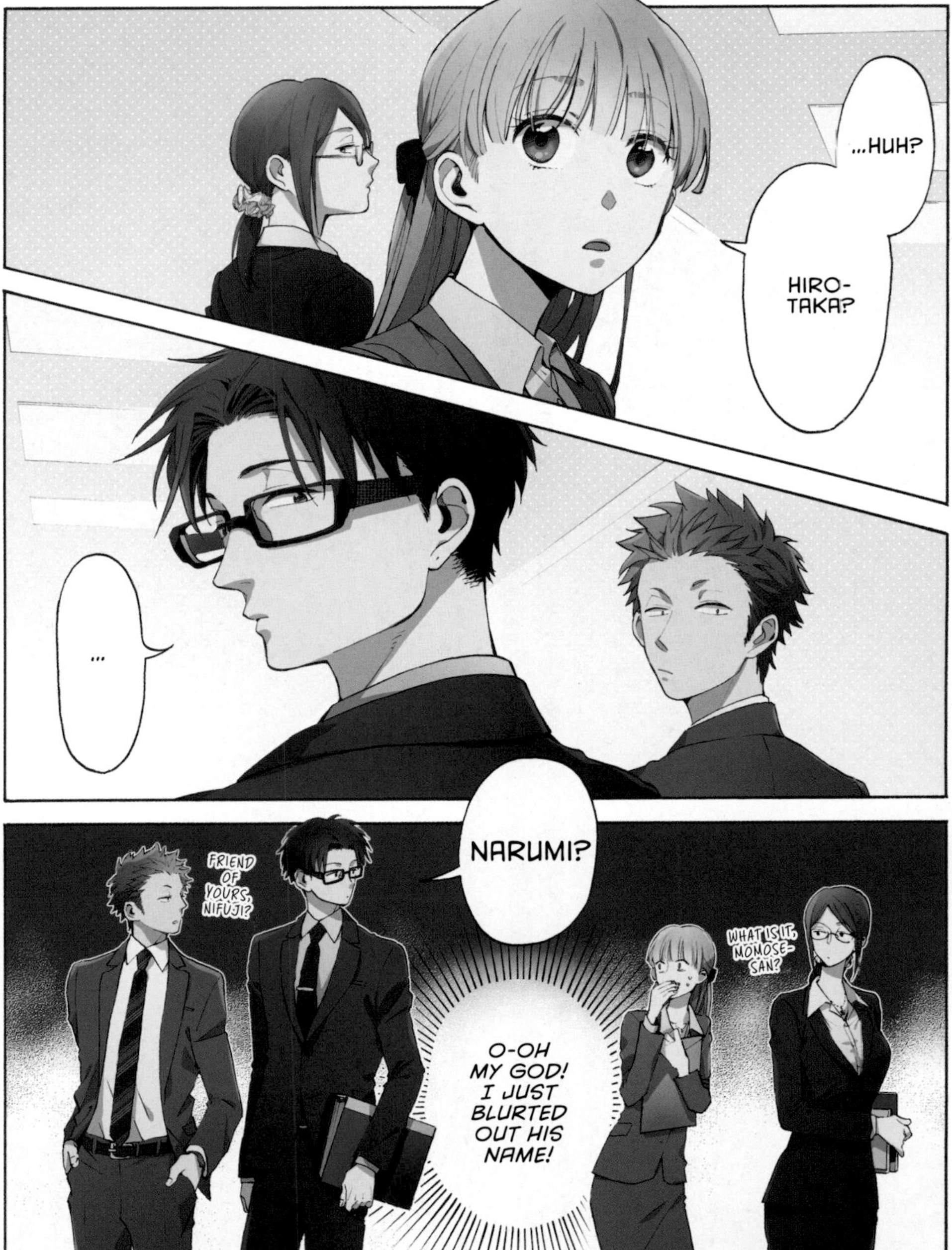
...HUH?
HIRO-TAKA?
...
NARUMI?
WHAT IS IT, MOMOSE-SAN?
O-OH MY GOD! I JUST BLURTED OUT HIS NAME!
FRIEND OF YOURS, NIFUJI?

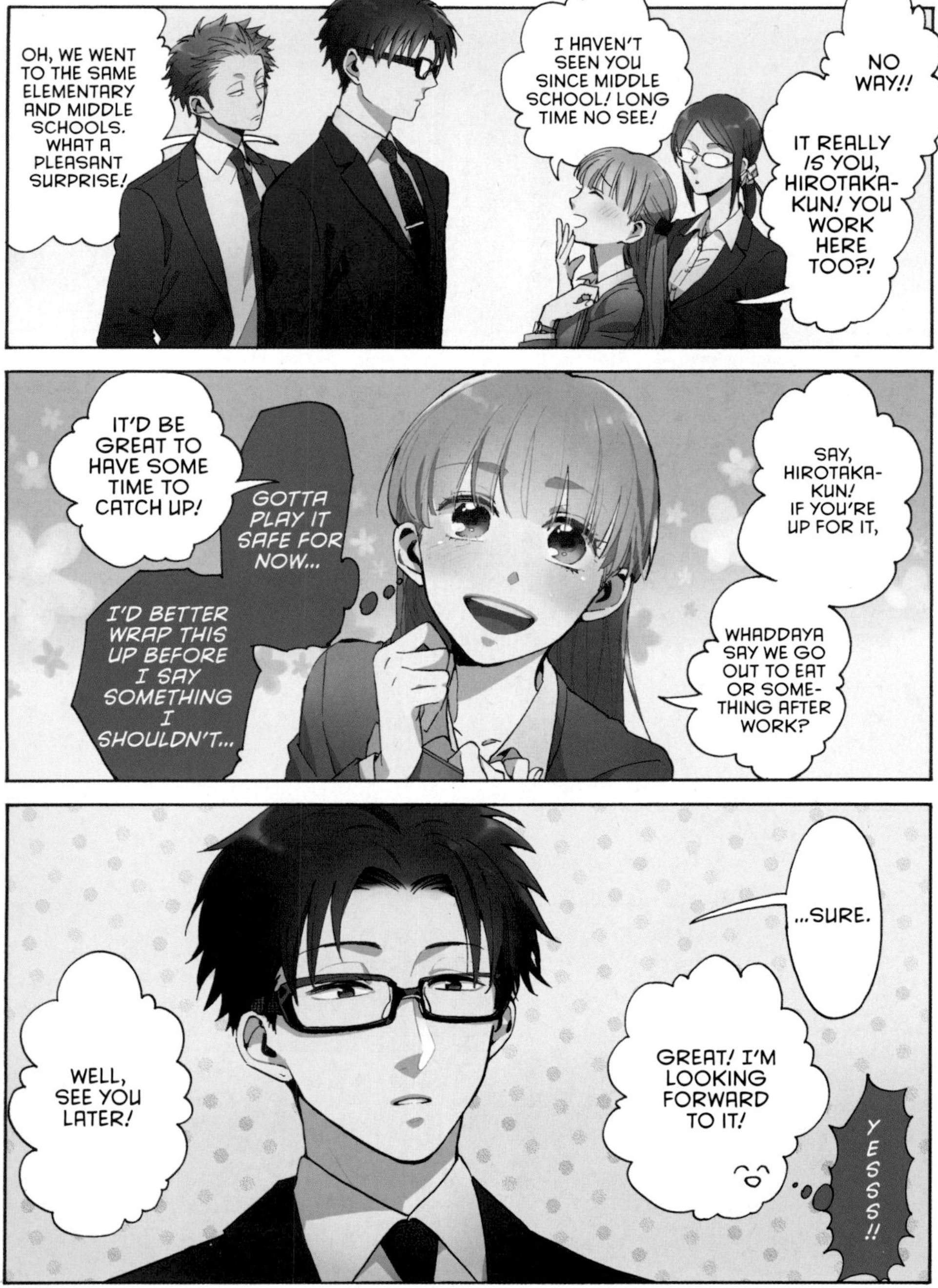
NO WAY!!
IT REALLY IS YOU, HIROTAKA-KUN! YOU WORK HERE TOO?!
I HAVEN'T SEEN YOU SINCE MIDDLE SCHOOL! LONG TIME NO SEE!
OH, WE WENT TO THE SAME ELEMENTARY AND MIDDLE SCHOOLS. WHAT A PLEASANT SURPRISE!
SAY, HIROTAKA-KUN! IF YOU'RE UP FOR IT,
WHADDAYA SAY WE GO OUT TO EAT OR SOME-THING AFTER WORK?
IT'D BE GREAT TO HAVE SOME TIME TO CATCH UP!
GOTTA PLAY IT SAFE FOR NOW...
I'D BETTER WRAP THIS UP BEFORE I SAY SOMETHING I SHOULDN'T...
...SURE.
GREAT! I'M LOOKING FORWARD TO IT!
YESSS!!
WELL, SEE YOU LATER!

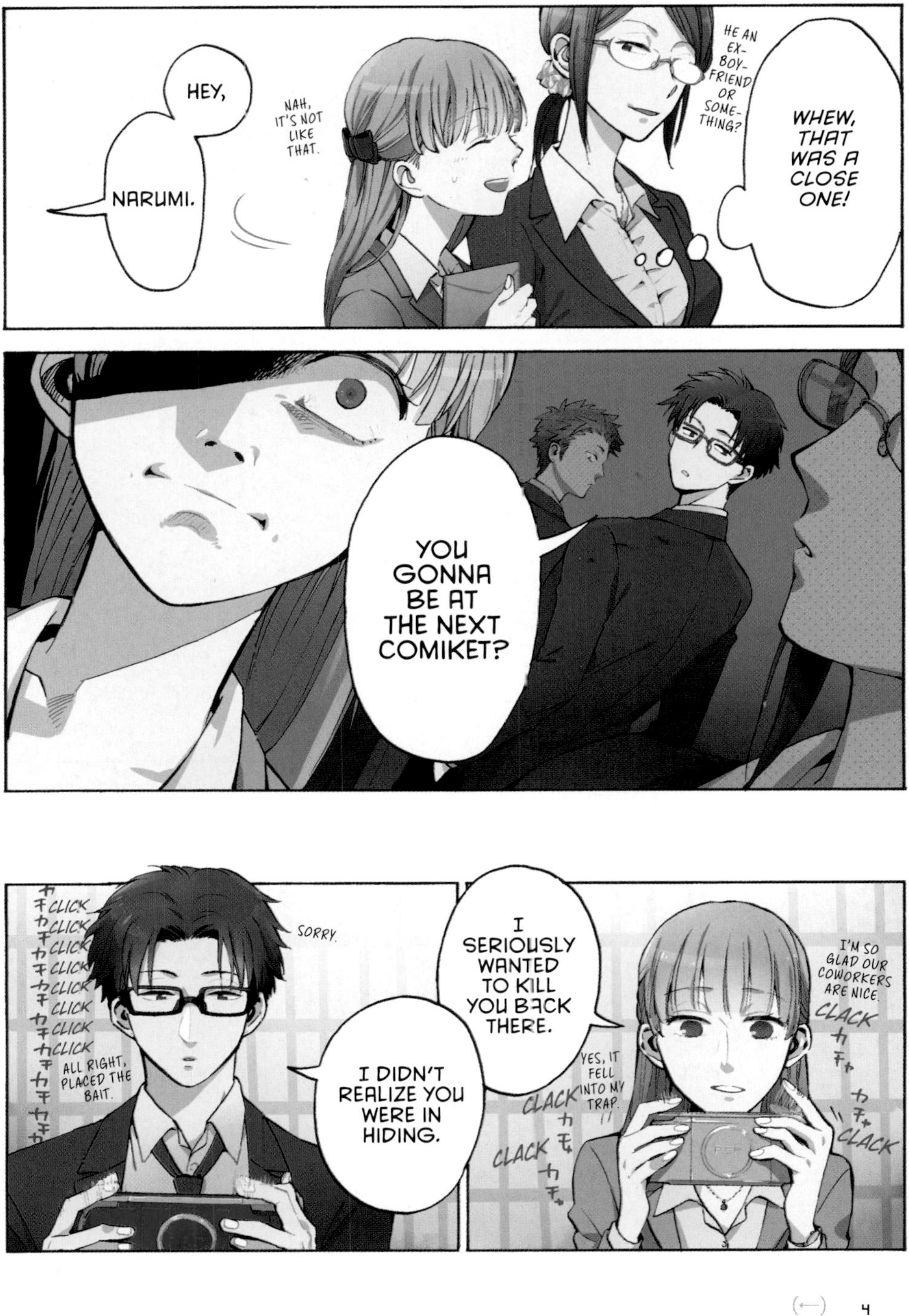

WHEW, THAT WAS A CLOSE ONE!
HE AN EX-BOYFRIEND OR SOMETHING?
NAH, IT'S NOT LIKE THAT.
HEY, NARUMI.
YOU GONNA BE AT THE NEXT COMIKET?
I'M SO GLAD OUR COWORKERS ARE NICE.
CLACK
CLACK
CLACK
CLACK
I SERIOUSLY WANTED TO KILL YOU BACK THERE.
YES, IT FELL INTO MY TRAP.
SORRY.
I DIDN'T REALIZE YOU WERE IN HIDING.
ALL RIGHT, PLACED THE BAIT.
CLICK
CLICK
CLICK
CLICK
CLICK
CLICK
CLICK
CLICK

(←)

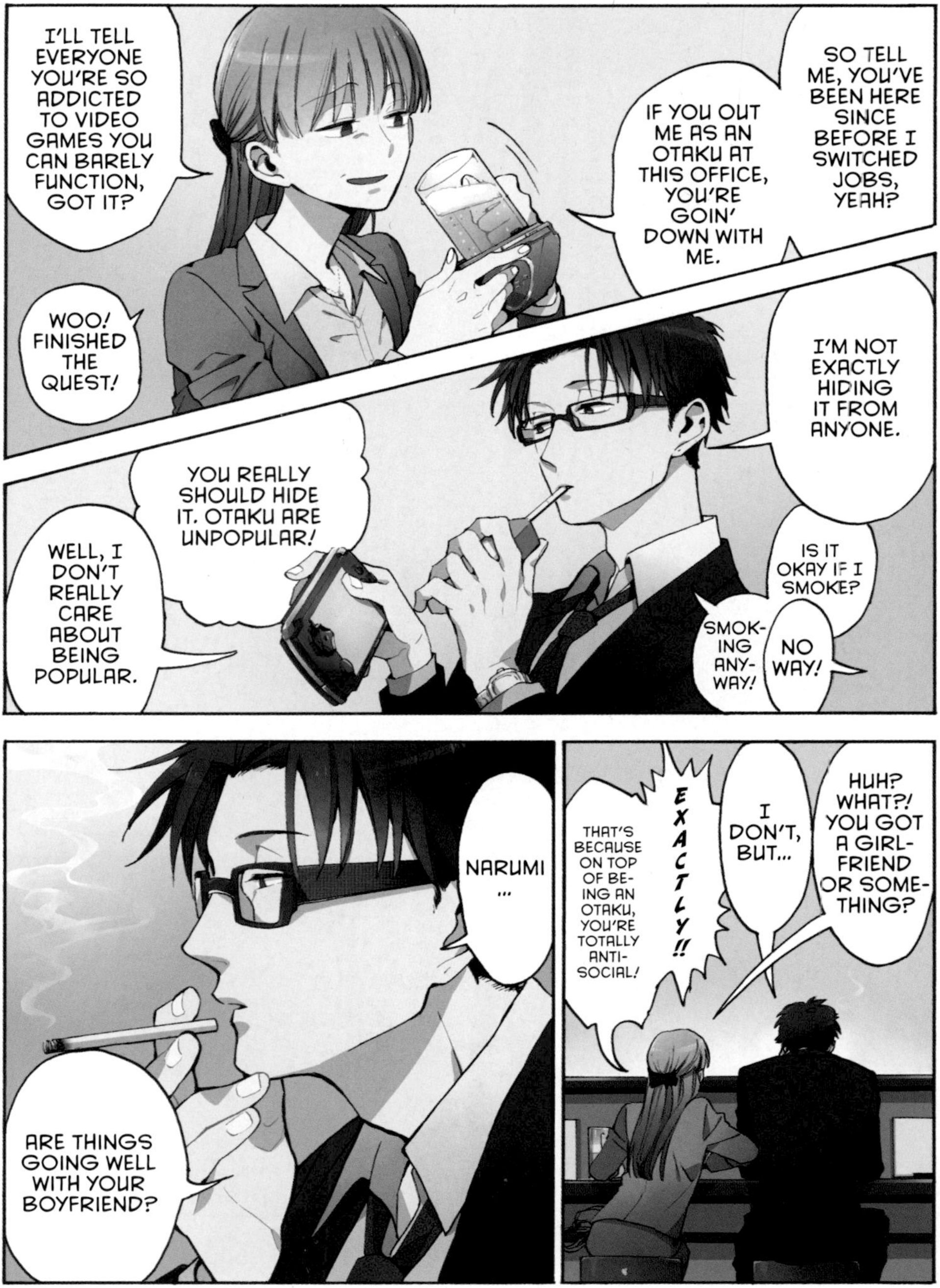
SO TELL ME, YOU'VE BEEN HERE SINCE BEFORE I SWITCHED JOBS, YEAH?
IF YOU OUT ME AS AN OTAKU AT THIS OFFICE, YOU'RE GOIN' DOWN WITH ME.
I'LL TELL EVERYONE YOU'RE SO ADDICTED TO VIDEO GAMES YOU CAN BARELY FUNCTION, GOT IT?
WOO! FINISHED THE QUEST!
I'M NOT EXACTLY HIDING IT FROM ANYONE.
YOU REALLY SHOULD HIDE IT. OTAKU ARE UNPOPULAR!
WELL, I DON'T REALLY CARE ABOUT BEING POPULAR.
IS IT OKAY IF I SMOKE?
NO WAY!
SMOKING ANYWAY!
HUH? WHAT?! YOU GOT A GIRLFRIEND OR SOMETHING?
I DON'T, BUT...
EXACTLY!!
THAT'S BECAUSE ON TOP OF BEING AN OTAKU, YOU'RE TOTALLY ANTISOCIAL!
NARUMI...
ARE THINGS GOING WELL WITH YOUR BOYFRIEND?

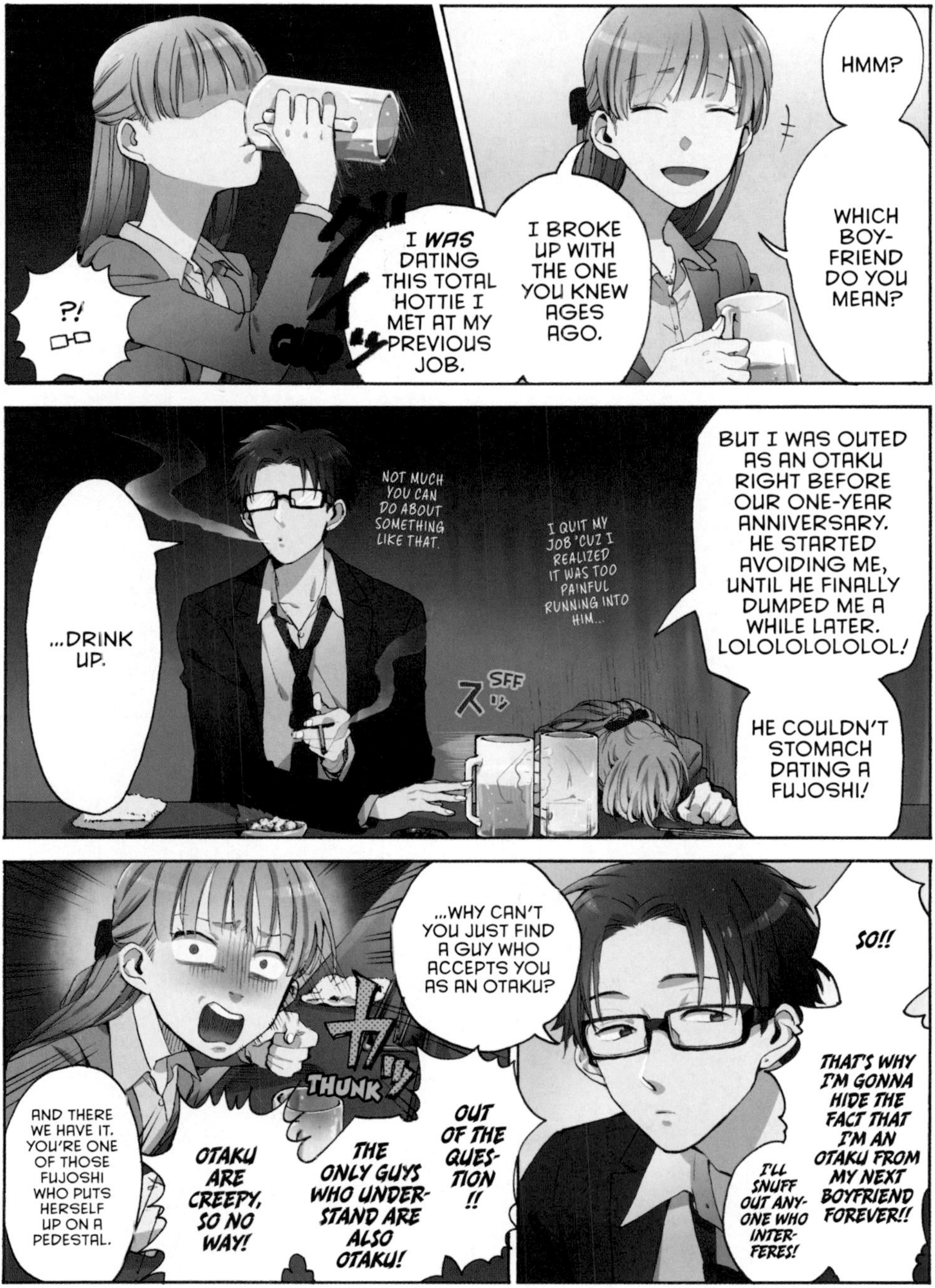
HMM?
WHICH BOY-FRIEND DO YOU MEAN?
I BROKE UP WITH THE ONE YOU KNEW AGES AGO.
I WAS DATING THIS TOTAL HOTTIE I MET AT MY PREVIOUS JOB.
?!
BUT I WAS OUTED AS AN OTAKU RIGHT BEFORE OUR ONE-YEAR ANNIVERSARY. HE STARTED AVOIDING ME, UNTIL HE FINALLY DUMPED ME A WHILE LATER. LOLOLOLOLOLOL!
HE COULDN'T STOMACH DATING A FUJOSHI!
I QUIT MY JOB 'CUZ I REALIZED IT WAS TOO PAINFUL RUNNING INTO HIM...
SFF
NOT MUCH YOU CAN DO ABOUT SOMETHING LIKE THAT.
...DRINK UP.
...WHY CAN'T YOU JUST FIND A GUY WHO ACCEPTS YOU AS AN OTAKU?
SO!!
THAT'S WHY I'M GONNA HIDE THE FACT THAT I'M AN OTAKU FROM MY NEXT BOYFRIEND FOREVER!!
I'LL SNUFF OUT ANY-ONE WHO INTER-FERES!
THUNK
OUT OF THE QUESTION!!
THE ONLY GUYS WHO UNDER-STAND ARE ALSO OTAKU!
OTAKU ARE CREEPY, SO NO WAY!
AND THERE WE HAVE IT. YOU'RE ONE OF THOSE FUJOSHI WHO PUTS HERSELF UP ON A PEDESTAL.

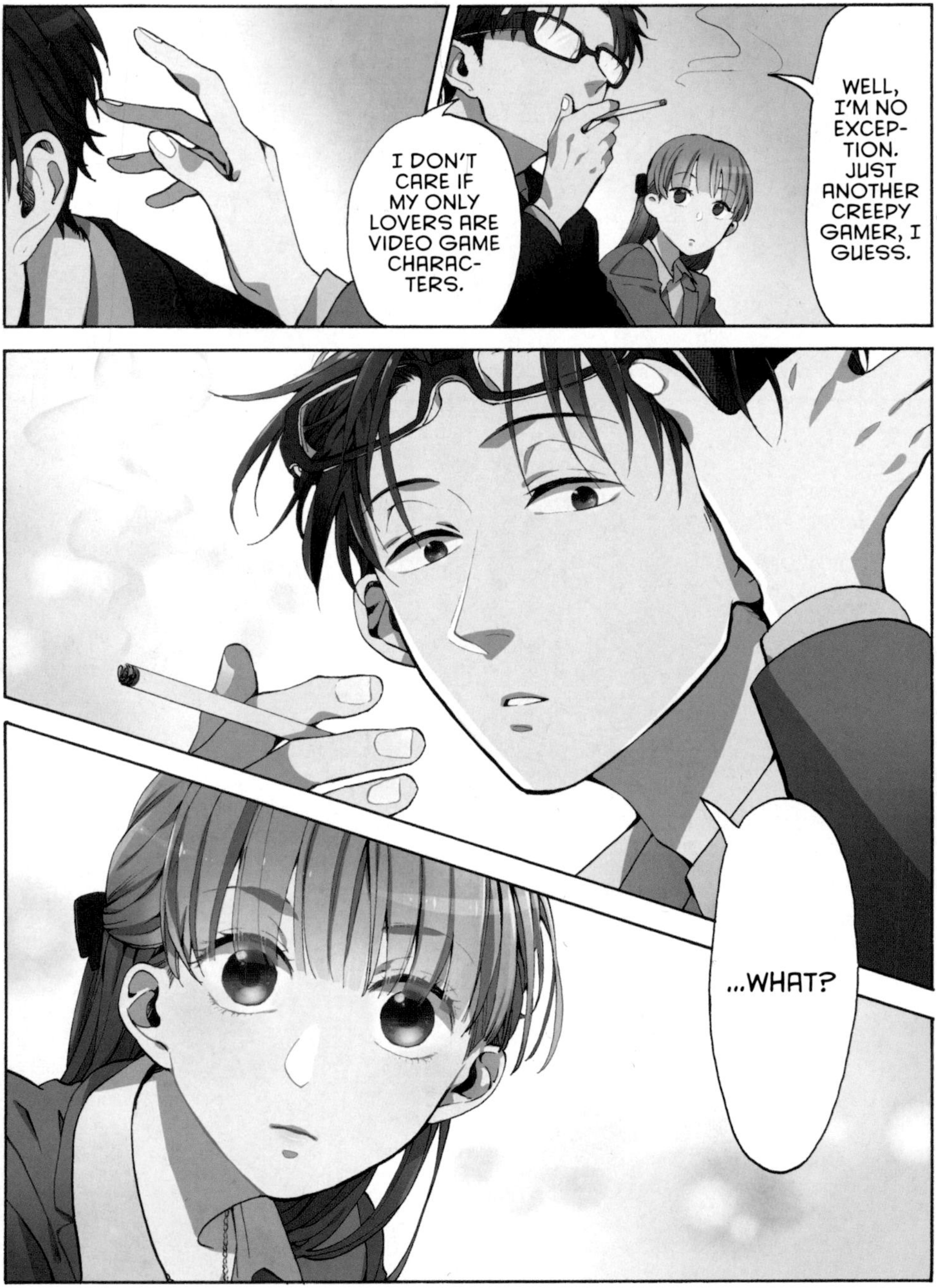
WELL, I'M NO EXCEPTION. JUST ANOTHER CREEPY GAMER, I GUESS.
I DON'T CARE IF MY ONLY LOVERS ARE VIDEO GAME CHARACTERS.
...WHAT?

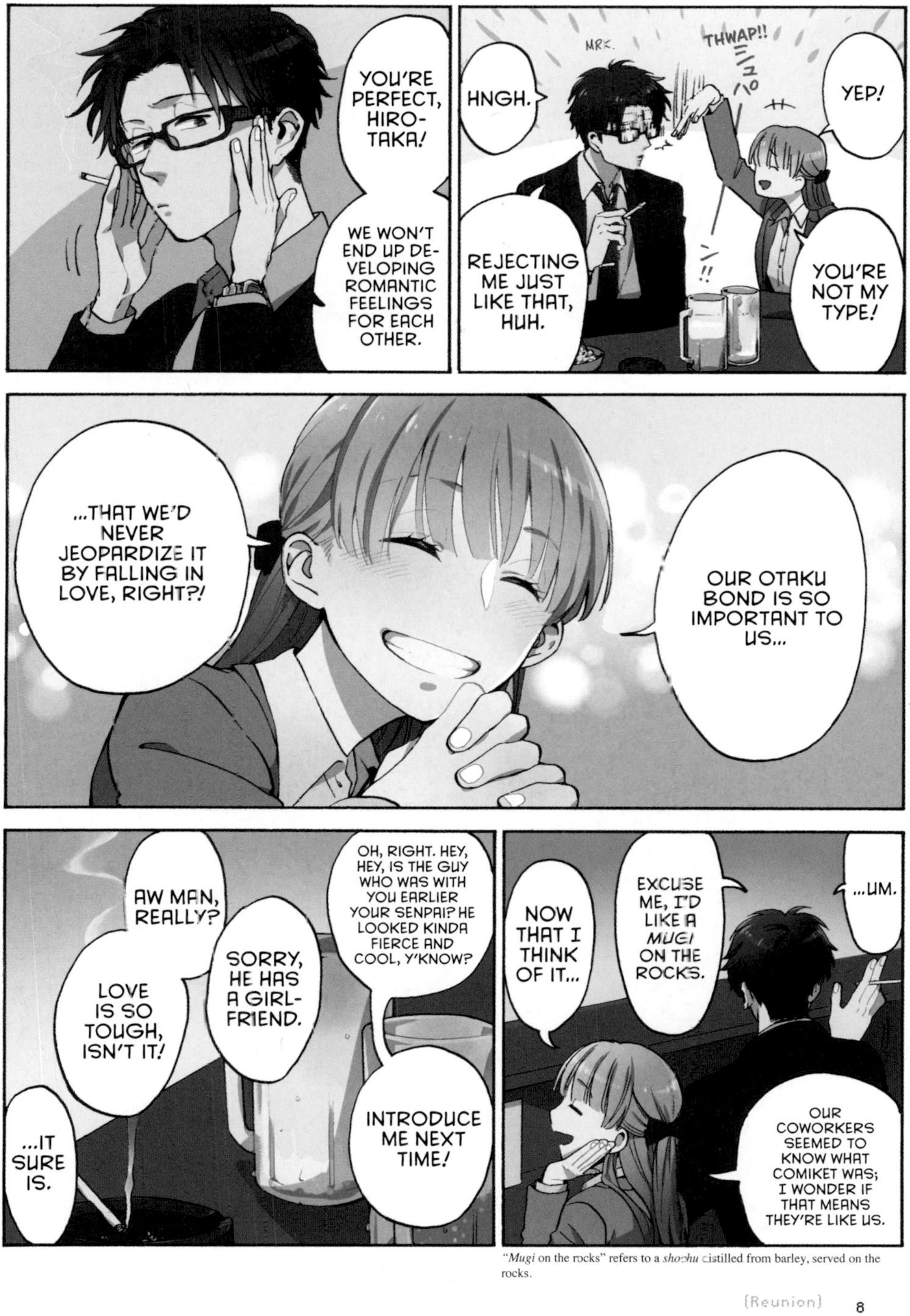
YEP!
THWAP!!
YOU'RE NOT MY TYPE!
MRK.
HNGH.
REJECTING ME JUST LIKE THAT, HUH.
YOU'RE PERFECT, HIRO-TAKA!
WE WON'T END UP DE-VELOPING ROMANTIC FEELINGS FOR EACH OTHER.
OUR OTAKU BOND IS SO IMPORTANT TO US...
...THAT WE'D NEVER JEOPARDIZE IT BY FALLING IN LOVE, RIGHT?!
...UM.
EXCUSE ME, I'D LIKE A *MUGI* ON THE ROCKS.
NOW THAT I THINK OF IT...
OUR COWORKERS SEEMED TO KNOW WHAT COMIKET WAS; I WONDER IF THAT MEANS THEY'RE LIKE US.
OH, RIGHT. HEY, HEY, IS THE GUY WHO WAS WITH YOU EARLIER YOUR SENPAI? HE LOOKED KINDA FIERCE AND COOL, Y'KNOW?
SORRY, HE HAS A GIRL-FRIEND.
INTRODUCE ME NEXT TIME!
AW MAN, REALLY?
LOVE IS SO TOUGH, ISN'T IT!
...IT SURE IS.

"*Mugi* on the rocks" refers to a *shochu* distilled from barley, served on the rocks.

Episode....**1**

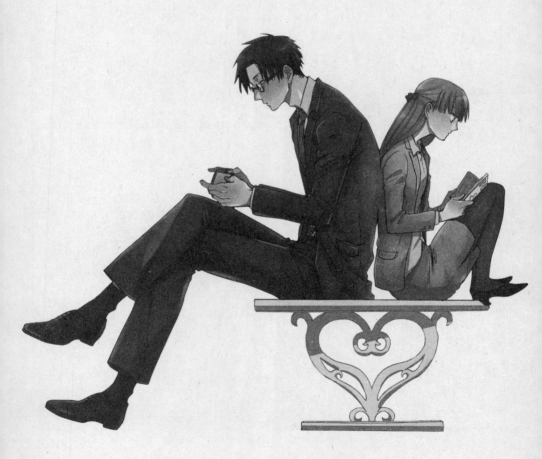

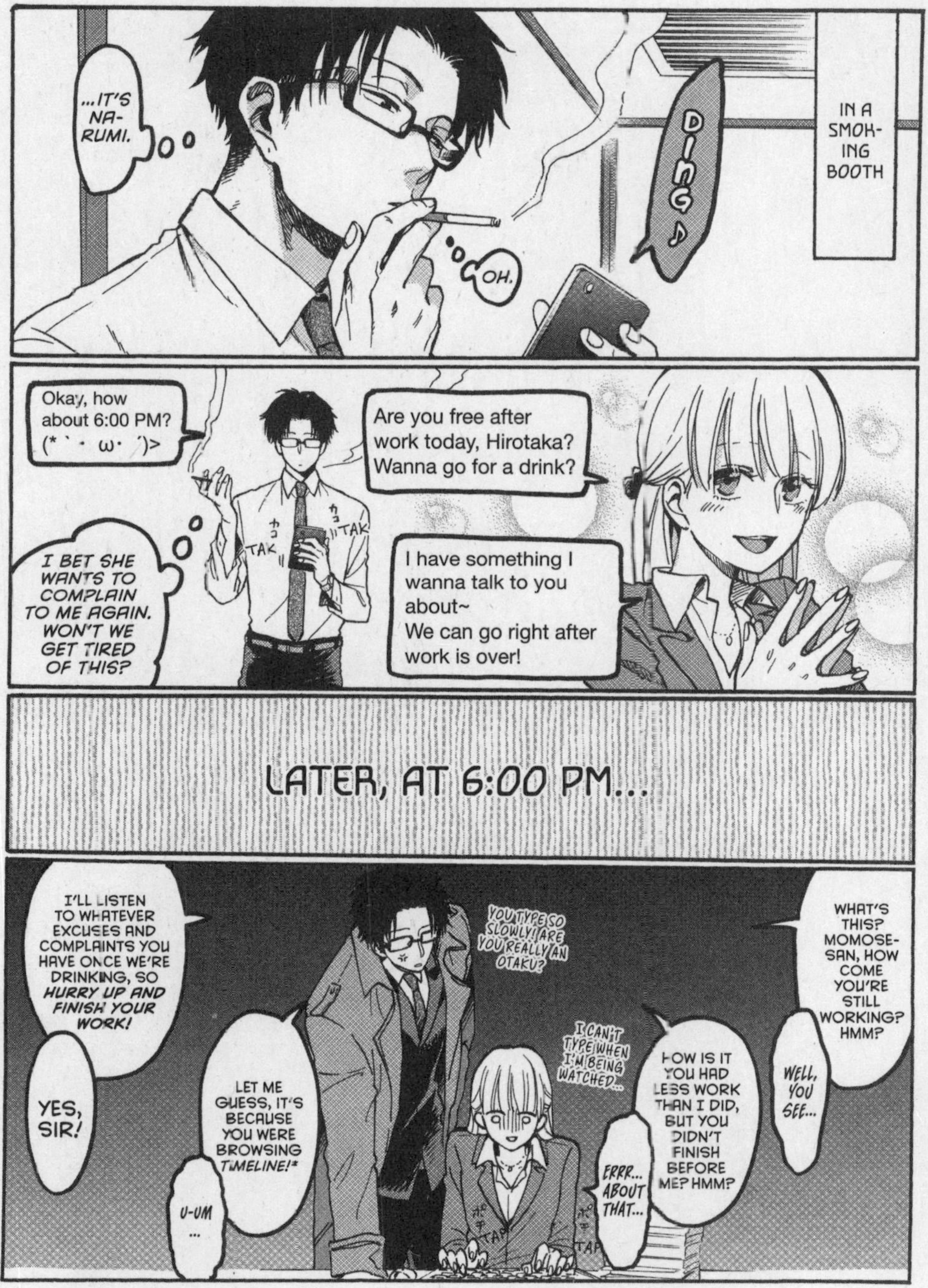
IN A SMOKING BOOTH
DING♪
OH.
...IT'S NARUMI.
Are you free after work today, Hirotaka? Wanna go for a drink?
I have something I wanna talk to you about~ We can go right after work is over!
Okay, how about 6:00 PM? (*`・ω・´)>
TAK TAK
I BET SHE WANTS TO COMPLAIN TO ME AGAIN. WON'T WE GET TIRED OF THIS?
LATER, AT 6:00 PM...
WHAT'S THIS? MOMOSE-SAN, HOW COME YOU'RE STILL WORKING? HMM?
WELL, YOU SEE...
HOW IS IT YOU HAD LESS WORK THAN I DID, BUT YOU DIDN'T FINISH BEFORE ME? HMM?
ERRR... ABOUT THAT...
I CAN'T TYPE WHEN I'M BEING WATCHED...
YOU TYPE SO SLOWLY! ARE YOU REALLY AN OTAKU?
LET ME GUESS, IT'S BECAUSE YOU WERE BROWSING TIMELINE!*
U-UM...
TAP TAP
I'LL LISTEN TO WHATEVER EXCUSES AND COMPLAINTS YOU HAVE ONCE WE'RE DRINKING, SO HURRY UP AND FINISH YOUR WORK!
YES, SIR!

*A Japanese message board with chat rooms that is similar to Twitter.

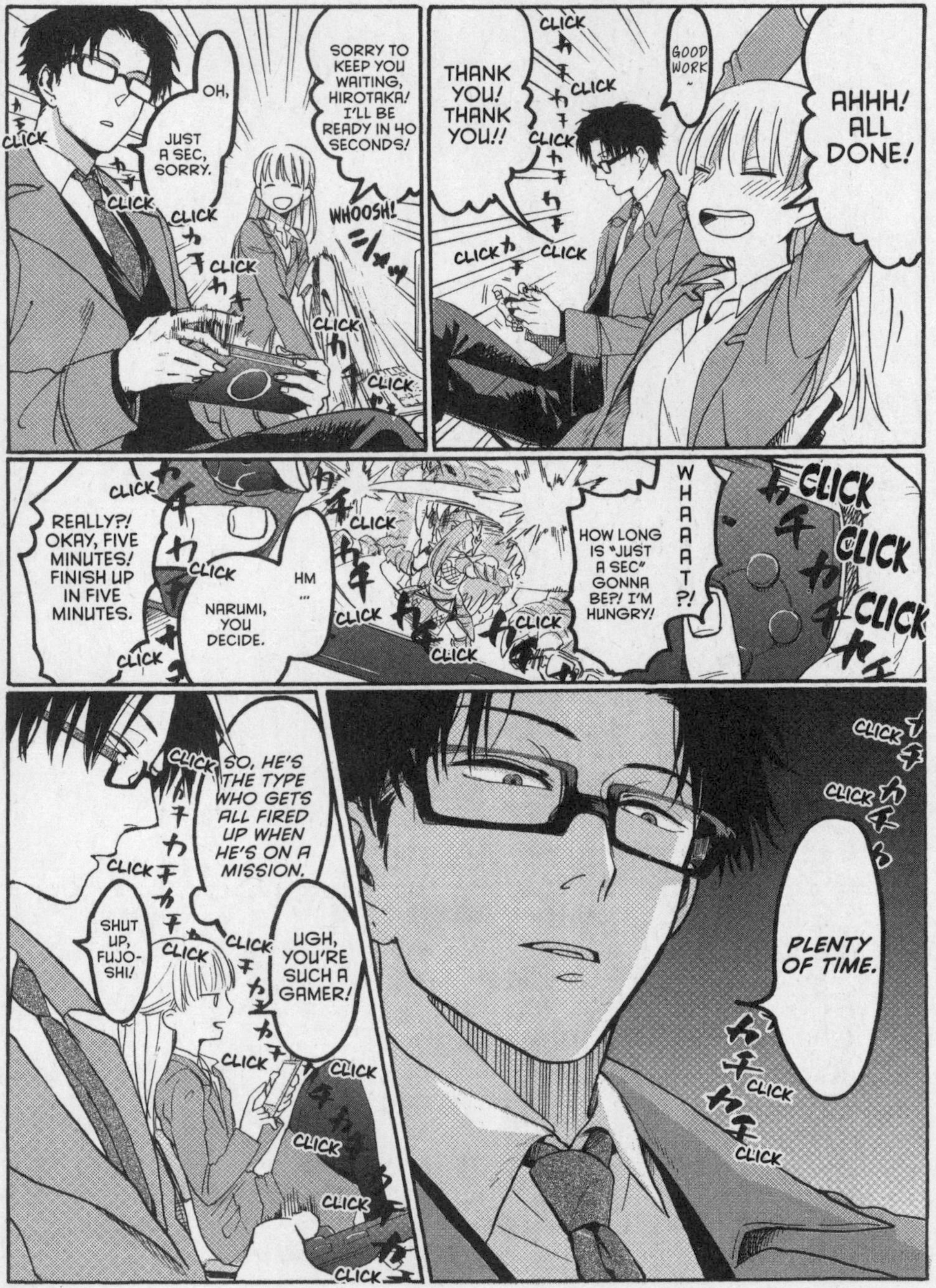
AHHH! ALL DONE!
GOOD WORK~
CLICK
CLICK
THANK YOU! THANK YOU!!
CLICK
CLICK
CLICK
SORRY TO KEEP YOU WAITING, HIROTAKA! I'LL BE READY IN 40 SECONDS!
WHOOSH!
OH,
JUST A SEC, SORRY.
CLICK
CLICK
CLICK
CLICK
CLICK
CLICK
CLICK
CLICK
CLICK
WHAAAAT?!
HOW LONG IS "JUST A SEC" GONNA BE?! I'M HUNGRY!
CLICK
CLICK
HM...
NARUMI, YOU DECIDE.
CLICK
CLICK
CLICK
REALLY?! OKAY, FIVE MINUTES! FINISH UP IN FIVE MINUTES.
CLICK
CLICK
CLICK
PLENTY OF TIME.
CLICK
CLICK
CLICK
SO, HE'S THE TYPE WHO GETS ALL FIRED UP WHEN HE'S ON A MISSION.
UGH, YOU'RE SUCH A GAMER!
CLICK
SHUT UP, FUJOSHI!
CLICK
CLICK
CLICK
CLICK
CLICK
CLICK

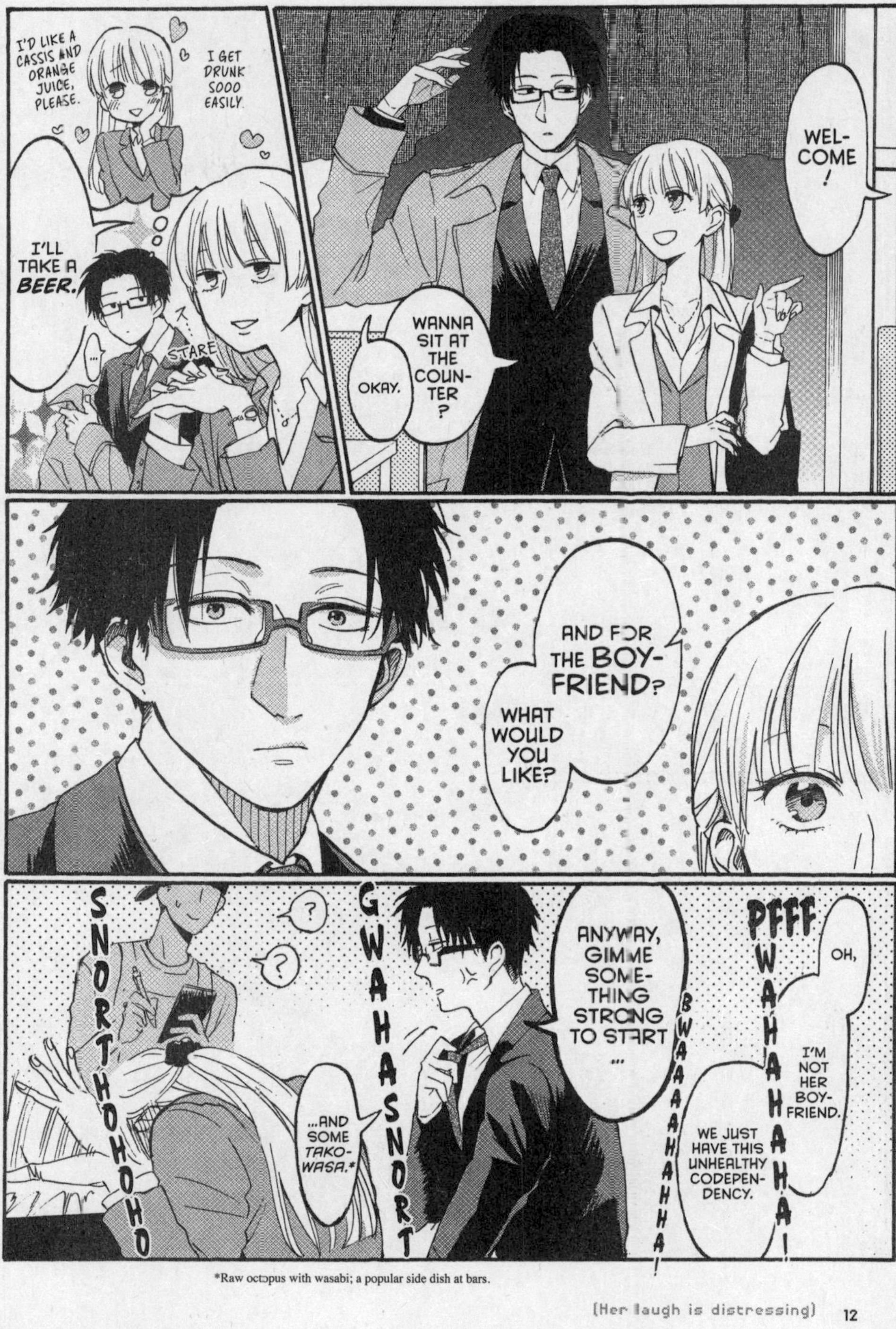
WEL-COME!
WANNA SIT AT THE COUNTER?
OKAY.
I'D LIKE A CASSIS AND ORANGE JUICE, PLEASE.
I GET DRUNK SOOO EASILY.
I'LL TAKE A BEER.
...
STARE
AND FOR THE BOY-FRIEND?
WHAT WOULD YOU LIKE?
PFFF
OH,
I'M NOT HER BOY-FRIEND.
WE JUST HAVE THIS UNHEALTHY CODEPEN-DENCY.
WAHAHAHA!
BWAAAAAHAHHA!
ANYWAY, GIMME SOME-THING STRONG TO START...
GWAHA SNORT
...AND SOME TAKO-WASA.*
?
?
SNORTHOHOHO

*Raw octopus with wasabi; a popular side dish at bars.

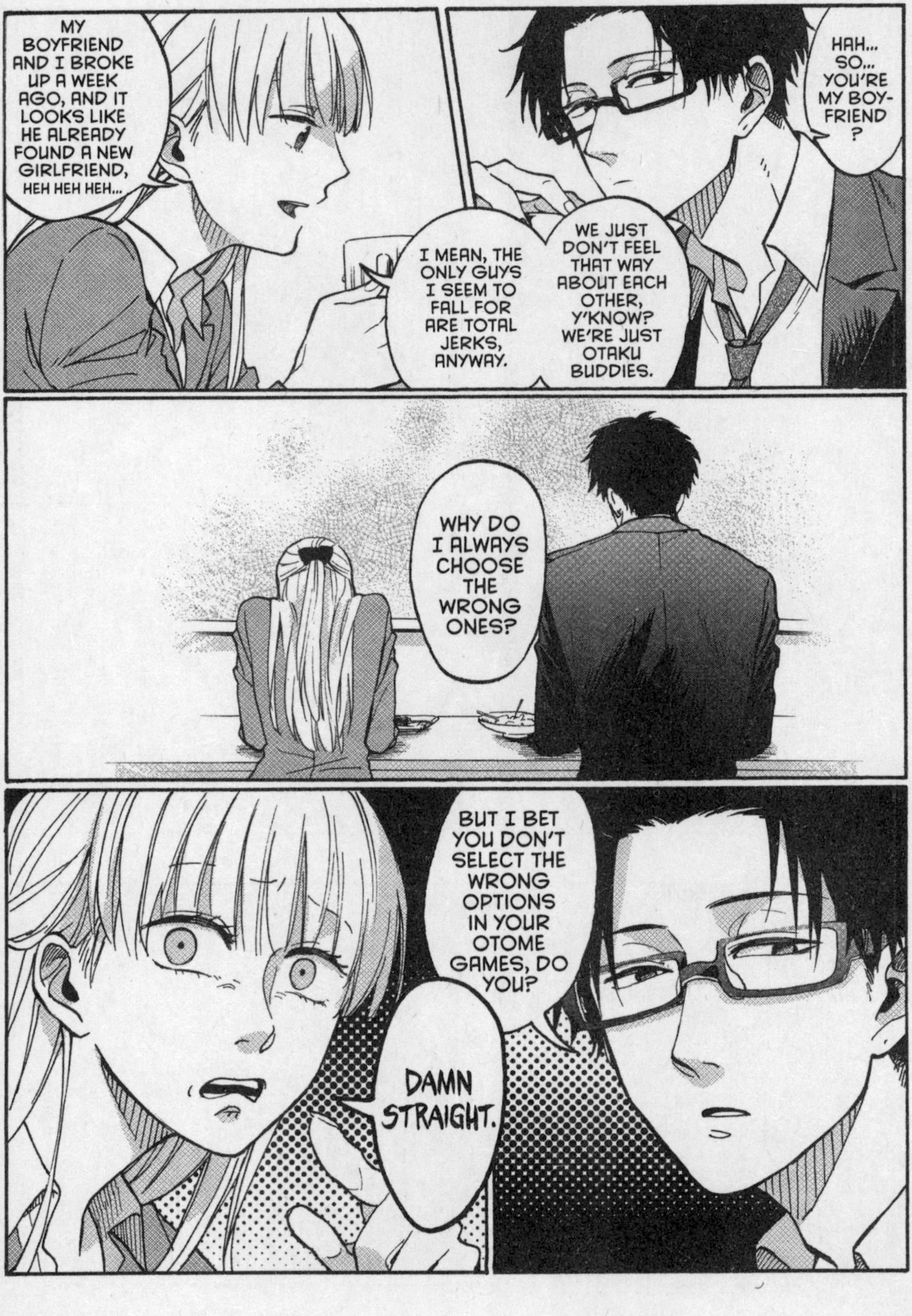
HAH... SO... YOU'RE MY BOY-FRIEND?
WE JUST DON'T FEEL THAT WAY ABOUT EACH OTHER, Y'KNOW? WE'RE JUST OTAKU BUDDIES.
I MEAN, THE ONLY GUYS I SEEM TO FALL FOR ARE TOTAL JERKS, ANYWAY.
MY BOYFRIEND AND I BROKE UP A WEEK AGO, AND IT LOOKS LIKE HE ALREADY FOUND A NEW GIRLFRIEND, HEH HEH HEH...
WHY DO I ALWAYS CHOOSE THE WRONG ONES?
BUT I BET YOU DON'T SELECT THE WRONG OPTIONS IN YOUR OTOME GAMES, DO YOU?
DAMN STRAIGHT.

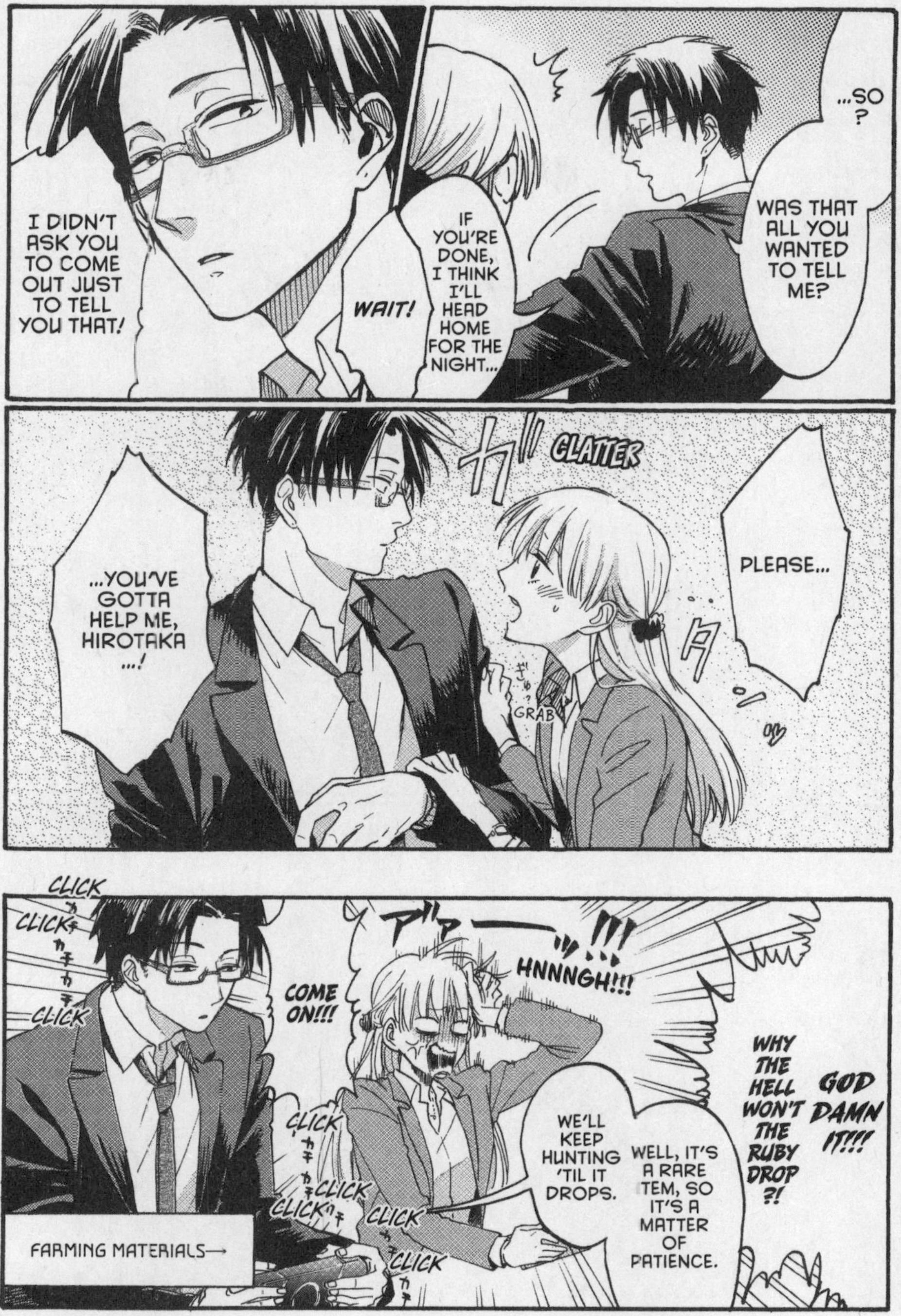
...SO?
WAS THAT ALL YOU WANTED TO TELL ME?
IF YOU'RE DONE, I THINK I'LL HEAD HOME FOR THE NIGHT...
WAIT!
I DIDN'T ASK YOU TO COME OUT JUST TO TELL YOU THAT!
CLATTER
PLEASE...
GRAB
...YOU'VE GOTTA HELP ME, HIROTAKA...!
GOD DAMN IT!!!
WHY THE HELL WON'T THE RUBY DROP?!
HNNNGH!!!
COME ON!!!
WELL, IT'S A RARE TEM, SO IT'S A MATTER OF PATIENCE.
WE'LL KEEP HUNTING 'TIL IT DROPS.
CLICK
CLICK
CLICK
CLICK
CLICK
CLICK
CLICK
CLICK
FARMING MATERIALS→

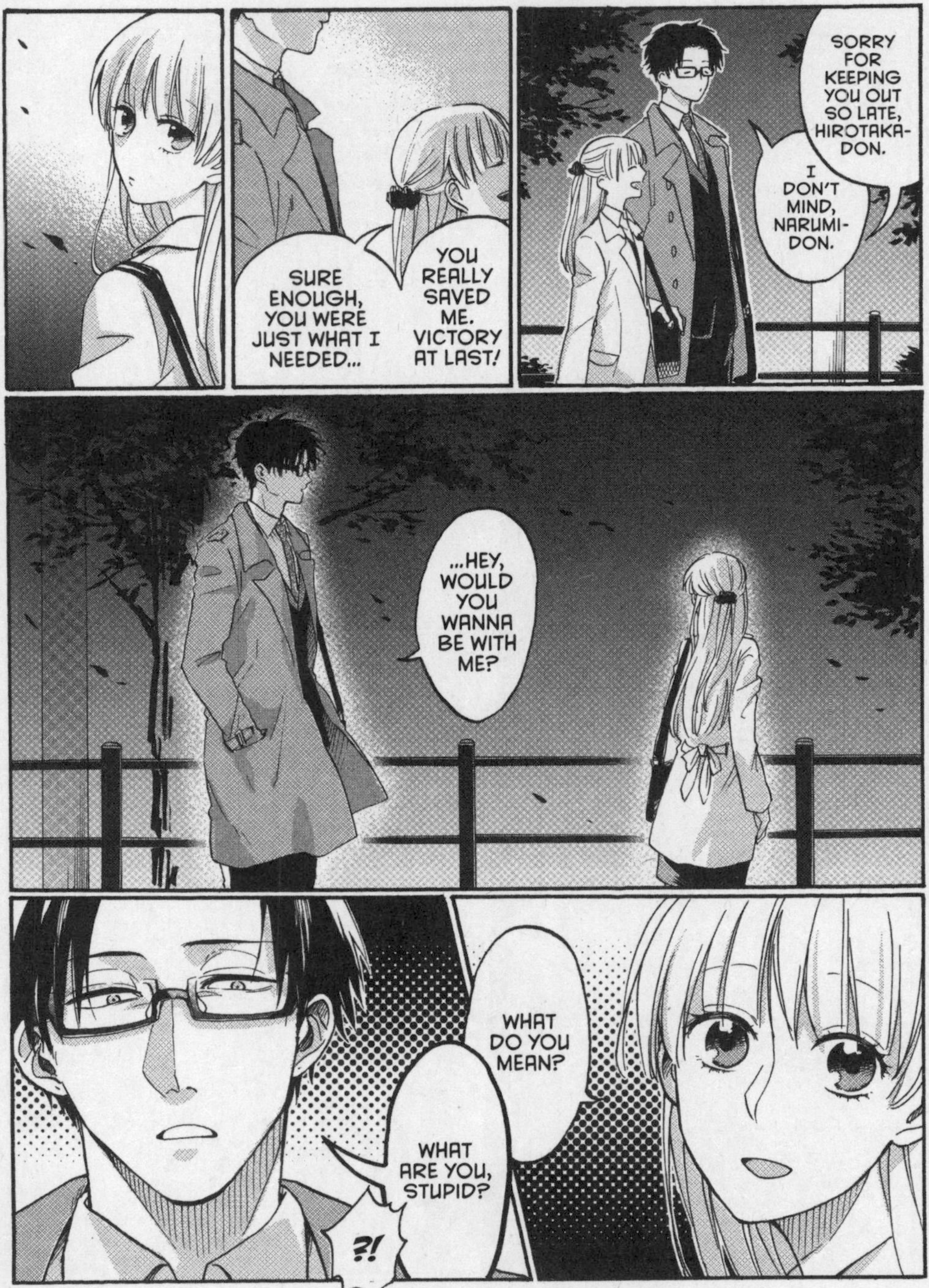
SORRY FOR KEEPING YOU OUT SO LATE, HIROTAKA-DON.
I DON'T MIND, NARUMI-DON.
YOU REALLY SAVED ME. VICTORY AT LAST!
SURE ENOUGH, YOU WERE JUST WHAT I NEEDED...
...HEY, WOULD YOU WANNA BE WITH ME?
WHAT DO YOU MEAN?
WHAT ARE YOU, STUPID?
?!

 (Why is he so upset?!)

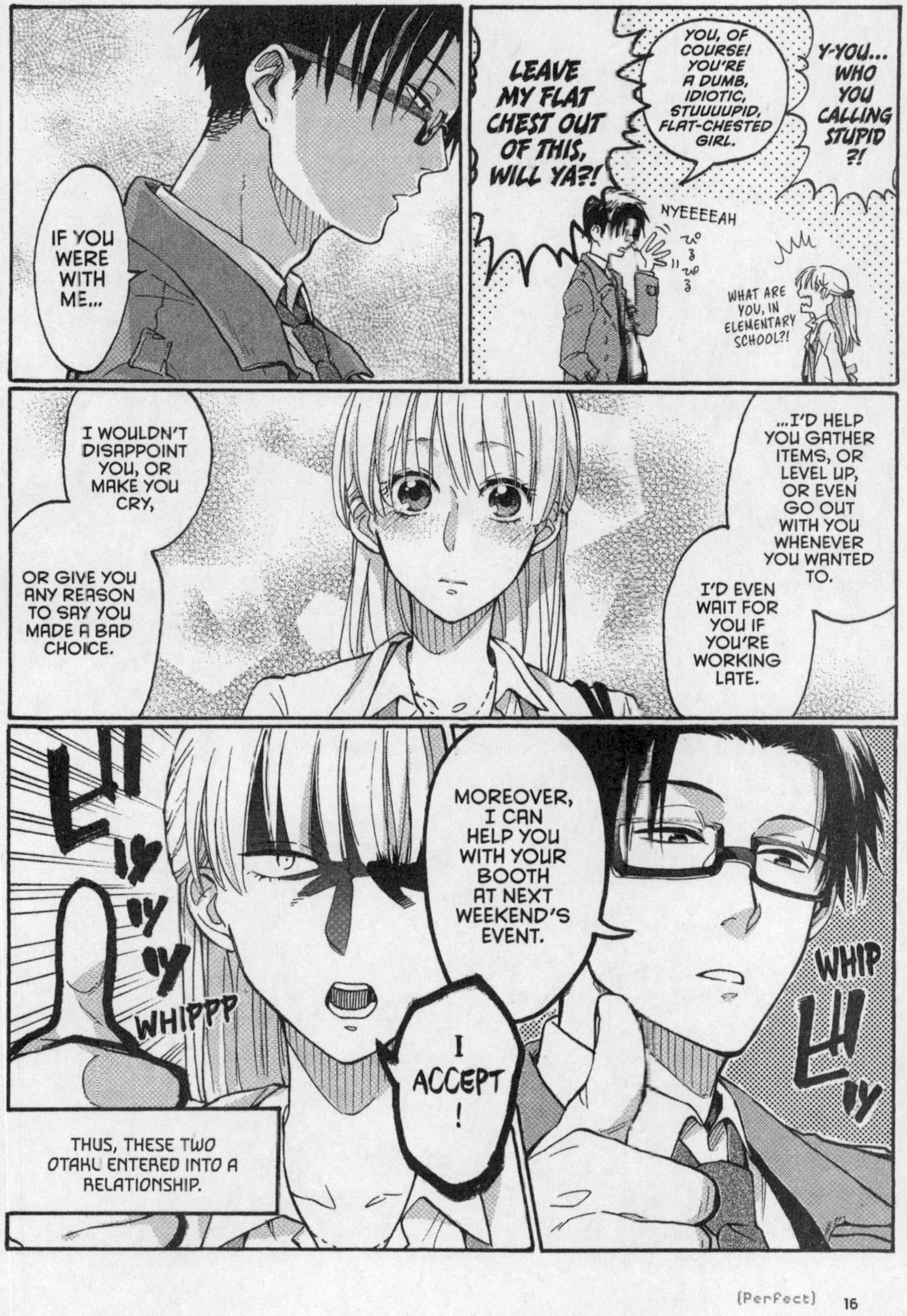
Y-YOU... WHO YOU CALLING STUPID?!
YOU, OF COURSE! YOU'RE A DUMB, IDIOTIC, STUUUUPID, FLAT-CHESTED GIRL.
LEAVE MY FLAT CHEST OUT OF THIS, WILL YA?!
NYEEEEAH
WHAT ARE YOU, IN ELEMENTARY SCHOOL?!
IF YOU WERE WITH ME...
...I'D HELP YOU GATHER ITEMS, OR LEVEL UP, OR EVEN GO OUT WITH YOU WHENEVER YOU WANTED TO.
I'D EVEN WAIT FOR YOU IF YOU'RE WORKING LATE.
I WOULDN'T DISAPPOINT YOU, OR MAKE YOU CRY,
OR GIVE YOU ANY REASON TO SAY YOU MADE A BAD CHOICE.
WHIP
MOREOVER, I CAN HELP YOU WITH YOUR BOOTH AT NEXT WEEKEND'S EVENT.
I ACCEPT!
WHIPPP
THUS, THESE TWO OTAKU ENTERED INTO A RELATIONSHIP.

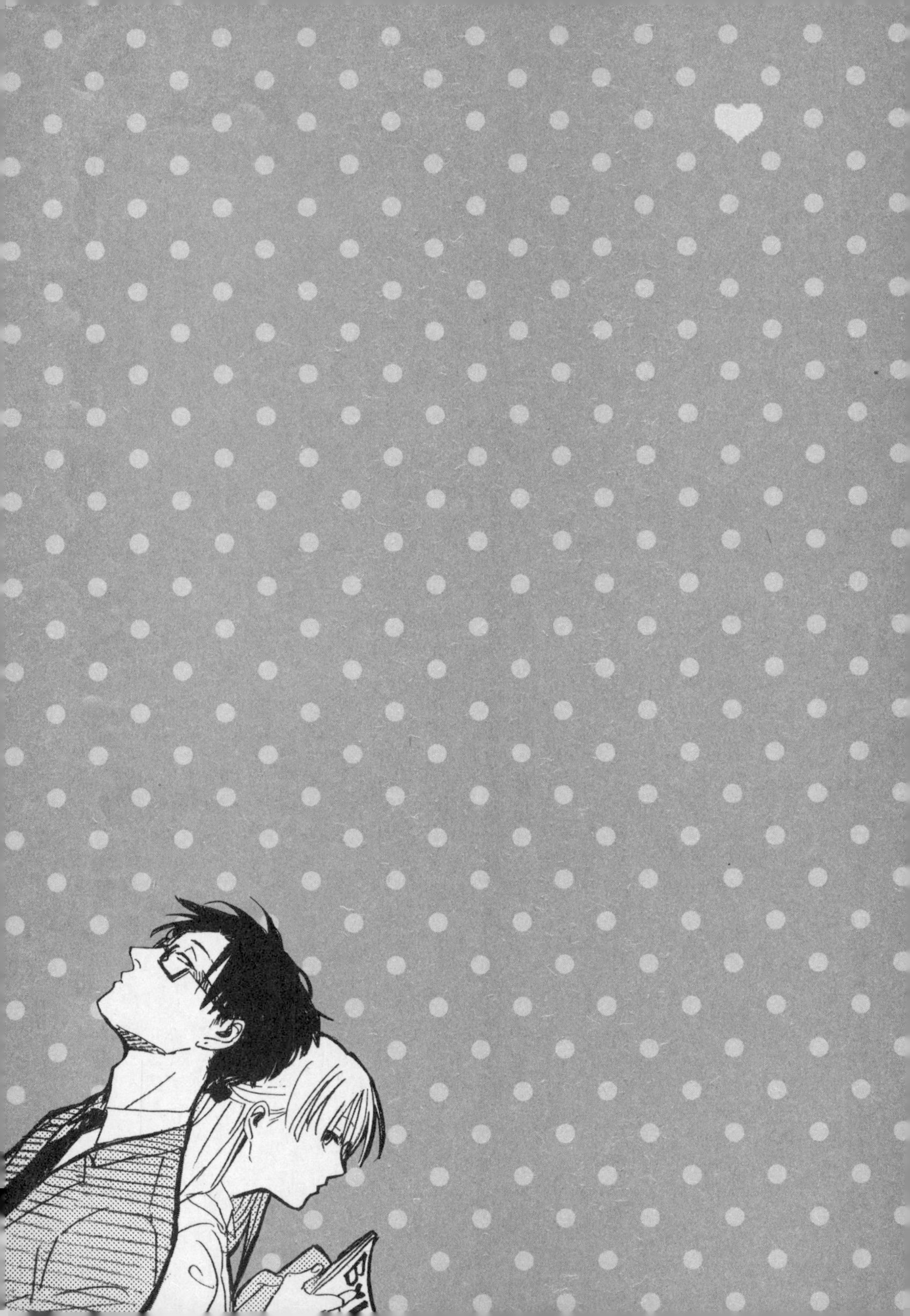

Narumi Momose

Birthday: 5/3
Age: 26
Height: 154 cm/5'
Blood Type: A
Zodiac: Taurus

A fan of manga, games, and all cosplay. She keeps up with all the current popular trends in each genre. She's a harem-type otaku who obsessively loves multiple waifu from several genres at a time.

Alcohol... Actually has a pretty high tolerance

Tobacco... Doesn't smoke, but likes people who do

A terrible OL who can't even serve tea properly, and a fujoshi to boot. She loves so many things, from cosplay, BL, and otome games to real-life idols, and she's totally insufferable about it. She puts all her effort into maintaining the appearance of being a normal person at work. She's coy, and acts in ways to earn the approval of potential boyfriends. Since she tries so hard to hide the fact that she's an otaku from newer friends and especially her family, her biggest fear is being outed. Narumi falls in love easily but has no luck with guys. She's always yearning for a dramatic romance. Despite having a wealth of romantic experience, she's completely oblivious when someone has feelings for her. She's been friends with Hirotaka since childhood (before she turned into an otaku). He's the only one she's confessed being an otaku to, so in a way, he's even more important to her than her boyfriends have been.

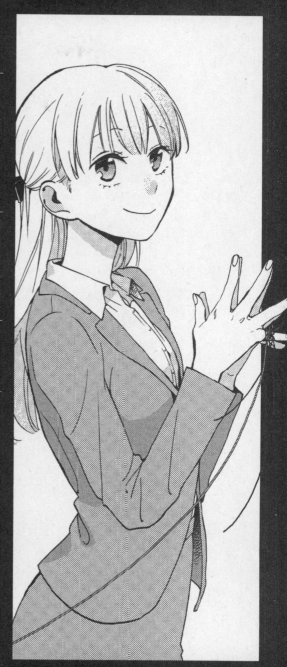

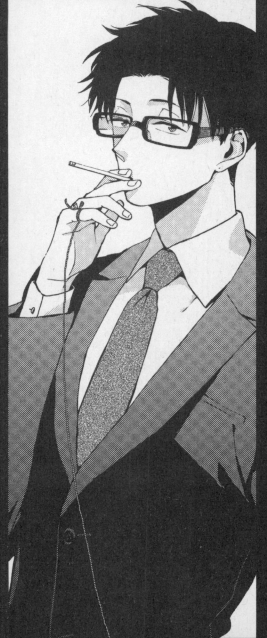

Hirotaka Nifuji

Birthday: 3/20
Age: 26
Height: 184 cm/6'
Weight: 70 kg/154 lbs
(sometimes less)
Blood Type: B
Zodiac: Pisces

Although he specializes in games, he also reads manga and watches anime a good deal. (He's good at all types of games, but he's particularly fond of games that don't require leveling up like first-person shooters, fighting games, and action games.) He has one waifu per genre and places more importance on stats than visuals.

Alcohol… Doesn't get drunk

Tobacco… Chain smoker

A hardcore gamer with high-spec glasses who's considered both good-looking and competent at his job. He would die without video games. He has almost no interest in other people, not because he hates them but because he'd rather be at home if he doesn't have any engagements. He doesn't really show his emotions outwardly, but it's not because he suppresses them; that's just his disposition. He spends more time playing video games than he does socializing, so he barely has any friends. He has neither the desire to hide that he's an otaku nor to change himself. He likes video games, cigarettes, and alcohol. (He doesn't get drunk because he doesn't drink a lot.) He loves girls with huge breasts. He'll strongly argue that every man is a breast man. He prefers to communicate by text, as he can express himself better and with more enthusiasm.

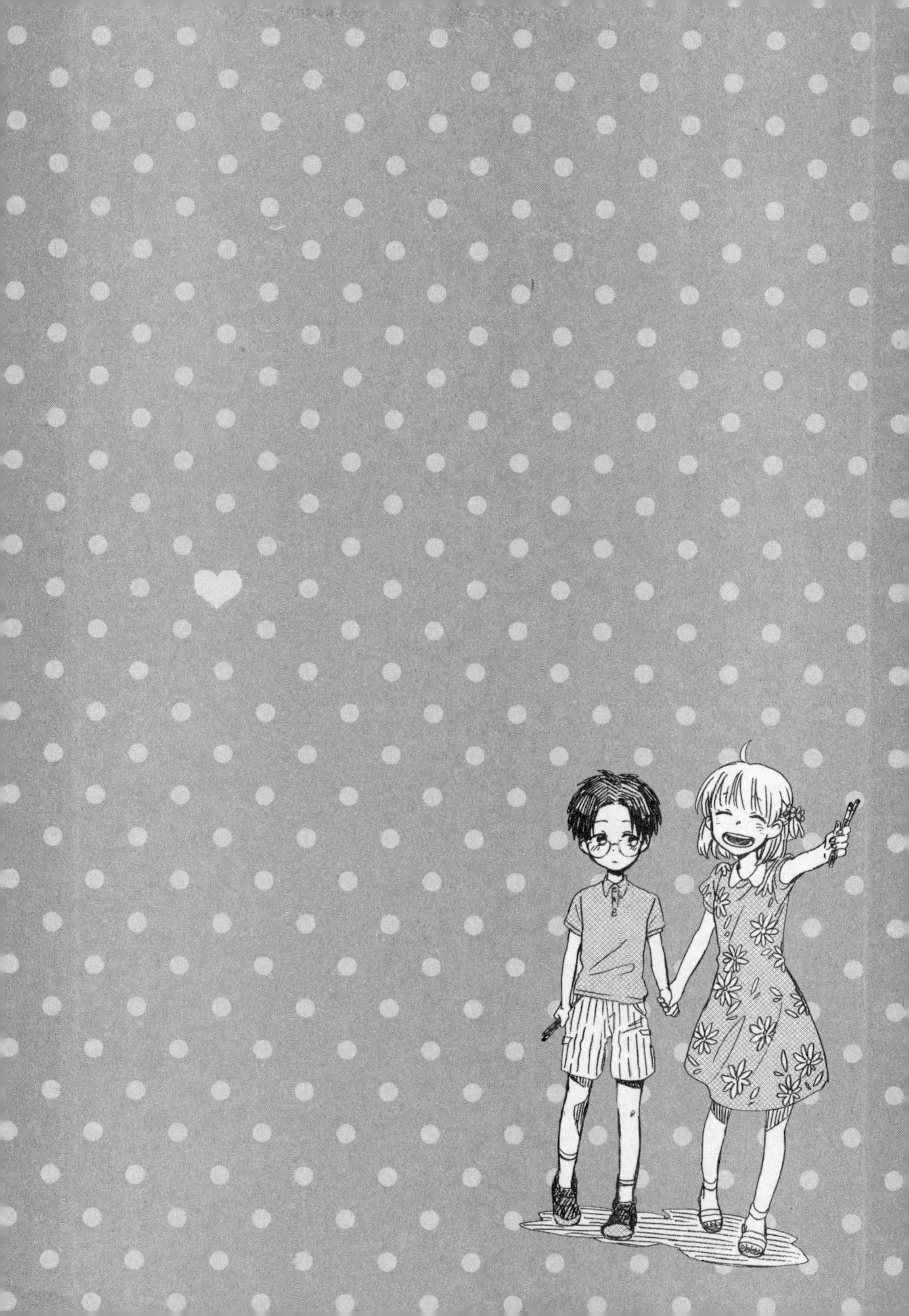

Episode.... 2

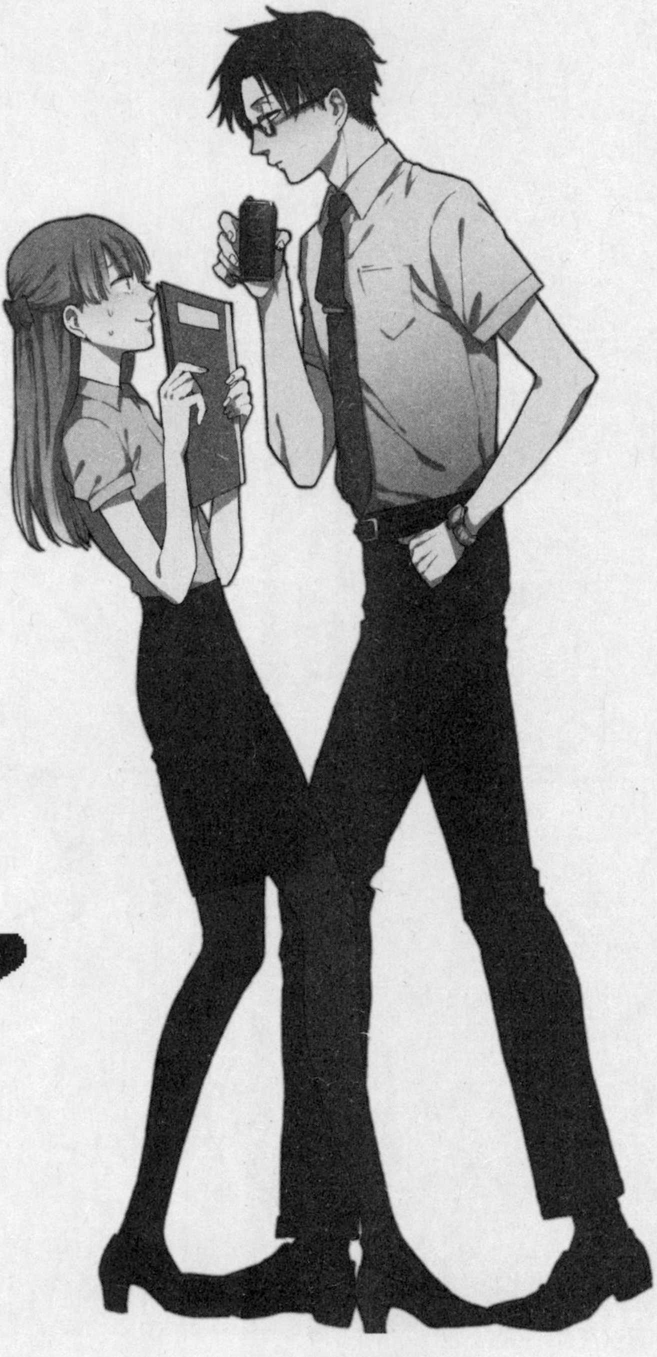

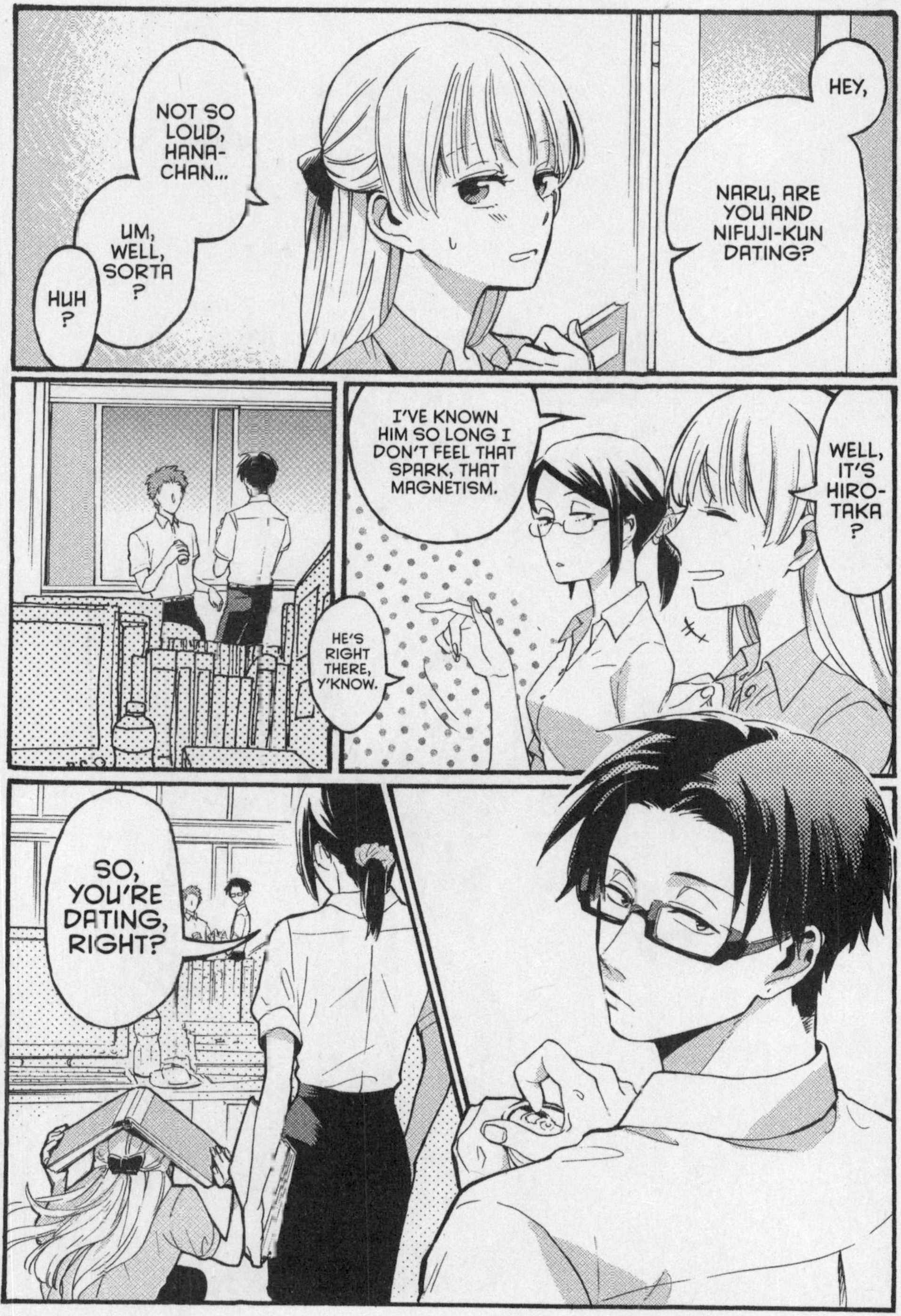
HEY,
NARU, ARE YOU AND NIFUJI-KUN DATING?
NOT SO LOUD, HANA-CHAN...
UM, WELL, SORTA ?
HUH ?
WELL, IT'S HIRO-TAKA ?
I'VE KNOWN HIM SO LONG I DON'T FEEL THAT SPARK, THAT MAGNETISM.
HE'S RIGHT THERE, Y'KNOW.
SO, YOU'RE DATING, RIGHT?

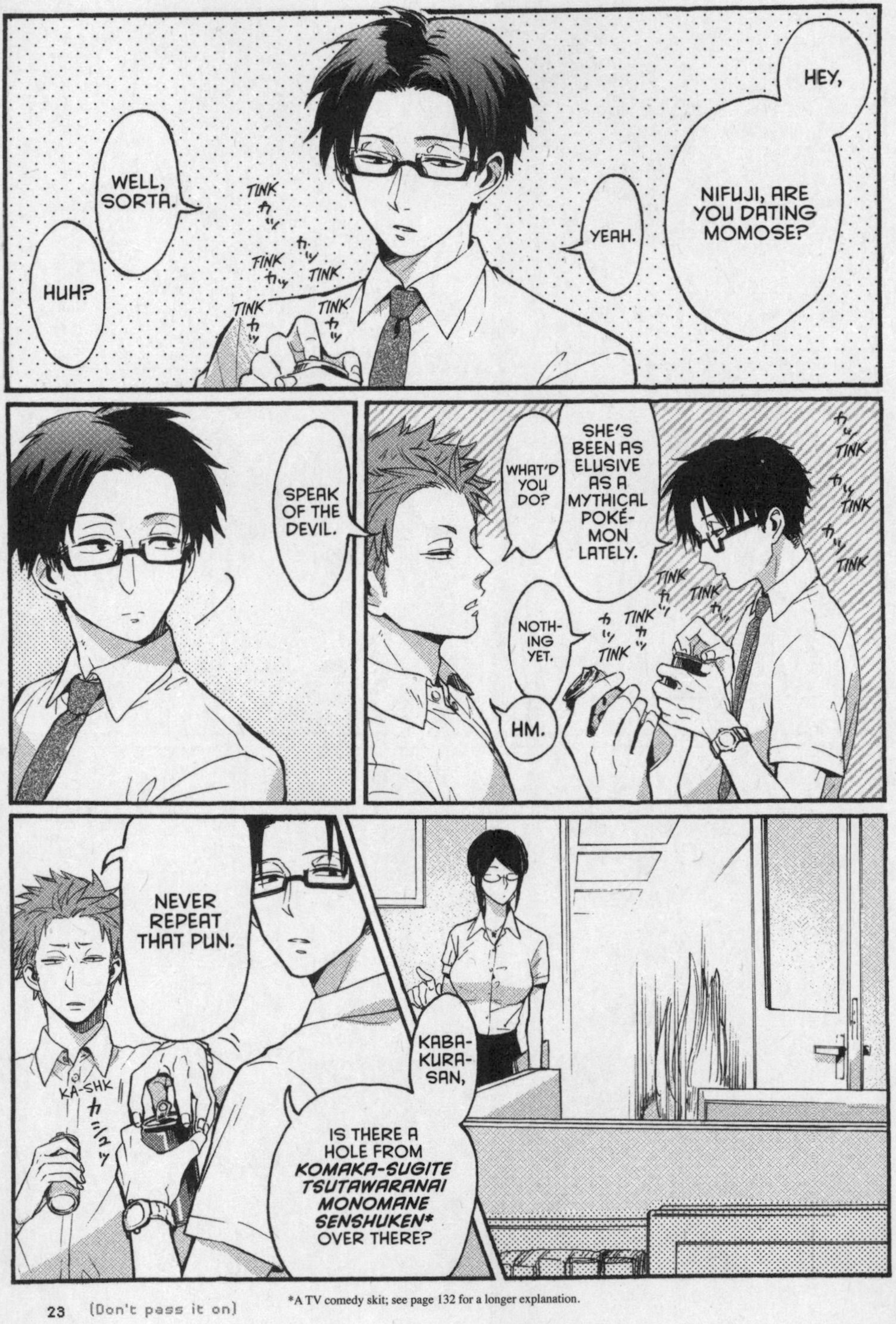
HEY,
NIFUJI, ARE YOU DATING MOMOSE?
YEAH.
TINK カッ
TINK カッ
TINK カッ
TINK カッ
TINK カッ
WELL, SORTA.
HUH?
カッ TINK
カッ TINK
カッ TINK
SHE'S BEEN AS ELUSIVE AS A MYTHICAL POKÉ-MON LATELY.
WHAT'D YOU DO?
TINK カッ
TINK カッ
TINK カッ
TINK カッ
NOTH-ING YET.
HM.
SPEAK OF THE DEVIL.
KABA-KURA-SAN,
IS THERE A HOLE FROM *KOMAKA-SUGITE TSUTAWARANAI MONOMANE SENSHUKEN** OVER THERE?
NEVER REPEAT THAT PUN.
KA-SHK カシュッ

*A TV comedy skit; see page 132 for a longer explanation.

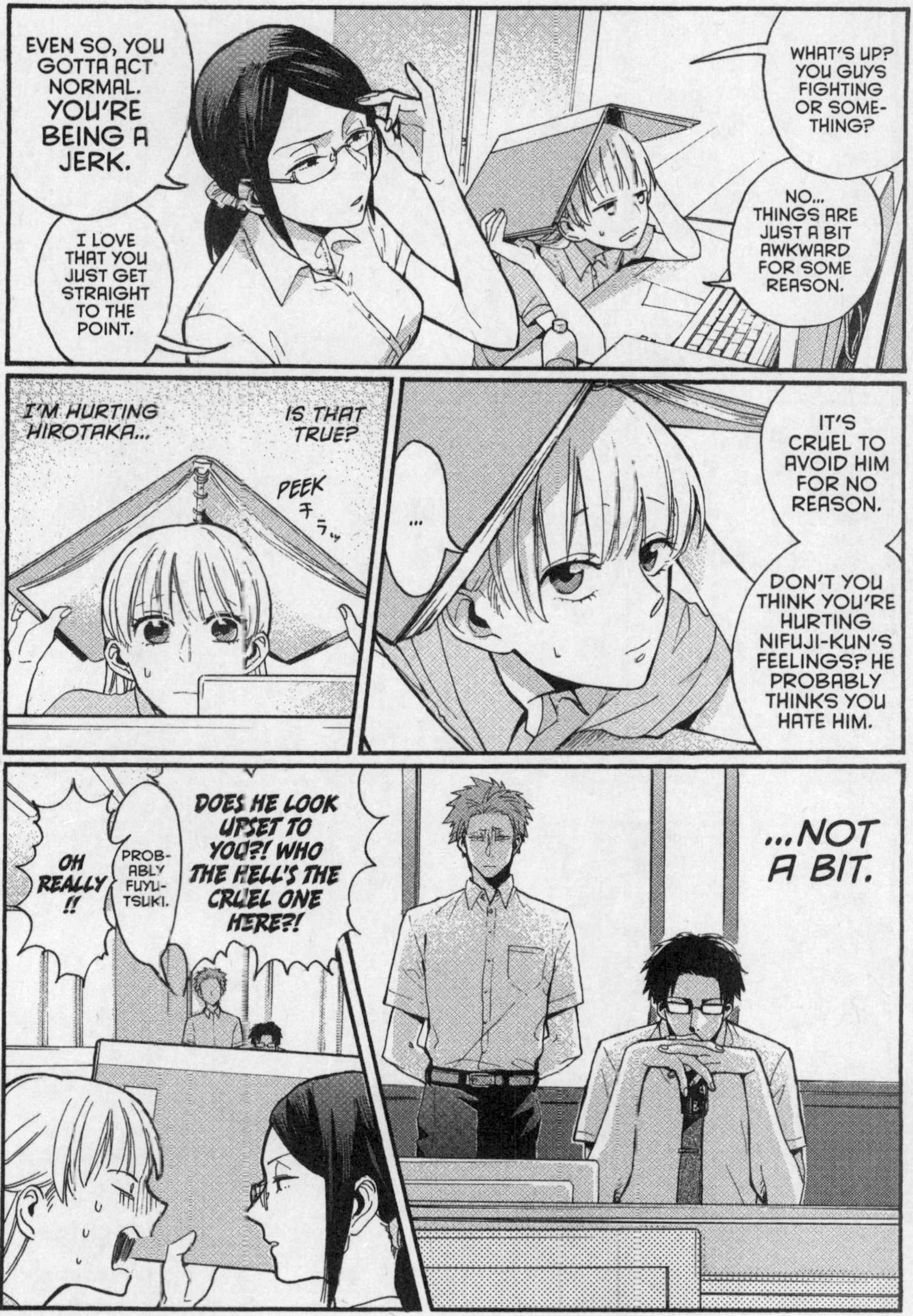
WHAT'S UP? YOU GUYS FIGHTING OR SOMETHING?
NO... THINGS ARE JUST A BIT AWKWARD FOR SOME REASON.
EVEN SO, YOU GOTTA ACT NORMAL. YOU'RE BEING A JERK.
I LOVE THAT YOU JUST GET STRAIGHT TO THE POINT.
IT'S CRUEL TO AVOID HIM FOR NO REASON.
DON'T YOU THINK YOU'RE HURTING NIFUJI-KUN'S FEELINGS? HE PROBABLY THINKS YOU HATE HIM.
...
I'M HURTING HIROTAKA...
IS THAT TRUE?
PEEK
チラッ
...NOT A BIT.
DOES HE LOOK UPSET TO YOU?! WHO THE HELL'S THE CRUEL ONE HERE?!
PROBABLY FUYUTSUKI.
OH REALLY!!

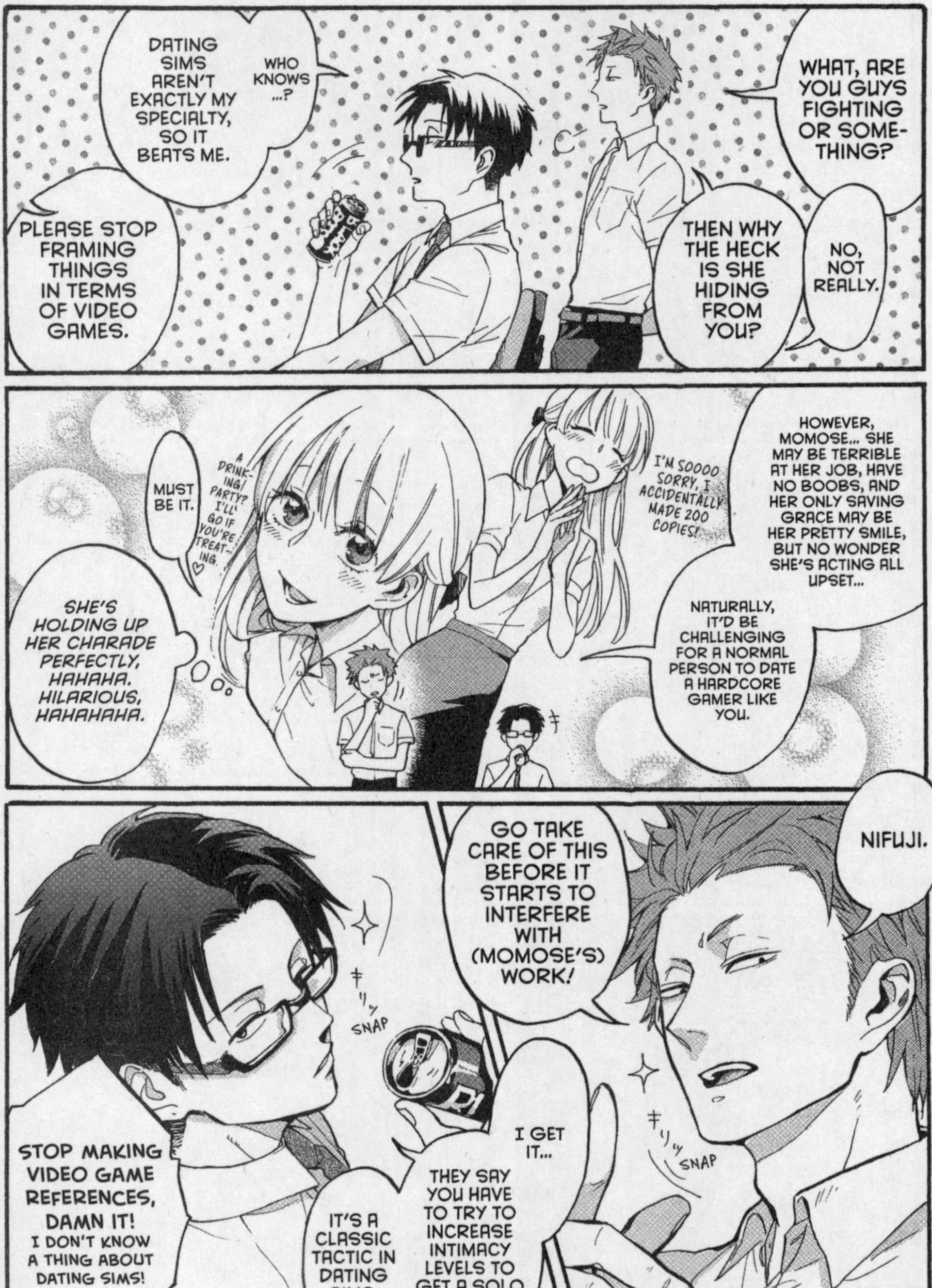
WHAT, ARE YOU GUYS FIGHTING OR SOMETHING?
NO, NOT REALLY.
THEN WHY THE HECK IS SHE HIDING FROM YOU?
WHO KNOWS ...?
DATING SIMS AREN'T EXACTLY MY SPECIALTY, SO IT BEATS ME.
PLEASE STOP FRAMING THINGS IN TERMS OF VIDEO GAMES.
HOWEVER, MOMOSE... SHE MAY BE TERRIBLE AT HER JOB, HAVE NO BOOBS, AND HER ONLY SAVING GRACE MAY BE HER PRETTY SMILE, BUT NO WONDER SHE'S ACTING ALL UPSET...
NATURALLY, IT'D BE CHALLENGING FOR A NORMAL PERSON TO DATE A HARDCORE GAMER LIKE YOU.
I'M SOOOO SORRY, I ACCIDENTALLY MADE 200 COPIES!
A DRINKING PARTY? I'LL GO IF YOU'RE TREATING. ♡
MUST BE IT.
SHE'S HOLDING UP HER CHARADE PERFECTLY, HAHAHA. HILARIOUS, HAHAHAHA.
NIFUJI.
GO TAKE CARE OF THIS BEFORE IT STARTS TO INTERFERE WITH (MOMOSE'S) WORK!
SNAP
I GET IT...
THEY SAY YOU HAVE TO TRY TO INCREASE INTIMACY LEVELS TO GET A SOLO EVENT.
IT'S A CLASSIC TACTIC IN DATING SIMS.
SNAP
STOP MAKING VIDEO GAME REFERENCES, DAMN IT! I DON'T KNOW A THING ABOUT DATING SIMS!

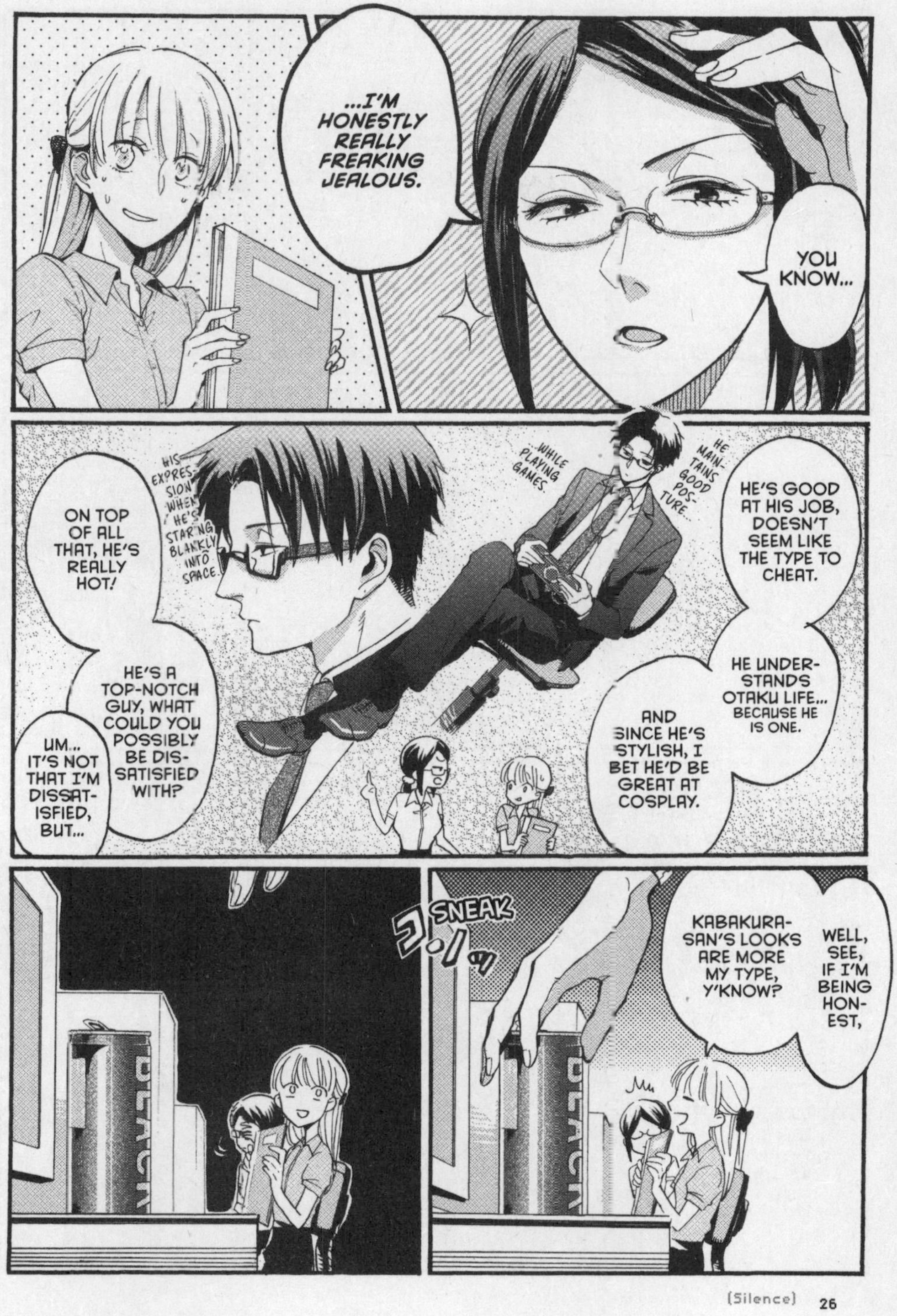
YOU KNOW...
...I'M HONESTLY REALLY FREAKING JEALOUS.
HE'S GOOD AT HIS JOB, DOESN'T SEEM LIKE THE TYPE TO CHEAT.
HE MAIN-TAINS GOOD POS-TURE...
...WHILE PLAYING GAMES.
HE UNDER-STANDS OTAKU LIFE... BECAUSE HE IS ONE.
AND SINCE HE'S STYLISH, I BET HE'D BE GREAT AT COSPLAY.
HIS EXPRES-SION WHEN HE'S STARING BLANKLY INTO SPACE.
ON TOP OF ALL THAT, HE'S REALLY HOT!
HE'S A TOP-NOTCH GUY, WHAT COULD YOU POSSIBLY BE DIS-SATISFIED WITH?
UM... IT'S NOT THAT I'M DISSAT-ISFIED, BUT...
WELL, SEE, IF I'M BEING HON-EST,
KABAKURA-SAN'S LOOKS ARE MORE MY TYPE, Y'KNOW?
SNEAK

(Silence)

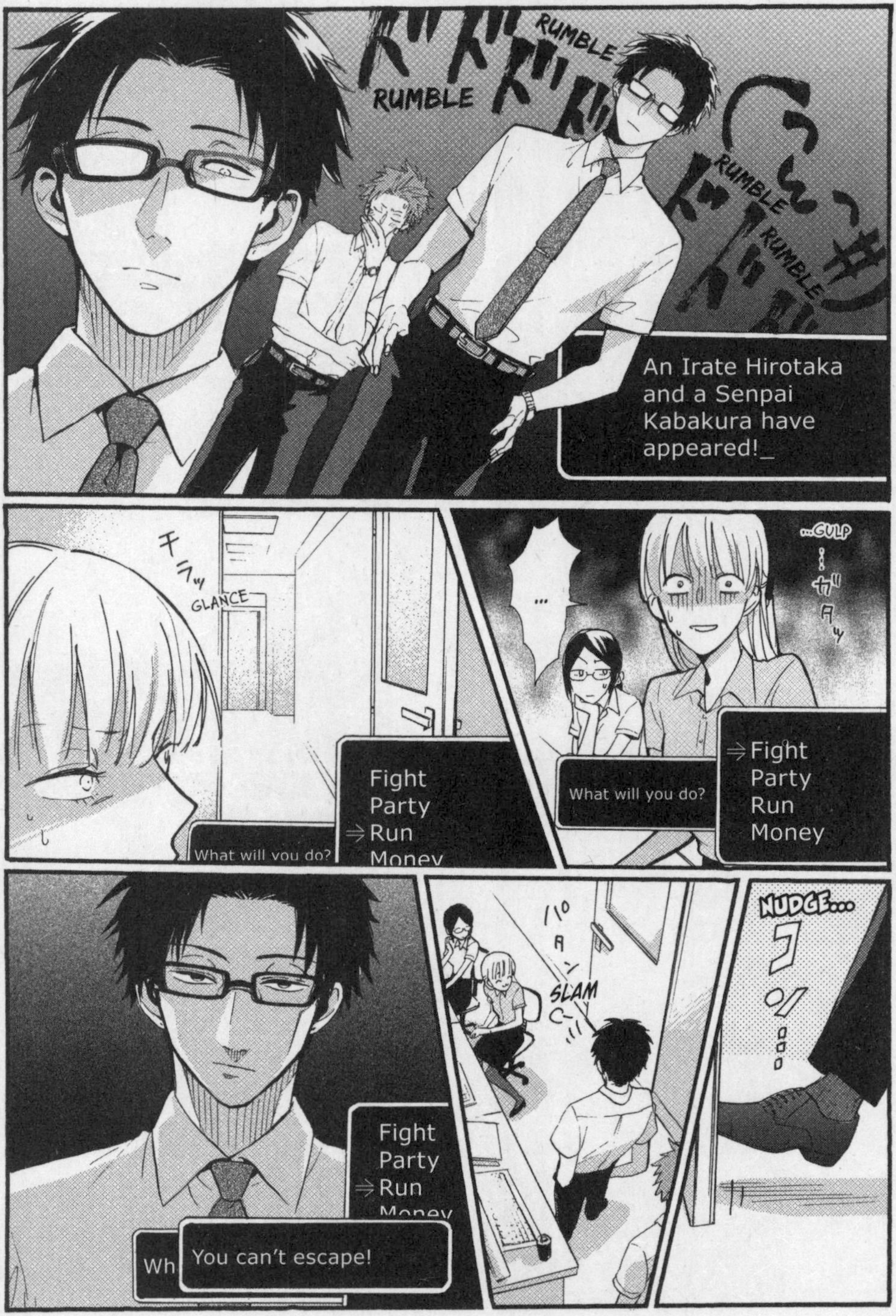
RUMBLE
RUMBLE
RUMBLE
RUMBLE
RUMBLE
An Irate Hirotaka and a Senpai Kabakura have appeared!_
...GULP
...
What will you do?
⇒ Fight
Party
Run
Money
GLANCE
What will you do?
Fight
Party
⇒ Run
Money
NUDGE...
SLAM
Fight
Party
⇒ Run
Money
You can't escape!

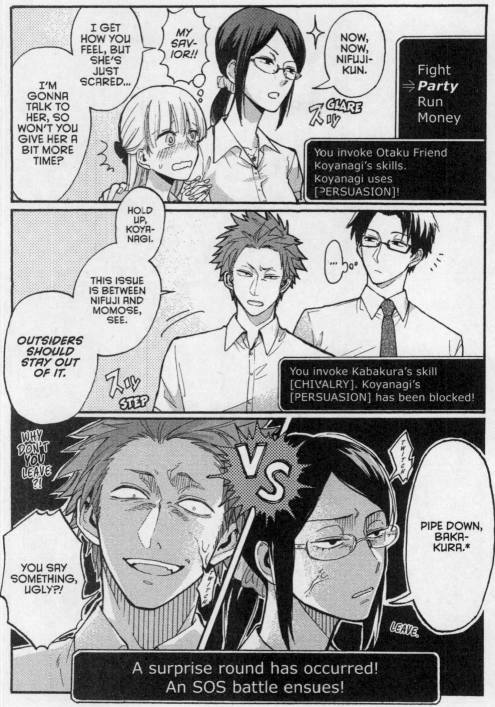

Fight
⇒**Party**
Run
Money
NOW, NOW, NIFUJI-KUN.
GLARE
MY SAVIOR!!
I GET HOW YOU FEEL, BUT SHE'S JUST SCARED...
I'M GONNA TALK TO HER, SO WON'T YOU GIVE HER A BIT MORE TIME?
You invoke Otaku Friend Koyanagi's skills. Koyanagi uses [PERSUASION]!
...
HOLD UP, KOYANAGI.
THIS ISSUE IS BETWEEN NIFUJI AND MOMOSE, SEE.
OUTSIDERS SHOULD STAY OUT OF IT.
STEP
You invoke Kabakura's skill [CHIVALRY]. Koyanagi's [PERSUASION] has been blocked!
TWITCH
PIPE DOWN, BAKAKURA.*
LEAVE.
VS
WHY DON'T YOU LEAVE?!
TWITCH
YOU SAY SOMETHING, UGLY?!
A surprise round has occurred! An SOS battle ensues!

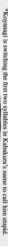

*Koyanagi is switching the first two syllables in Kabakura's name to call him stupid.

(Background music: "Sunrise")

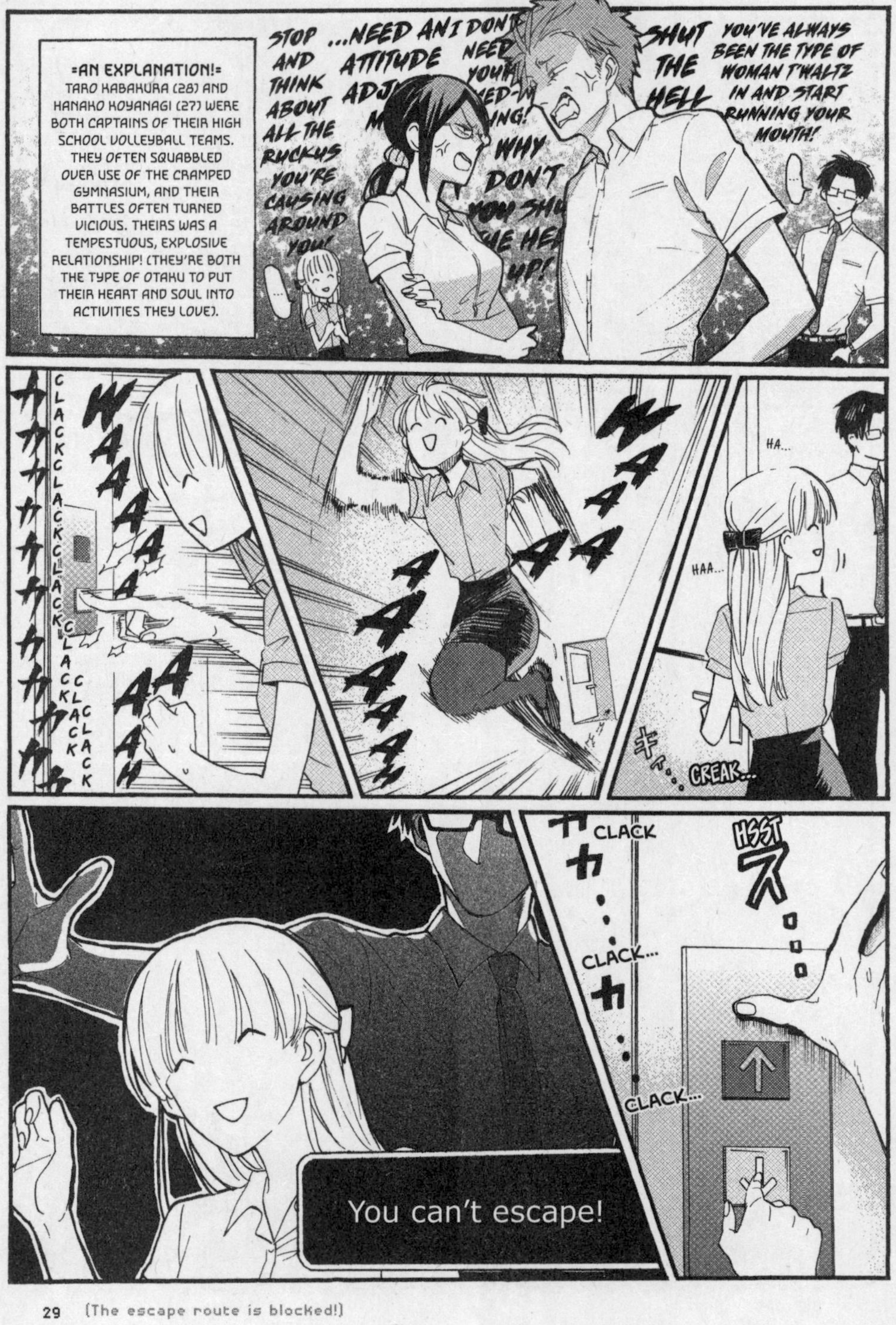
YOU'VE ALWAYS BEEN THE TYPE OF WOMAN T'WALTZ IN AND START RUNNING YOUR MOUTH!
SHUT THE HELL
I DON'T NEED YOUR
...NEED AN ATTITUDE
STOP AND THINK ABOUT ALL THE RUCKUS YOU'RE CAUSING AROUND YOU!
WHY DON'T
UP!
...
=AN EXPLANATION!=
TARO KABAKURA (28) AND HANAKO KOYANAGI (27) WERE BOTH CAPTAINS OF THEIR HIGH SCHOOL VOLLEYBALL TEAMS. THEY OFTEN SQUABBLED OVER USE OF THE CRAMPED GYMNASIUM, AND THEIR BATTLES OFTEN TURNED VICIOUS. THEIRS WAS A TEMPESTUOUS, EXPLOSIVE RELATIONSHIP! (THEY'RE BOTH THE TYPE OF OTAKU TO PUT THEIR HEART AND SOUL INTO ACTIVITIES THEY LOVE).
...
HA...
HAA...
CREAK...
WAAAAAAAAAAAA
WAAAAAAAAAH
CLACK CLACK CLACK CLACK CLACK CLACK CLACK
HSST
CLACK
CLACK...
CLACK...
You can't escape!

 (The escape route is blocked!)

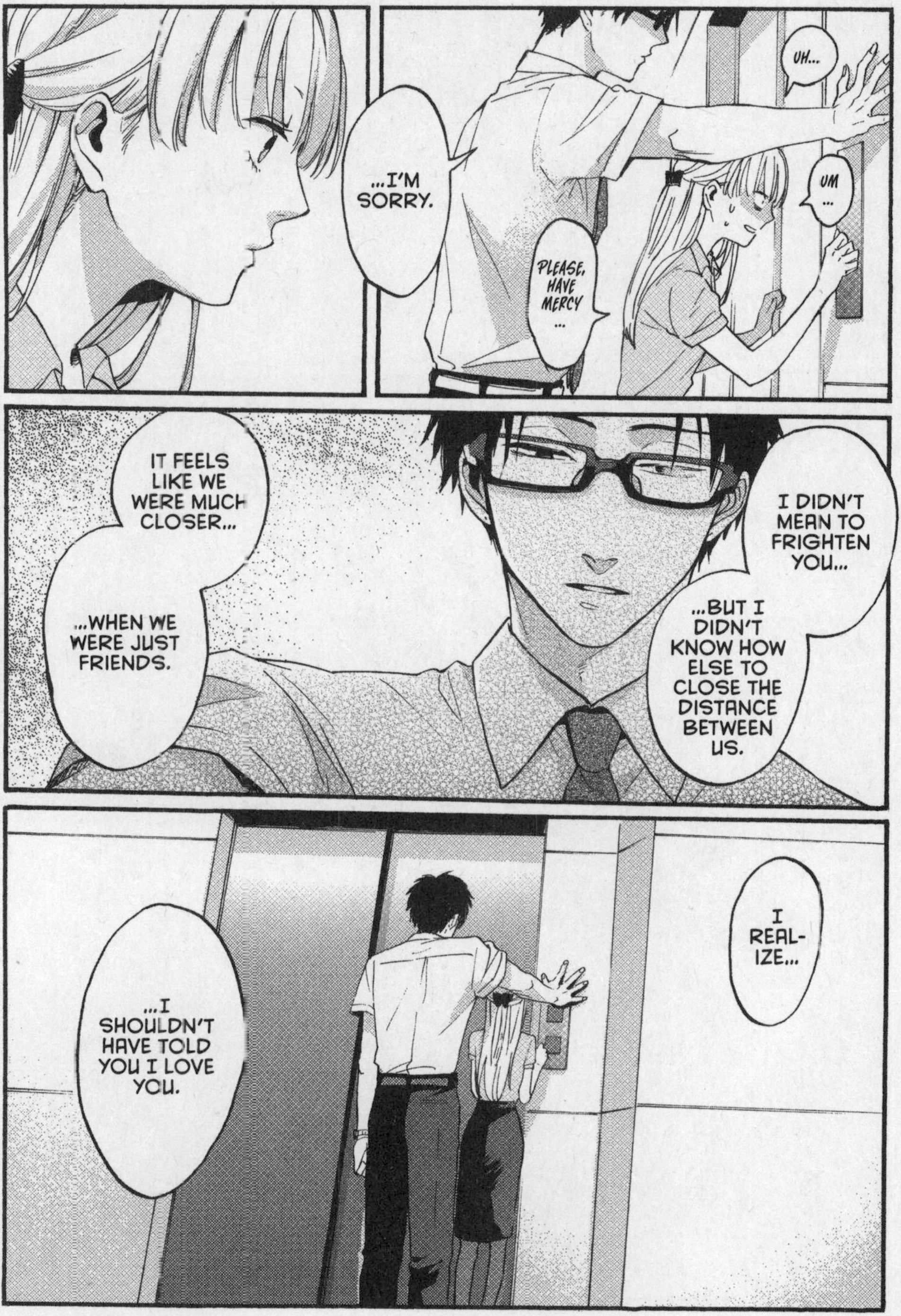
UH...
UM...
PLEASE, HAVE MERCY...
...I'M SORRY.
I DIDN'T MEAN TO FRIGHTEN YOU...
...BUT I DIDN'T KNOW HOW ELSE TO CLOSE THE DISTANCE BETWEEN US.
IT FEELS LIKE WE WERE MUCH CLOSER...
...WHEN WE WERE JUST FRIENDS.
I REAL-IZE...
...I SHOULDN'T HAVE TOLD YOU I LOVE YOU.

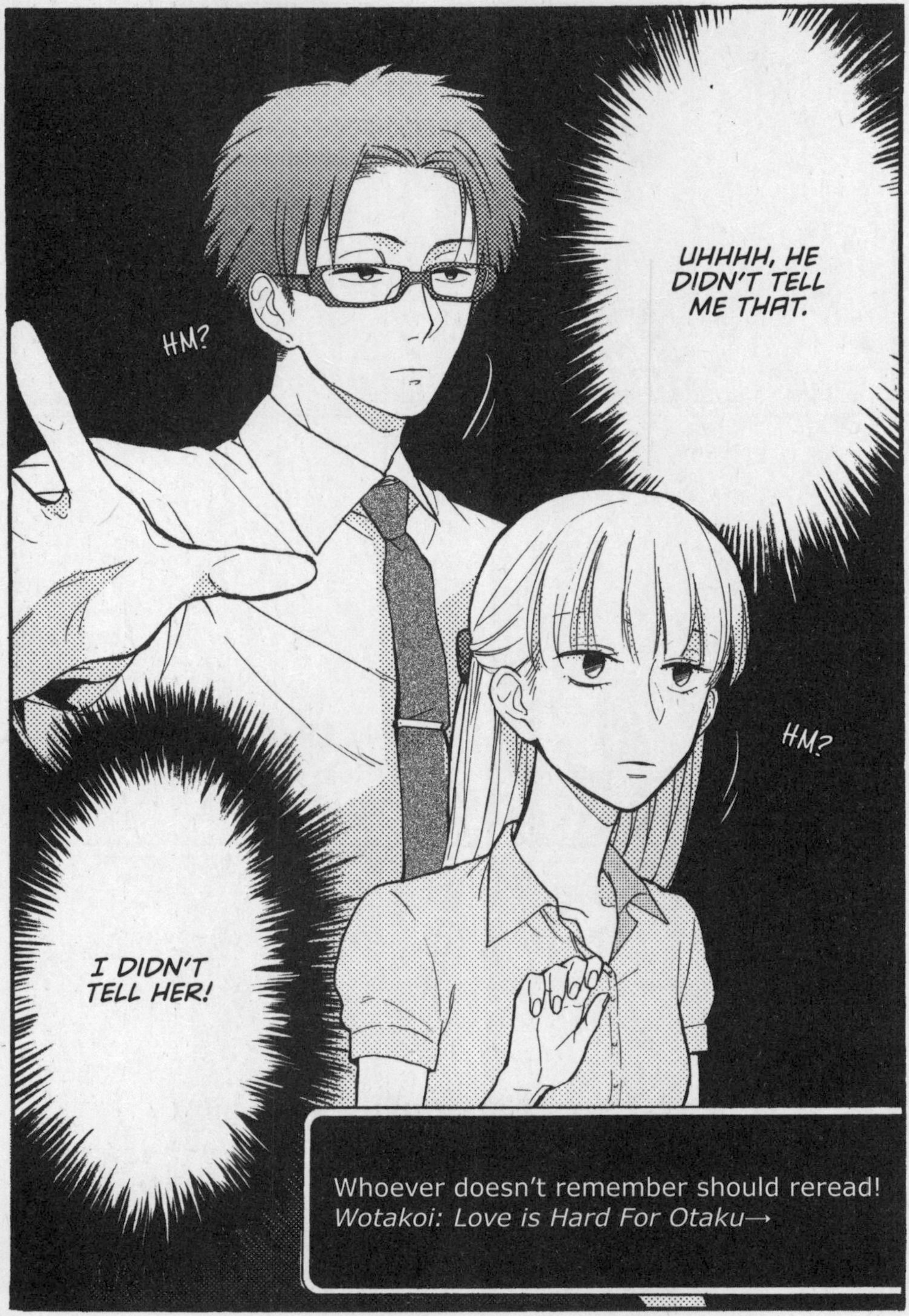
UHHHH, HE DIDN'T TELL ME THAT.
HM?
HM?
I DIDN'T TELL HER!
Whoever doesn't remember should reread!
Wotakoi: Love is Hard For Otaku→

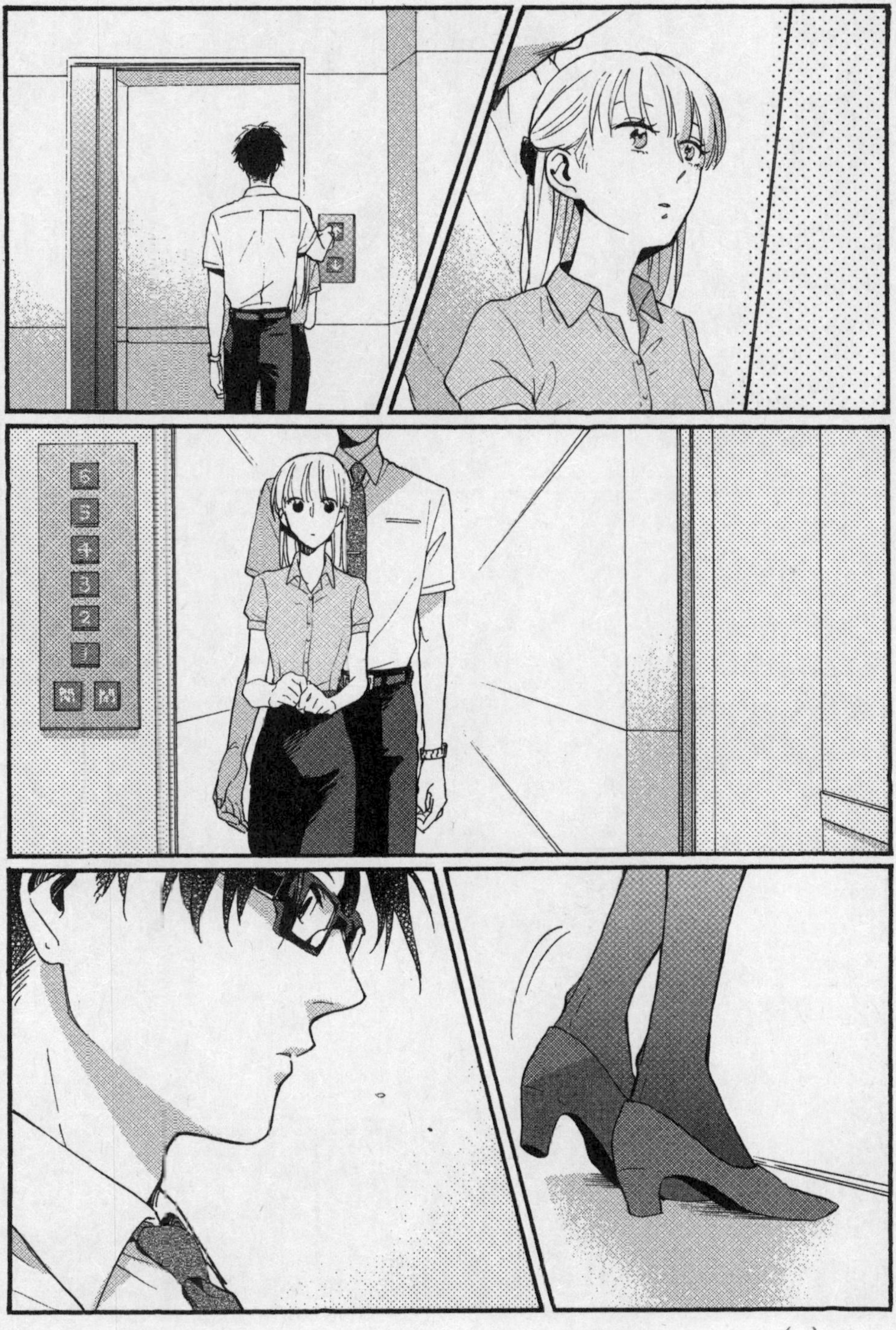

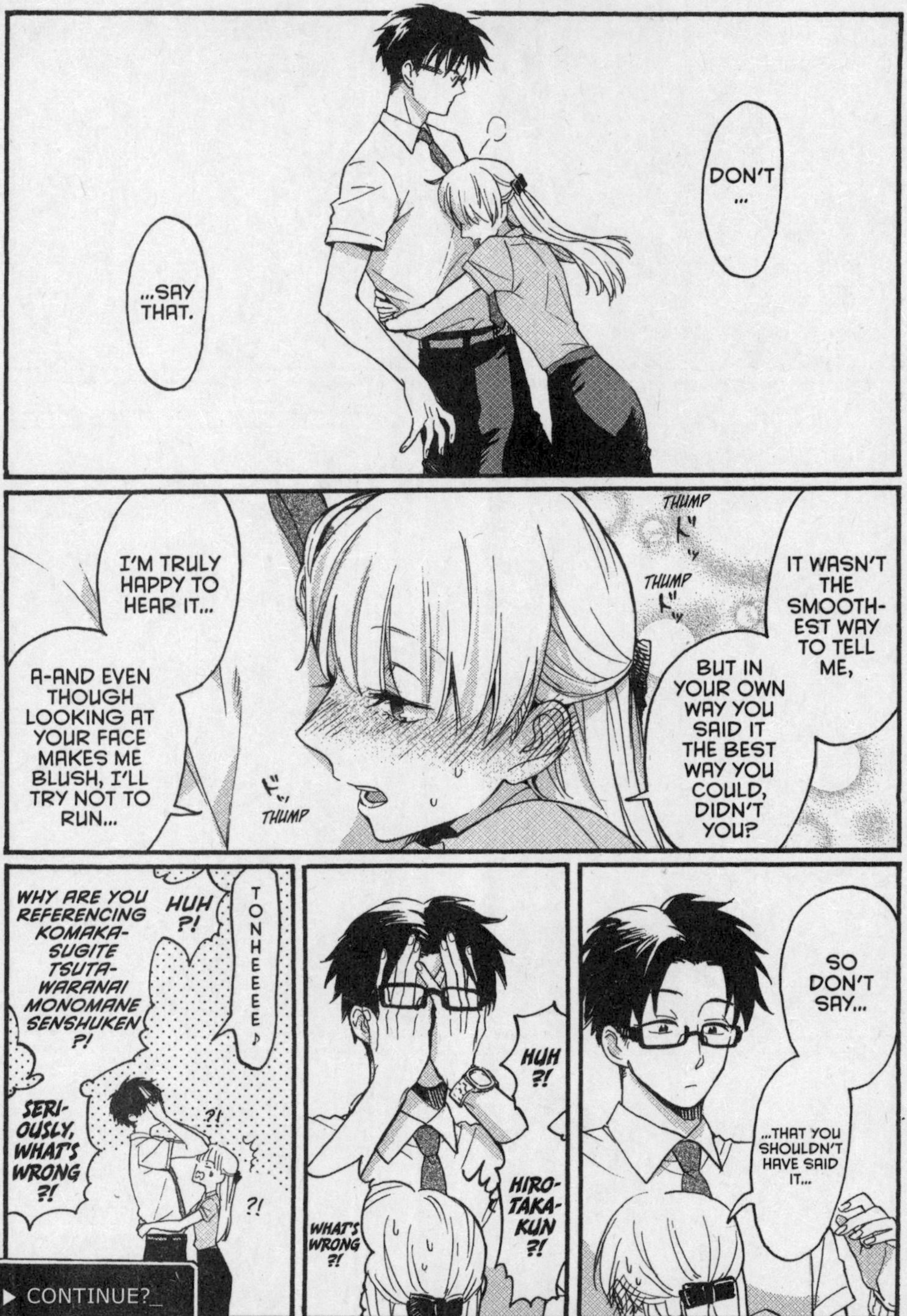
DON'T ...
...SAY THAT.
THUMP ドッ
THUMP ドッ
IT WASN'T THE SMOOTH-EST WAY TO TELL ME,
BUT IN YOUR OWN WAY YOU SAID IT THE BEST WAY YOU COULD, DIDN'T YOU?
I'M TRULY HAPPY TO HEAR IT...
A-AND EVEN THOUGH LOOKING AT YOUR FACE MAKES ME BLUSH, I'LL TRY NOT TO RUN...
ドッ THUMP
SO DON'T SAY...
...THAT YOU SHOULDN'T HAVE SAID IT...
HUH ?!
HIRO-TAKA-KUN ?!
WHAT'S WRONG ?!
TONHEEEEE♪
HUH ?!
WHY ARE YOU REFERENCING KOMAKA-SUGITE TSUTA-WARANAI MONOMANE SENSHUKEN ?!
?!
SERI-OUSLY, WHAT'S WRONG ?!
?!
▶ CONTINUE?_

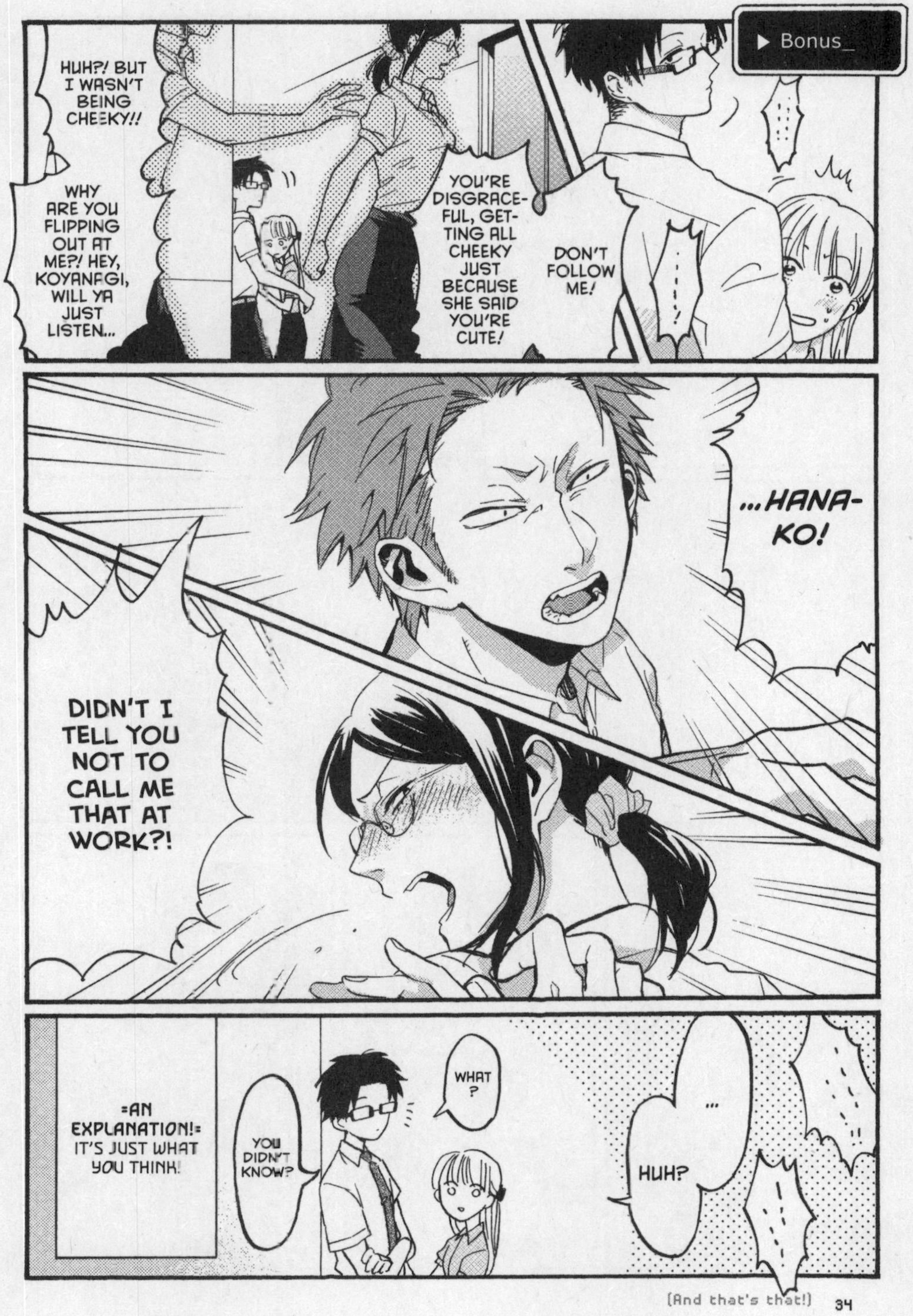
▶ Bonus_
...
DON'T FOLLOW ME!
YOU'RE DISGRACEFUL, GETTING ALL CHEEKY JUST BECAUSE SHE SAID YOU'RE CUTE!
HUH?! BUT I WASN'T BEING CHEEKY!!
WHY ARE YOU FLIPPING OUT AT ME?! HEY, KOYANAGI, WILL YA JUST LISTEN...
...HANAKO!
DIDN'T I TELL YOU NOT TO CALL ME THAT AT WORK?!
...
HUH?
WHAT?
YOU DIDN'T KNOW?
=AN EXPLANATION!= IT'S JUST WHAT YOU THINK!

(And that's that!)

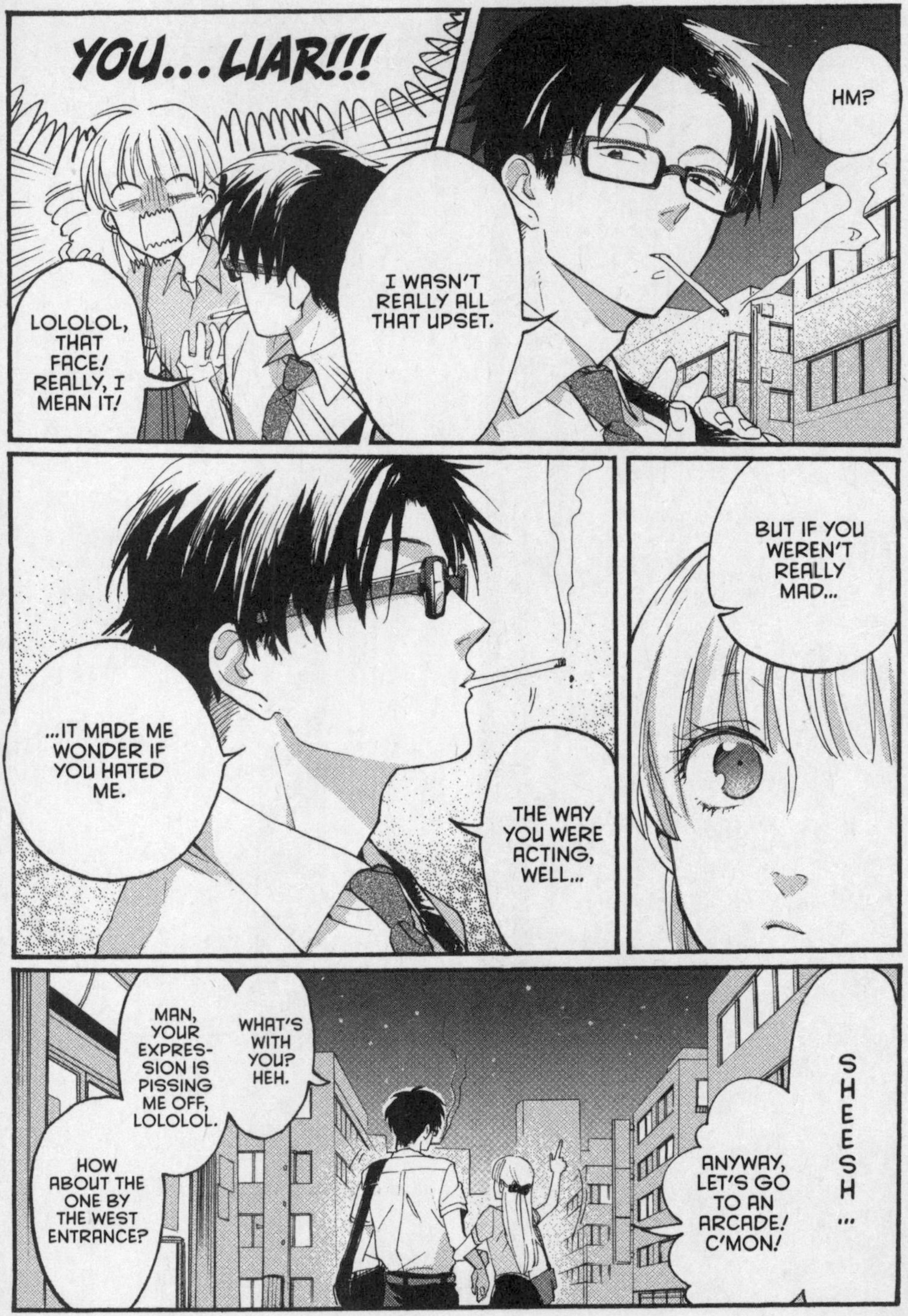
HM?
I WASN'T REALLY ALL THAT UPSET.
YOU... LIAR!!!
LOLOLOL, THAT FACE! REALLY, I MEAN IT!
BUT IF YOU WEREN'T REALLY MAD...
THE WAY YOU WERE ACTING, WELL...
...IT MADE ME WONDER IF YOU HATED ME.
SHEESH...
ANYWAY, LET'S GO TO AN ARCADE! C'MON!
WHAT'S WITH YOU? HEH.
MAN, YOUR EXPRES-SION IS PISSING ME OFF, LOLOLOL.
HOW ABOUT THE ONE BY THE WEST ENTRANCE?

Taro Kabakura

Birthday: 11/9
Age: 28
Height: 180 cm/5'9"
Weight: 72 kg/158 lbs
Blood Type: O
Zodiac: Scorpio

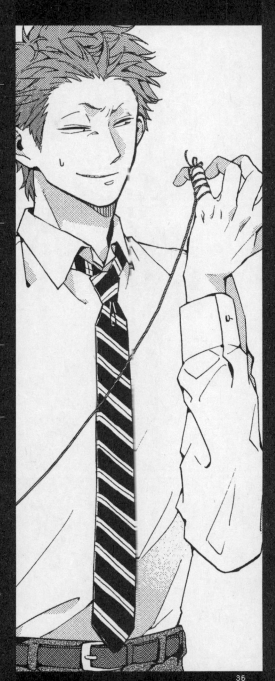

He's familiar with the mainstream manga and video games, and has a good amount of merchandise. While he's more into this stuff than the average person, he's not a full-blown otaku. He's the type who remembers previous waifu with pangs of guilt anytime he becomes obsessed with a new character, so he has a system of memorializing them in his waifu hall of fame.

Alcohol... Gets sleepy if he drinks more than his usual limit

Tobacco... Quit after he heard they were raising cigarette taxes

Hirotaka's senpai. His face is pretty scary, but behind the face lies a serious, dependable guy who takes care of others. He loves stories about heroes and beautiful damsels, and is more or less a typical otaku. While not as bad as Narumi, he still feels ashamed about being an otaku, and tries to hide his hobbies from his friends. Whenever he's around Narumi or Hirotaka he feels relieved, thinking "Hey, I'm not an otaku at all," except he totally is. He keeps a watchful, parental eye over Hirotaka and Narumi's relationship. He worries a little because they're not good at opening up to others. He's had a tempestuous rapport with Koyanagi since their school days, but somehow, they're in a relationship of sorts despite that.

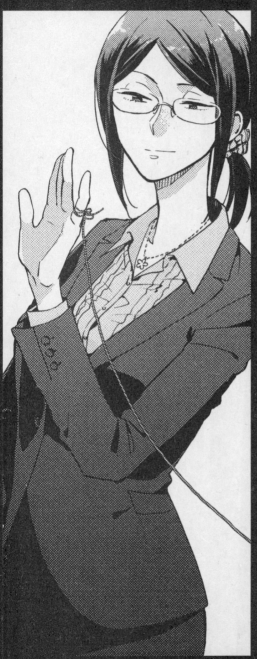

Hanako Koyanagi

Birthday: 8/28
Age: 27
Height: 167 cm/5'5"
Blood Type: AB
Zodiac: Virgo

Likes real-life art forms like the theater. Also has a taste for anime and manga to some extent. She's a fan of BL as well. For some reason she always falls for the minor characters, but she nevertheless loves her darling waifu with all her heart.

Alcohol... Loves to drink but has a low tolerance, so she shouldn't be given any

Tobacco... Rarely

Narumi's senpai and friend. She has a plain face that projects a cool demeanor, but she's stylish. She's fairly well-known in the cosplaying community for her talent for crossplay. She may look laid-back, but she's actually a meddlesome busybody. She speaks harshly but doesn't mean to push people away. After finding out Narumi was an otaku she came out as well, and now they're so close they call each other "Naru" and "Hana-chan." She finds Narumi and Hirotaka's relationship part lovely, part irritating, so she's watching over them. She's had a tempestuous rapport with Kabakura since their school days, but somehow, they're in a relationship of sorts despite that. In public she's standoffish with Kabakura, but she dotes on him when they're alone. It's annoying.

(*・∀-)b

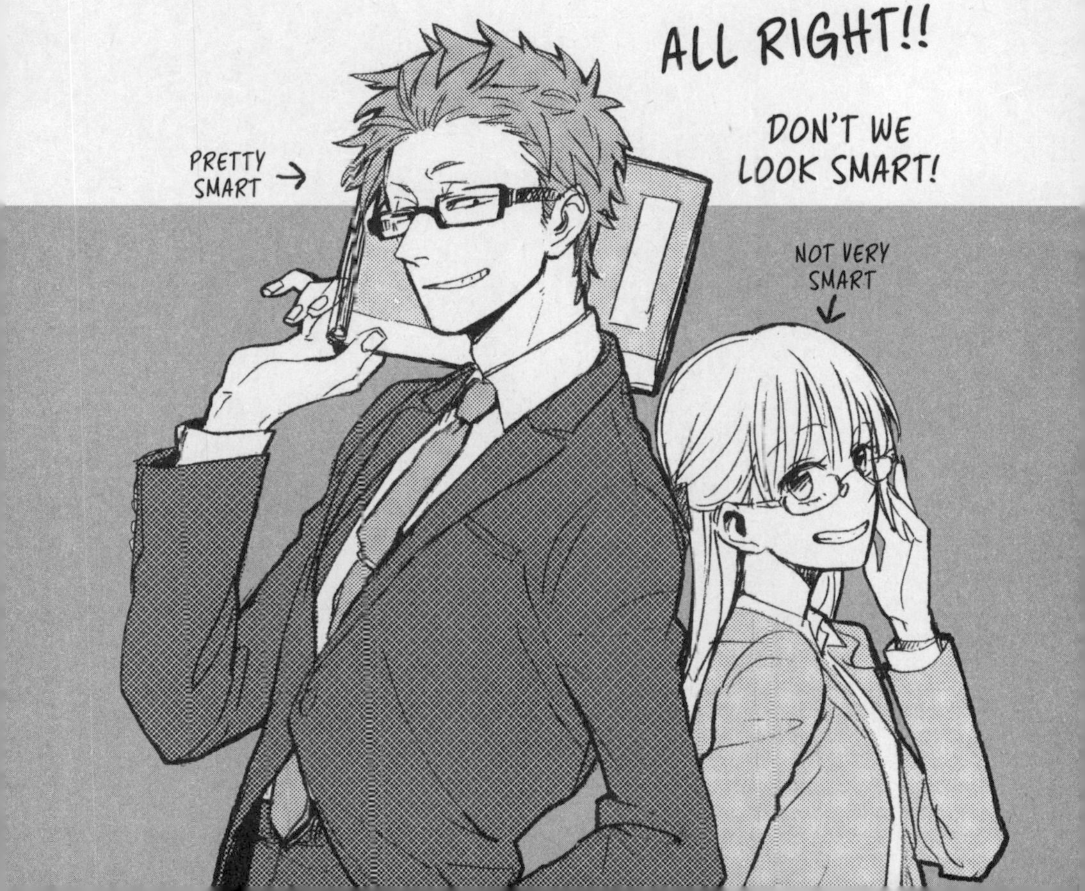
ALL RIGHT!!
DON'T WE LOOK SMART!
PRETTY SMART
NOT VERY SMART

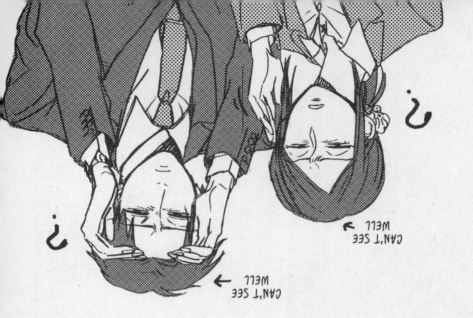

CAN'T SEE
WELL

CAN'T SEE
WELL

Wotakoi: Love is Hard For Otaku

▶ CONTINUE

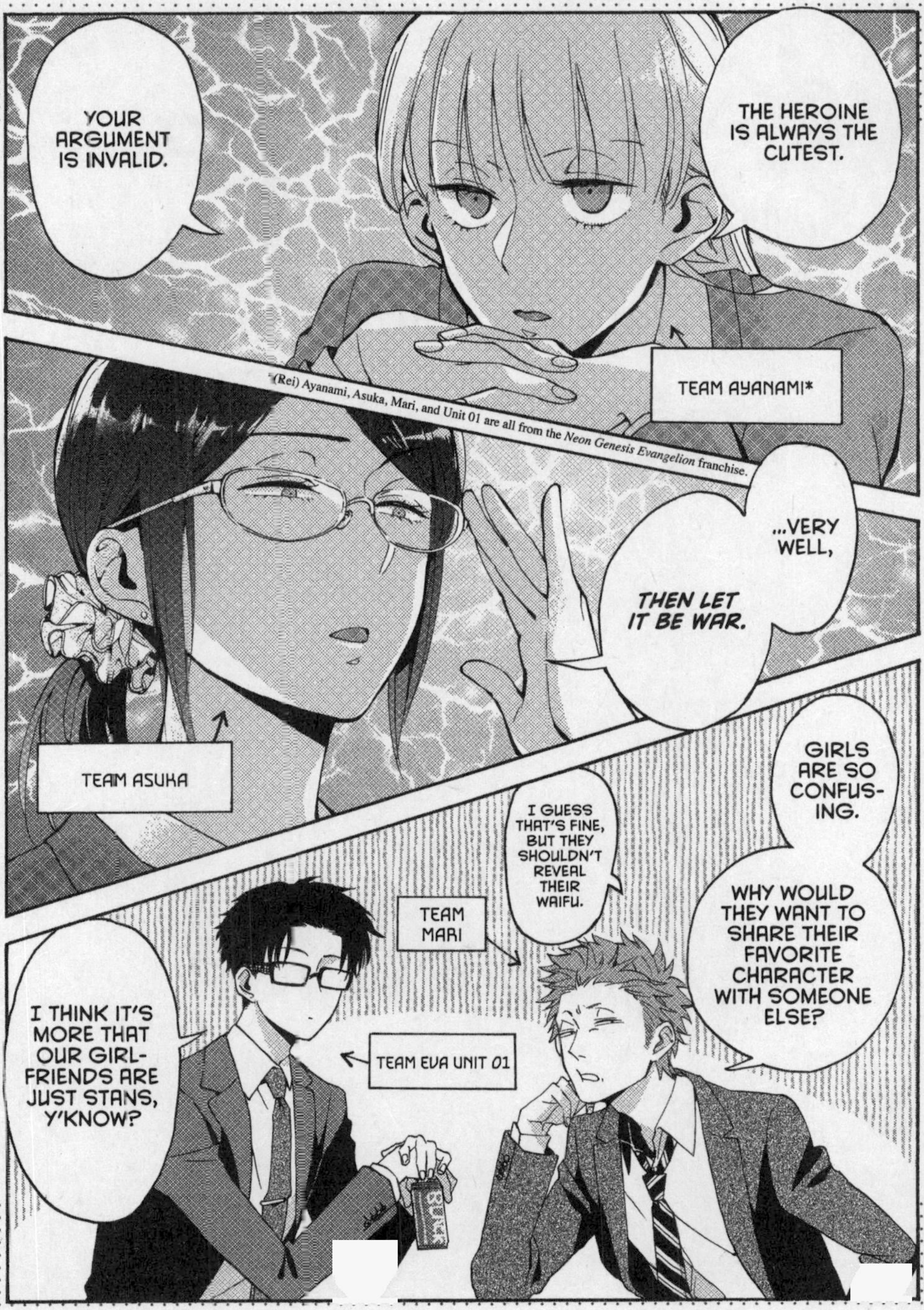
THE HEROINE IS ALWAYS THE CUTEST.
YOUR ARGUMENT IS INVALID.
TEAM AYANAMI*
...VERY WELL, *THEN LET IT BE WAR.*
TEAM ASUKA
GIRLS ARE SO CONFUS-ING.
WHY WOULD THEY WANT TO SHARE THEIR FAVORITE CHARACTER WITH SOMEONE ELSE?
I GUESS THAT'S FINE, BUT THEY SHOULDN'T REVEAL THEIR WAIFU.
TEAM MARI
TEAM EVA UNIT 01
I THINK IT'S MORE THAT OUR GIRL-FRIENDS ARE JUST STANS, Y'KNOW?

*(Rei) Ayanami, Asuka, Mari, and Unit 01 are all from the *Neon Genesis Evangelion* franchise.

What squicks you out?

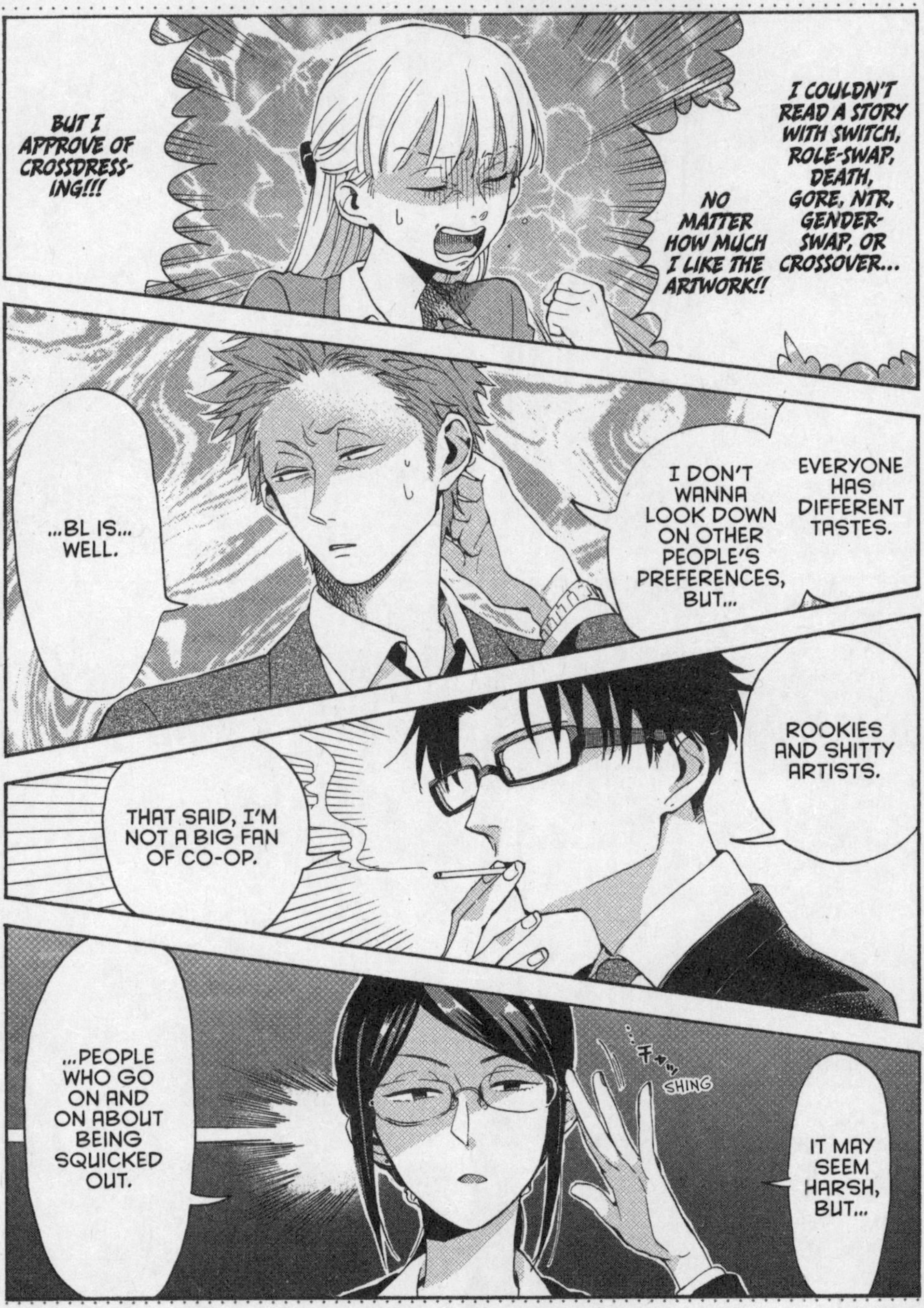
I COULDN'T READ A STORY WITH SWITCH, ROLE-SWAP, DEATH, GORE, NTR, GENDER-SWAP, OR CROSSOVER...
NO MATTER HOW MUCH I LIKE THE ARTWORK!!
BUT I APPROVE OF CROSSDRESS-ING!!!
EVERYONE HAS DIFFERENT TASTES.
I DON'T WANNA LOOK DOWN ON OTHER PEOPLE'S PREFERENCES, BUT...
...BL IS... WELL.
ROOKIES AND SHITTY ARTISTS.
THAT SAID, I'M NOT A BIG FAN OF CO-OP.
SHING
IT MAY SEEM HARSH, BUT...
...PEOPLE WHO GO ON AND ON ABOUT BEING SQUICKED OUT.

I...
...CAN'T WINK AT ALL.
THANKS FOR SHARING SUCH TRIVIAL INFORMATION OUT OF THE BLUE!
I CAN ONLY DO IT IF I CLOSE BOTH MY EYES.
THAT'S CALLED BLINK-ING.
THAT'S KINDA CUTE...
BUT WINKING IS SOOOO EASY.
LIKE THIS!
SO CUTE.
HER CUTENESS COMES SO NATURALLY TO HER...
YOU GOT THIS, NIFUJI-KUN!
GOOD LUCK, NIFUJI.
OKAY, OKAY, TRY IT, TRY IT ♪ HI! RO! TA! KA! ♪
...
...
HNGH...
HUH?!
SORRY!! I'M SORRY TO SAY THIS, HIROTAKA, BUT IT'S IMPOS-SIBLE!!!
AUGH!!!

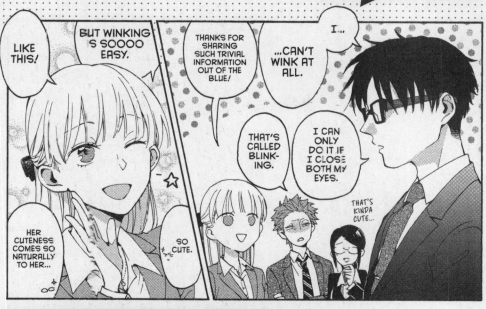

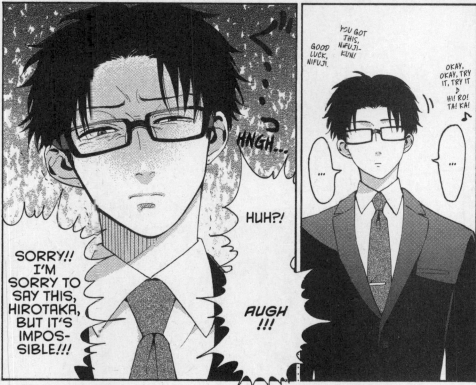

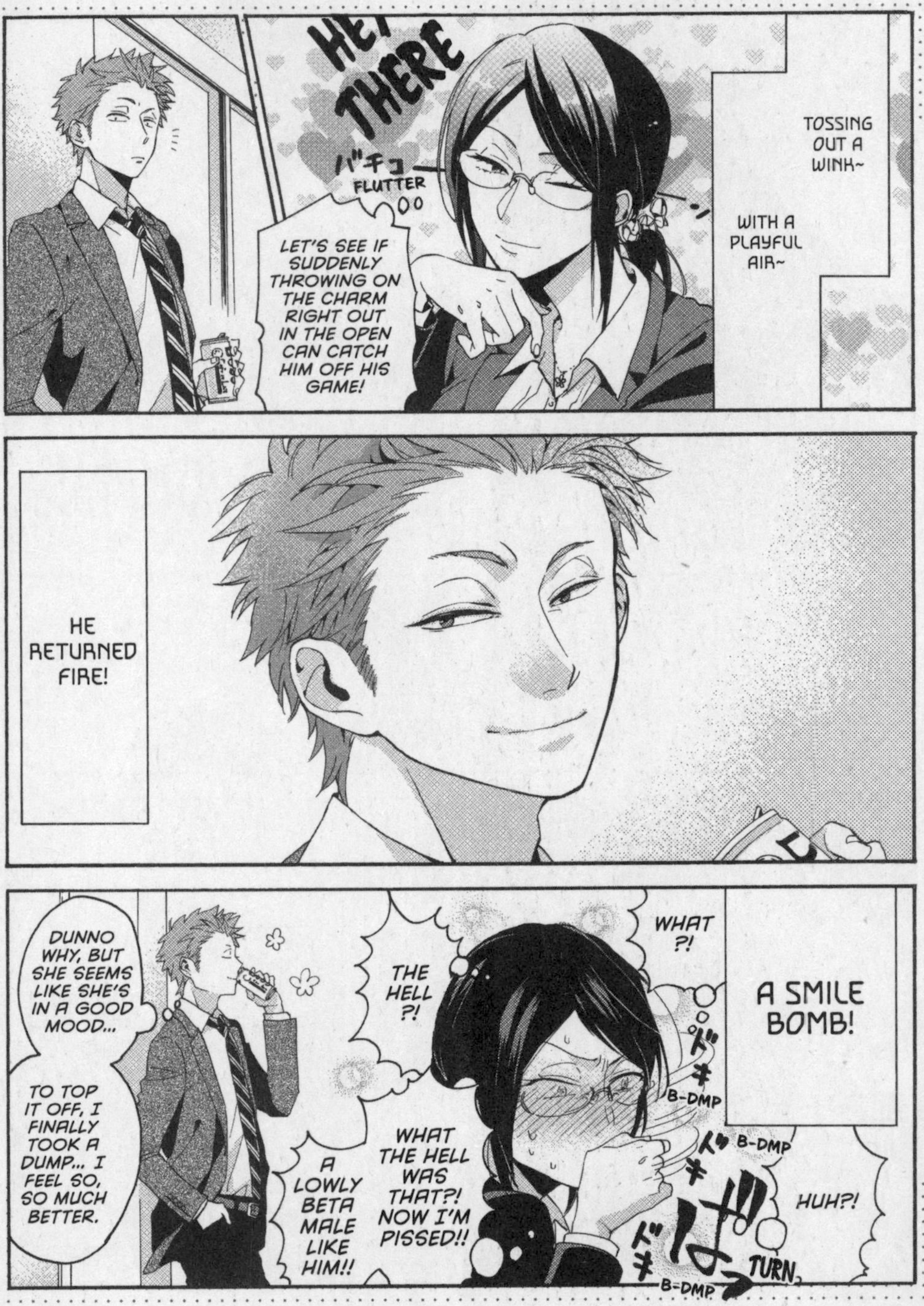
TOSSING OUT A WINK~
WITH A PLAYFUL AIR~
HEY THERE
バチコー
FLUTTER
LET'S SEE IF SUDDENLY THROWING ON THE CHARM RIGHT OUT IN THE OPEN CAN CATCH HIM OFF HIS GAME!
HE RETURNED FIRE!
A SMILE BOMB!
WHAT?!
HUH?!
ドキ B-DMP
ドキ B-DMP
ば TURN
ドキ B-DMP
THE HELL?!
WHAT THE HELL WAS THAT?! NOW I'M PISSED!!
A LOWLY BETA MALE LIKE HIM!!
DUNNO WHY, BUT SHE SEEMS LIKE SHE'S IN A GOOD MOOD...
TO TOP IT OFF, I FINALLY TOOK A DUMP... I FEEL SO, SO MUCH BETTER.

Fan service (for the girls)

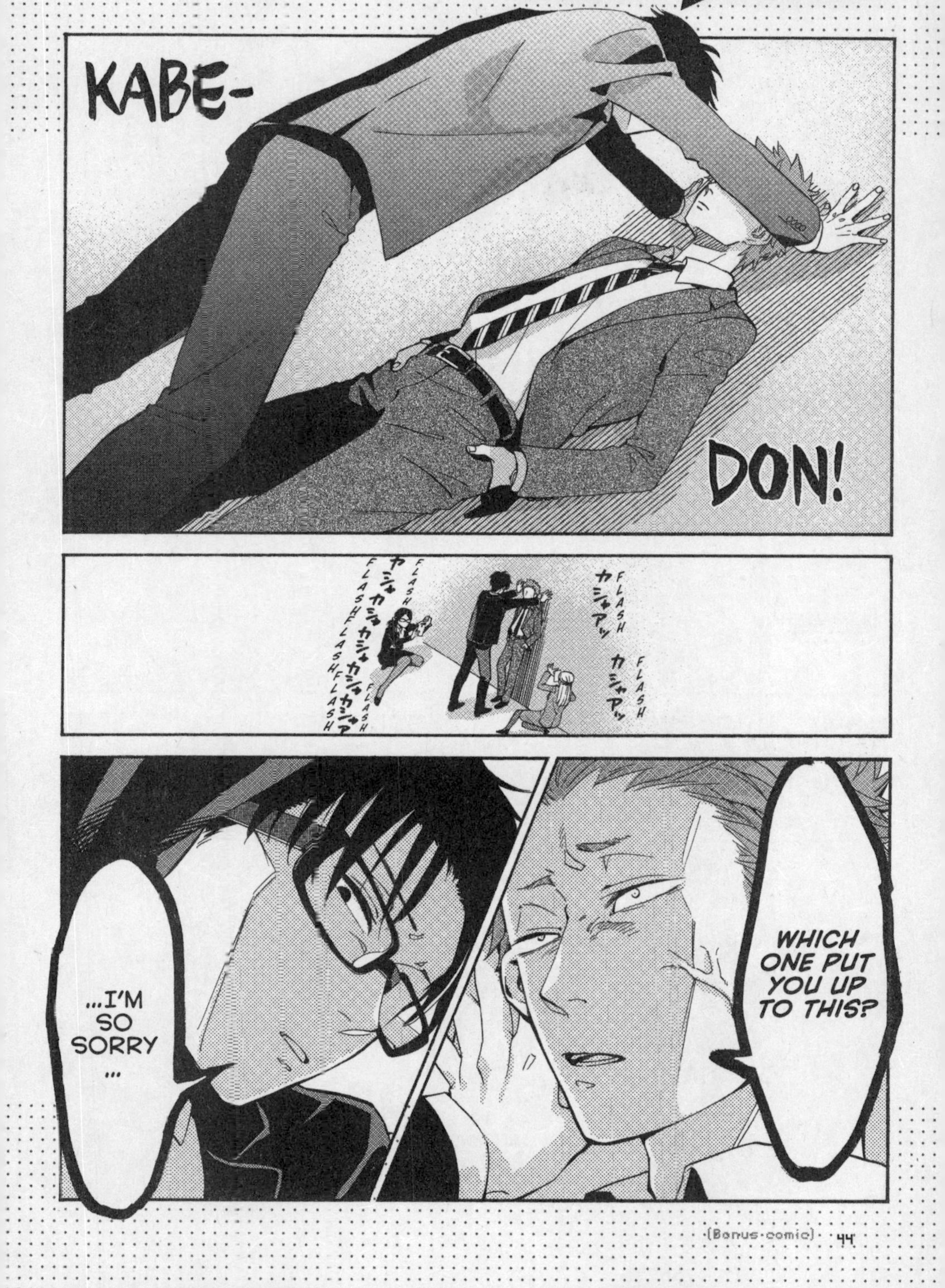
KABE-
DON!
カシャッ FLASH
カシャッ FLASH
カシャカシャカシャカシャ FLASH FLASH FLASH
カシャカシャカシャカシャ FLASH FLASH FLASH
WHICH ONE PUT YOU UP TO THIS?
...I'M SO SORRY ...

Fan service (for the guys)

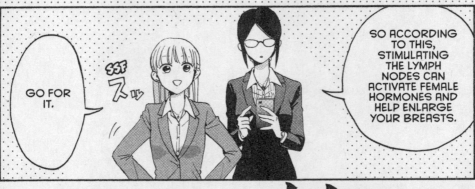

SO ACCORDING TO THIS, STIMULATING THE LYMPH NODES CAN ACTIVATE FEMALE HORMONES AND HELP ENLARGE YOUR BREASTS.
SSF
GO FOR IT.
AWWWW! ♥♥♥ YOUR BOOBS ARE SO TEENY!! NARU'S TINY BOOBS!
ADORABLE TINY BOOBS! KYAAA! SO CUTE, NARU~ ♥♥
NARU'S BOOBS ARE ADORABLE! ♥
GRAB
HUFF
MMMM ♥
HUFF
AAAAH HA HA HA HA HA HA HA HA
MY BOOBS ARE GROWING! NOW! RIGHT THIS INSTANT! EVEN BETTER, THIS IS GREAT FAN SERVICE FOR OUR MALE READERS! WORTH IT!
SQUEAK
SQUEAK
SQUEAK
SQUEAK

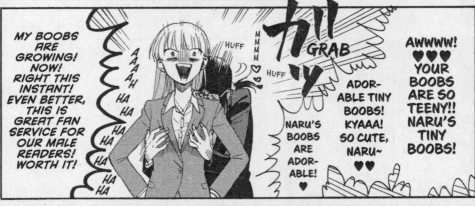

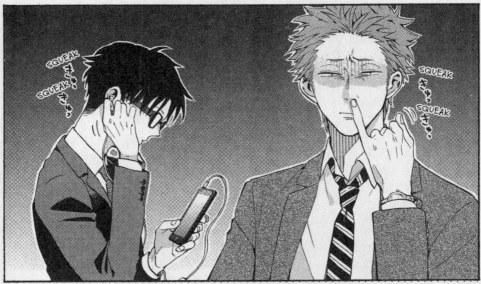

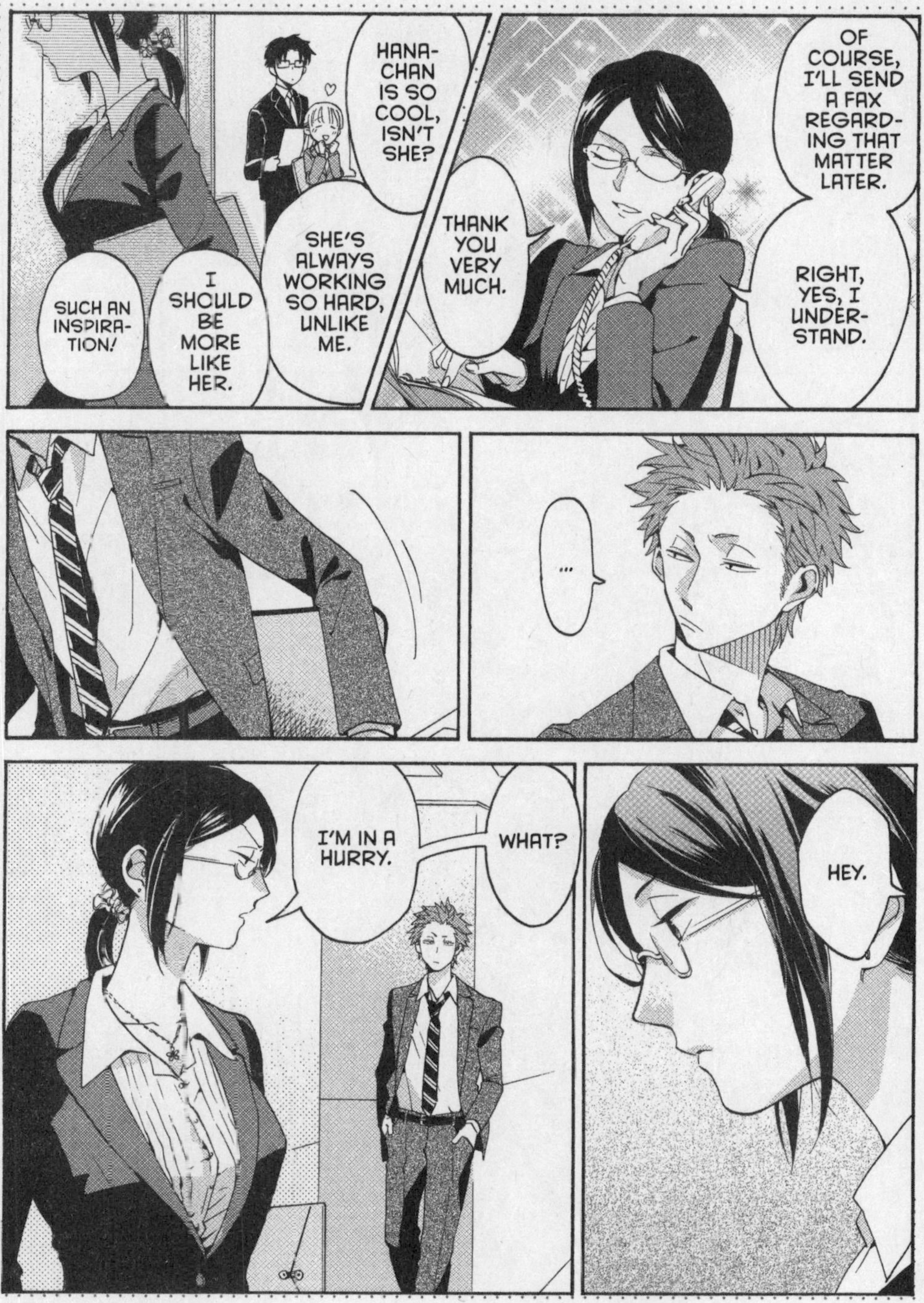
OF COURSE, I'LL SEND A FAX REGARDING THAT MATTER LATER.
RIGHT, YES, I UNDERSTAND.
THANK YOU VERY MUCH.
HANA-CHAN IS SO COOL, ISN'T SHE?
SHE'S ALWAYS WORKING SO HARD, UNLIKE ME.
I SHOULD BE MORE LIKE HER.
SUCH AN INSPIRATION!
...
HEY.
WHAT?
I'M IN A HURRY.

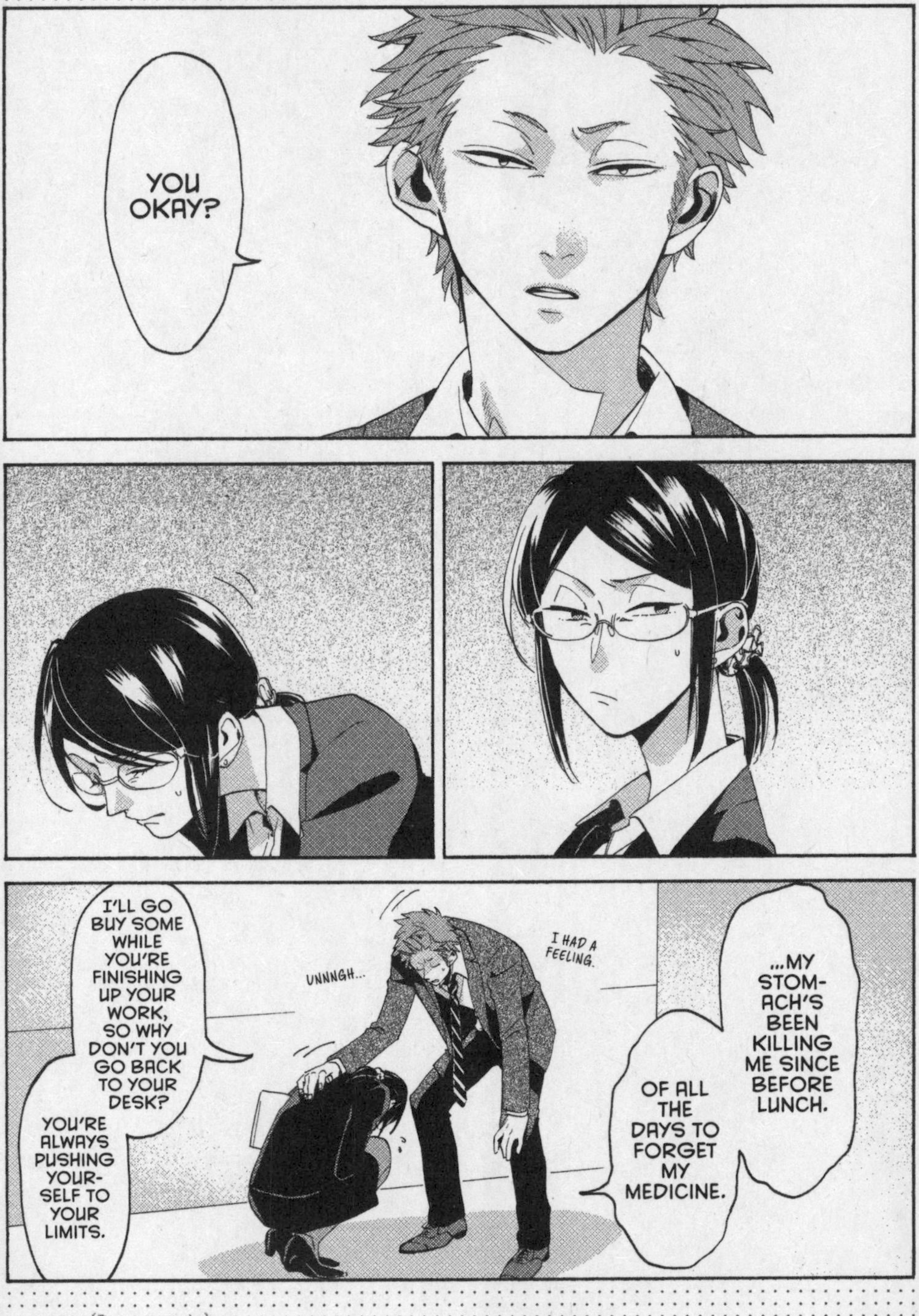
YOU OKAY?
...MY STOMACH'S BEEN KILLING ME SINCE BEFORE LUNCH.
OF ALL THE DAYS TO FORGET MY MEDICINE.
I HAD A FEELING.
UNNNGH...
I'LL GO BUY SOME WHILE YOU'RE FINISHING UP YOUR WORK, SO WHY DON'T YOU GO BACK TO YOUR DESK?
YOU'RE ALWAYS PUSHING YOURSELF TO YOUR LIMITS.

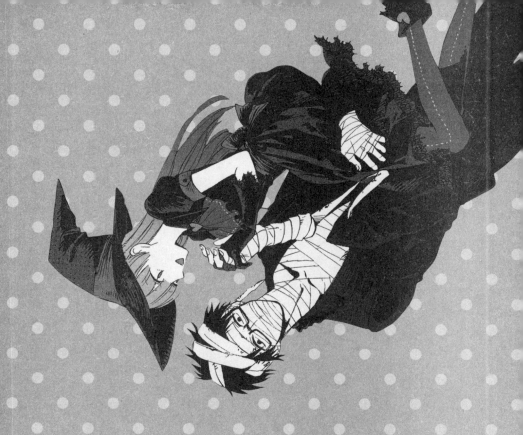

Wotakoi: Love is Hard for Otaku

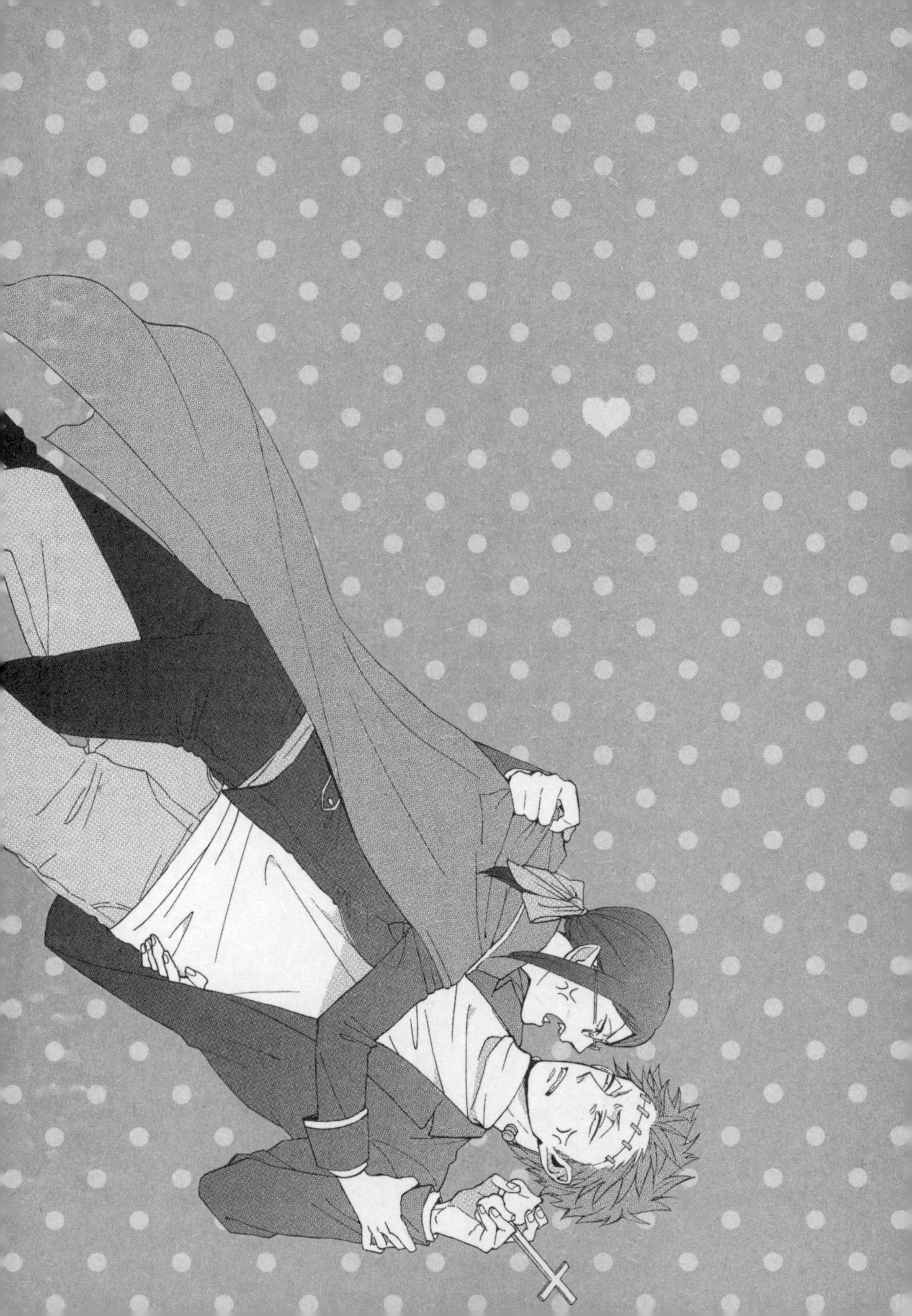

Episode....3

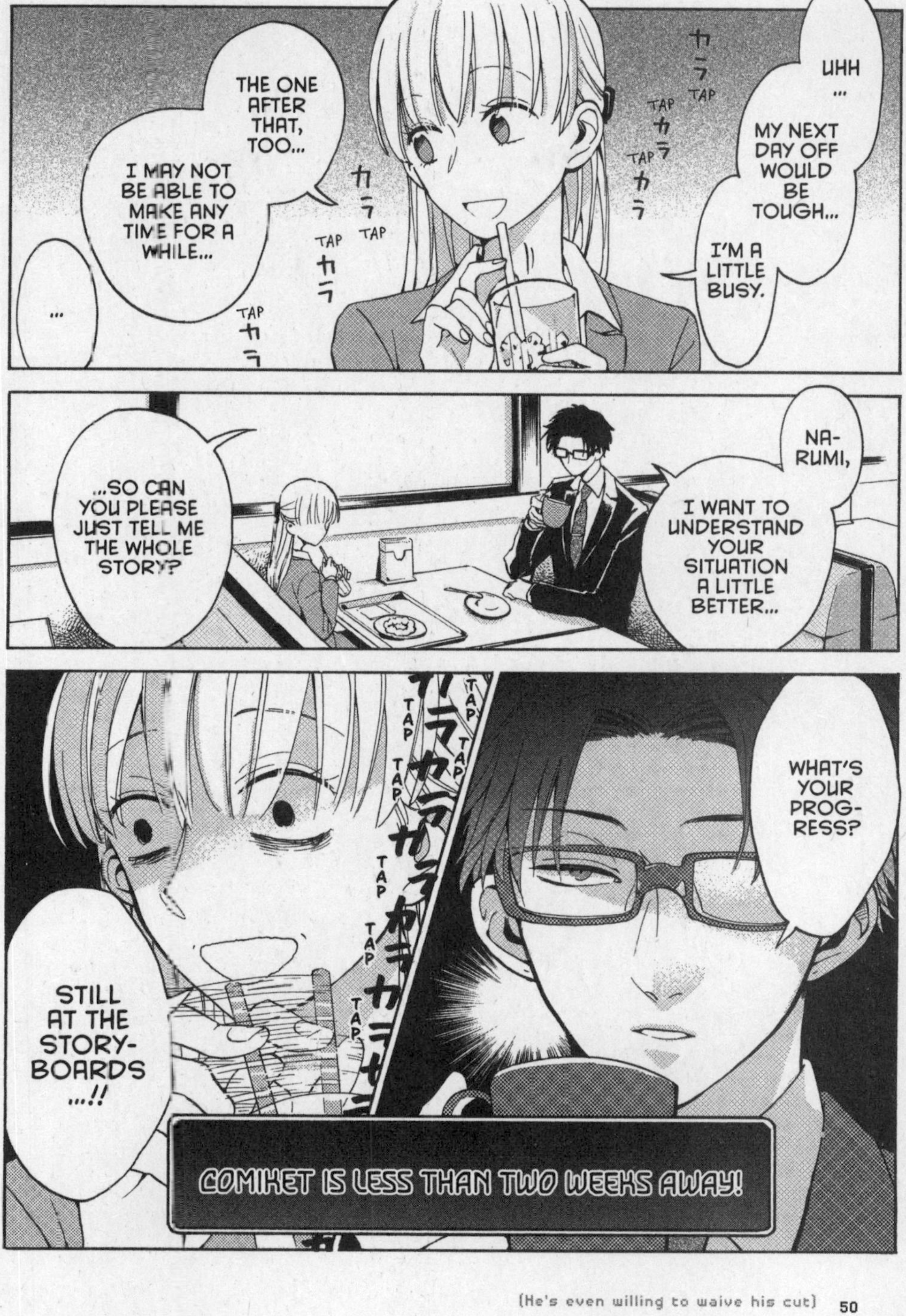
UHH ... MY NEXT DAY OFF WOULD BE TOUGH...
I'M A LITTLE BUSY.
カラ TAP
THE ONE AFTER THAT, TOO...
I MAY NOT BE ABLE TO MAKE ANY TIME FOR A WHILE...
...
NARUMI,
I WANT TO UNDERSTAND YOUR SITUATION A LITTLE BETTER...
...SO CAN YOU PLEASE JUST TELL ME THE WHOLE STORY?
WHAT'S YOUR PROGRESS?
カラ TAP
STILL AT THE STORYBOARDS ...!!
COMIKET IS LESS THAN TWO WEEKS AWAY!

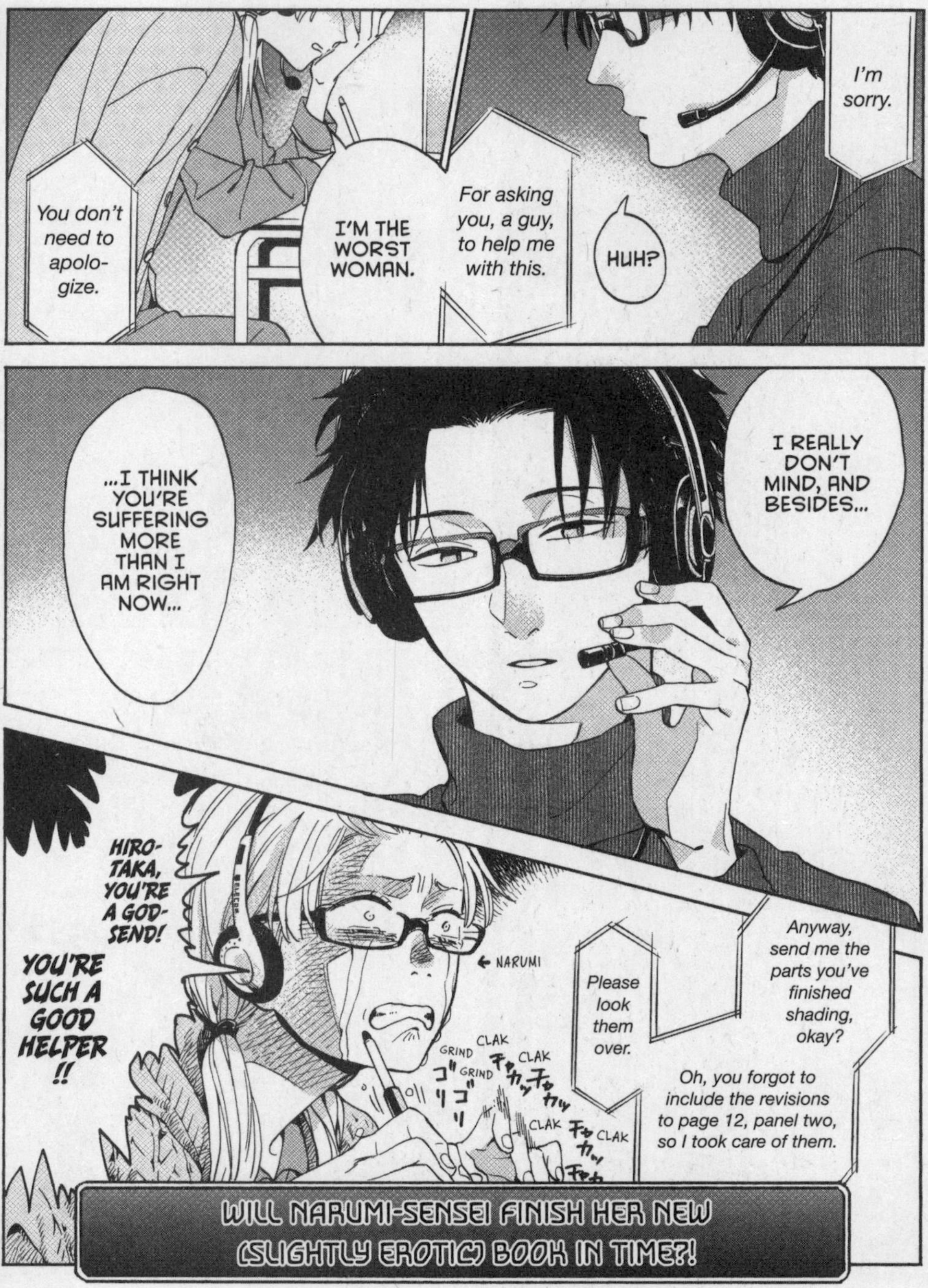

I'm sorry.
HUH?
For asking you, a guy, to help me with this.
I'M THE WORST WOMAN.
You don't need to apologize.
I REALLY DON'T MIND, AND BESIDES...
...I THINK YOU'RE SUFFERING MORE THAN I AM RIGHT NOW...
Anyway, send me the parts you've finished shading, okay?
Oh, you forgot to include the revisions to page 12, panel two, so I took care of them.
Please look them over.
CLAK CLAK CLAK CLAK
GRIND GRIND
← NARUMI
HIRO-TAKA, YOU'RE A GOD-SEND!
YOU'RE SUCH A GOOD HELPER!!
WILL NARUMI-SENSEI FINISH HER NEW (SLIGHTLY EROTIC) BOOK IN TIME?!

 (The deadline is only three hours away)

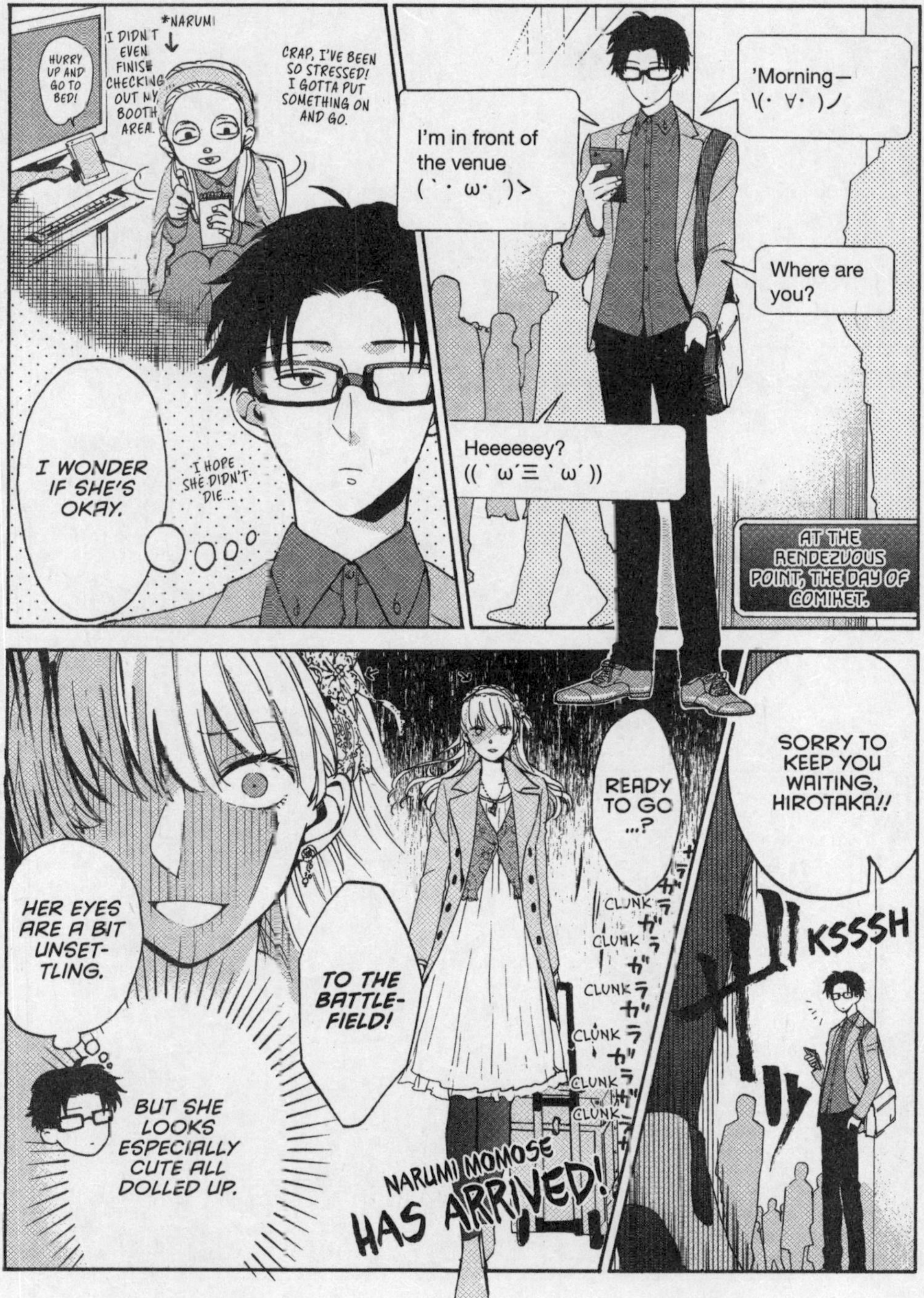

'Morning— \(・∀・)ノ
I'm in front of the venue (`・ω・´)>
Where are you?
Heeeeeey? ((`ω´三`ω´))
AT THE RENDEZVOUS POINT, THE DAY OF COMIKET.
*NARUMI
CRAP, I'VE BEEN SO STRESSED! I GOTTA PUT SOMETHING ON AND GO.
I DIDN'T EVEN FINISH CHECKING OUT MY BOOTH AREA.
HURRY UP AND GO TO BED!
I HOPE SHE DIDN'T DIE...
I WONDER IF SHE'S OKAY.
SORRY TO KEEP YOU WAITING, HIROTAKA!!
KSSSH
READY TO GO ...?
CLUNK CLUNK CLUNK CLUNK CLUNK CLUNK
TO THE BATTLE-FIELD!
HER EYES ARE A BIT UNSET-TLING.
BUT SHE LOOKS ESPECIALLY CUTE ALL DOLLED UP.
NARUMI MOMOSE HAS ARRIVED!

(Off to battle)

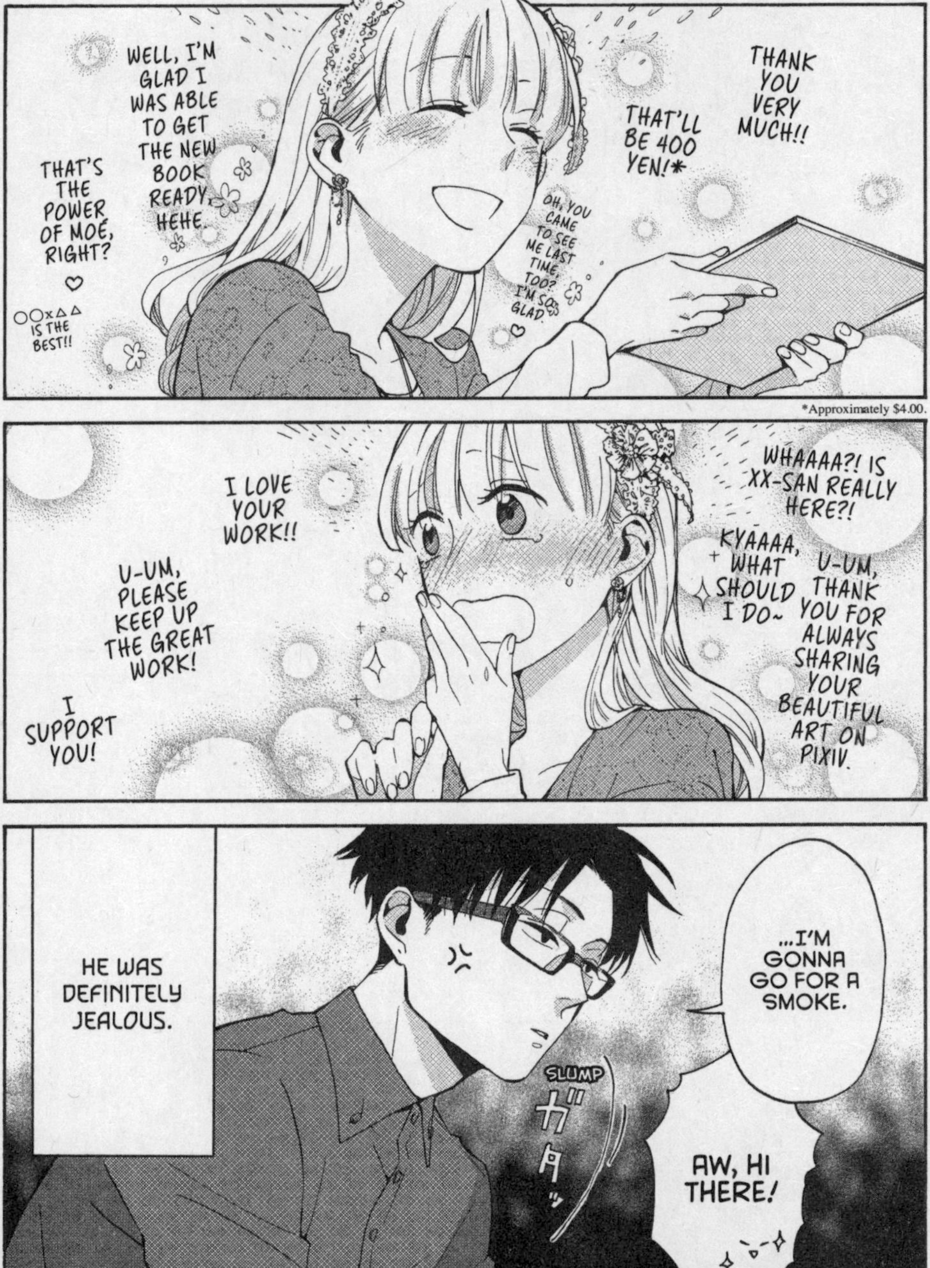
THANK YOU VERY MUCH!!
THAT'LL BE 400 YEN!*
OH, YOU CAME TO SEE ME LAST TIME, TOO? I'M SO GLAD. ♡
WELL, I'M GLAD I WAS ABLE TO GET THE NEW BOOK READY, HEHE.
THAT'S THE POWER OF MOÉ, RIGHT? ♡
○○x△△ IS THE BEST!!
WHAAAA?! IS XX-SAN REALLY HERE?!
KYAAAA, WHAT SHOULD I DO~
U-UM, THANK YOU FOR ALWAYS SHARING YOUR BEAUTIFUL ART ON PIXIV.
I LOVE YOUR WORK!!
U-UM, PLEASE KEEP UP THE GREAT WORK!
I SUPPORT YOU!
...I'M GONNA GO FOR A SMOKE.
SLUMP
ガタッ
HE WAS DEFINITELY JEALOUS.
AW, HI THERE!

*Approximately $4.00.

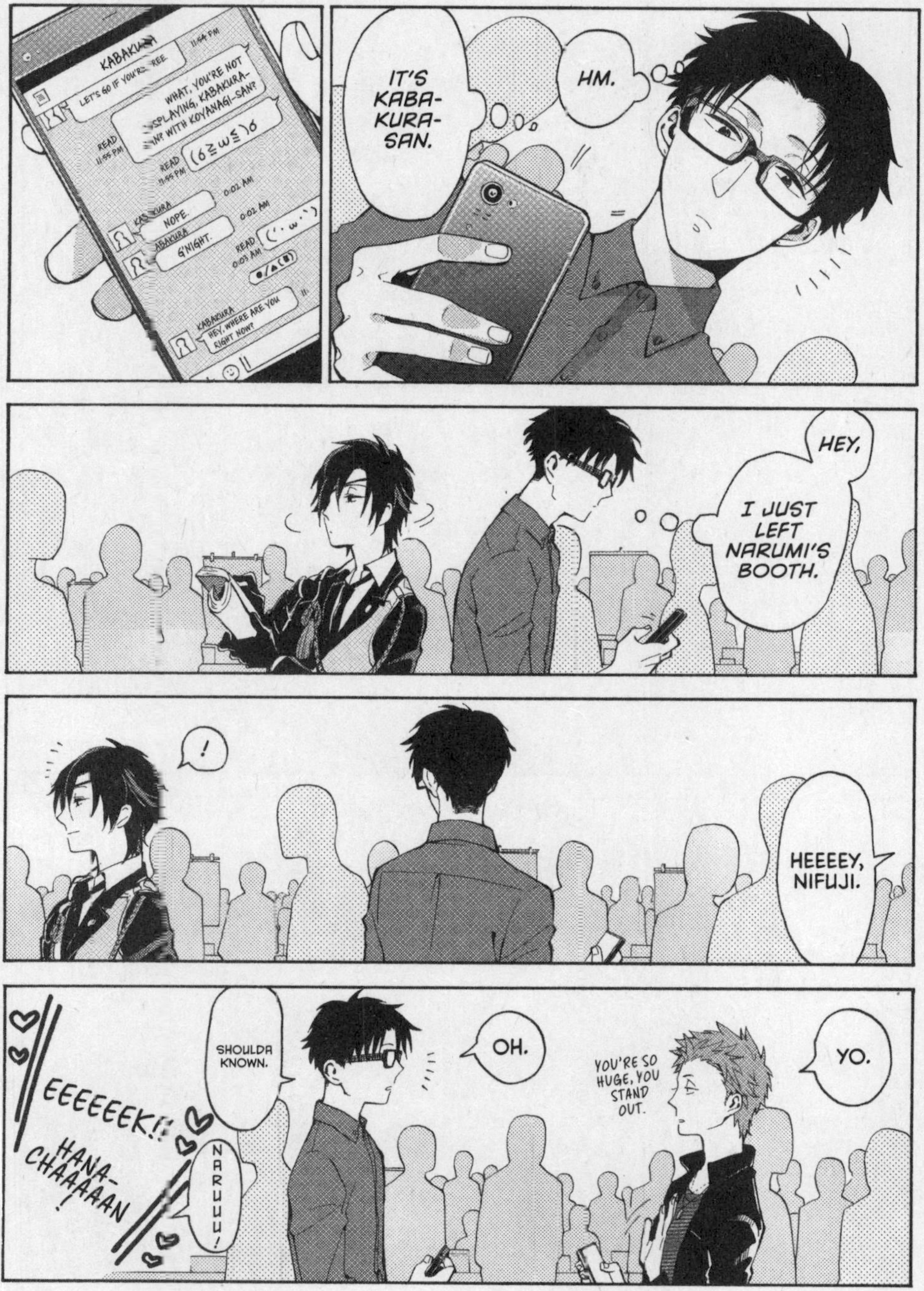
HM.
IT'S KABAKURA-SAN.
KABAKU
11:54 PM
LET'S GO IF YOU'R REE.
WHAT, YOU'RE NOT
SPLAYING, KABAKURA-
WITH KOYANAGI-SAN?
READ 11:55 PM
(6≧ω≦)6
READ 11:55 PM
0:02 AM
NOPE.
0:02 AM
ABAKURA
G'NIGHT.
(´・ω・`)
READ 0:03 AM
●/▲(■)
KABAKURA
HEY, WHERE ARE YOU RIGHT NOW?
HEY, I JUST LEFT NARUMI'S BOOTH.
!
HEEEEY, NIFUJI.
YO.
YOU'RE SO HUGE, YOU STAND OUT.
OH.
SHOULDA KNOWN.
NARUUU!
EEEEEEK!!
HANA-CHAAAAAN!

(That hot guy looks familiar)

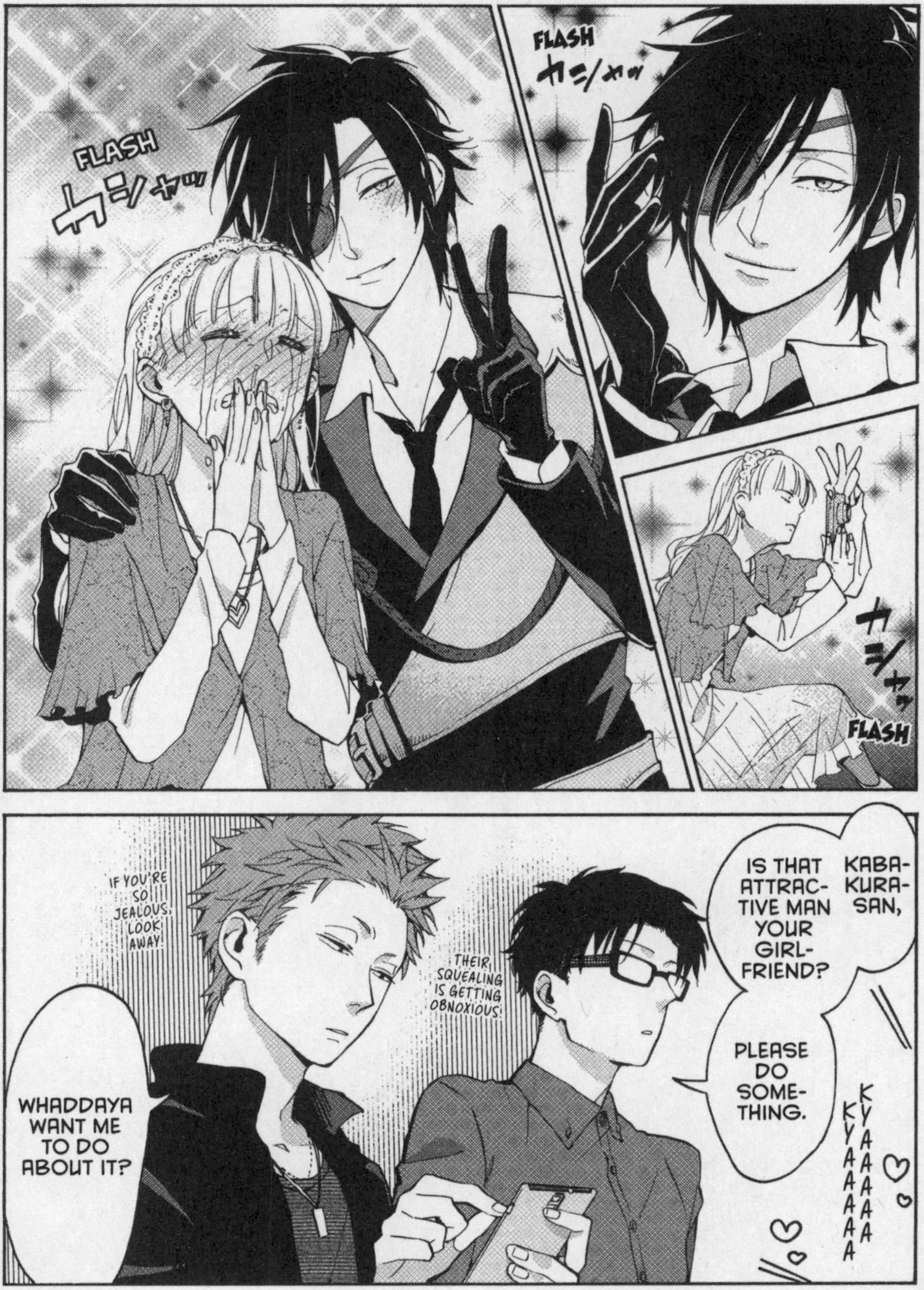
FLASH
カシャッ
カシャッ
FLASH
FLASH
カシャッ
KABA-KURA-SAN,
IS THAT ATTRACTIVE MAN YOUR GIRLFRIEND?
PLEASE DO SOMETHING.
KYAAAAAAA
KYAAAAAAA
THEIR SQUEALING IS GETTING OBNOXIOUS.
IF YOU'RE SO JEALOUS, LOOK AWAY.
WHADDAYA WANT ME TO DO ABOUT IT?

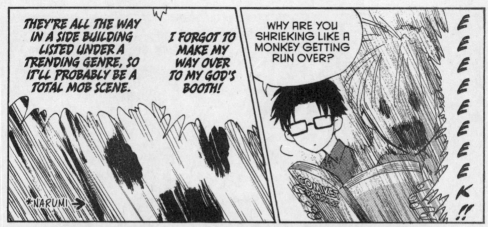

EEEEEEEEK!!
WHY ARE YOU SHRIEKING LIKE A MONKEY GETTING RUN OVER?
COMIKET PAMPHLET
I FORGOT TO MAKE MY WAY OVER TO MY GOD'S BOOTH!
THEY'RE ALL THE WAY IN A SIDE BUILDING LISTED UNDER A TRENDING GENRE, SO IT'LL PROBABLY BE A TOTAL MOB SCENE.
*NARUMI
IT'S NO USE, I SHOULD JUST FORGET ABOUT IT...
THEY PROBABLY ALREADY SOLD OUT TODAY...
I CAN BUY DOJINSHI ANYTIME, AFTER ALL...
YOU SHOULD GO.
SOME OF THEIR BOOKS ARE ONLY AVAILABLE TODAY, RIGHT?
I'LL WATCH OVER YOUR BOOTH.
JUST BRING ME BACK SOME TEA.
SHE THOUGHT HE MIGHT BE A GOD.

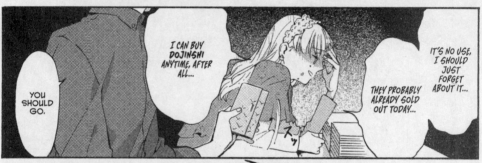

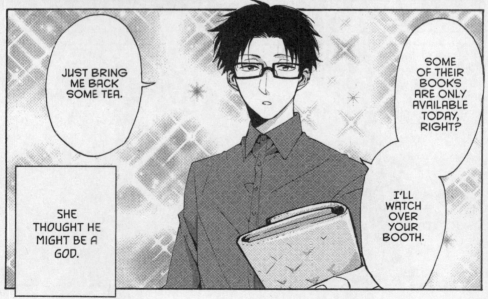

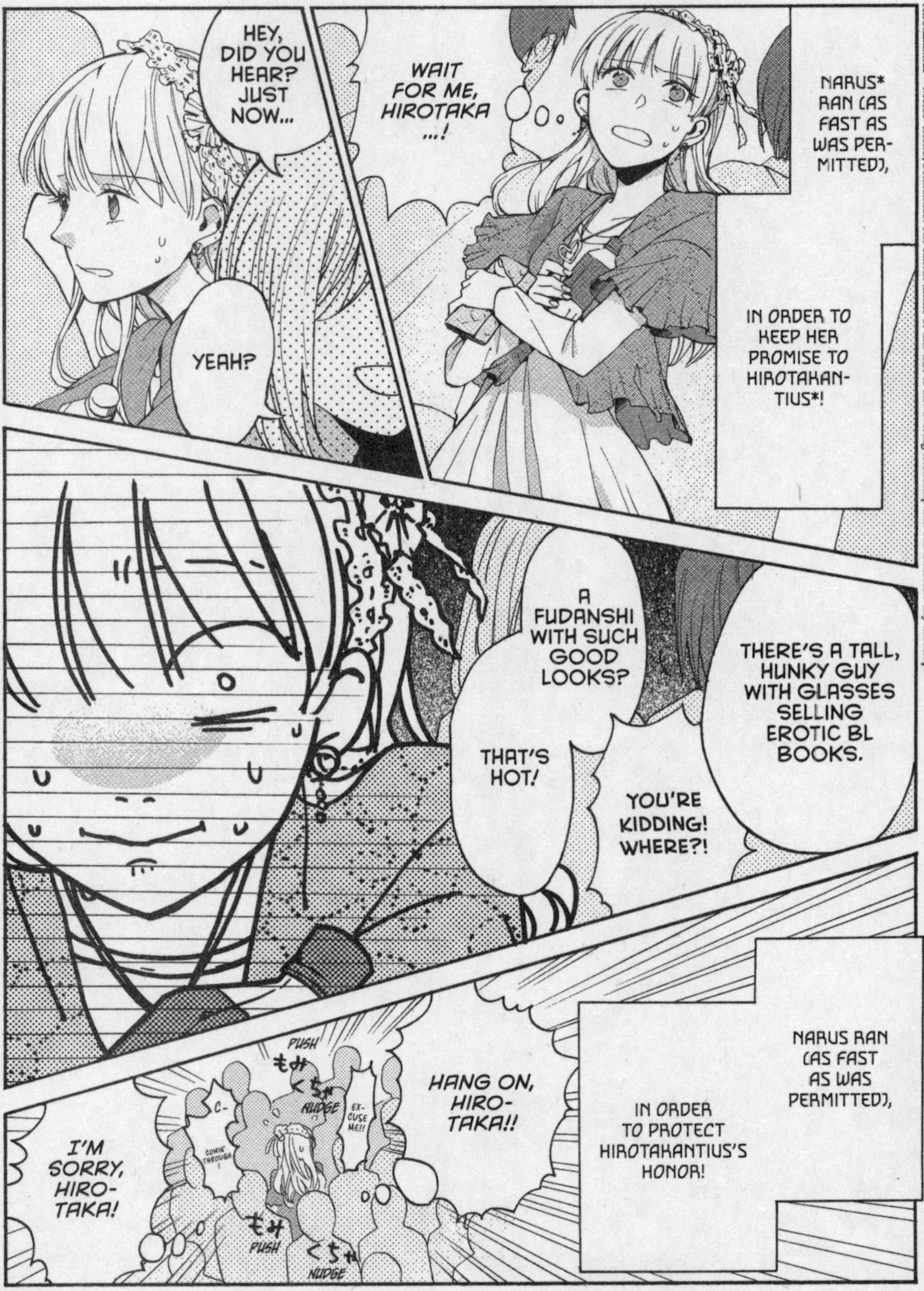
NARUS* RAN (AS FAST AS WAS PER-MITTED),
IN ORDER TO KEEP HER PROMISE TO HIROTAKAN-TIUS*!
WAIT FOR ME, HIROTAKA ...!
HEY, DID YOU HEAR? JUST NOW...
YEAH?
THERE'S A TALL, HUNKY GUY WITH GLASSES SELLING EROTIC BL BOOKS.
A FUDANSHI WITH SUCH GOOD LOOKS?
THAT'S HOT!
YOU'RE KIDDING! WHERE?!
NARUS RAN (AS FAST AS WAS PERMITTED),
IN ORDER TO PROTECT HIROTAKANTIUS'S HONOR!
HANG ON, HIRO-TAKA!!
PUSH
NUDGE
EX-CUSE ME!!
C-
COMIN' THROUGH!
I'M SORRY, HIRO-TAKA!
PUSH
NUDGE

*An homage to the short story and anime film, *Run, Melos!*, written by Osamu Dazai. Narumi as Narus = Melos, and Hirotaka as Hirotakantius = Melos' friend, Selinuntius. The salient theme of this title is unwavering friendship that can transcend any hardship.

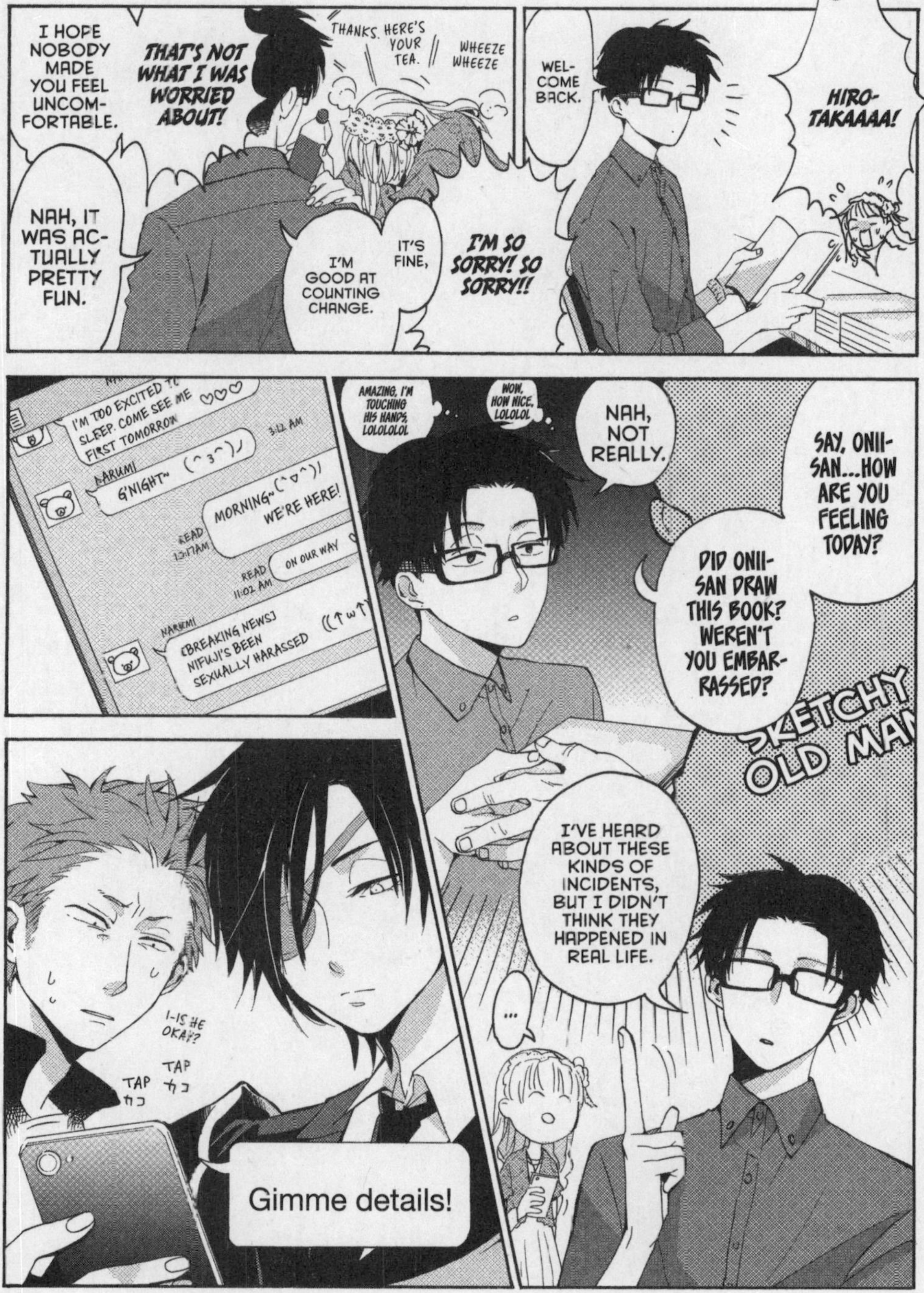
HIRO-TAKAAAA!
WEL-COME BACK.
I'M SO SORRY! SO SORRY!!
IT'S FINE,
I'M GOOD AT COUNTING CHANGE.
THANKS. HERE'S YOUR TEA.
WHEEZE WHEEZE
THAT'S NOT WHAT I WAS WORRIED ABOUT!
I HOPE NOBODY MADE YOU FEEL UNCOM-FORTABLE.
NAH, IT WAS AC-TUALLY PRETTY FUN.
SAY, ONII-SAN...HOW ARE YOU FEELING TODAY?
NAH, NOT REALLY.
WOW, HOW NICE, LOLOLOL
AMAZING, I'M TOUCHING HIS HANDS, LOLOLOLOL
DID ONII-SAN DRAW THIS BOOK? WEREN'T YOU EMBAR-RASSED?
SKETCHY OLD MAN
I'VE HEARD ABOUT THESE KINDS OF INCIDENTS, BUT I DIDN'T THINK THEY HAPPENED IN REAL LIFE.
...
I'M TOO EXCITED TO SLEEP. COME SEE ME FIRST TOMORROW ♡♡♡
3:12 AM
NARUMI
G'NIGHT~ (^3^)ノ
MORNING~(^▽^)ノ WE'RE HERE!
READ 10:17 AM
ON OUR WAY
READ 11:02 AM
NARUMI
[BREAKING NEWS] NIFUJI'S BEEN SEXUALLY HARASSED ((↑w↑))
I-IS HE OKAY?
TAP
TAP
Gimme details!

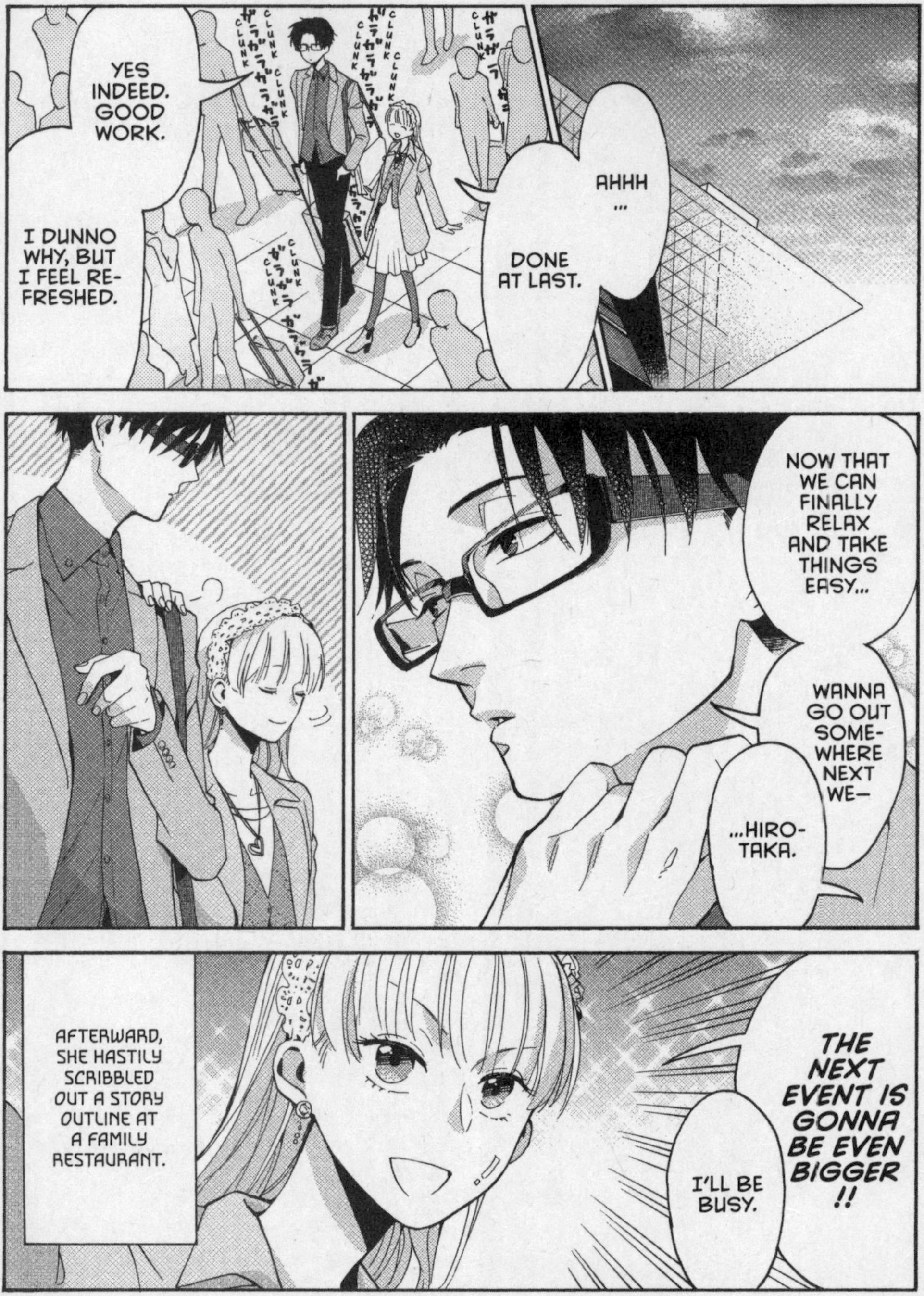
AHHH...
DONE AT LAST.
YES INDEED. GOOD WORK.
I DUNNO WHY, BUT I FEEL REFRESHED.
CLUNK CLUNK
NOW THAT WE CAN FINALLY RELAX AND TAKE THINGS EASY...
WANNA GO OUT SOMEWHERE NEXT WE—
...HIROTAKA.
THE NEXT EVENT IS GONNA BE EVEN BIGGER!!
I'LL BE BUSY.
AFTERWARD, SHE HASTILY SCRIBBLED OUT A STORY OUTLINE AT A FAMILY RESTAURANT.

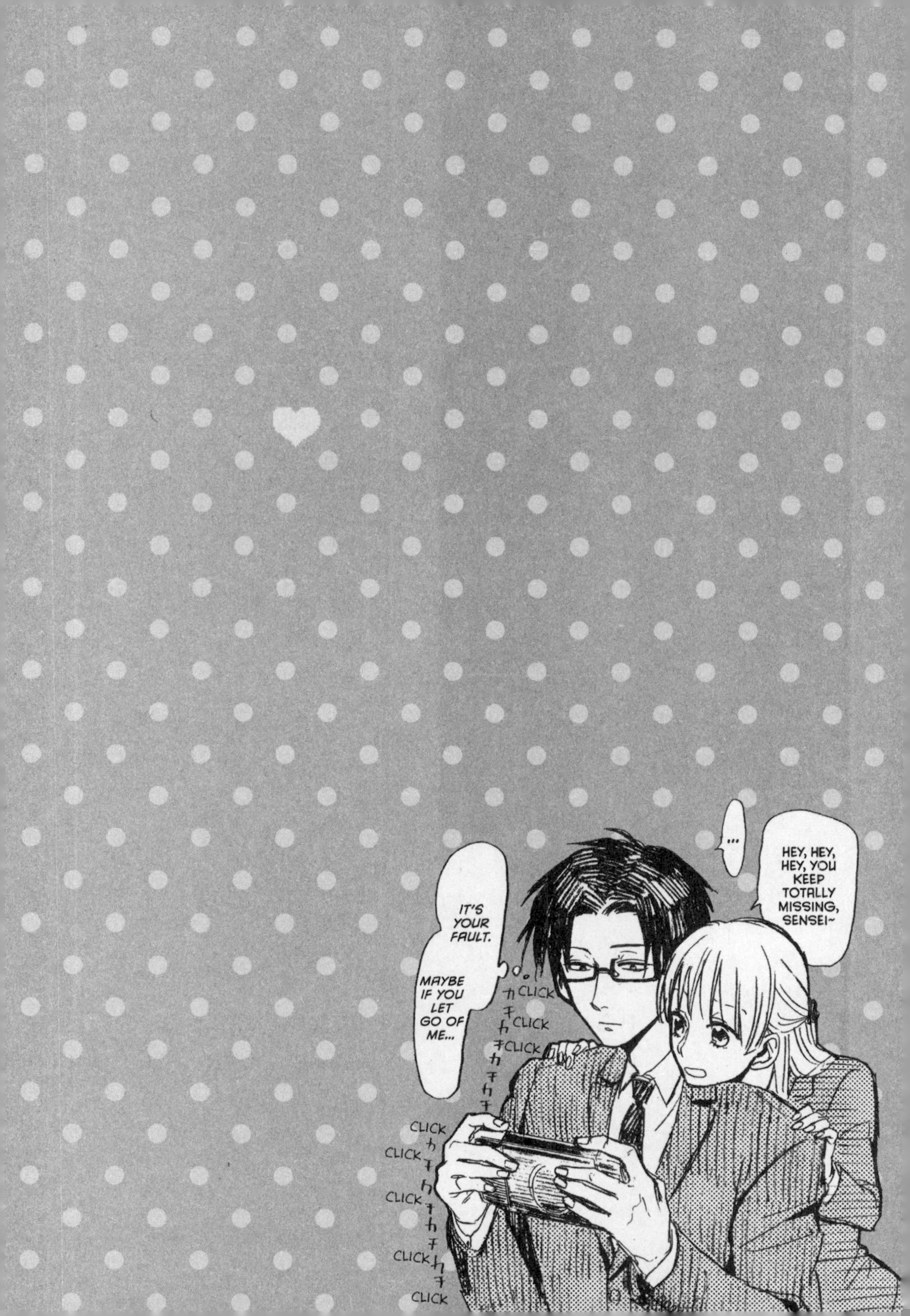
...
HEY, HEY, HEY, YOU KEEP TOTALLY MISSING, SENSEI~
IT'S YOUR FAULT.
MAYBE IF YOU LET GO OF ME...
CLICK
CLICK
CLICK
CLICK
CLICK
CLICK
CLICK
CLICK

Episode.... 4

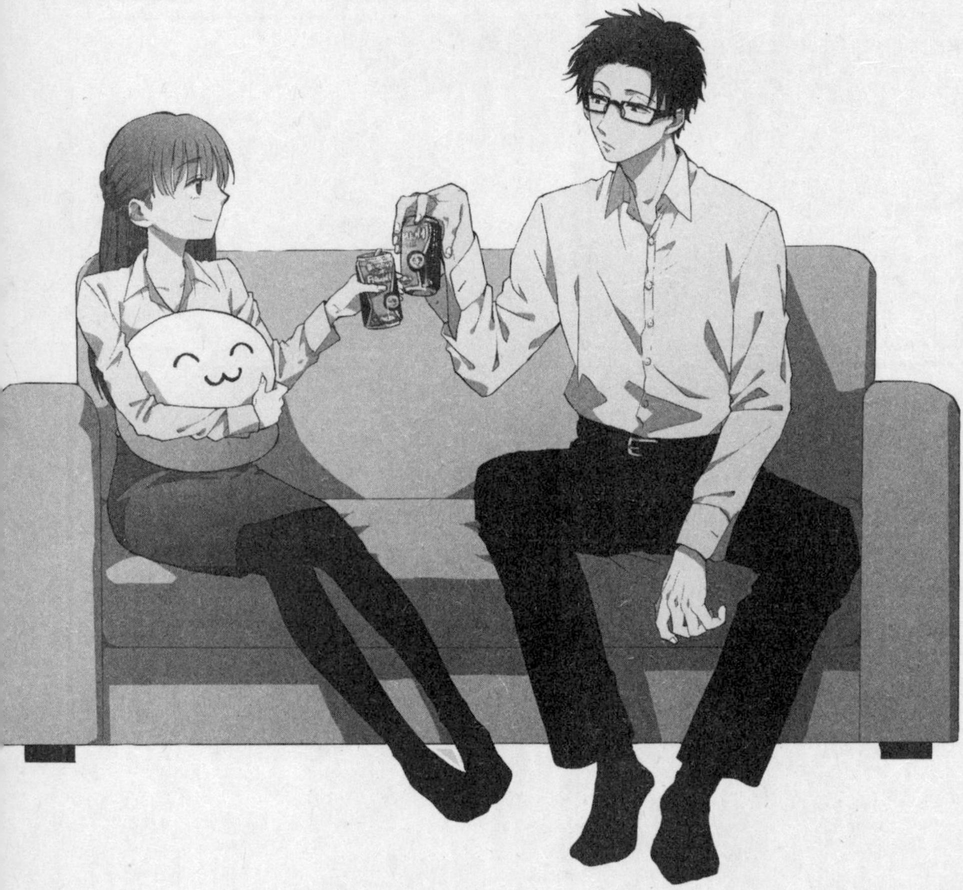

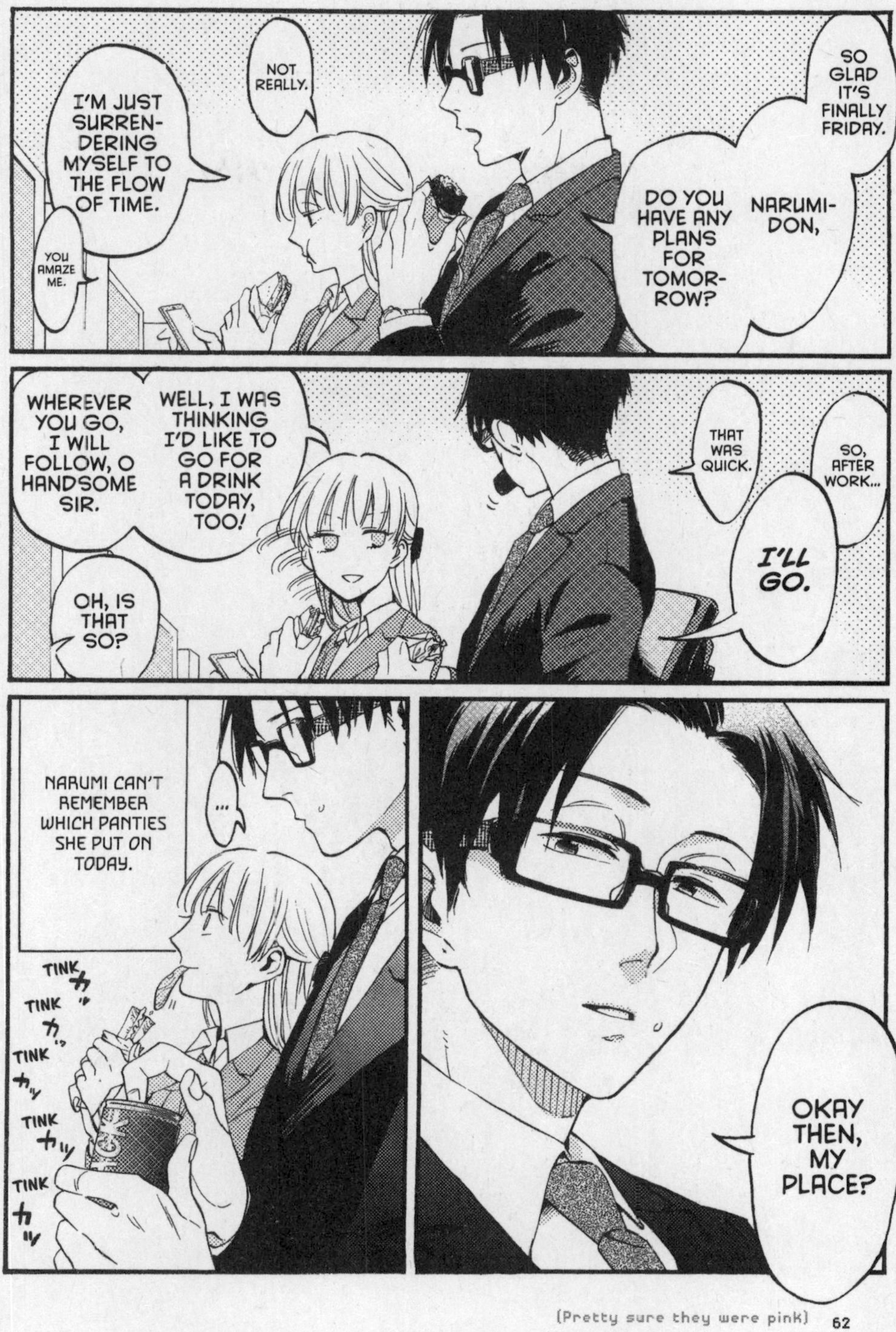
SO GLAD IT'S FINALLY FRIDAY.
NARUMI-DON, DO YOU HAVE ANY PLANS FOR TOMORROW?
NOT REALLY.
I'M JUST SURRENDERING MYSELF TO THE FLOW OF TIME.
YOU AMAZE ME.
SO, AFTER WORK...
I'LL GO.
THAT WAS QUICK.
WELL, I WAS THINKING I'D LIKE TO GO FOR A DRINK TODAY, TOO!
WHEREVER YOU GO, I WILL FOLLOW, O HANDSOME SIR.
OH, IS THAT SO?
OKAY THEN, MY PLACE?
...
NARUMI CAN'T REMEMBER WHICH PANTIES SHE PUT ON TODAY.
TINK
TINK
TINK
TINK
TINK

(Pretty sure they were pink)

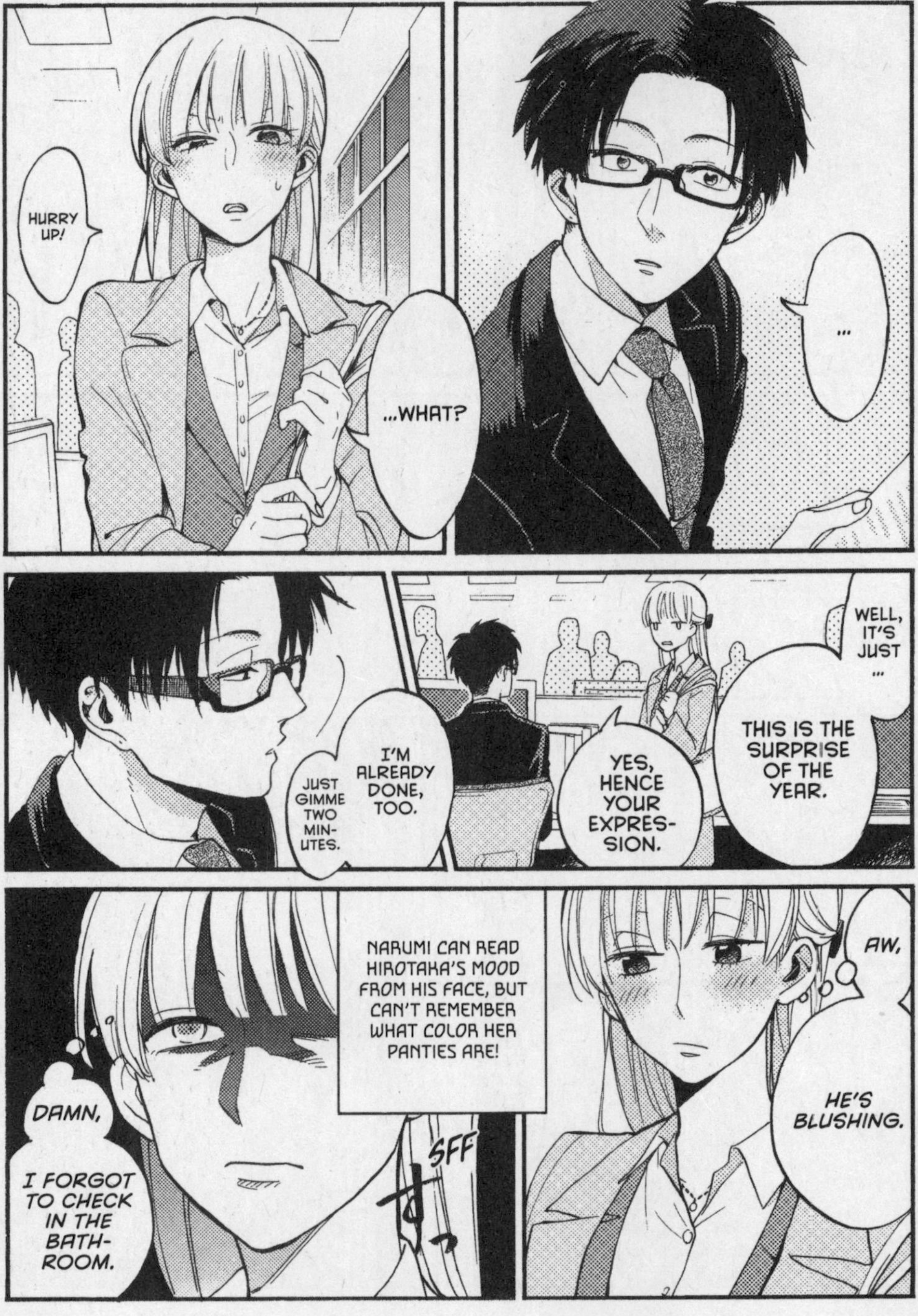
...
...WHAT?
HURRY UP!
WELL, IT'S JUST ...
THIS IS THE SURPRISE OF THE YEAR.
YES, HENCE YOUR EXPRES-SION.
I'M ALREADY DONE, TOO.
JUST GIMME TWO MIN-UTES.
AW,
HE'S BLUSHING.
NARUMI CAN READ HIROTAKA'S MOOD FROM HIS FACE, BUT CAN'T REMEMBER WHAT COLOR HER PANTIES ARE!
SFF
DAMN,
I FORGOT TO CHECK IN THE BATH-ROOM.

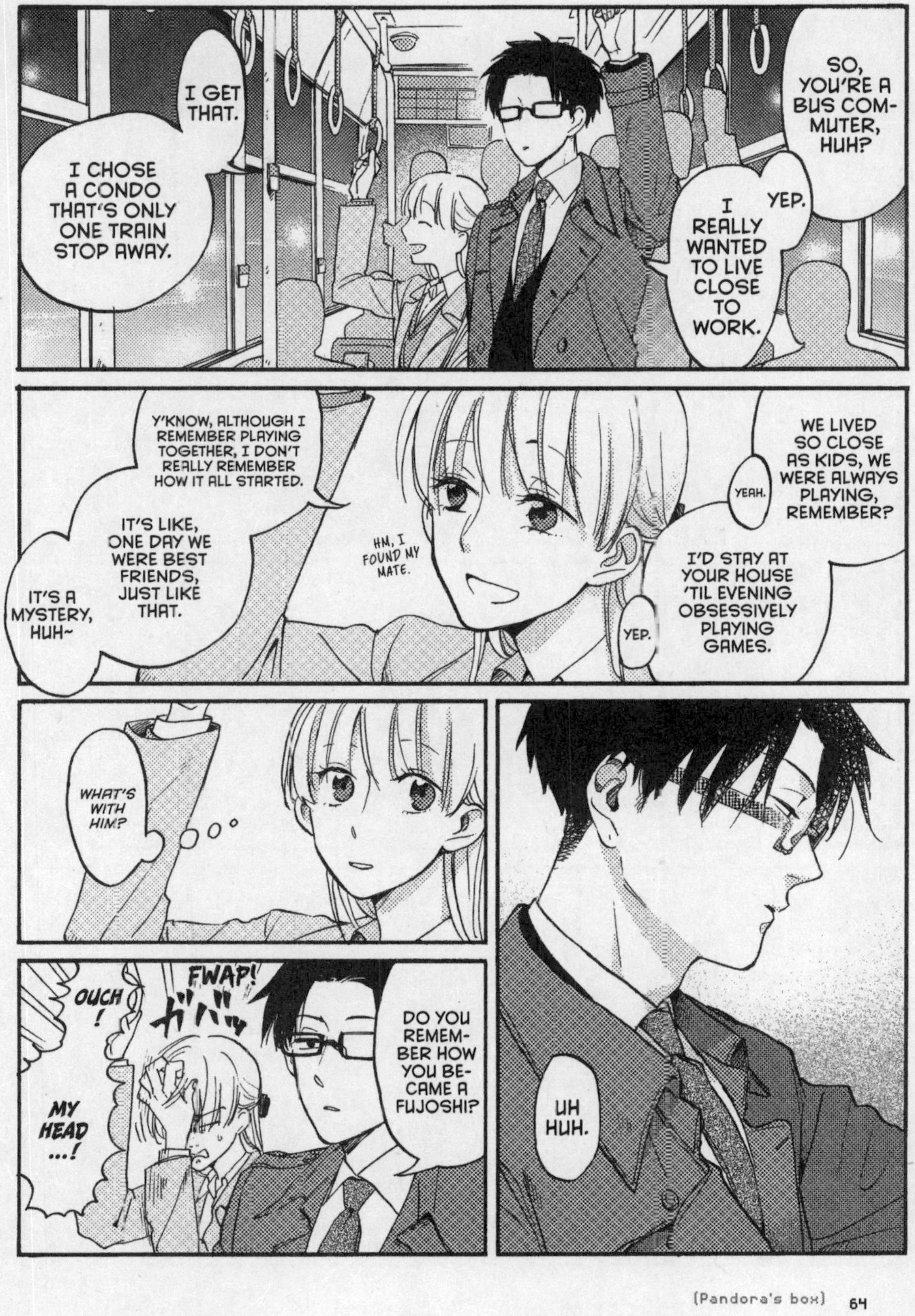
SO, YOU'RE A BUS COM-MUTER, HUH?
YEP.
I REALLY WANTED TO LIVE CLOSE TO WORK.
I GET THAT.
I CHOSE A CONDO THAT'S ONLY ONE TRAIN STOP AWAY.
WE LIVED SO CLOSE AS KIDS, WE WERE ALWAYS PLAYING, REMEMBER?
YEAH.
I'D STAY AT YOUR HOUSE 'TIL EVENING OBSESSIVELY PLAYING GAMES.
YEP.
Y'KNOW, ALTHOUGH I REMEMBER PLAYING TOGETHER, I DON'T REALLY REMEMBER HOW IT ALL STARTED.
HM, I FOUND MY MATE.
IT'S LIKE, ONE DAY WE WERE BEST FRIENDS, JUST LIKE THAT.
IT'S A MYSTERY, HUH~
UH HUH.
WHAT'S WITH HIM?
DO YOU REMEM-BER HOW YOU BE-CAME A FUJOSHI?
FWAP!
ガバッ
OUCH!
MY HEAD ...!

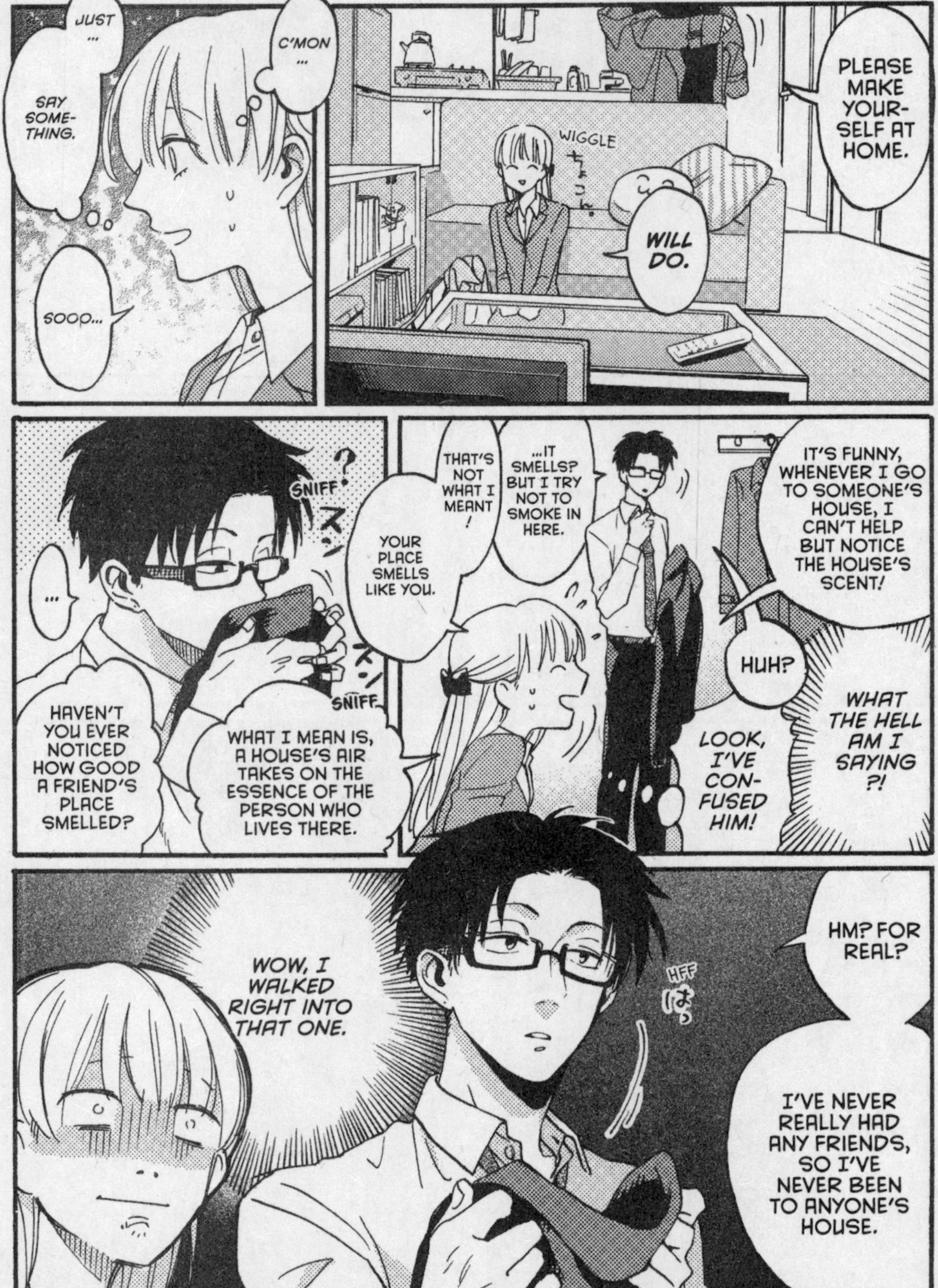
PLEASE MAKE YOURSELF AT HOME.
WIGGLE
WILL DO.
C'MON ...
JUST ... SAY SOMETHING.
SOOO...
IT'S FUNNY, WHENEVER I GO TO SOMEONE'S HOUSE, I CAN'T HELP BUT NOTICE THE HOUSE'S SCENT!
...IT SMELLS? BUT I TRY NOT TO SMOKE IN HERE.
THAT'S NOT WHAT I MEANT!
YOUR PLACE SMELLS LIKE YOU.
HUH?
WHAT THE HELL AM I SAYING?!
LOOK, I'VE CONFUSED HIM!
SNIFF
...
SNIFF
WHAT I MEAN IS, A HOUSE'S AIR TAKES ON THE ESSENCE OF THE PERSON WHO LIVES THERE.
HAVEN'T YOU EVER NOTICED HOW GOOD A FRIEND'S PLACE SMELLED?
HM? FOR REAL?
HFF
I'VE NEVER REALLY HAD ANY FRIENDS, SO I'VE NEVER BEEN TO ANYONE'S HOUSE.
WOW, I WALKED RIGHT INTO THAT ONE.

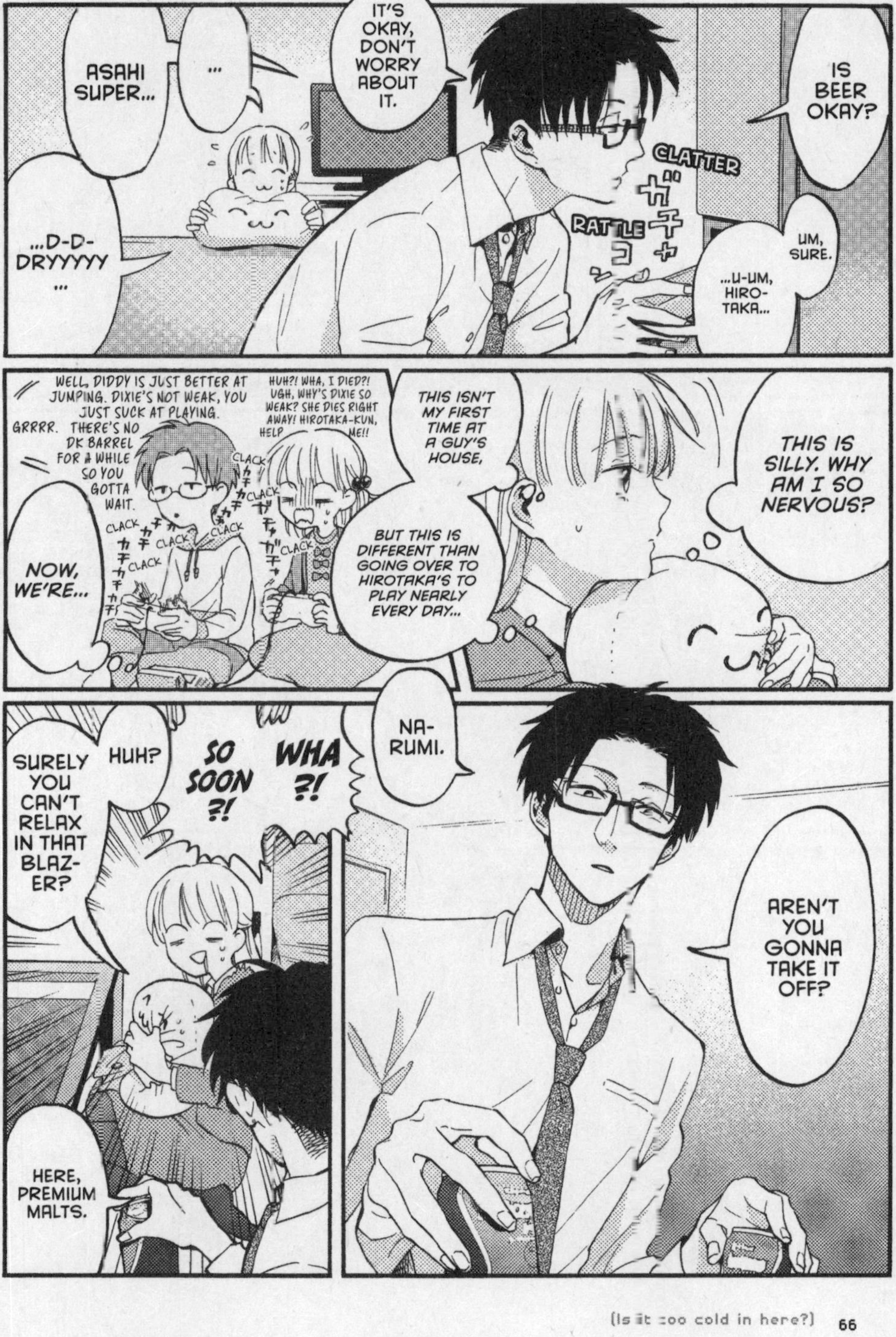
IS BEER OKAY?
CLATTER
RATTLE
UM, SURE.
...U-UM, HIRO-TAKA...
IT'S OKAY, DON'T WORRY ABOUT IT.
...
ASAHI SUPER...
...D-D-DRYYYYY ...
THIS IS SILLY. WHY AM I SO NERVOUS?
THIS ISN'T MY FIRST TIME AT A GUY'S HOUSE,
BUT THIS IS DIFFERENT THAN GOING OVER TO HIROTAKA'S TO PLAY NEARLY EVERY DAY...
HUH?! WHA, I DIED?! UGH, WHY'S DIXIE SO WEAK? SHE DIES RIGHT AWAY! HIROTAKA-KUN, HELP ME!!
WELL, DIDDY IS JUST BETTER AT JUMPING. DIXIE'S NOT WEAK, YOU JUST SUCK AT PLAYING.
GRRRR. THERE'S NO DK BARREL FOR A WHILE SO YOU GOTTA WAIT.
CLACK
CLACK
CLACK
CLACK
CLACK
CLACK
NOW, WE'RE...
NA-RUMI.
AREN'T YOU GONNA TAKE IT OFF?
WHA ?!
SO SOON ?!
HUH?
SURELY YOU CAN'T RELAX IN THAT BLAZER?
HERE, PREMIUM MALTS.

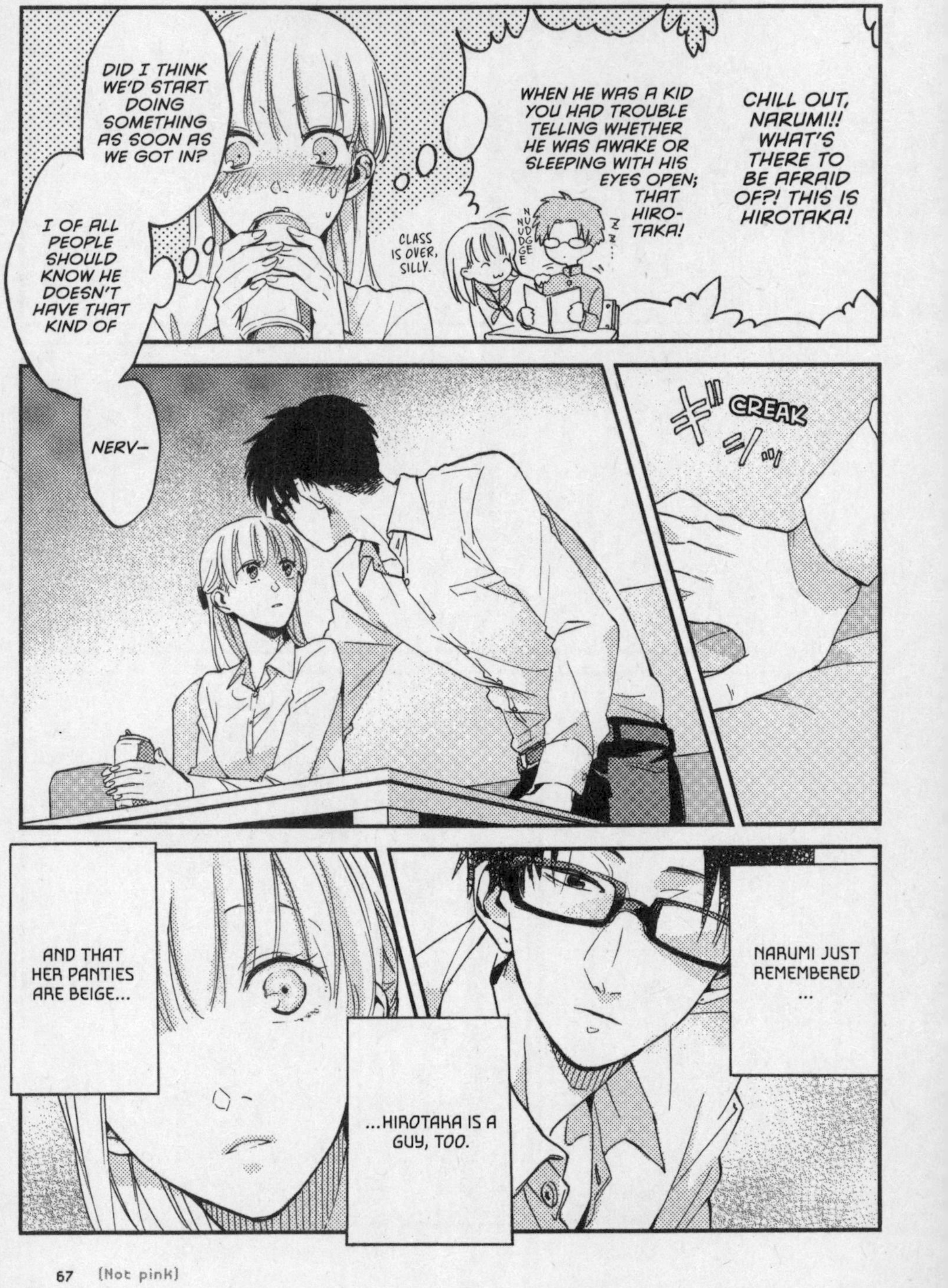
CHILL OUT, NARUMI!! WHAT'S THERE TO BE AFRAID OF?! THIS IS HIROTAKA!
WHEN HE WAS A KID YOU HAD TROUBLE TELLING WHETHER HE WAS AWAKE OR SLEEPING WITH HIS EYES OPEN; THAT HIRO-TAKA!
Z Z...
NUDGE
CLASS IS OVER, SILLY.
DID I THINK WE'D START DOING SOMETHING AS SOON AS WE GOT IN?
I OF ALL PEOPLE SHOULD KNOW HE DOESN'T HAVE THAT KIND OF
NERV—
CREAK
NARUMI JUST REMEMBERED ...
...HIROTAKA IS A GUY, TOO.
AND THAT HER PANTIES ARE BEIGE...

 (Not pink)

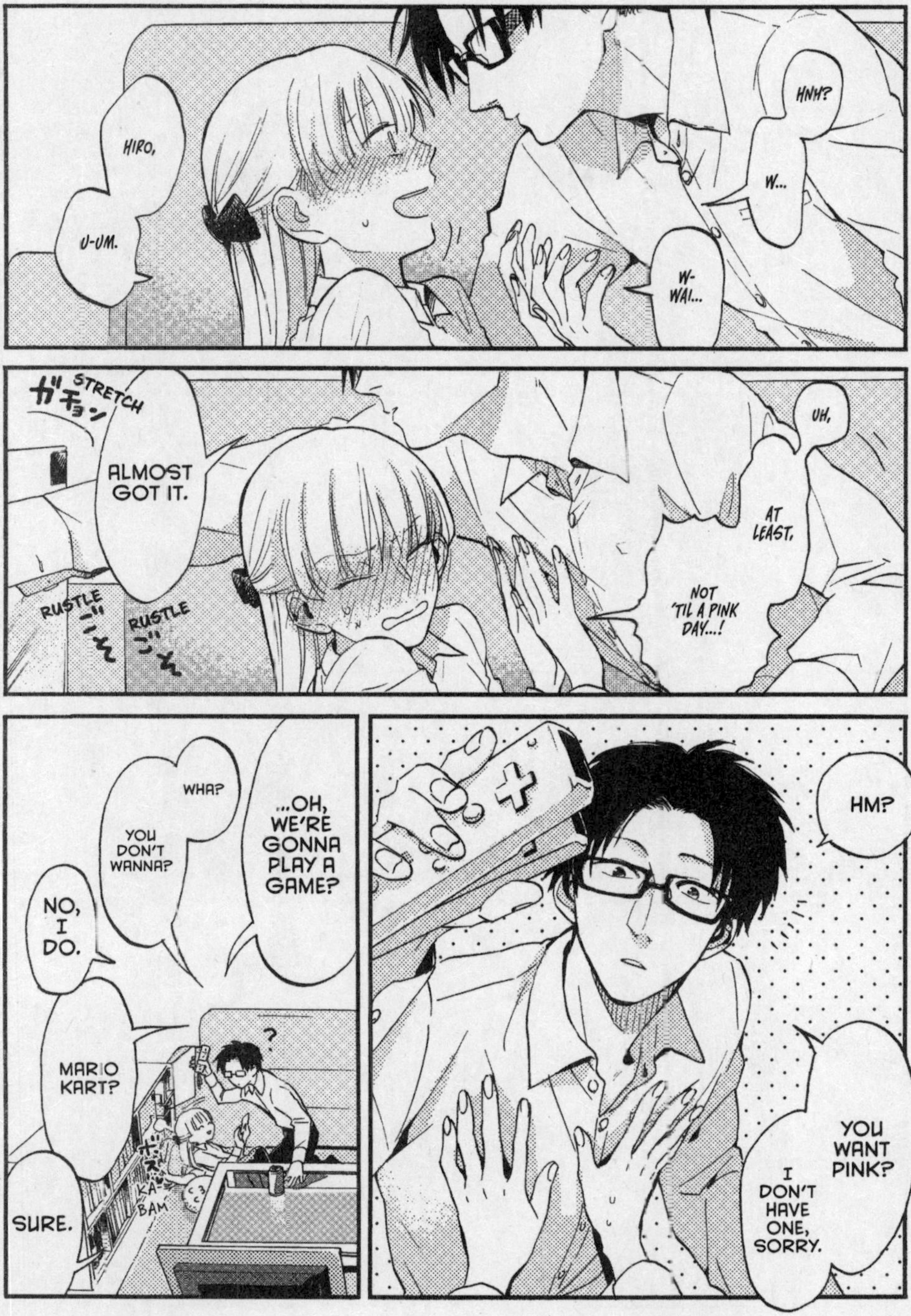
HNH?
W...
W-WAI...
HIRO,
U-UM.
UH,
AT LEAST.
NOT 'TIL A PINK DAY...!
ALMOST GOT IT.
ガチョン
STRETCH
RUSTLE
ごそ
RUSTLE
ごそ
HM?
YOU WANT PINK?
I DON'T HAVE ONE, SORRY.
...OH, WE'RE GONNA PLAY A GAME?
WHA?
YOU DON'T WANNA?
NO, I DO.
MARIO KART?
KA-BAM
SURE.

(There was no pink)

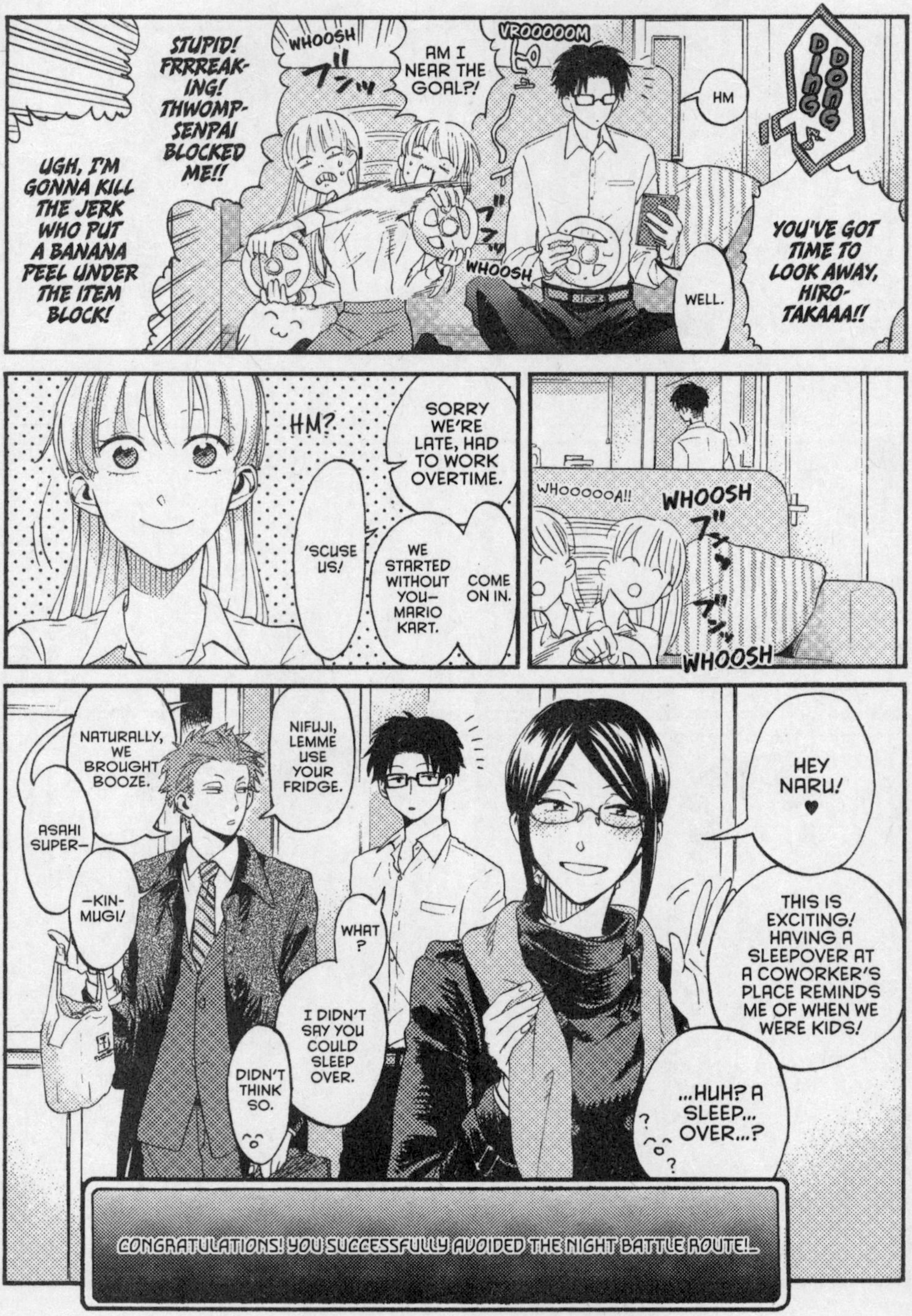
DING DONG
YOU'VE GOT TIME TO LOOK AWAY, HIRO-TAKAAA!!
HM
WELL.
VROOOOOM
AM I NEAR THE GOAL?!
WHOOSH
WHOOSH
STUPID! FRRREAK-ING! THWOMP-SENPAI BLOCKED ME!!
UGH, I'M GONNA KILL THE JERK WHO PUT A BANANA PEEL UNDER THE ITEM BLOCK!
WHOOOOOA!!
WHOOSH
WHOOSH
SORRY WE'RE LATE, HAD TO WORK OVERTIME.
HM?
COME ON IN.
WE STARTED WITHOUT YOU—MARIO KART.
'SCUSE US!
HEY NARU! ♥
THIS IS EXCITING! HAVING A SLEEPOVER AT A COWORKER'S PLACE REMINDS ME OF WHEN WE WERE KIDS!
...HUH? A SLEEP... OVER...?
NIFUJI, LEMME USE YOUR FRIDGE.
WHAT?
I DIDN'T SAY YOU COULD SLEEP OVER.
NATURALLY, WE BROUGHT BOOZE.
ASAHI SUPER—
—KIN-MUGI!
DIDN'T THINK SO.
CONGRATULATIONS! YOU SUCCESSFULLY AVOIDED THE NIGHT BATTLE ROUTE!...

 (And so, back to the checkpoint)

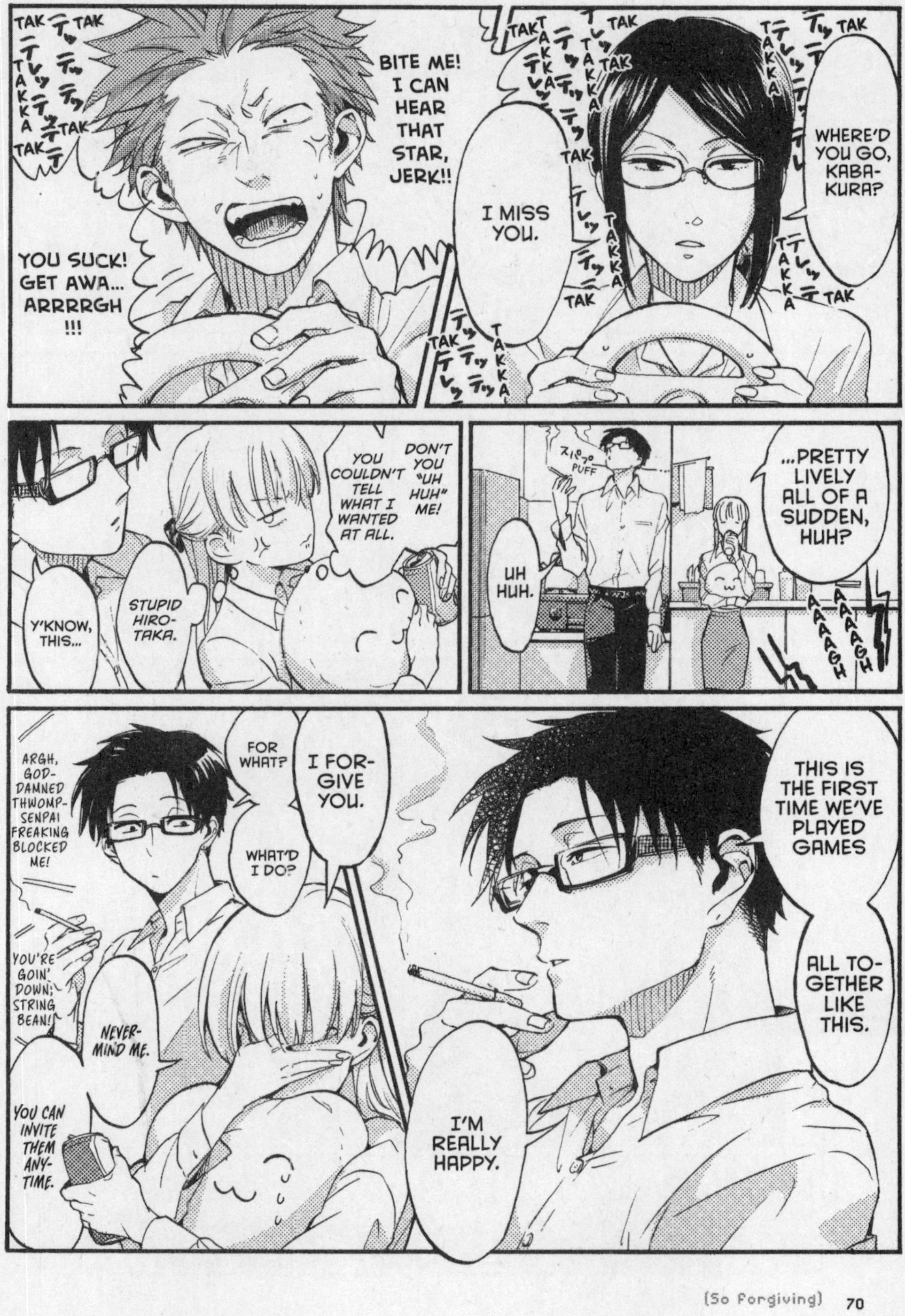
TAK TAKKA TAK
WHERE'D YOU GO, KABA-KURA?
I MISS YOU.
TAK TAKKA TAK
BITE ME! I CAN HEAR THAT STAR, JERK!!
YOU SUCK! GET AWA... ARRRRGH !!!
...PRETTY LIVELY ALL OF A SUDDEN, HUH?
AAAAAGH
AAAAAGH
スパー PUFF
UH HUH.
DON'T YOU "UH HUH" ME!
YOU COULDN'T TELL WHAT I WANTED AT ALL.
STUPID HIRO-TAKA.
Y'KNOW, THIS...
THIS IS THE FIRST TIME WE'VE PLAYED GAMES
ALL TO-GETHER LIKE THIS.
I'M REALLY HAPPY.
I FOR-GIVE YOU.
FOR WHAT?
WHAT'D I DO?
ARGH, GOD-DAMNED THWOMP-SENPAI FREAKING BLOCKED ME!
NEVER-MIND ME.
YOU'RE GOIN' DOWN, STRING BEAN!
YOU CAN INVITE THEM ANY-TIME.

(So Forgiving)

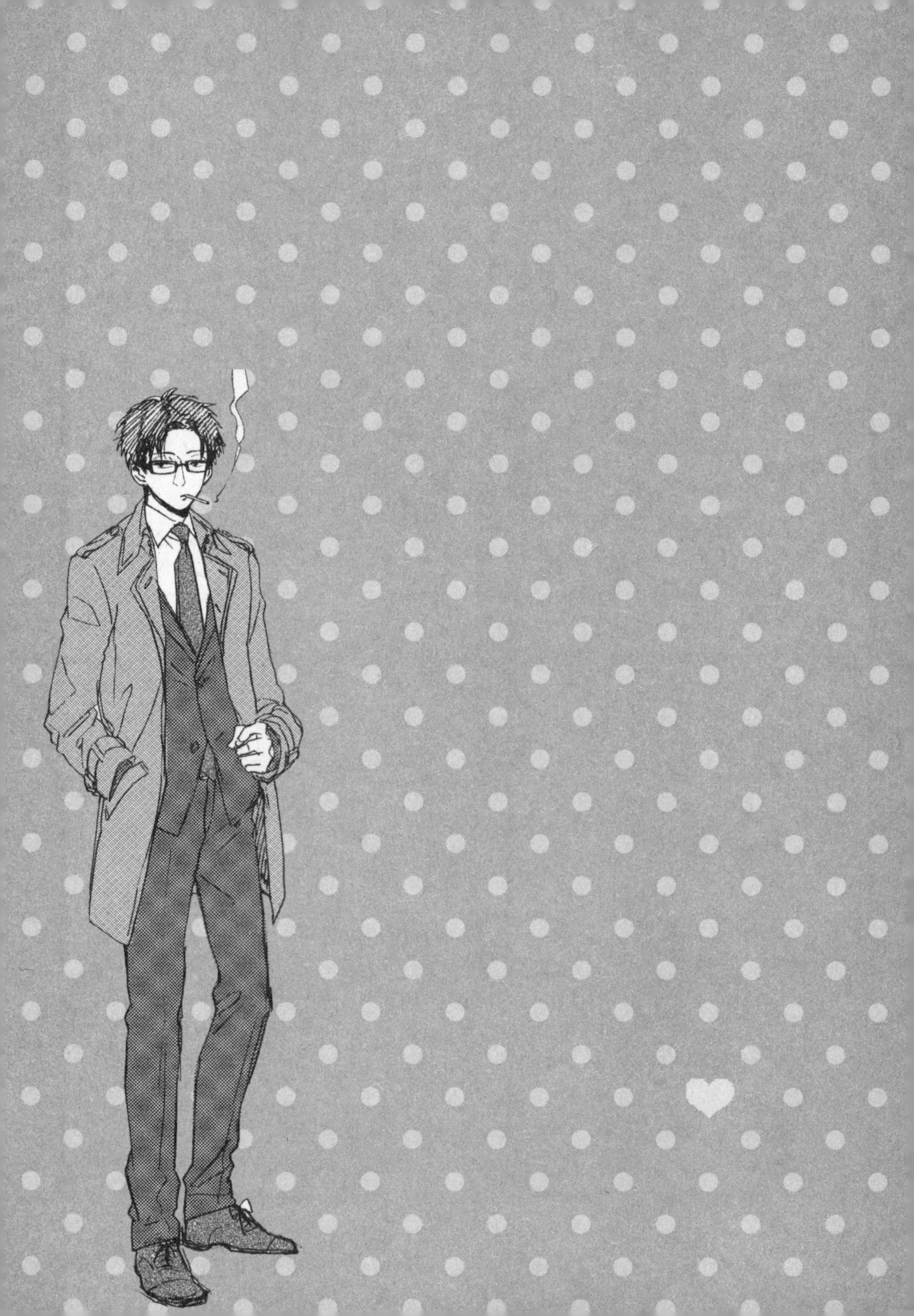

▼ HOW THEY ARE OUTSIDE OF WORK

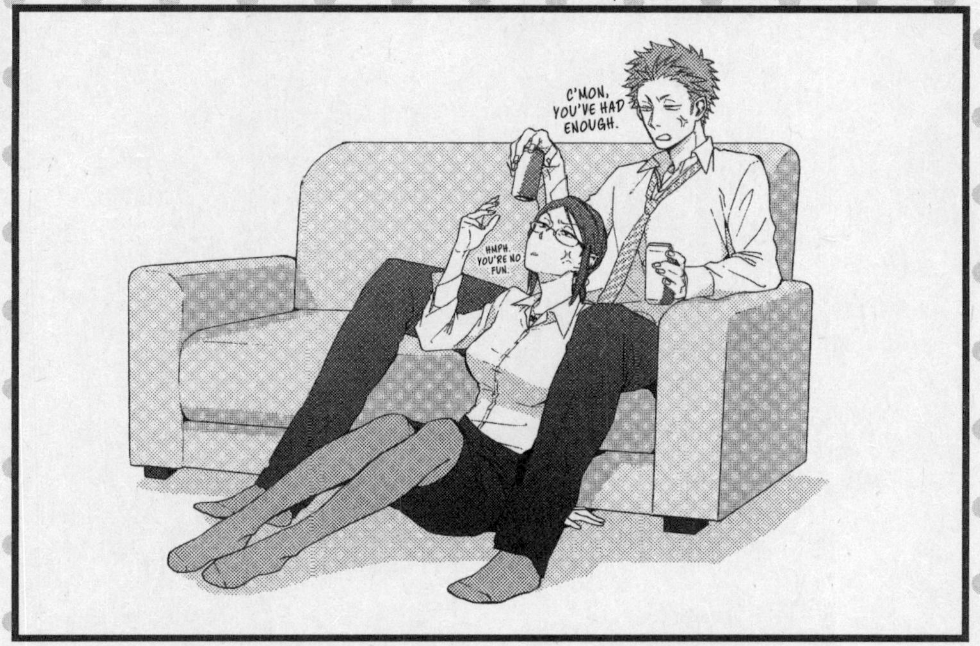
C'MON, YOU'VE HAD ENOUGH.
HMPH. YOU'RE NO FUN.

▼ NO, THAT'S NOT IT

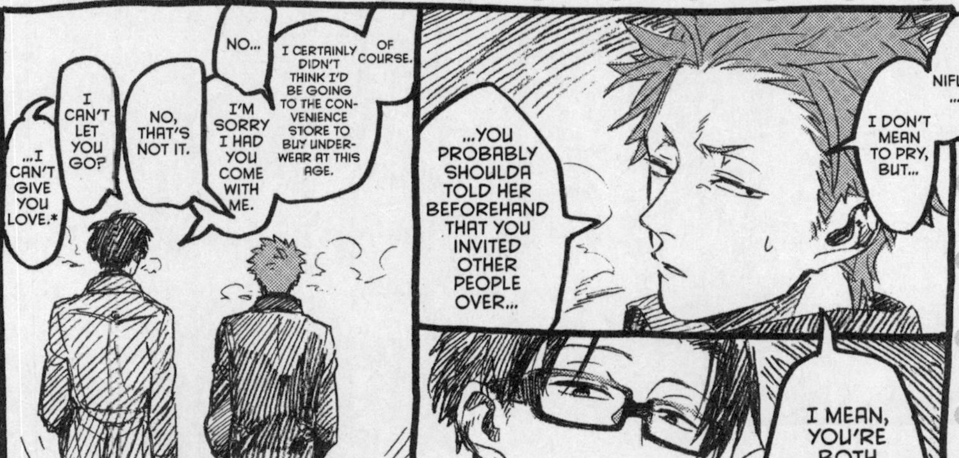
NIFUJI... I DON'T MEAN TO PRY, BUT...
...YOU PROBABLY SHOULDA TOLD HER BEFOREHAND THAT YOU INVITED OTHER PEOPLE OVER...
I MEAN, YOU'RE BOTH ADULTS AND ALL, IF YOU CATCH MY DRIFT.
OF COURSE.
I CERTAINLY DIDN'T THINK I'D BE GOING TO THE CONVENIENCE STORE TO BUY UNDERWEAR AT THIS AGE.
NO...
I'M SORRY I HAD YOU COME WITH ME.
NO, THAT'S NOT IT.
I CAN'T LET YOU GO?
...I CAN'T GIVE YOU LOVE.*

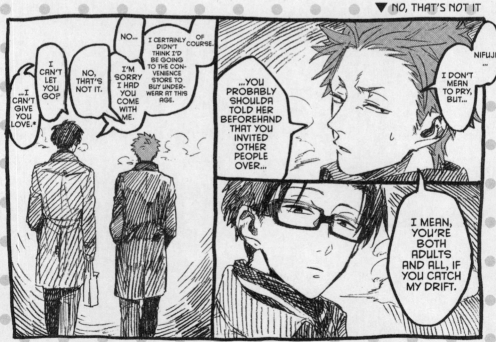

* They're citing lines from a song titled *"Chigau, sō ja naï"* ("No, That's Not It") by Suzuki Masayuki.

▼ WHOA, HUGE

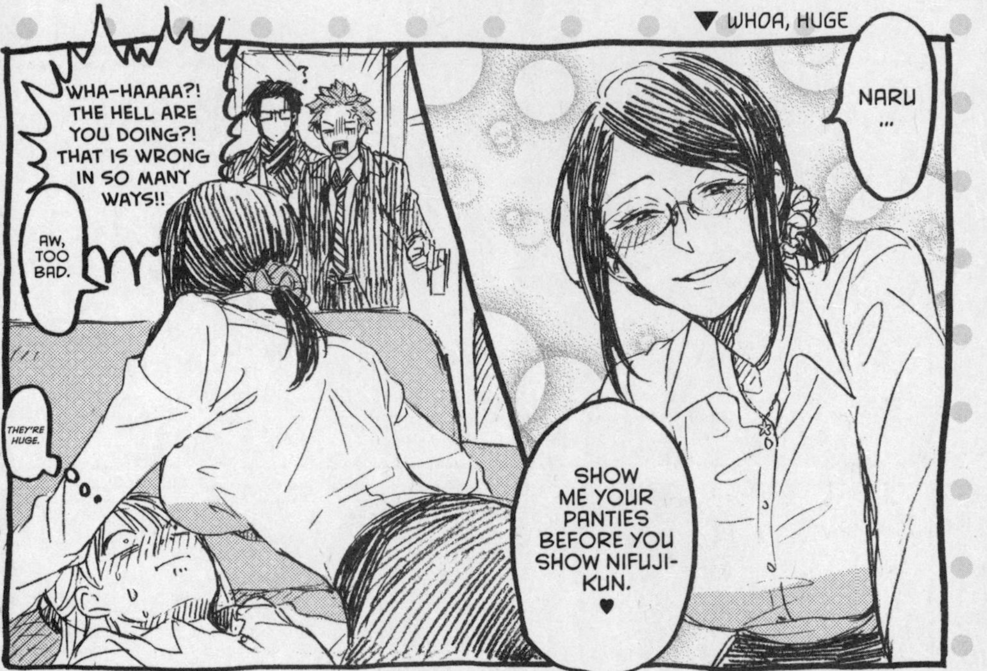
NARU …
SHOW ME YOUR PANTIES BEFORE YOU SHOW NIFUJI-KUN. ♥
WHA-HAAAA?! THE HELL ARE YOU DOING?! THAT IS WRONG IN SO MANY WAYS!!
?
AW, TOO BAD.
THEY'RE HUGE.

▼ BARE-FACED BEAUTIES

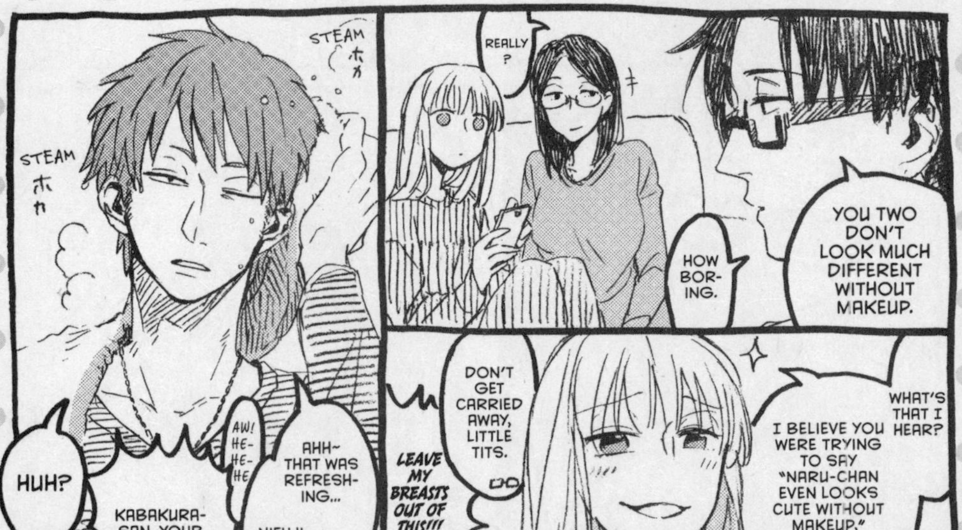
YOU TWO DON'T LOOK MUCH DIFFERENT WITHOUT MAKEUP.
REALLY?
HOW BOR-ING.
WHAT'S THAT I HEAR?
I BELIEVE YOU WERE TRYING TO SAY "NARU-CHAN EVEN LOOKS CUTE WITHOUT MAKEUP," RIGHT, M'DEAR?
DON'T GET CARRIED AWAY, LITTLE TITS.
LEAVE MY BREASTS OUT OF THIS!!!
STEAM
STEAM
AHH~ THAT WAS REFRESH-ING…
NIFUJI, SORRY I TOOK SO LONG~
AW! HE-HE-HE
KABAKURA-SAN, YOUR BARE FACE IS SO CUTE!!
HUH?
WHO? HAHA-HA

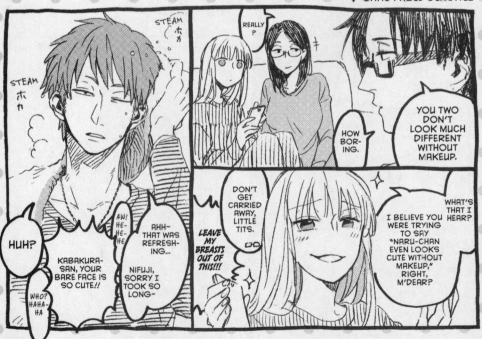

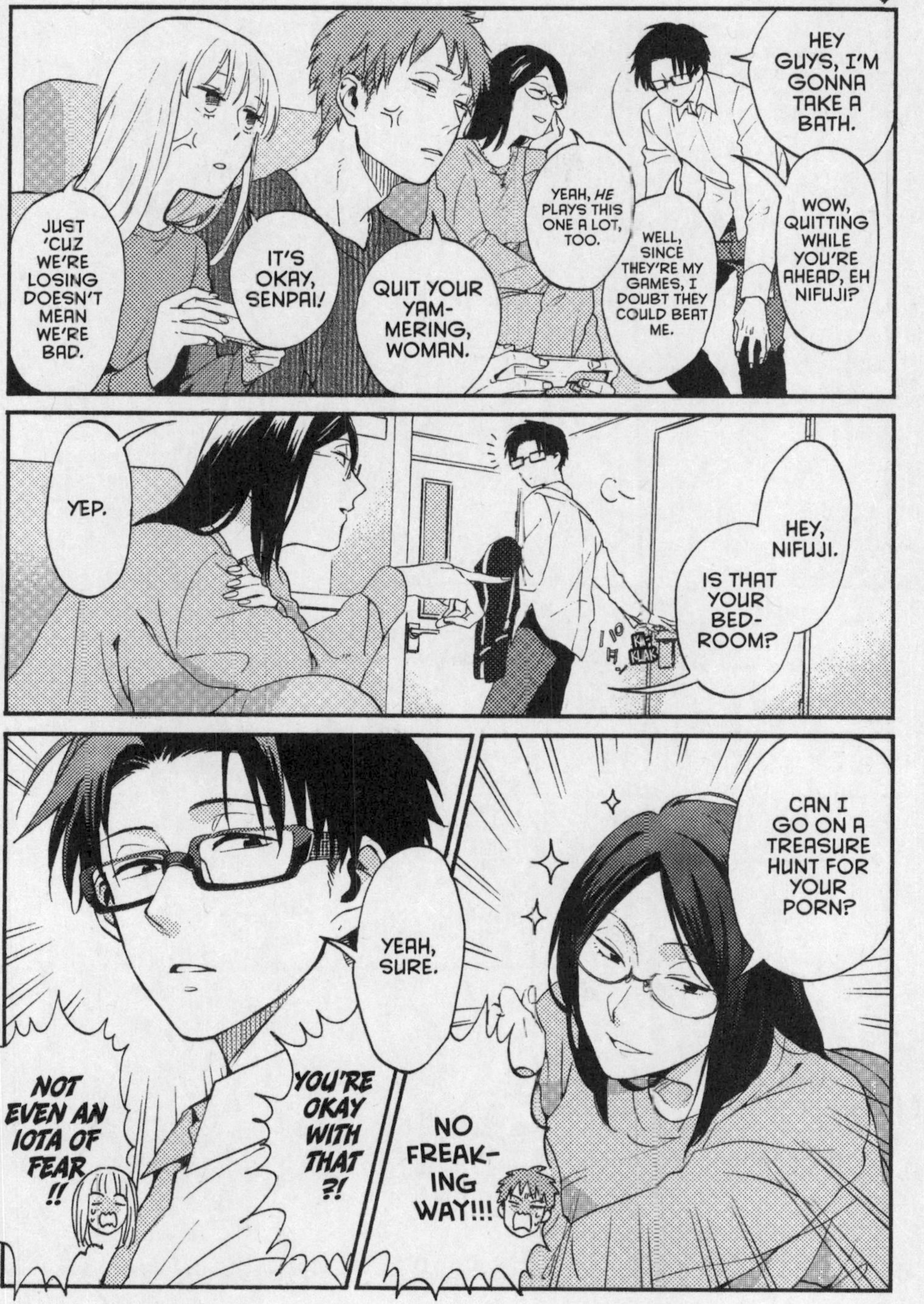
HEY GUYS, I'M GONNA TAKE A BATH.
WOW, QUITTING WHILE YOU'RE AHEAD, EH NIFUJI?
WELL, SINCE THEY'RE MY GAMES, I DOUBT THEY COULD BEAT ME.
YEAH, *HE* PLAYS THIS ONE A LOT, TOO.
QUIT YOUR YAM-MERING, WOMAN.
IT'S OKAY, SENPAI!
JUST 'CUZ WE'RE LOSING DOESN'T MEAN WE'RE BAD.
HEY, NIFUJI.
IS THAT YOUR BED-ROOM?
KI-KLAK
YEP.
CAN I GO ON A TREASURE HUNT FOR YOUR PORN?
NO FREAK-ING WAY!!!
YEAH, SURE.
YOU'RE OKAY WITH THAT ?!
NOT EVEN AN IOTA OF FEAR !!

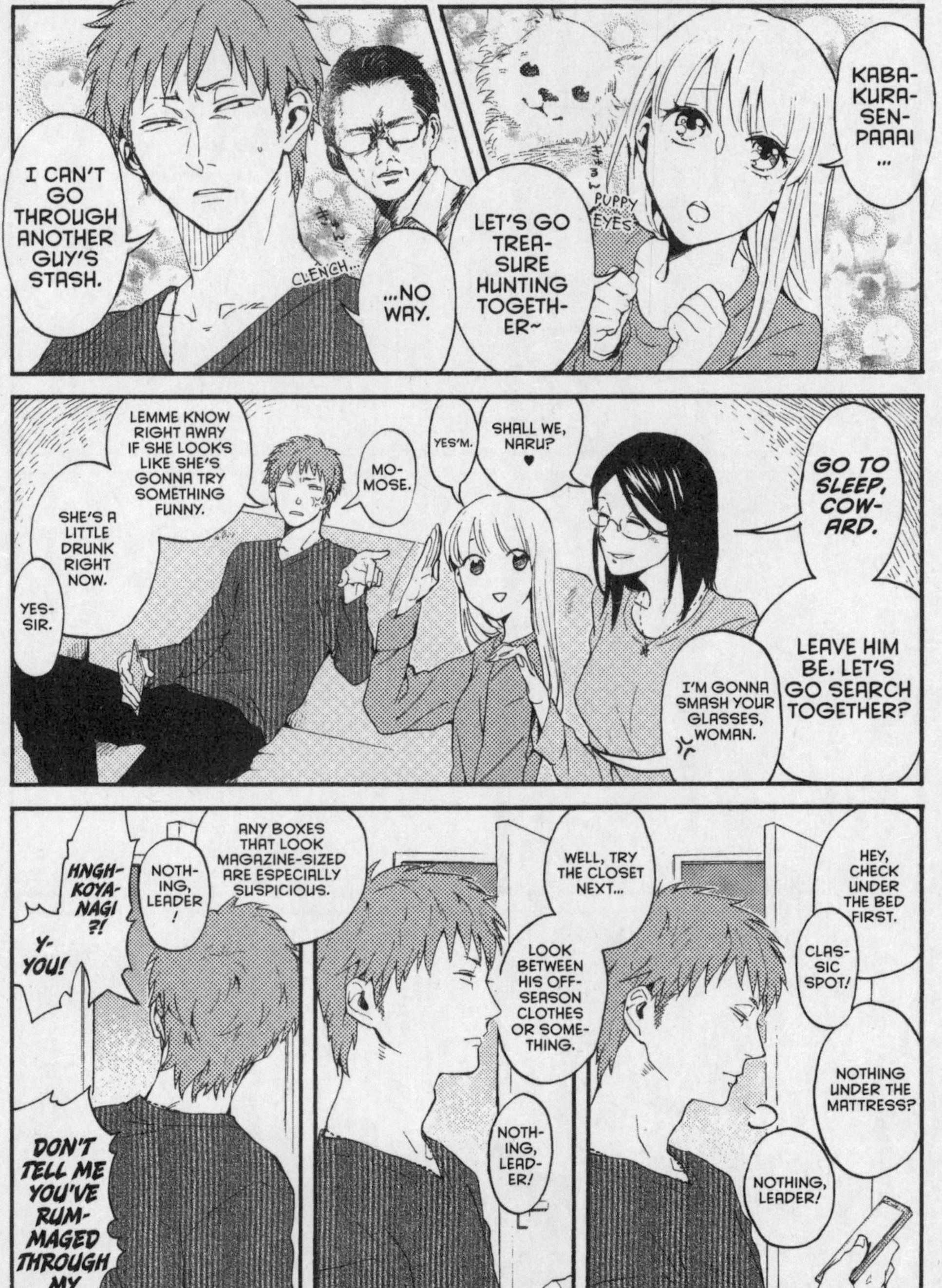

KABA-KURA-SEN-PAAAI ...
PUPPY EYES
LET'S GO TREA-SURE HUNTING TOGETH-ER~
...NO WAY.
CLENCH...
I CAN'T GO THROUGH ANOTHER GUY'S STASH.
GO TO SLEEP, COW-ARD.
LEAVE HIM BE. LET'S GO SEARCH TOGETHER?
I'M GONNA SMASH YOUR GLASSES, WOMAN.
SHALL WE, NARU? ♥
YES'M.
MO-MOSE.
LEMME KNOW RIGHT AWAY IF SHE LOOKS LIKE SHE'S GONNA TRY SOMETHING FUNNY.
SHE'S A LITTLE DRUNK RIGHT NOW.
YES-SIR.
HEY, CHECK UNDER THE BED FIRST.
CLAS-SIC SPOT!
NOTHING UNDER THE MATTRESS?
NOTHING, LEADER!
WELL, TRY THE CLOSET NEXT...
LOOK BETWEEN HIS OFF-SEASON CLOTHES OR SOME-THING.
NOTH-ING, LEAD-ER!
ANY BOXES THAT LOOK MAGAZINE-SIZED ARE ESPECIALLY SUSPICIOUS.
NOTH-ING, LEADER!
HNGH-KOYA-NAGI?!
Y-YOU!
DON'T TELL ME YOU'VE RUM-MAGED THROUGH MY

 (Conquest completed)

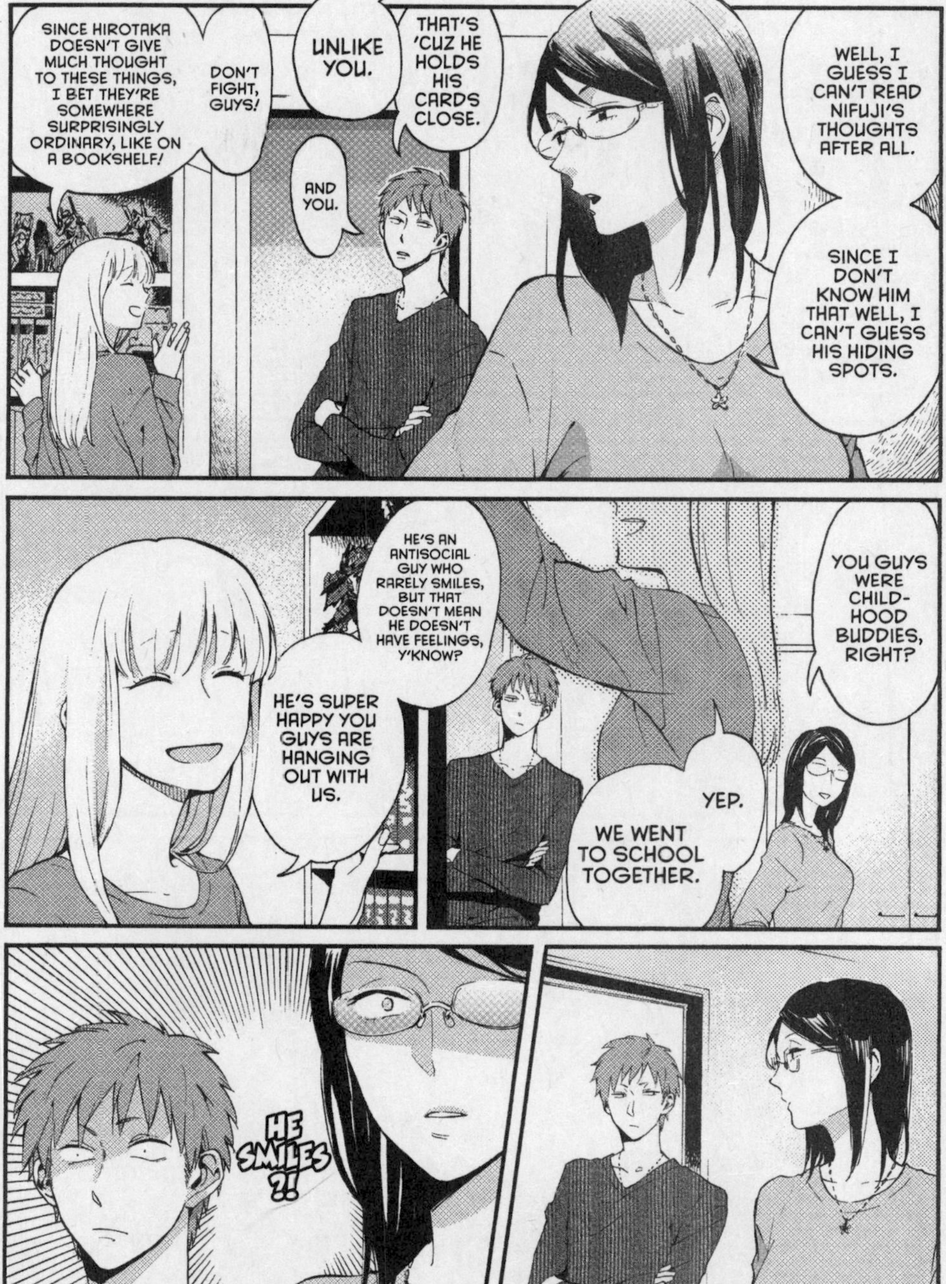
WELL, I GUESS I CAN'T READ NIFUJI'S THOUGHTS AFTER ALL.
SINCE I DON'T KNOW HIM THAT WELL, I CAN'T GUESS HIS HIDING SPOTS.
THAT'S 'CUZ HE HOLDS HIS CARDS CLOSE.
UNLIKE YOU.
DON'T FIGHT, GUYS!
SINCE HIROTAKA DOESN'T GIVE MUCH THOUGHT TO THESE THINGS, I BET THEY'RE SOMEWHERE SURPRISINGLY ORDINARY, LIKE ON A BOOKSHELF!
AND YOU.
YOU GUYS WERE CHILD-HOOD BUDDIES, RIGHT?
YEP.
WE WENT TO SCHOOL TOGETHER.
HE'S AN ANTISOCIAL GUY WHO RARELY SMILES, BUT THAT DOESN'T MEAN HE DOESN'T HAVE FEELINGS, Y'KNOW?
HE'S SUPER HAPPY YOU GUYS ARE HANGING OUT WITH US.
HE SMILES ?!

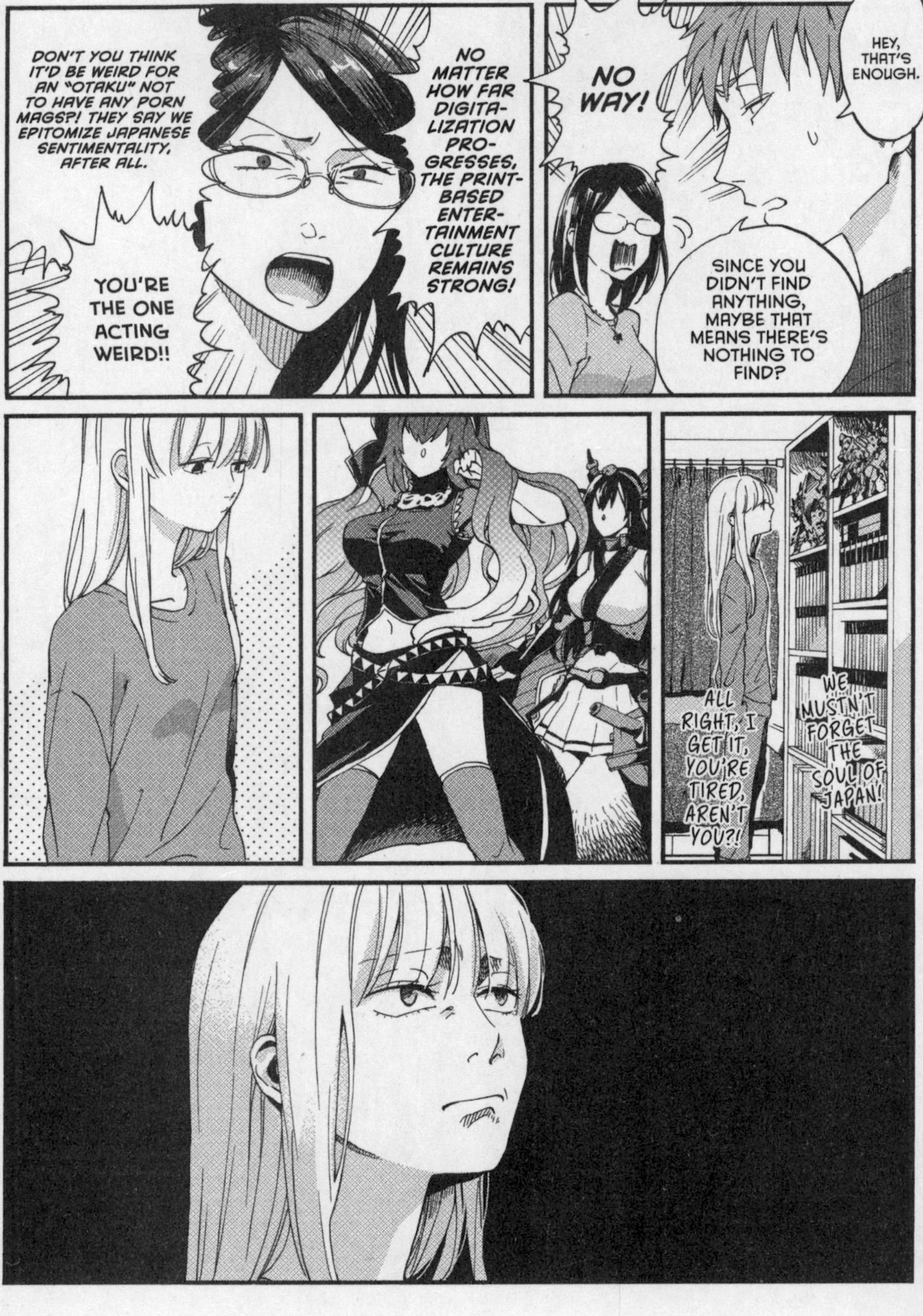
HEY, THAT'S ENOUGH.
NO WAY!
SINCE YOU DIDN'T FIND ANYTHING, MAYBE THAT MEANS THERE'S NOTHING TO FIND?
NO MATTER HOW FAR DIGITALIZATION PROGRESSES, THE PRINT-BASED ENTERTAINMENT CULTURE REMAINS STRONG!
DON'T YOU THINK IT'D BE WEIRD FOR AN "OTAKU" NOT TO HAVE ANY PORN MAGS?! THEY SAY WE EPITOMIZE JAPANESE SENTIMENTALITY, AFTER ALL.
YOU'RE THE ONE ACTING WEIRD!!
WE MUSTN'T FORGET THE SOUL OF JAPAN!
ALL RIGHT, I GET IT, YOU'RE TIRED, AREN'T YOU?!

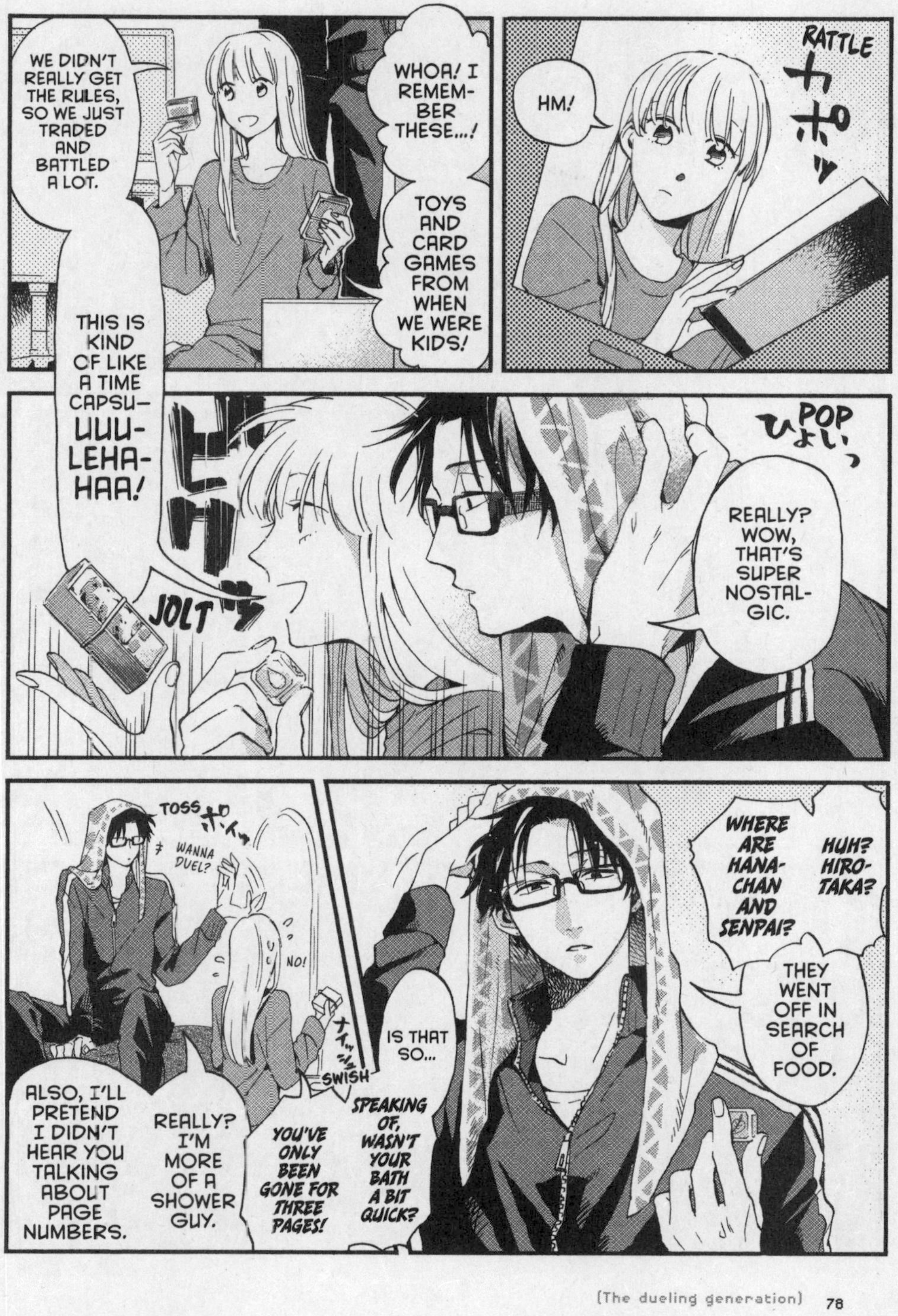
RATTLE
HM!
WHOA! I REMEMBER THESE...!
TOYS AND CARD GAMES FROM WHEN WE WERE KIDS!
WE DIDN'T REALLY GET THE RULES, SO WE JUST TRADED AND BATTLED A LOT.
THIS IS KIND OF LIKE A TIME CAPSU-UUU-LEHA-HAA!
POP
REALLY? WOW, THAT'S SUPER NOSTALGIC.
JOLT
HUH? HIROTAKA?
WHERE ARE HANA-CHAN AND SENPAI?
THEY WENT OFF IN SEARCH OF FOOD.
IS THAT SO...
TOSS
WANNA DUEL?
NO!
SWISH
SPEAKING OF, WASN'T YOUR BATH A BIT QUICK?
YOU'VE ONLY BEEN GONE FOR THREE PAGES!
REALLY? I'M MORE OF A SHOWER GUY.
ALSO, I'LL PRETEND I DIDN'T HEAR YOU TALKING ABOUT PAGE NUMBERS.

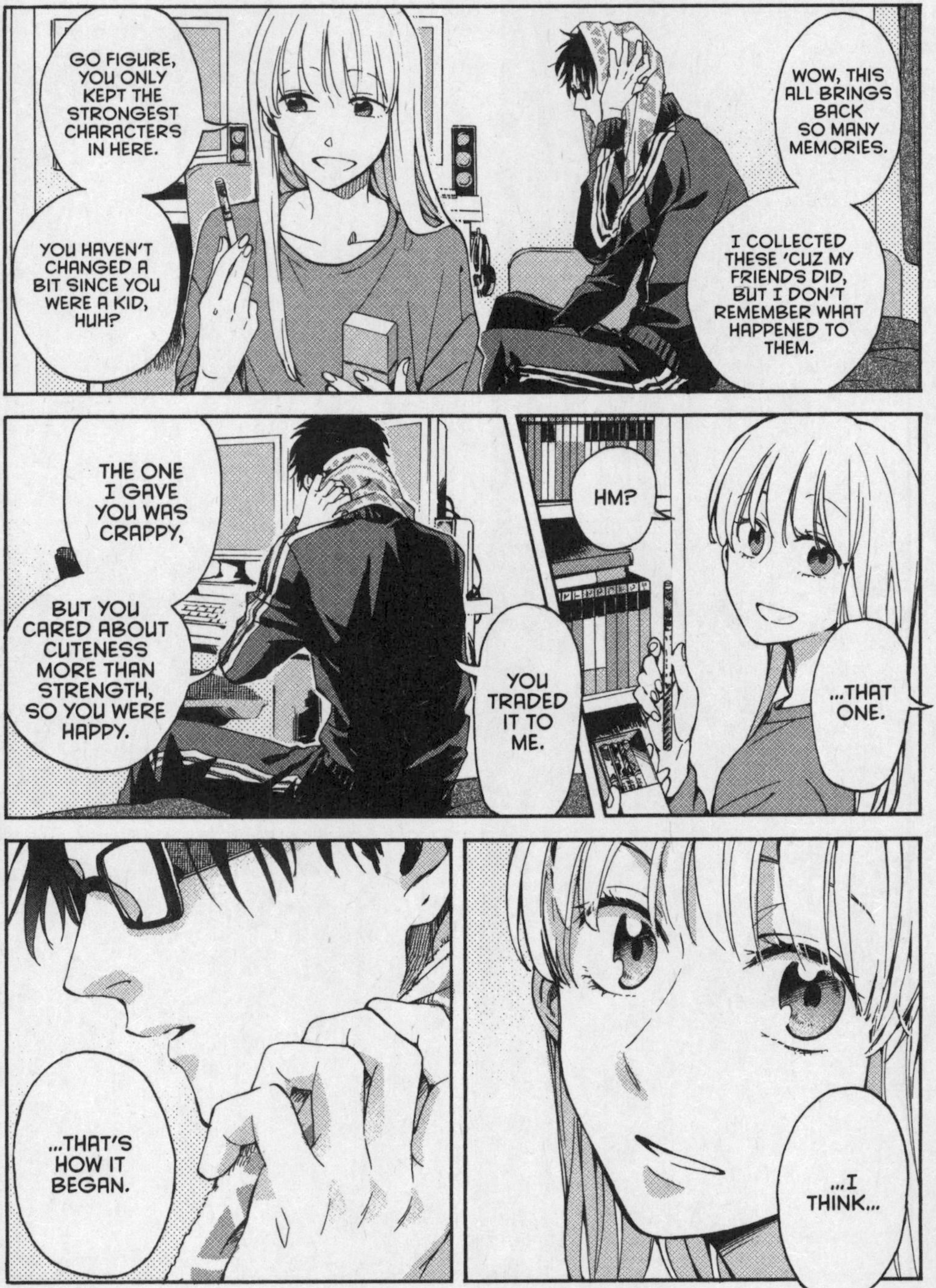
WOW, THIS ALL BRINGS BACK SO MANY MEMORIES.
I COLLECTED THESE 'CUZ MY FRIENDS DID, BUT I DON'T REMEMBER WHAT HAPPENED TO THEM.
GO FIGURE, YOU ONLY KEPT THE STRONGEST CHARACTERS IN HERE.
YOU HAVEN'T CHANGED A BIT SINCE YOU WERE A KID, HUH?
...THAT ONE.
HM?
YOU TRADED IT TO ME.
THE ONE I GAVE YOU WAS CRAPPY,
BUT YOU CARED ABOUT CUTENESS MORE THAN STRENGTH, SO YOU WERE HAPPY.
...I THINK...
...THAT'S HOW IT BEGAN.

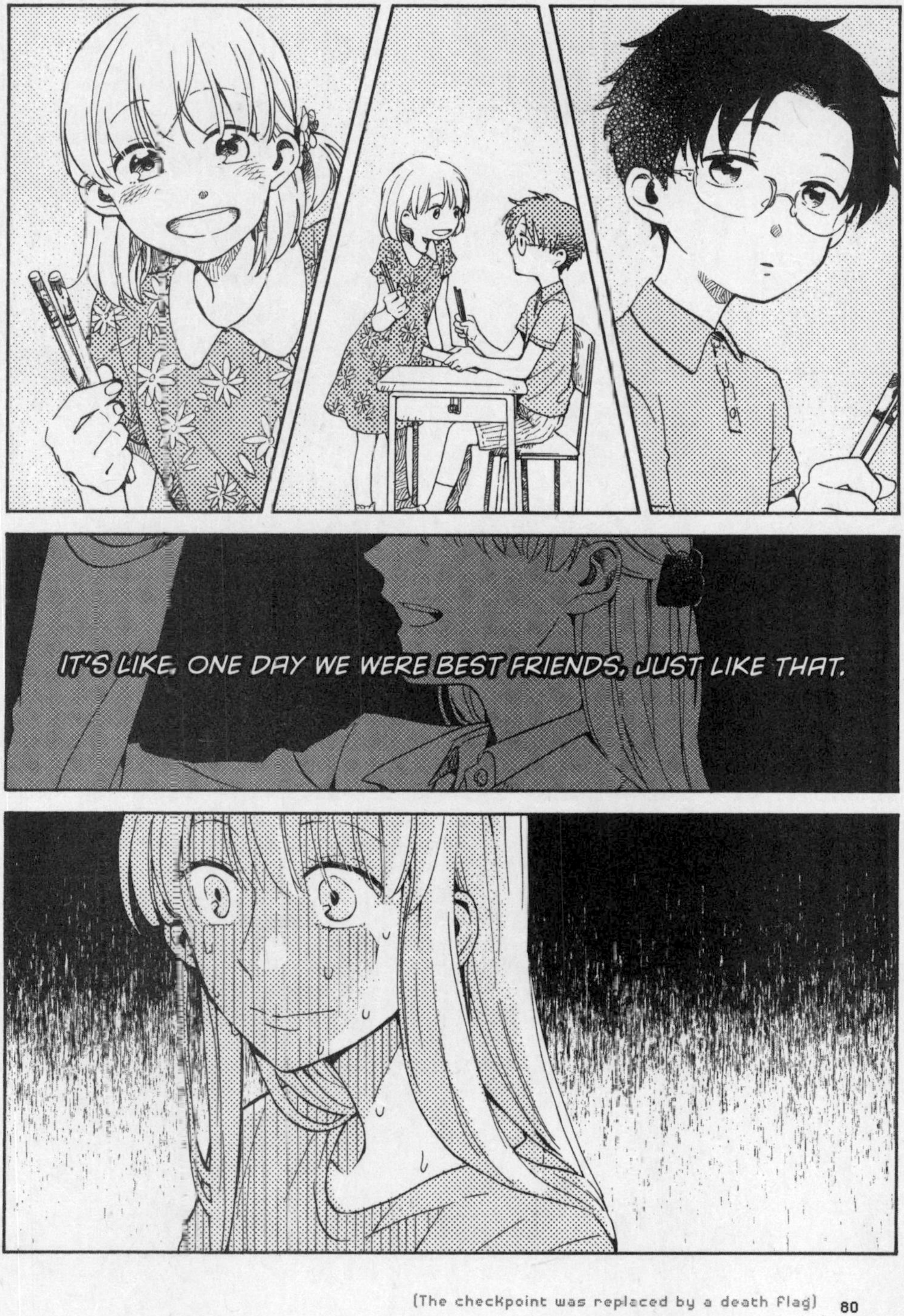
IT'S LIKE, ONE DAY WE WERE BEST FRIENDS, JUST LIKE THAT.

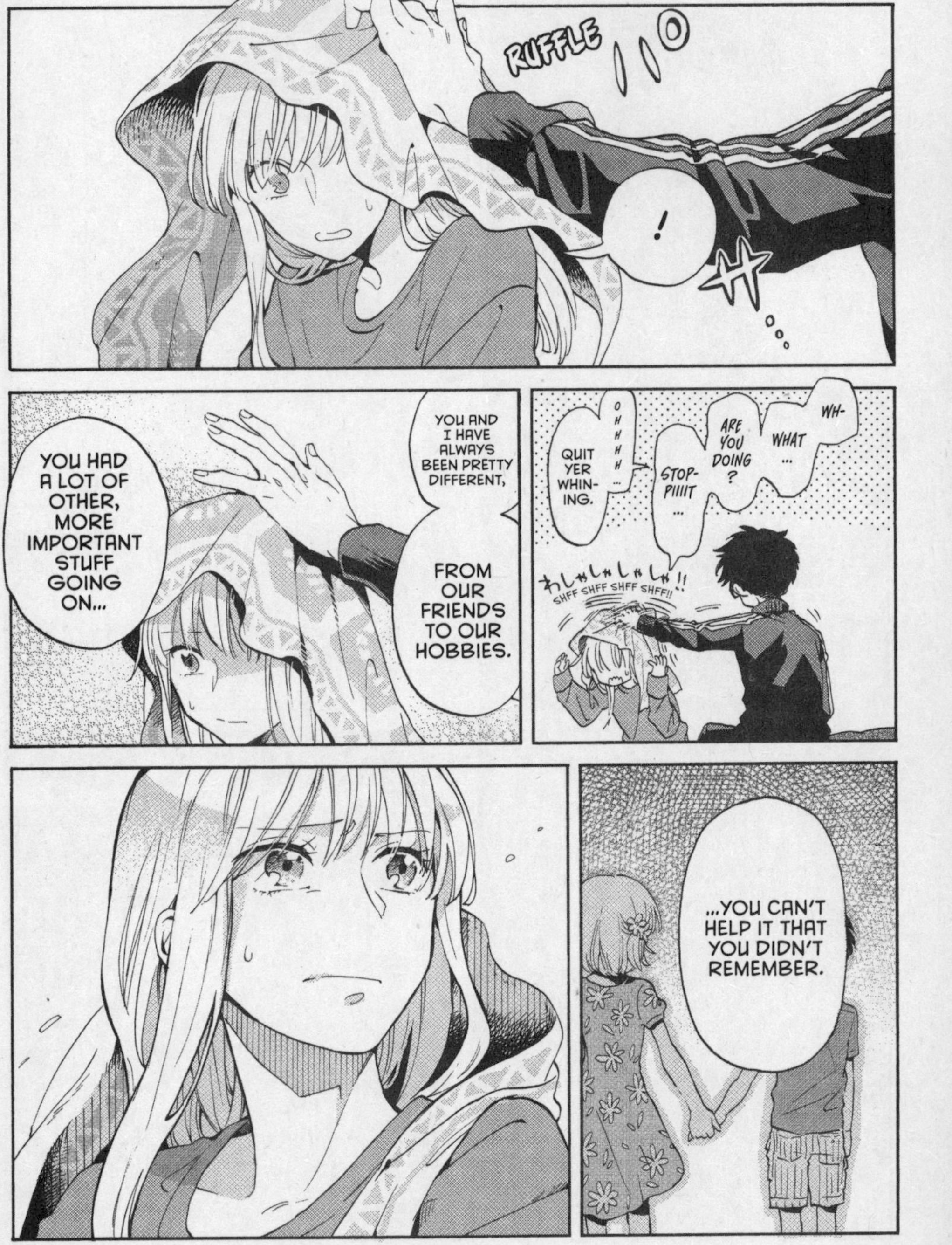
RUFFLE
!
WH- WHAT ...
ARE YOU DOING?
STOP-PIIIIT ...
OHHHH...
QUIT YER WHINING.
わしゃしゃしゃ!! SHFF SHFF SHFF SHFF!!
YOU AND I HAVE ALWAYS BEEN PRETTY DIFFERENT,
FROM OUR FRIENDS TO OUR HOBBIES.
YOU HAD A LOT OF OTHER, MORE IMPORTANT STUFF GOING ON...
...YOU CAN'T HELP IT THAT YOU DIDN'T REMEMBER.

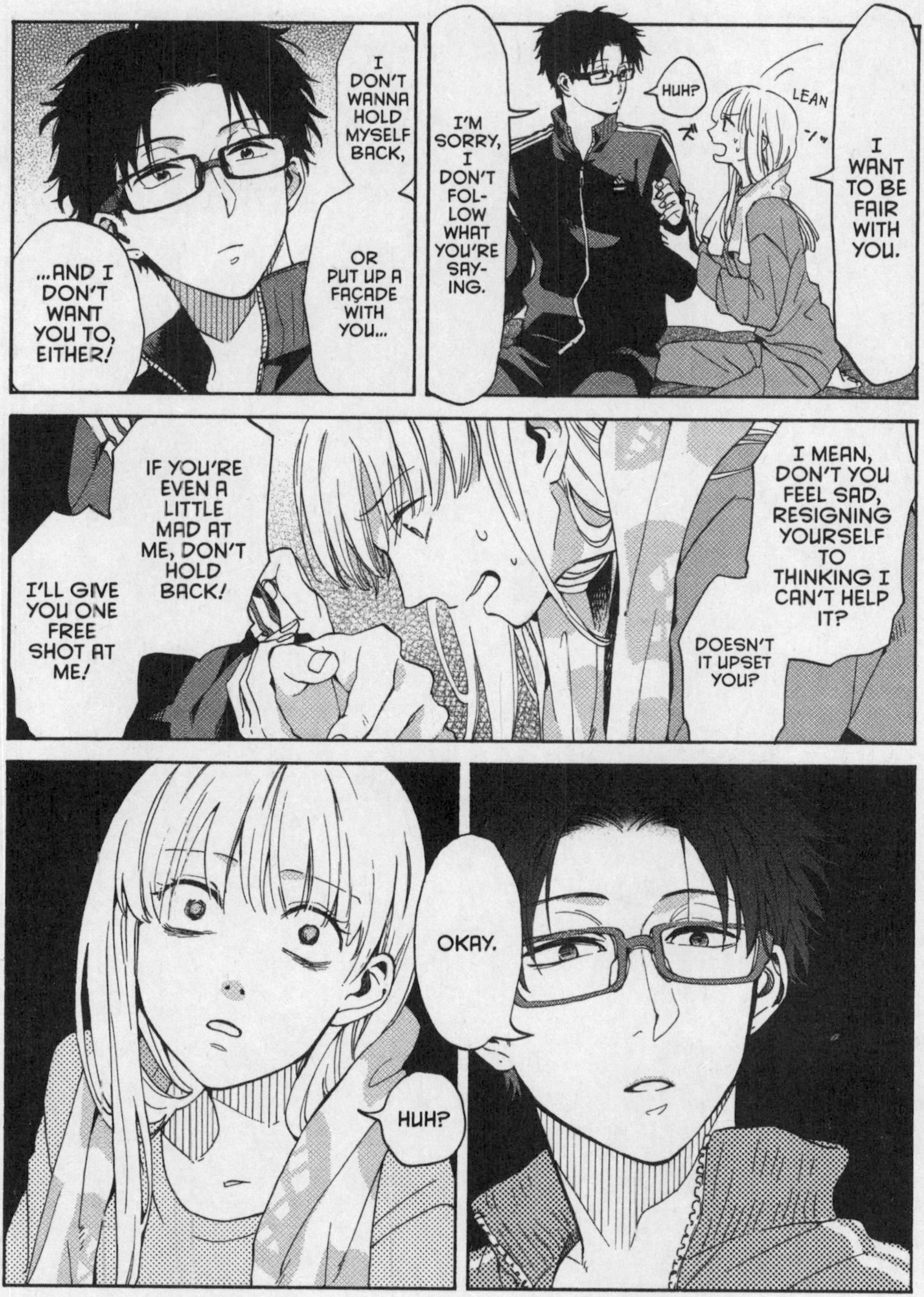
I WANT TO BE FAIR WITH YOU.
LEAN
HUH?
I'M SORRY, I DON'T FOL-LOW WHAT YOU'RE SAY-ING.
I DON'T WANNA HOLD MYSELF BACK,
OR PUT UP A FAÇADE WITH YOU...
...AND I DON'T WANT YOU TO, EITHER!
I MEAN, DON'T YOU FEEL SAD, RESIGNING YOURSELF TO THINKING I CAN'T HELP IT?
DOESN'T IT UPSET YOU?
IF YOU'RE EVEN A LITTLE MAD AT ME, DON'T HOLD BACK!
I'LL GIVE YOU ONE FREE SHOT AT ME!
OKAY.
HUH?

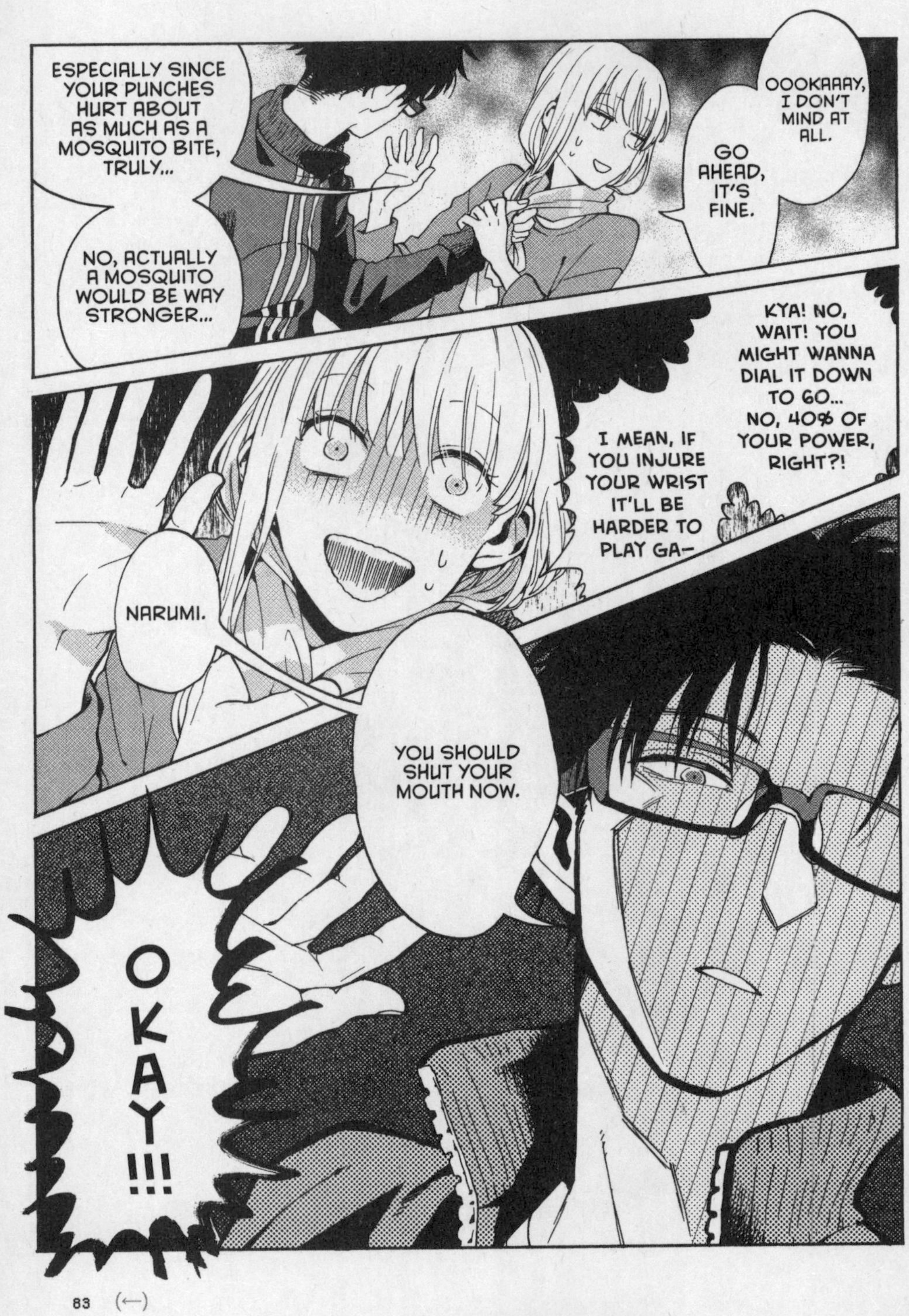
OOOKAAAY, I DON'T MIND AT ALL.
GO AHEAD, IT'S FINE.
ESPECIALLY SINCE YOUR PUNCHES HURT ABOUT AS MUCH AS A MOSQUITO BITE, TRULY...
NO, ACTUALLY A MOSQUITO WOULD BE WAY STRONGER...
KYA! NO, WAIT! YOU MIGHT WANNA DIAL IT DOWN TO 60... NO, 40% OF YOUR POWER, RIGHT?!
I MEAN, IF YOU INJURE YOUR WRIST IT'LL BE HARDER TO PLAY GA–
NARUMI.
YOU SHOULD SHUT YOUR MOUTH NOW.
OKAY!!!

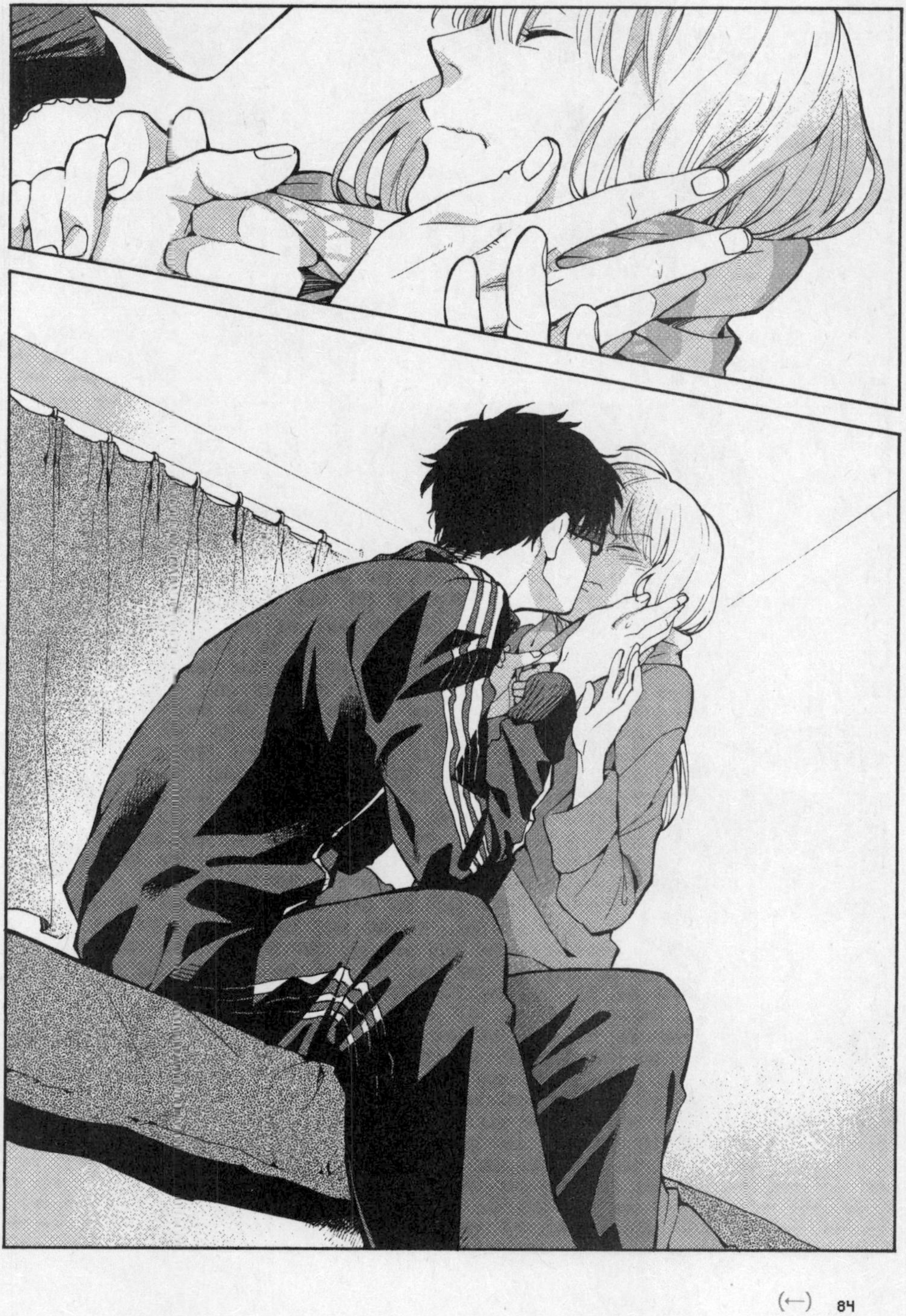

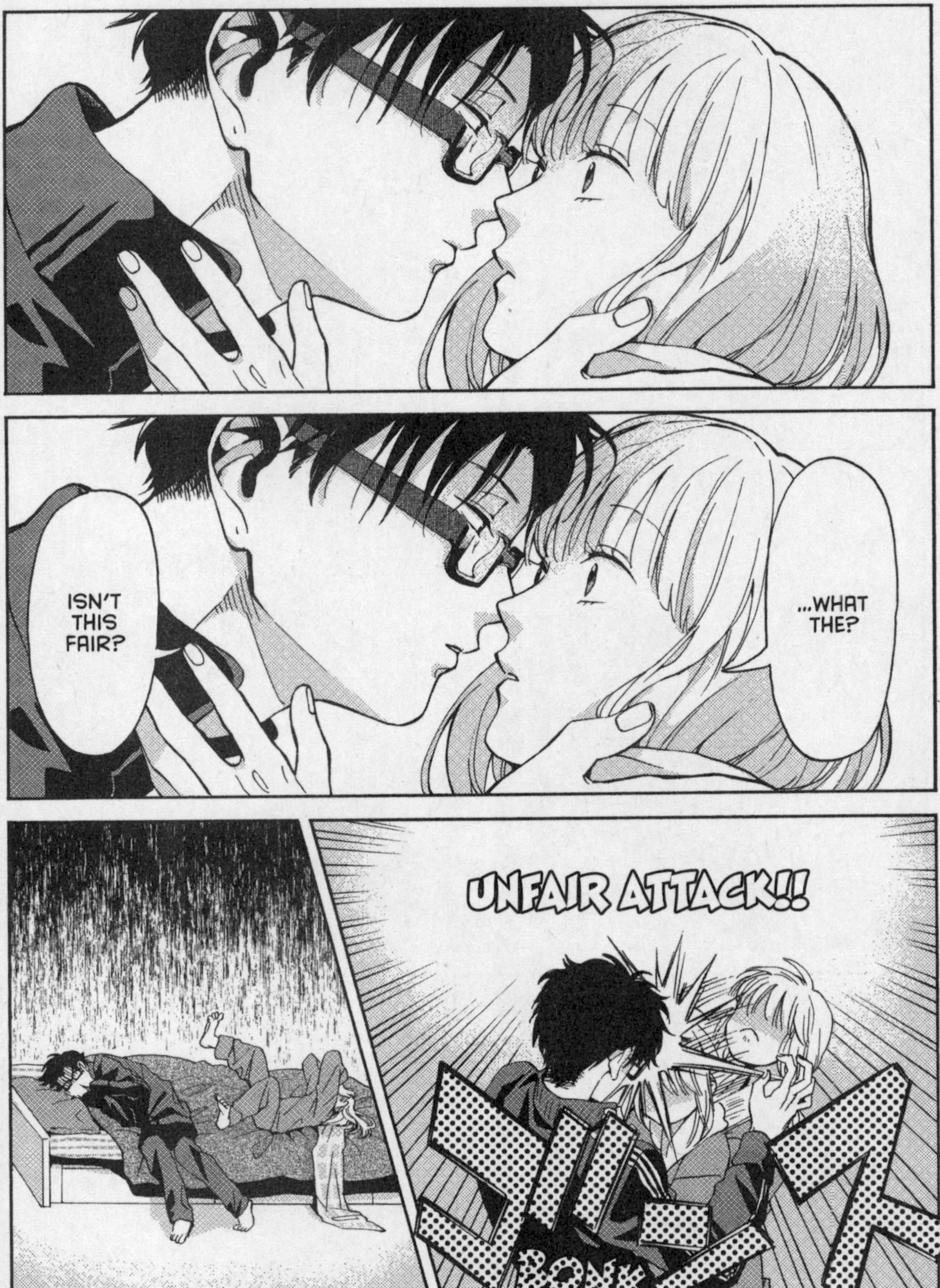
...WHAT THE?
ISN'T THIS FAIR?
UNFAIR ATTACK!!
BONK

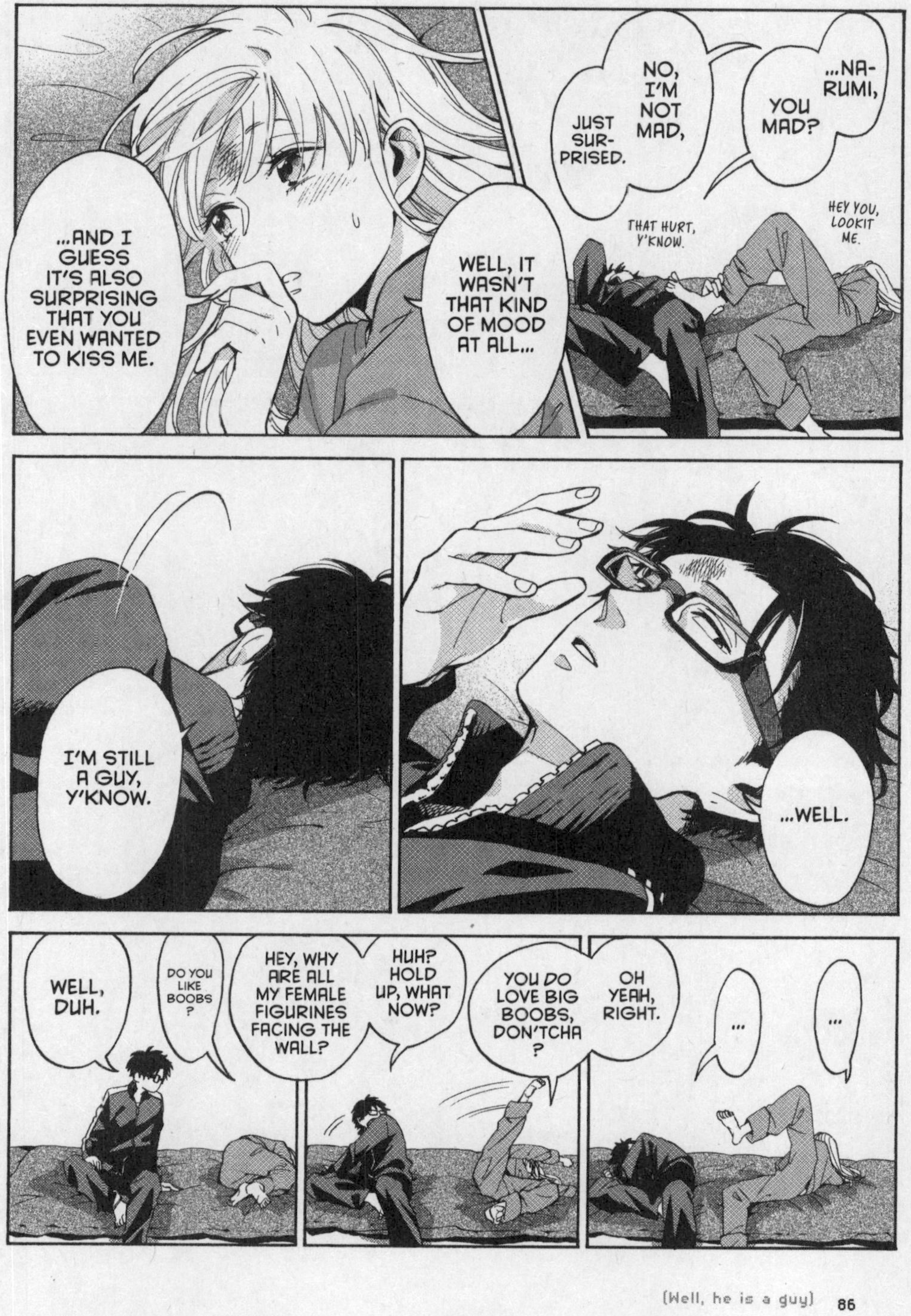
...NA-RUMI, YOU MAD?
NO, I'M NOT MAD, JUST SUR-PRISED.
HEY YOU, LOOKIT ME.
THAT HURT, Y'KNOW.
WELL, IT WASN'T THAT KIND OF MOOD AT ALL...
...AND I GUESS IT'S ALSO SURPRISING THAT YOU EVEN WANTED TO KISS ME.
...WELL.
I'M STILL A GUY, Y'KNOW.
...
...
OH YEAH, RIGHT.
YOU *DO* LOVE BIG BOOBS, DON'TCHA?
HUH? HOLD UP, WHAT NOW?
HEY, WHY ARE ALL MY FEMALE FIGURINES FACING THE WALL?
DO YOU LIKE BOOBS?
WELL, DUH.

(Well, he is a guy)

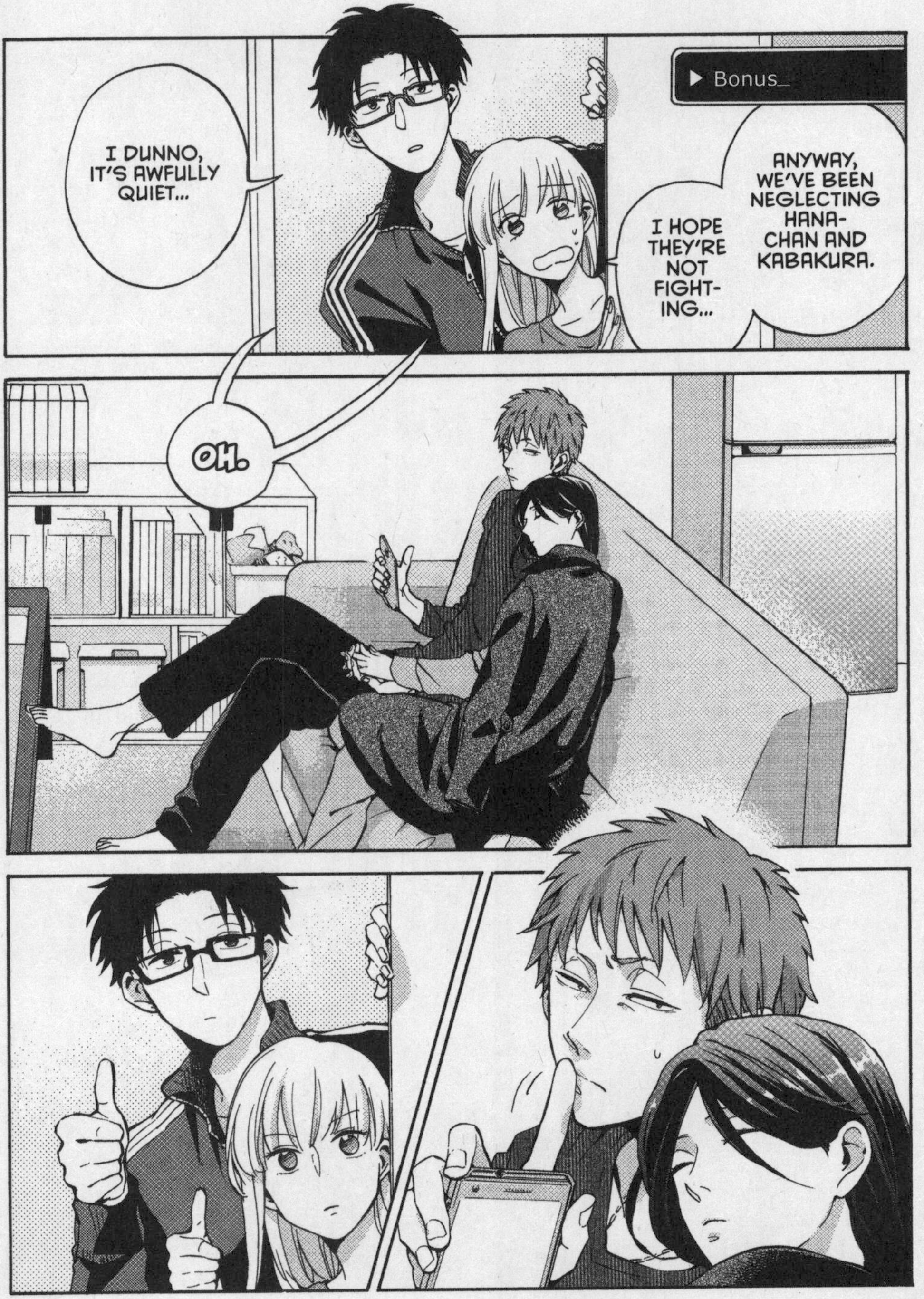
▶ Bonus_
ANYWAY, WE'VE BEEN NEGLECTING HANA-CHAN AND KABAKURA.
I HOPE THEY'RE NOT FIGHTING...
I DUNNO, IT'S AWFULLY QUIET...
OH.

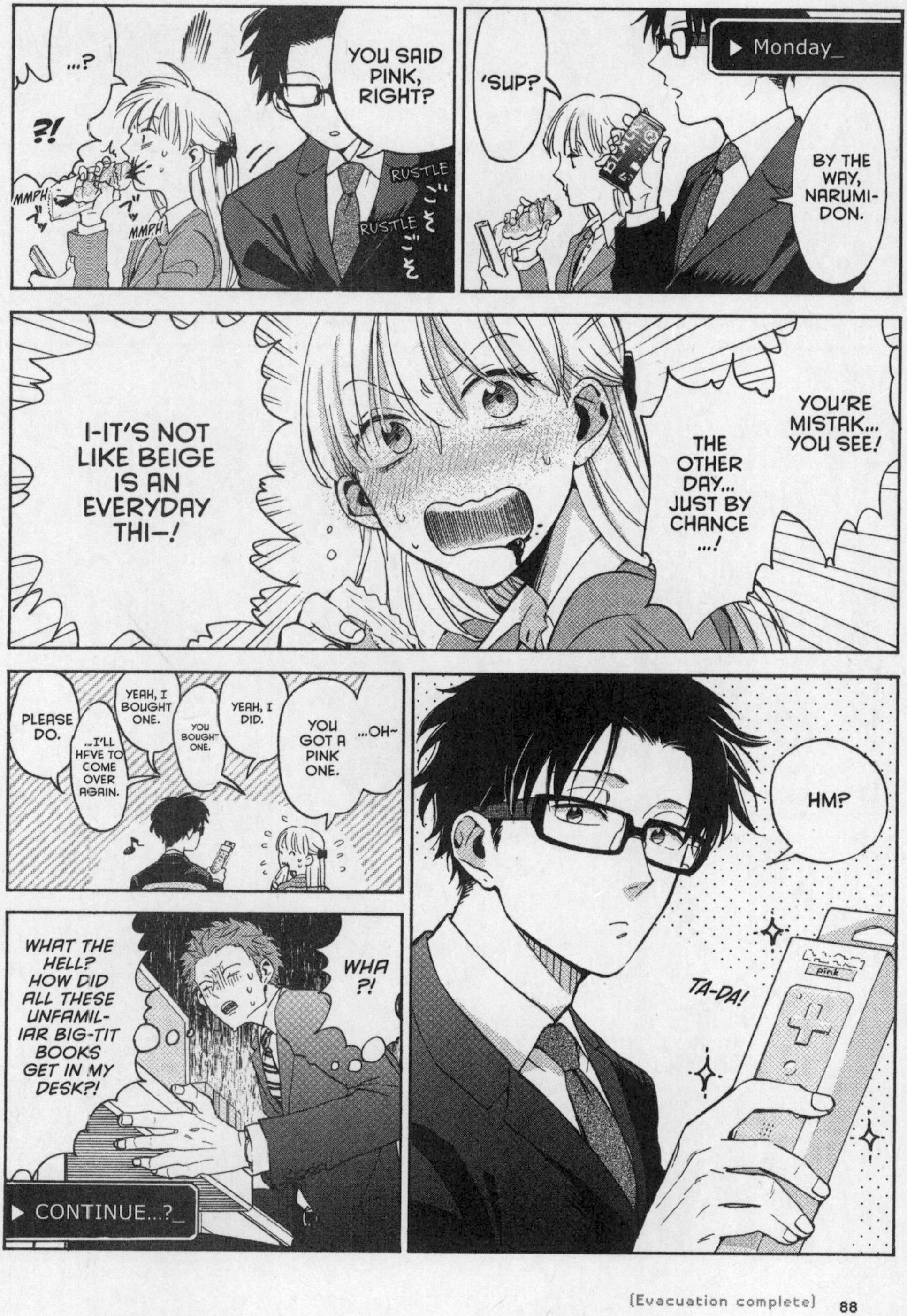
▶ Monday_
BY THE WAY, NARUMI-DON.
'SUP?
YOU SAID PINK, RIGHT?
RUSTLE
RUSTLE
...?
?!
MMPH
MMPH
YOU'RE MISTAK... YOU SEE!
THE OTHER DAY... JUST BY CHANCE ...!
I-IT'S NOT LIKE BEIGE IS AN EVERYDAY THI—!
HM?
TA-DA!
pink
...OH~
YOU GOT A PINK ONE.
YEAH, I DID.
YOU BOUGHT ONE.
YEAH, I BOUGHT ONE.
...I'LL HAVE TO COME OVER AGAIN.
PLEASE DO.
WHA?!
WHAT THE HELL? HOW DID ALL THESE UNFAMILIAR BIG-TIT BOOKS GET IN MY DESK?!
▶ CONTINUE...?_

▼ DÉJÀ VU

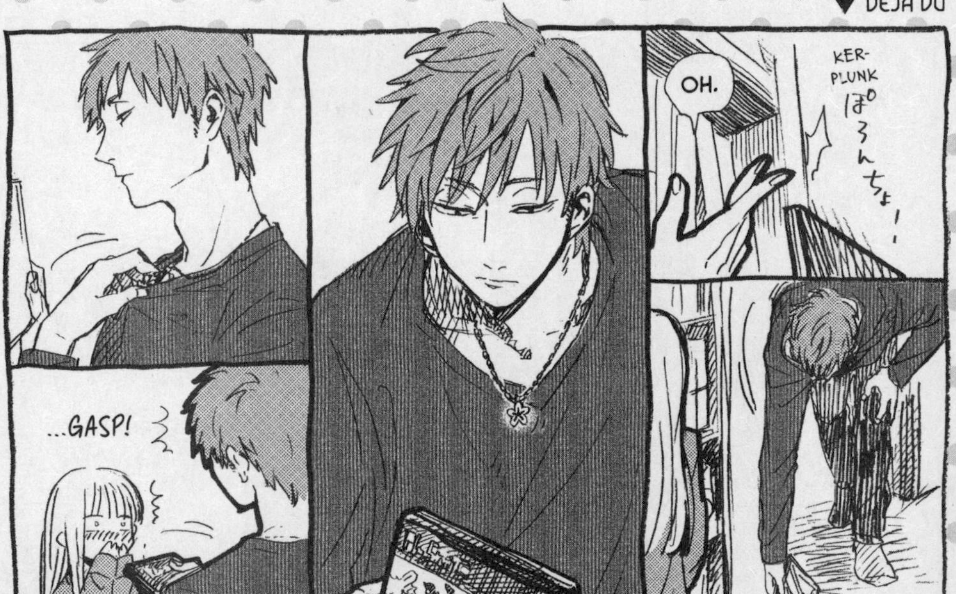
OH.
KER-PLUNK
ぽろんちょ!!
...GASP!

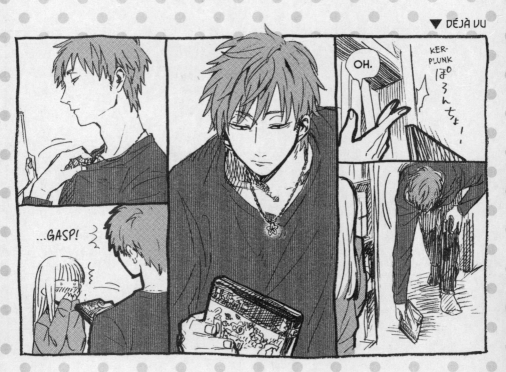

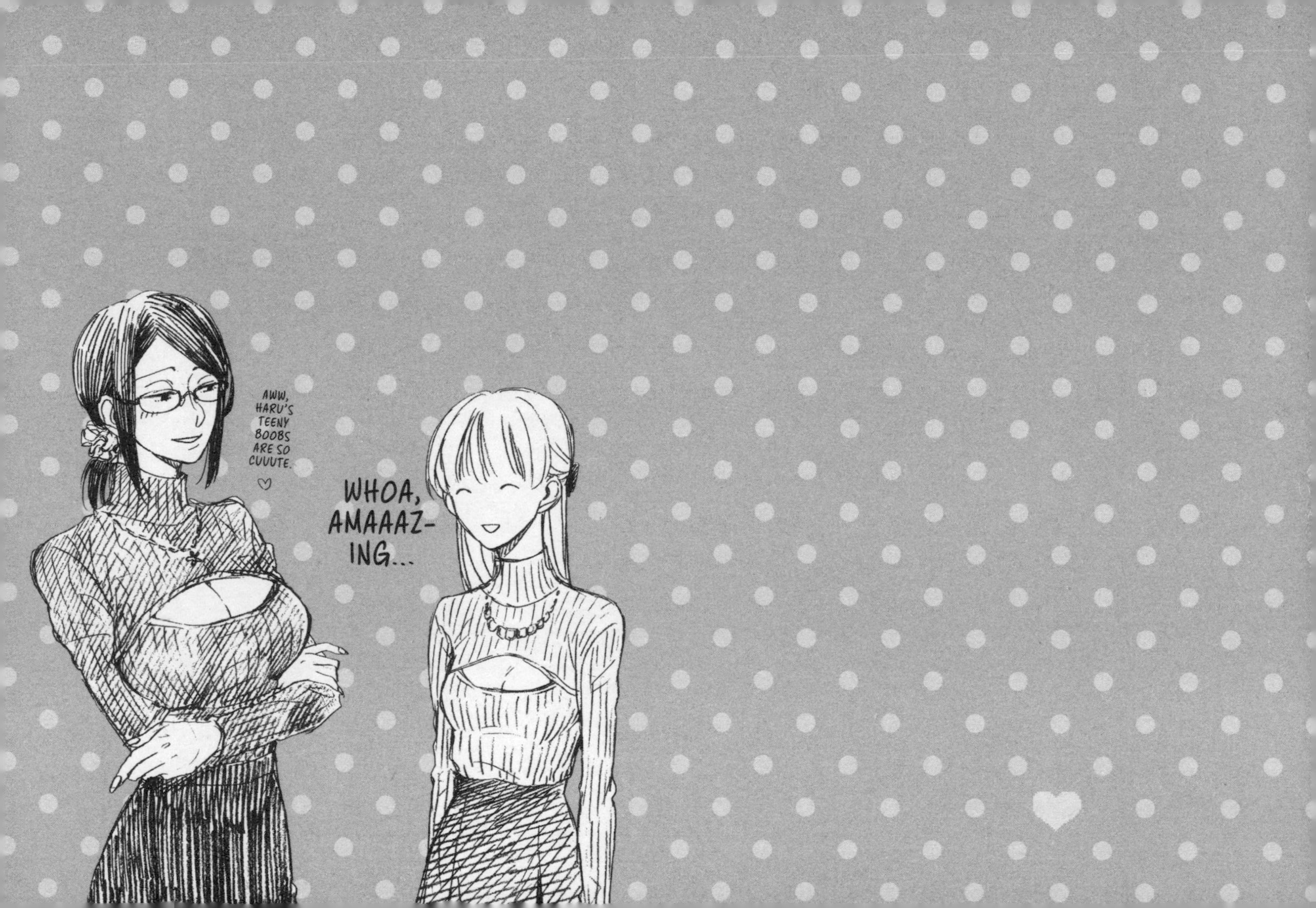
WHOA, AMAAAZ-ING...
AWW, HARU'S TEENY BOOBS ARE SO CUUUTE. ♡

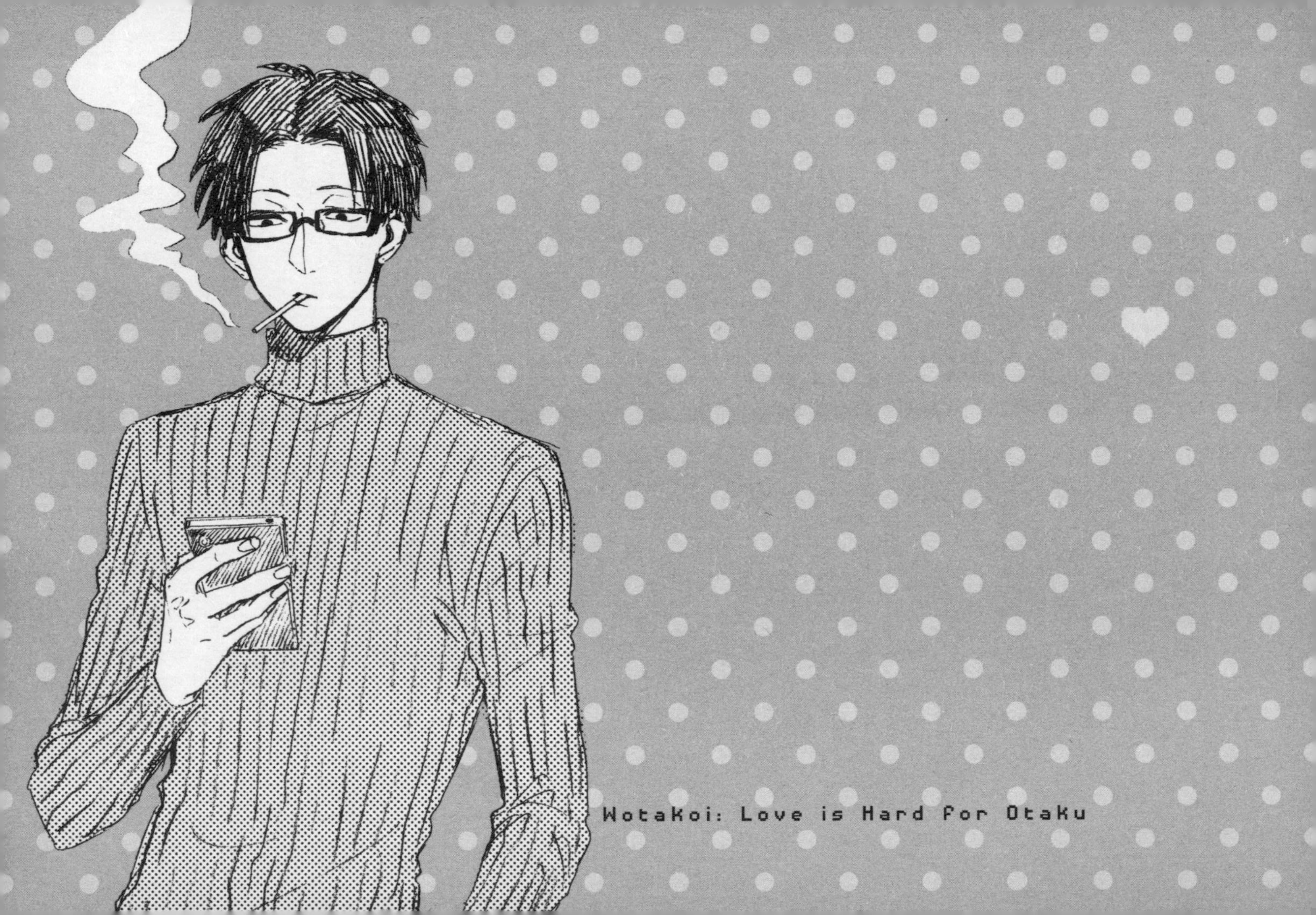
WotaKoi: Love is Hard for Otaku

Let's mess with our boyfriends!

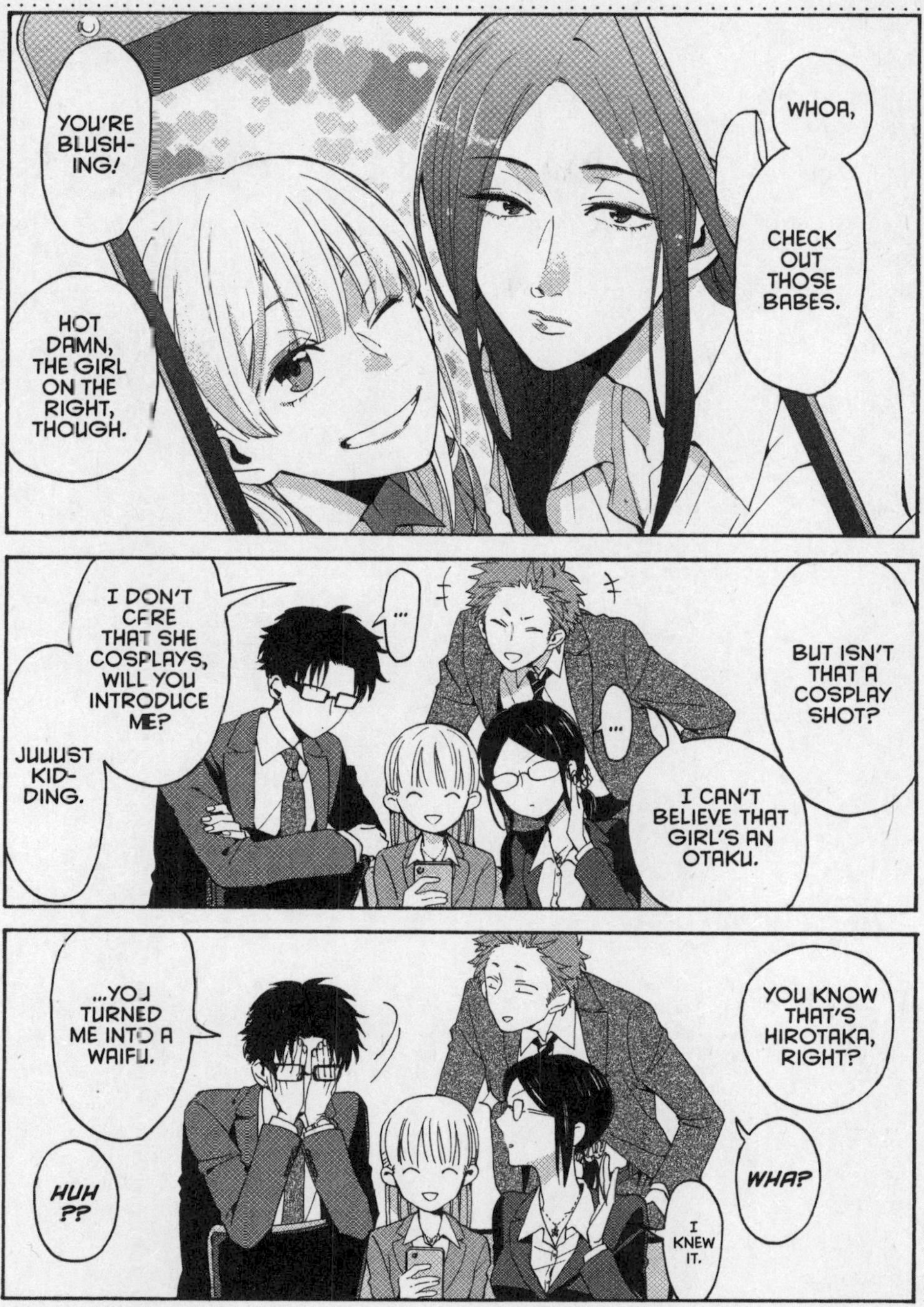
WHOA, CHECK OUT THOSE BABES.
YOU'RE BLUSHING!
HOT DAMN, THE GIRL ON THE RIGHT, THOUGH.
BUT ISN'T THAT A COSPLAY SHOT?
I CAN'T BELIEVE THAT GIRL'S AN OTAKU.
...
...
I DON'T CARE THAT SHE COSPLAYS, WILL YOU INTRODUCE ME?
JUUUST KIDDING.
YOU KNOW THAT'S HIROTAKA, RIGHT?
WHA?
I KNEW IT.
...YOU TURNED ME INTO A WAIFU.
HUH ??

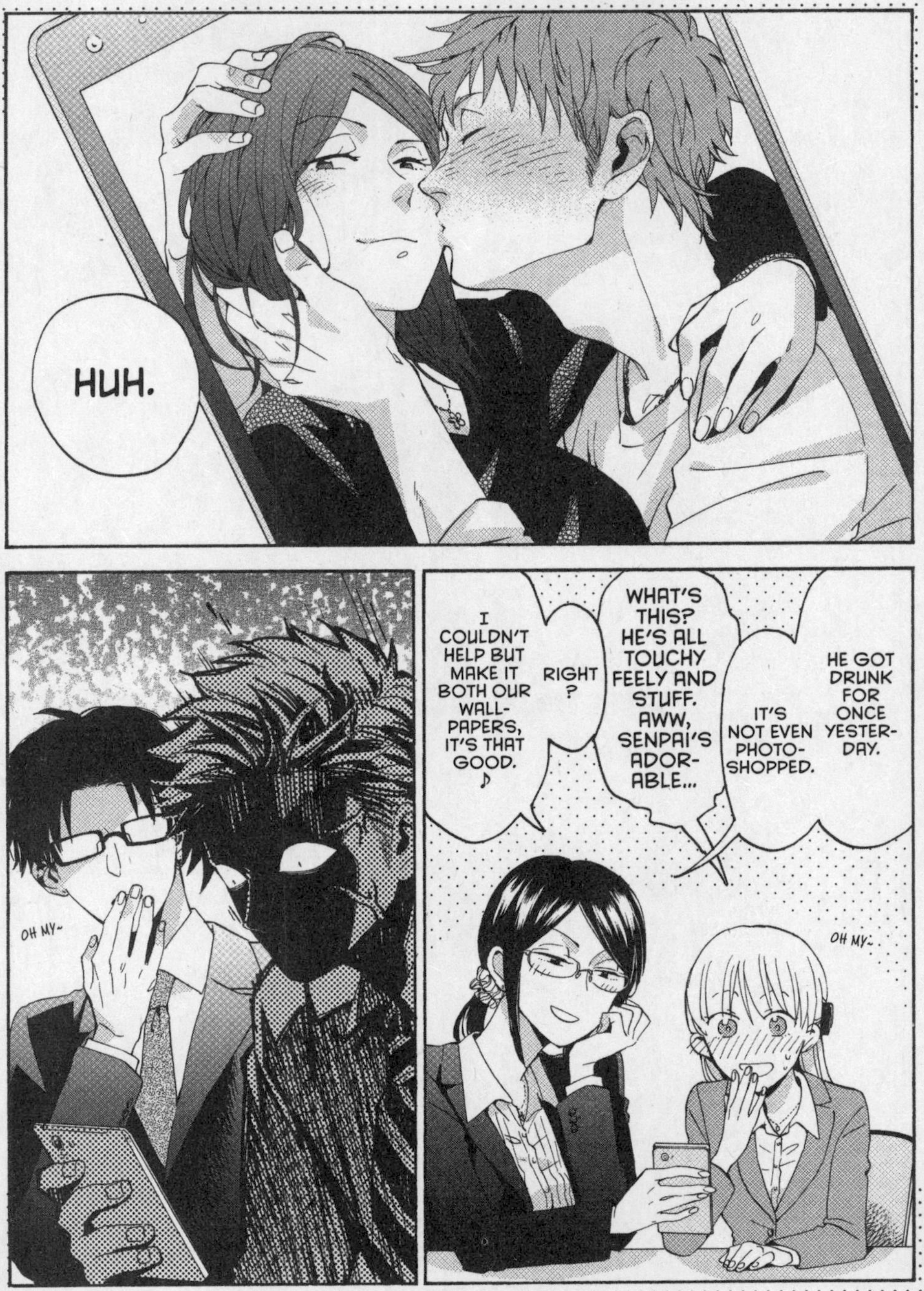
HUH.
HE GOT DRUNK FOR ONCE YESTER-DAY.
IT'S NOT EVEN PHOTO-SHOPPED.
WHAT'S THIS? HE'S ALL TOUCHY FEELY AND STUFF. AWW, SENPAI'S ADOR-ABLE...
RIGHT?
I COULDN'T HELP BUT MAKE IT BOTH OUR WALL-PAPERS, IT'S THAT GOOD. ♪
OH MY~
OH MY~

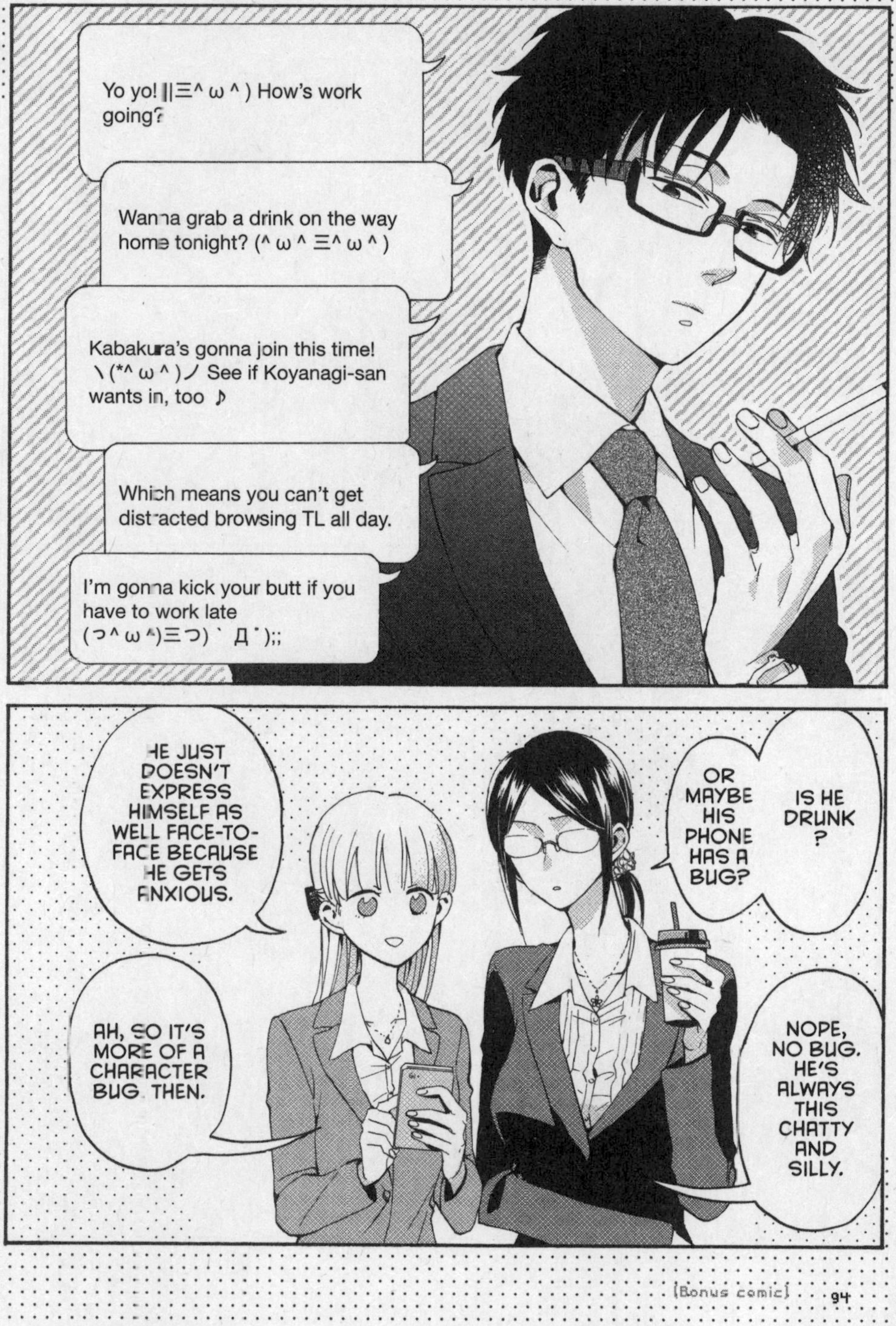
Yo yo! ||三^ ω ^) How's work going?
Wanna grab a drink on the way home tonight? (^ ω ^ 三^ ω ^)
Kabakura's gonna join this time! \(*^ ω ^)ノ See if Koyanagi-san wants in, too ♪
Which means you can't get distracted browsing TL all day.
I'm gonna kick your butt if you have to work late (つ^ ω ^)三つ) ` Д ´);;
IS HE DRUNK?
OR MAYBE HIS PHONE HAS A BUG?
HE JUST DOESN'T EXPRESS HIMSELF AS WELL FACE-TO-FACE BECAUSE HE GETS ANXIOUS.
NOPE, NO BUG. HE'S ALWAYS THIS CHATTY AND SILLY.
AH, SO IT'S MORE OF A CHARACTER BUG, THEN.

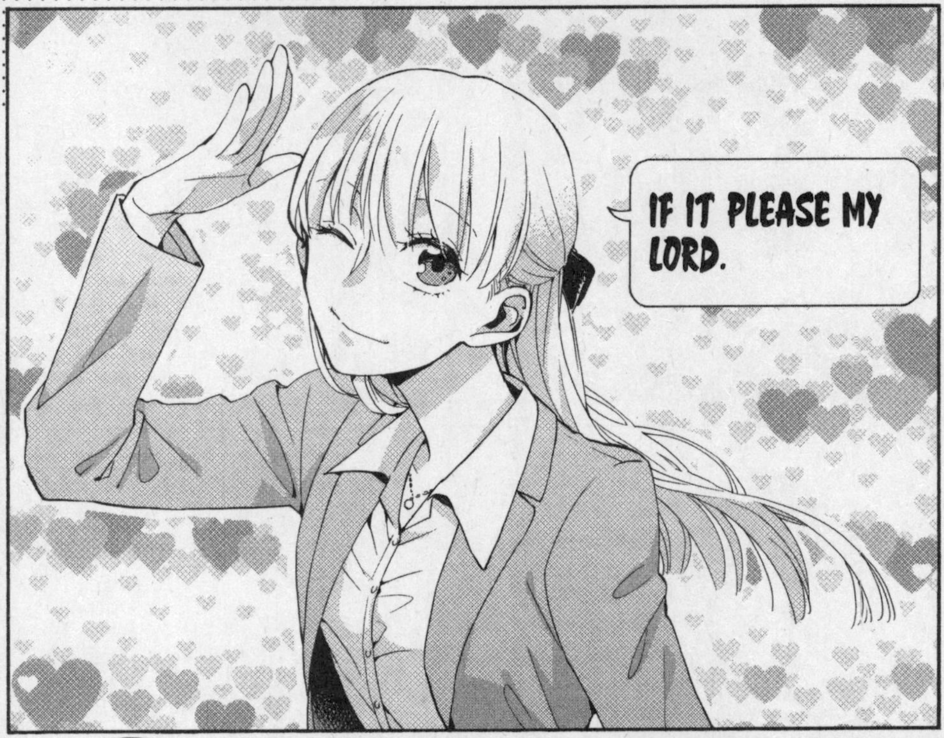
IF IT PLEASE MY LORD.

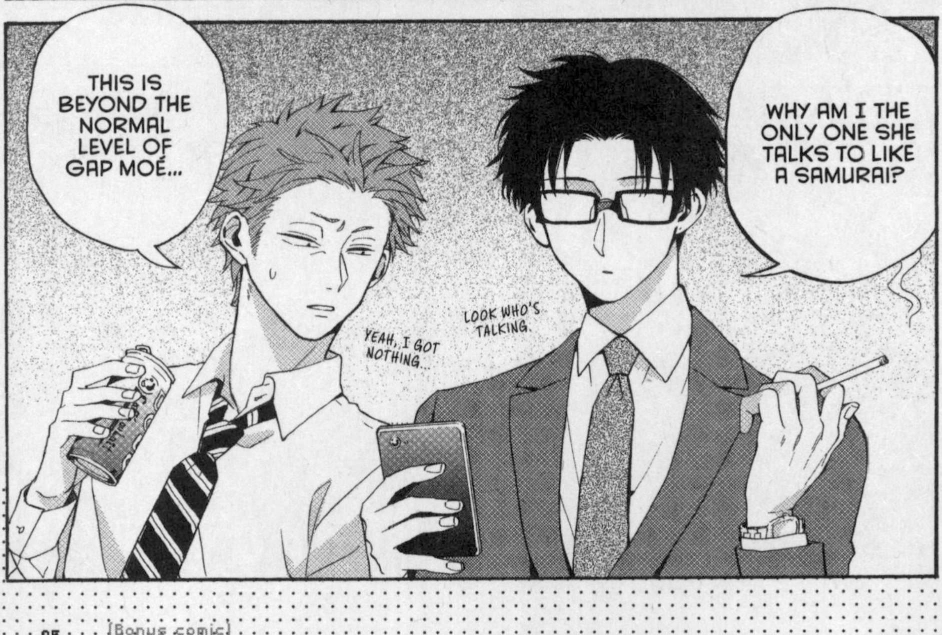
WHY AM I THE ONLY ONE SHE TALKS TO LIKE A SAMURAI?
THIS IS BEYOND THE NORMAL LEVEL OF GAP MOÉ...
LOOK WHO'S TALKING.
YEAH, I GOT NOTHING...

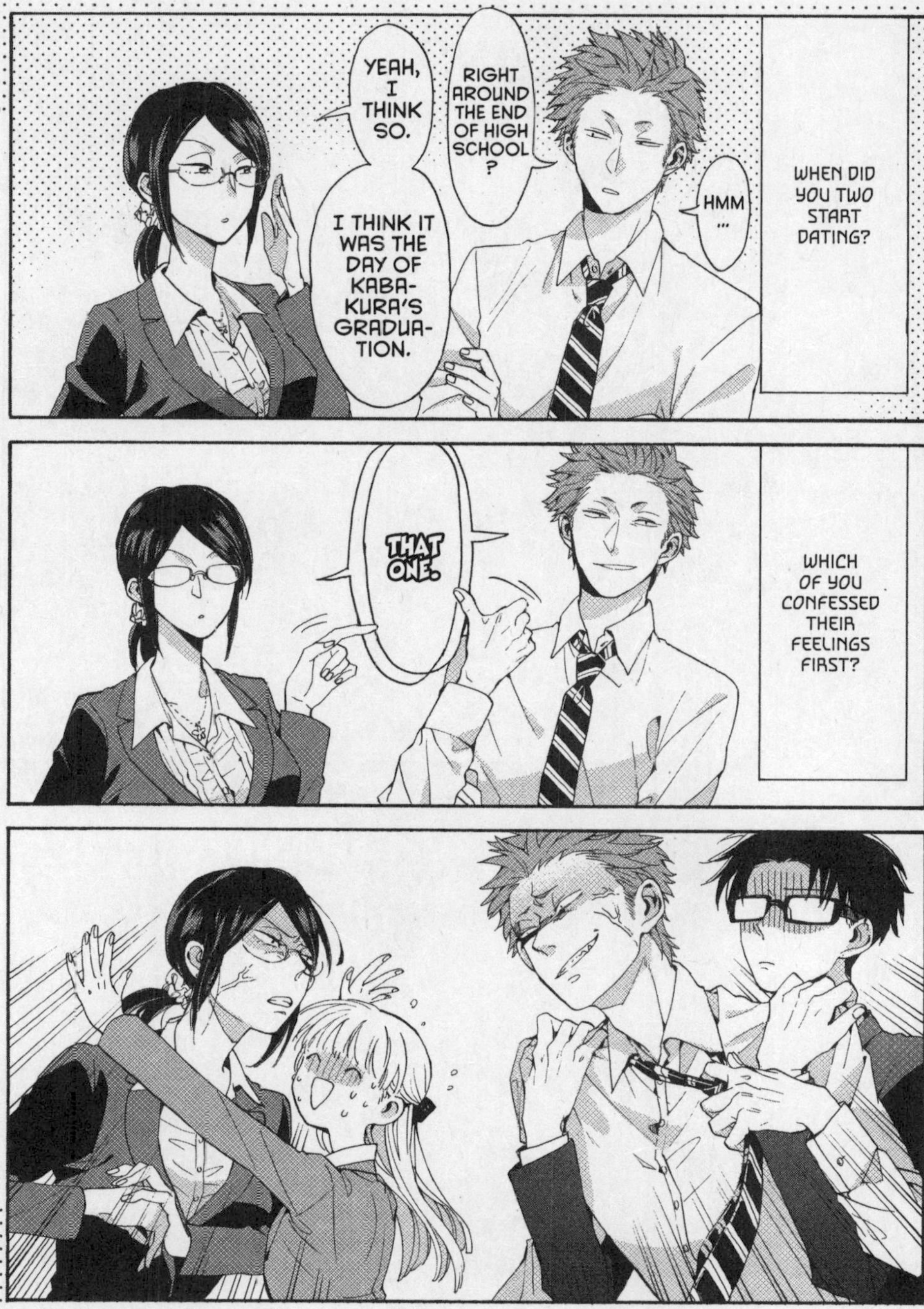
WHEN DID YOU TWO START DATING?
HMM...
RIGHT AROUND THE END OF HIGH SCHOOL?
YEAH, I THINK SO.
I THINK IT WAS THE DAY OF KABA-KURA'S GRADUA-TION.
WHICH OF YOU CONFESSED THEIR FEELINGS FIRST?
THAT ONE.

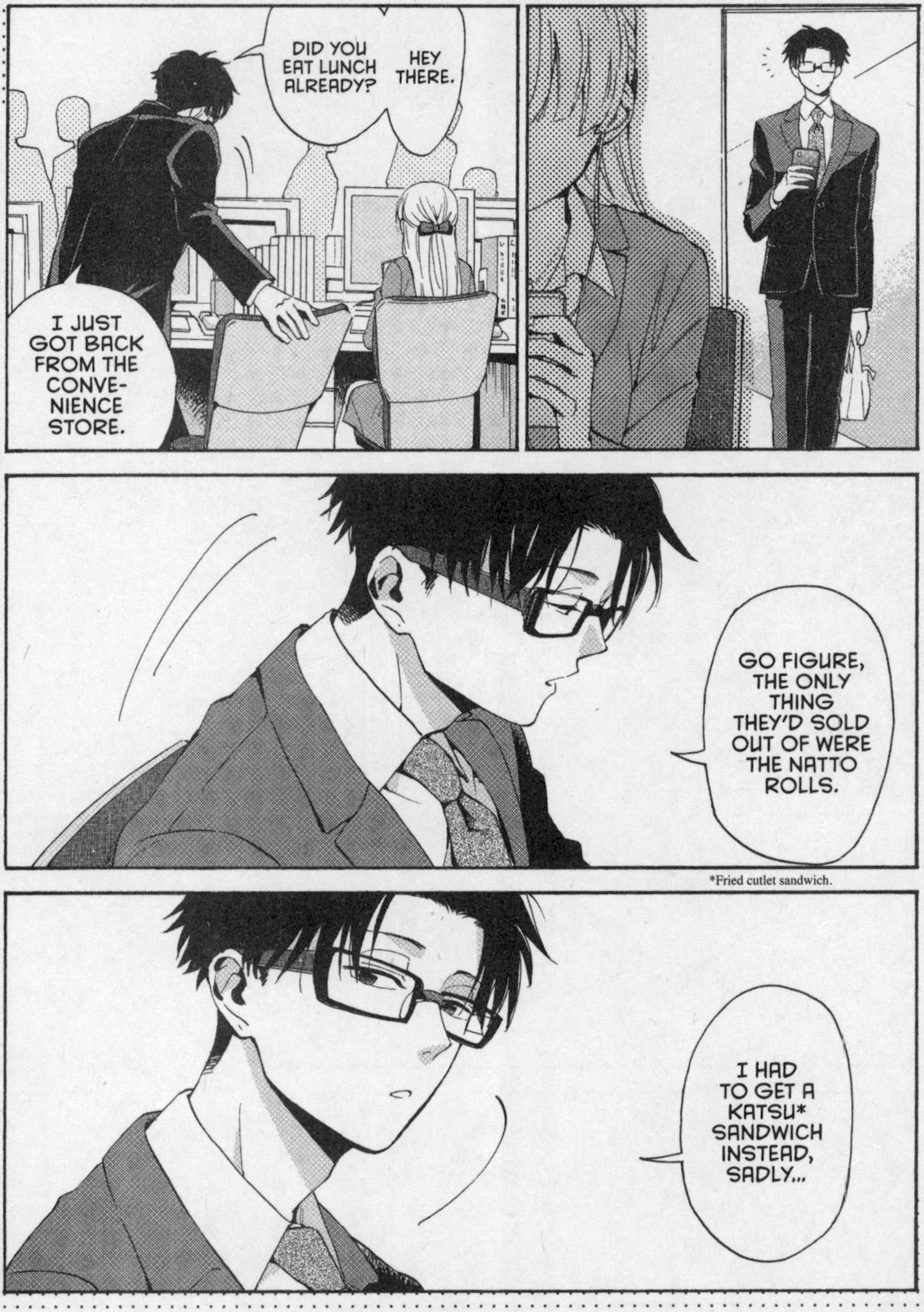
HEY THERE.
DID YOU EAT LUNCH ALREADY?
I JUST GOT BACK FROM THE CONVENIENCE STORE.
GO FIGURE, THE ONLY THING THEY'D SOLD OUT OF WERE THE NATTO ROLLS.
I HAD TO GET A KATSU* SANDWICH INSTEAD, SADLY...

*Fried cutlet sandwich.

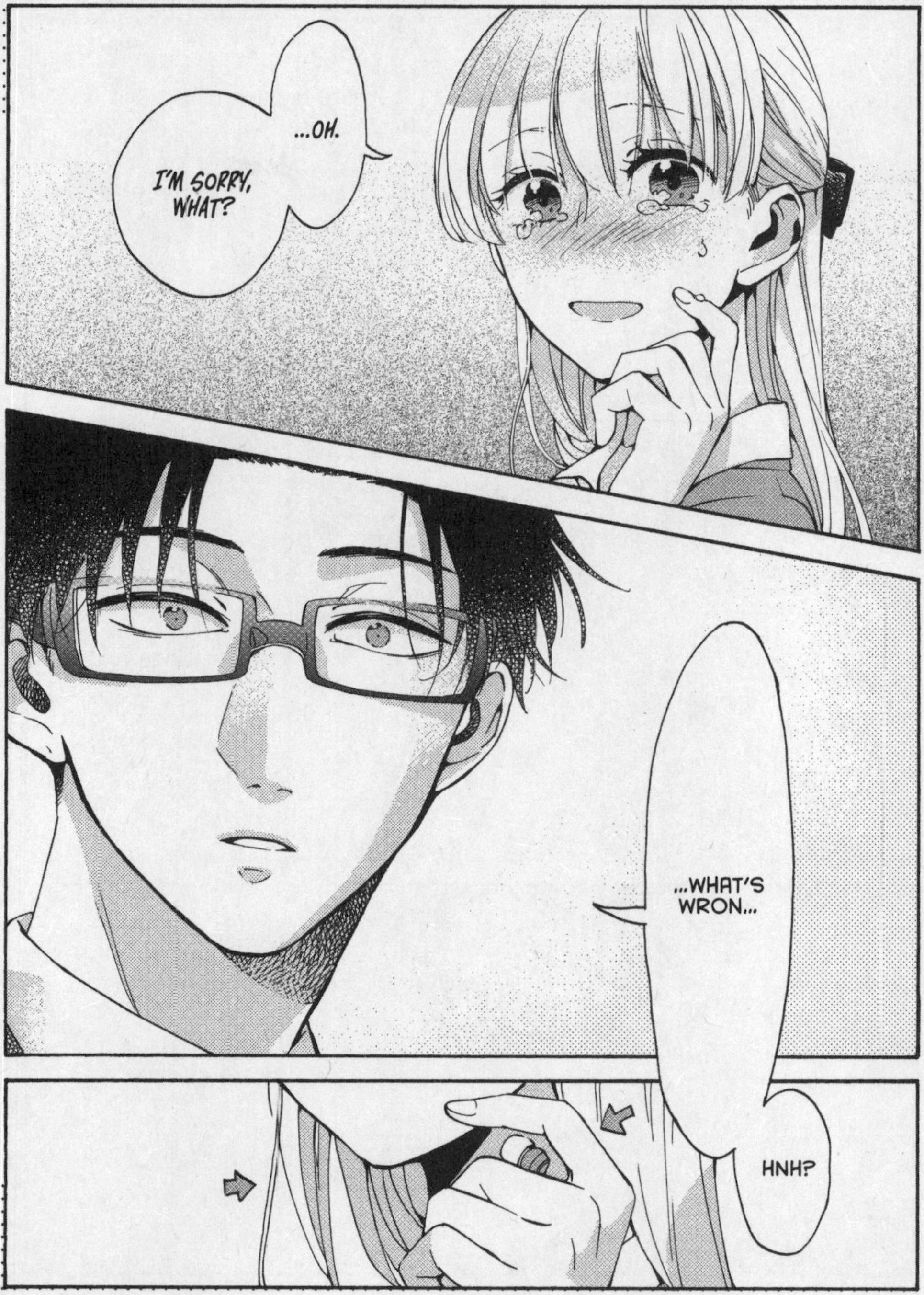
...OH.
I'M SORRY, WHAT?
...WHAT'S WRON...
HNH?

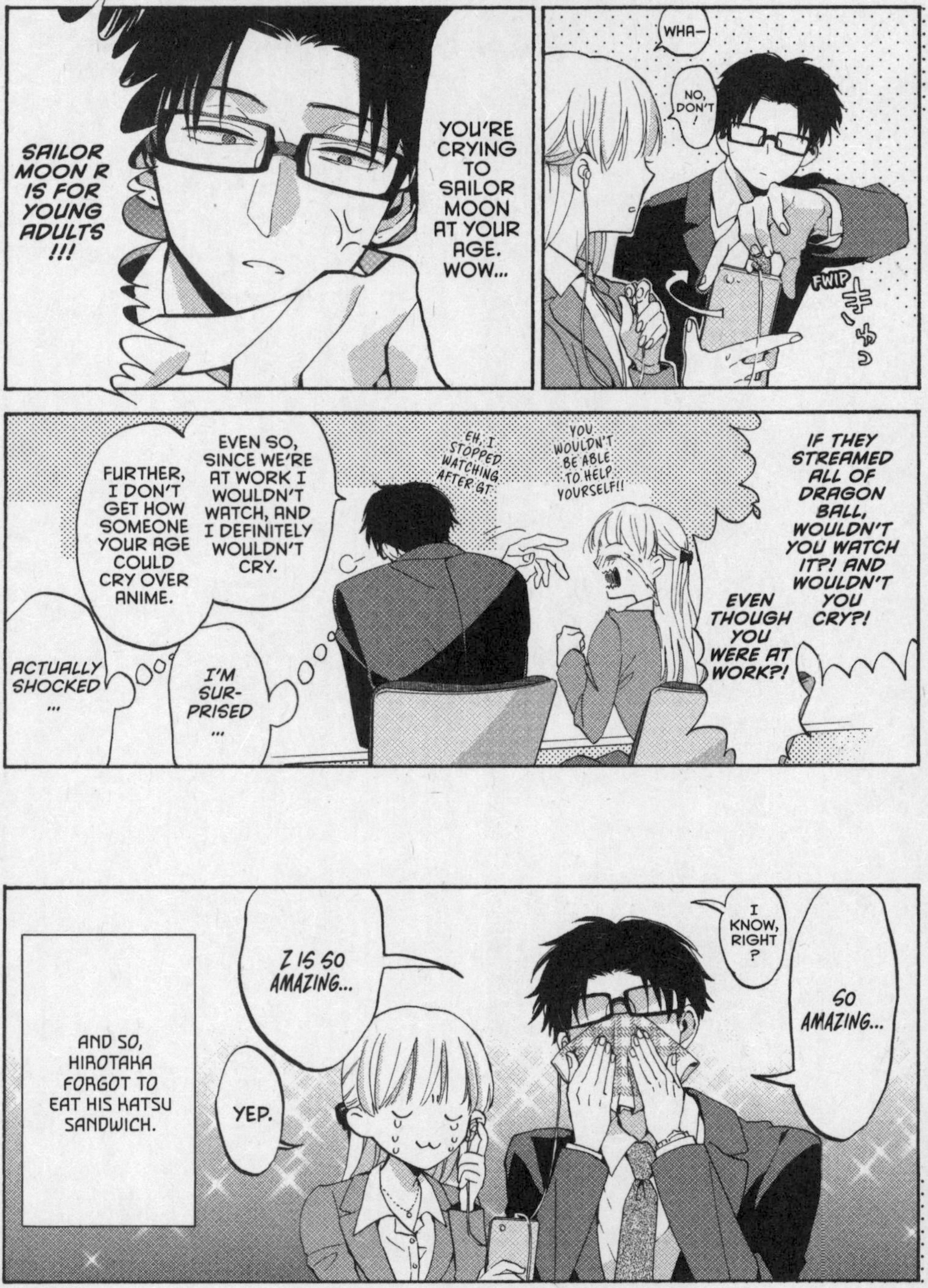
WHA—
NO, DON'T!
FWIP
きゅっ
YOU'RE CRYING TO SAILOR MOON AT YOUR AGE. WOW...
SAILOR MOON R IS FOR YOUNG ADULTS!!!
IF THEY STREAMED ALL OF DRAGON BALL, WOULDN'T YOU WATCH IT?! AND WOULDN'T YOU CRY?!
EVEN THOUGH YOU WERE AT WORK?!
YOU WOULDN'T BE ABLE TO HELP YOURSELF!!
EH, I STOPPED WATCHING AFTER GT
EVEN SO, SINCE WE'RE AT WORK I WOULDN'T WATCH, AND I DEFINITELY WOULDN'T CRY.
FURTHER, I DON'T GET HOW SOMEONE YOUR AGE COULD CRY OVER ANIME.
I'M SUR-PRISED...
ACTUALLY SHOCKED...
I KNOW, RIGHT?
SO AMAZING...
Z IS SO AMAZING...
YEP.
AND SO, HIROTAKA FORGOT TO EAT HIS KATSU SANDWICH.

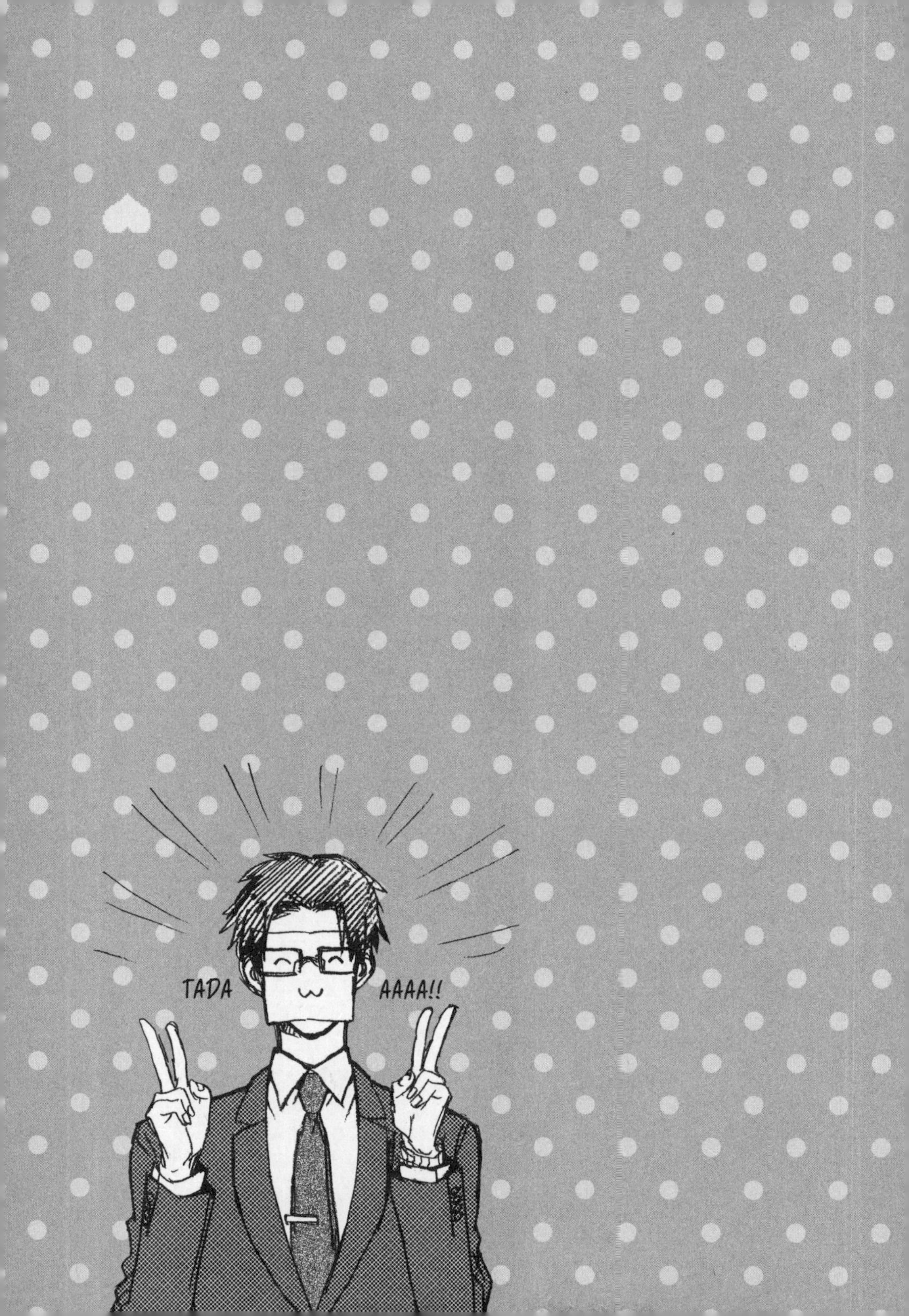
TADA
AAAA!!

Wotakoi: Love is Hard for Otaku

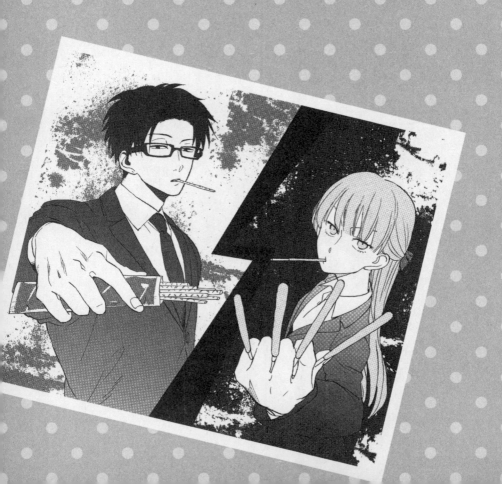

Episode.... 5

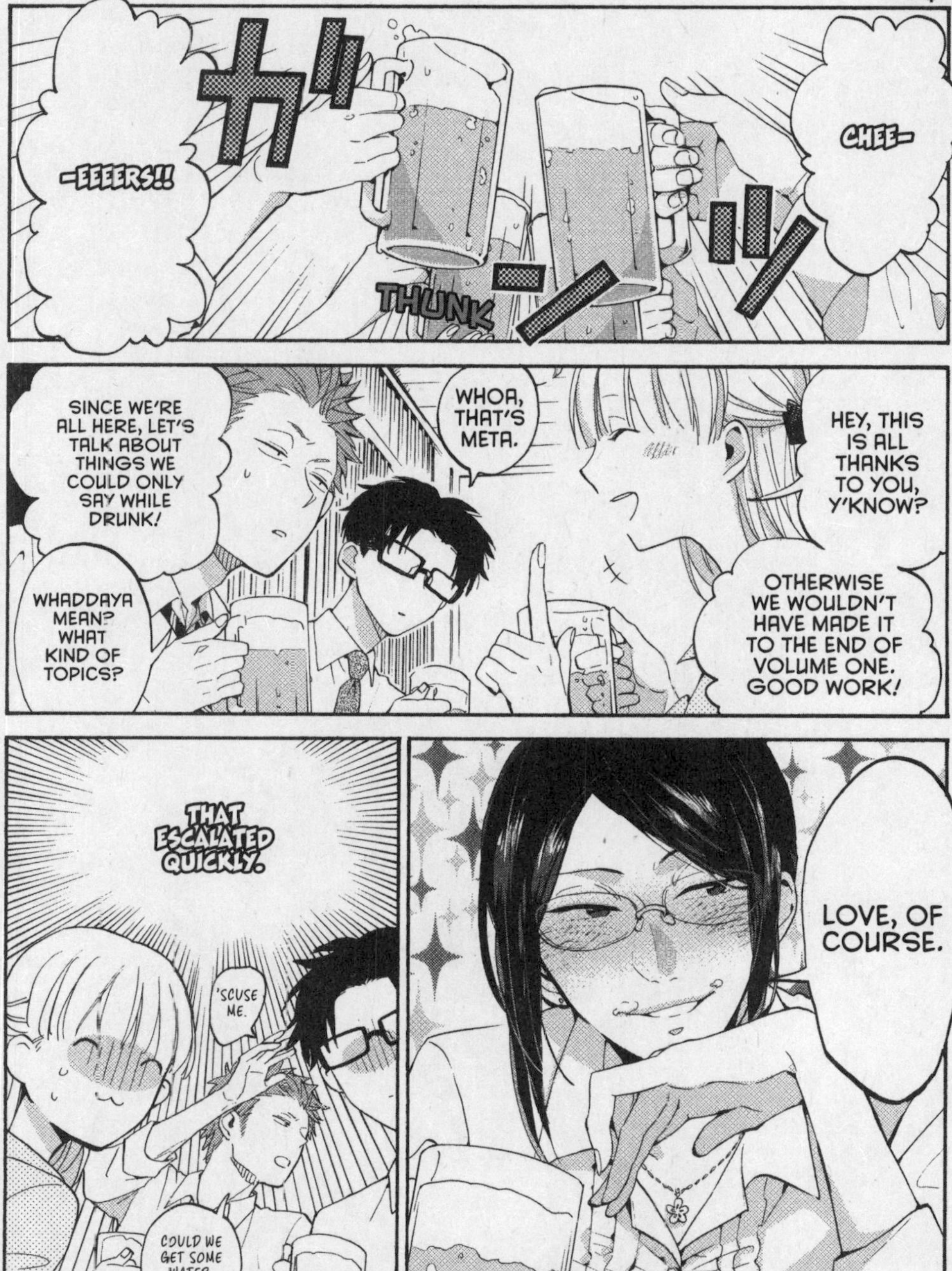
CHEE-
-EEEERS!!
THUNK
HEY, THIS IS ALL THANKS TO YOU, Y'KNOW?
OTHERWISE WE WOULDN'T HAVE MADE IT TO THE END OF VOLUME ONE. GOOD WORK!
WHOA, THAT'S META.
SINCE WE'RE ALL HERE, LET'S TALK ABOUT THINGS WE COULD ONLY SAY WHILE DRUNK!
WHADDAYA MEAN? WHAT KIND OF TOPICS?
LOVE, OF COURSE.
THAT ESCALATED QUICKLY.
'SCUSE ME.
COULD WE GET SOME WATER, PLEASE?

(An overpowering running start)

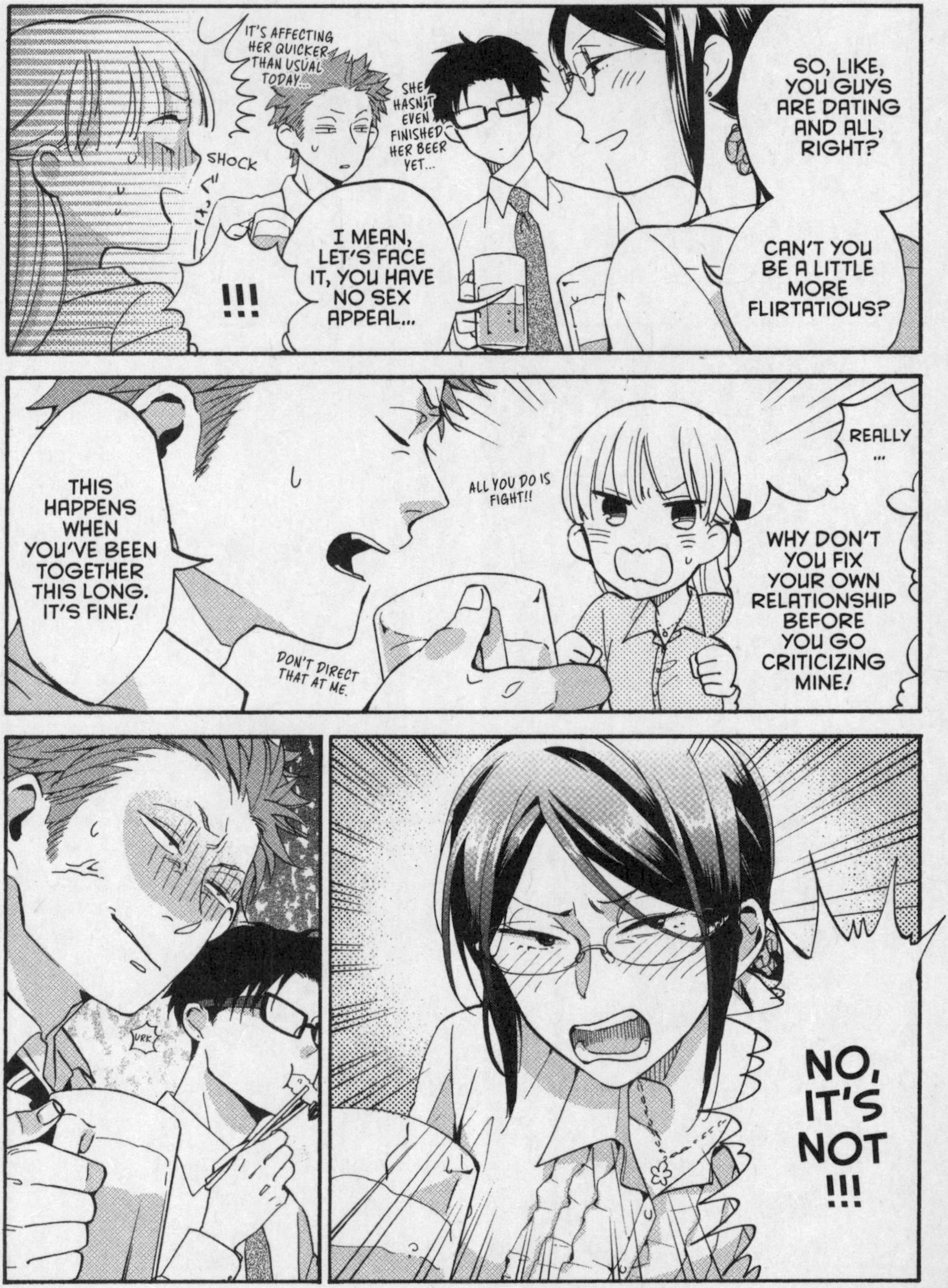
SO, LIKE, YOU GUYS ARE DATING AND ALL, RIGHT?
CAN'T YOU BE A LITTLE MORE FLIRTATIOUS?
SHE HASN'T EVEN FINISHED HER BEER YET...
I MEAN, LET'S FACE IT, YOU HAVE NO SEX APPEAL...
IT'S AFFECTING HER QUICKER THAN USUAL TODAY...
SHOCK
!!!
REALLY ...
WHY DON'T YOU FIX YOUR OWN RELATIONSHIP BEFORE YOU GO CRITICIZING MINE!
ALL YOU DO IS FIGHT!!
THIS HAPPENS WHEN YOU'VE BEEN TOGETHER THIS LONG. IT'S FINE!
DON'T DIRECT THAT AT ME.
NO, IT'S NOT !!!
URK

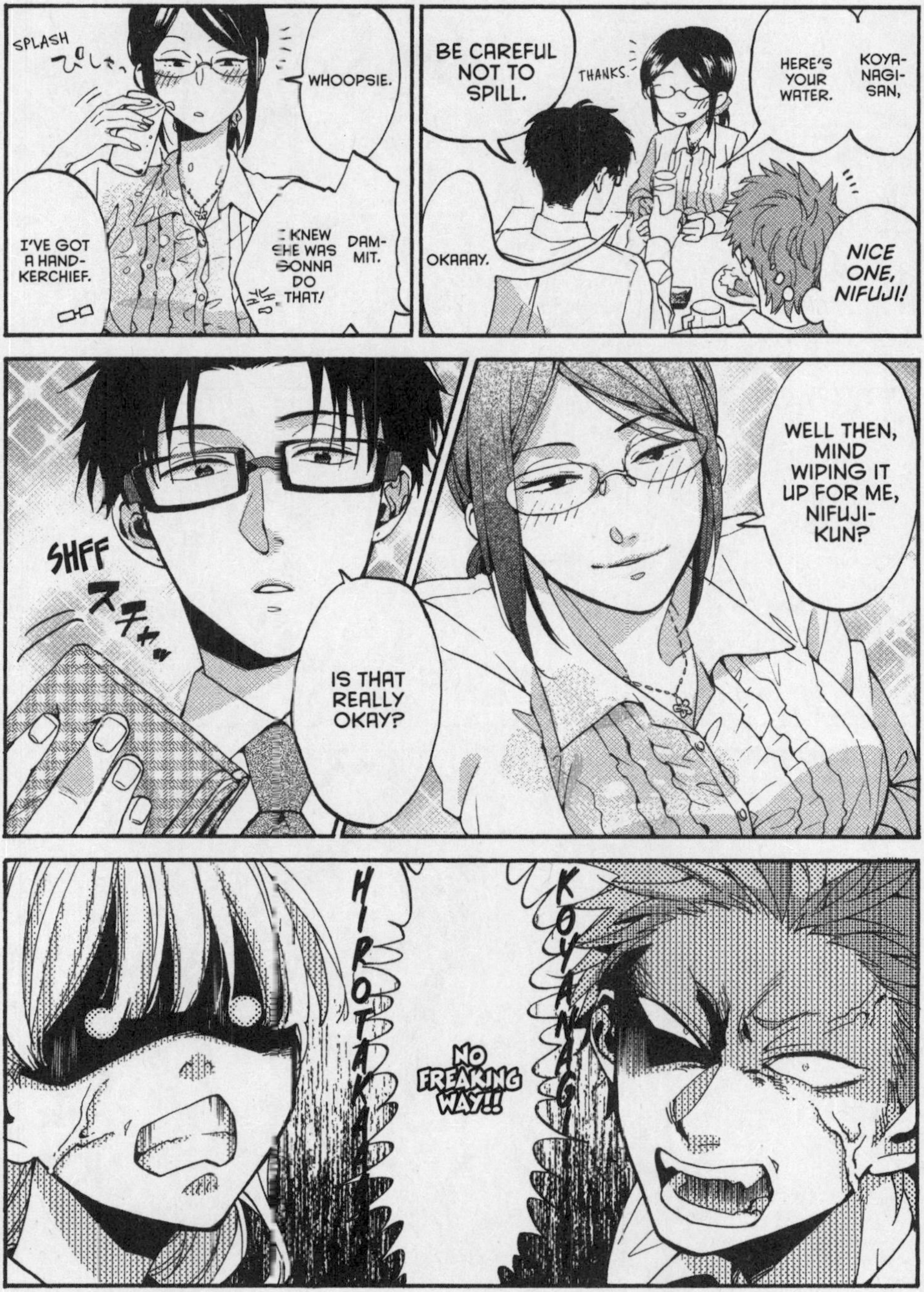
KOYA-NAGI-SAN,
HERE'S YOUR WATER.
THANKS.
BE CAREFUL NOT TO SPILL.
NICE ONE, NIFUJI!
OKAAAY.
WHOOPSIE.
SPLASH
DAM-MIT.
I KNEW SHE WAS GONNA DO THAT!
I'VE GOT A HAND-KERCHIEF.
WELL THEN, MIND WIPING IT UP FOR ME, NIFUJI-KUN?
IS THAT REALLY OKAY?
SHFF
KOYANAGI
NO FREAKING WAY!!
HIROTAKA

[They're super angry]

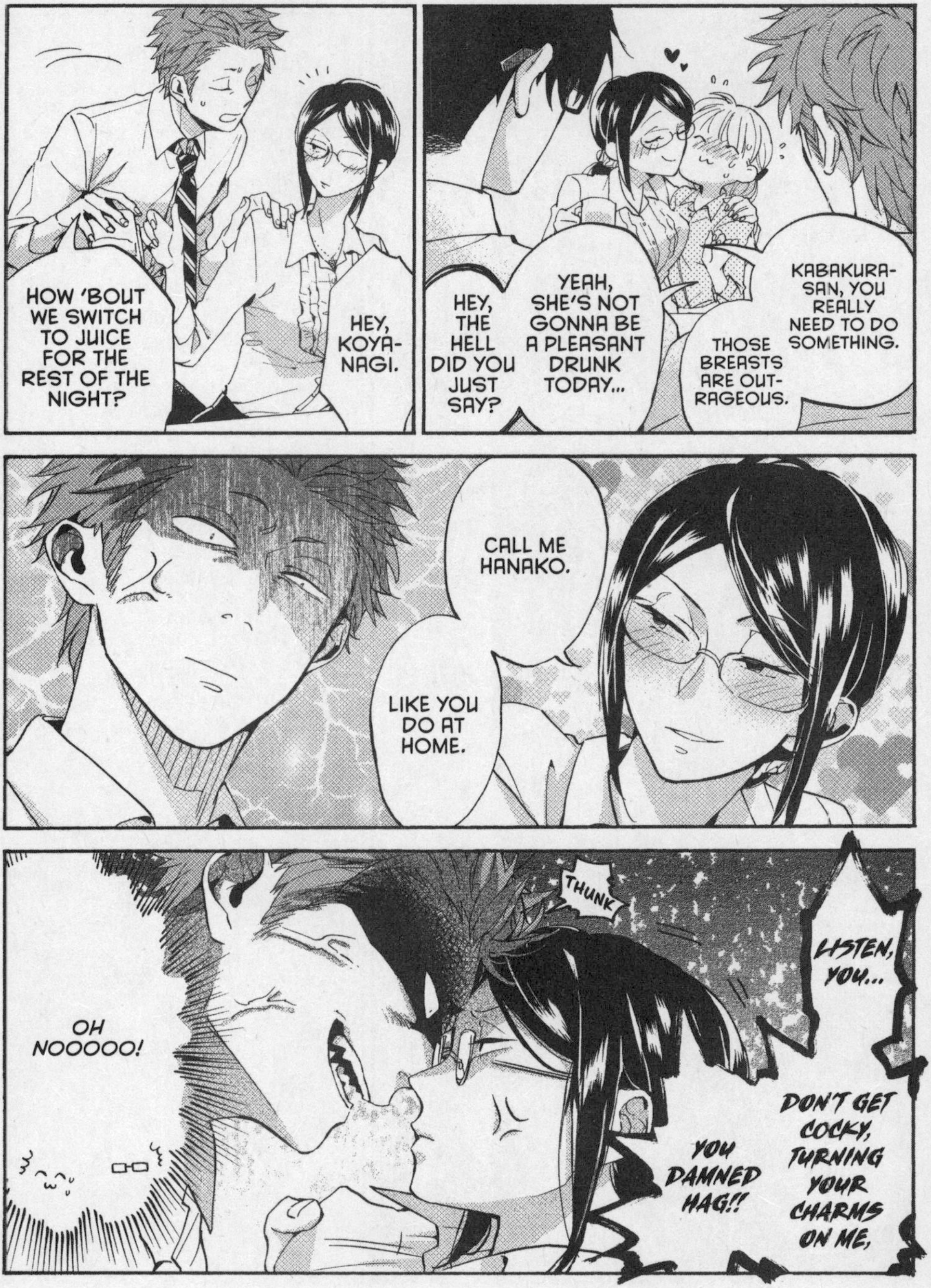
KABAKURA-SAN, YOU REALLY NEED TO DO SOMETHING.
THOSE BREASTS ARE OUT-RAGEOUS.
YEAH, SHE'S NOT GONNA BE A PLEASANT DRUNK TODAY...
HEY, THE HELL DID YOU JUST SAY?
HEY, KOYA-NAGI.
HOW 'BOUT WE SWITCH TO JUICE FOR THE REST OF THE NIGHT?
CALL ME HANAKO.
LIKE YOU DO AT HOME.
THUNK
LISTEN, YOU...
DON'T GET COCKY, TURNING YOUR CHARMS ON ME,
YOU DAMNED HAG!!
OH NOOOOO!

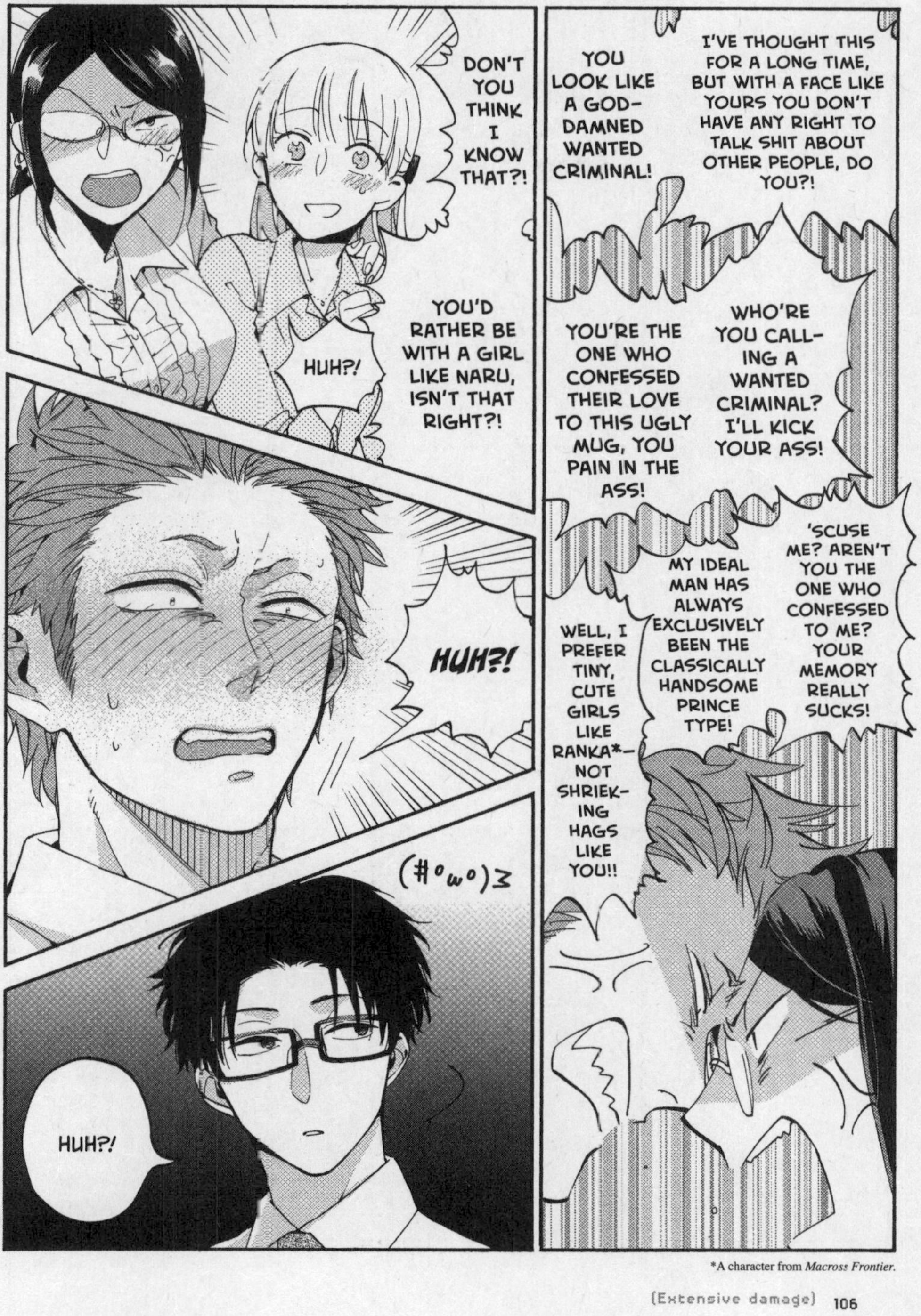

I'VE THOUGHT THIS FOR A LONG TIME, BUT WITH A FACE LIKE YOURS YOU DON'T HAVE ANY RIGHT TO TALK SHIT ABOUT OTHER PEOPLE, DO YOU?!
YOU LOOK LIKE A GOD-DAMNED WANTED CRIMINAL!
WHO'RE YOU CALLING A WANTED CRIMINAL? I'LL KICK YOUR ASS!
YOU'RE THE ONE WHO CONFESSED THEIR LOVE TO THIS UGLY MUG, YOU PAIN IN THE ASS!
'SCUSE ME? AREN'T YOU THE ONE WHO CONFESSED TO ME? YOUR MEMORY REALLY SUCKS!
MY IDEAL MAN HAS ALWAYS EXCLUSIVELY BEEN THE CLASSICALLY HANDSOME PRINCE TYPE!
WELL, I PREFER TINY, CUTE GIRLS LIKE RANKA*—NOT SHRIEKING HAGS LIKE YOU!!
DON'T YOU THINK I KNOW THAT?!
YOU'D RATHER BE WITH A GIRL LIKE NARU, ISN'T THAT RIGHT?!
HUH?!
HUH?!
(#ºωº)ɜ
HUH?!

*A character from *Macross Frontier*.

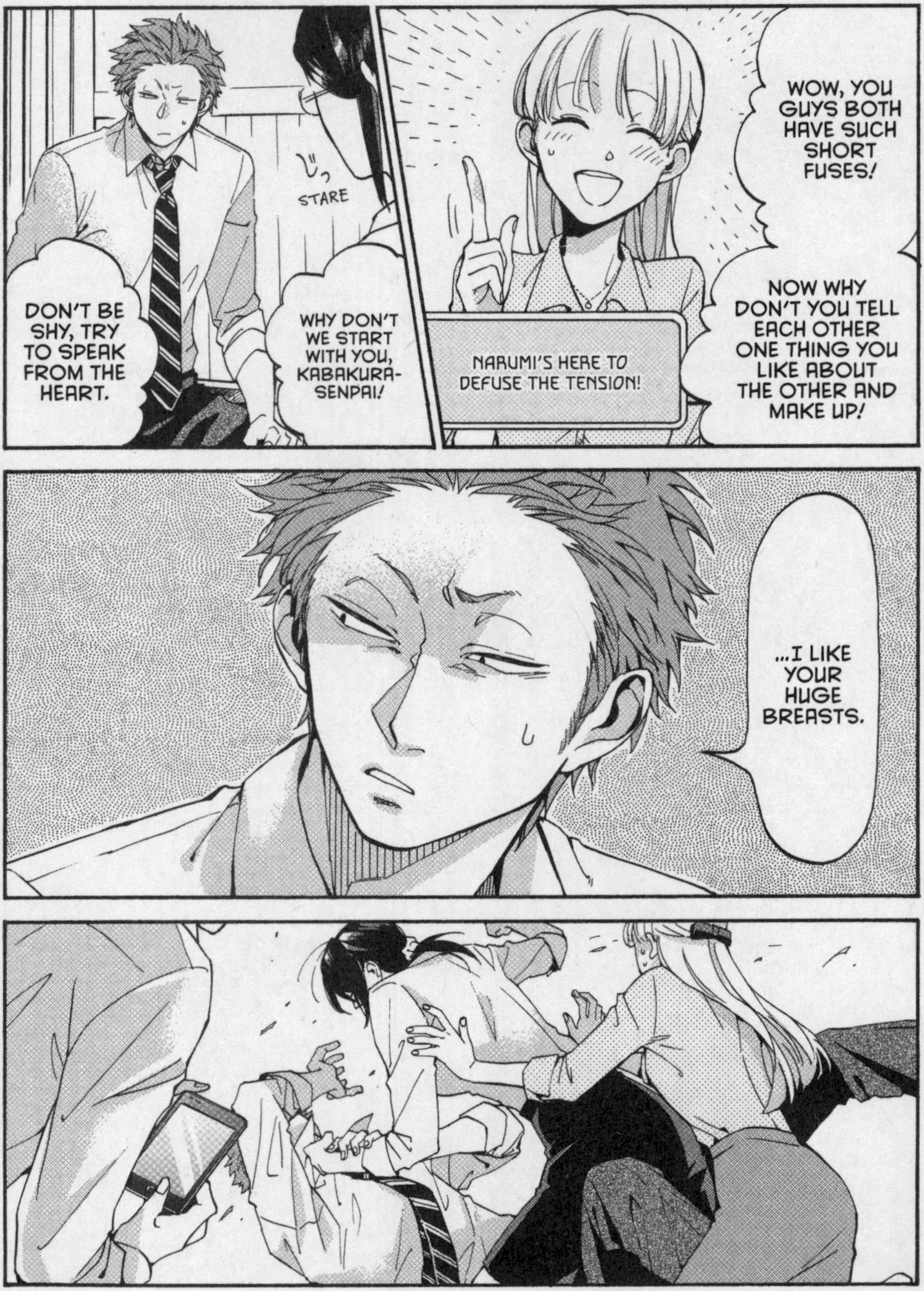
WOW, YOU GUYS BOTH HAVE SUCH SHORT FUSES!
NOW WHY DON'T YOU TELL EACH OTHER ONE THING YOU LIKE ABOUT THE OTHER AND MAKE UP!
NARUMI'S HERE TO DEFUSE THE TENSION!
じっ
STARE
WHY DON'T WE START WITH YOU, KABAKURA-SENPAI!
DON'T BE SHY, TRY TO SPEAK FROM THE HEART.
...I LIKE YOUR HUGE BREASTS.

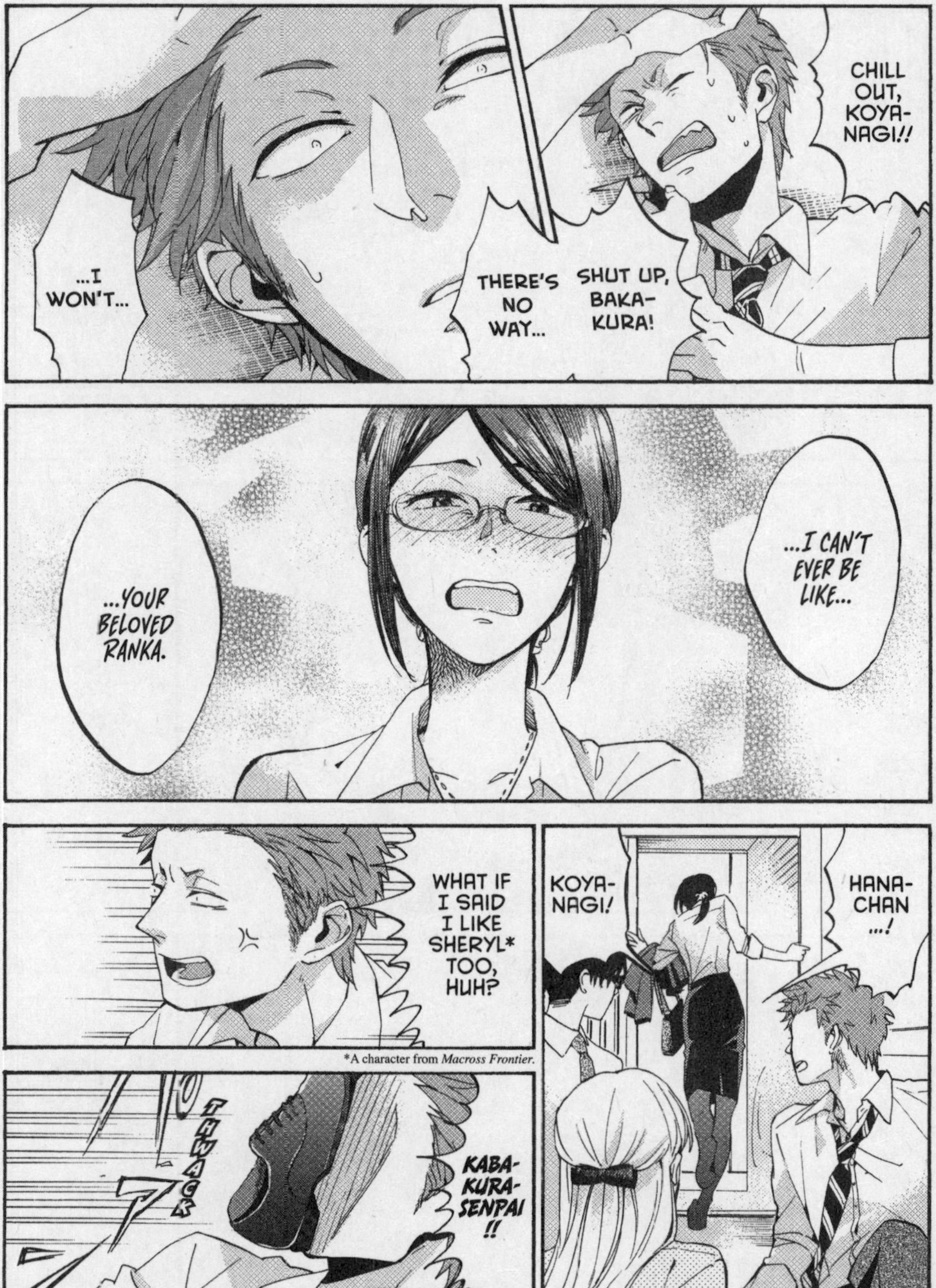
CHILL OUT, KOYA-NAGI!!
SHUT UP, BAKA-KURA!
THERE'S NO WAY...
...I WON'T...
...I CAN'T EVER BE LIKE...
...YOUR BELOVED RANKA.
HANA-CHAN ...!
KOYA-NAGI!
WHAT IF I SAID I LIKE SHERYL* TOO, HUH?
THWACK
KABA-KURA-SENPAI !!
*A character from *Macross Frontier.*

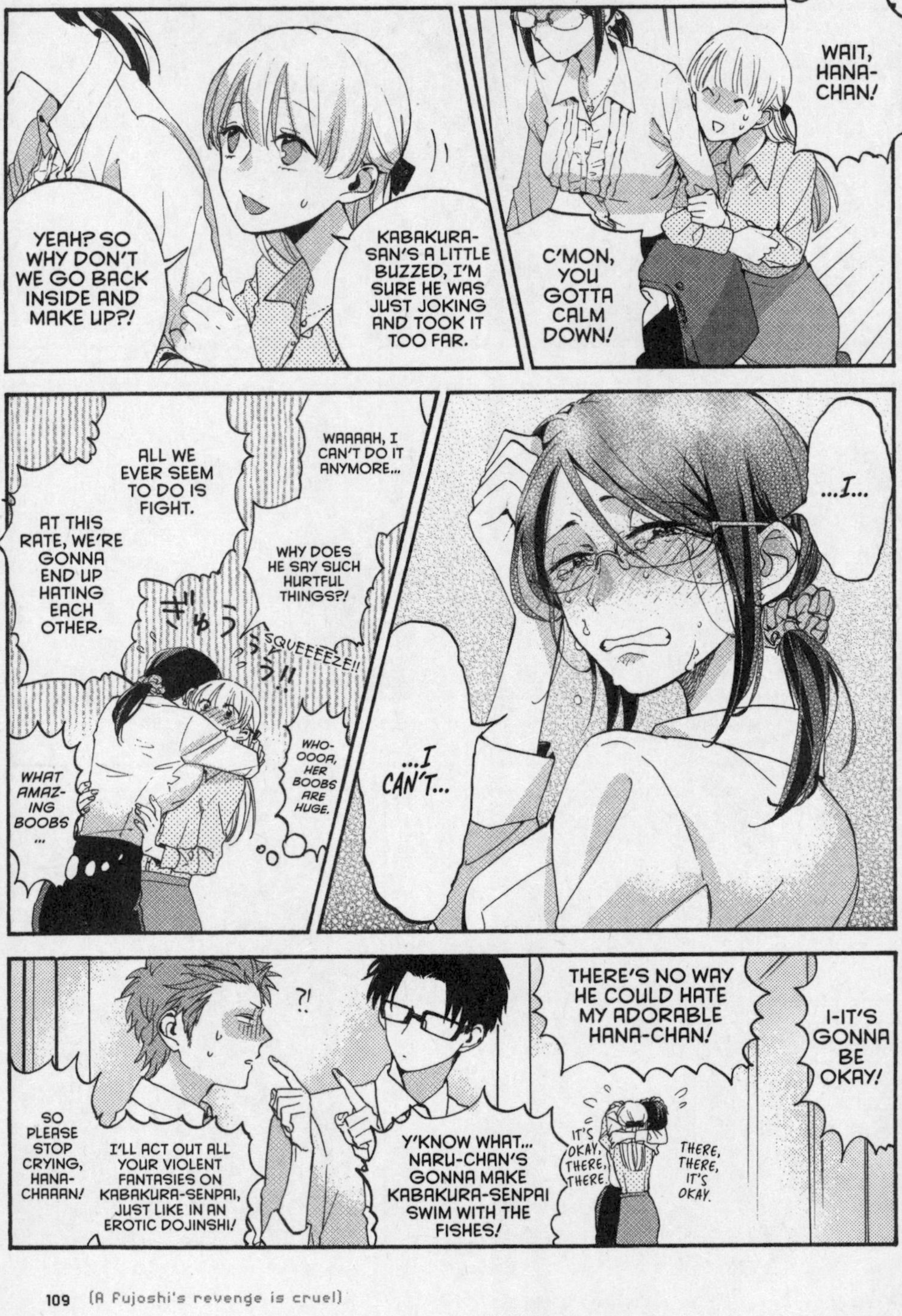
WAIT, HANA-CHAN!
C'MON, YOU GOTTA CALM DOWN!
KABAKURA-SAN'S A LITTLE BUZZED, I'M SURE HE WAS JUST JOKING AND TOOK IT TOO FAR.
YEAH? SO WHY DON'T WE GO BACK INSIDE AND MAKE UP?!
...I...
...I CAN'T...
WAAAAH, I CAN'T DO IT ANYMORE...
ALL WE EVER SEEM TO DO IS FIGHT.
WHY DOES HE SAY SUCH HURTFUL THINGS?!
AT THIS RATE, WE'RE GONNA END UP HATING EACH OTHER.
ぎゅうう
SQUEEEEEZE!!
WHO-OOOA, HER BOOBS ARE HUGE.
WHAT AMAZ-ING BOOBS ...
THERE'S NO WAY HE COULD HATE MY ADORABLE HANA-CHAN!
I-IT'S GONNA BE OKAY!
THERE, THERE, IT'S OKAY.
IT'S OKAY, THERE, THERE.
Y'KNOW WHAT... NARU-CHAN'S GONNA MAKE KABAKURA-SENPAI SWIM WITH THE FISHES!
?!
I'LL ACT OUT ALL YOUR VIOLENT FANTASIES ON KABAKURA-SENPAI, JUST LIKE IN AN EROTIC DOJINSHI!
SO PLEASE STOP CRYING, HANA-CHAAAN!

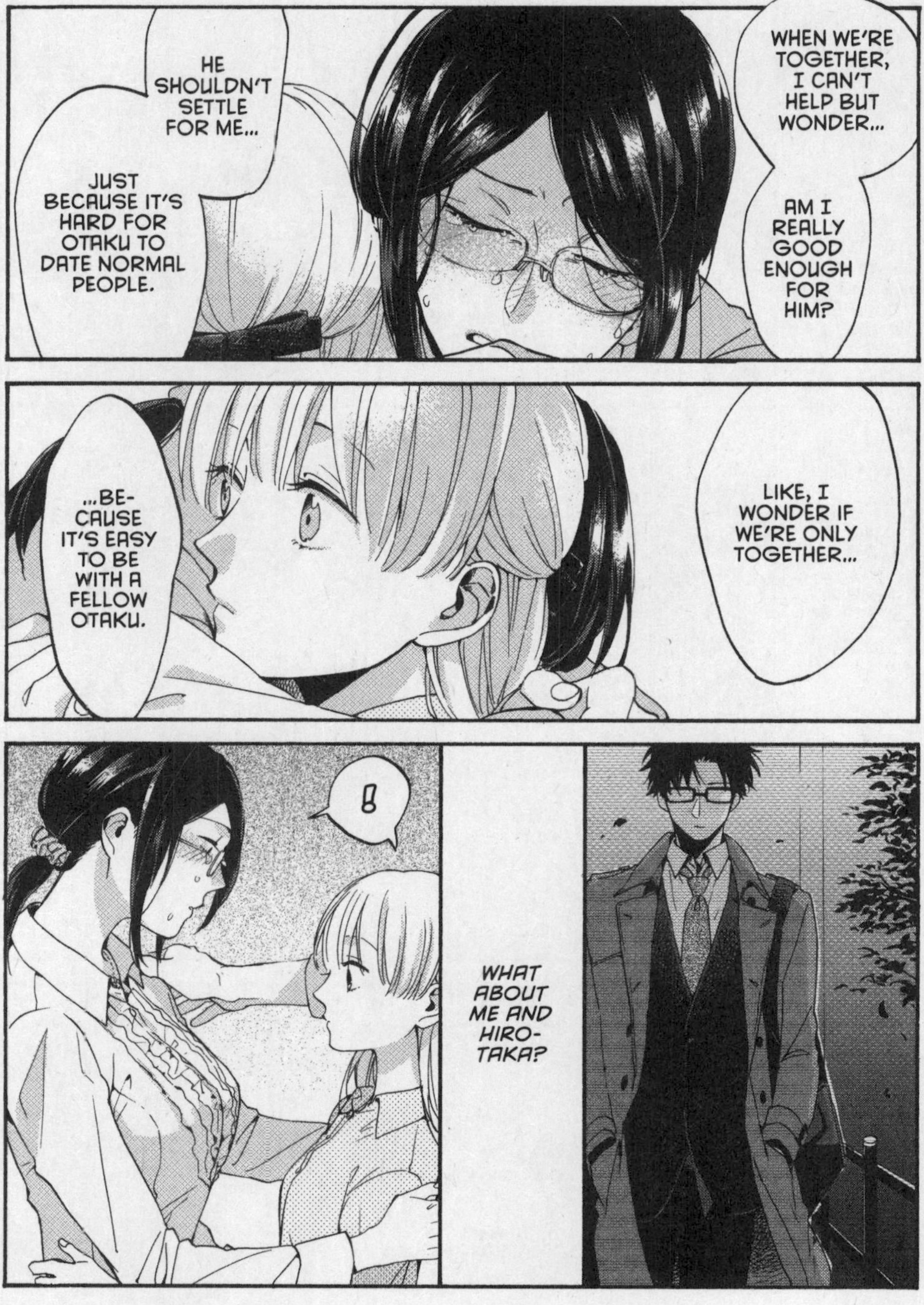
WHEN WE'RE TOGETHER, I CAN'T HELP BUT WONDER...
AM I REALLY GOOD ENOUGH FOR HIM?
HE SHOULDN'T SETTLE FOR ME...
JUST BECAUSE IT'S HARD FOR OTAKU TO DATE NORMAL PEOPLE.
LIKE, I WONDER IF WE'RE ONLY TOGETHER...
...BE-CAUSE IT'S EASY TO BE WITH A FELLOW OTAKU.
WHAT ABOUT ME AND HIRO-TAKA?
!

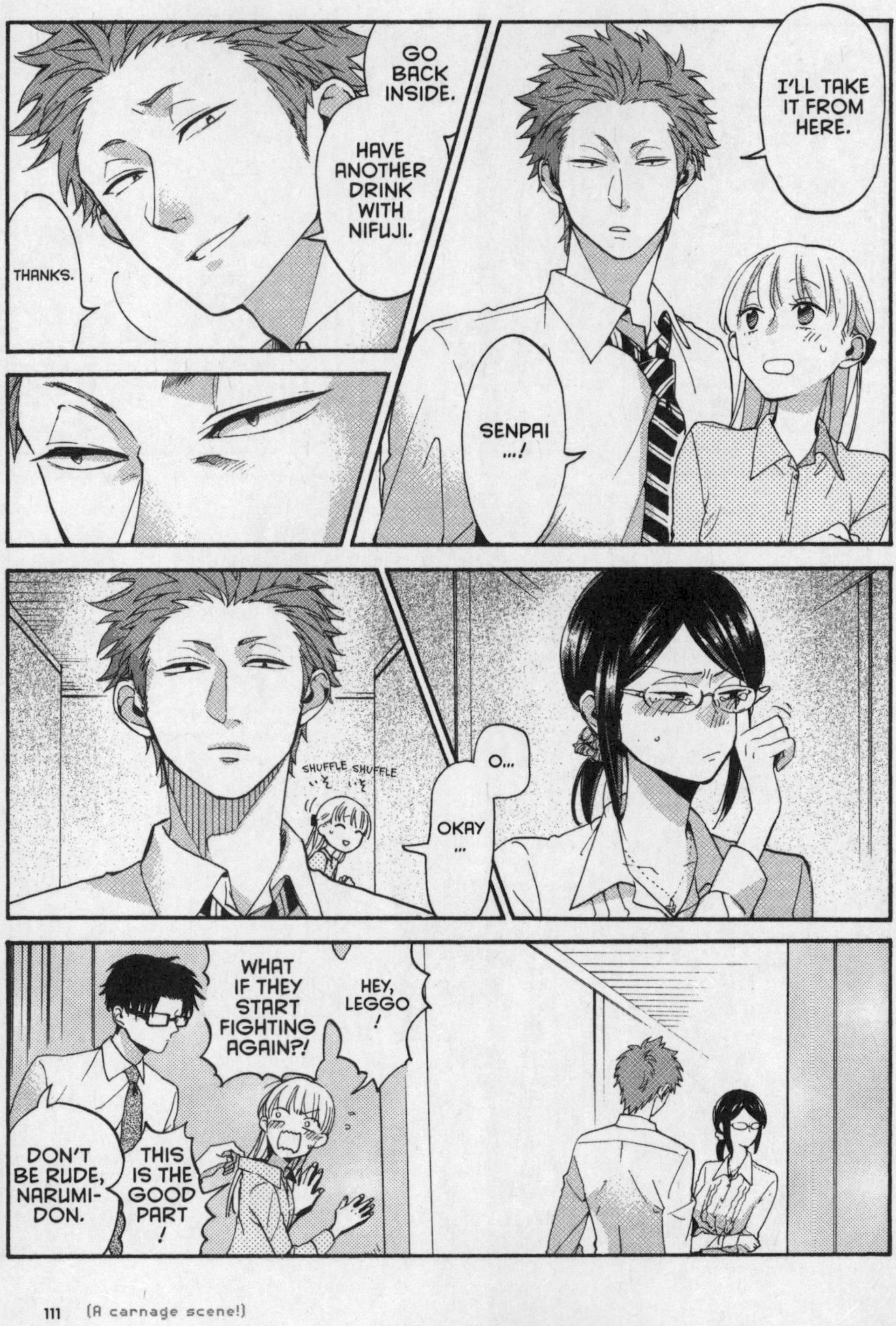
I'LL TAKE IT FROM HERE.
SENPAI ...!
GO BACK INSIDE.
HAVE ANOTHER DRINK WITH NIFUJI.
THANKS.
O...
OKAY ...
SHUFFLE SHUFFLE
HEY, LEGGO!
WHAT IF THEY START FIGHTING AGAIN?!
THIS IS THE GOOD PART!
DON'T BE RUDE, NARUMIDON.

 (A carnage scene!)

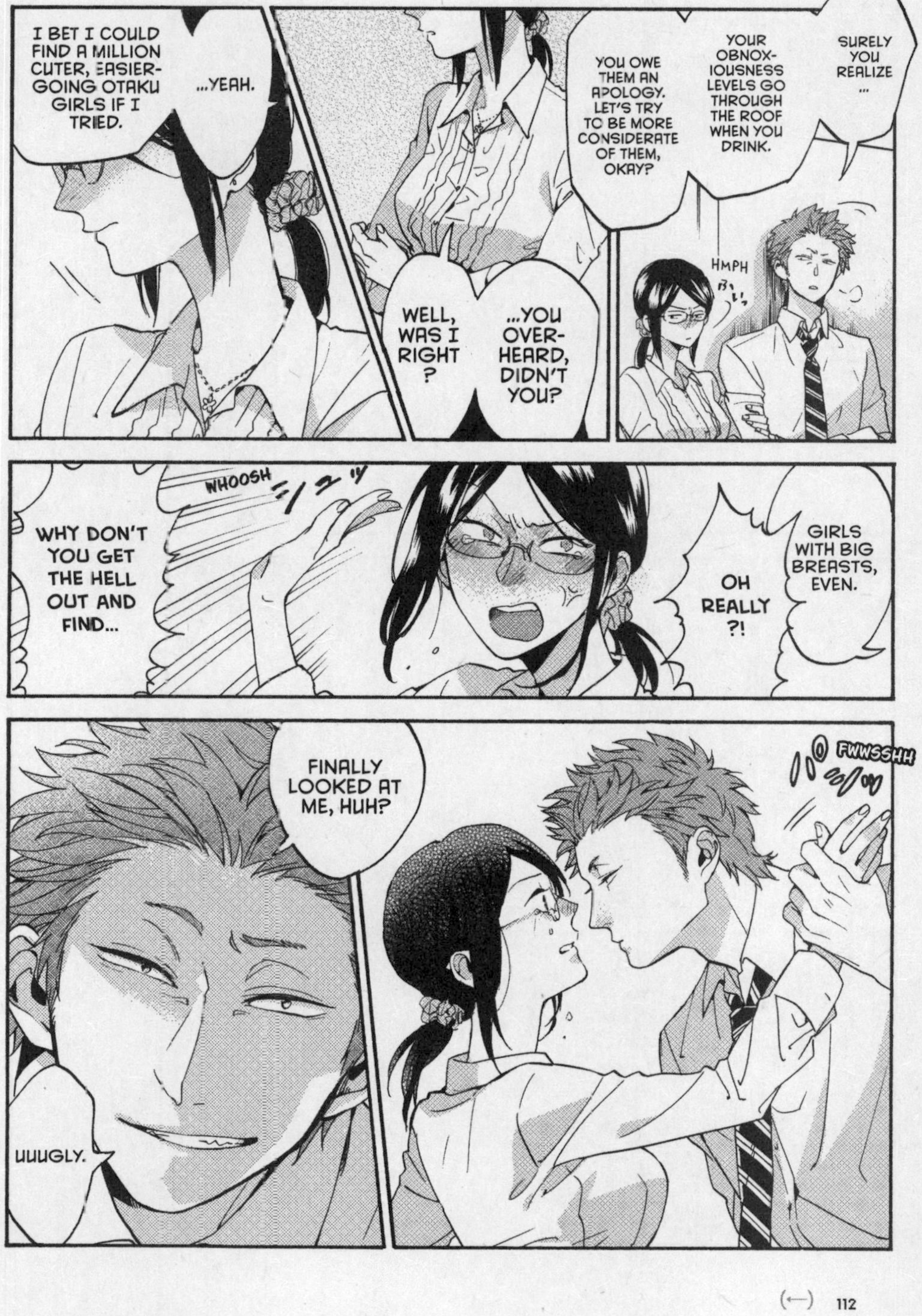

SURELY YOU REALIZE ...
YOUR OBNOX-IOUSNESS LEVELS GO THROUGH THE ROOF WHEN YOU DRINK.
YOU OWE THEM AN APOLOGY. LET'S TRY TO BE MORE CONSIDERATE OF THEM, OKAY?
HMPH
...YOU OVER-HEARD, DIDN'T YOU?
WELL, WAS I RIGHT ?
...YEAH.
I BET I COULD FIND A MILLION CUTER, EASIER-GOING OTAKU GIRLS IF I TRIED.
GIRLS WITH BIG BREASTS, EVEN.
OH REALLY ?!
WHOOSH
WHY DON'T YOU GET THE HELL OUT AND FIND...
FWWSSHH
FINALLY LOOKED AT ME, HUH?
UUUGLY.

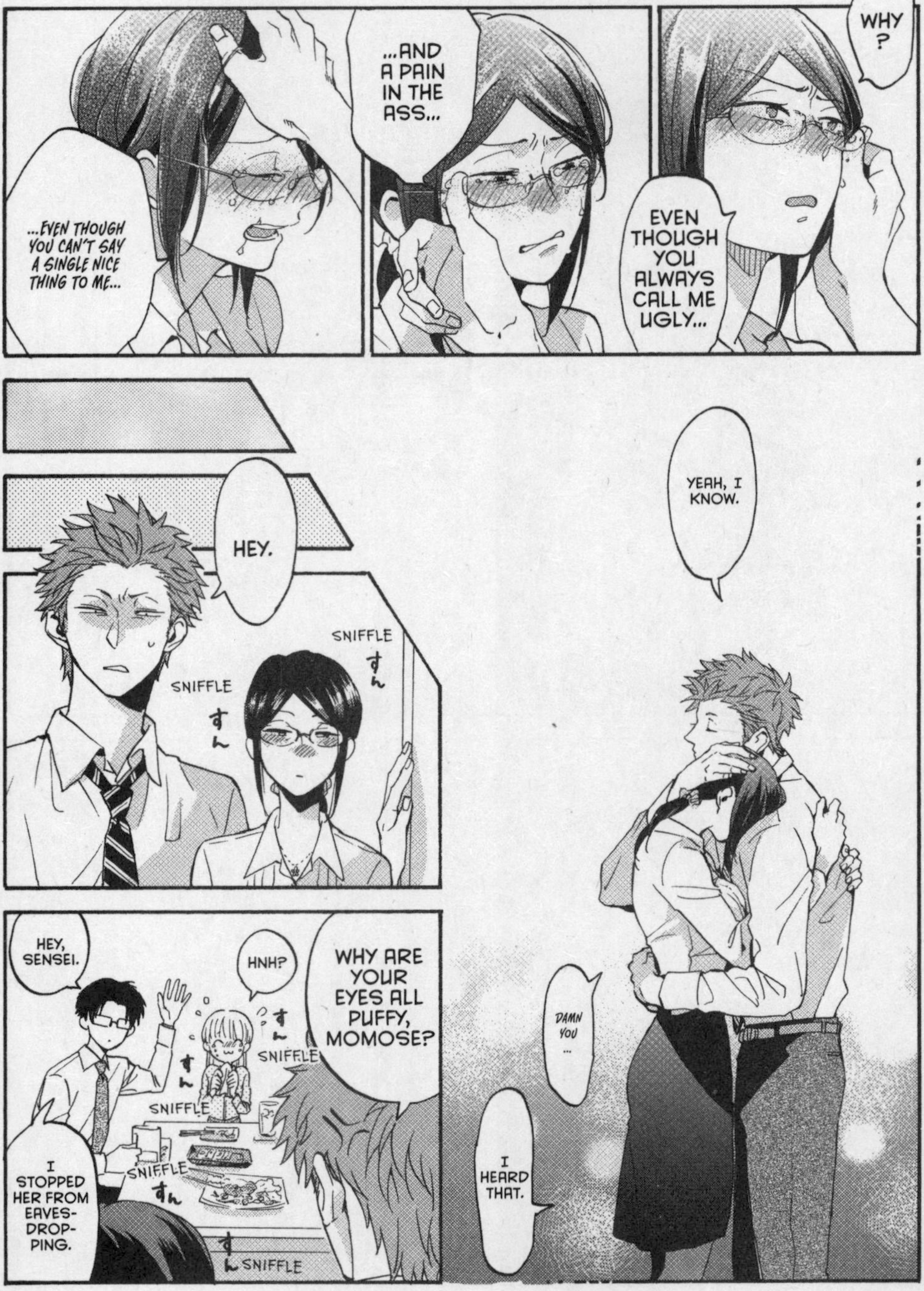
WHY?
EVEN THOUGH YOU ALWAYS CALL ME UGLY...
...AND A PAIN IN THE ASS...
...EVEN THOUGH YOU CAN'T SAY A SINGLE NICE THING TO ME...
YEAH, I KNOW.
DAMN YOU ...
I HEARD THAT.
HEY.
SNIFFLE すん
SNIFFLE すん
WHY ARE YOUR EYES ALL PUFFY, MOMOSE?
HNH?
HEY, SENSEI.
すん SNIFFLE
すん SNIFFLE
I STOPPED HER FROM EAVES-DROPPING.
SNIFFLE すん
すん SNIFFLE

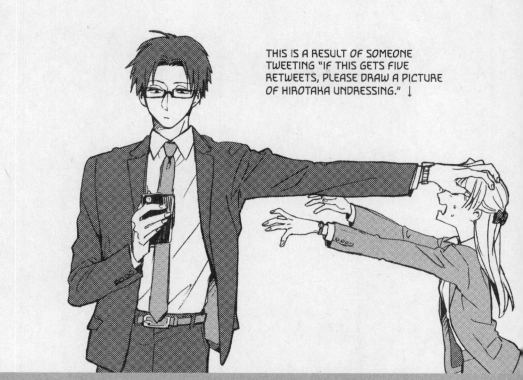

THIS IS A RESULT OF SOMEONE
TWEETING "IF THIS GETS FIVE
RETWEETS, PLEASE DRAW A PICTURE
OF HIROTAKA UNDRESSING." ↓

▶ CONTINUE

\(ˊᵕˋ)/

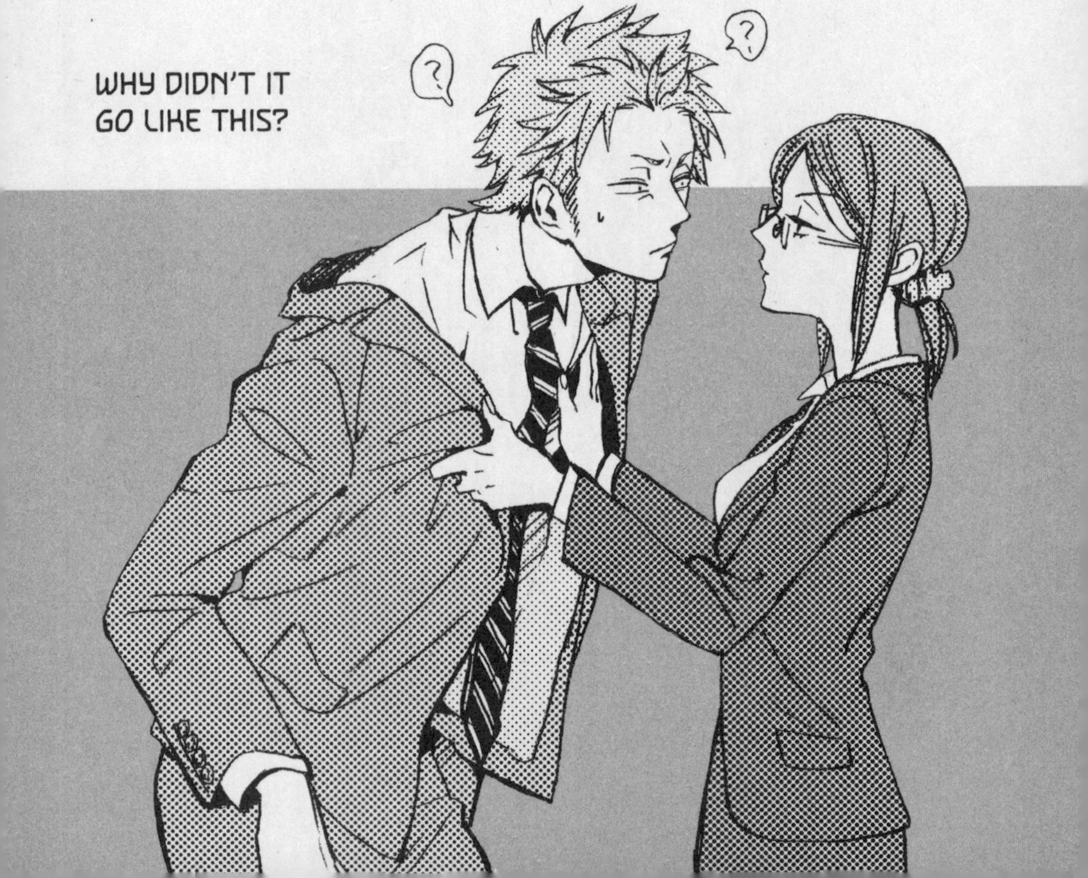
WHY DIDN'T IT GO LIKE THIS?
?
?

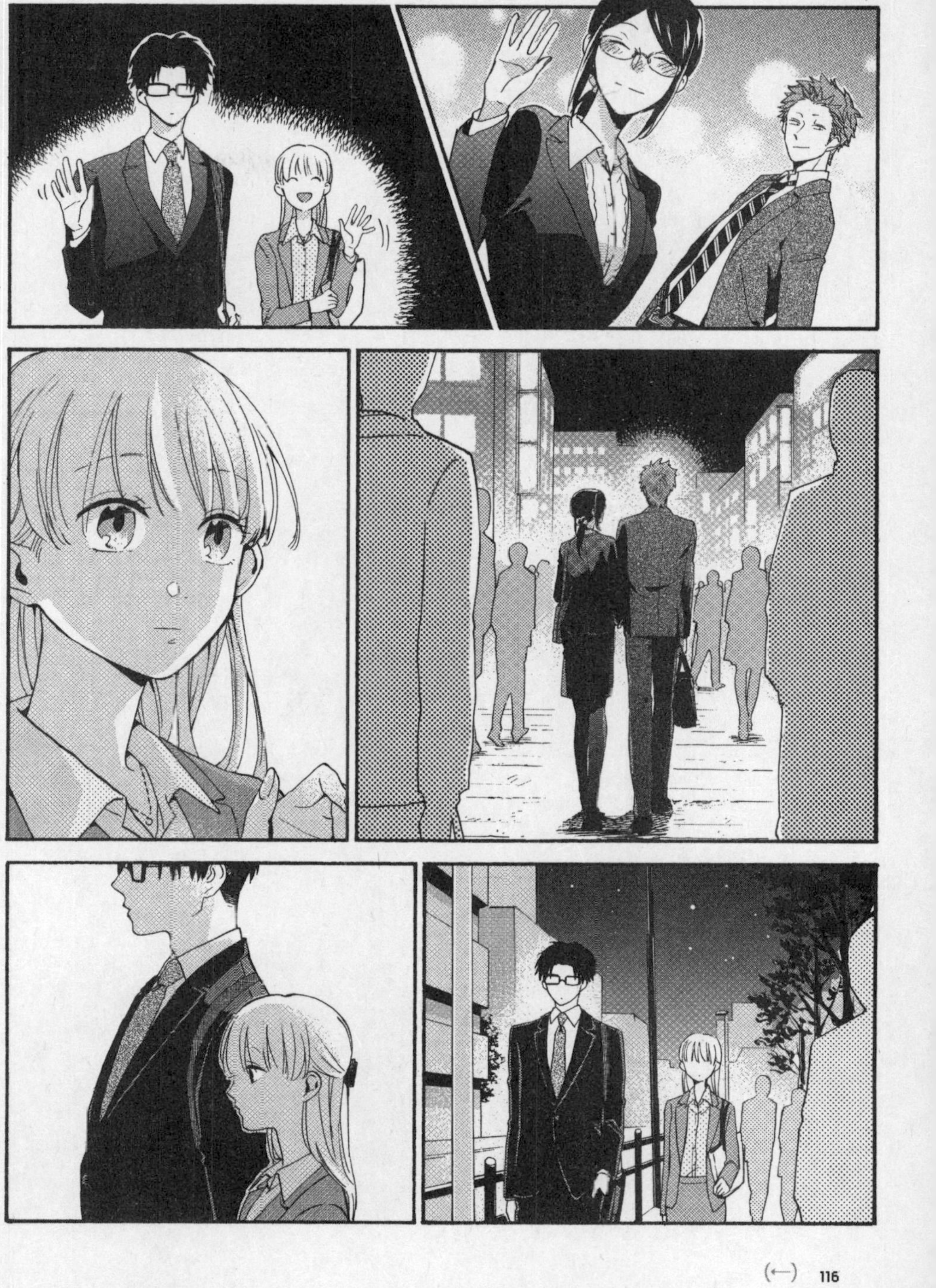

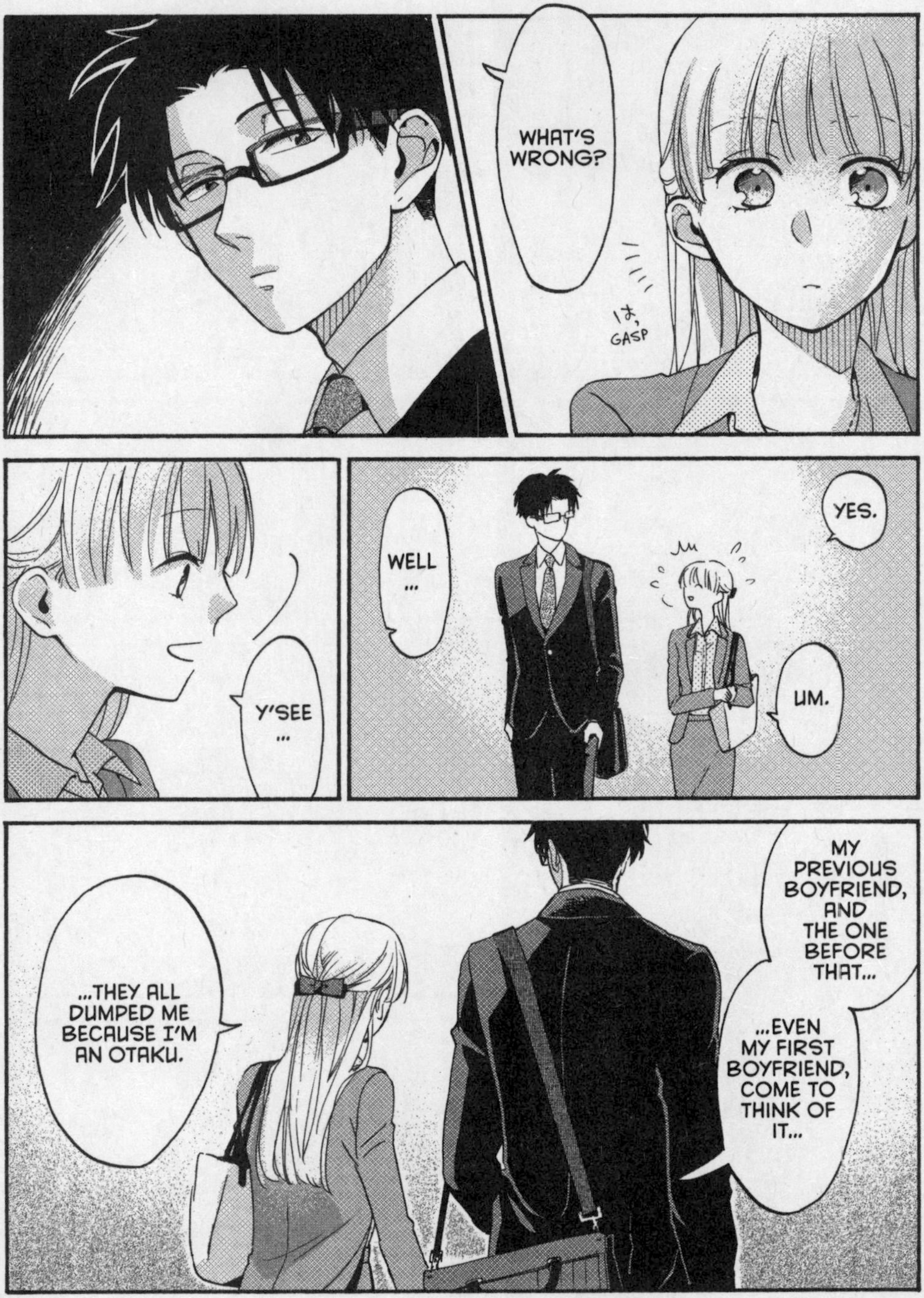
WHAT'S WRONG?
は, GASP
YES.
WELL...
UM.
Y'SEE...
MY PREVIOUS BOYFRIEND, AND THE ONE BEFORE THAT...
...EVEN MY FIRST BOYFRIEND, COME TO THINK OF IT...
...THEY ALL DUMPED ME BECAUSE I'M AN OTAKU.

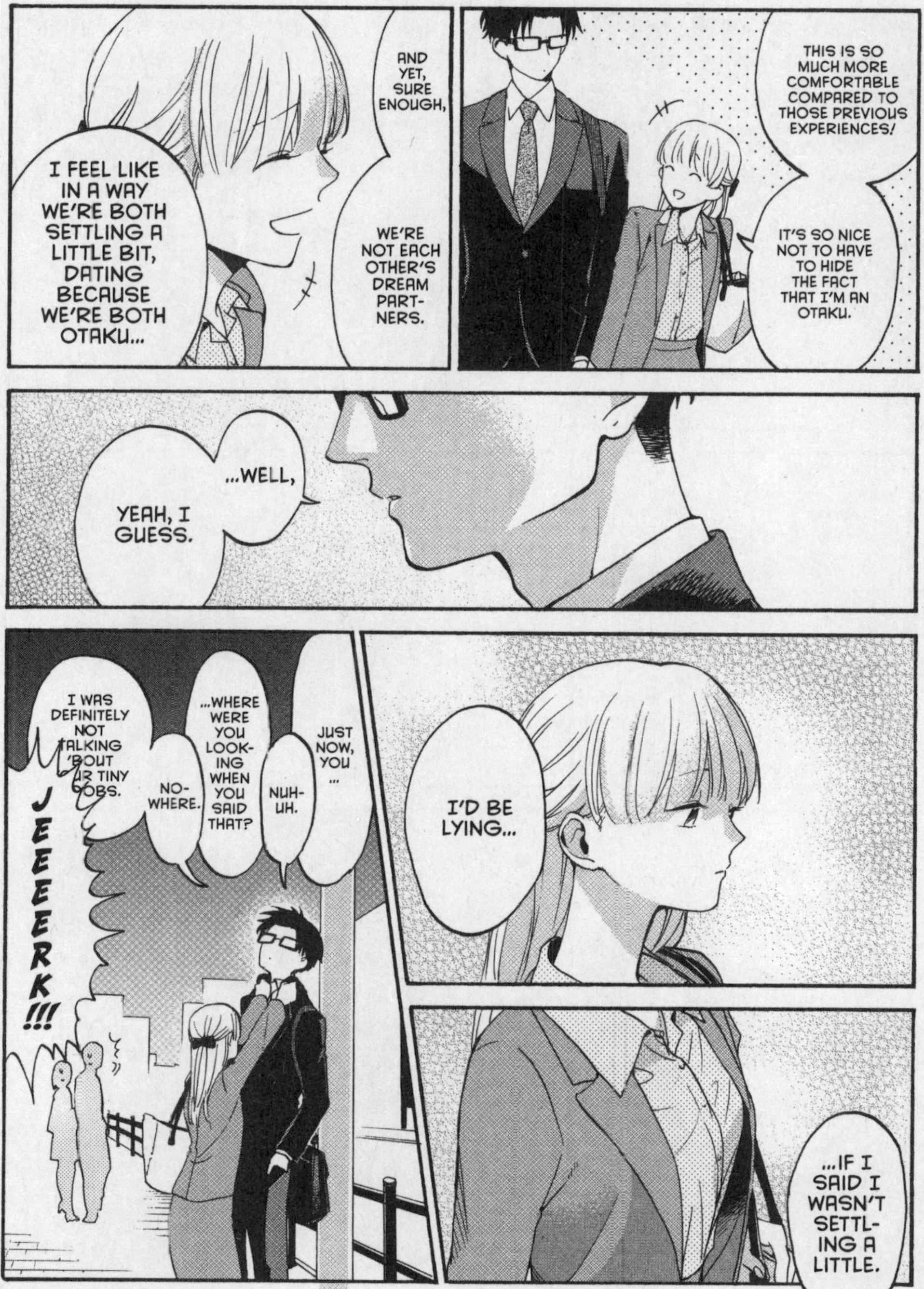
THIS IS SO MUCH MORE COMFORTABLE COMPARED TO THOSE PREVIOUS EXPERIENCES!
IT'S SO NICE NOT TO HAVE TO HIDE THE FACT THAT I'M AN OTAKU.
AND YET, SURE ENOUGH,
WE'RE NOT EACH OTHER'S DREAM PART-NERS.
I FEEL LIKE IN A WAY WE'RE BOTH SETTLING A LITTLE BIT, DATING BECAUSE WE'RE BOTH OTAKU...
...WELL,
YEAH, I GUESS.
I'D BE LYING...
...IF I SAID I WASN'T SETTL-ING A LITTLE.
JUST NOW, YOU ...
NUH-UH.
...WHERE WERE YOU LOOK-ING WHEN YOU SAID THAT?
NO-WHERE.
I WAS DEFINITELY NOT TALKING 'BOUT UR TINY BOBS.
JEEEERK!!!

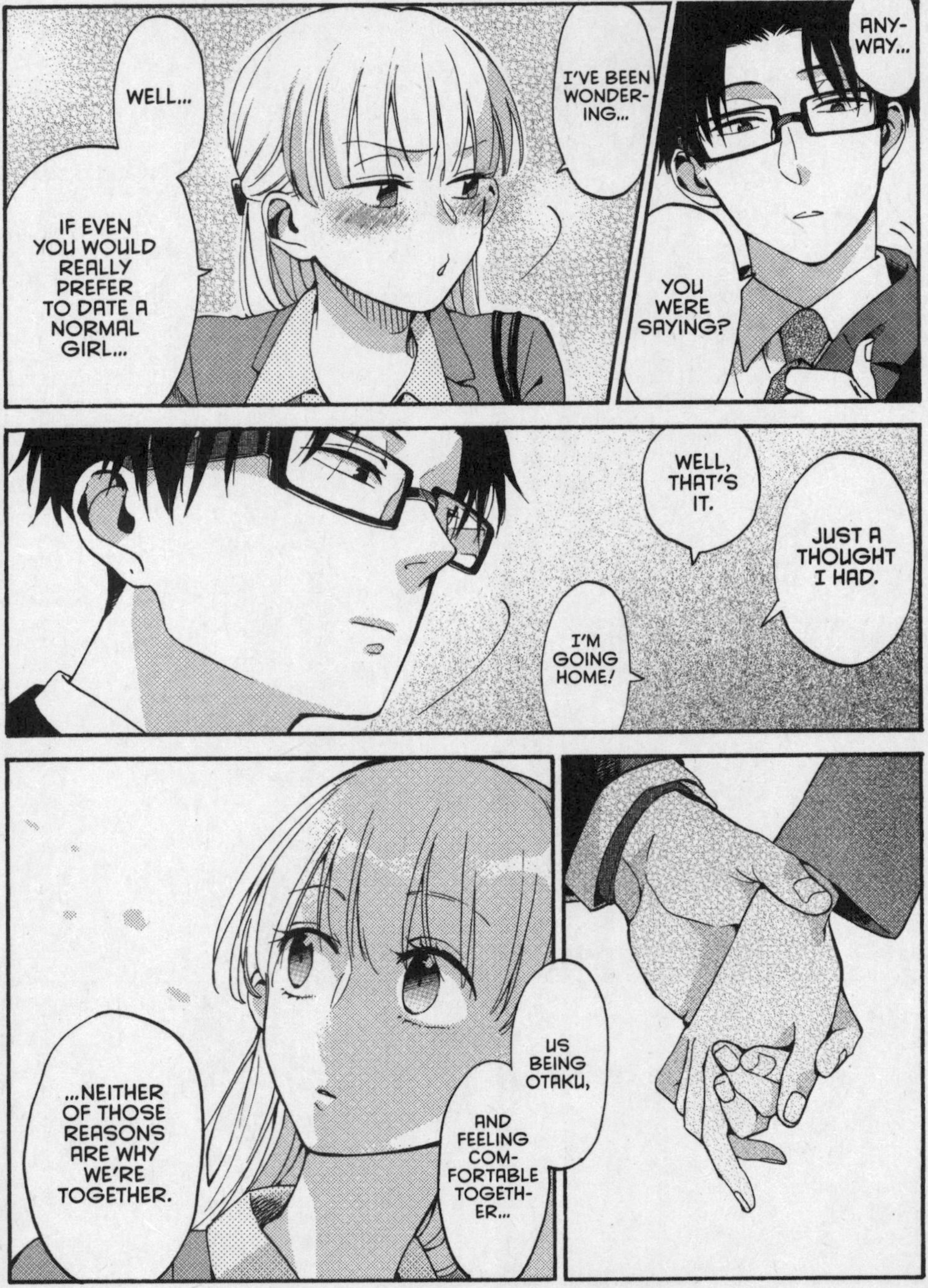
ANY-WAY...
YOU WERE SAYING?
I'VE BEEN WONDER-ING...
WELL...
IF EVEN YOU WOULD REALLY PREFER TO DATE A NORMAL GIRL...
WELL, THAT'S IT.
JUST A THOUGHT I HAD.
I'M GOING HOME!
US BEING OTAKU,
AND FEELING COM-FORTABLE TOGETH-ER...
...NEITHER OF THOSE REASONS ARE WHY WE'RE TOGETHER.

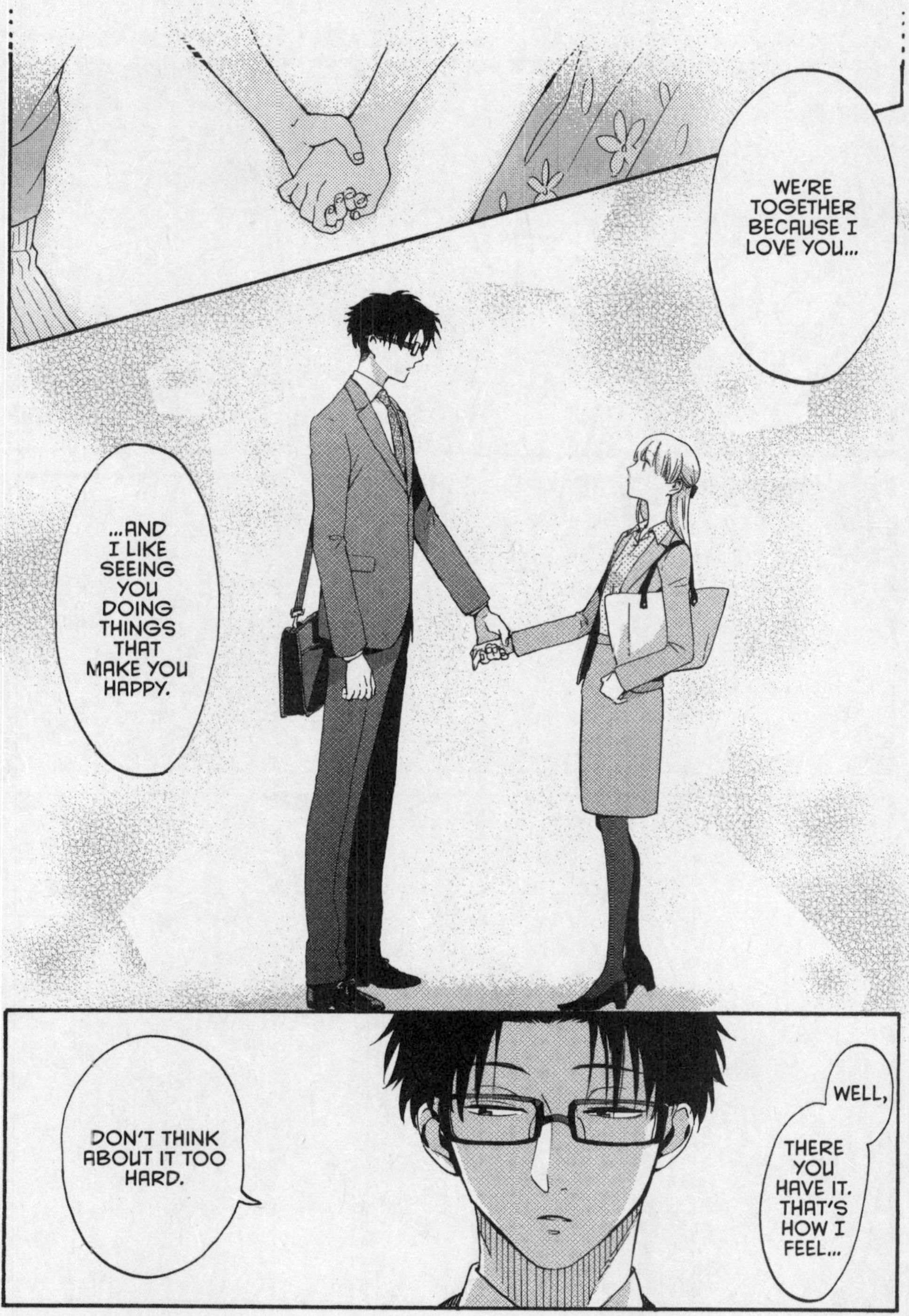
WE'RE TOGETHER BECAUSE I LOVE YOU...
...AND I LIKE SEEING YOU DOING THINGS THAT MAKE YOU HAPPY.
WELL,
THERE YOU HAVE IT. THAT'S HOW I FEEL...
DON'T THINK ABOUT IT TOO HARD.

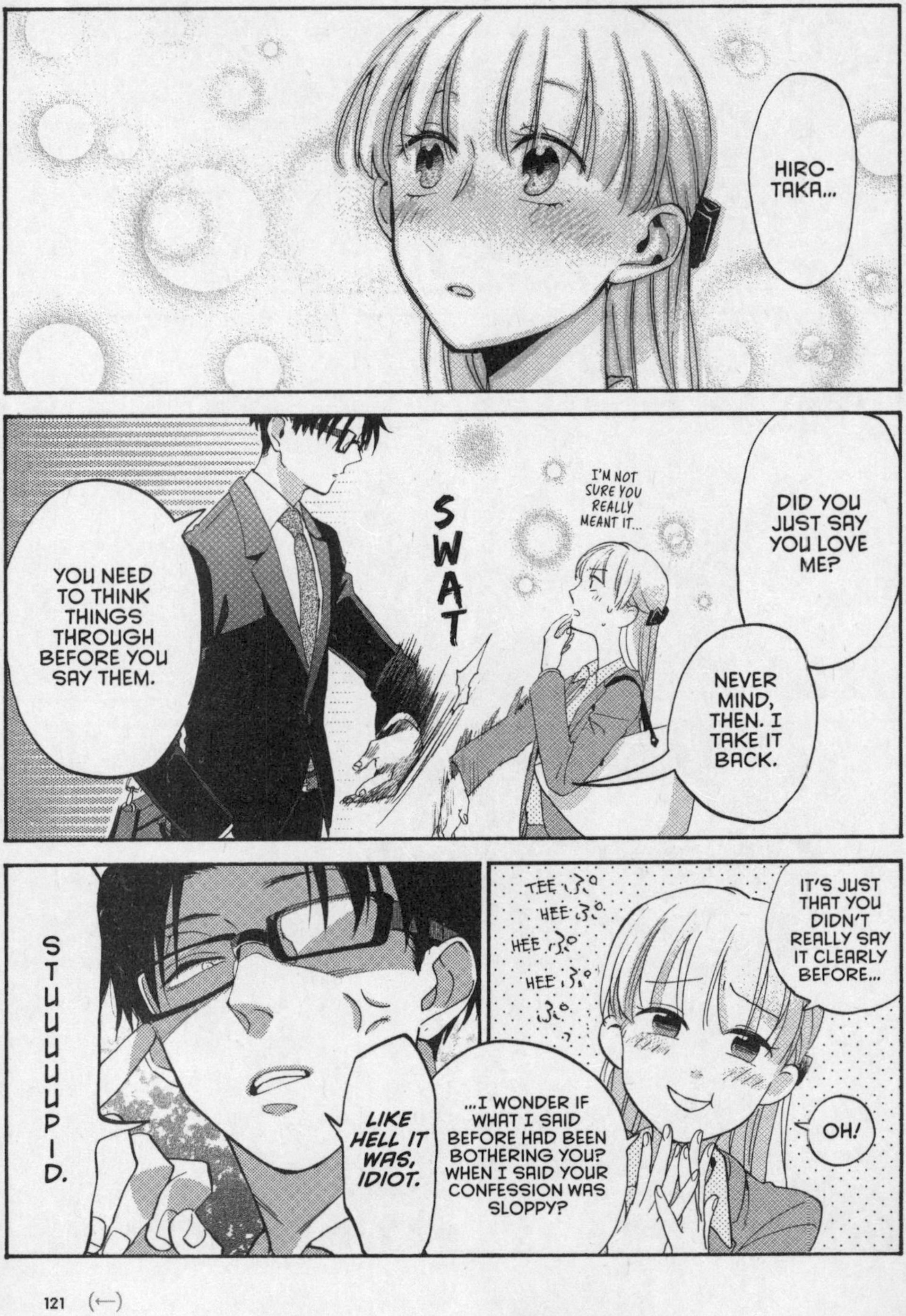
HIRO-TAKA...
DID YOU JUST SAY YOU LOVE ME?
I'M NOT SURE YOU REALLY MEANT IT...
NEVER MIND, THEN. I TAKE IT BACK.
SWAT
YOU NEED TO THINK THINGS THROUGH BEFORE YOU SAY THEM.
IT'S JUST THAT YOU DIDN'T REALLY SAY IT CLEARLY BEFORE...
TEE HEE HEE HEE
OH!
...I WONDER IF WHAT I SAID BEFORE HAD BEEN BOTHERING YOU? WHEN I SAID YOUR CONFESSION WAS SLOPPY?
LIKE HELL IT WAS, IDIOT.
STUUUUUPID.

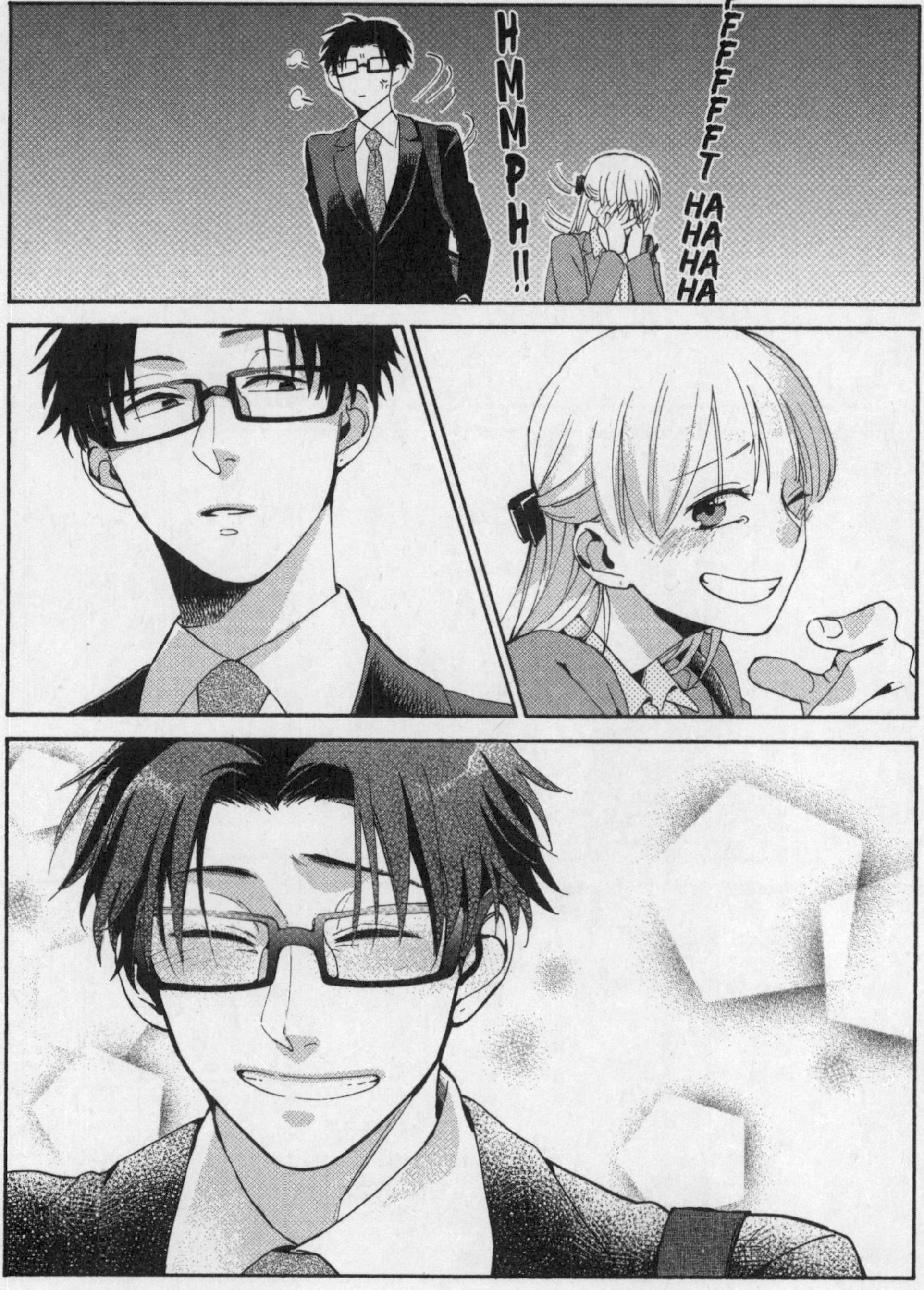
PFFFFFFT HAHAHAHA
HMMPH!!

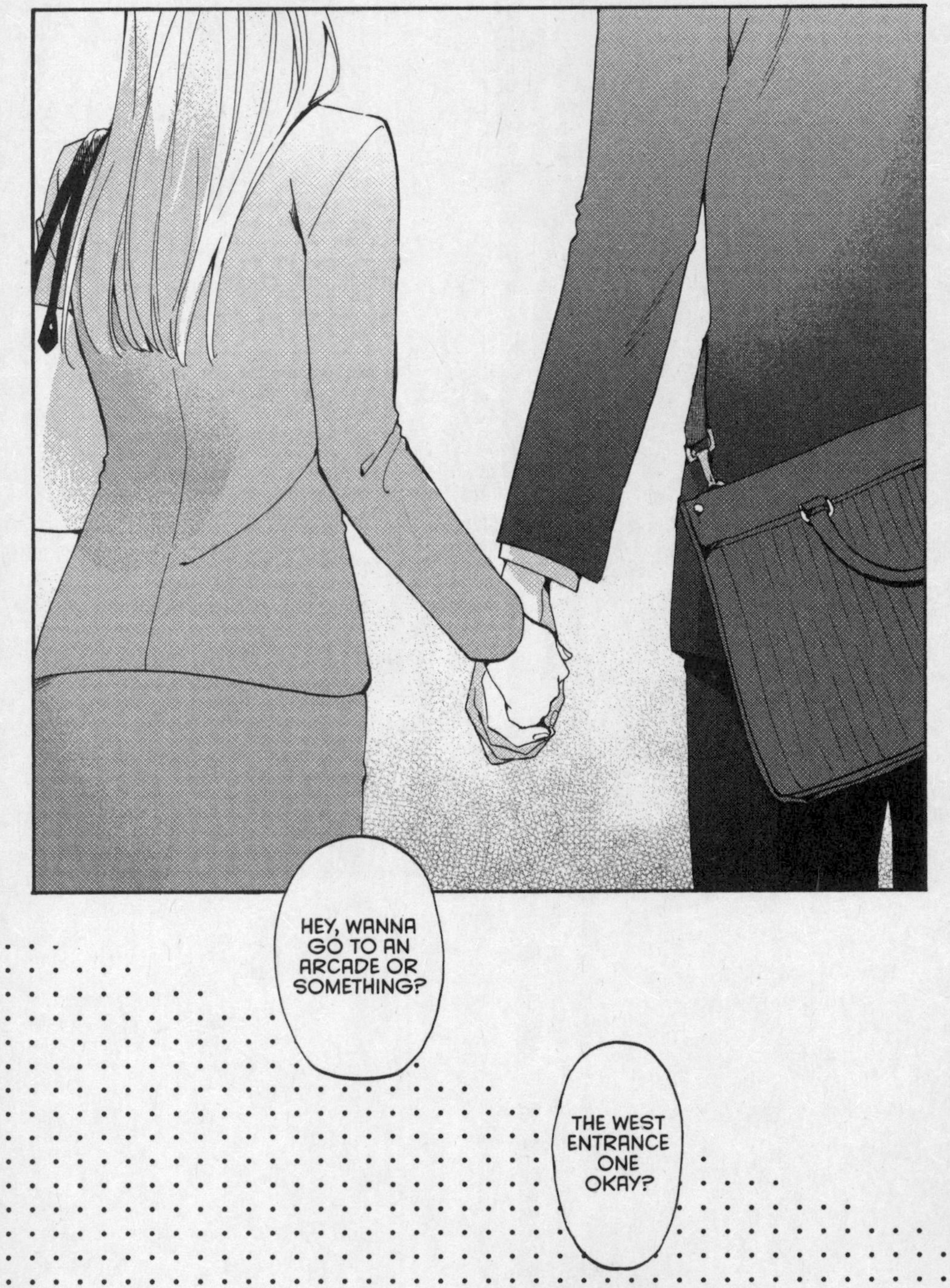
HEY, WANNA GO TO AN ARCADE OR SOMETHING?
THE WEST ENTRANCE ONE OKAY?

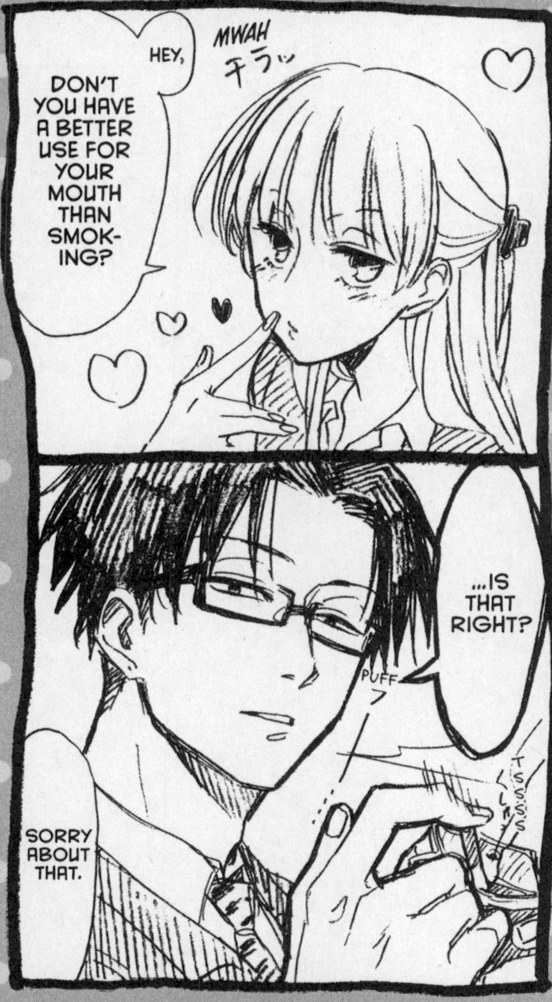
MWAH
チラッ
HEY, DON'T YOU HAVE A BETTER USE FOR YOUR MOUTH THAN SMOKING?
...IS THAT RIGHT?
PUFF
SORRY ABOUT THAT.

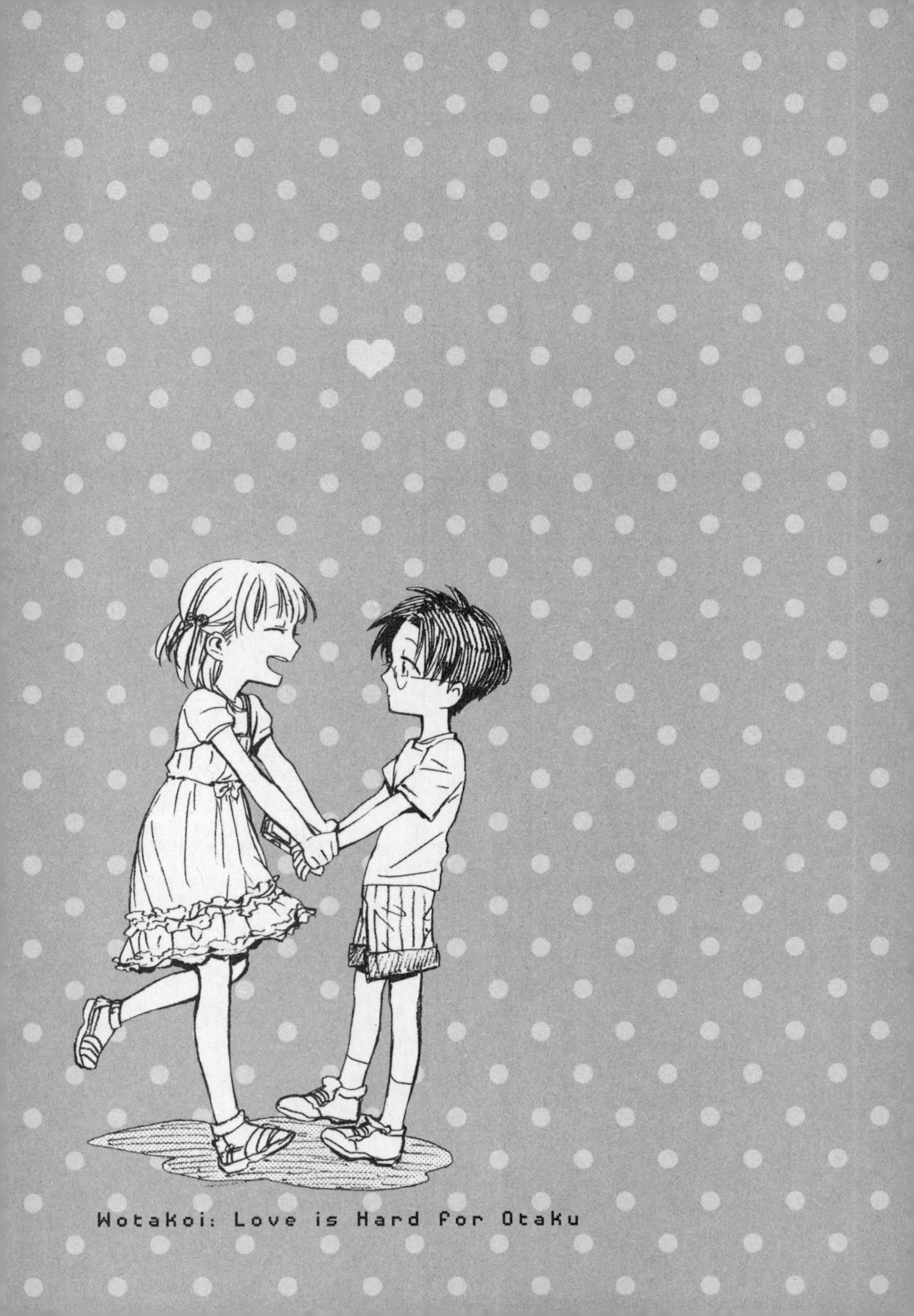

Wotakoi: Love is Hard for Otaku

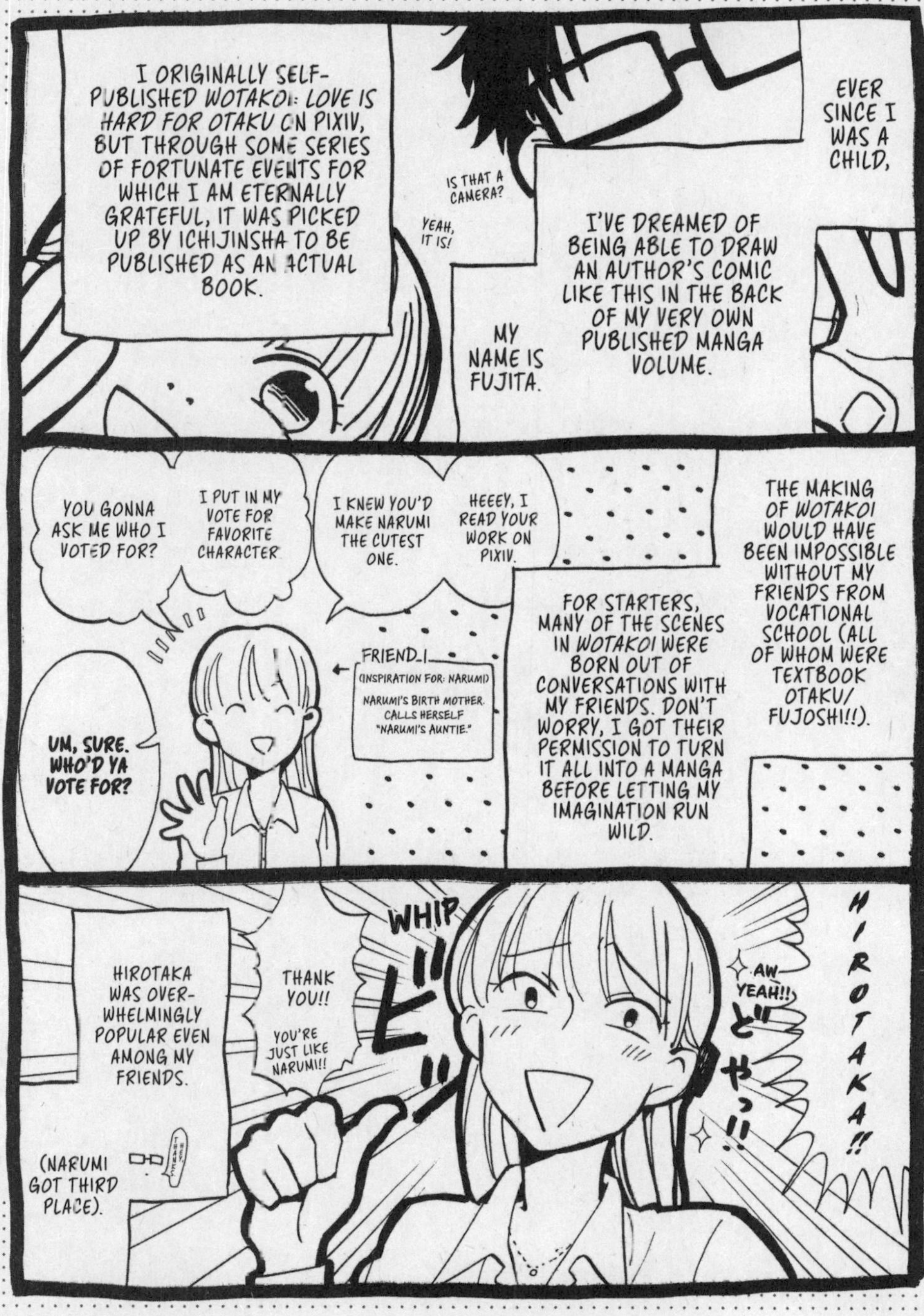
EVER SINCE I WAS A CHILD,
I'VE DREAMED OF BEING ABLE TO DRAW AN AUTHOR'S COMIC LIKE THIS IN THE BACK OF MY VERY OWN PUBLISHED MANGA VOLUME.
MY NAME IS FUJITA.
IS THAT A CAMERA?
YEAH, IT IS!
I ORIGINALLY SELF-PUBLISHED *WOTAKOI: LOVE IS HARD FOR OTAKU* ON PIXIV, BUT THROUGH SOME SERIES OF FORTUNATE EVENTS FOR WHICH I AM ETERNALLY GRATEFUL, IT WAS PICKED UP BY ICHIJINSHA TO BE PUBLISHED AS AN ACTUAL BOOK.
THE MAKING OF *WOTAKOI* WOULD HAVE BEEN IMPOSSIBLE WITHOUT MY FRIENDS FROM VOCATIONAL SCHOOL (ALL OF WHOM WERE TEXTBOOK OTAKU/FUJOSHI!!).
FOR STARTERS, MANY OF THE SCENES IN *WOTAKOI* WERE BORN OUT OF CONVERSATIONS WITH MY FRIENDS. DON'T WORRY, I GOT THEIR PERMISSION TO TURN IT ALL INTO A MANGA BEFORE LETTING MY IMAGINATION RUN WILD.
HEEEY, I READ YOUR WORK ON PIXIV.
I KNEW YOU'D MAKE NARUMI THE CUTEST ONE.
I PUT IN MY VOTE FOR FAVORITE CHARACTER
YOU GONNA ASK ME WHO I VOTED FOR?
FRIEND I
(INSPIRATION FOR: NARUMI)
NARUMI'S BIRTH MOTHER. CALLS HERSELF "NARUMI'S AUNTIE."
UM, SURE. WHO'D YA VOTE FOR?
HIROTAKA!!
AW YEAH!!
どやっ!!
WHIP
ビッ
THANK YOU!!
YOU'RE JUST LIKE NARUMI!!
HIROTAKA WAS OVERWHELMINGLY POPULAR EVEN AMONG MY FRIENDS.
(NARUMI GOT THIRD PLACE).

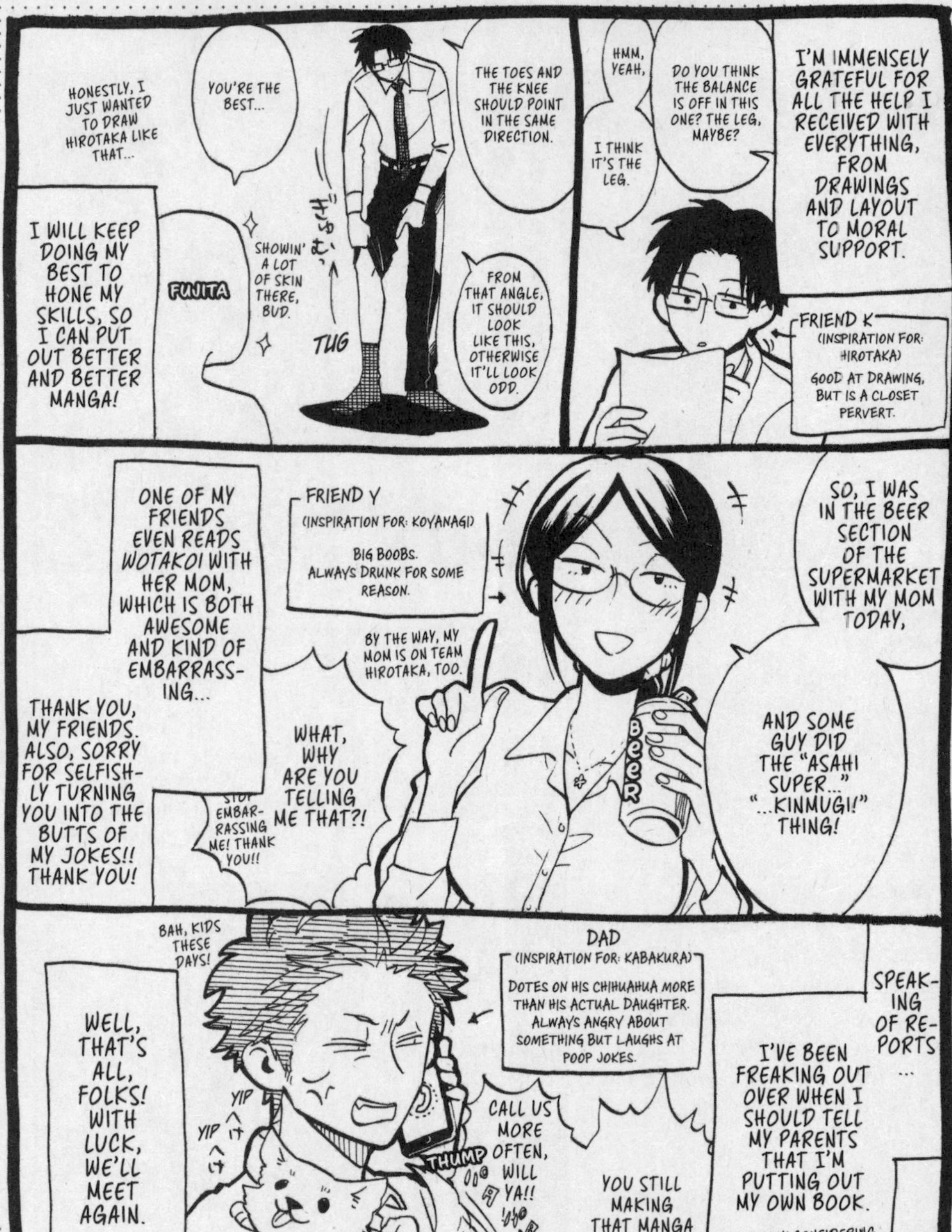

I'M IMMENSELY GRATEFUL FOR ALL THE HELP I RECEIVED WITH EVERYTHING, FROM DRAWINGS AND LAYOUT TO MORAL SUPPORT.
DO YOU THINK THE BALANCE IS OFF IN THIS ONE? THE LEG, MAYBE?
HMM, YEAH,
I THINK IT'S THE LEG.
FRIEND K (INSPIRATION FOR: HIROTAKA) GOOD AT DRAWING, BUT IS A CLOSET PERVERT.
THE TOES AND THE KNEE SHOULD POINT IN THE SAME DIRECTION.
YOU'RE THE BEST...
HONESTLY, I JUST WANTED TO DRAW HIROTAKA LIKE THAT...
FROM THAT ANGLE, IT SHOULD LOOK LIKE THIS, OTHERWISE IT'LL LOOK ODD.
TUG
SHOWIN' A LOT OF SKIN THERE, BUD.
FUJITA
I WILL KEEP DOING MY BEST TO HONE MY SKILLS, SO I CAN PUT OUT BETTER AND BETTER MANGA!
SO, I WAS IN THE BEER SECTION OF THE SUPERMARKET WITH MY MOM TODAY,
AND SOME GUY DID THE "ASAHI SUPER..." "...KINMUGI!" THING!
BEER
FRIEND Y (INSPIRATION FOR: KOYANAGI) BIG BOOBS. ALWAYS DRUNK FOR SOME REASON.
BY THE WAY, MY MOM IS ON TEAM HIROTAKA, TOO.
WHAT, WHY ARE YOU TELLING ME THAT?!
STOP EMBARRASSING ME! THANK YOU!!
ONE OF MY FRIENDS EVEN READS WOTAKOI WITH HER MOM, WHICH IS BOTH AWESOME AND KIND OF EMBARRASSING...
THANK YOU, MY FRIENDS. ALSO, SORRY FOR SELFISHLY TURNING YOU INTO THE BUTTS OF MY JOKES!! THANK YOU!
SPEAKING OF REPORTS...
I'VE BEEN FREAKING OUT OVER WHEN I SHOULD TELL MY PARENTS THAT I'M PUTTING OUT MY OWN BOOK.
ESPECIALLY CONSIDERING THE CONTENTS OF SAID BOOK, I DON'T REALLY WANNA TELL THEM.
DAD (INSPIRATION FOR: KABAKURA) DOTES ON HIS CHIHUAHUA MORE THAN HIS ACTUAL DAUGHTER. ALWAYS ANGRY ABOUT SOMETHING BUT LAUGHS AT POOP JOKES.
YOU STILL MAKING THAT MANGA THING?!
CALL US MORE OFTEN, WILL YA!!
BAH, KIDS THESE DAYS!
YIP
YIP
THUMP
THUMP
THUMP
WELL, THAT'S ALL, FOLKS! WITH LUCK, WE'LL MEET AGAIN.
FUJITA, 04/2015

TRANSLATION NOTES

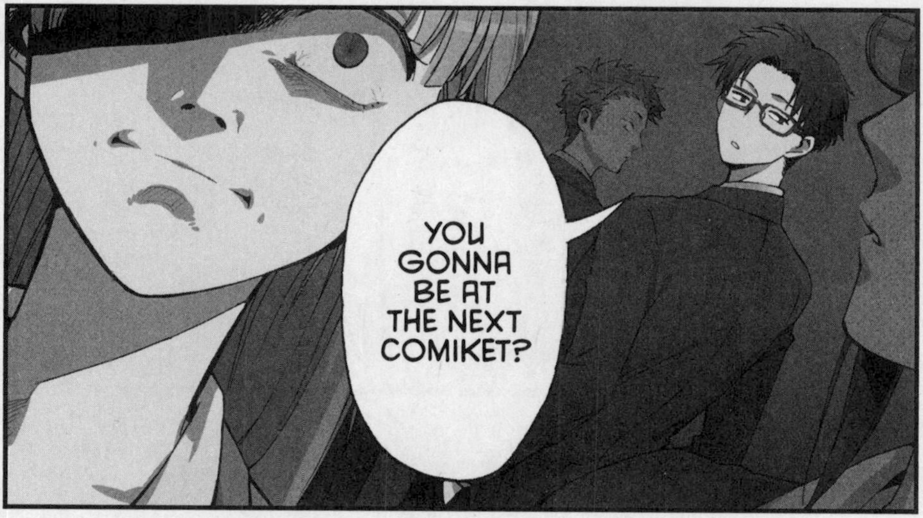
YOU GONNA BE AT THE NEXT COMIKET?

▲COMIKET,
PAGE 4
Also known as the Comic Market, *Comiket* is the largest fair for *dojinshi*, or amateur comic books, in the world. They are held twice a year in Tokyo.

▶OTAKU,
PAGE 5
Someone who is obsessed with aspects of popular culture such as video games, anime, manga, computers, etc., to the point that they are socially awkward and don't fit in well with society at large.

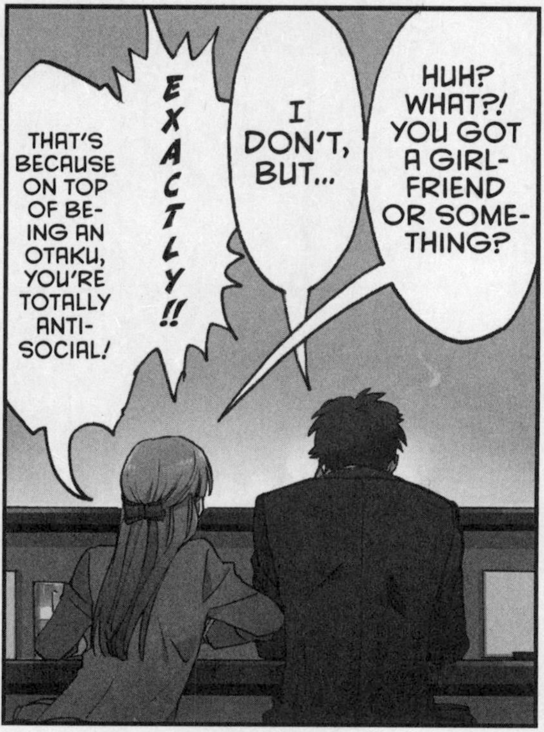
HUH? WHAT?! YOU GOT A GIRLFRIEND OR SOMETHING?
I DON'T, BUT...
EXACTLY!!
THAT'S BECAUSE ON TOP OF BEING AN OTAKU, YOU'RE TOTALLY ANTI-SOCIAL!

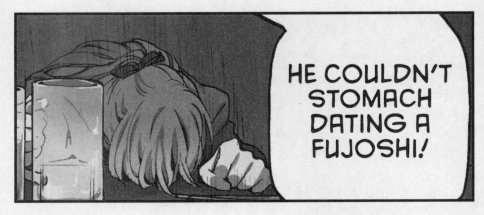

HE COULDN'T STOMACH DATING A FUJOSHI!

▲FUJOSHI,
PAGE 6
Girls/women who enjoy *yaoi* and BL (boys' love) (genres of anime and manga centered around romance between two men); literally translated, the term means "rotten girl." The male equivalent is fudanshi.

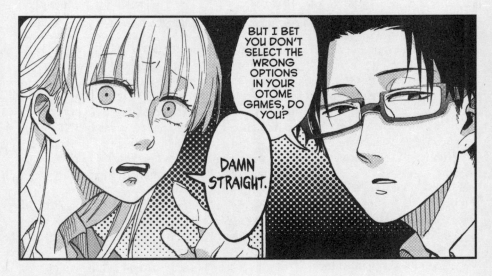

BUT I BET YOU DON'T SELECT THE WRONG OPTIONS IN YOUR OTOME GAMES, DO YOU?

DAMN STRAIGHT.

▲OTOME GAMES,
PAGE 13
Video games geared toward women, especially dating simulations. Otome dating simulations usually have the main character play as a woman or girl who is presented with many options of characters to date, and must choose one to pursue (by choosing their "route"). In order to get a happily-ever-after ending with their chosen, players must respond to certain prompts in such a way that most pleases their fictional beau.

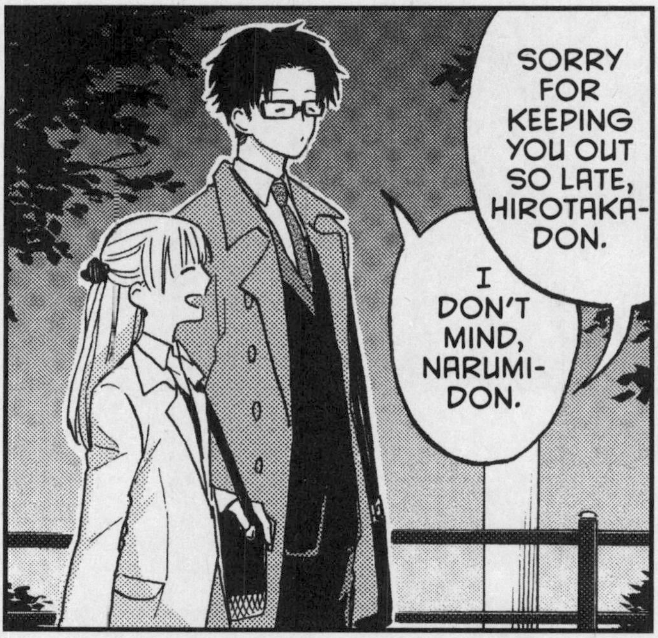
SORRY FOR KEEPING YOU OUT SO LATE, HIROTAKA-DON.
I DON'T MIND, NARUMI-DON.

◂-DON, HONORIFICS, PAGE 15

Don is an honorific suffix often used to address an apprentice, although it has much broader use in southern Kyushu.

Honorific suffixes, which go at the end of a person's name, are nearly always used when addressing someone directly as a way to be polite. Different honorifics are used depending on the person's status, and how well the speaker knows them. Following are some of the most commonly used honorifics and their use.

- -sama: A very polite suffix that is used for someone who is above the speaker's station such as a boss, or for customers and guests in a retail/business setting.
- -san: The most commonly used honorific, it is a title denoting respect used among equals of any age.
- -kun: Almost exclusively used for younger males, usually by older people, though it can also be used to address women in an office. Younger people might also use -kun if they have a close relationship.
- -chan: A diminutive suffix used to express a fondness for the person or to indicate the speaker thinks the person is cute/endearing. Frequently used for babies, lovers, young girls, and between close friends. It can also be used when someone is trying to be condescending.
- -sensei: A suffix used for teachers, but also for experts in a field, including doctors and manga artists.

▼WAIFU, PAGE 18

In *Wotakoi*, we use the term "waifu" to represent the fictional or otherwise unattainable love interests of our heroes. These can be characters of any gender, from games, manga, anime, idol groups, or any other otaku realms. Waifu itself is a term used primarily by U.S.-based, English-speaking otaku to refer to female fictional characters, with male characters referred to as "husbando." From the Japanese *yomé*, meaning "wife" or "bride."

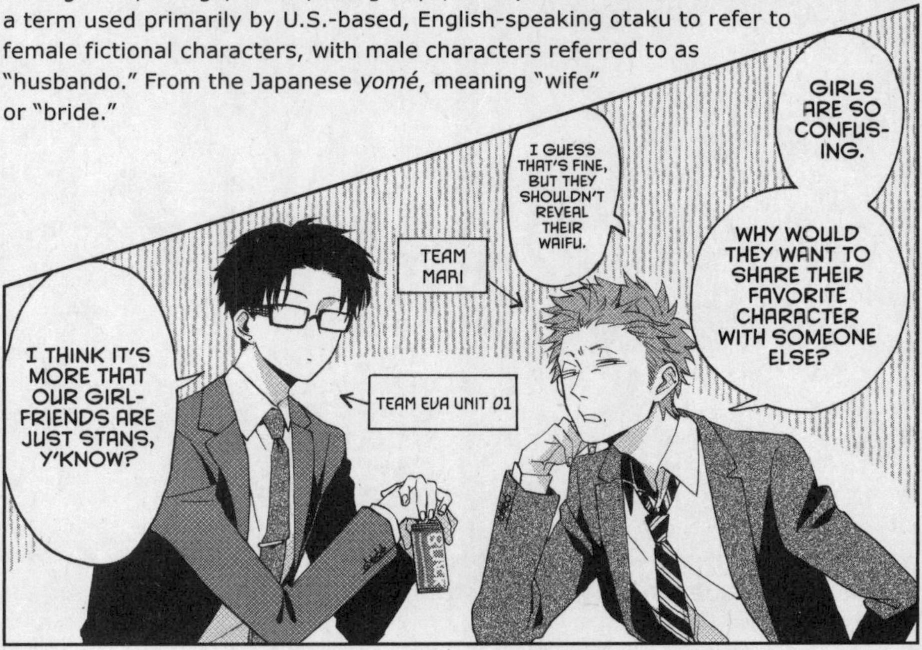
GIRLS ARE SO CONFUS-ING.
WHY WOULD THEY WANT TO SHARE THEIR FAVORITE CHARACTER WITH SOMEONE ELSE?
I GUESS THAT'S FINE, BUT THEY SHOULDN'T REVEAL THEIR WAIFU.
TEAM MARI
TEAM EVA UNIT 01
I THINK IT'S MORE THAT OUR GIRL-FRIENDS ARE JUST STANS, Y'KNOW?

▶OL, PAGE 18

An abbreviation for Office Lady, which refers to a female office worker in Japan who performs general secretarial/support work such as serving tea, making copies, etc. There is usually little opportunity for promotion as it is implicitly understood that an OL will leave her job once she marries.

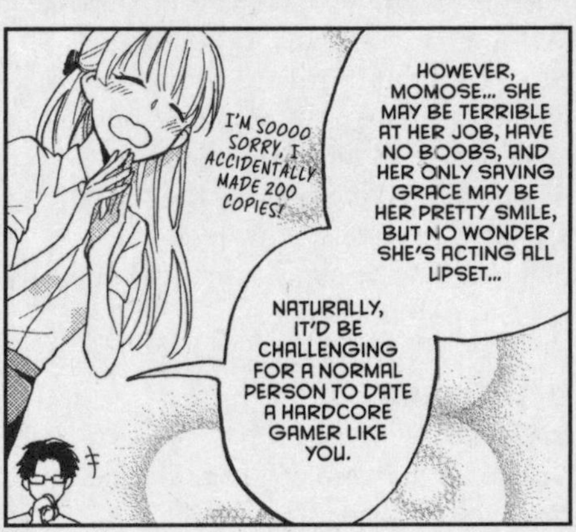
HOWEVER, MOMOSE... SHE MAY BE TERRIBLE AT HER JOB, HAVE NO BOOBS, AND HER ONLY SAVING GRACE MAY BE HER PRETTY SMILE, BUT NO WONDER SHE'S ACTING ALL UPSET...
NATURALLY, IT'D BE CHALLENGING FOR A NORMAL PERSON TO DATE A HARDCORE GAMER LIKE YOU.
I'M SOOOO SORRY, I ACCIDENTALLY MADE 200 COPIES!

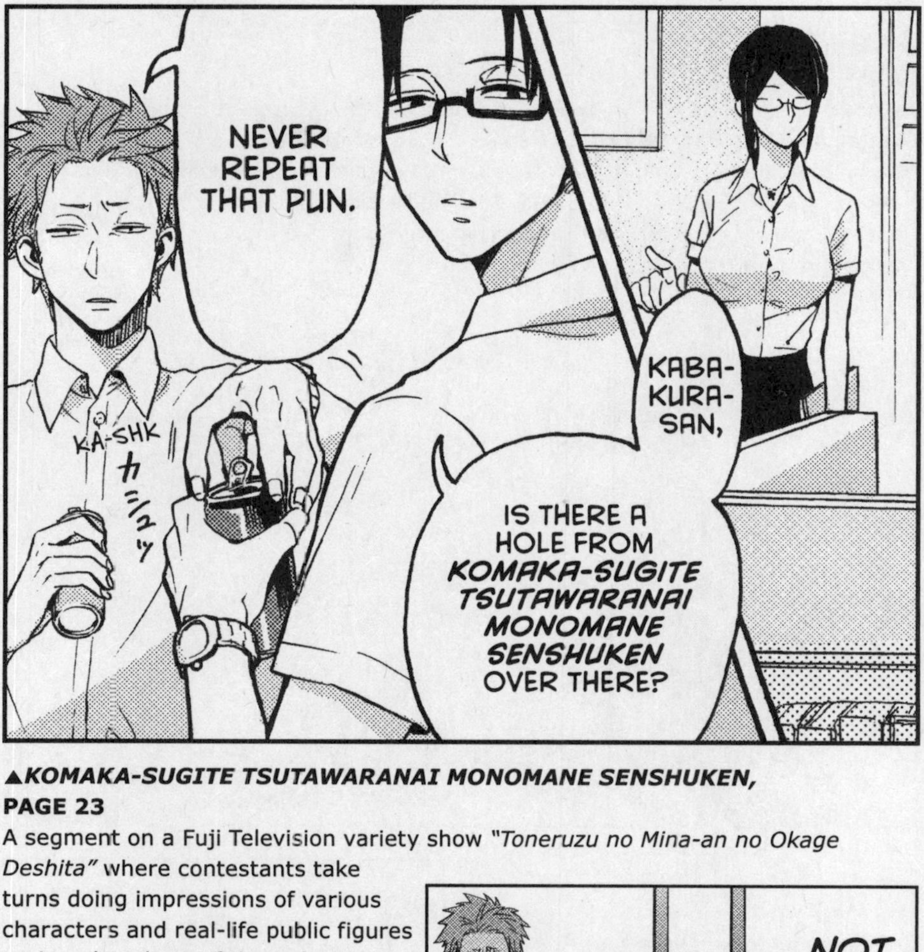
KABA-KURA-SAN,
IS THERE A HOLE FROM *KOMAKA-SUGITE TSUTAWARANAI MONOMANE SENSHUKEN* OVER THERE?
NEVER REPEAT THAT PUN.
KA-SHK

▲*KOMAKA-SUGITE TSUTAWARANAI MONOMANE SENSHUKEN*, PAGE 23

A segment on a Fuji Television variety show *"Toneruzu no Mina-an no Okage Deshita"* where contestants take turns doing impressions of various characters and real-life public figures assigned to them; if the judges don't like the impression, they press a button to release a trap door underneath the contestant, and they fall through the stage.

▶FUYUTSUKI, PAGE 24

This is an homage to an iconic image from Neon Genesis Evangelion, wherein Fuyutsuki is standing rigidly with his hands behind his back while Gendo sits, leaning forward, with his hands folded together.

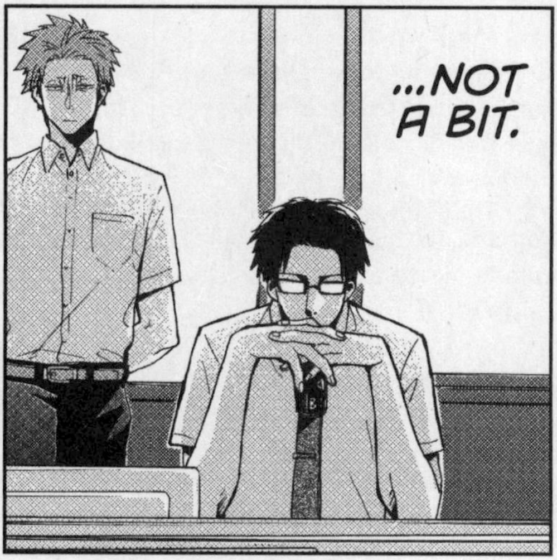
...NOT A BIT.

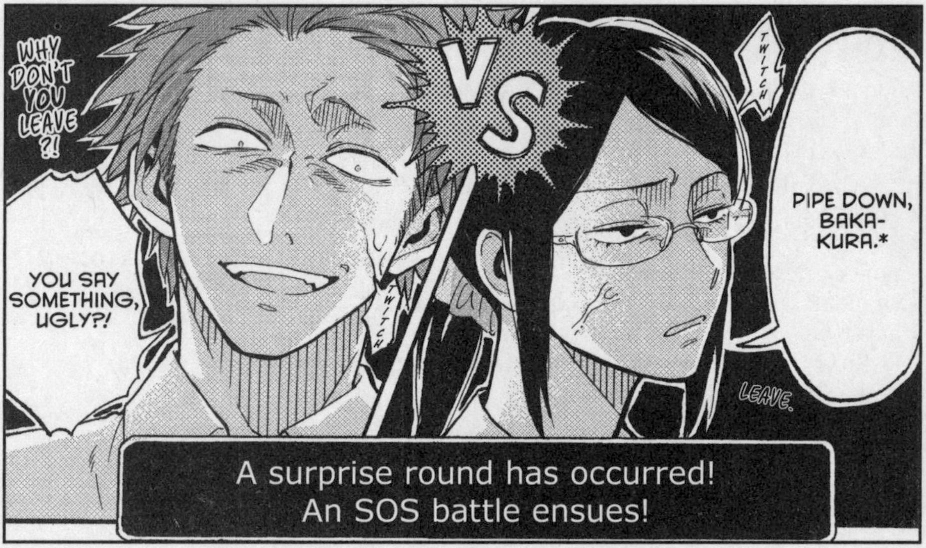
PIPE DOWN, BAKA-KURA.*
TWITCH
LEAVE.
VS
WHY DON'T YOU LEAVE?!
TWITCH
YOU SAY SOMETHING, UGLY?!
A surprise round has occurred!
An SOS battle ensues!

▲SUNRISE,
PAGE 28

"Sunrise" was the entrance theme used by pro wrestler Stan Hansen. Far more renowned in Japan than in the US, he was cast as a villain character. Variety TV shows also use "Sunrise" as background music for debates and arguments.

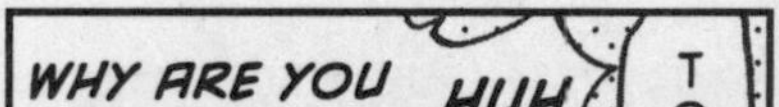
TONHEEEE♪
HUH?!
WHY ARE YOU REFERENCING KOMAKA-SUGITE TSUTA-WARANAI MONOMANE SENSHUKEN?!
?!
SERI-OUSLY, WHAT'S WRONG?!
?!

▶TONHE,
PAGE 33

This is a repeat joke from *Komaka-sugite Tsutawaranai Monomane Senshuken.* Japanese comedian Myo-chan routinely impersonates a Korean soldier who finds himself in various situations in which he is on the brink of death. He then melodramatically belts out the first word of the South Korean national anthem. In this scenario, Hirotaka is trying to communicate a feeling of relief after a tense moment.

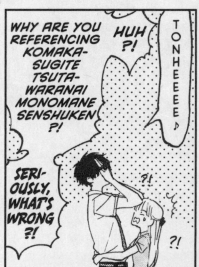

CROSSPLAY,
PAGE 37

Crossplay is when a person cosplays a character whose sex is different from their own. This can include using makeup, binders, padding, and other means to add the effect of the character's biology.

▶NTR,
PAGE 41

Short for *netorare* and translated as "cuckold" in English, NTR is a subgenre of erotic manga and anime centered around infidelity, whereby a character in a relationship is stolen away from their partner by another person. Usually the cheating partner is female, but in some cases it can be the male.

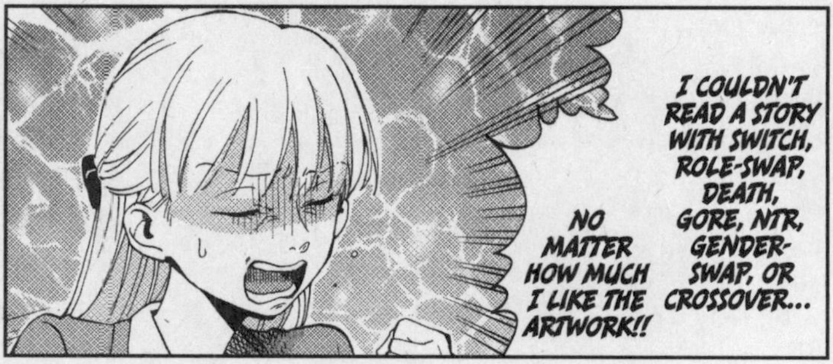
I COULDN'T READ A STORY WITH SWITCH, ROLE-SWAP, DEATH, GORE, NTR, GENDER-SWAP, OR CROSSOVER...
NO MATTER HOW MUCH I LIKE THE ARTWORK!!

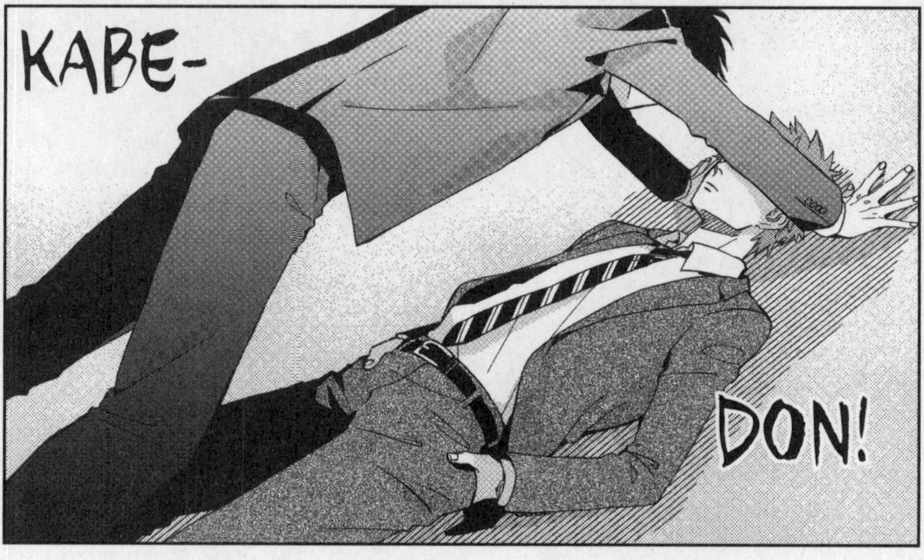
KABE-
DON!

▲KABE-DON,
PAGE 44

Kabe-don is a combination of *kabe*, or "wall" and *don*, the onomatopoeia for a thudding slam, and is a common scenario in anime, manga, and dramas, whereby a character (usually a dominant-type male) slams his hand(s) against a wall, pinning their partner against it. The character initiating the kabe-don usually does so out of anger, jealousy, or a more aggressive style of flirting. Either way, it often leads to lots of blushing and romantic dialogue as they end up in close proximity to one another.

▼GAP MOÉ, PAGE 95

Moé is a hard-to-define term that basically covers feelings of adoration and affection one feels towards (in the otaku's case) a character from anime, manga, or games; and a gap moé is specifically a character whose appeal comes from the difference between expectation and reality. In Narumi's case, Taro would expect a cute woman to use feminine language, not that of a feudal lord.

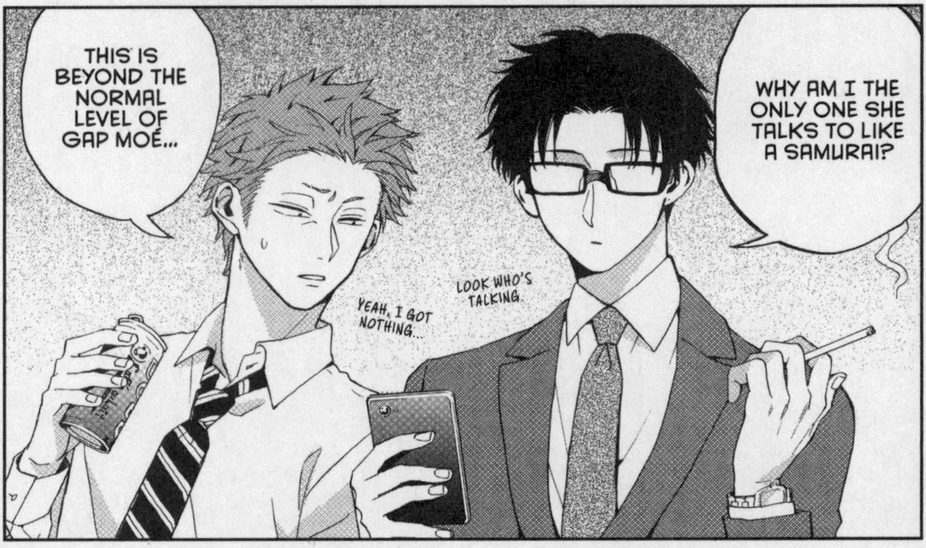
WHY AM I THE ONLY ONE SHE TALKS TO LIKE A SAMURAI?
THIS IS BEYOND THE NORMAL LEVEL OF GAP MOÉ...
LOOK WHO'S TALKING.
YEAH, I GOT NOTHING...

WEST ENTRANCE, PAGE 123

Train stations in Japan, especially in Tokyo, can be utterly sprawling affairs, and to navigate them without getting lost, one should become well-aquainted with the different exits/entrances. Here, Narumi and Hirotaka are likely referring to a station close to their office with an arcade by the West Entrance.

▶PIXIV, PAGE 126

Launched in 2007, Pixiv is an online community for Japanese artists to share their artwork. Artists can get feedback through a rating system and comments from users. *Wotakoi* got its start as a webcomic on Pixiv.

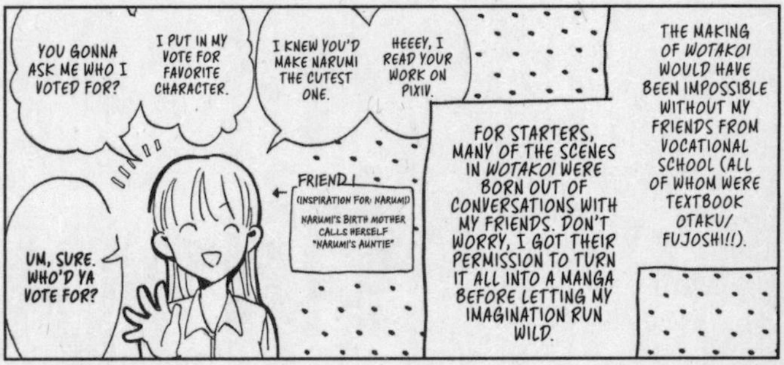
THE MAKING OF *WOTAKOI* WOULD HAVE BEEN IMPOSSIBLE WITHOUT MY FRIENDS FROM VOCATIONAL SCHOOL (ALL OF WHOM WERE TEXTBOOK OTAKU/FUJOSHI!!).
FOR STARTERS, MANY OF THE SCENES IN *WOTAKOI* WERE BORN OUT OF CONVERSATIONS WITH MY FRIENDS. DON'T WORRY, I GOT THEIR PERMISSION TO TURN IT ALL INTO A MANGA BEFORE LETTING MY IMAGINATION RUN WILD.
HEEEY, I READ YOUR WORK ON PIXIV.
I KNEW YOU'D MAKE NARUMI THE CUTEST ONE.
I PUT IN MY VOTE FOR FAVORITE CHARACTER.
YOU GONNA ASK ME WHO I VOTED FOR?
FRIEND!
(INSPIRATION FOR: NARUMI)
NARUMI'S BIRTH MOTHER CALLS HERSELF "NARUMI'S AUNTIE"
UM, SURE. WHO'D YA VOTE FOR?

◀ WOTAKOI: LOVE IS HARD FOR OTAKU, COVER

On the *Wotakoi* covers, the characters tend to point to whichever part of the Japanese title is most relevant to them. As Japanese grammar works in a different order from English, the Japanese and English titles do not match one-for-one. Here is a breakdown of each word, so non-Japanese speakers can see which part is which!

ヲタク — (*W*)*otaku* (The w in *wotaku* comes from Fujita's use of the character ヲ (*wo*), which has fallen out of use in modern Japanese.)

恋 — *Koi* (Love)

難しい — *Muzukashii* (Hard)

WOTAKOI:

LOVE IS HARD FOR OTAKU

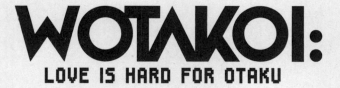

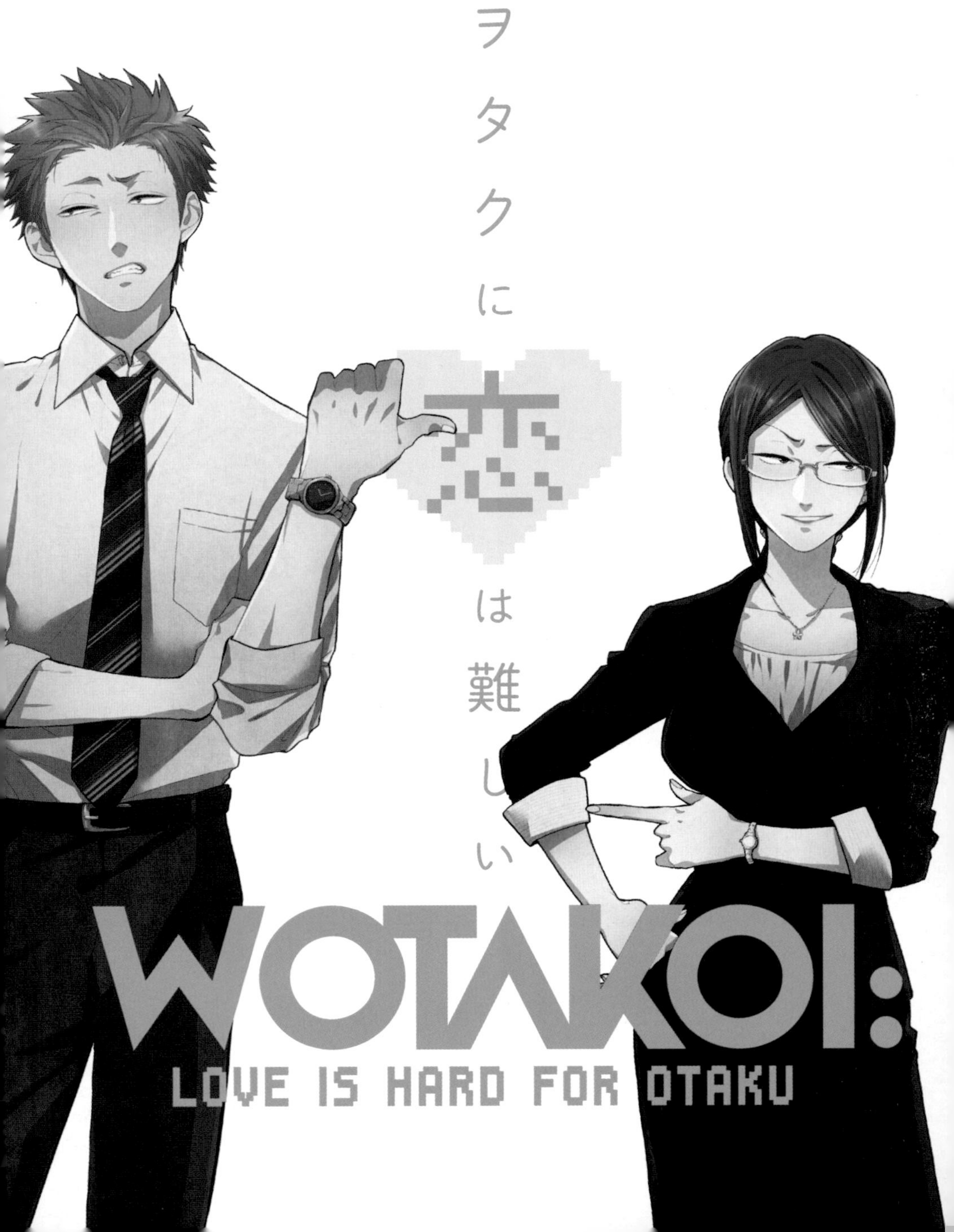
ヲタクに恋は難しい
WOTAKOI:
LOVE IS HARD FOR OTAKU

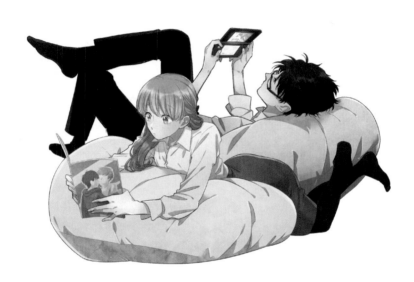

WOTAKOI:
LOVE IS HARD FOR OTAKU

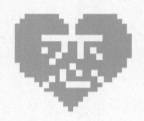

②

FUJITA

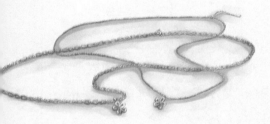

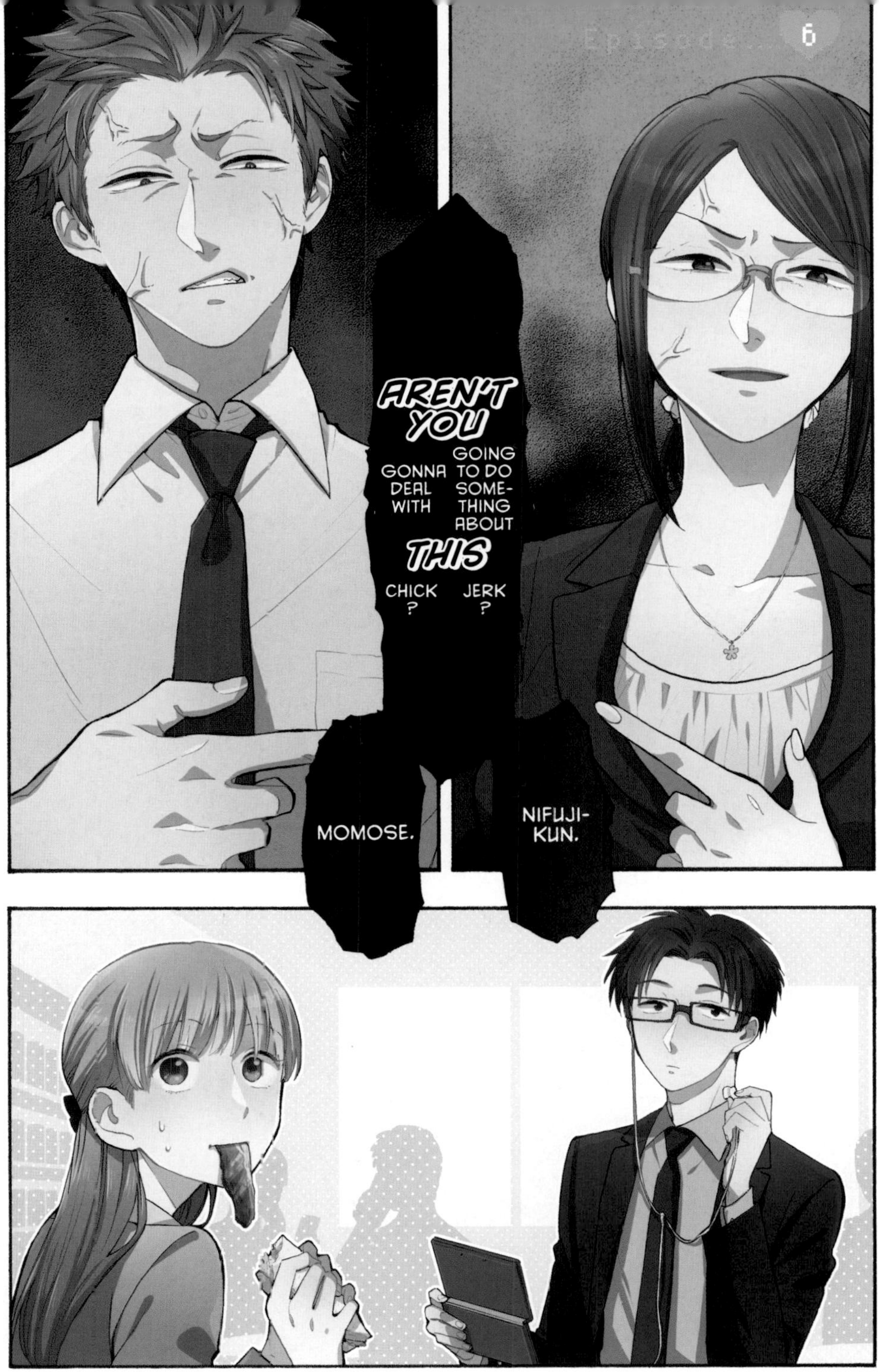
Episode 6
AREN'T YOU
GOING TO DO SOMETHING ABOUT
GONNA DEAL WITH
THIS
JERK?
CHICK?
NIFUJI-KUN.
MOMOSE.

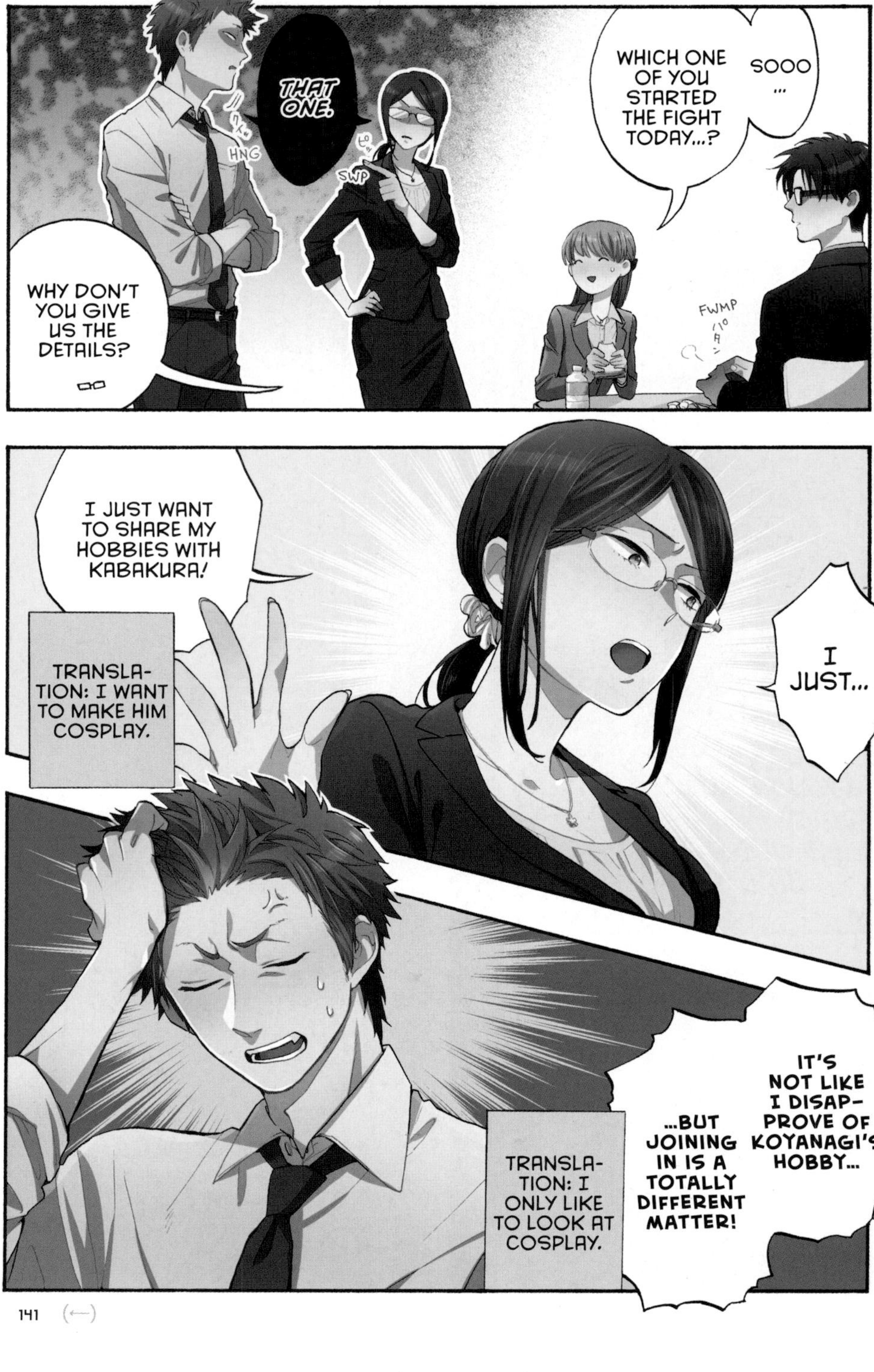
SOOO ...
WHICH ONE OF YOU STARTED THE FIGHT TODAY...?
THAT ONE.
SWP
HNG
WHY DON'T YOU GIVE US THE DETAILS?
FWMP
I JUST...
I JUST WANT TO SHARE MY HOBBIES WITH KABAKURA!
TRANSLA- TION: I WANT TO MAKE HIM COSPLAY.
IT'S NOT LIKE I DISAP- PROVE OF KOYANAGI'S HOBBY...
...BUT JOINING IN IS A TOTALLY DIFFERENT MATTER!
TRANSLA- TION: I ONLY LIKE TO LOOK AT COSPLAY.

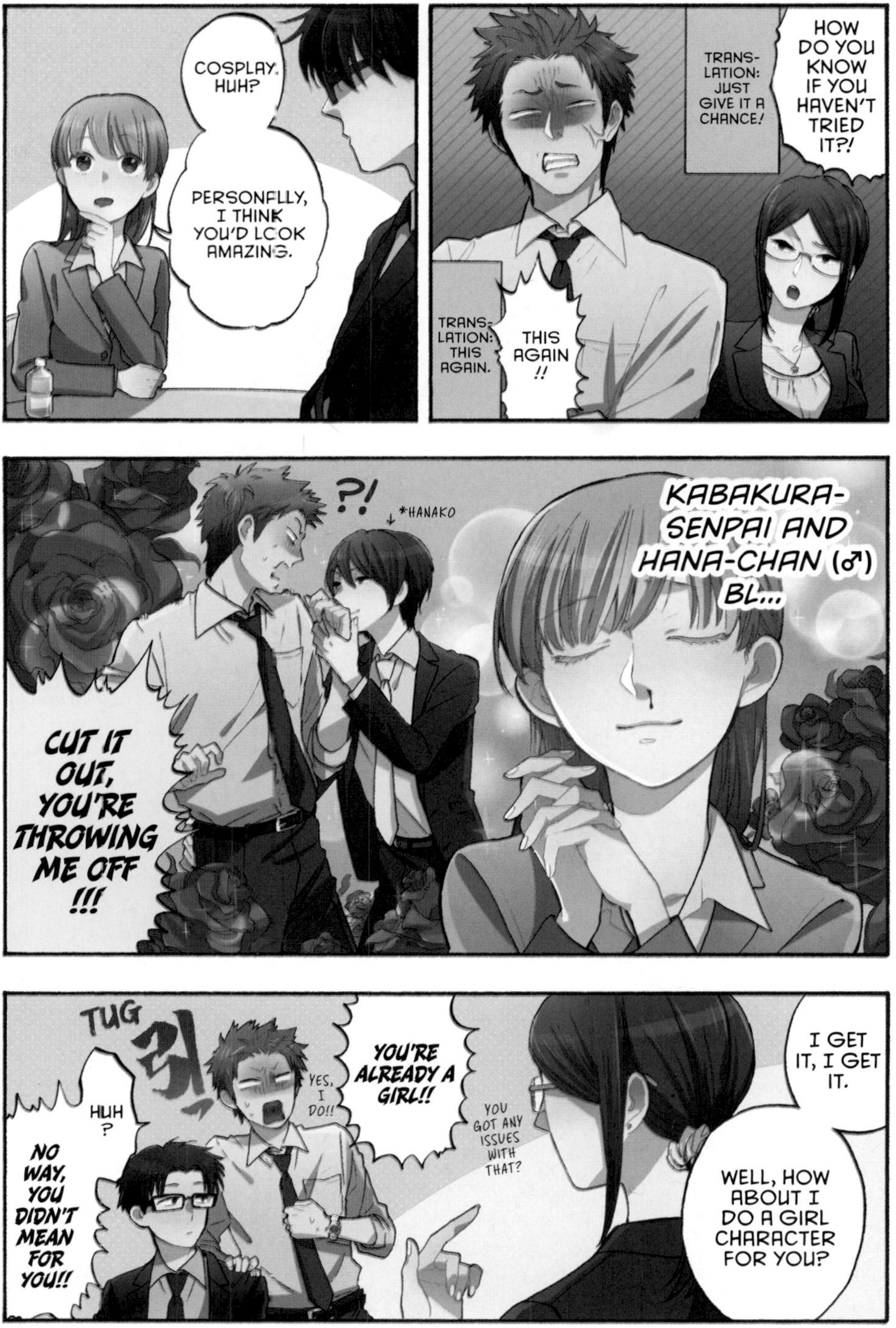
HOW DO YOU KNOW IF YOU HAVEN'T TRIED IT?!
TRANSLATION: JUST GIVE IT A CHANCE!
THIS AGAIN!!
TRANSLATION: THIS AGAIN.
COSPLAY, HUH?
PERSONALLY, I THINK YOU'D LOOK AMAZING.
KABAKURA-SENPAI AND HANA-CHAN (♂) BL...
?!
*HANAKO
CUT IT OUT, YOU'RE THROWING ME OFF!!!
I GET IT, I GET IT.
WELL, HOW ABOUT I DO A GIRL CHARACTER FOR YOU?
YOU GOT ANY ISSUES WITH THAT?
YOU'RE ALREADY A GIRL!!
YES, I DO!!
TUG
HUH?
NO WAY, YOU DIDN'T MEAN FOR YOU!!

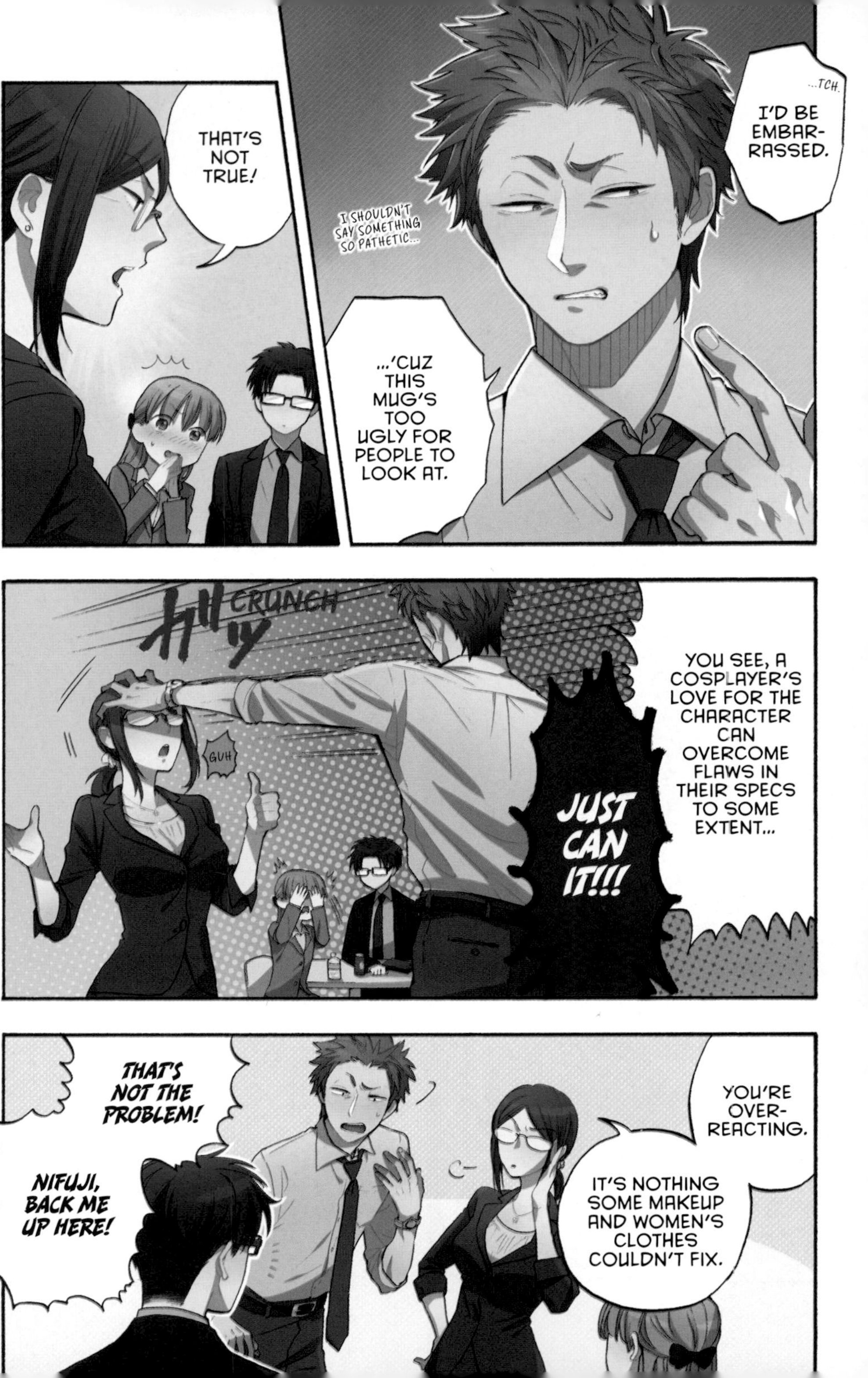
...TCH.
I'D BE EMBAR-RASSED.
I SHOULDN'T SAY SOMETHING SO PATHETIC...
...'CUZ THIS MUG'S TOO UGLY FOR PEOPLE TO LOOK AT.
THAT'S NOT TRUE!
YOU SEE, A COSPLAYER'S LOVE FOR THE CHARACTER CAN OVERCOME FLAWS IN THEIR SPECS TO SOME EXTENT...
JUST CAN IT!!!
CRUNCH
GUH
YOU'RE OVER-REACTING.
IT'S NOTHING SOME MAKEUP AND WOMEN'S CLOTHES COULDN'T FIX.
THAT'S NOT THE PROBLEM!
NIFUJI, BACK ME UP HERE!

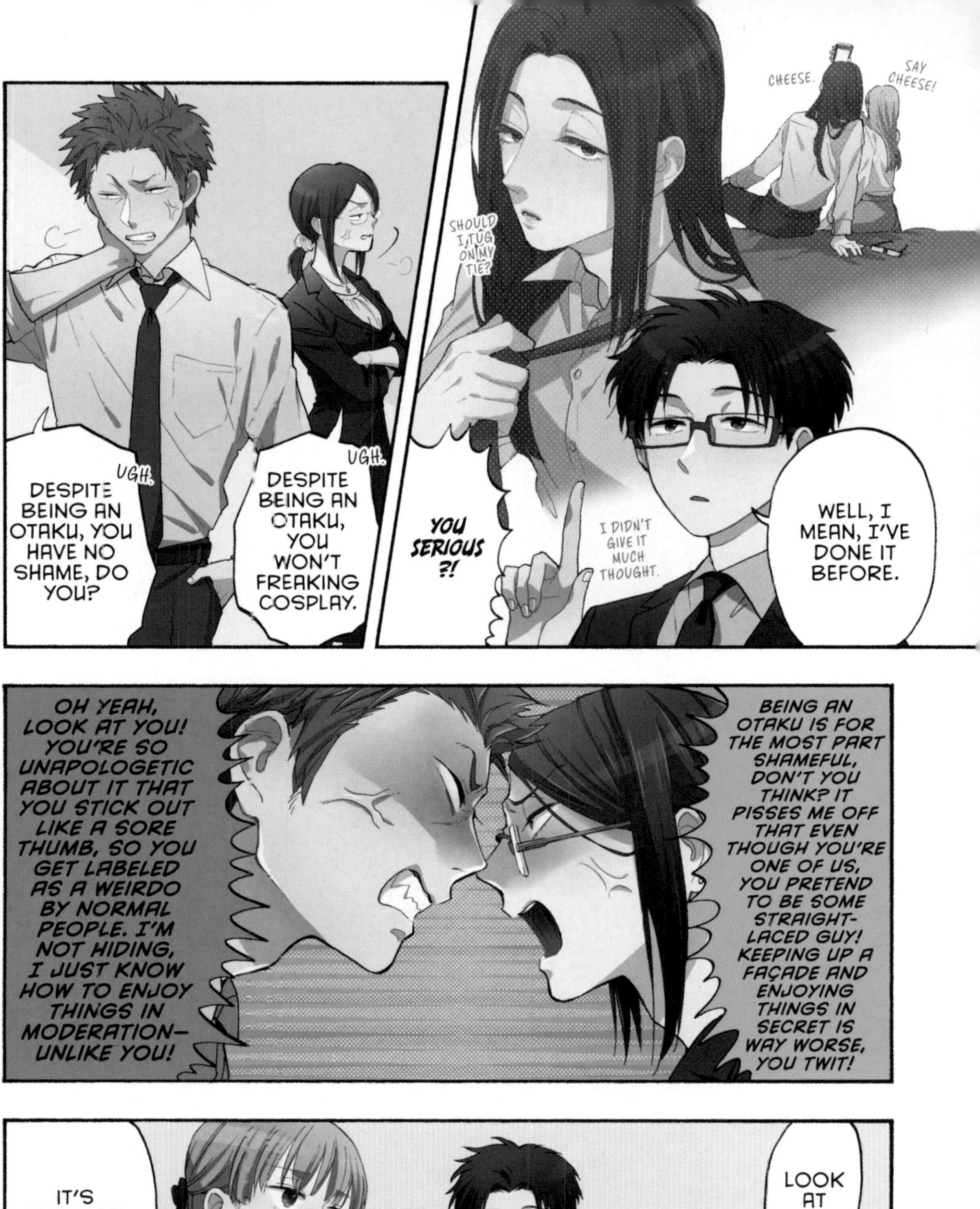
SAY CHEESE!
CHEESE.
SHOULD I TUG ON MY TIE?
WELL, I MEAN, I'VE DONE IT BEFORE.
I DIDN'T GIVE IT MUCH THOUGHT.
YOU SERIOUS?!
UGH.
DESPITE BEING AN OTAKU, YOU WON'T FREAKING COSPLAY.
UGH.
DESPITE BEING AN OTAKU, YOU HAVE NO SHAME, DO YOU?
BEING AN OTAKU IS FOR THE MOST PART SHAMEFUL, DON'T YOU THINK? IT PISSES ME OFF THAT EVEN THOUGH YOU'RE ONE OF US, YOU PRETEND TO BE SOME STRAIGHT-LACED GUY! KEEPING UP A FAÇADE AND ENJOYING THINGS IN SECRET IS WAY WORSE, YOU TWIT!
OH YEAH, LOOK AT YOU! YOU'RE SO UNAPOLOGETIC ABOUT IT THAT YOU STICK OUT LIKE A SORE THUMB, SO YOU GET LABELED AS A WEIRDO BY NORMAL PEOPLE. I'M NOT HIDING, I JUST KNOW HOW TO ENJOY THINGS IN MODERATION—UNLIKE YOU!
LOOK AT THEM.
FIGHTING LIKE THAT GOES TO SHOW HOW GOOD THEIR RELATION-SHIP IS.
SLURP...
ちゅる...
IT'S AMAZING YOU CAN SAY THAT ABOUT THIS SITUATION.

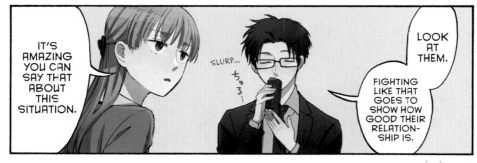

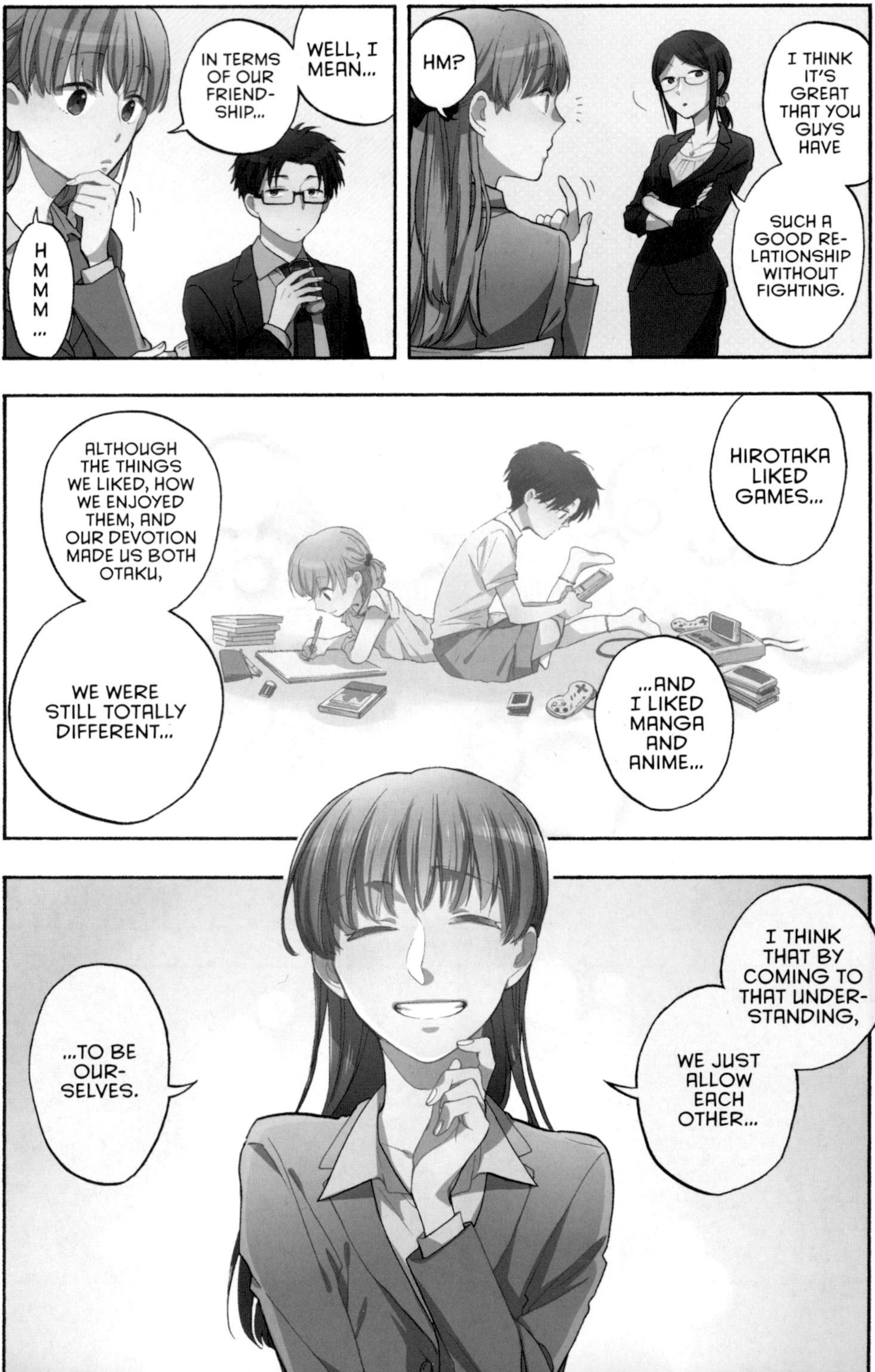
I THINK IT'S GREAT THAT YOU GUYS HAVE
SUCH A GOOD RE-LATIONSHIP WITHOUT FIGHTING.
HM?
WELL, I MEAN...
IN TERMS OF OUR FRIEND-SHIP...
HMMM...
HIROTAKA LIKED GAMES...
...AND I LIKED MANGA AND ANIME...
ALTHOUGH THE THINGS WE LIKED, HOW WE ENJOYED THEM, AND OUR DEVOTION MADE US BOTH OTAKU,
WE WERE STILL TOTALLY DIFFERENT...
I THINK THAT BY COMING TO THAT UNDER-STANDING,
WE JUST ALLOW EACH OTHER...
...TO BE OUR-SELVES.

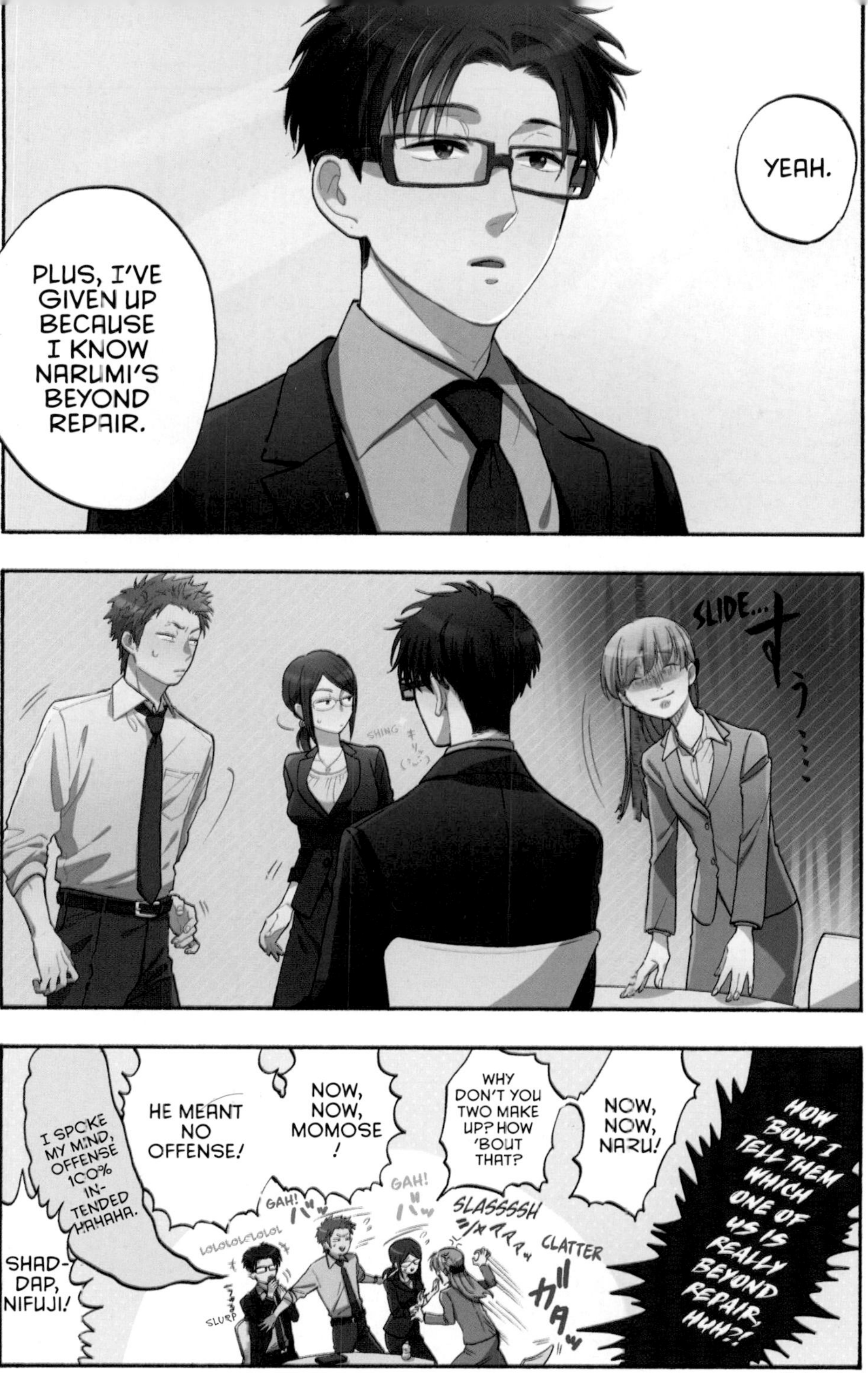
YEAH.
PLUS, I'VE GIVEN UP BECAUSE I KNOW NARUMI'S BEYOND REPAIR.
SLIDE...
SHING
HOW 'BOUT I TELL THEM WHICH ONE OF US IS REALLY BEYOND REPAIR, HUH?!
NOW, NOW, NARU!
WHY DON'T YOU TWO MAKE UP? HOW 'BOUT THAT?
NOW, NOW, MOMOSE!
HE MEANT NO OFFENSE!
I SPOKE MY MIND, OFFENSE 100% IN-TENDED HAHAHA.
CLATTER
SLASSSSH
GAH!
GAH!
LOLOLOLOLOL
SHAD-DAP, NIFUJI!
SLURP

Episode 7

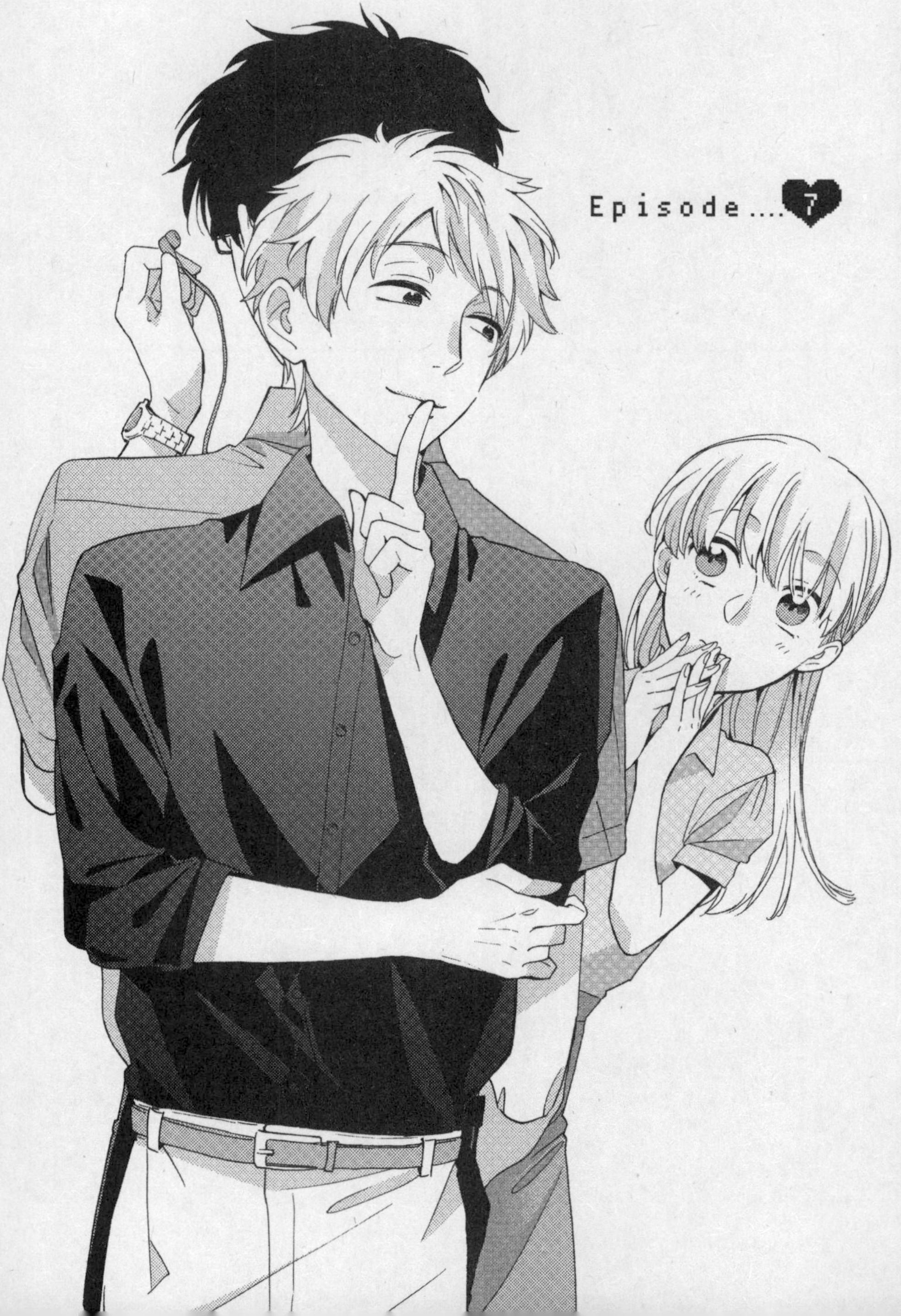

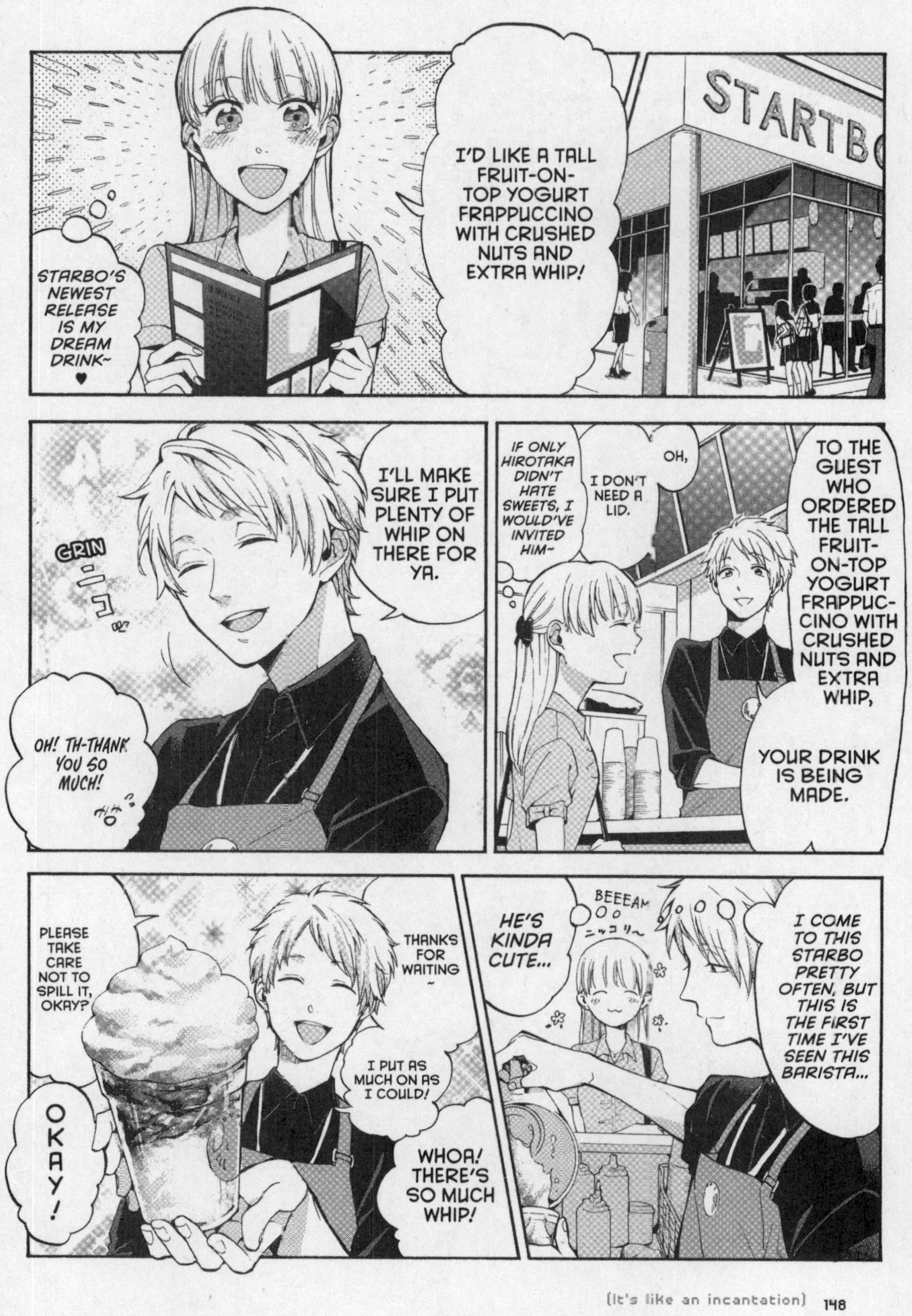
STARTBO
I'D LIKE A TALL FRUIT-ON-TOP YOGURT FRAPPUCCINO WITH CRUSHED NUTS AND EXTRA WHIP!
STARBO'S NEWEST RELEASE IS MY DREAM DRINK~ ♥
TO THE GUEST WHO ORDERED THE TALL FRUIT-ON-TOP YOGURT FRAPPUC-CINO WITH CRUSHED NUTS AND EXTRA WHIP,
OH,
I DON'T NEED A LID.
IF ONLY HIROTAKA DIDN'T HATE SWEETS, I WOULD'VE INVITED HIM~
YOUR DRINK IS BEING MADE.
I'LL MAKE SURE I PUT PLENTY OF WHIP ON THERE FOR YA.
GRIN
OH! TH-THANK YOU SO MUCH!
I COME TO THIS STARBO PRETTY OFTEN, BUT THIS IS THE FIRST TIME I'VE SEEN THIS BARISTA...
BEEEAM
HE'S KINDA CUTE...
THANKS FOR WAITING ~
PLEASE TAKE CARE NOT TO SPILL IT, OKAY?
I PUT AS MUCH ON AS I COULD!
WHOA! THERE'S SO MUCH WHIP!
OKAY!

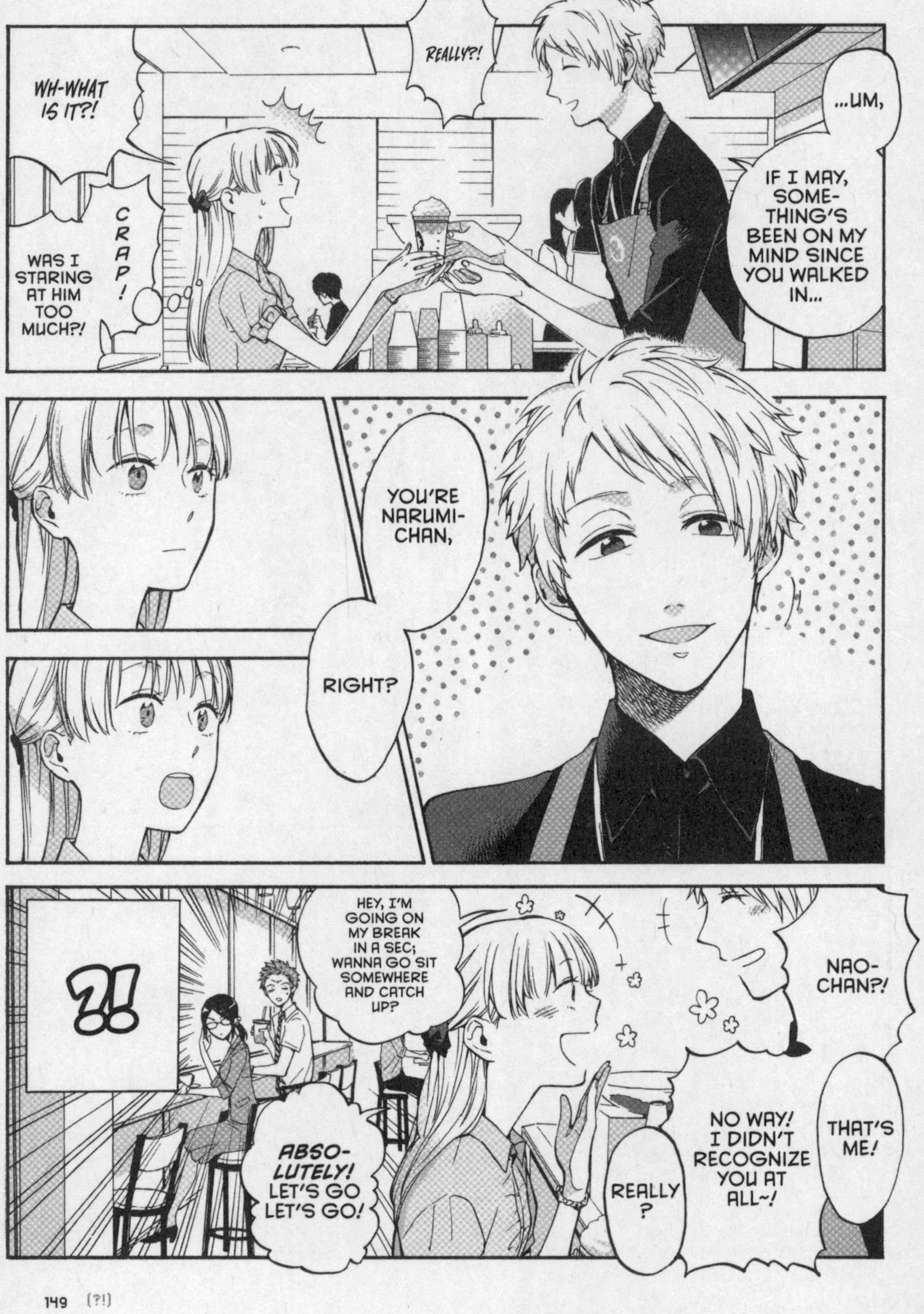
...UM,
IF I MAY, SOME-THING'S BEEN ON MY MIND SINCE YOU WALKED IN...
REALLY?!
WH-WHAT IS IT?!
CRAP!
WAS I STARING AT HIM TOO MUCH?!
YOU'RE NARUMI-CHAN,
RIGHT?
NAO-CHAN?!
THAT'S ME!
NO WAY! I DIDN'T RECOGNIZE YOU AT ALL~!
REALLY?
HEY, I'M GOING ON MY BREAK IN A SEC; WANNA GO SIT SOMEWHERE AND CATCH UP?
ABSO-LUTELY! LET'S GO LET'S GO!
?!

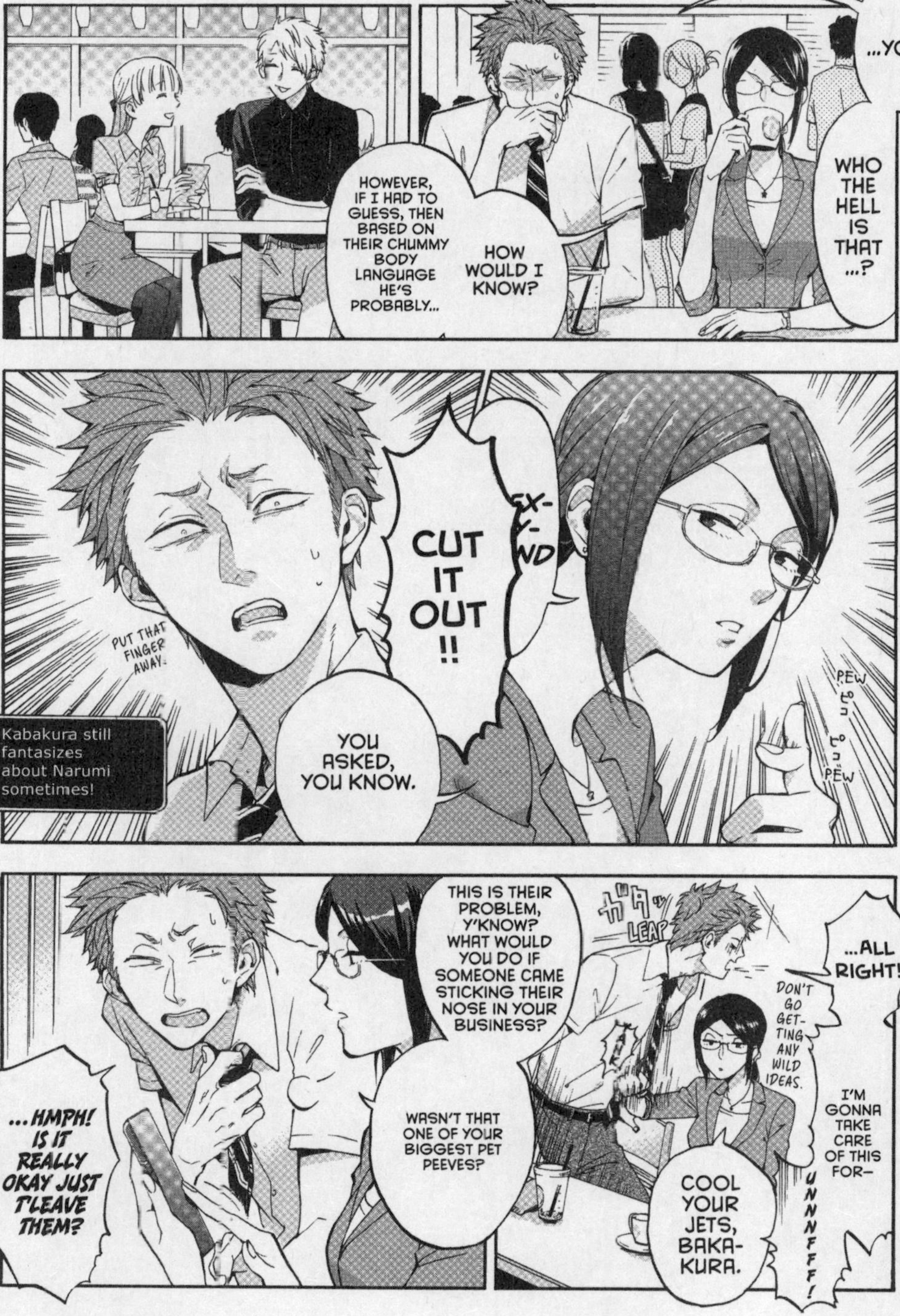
...YO.
WHO THE HELL IS THAT ...?
HOW WOULD I KNOW?
HOWEVER, IF I HAD TO GUESS, THEN BASED ON THEIR CHUMMY BODY LANGUAGE HE'S PROBABLY...
CUT IT OUT !!
PEW
PEW
YOU ASKED, YOU KNOW.
PUT THAT FINGER AWAY.
Kabakura still fantasizes about Narumi sometimes!
...ALL RIGHT!
I'M GONNA TAKE CARE OF THIS FOR—
LEAP
DON'T GO GETTING ANY WILD IDEAS.
COOL YOUR JETS, BAKAKURA.
UNNNFFF!
THIS IS THEIR PROBLEM, Y'KNOW? WHAT WOULD YOU DO IF SOMEONE CAME STICKING THEIR NOSE IN YOUR BUSINESS?
WASN'T THAT ONE OF YOUR BIGGEST PET PEEVES?
...HMPH! IS IT REALLY OKAY JUST T'LEAVE THEM?

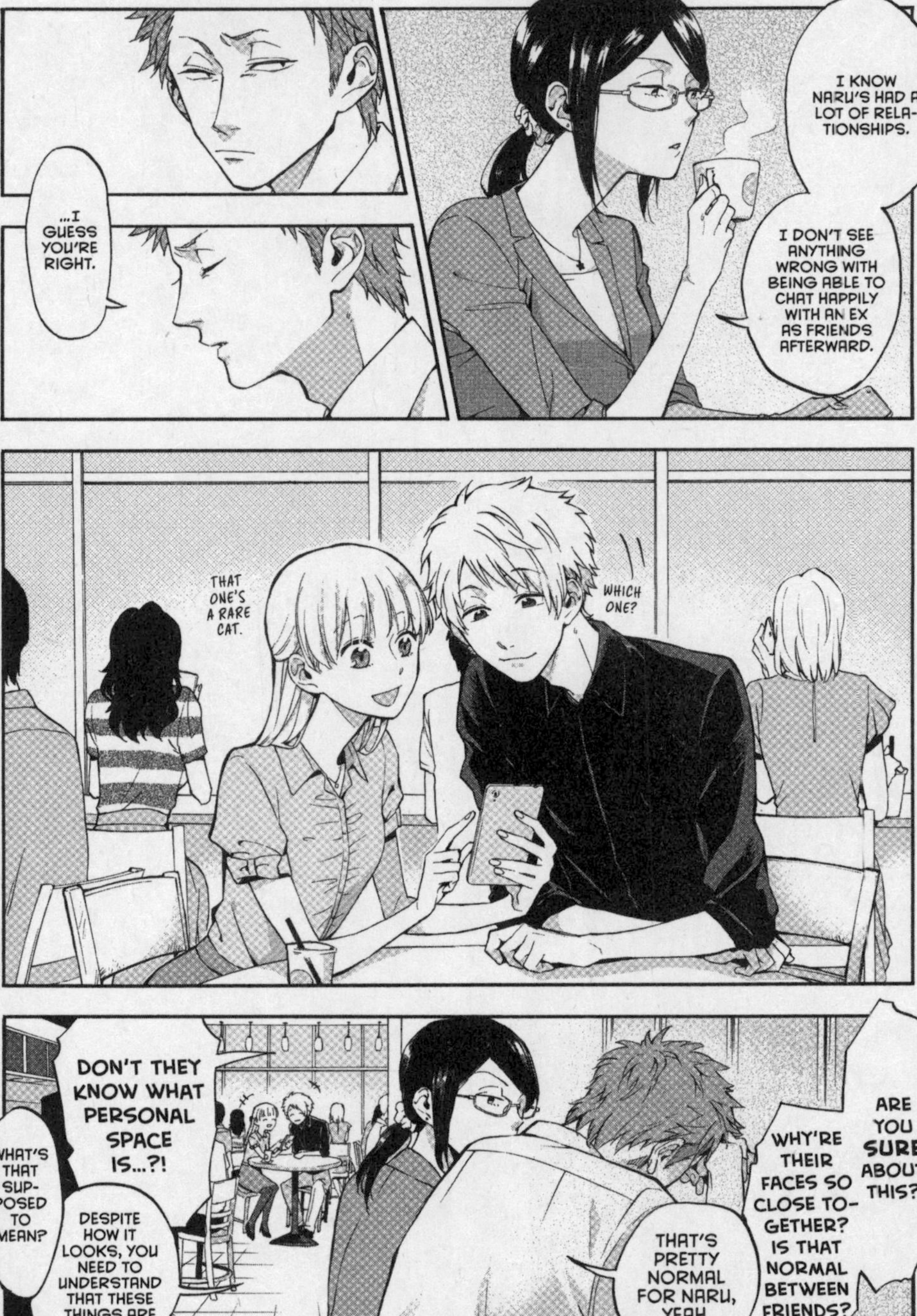
I KNOW NARU'S HAD A LOT OF RELATIONSHIPS.
I DON'T SEE ANYTHING WRONG WITH BEING ABLE TO CHAT HAPPILY WITH AN EX AS FRIENDS AFTERWARD.
...I GUESS YOU'RE RIGHT.
WHICH ONE?
THAT ONE'S A RARE CAT.
ARE YOU **SURE** ABOUT THIS?
WHY'RE THEIR FACES SO CLOSE TOGETHER? IS THAT NORMAL BETWEEN FRIENDS?
THAT'S PRETTY NORMAL FOR NARU, YEAH.
DON'T THEY KNOW WHAT PERSONAL SPACE IS...?!
WHAT'S THAT SUPPOSED TO MEAN?
DESPITE HOW IT LOOKS, YOU NEED TO UNDERSTAND THAT THESE THINGS ARE DELICATE.

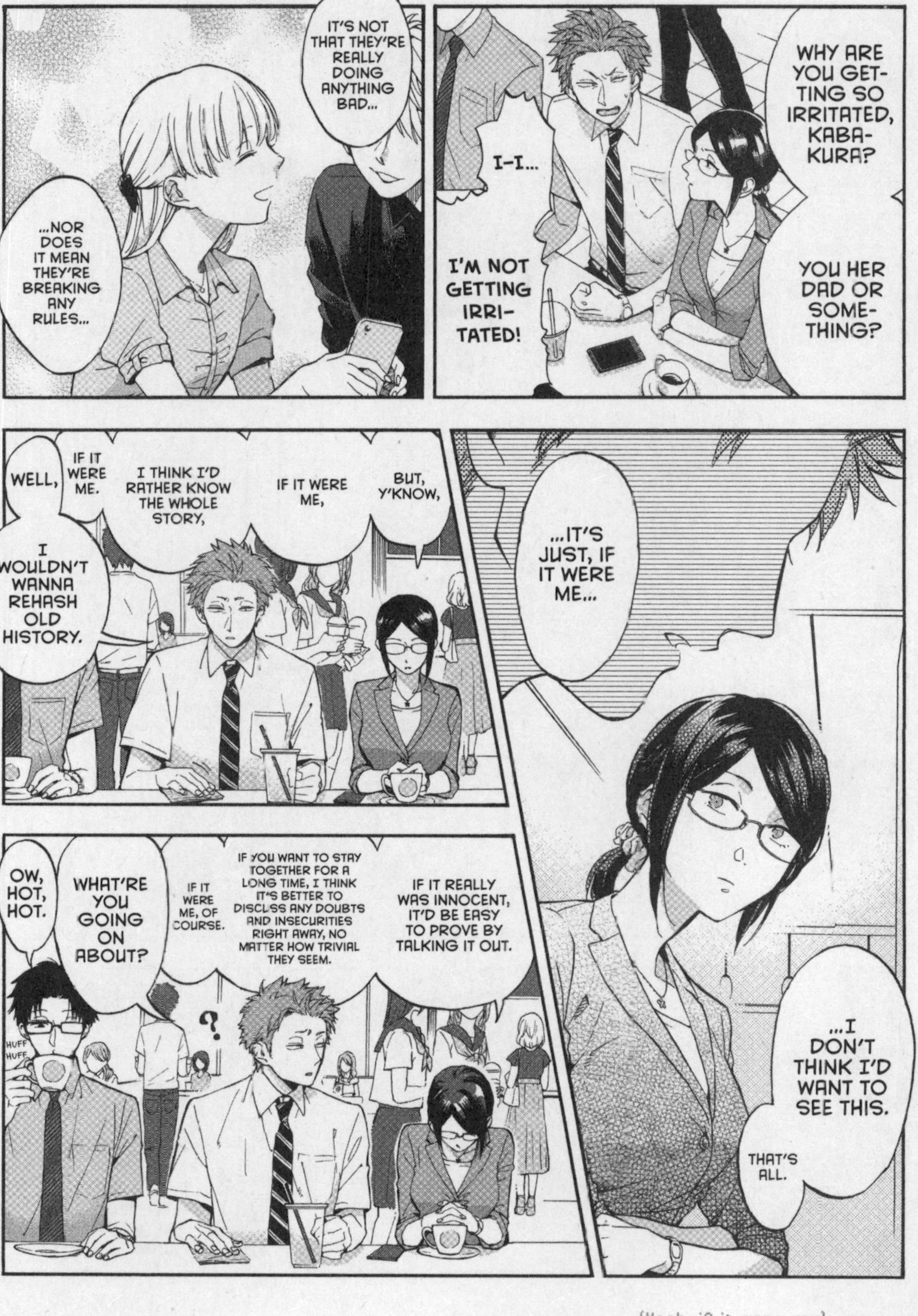
WHY ARE YOU GETTING SO IRRITATED, KABAKURA?
YOU HER DAD OR SOMETHING?
I-I...
I'M NOT GETTING IRRITATED!
IT'S NOT THAT THEY'RE REALLY DOING ANYTHING BAD...
...NOR DOES IT MEAN THEY'RE BREAKING ANY RULES...
...IT'S JUST, IF IT WERE ME...
...I DON'T THINK I'D WANT TO SEE THIS.
THAT'S ALL.
BUT, Y'KNOW,
IF IT WERE ME,
I THINK I'D RATHER KNOW THE WHOLE STORY,
IF IT WERE ME.
WELL,
I WOULDN'T WANNA REHASH OLD HISTORY.
IF IT REALLY WAS INNOCENT, IT'D BE EASY TO PROVE BY TALKING IT OUT.
IF YOU WANT TO STAY TOGETHER FOR A LONG TIME, I THINK IT'S BETTER TO DISCUSS ANY DOUBTS AND INSECURITIES RIGHT AWAY, NO MATTER HOW TRIVIAL THEY SEEM.
IF IT WERE ME, OF COURSE.
WHAT'RE YOU GOING ON ABOUT?
OW, HOT, HOT.
?
HUFF HUFF

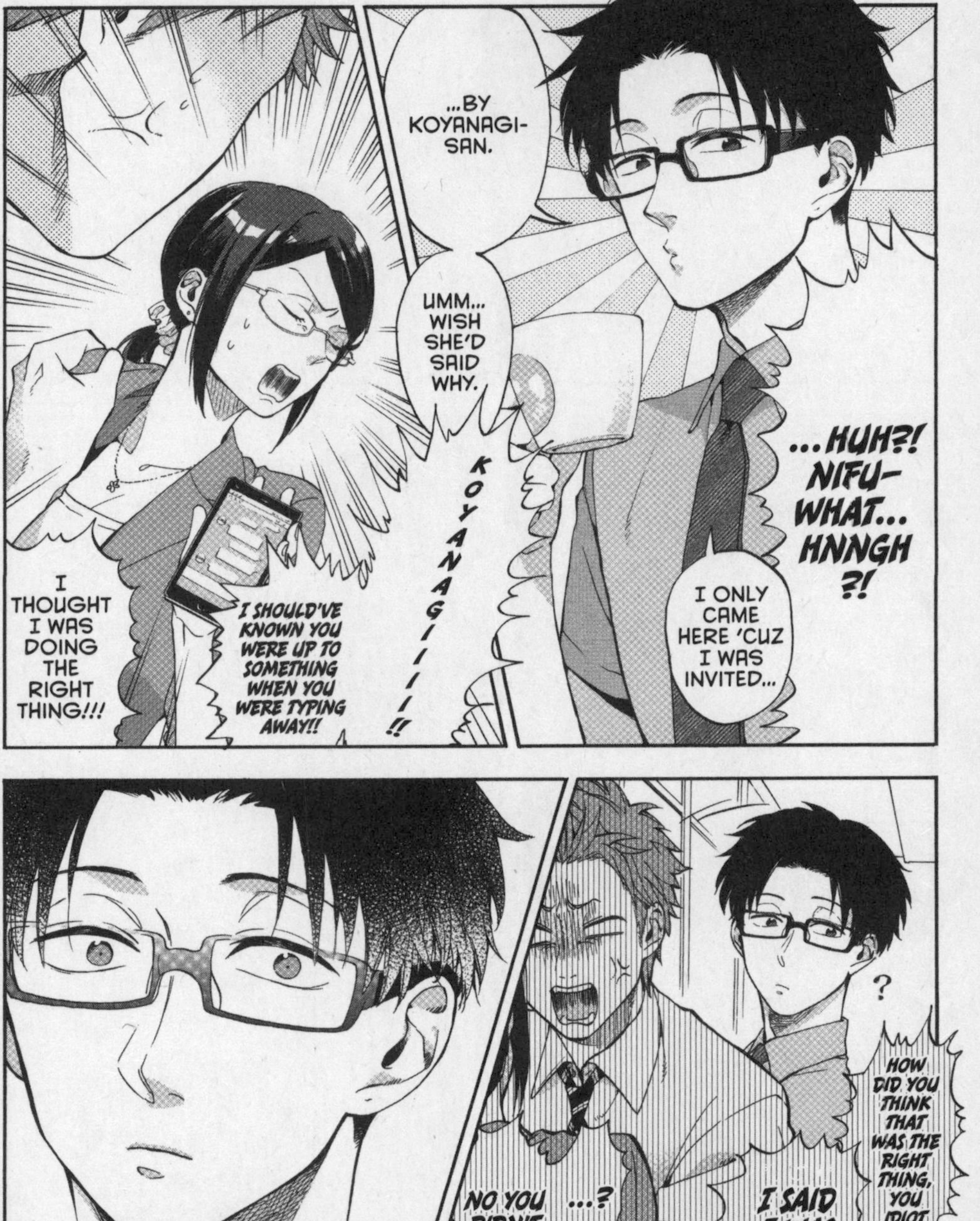
I ONLY CAME HERE 'CUZ I WAS INVITED...
...BY KOYANAGI-SAN.
...HUH?! NIFU-WHAT... HNNGH ?!
UMM... WISH SHE'D SAID WHY.
KOYANAGIIIII!!
I SHOULD'VE KNOWN YOU WERE UP TO SOMETHING WHEN YOU WERE TYPING AWAY!!
I THOUGHT I WAS DOING THE RIGHT THING!!!
HOW DID YOU THINK THAT WAS THE RIGHT THING, YOU IDIOT ?!
I SAID I WAS SORRY!
...?
NO YOU DIDN'T !!
?

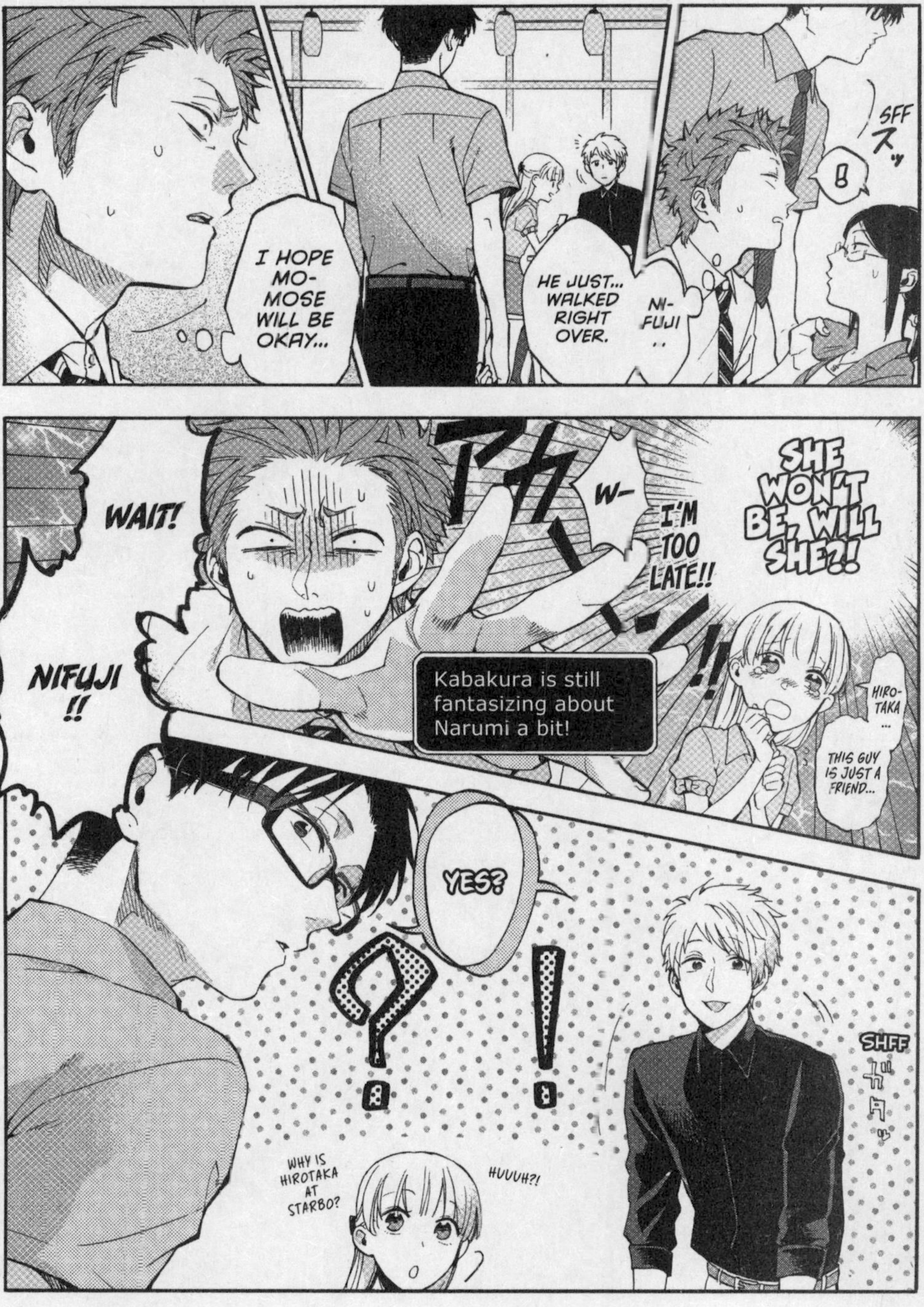
SFF
スッ
!
NI-FUJI..
HE JUST... WALKED RIGHT OVER.
I HOPE MO-MOSE WILL BE OKAY...
SHE WON'T BE, WILL SHE?!
I'M TOO LATE!!
W-
WAIT!
NIFUJI!!
HIRO-TAKA...
THIS GUY IS JUST A FRIEND...
Kabakura is still fantasizing about Narumi a bit!
SHFF
YES?
HUUUH?!
WHY IS HIROTAKA AT STARBO?

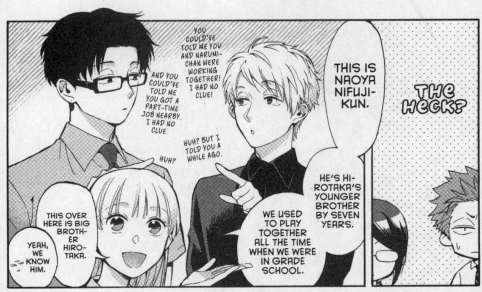

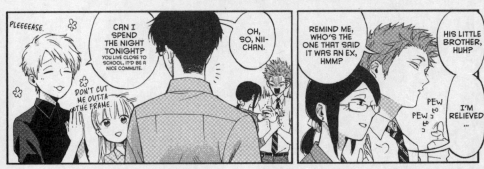

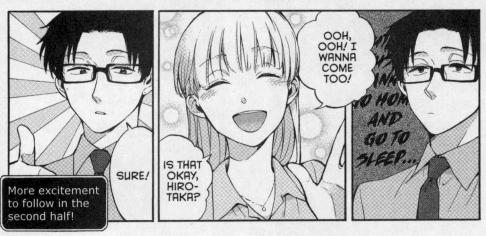

THE HECK?
THIS IS NAOYA NIFUJI-KUN.
YOU COULD'VE TOLD ME YOU AND NARUMI-CHAN WERE WORKING TOGETHER! I HAD NO CLUE!
AND YOU COULD'VE TOLD ME YOU GOT A PART-TIME JOB NEARBY. I HAD NO CLUE.
HUH? BUT I TOLD YOU A WHILE AGO.
HUH?
HE'S HI-ROTAKA'S YOUNGER BROTHER BY SEVEN YEARS.
WE USED TO PLAY TOGETHER ALL THE TIME WHEN WE WERE IN GRADE SCHOOL.
THIS OVER HERE IS BIG BROTH-ER HIRO-TAKA.
YEAH, WE KNOW HIM.
HIS LITTLE BROTHER, HUH?
REMIND ME, WHO'S THE ONE THAT SAID IT WAS AN EX, HMM?
I'M RELIEVED...
PEW PEW
OH, SO, NII-CHAN.
CAN I SPEND THE NIGHT TONIGHT? YOU LIVE CLOSE TO SCHOOL, IT'D BE A NICE COMMUTE.
PLEEEEASE.
DON'T CUT ME OUTTA THE FRAME.
OOH, OOH! I WANNA COME TOO!
AND GO TO SLEEP...
IS THAT OKAY, HIRO-TAKA?
SURE!
More excitement to follow in the second half!

Narumi Momose

▽ Sunday morning
Only realizes it's not a workday when she gets to her front door.

Waking up... Hits snooze a lot.
Staying up late... No longer young, so whenever she stays up all night, the next day is miserable.

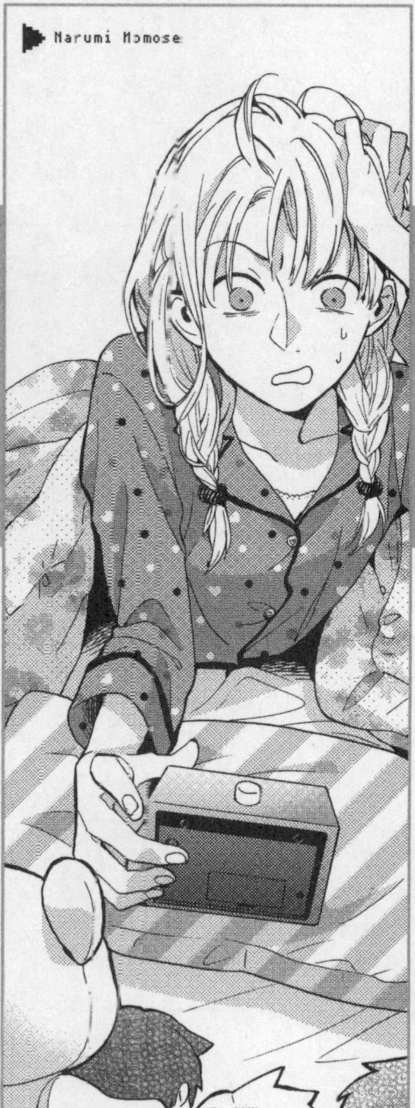
Narumi Momose

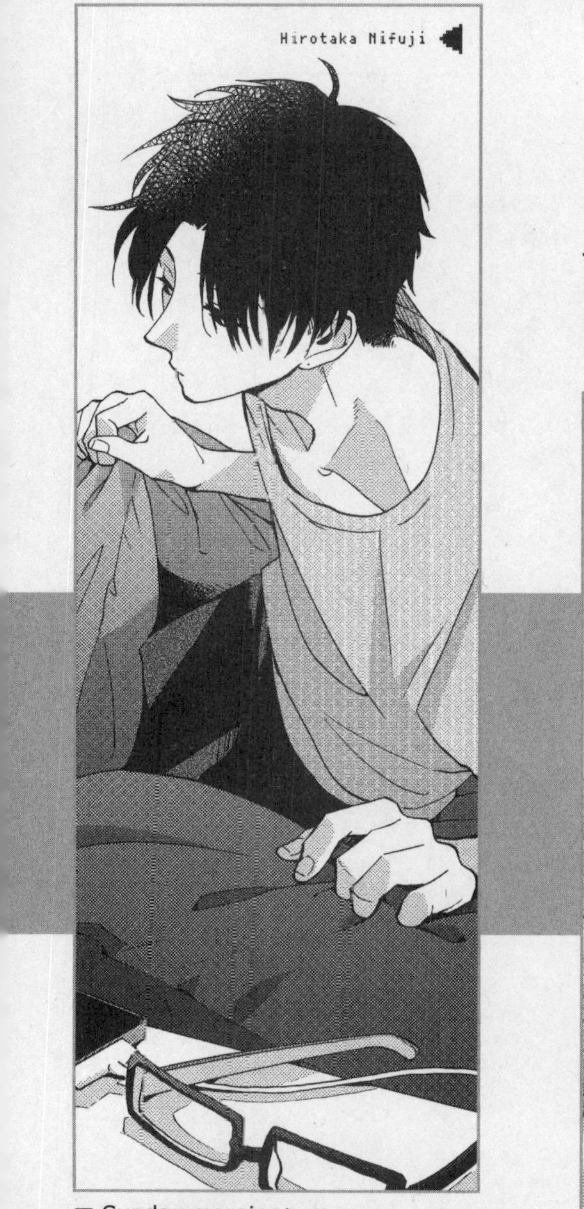
Hirotaka Nifuji

▽ Sunday morning
Just going to sleep.

Hirotaka Nifuji

Waking up... Totally useless for 10 minutes after waking up.
Staying up late... Regardless of the time of day, when he operates beyond his limits he suffers from intense fatigue.

Taro Kabakura

▽ Sunday morning
He always wakes up on time, even without an alarm clock.

Waking up... He wakes up at the slightest sound. Usually feels a little sleep deprived.
Staying up late... He can't do it, so he records all the late-night anime and binge-watches them on the weekends.

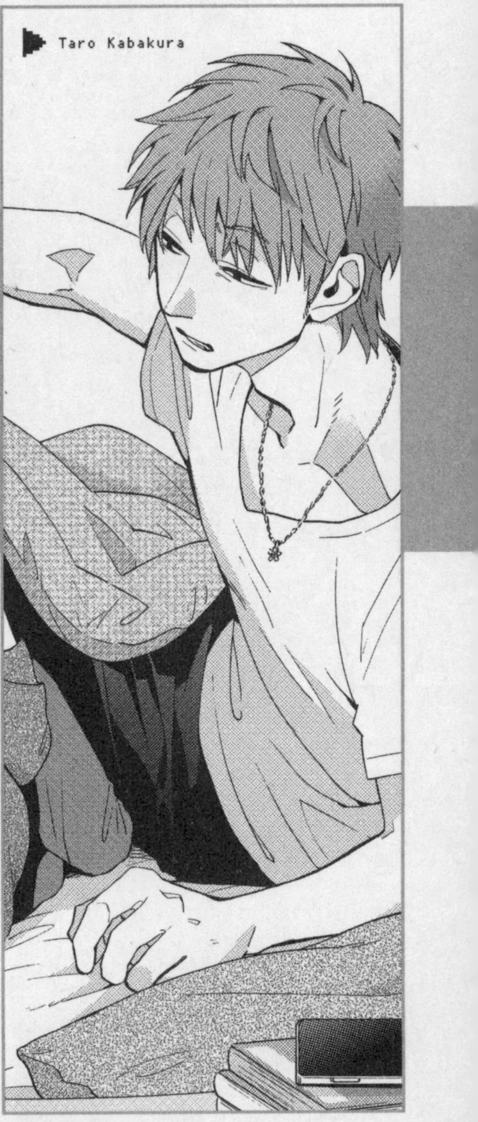
Taro Kabakura

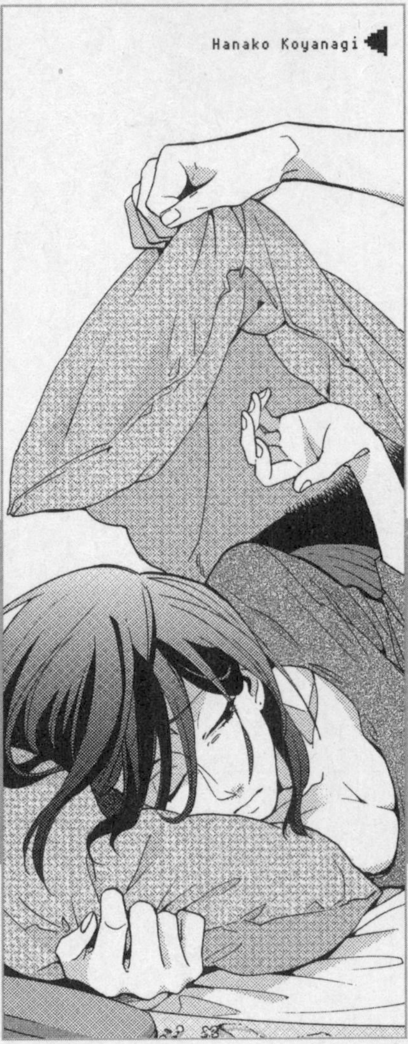
Hanako Koyanagi

Hanako Koyanagi

▽ Sunday morning
When she gets woken up, she wants to keep sleeping out of stubbornness.

Waking up... She can wake up on work days, but on other days she takes her time.
Staying up late... When she does, she's full of energy one moment, then suddenly crashes.

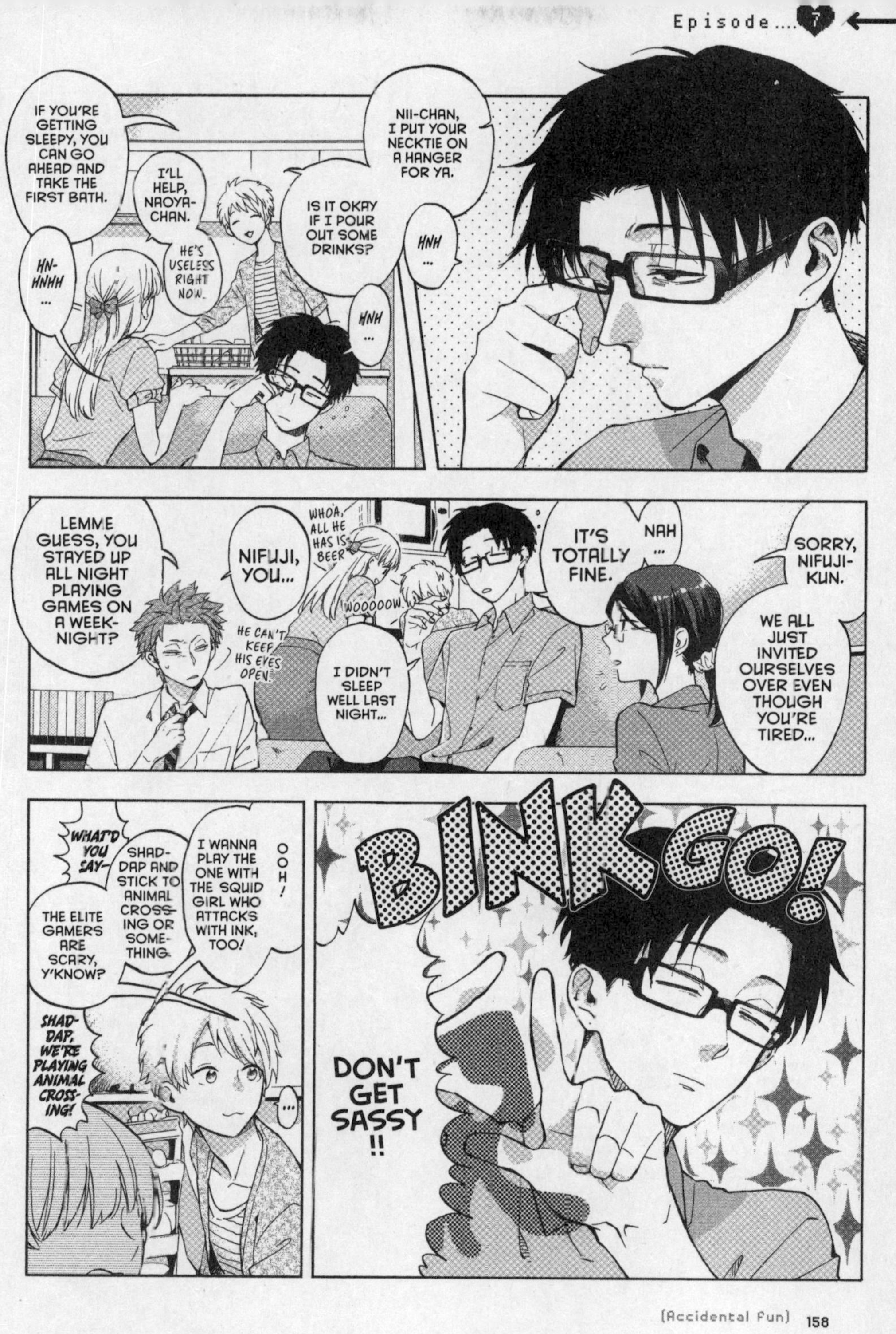
NII-CHAN, I PUT YOUR NECKTIE ON A HANGER FOR YA.
HNH...
IS IT OKAY IF I POUR OUT SOME DRINKS?
HNH...
I'LL HELP, NAOYA-CHAN.
HE'S USELESS RIGHT NOW.
IF YOU'RE GETTING SLEEPY, YOU CAN GO AHEAD AND TAKE THE FIRST BATH.
HN-HNHH...
SORRY, NIFUJI-KUN.
WE ALL JUST INVITED OURSELVES OVER EVEN THOUGH YOU'RE TIRED...
NAH...
IT'S TOTALLY FINE.
WHOA, ALL HE HAS IS BEER.
WOOOOOW.
NIFUJI, YOU...
I DIDN'T SLEEP WELL LAST NIGHT...
HE CAN'T KEEP HIS EYES OPEN.
LEMME GUESS, YOU STAYED UP ALL NIGHT PLAYING GAMES ON A WEEK-NIGHT?
BINKGO!
DON'T GET SASSY!!
OOH!
I WANNA PLAY THE ONE WITH THE SQUID GIRL WHO ATTACKS WITH INK, TOO!
SHAD-DAP AND STICK TO ANIMAL CROSSING OR SOMETHING.
WHAT'D YOU SAY-
THE ELITE GAMERS ARE SCARY, Y'KNOW?
SHAD-DAP, WE'RE PLAYING ANIMAL CROSSING!
...

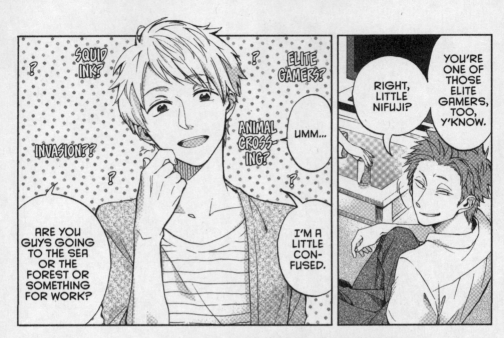

YOU'RE ONE OF THOSE ELITE GAMERS, TOO, Y'KNOW.
RIGHT, LITTLE NIFUJI?
ELITE GAMERS?
UMM...
ANIMAL CROSS-ING?
SQUID INK?
I'M A LITTLE CON-FUSED.
INVASION??
ARE YOU GUYS GOING TO THE SEA OR THE FOREST OR SOMETHING FOR WORK?
HUH? SOME-THING ELSE ?!
I'M SORRY, I'M LIKE,
NOT FAMILIAR WITH ANY OF THOSE FANCY TECHNICAL TERMS YOU PEOPLE IN THE WORKFORCE USE...
BUT IT'S PRETTY COOL... IT'S LIKE YOU'RE ALL HAVING AN OFFICE CONVERSA-TION! I AD-MIRE YOU ALL SO MUCH...
CODE BLUE: IT'S A NON-OTAKU!!

 (All hands to report to class one combat stations)

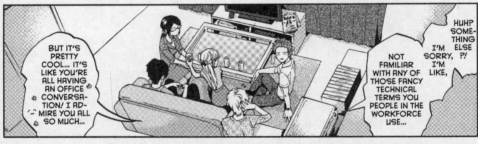

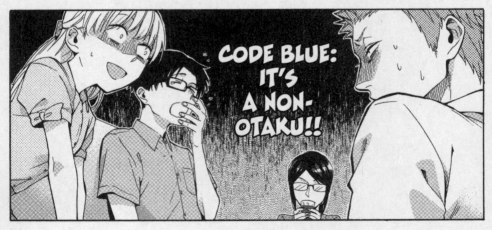

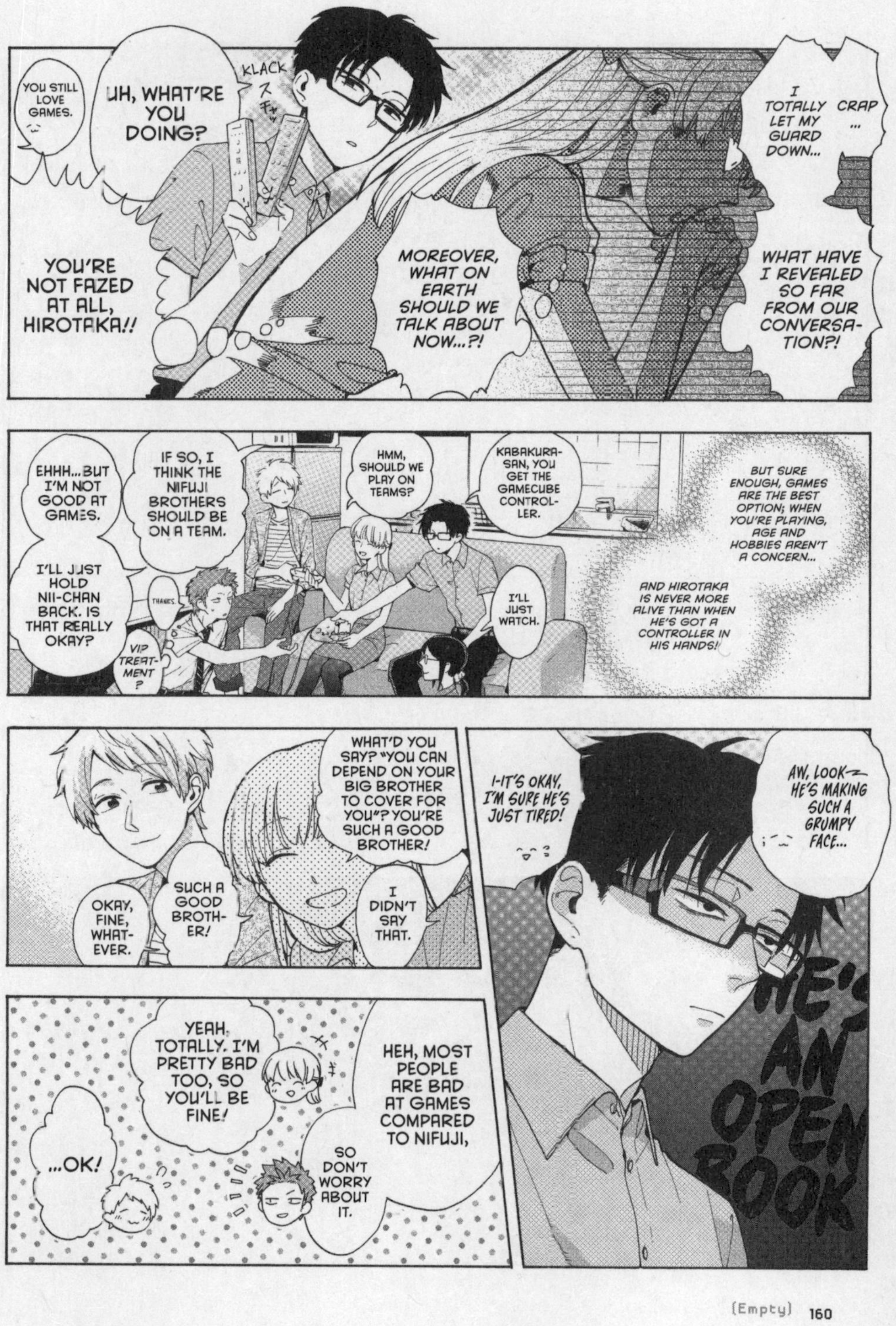
CRAP...
I TOTALLY LET MY GUARD DOWN...
WHAT HAVE I REVEALED SO FAR FROM OUR CONVERSATION?!
MOREOVER, WHAT ON EARTH SHOULD WE TALK ABOUT NOW...?!
UH, WHAT'RE YOU DOING?
KLACK
YOU STILL LOVE GAMES.
YOU'RE NOT FAZED AT ALL, HIROTAKA!!
BUT SURE ENOUGH, GAMES ARE THE BEST OPTION; WHEN YOU'RE PLAYING, AGE AND HOBBIES AREN'T A CONCERN...
AND HIROTAKA IS NEVER MORE ALIVE THAN WHEN HE'S GOT A CONTROLLER IN HIS HANDS!
KABAKURA-SAN, YOU GET THE GAMECUBE CONTROLLER.
I'LL JUST WATCH.
HMM, SHOULD WE PLAY ON TEAMS?
IF SO, I THINK THE NIFUJI BROTHERS SHOULD BE ON A TEAM.
EHHH...BUT I'M NOT GOOD AT GAMES.
I'LL JUST HOLD NII-CHAN BACK. IS THAT REALLY OKAY?
THANKS.
VIP TREATMENT?
AW, LOOK— HE'S MAKING SUCH A GRUMPY FACE...
I-IT'S OKAY, I'M SURE HE'S JUST TIRED!
HE'S AN OPEN BOOK
WHAT'D YOU SAY? "YOU CAN DEPEND ON YOUR BIG BROTHER TO COVER FOR YOU"? YOU'RE SUCH A GOOD BROTHER!
I DIDN'T SAY THAT.
SUCH A GOOD BROTHER!
OKAY, FINE, WHATEVER.
HEH, MOST PEOPLE ARE BAD AT GAMES COMPARED TO NIFUJI,
SO DON'T WORRY ABOUT IT.
YEAH, TOTALLY. I'M PRETTY BAD TOO, SO YOU'LL BE FINE!
...OK!

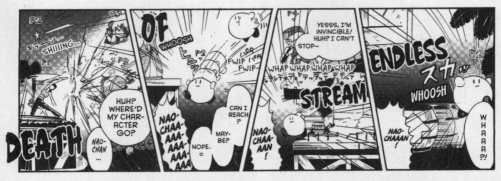

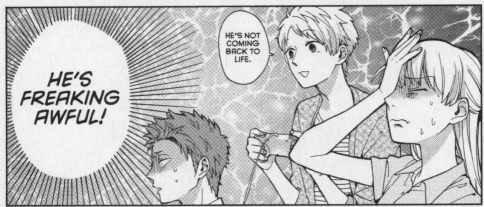

ENDLESS
スカッ
WHOOSH
NAO-CHAAAN!
WHAAAA?!
YESSS, I'M INVINCIBLE! HUH? I CAN'T STOP—
WHAP WHAP WHAP WHAP
STREAM
NAO-CHAAAAN!
OF
WHOOSH
FWIP FWIP
CAN I REACH?
MAY-BE?
NOPE. ☆
NAO-CHAA-AAA-AAA-AAA-AAA
キラーン… SHIIIING…
HUH? WHERE'D MY CHAR-ACTER GO?
NAO-CHAN…
DEATH
HE'S NOT COMING BACK TO LIFE.
HE'S FREAKING AWFUL!
THIS ARENA IS A LITTLE TOUGH, THAT'S ALL!
SOOOORRY, NII-CHAN...
WE'LL CHOOSE AN ARENA THAT'S HARDER TO FALL FROM NEXT...
IT'S TOTALLY FINE.
IF ANYTHING, NOW THAT YOU'RE DEAD IT'S EASIER TO PLAY.
CLACK CLACK CLACK CLACK CLACK CLACK CLACK CLACK CLACK
HIROTAKA!! THAT'S MEAN!
WELL, AH, I'M GLAD IT TURNED OUT WELL?
PHEW
NAO-CHAN, YOU SHOULD BE ANGRIER, Y'KNOW?!
And as a result, Hirotaka ended up winning on his own!

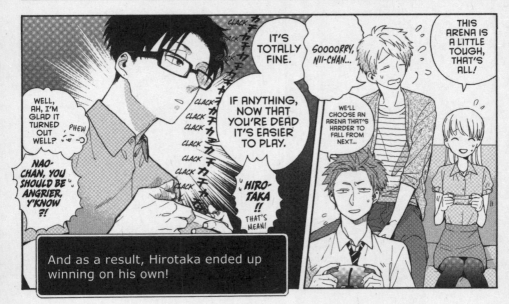

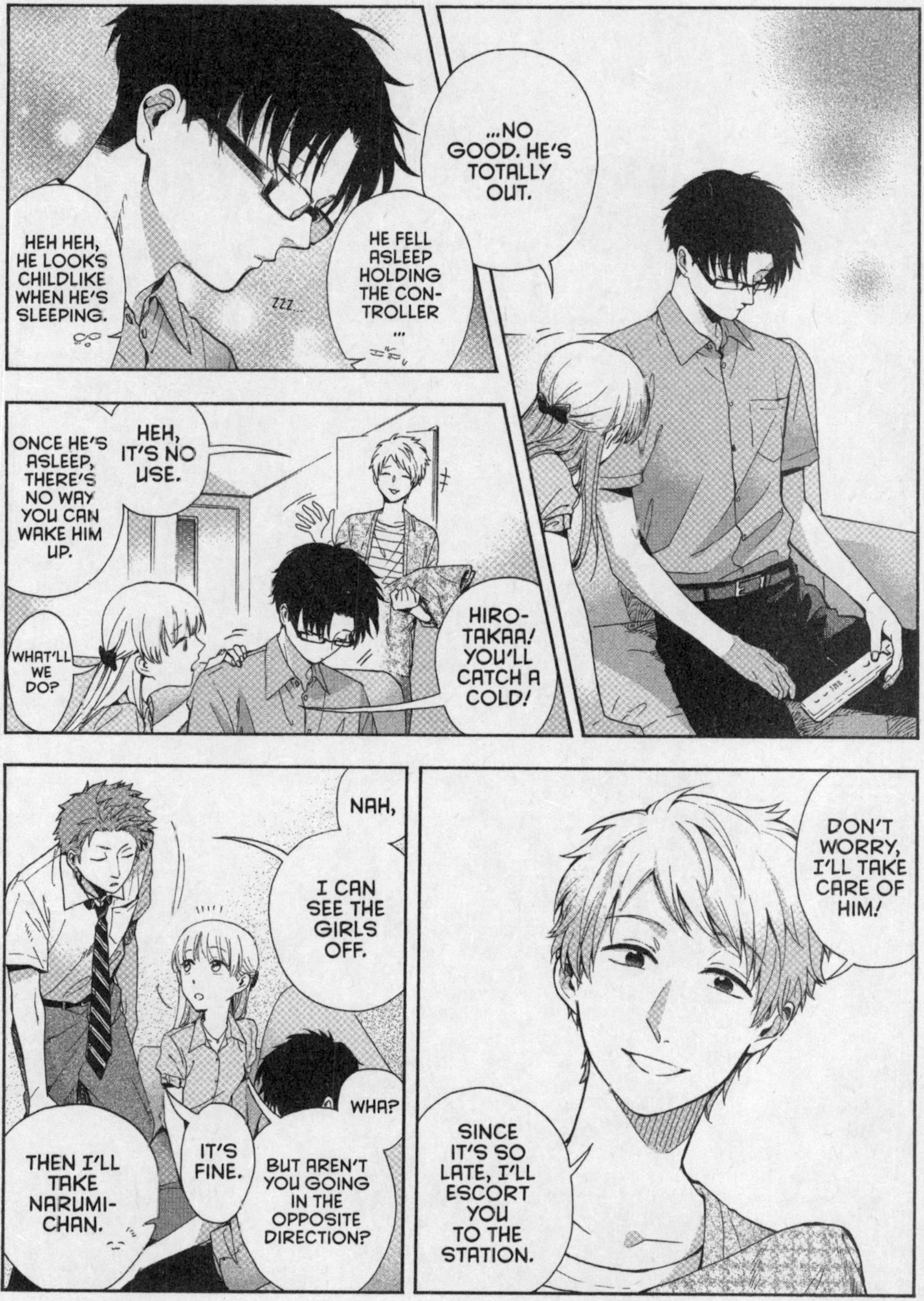
...NO GOOD. HE'S TOTALLY OUT.
HE FELL ASLEEP HOLDING THE CON- TROLLER ...
ZZZ...
HEH HEH, HE LOOKS CHILDLIKE WHEN HE'S SLEEPING.
HEH, IT'S NO USE.
ONCE HE'S ASLEEP, THERE'S NO WAY YOU CAN WAKE HIM UP.
HIRO- TAKAA! YOU'LL CATCH A COLD!
WHAT'LL WE DO?
DON'T WORRY, I'LL TAKE CARE OF HIM!
SINCE IT'S SO LATE, I'LL ESCORT YOU TO THE STATION.
NAH,
I CAN SEE THE GIRLS OFF.
WHA?
BUT AREN'T YOU GOING IN THE OPPOSITE DIRECTION?
IT'S FINE.
THEN I'LL TAKE NARUMI- CHAN.

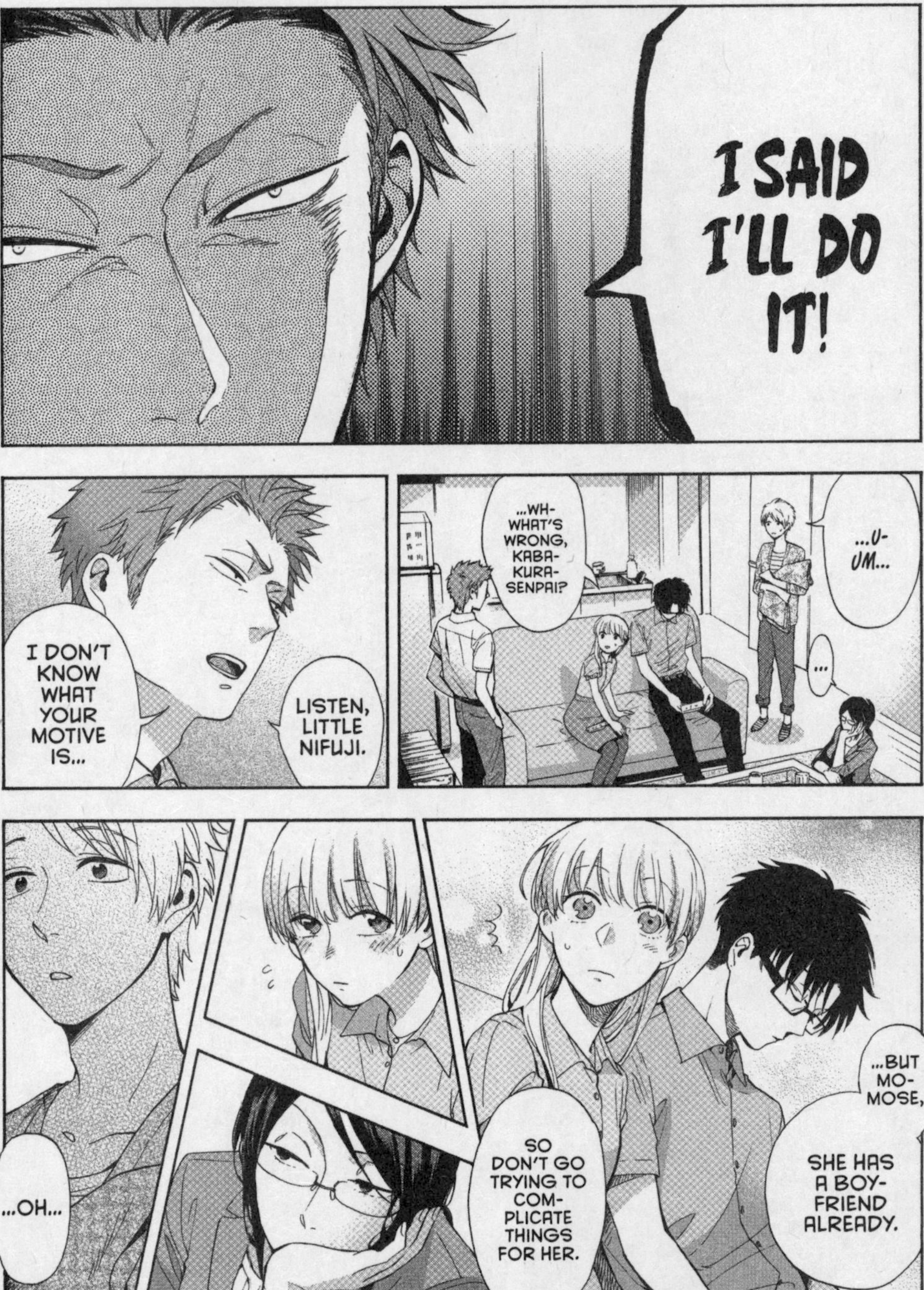
I SAID I'LL DO IT!
...U-UM...
...WH-WHAT'S WRONG, KABA-KURA-SENPAI?
...
LISTEN, LITTLE NIFUJI.
I DON'T KNOW WHAT YOUR MOTIVE IS...
...BUT MO-MOSE,
SHE HAS A BOY-FRIEND ALREADY.
SO DON'T GO TRYING TO COM-PLICATE THINGS FOR HER.
...OH...

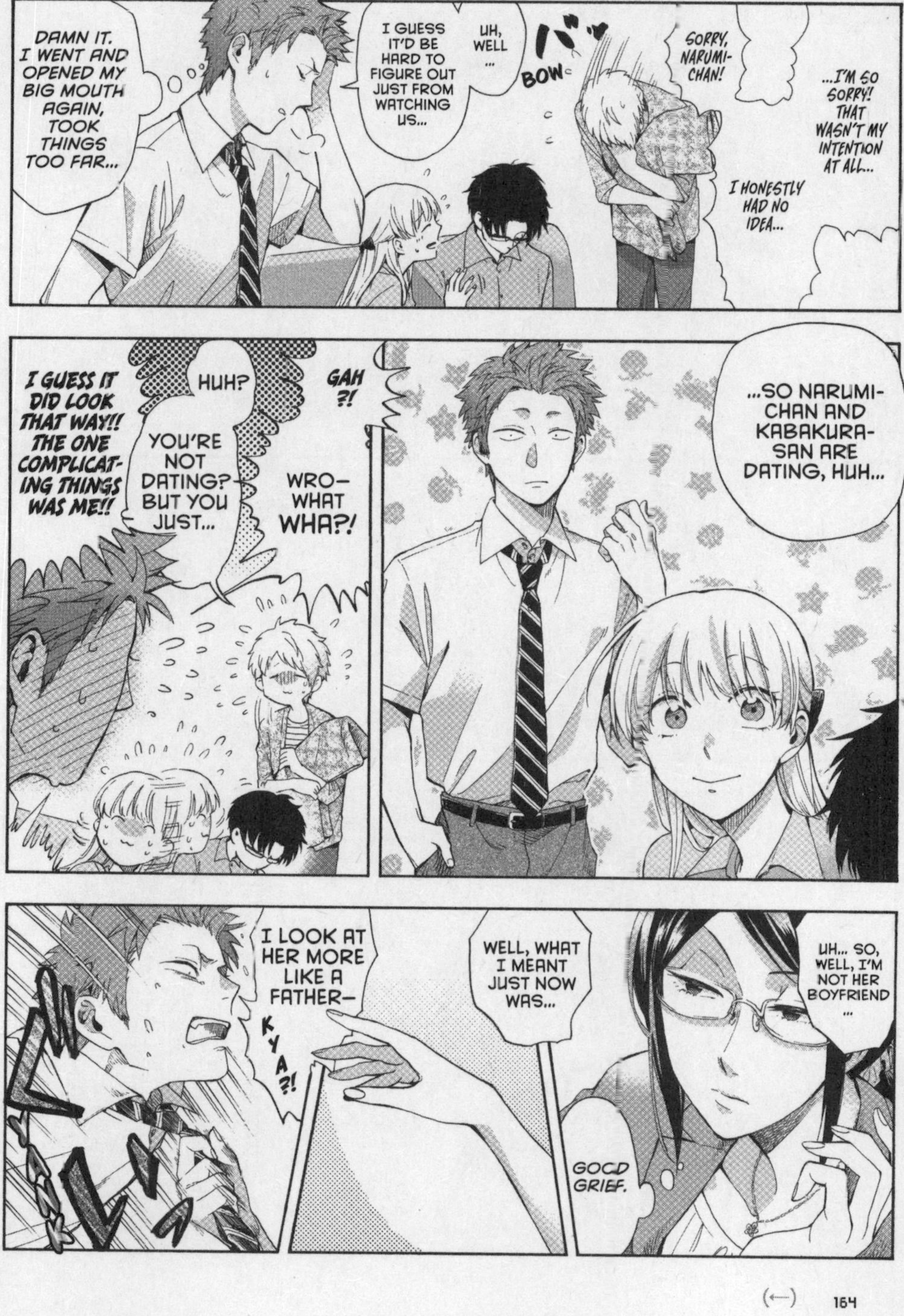
...I'M SO SORRY! THAT WASN'T MY INTENTION AT ALL...
SORRY, NARUMI-CHAN!
I HONESTLY HAD NO IDEA...
BOW
UH, WELL ...
I GUESS IT'D BE HARD TO FIGURE OUT JUST FROM WATCHING US...
DAMN IT. I WENT AND OPENED MY BIG MOUTH AGAIN, TOOK THINGS TOO FAR...
...SO NARUMI-CHAN AND KABAKURA-SAN ARE DATING, HUH...
GAH ?!
WRO— WHAT WHA?!
HUH?
YOU'RE NOT DATING? BUT YOU JUST...
I GUESS IT DID LOOK THAT WAY!! THE ONE COMPLICATING THINGS WAS ME!!
UH... SO, WELL, I'M NOT HER BOYFRIEND ...
WELL, WHAT I MEANT JUST NOW WAS...
GOOD GRIEF.
I LOOK AT HER MORE LIKE A FATHER—
KYA?!

(←)

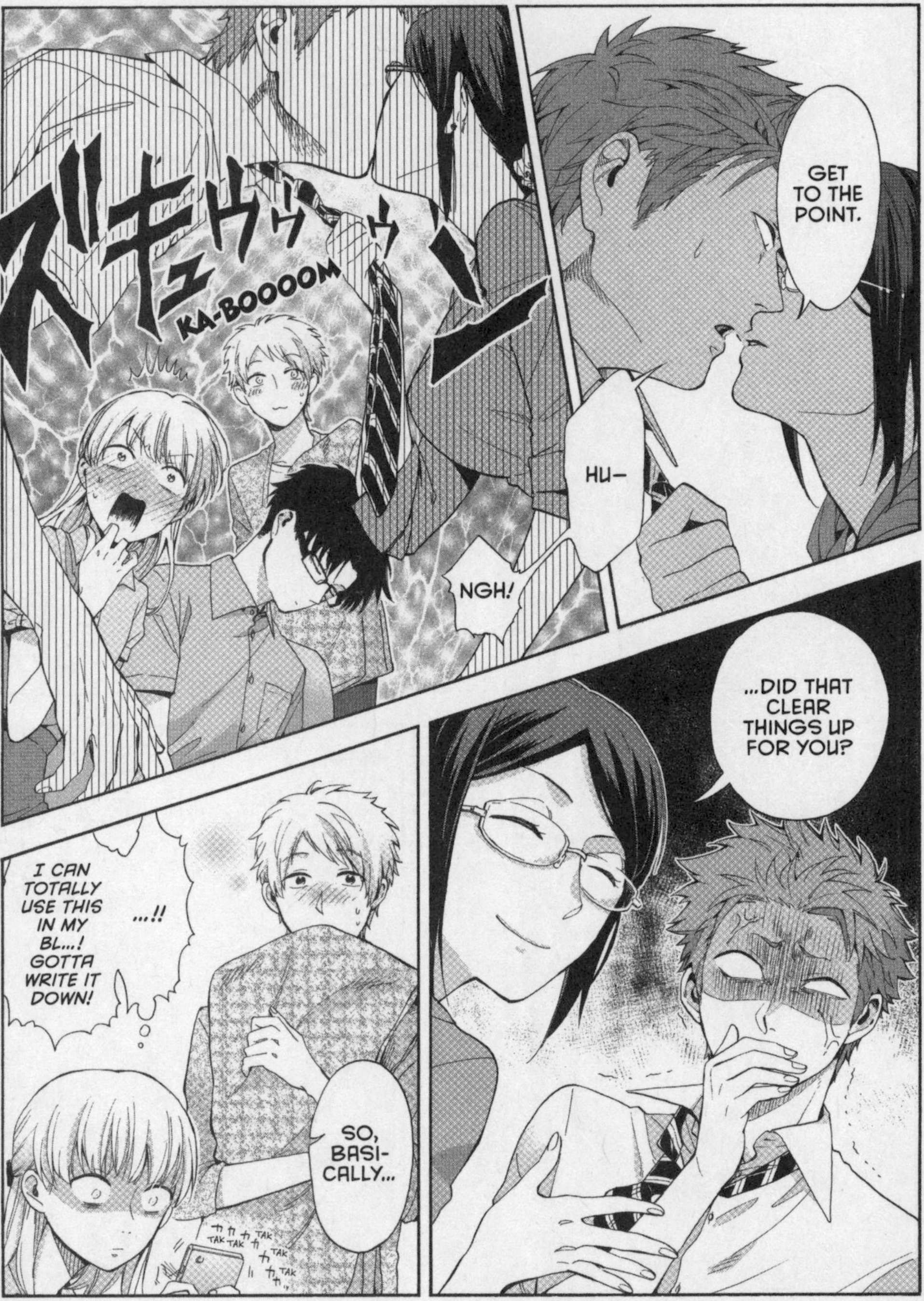
GET TO THE POINT.
HU–
KA-BOOOM
NGH!
...DID THAT CLEAR THINGS UP FOR YOU?
I CAN TOTALLY USE THIS IN MY BL...! GOTTA WRITE IT DOWN!
...!!
SO, BASICALLY...
TAK TAK TAK TAK TAK TAK

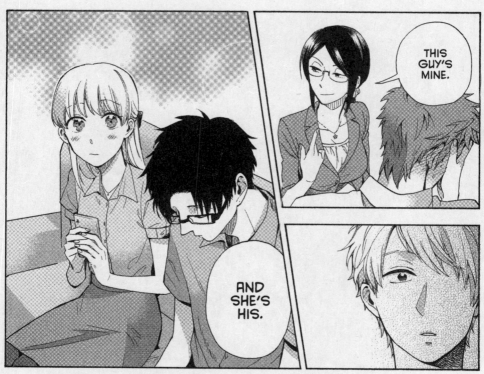

THIS GUY'S MINE.
AND SHE'S HIS.
HUH?
NARUMI-CHAN AND...NII-CHAN?
AHAHA... YEP, THAT'S RIGHT. WEIRD, HUH?
REALLY?
BUT, WELL, YEAH...
...WE ARE INDEED GOING OUT.
THOUGH REALLY, NOT MUCH HAS CHANGED BETWEEN US SINCE WE STARTED DATING...

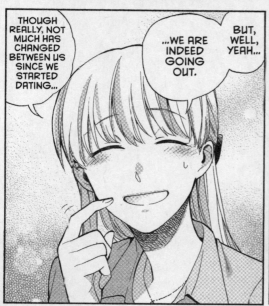

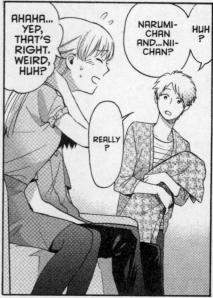

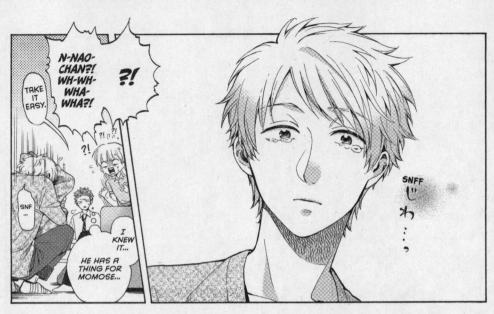

SNFF
じわ…っ
N-NAO-CHAN?! WH-WH-WHA-WHA?!
?!
TAKE IT EASY.
?! ?!
?!
SNF...
I KNEW IT...
HE HAS A THING FOR MOMOSE...
...I'M SO GLAD...
SORRY, IT'S JUST...
...I'VE ALWAYS WORRIED...
THE WAY NII-CHAN IS, NEVER CARING WHETHER HE'S ALONE, I THOUGHT HE'D NEVER FIND SOMEONE...
BUT I'VE ALWAYS KIND OF THOUGHT...
...IT'D BE GREAT IF YOU ENDED UP TOGETHER.

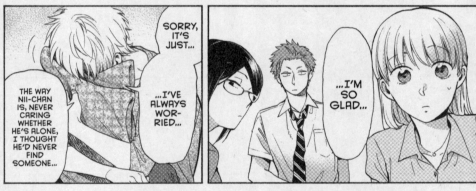

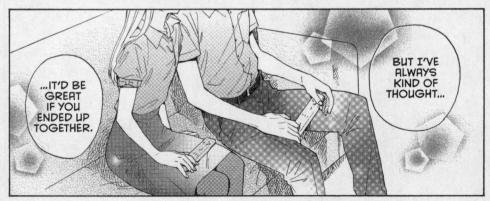

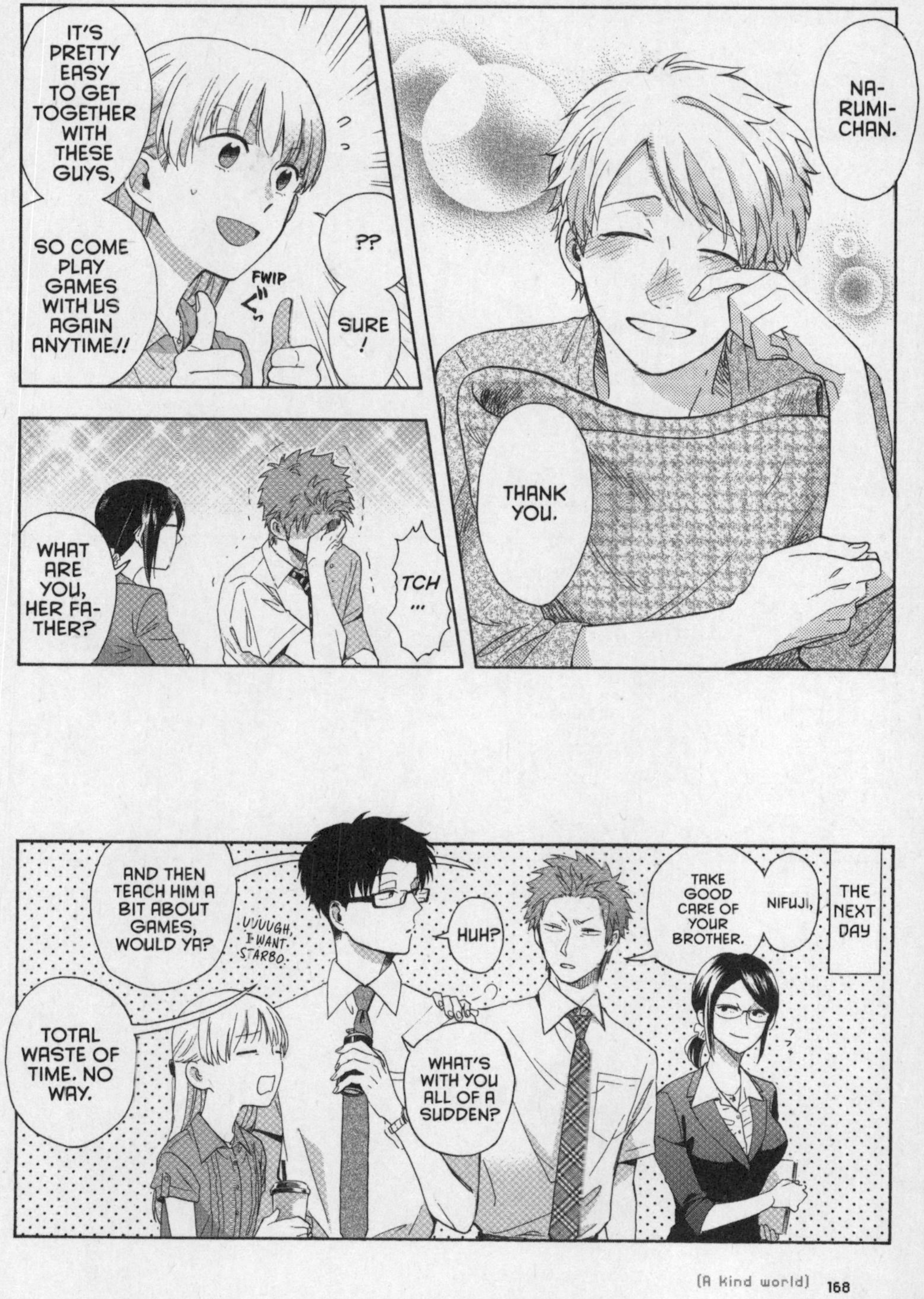
NARUMI-CHAN.
THANK YOU.
IT'S PRETTY EASY TO GET TOGETHER WITH THESE GUYS,
SO COME PLAY GAMES WITH US AGAIN ANYTIME!!
FWIP
??
SURE!
TCH...
WHAT ARE YOU, HER FATHER?
THE NEXT DAY
NIFUJI,
TAKE GOOD CARE OF YOUR BROTHER.
HUH?
AND THEN TEACH HIM A BIT ABOUT GAMES, WOULD YA?
UUUUGH, I WANT STARBO.
WHAT'S WITH YOU ALL OF A SUDDEN?
TOTAL WASTE OF TIME. NO WAY.

(A kind world)

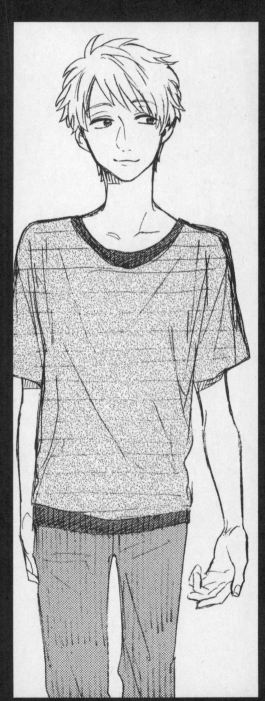

Naoya Nifuji

Birthday: 4/21
Age: 19
Height: 177 cm/5'9"
Blood Type: AB
Zodiac: Taurus

He's only really borrowed manga and anime from his friends. He prefers watching others play video games than to play himseif. For some reason he thinks otaku terms are business terms.

Hirotaka's younger brother by seven years. He's left-handed. Unlike his brother, he's eloquent, social, expressive, and terrible at games. He remembers Hirotaka's (only) childhood friend, Narumi, pretty well because she came over to play a lot when they were young, and he fully supports their relationship. (He always worried they'd be stuck as just "good friends," so he's ecstatic they're dating.) He perceives things in an accepting and positive way. An extreme optimist who smiles at other people's happiness. Not even his older brother Hirotaka has ever really seen Naoya look serious. He's easygoing but is also well put together, so he occasionally visits his brother from college to make sure he's taking care of himself. He's been really into making sweets lately. Not really sure what else to say here.

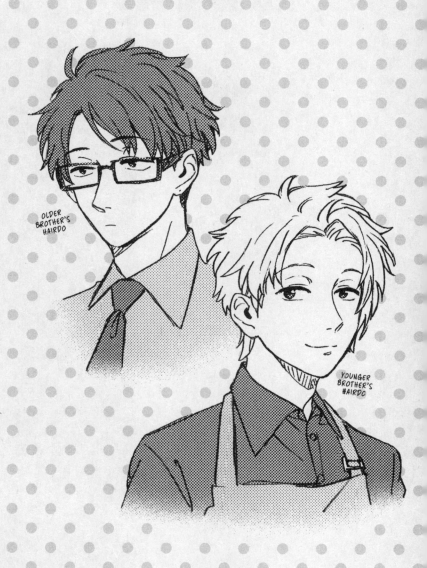

OLDER BROTHER'S HAIRDO

YOUNGER BROTHER'S HAIRDO

Wotakoi: Love is Hard for Otaku

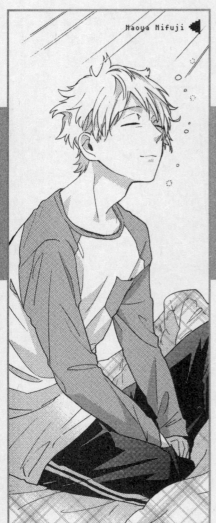

Naoya Nifuji

▽ Sunday Morning
If he sleeps even an hour longer than usual, his bed head gets three times worse.

Waking up… He wakes up fairly quickly, but he's useless for the first 10 minutes.
Staying up late… Sleepiness oozes out from every fiber of his being.

Brothers with too much free time at play

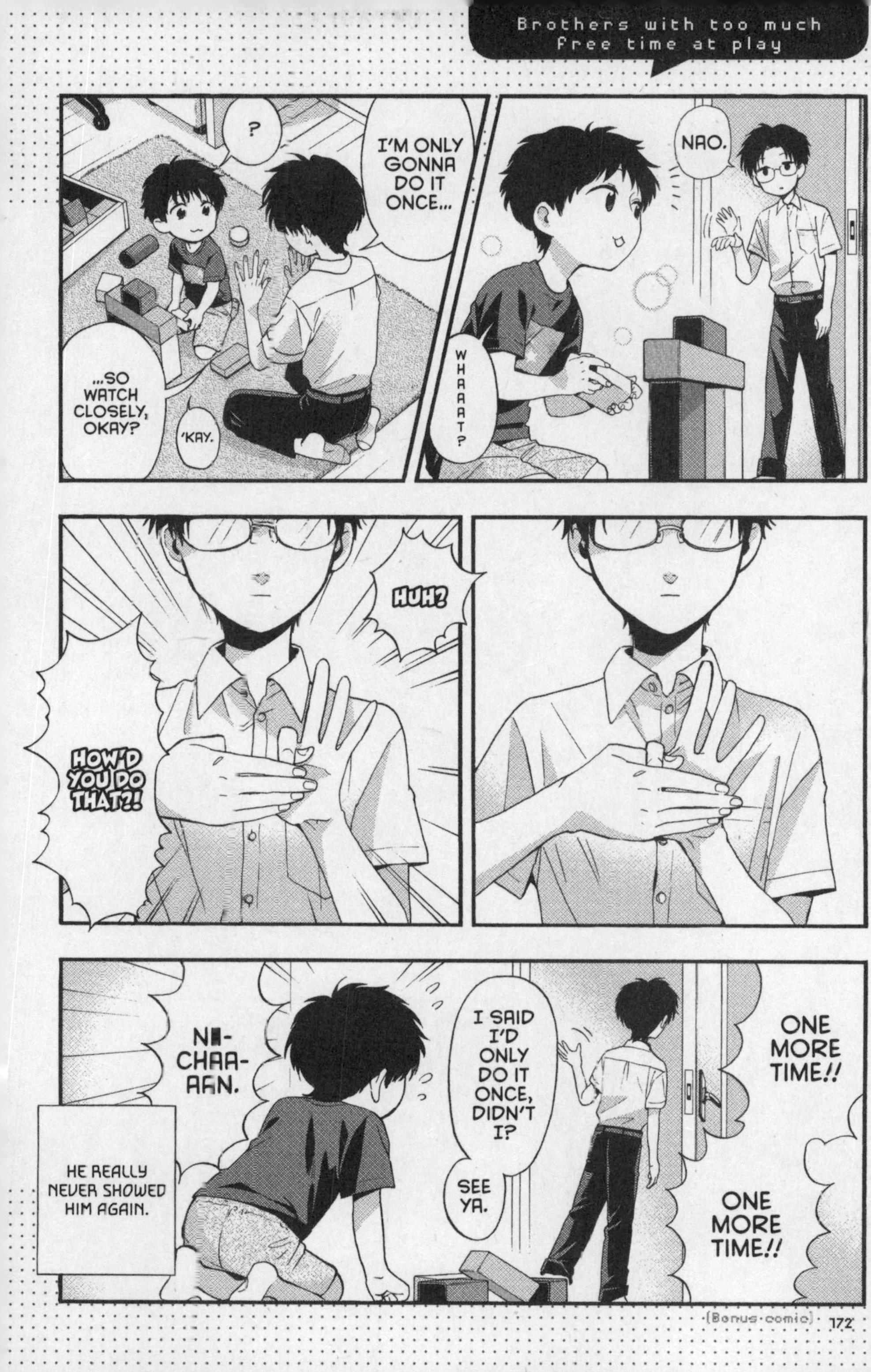
NAO.
WHAAAT?
I'M ONLY GONNA DO IT ONCE...
?
...SO WATCH CLOSELY, OKAY?
'KAY.
HUH?
HOW'D YOU DO THAT?!
ONE MORE TIME!!
ONE MORE TIME!!
I SAID I'D ONLY DO IT ONCE, DIDN'T I?
SEE YA.
NI-CHAAAN.
HE REALLY NEVER SHOWED HIM AGAIN.

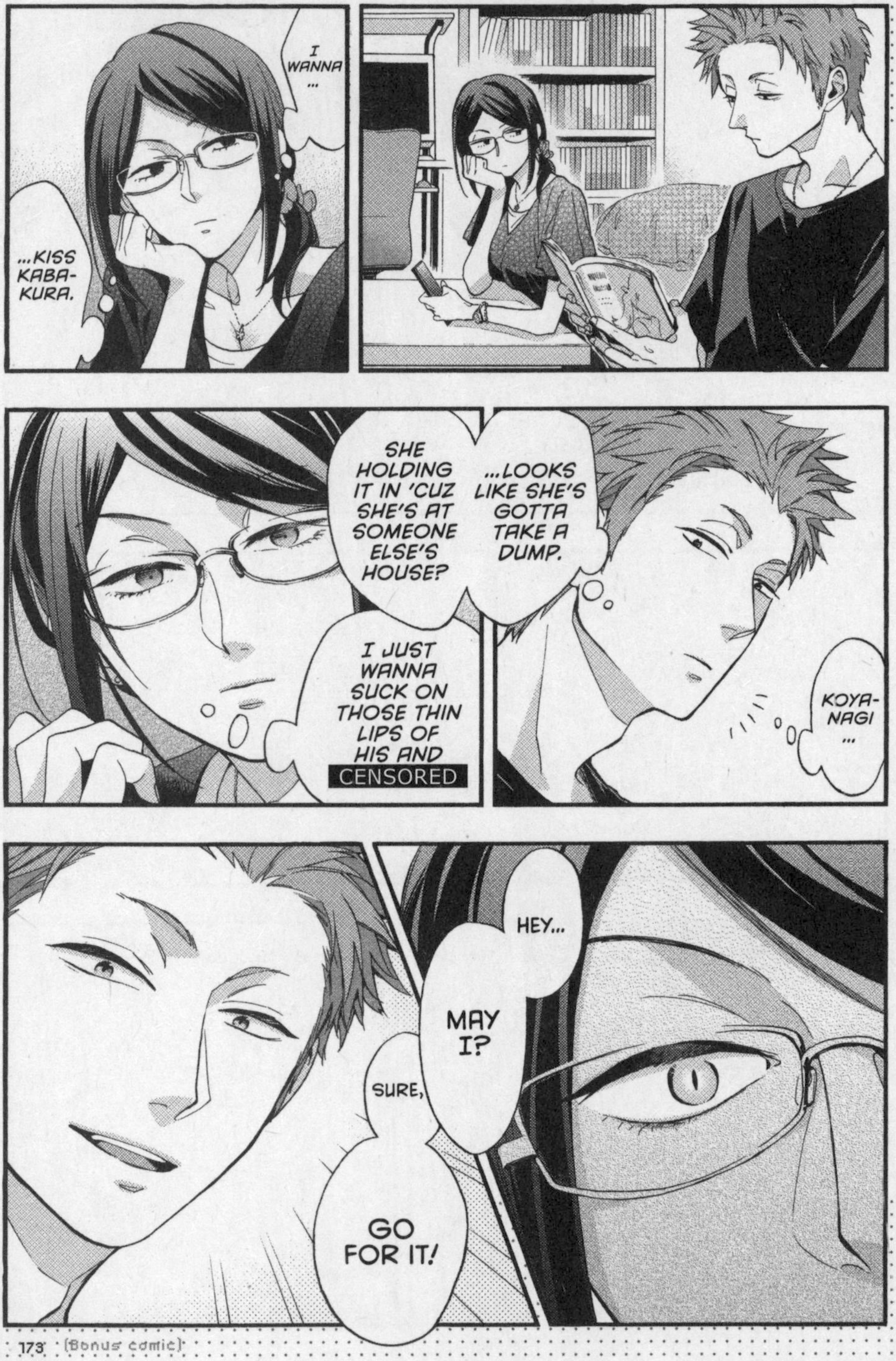
I WANNA ...
...KISS KABAKURA.
...LOOKS LIKE SHE'S GOTTA TAKE A DUMP.
KOYANAGI ...
SHE HOLDING IT IN 'CUZ SHE'S AT SOMEONE ELSE'S HOUSE?
I JUST WANNA SUCK ON THOSE THIN LIPS OF HIS AND CENSORED
HEY...
MAY I?
SURE,
GO FOR IT!

The Story Behind his Piercing (1)

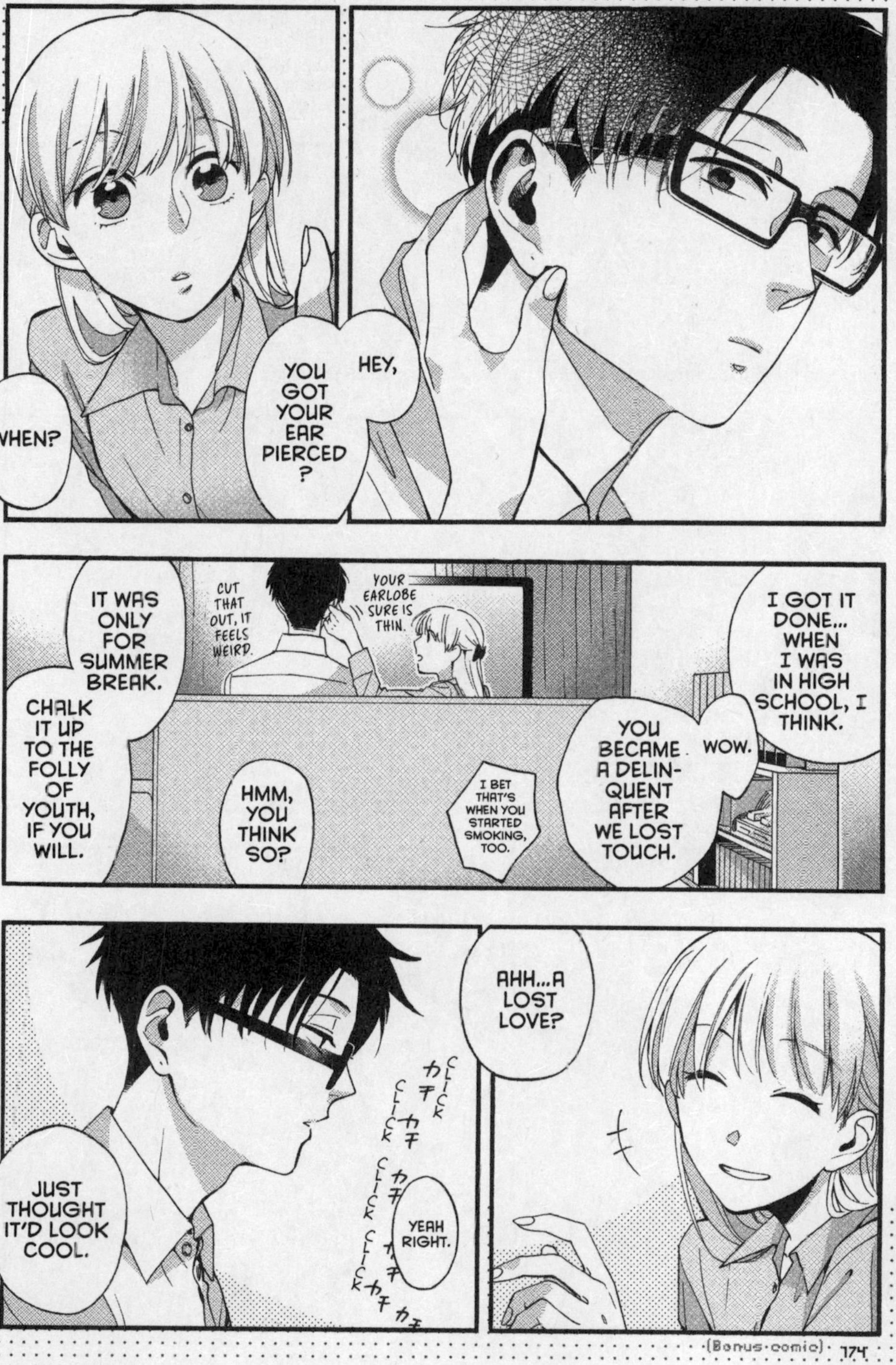
HEY, YOU GOT YOUR EAR PIERCED?
WHEN?
I GOT IT DONE... WHEN I WAS IN HIGH SCHOOL, I THINK.
WOW.
YOU BECAME A DELINQUENT AFTER WE LOST TOUCH.
I BET THAT'S WHEN YOU STARTED SMOKING, TOO.
YOUR EARLOBE SURE IS THIN.
CUT THAT OUT, IT FEELS WEIRD.
HMM, YOU THINK SO?
IT WAS ONLY FOR SUMMER BREAK.
CHALK IT UP TO THE FOLLY OF YOUTH, IF YOU WILL.
AHH...A LOST LOVE?
CLICK カチ
CLICK カチ
CLICK カチ
CLICK カチ
CLICK カチ
カチ
YEAH RIGHT.
JUST THOUGHT IT'D LOOK COOL.

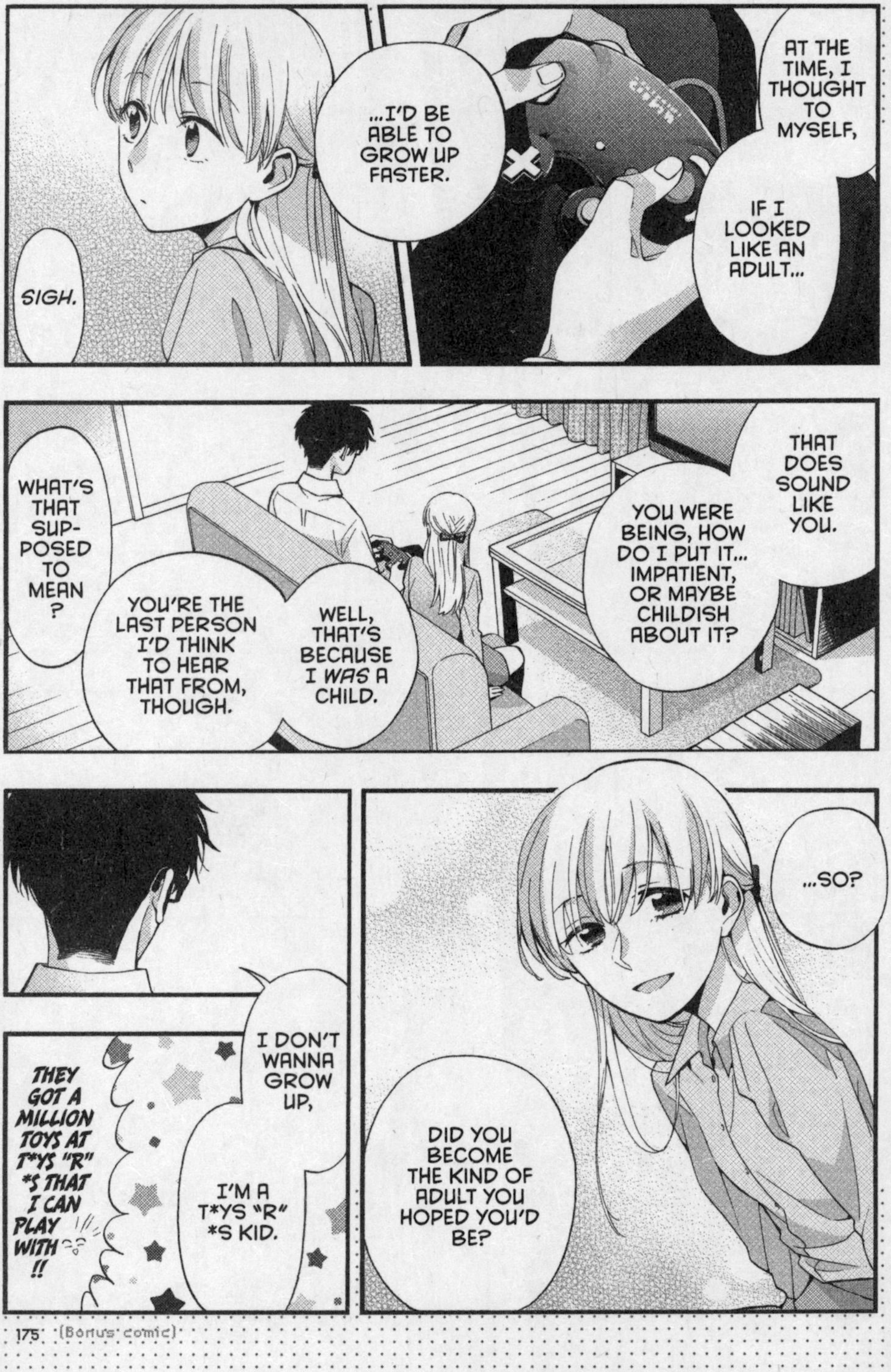
AT THE TIME, I THOUGHT TO MYSELF,
IF I LOOKED LIKE AN ADULT...
...I'D BE ABLE TO GROW UP FASTER.
SIGH.
THAT DOES SOUND LIKE YOU.
YOU WERE BEING, HOW DO I PUT IT... IMPATIENT, OR MAYBE CHILDISH ABOUT IT?
WELL, THAT'S BECAUSE I *WAS* A CHILD.
YOU'RE THE LAST PERSON I'D THINK TO HEAR THAT FROM, THOUGH.
WHAT'S THAT SUP-POSED TO MEAN?
...SO?
DID YOU BECOME THE KIND OF ADULT YOU HOPED YOU'D BE?
I DON'T WANNA GROW UP,
I'M A T*YS "R" *S KID.
THEY GOT A MILLION TOYS AT T*YS "R" *S THAT I CAN PLAY WITH!!

Photo (1)

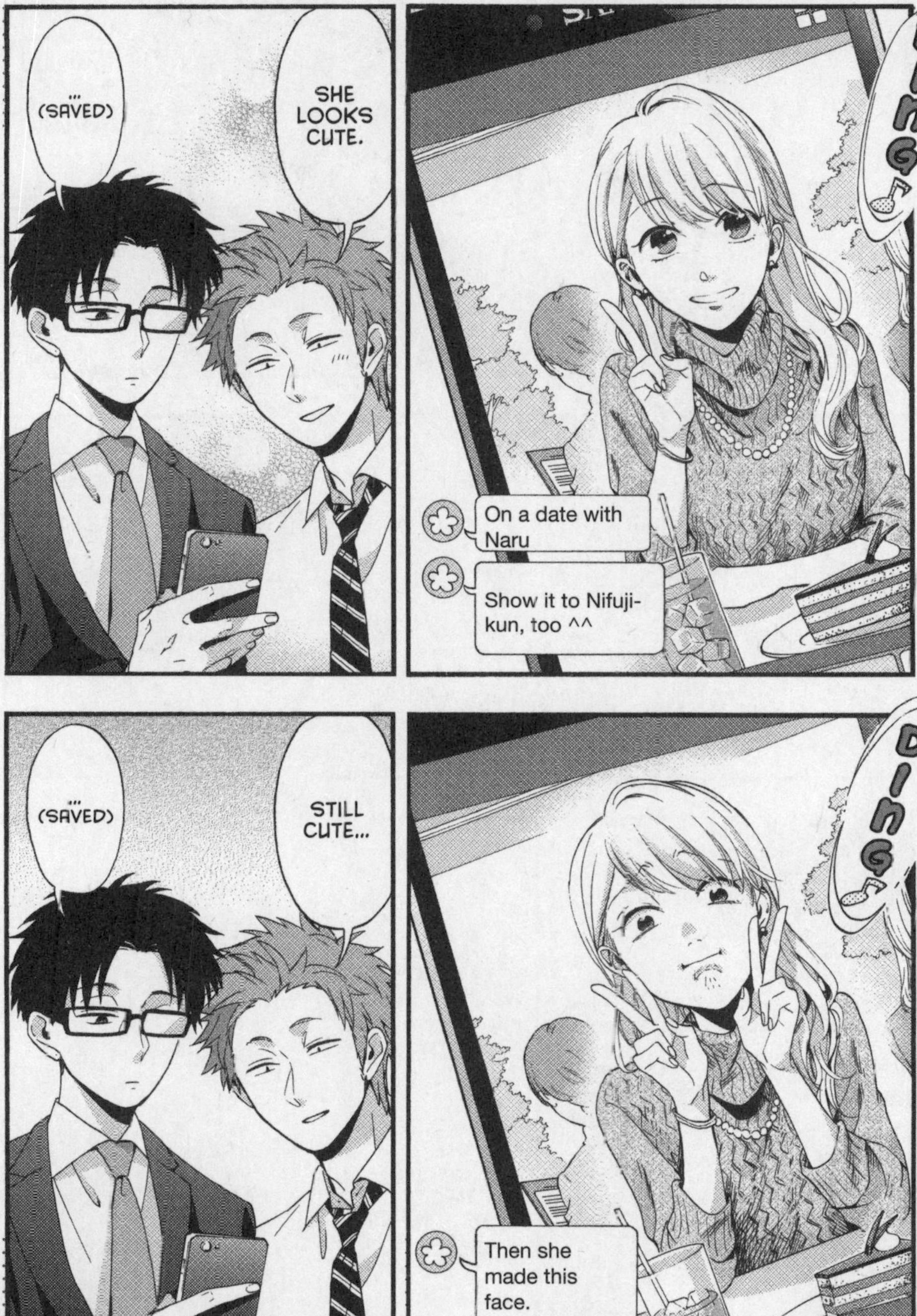
DING
On a date with Naru
Show it to Nifuji-kun, too ^^
SHE LOOKS CUTE.
... (SAVED)
DING
Then she made this face.
STILL CUTE...
... (SAVED)

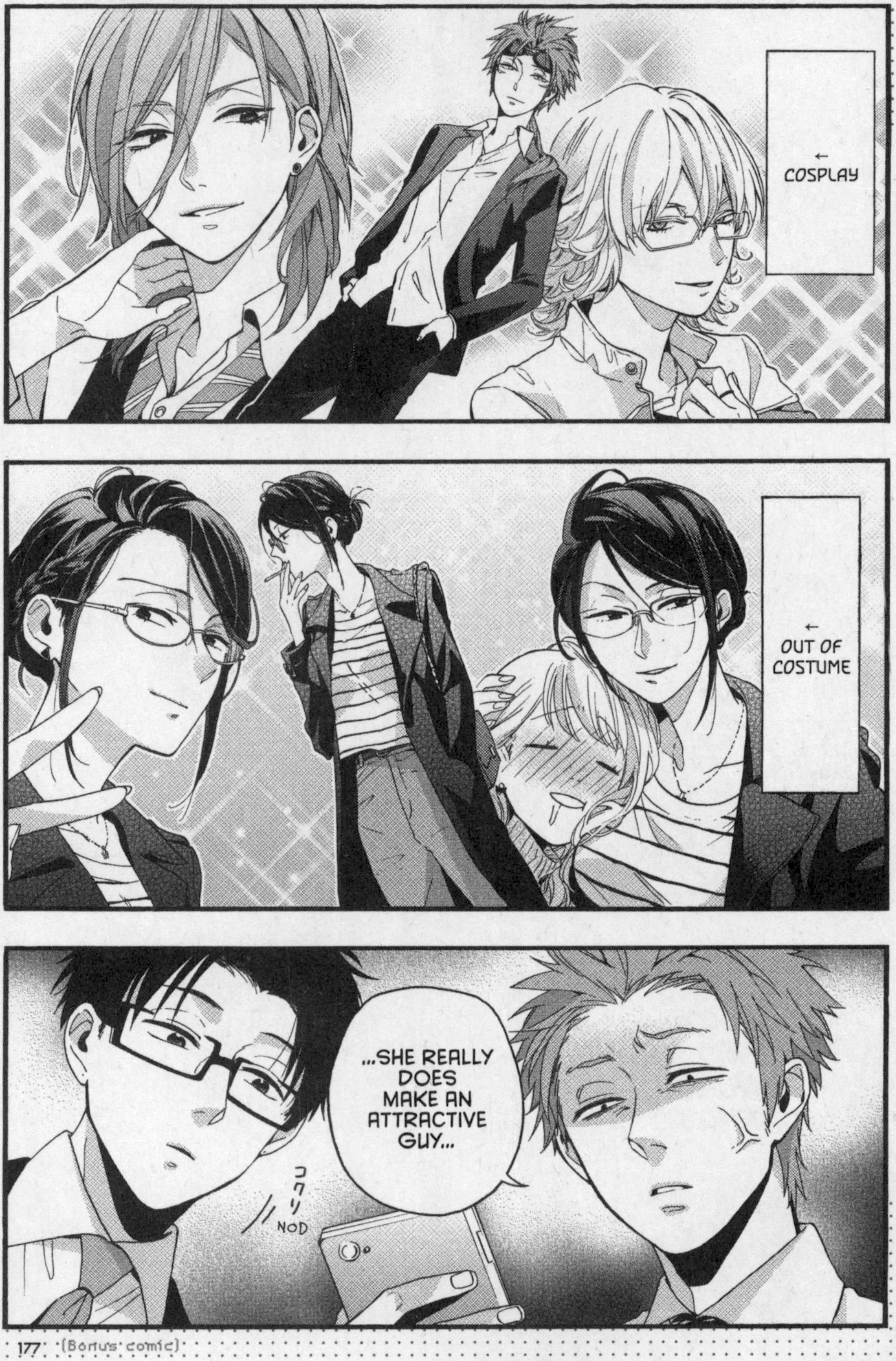
← COSPLAY
← OUT OF COSTUME
...SHE REALLY DOES MAKE AN ATTRACTIVE GUY...
コクリ NOD

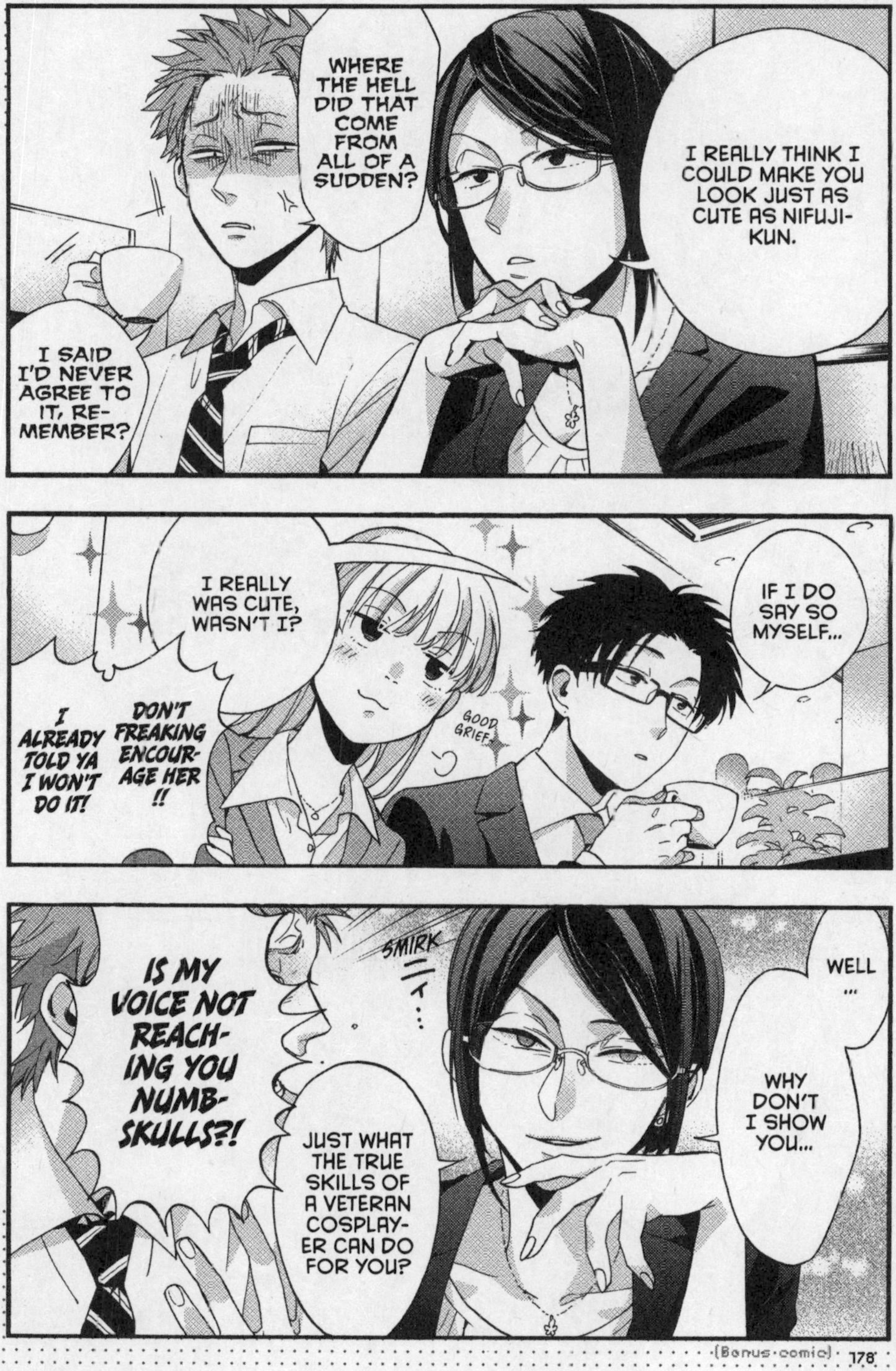
I REALLY THINK I COULD MAKE YOU LOOK JUST AS CUTE AS NIFUJI-KUN.
WHERE THE HELL DID THAT COME FROM ALL OF A SUDDEN?
I SAID I'D NEVER AGREE TO IT, RE-MEMBER?
IF I DO SAY SO MYSELF...
I REALLY WAS CUTE, WASN'T I?
GOOD GRIEF.
DON'T FREAKING ENCOUR-AGE HER !!
I ALREADY TOLD YA I WON'T DO IT!
WELL ...
WHY DON'T I SHOW YOU...
SMIRK
JUST WHAT THE TRUE SKILLS OF A VETERAN COSPLAY-ER CAN DO FOR YOU?
IS MY VOICE NOT REACH-ING YOU NUMB-SKULLS?!

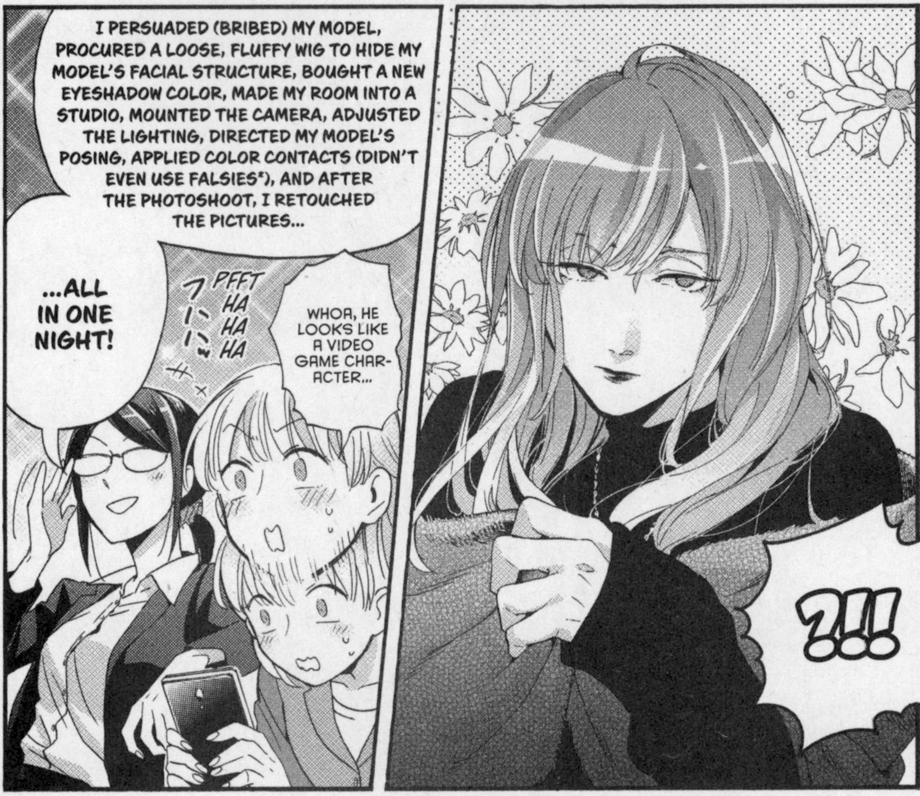
?!!
I PERSUADED (BRIBED) MY MODEL, PROCURED A LOOSE, FLUFFY WIG TO HIDE MY MODEL'S FACIAL STRUCTURE, BOUGHT A NEW EYESHADOW COLOR, MADE MY ROOM INTO A STUDIO, MOUNTED THE CAMERA, ADJUSTED THE LIGHTING, DIRECTED MY MODEL'S POSING, APPLIED COLOR CONTACTS (DIDN'T EVEN USE FALSIES*), AND AFTER THE PHOTOSHOOT, I RETOUCHED THE PICTURES...
WHOA, HE LOOKS LIKE A VIDEO GAME CHAR-ACTER...
PFFT HA HA HA
...ALL IN ONE NIGHT!

*False eyelashes.

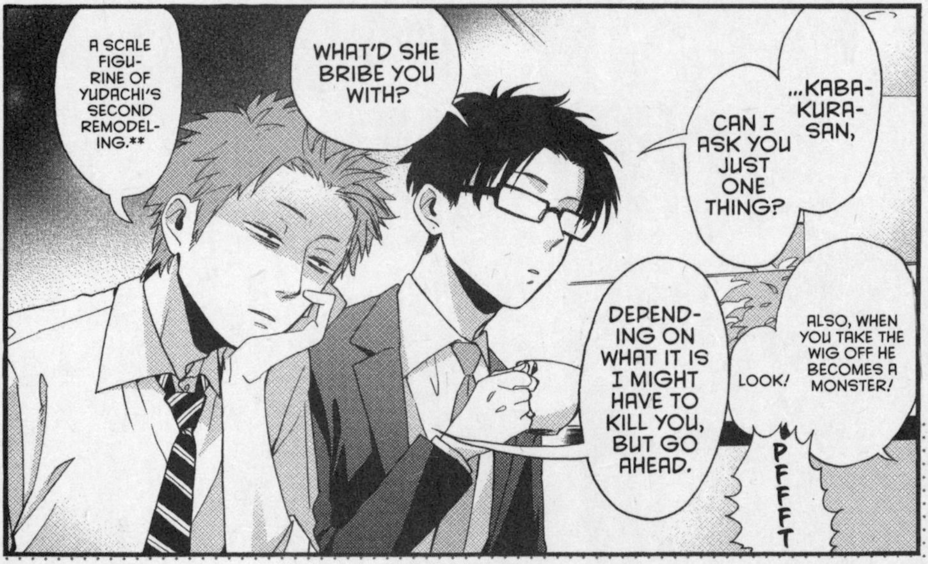
...KABA-KURA-SAN, CAN I ASK YOU JUST ONE THING?
ALSO, WHEN YOU TAKE THE WIG OFF HE BECOMES A MONSTER!
LOOK!
PFFFT
DEPEND-ING ON WHAT IT IS I MIGHT HAVE TO KILL YOU, BUT GO AHEAD.
WHAT'D SHE BRIBE YOU WITH?
A SCALE FIGU-RINE OF YUDACHI'S SECOND REMODEL-ING.**

**A character from the *Kantai Collection.*

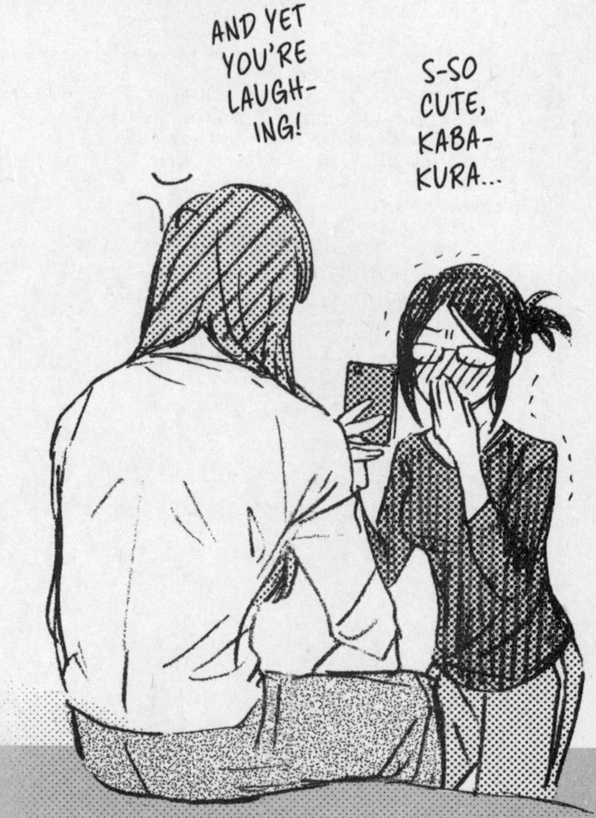
S-SO CUTE, KABAKURA...
AND YET YOU'RE LAUGHING!

(*·∀-)b

Wotakoi: Love is Hard for Otaku

▶CONTINUE

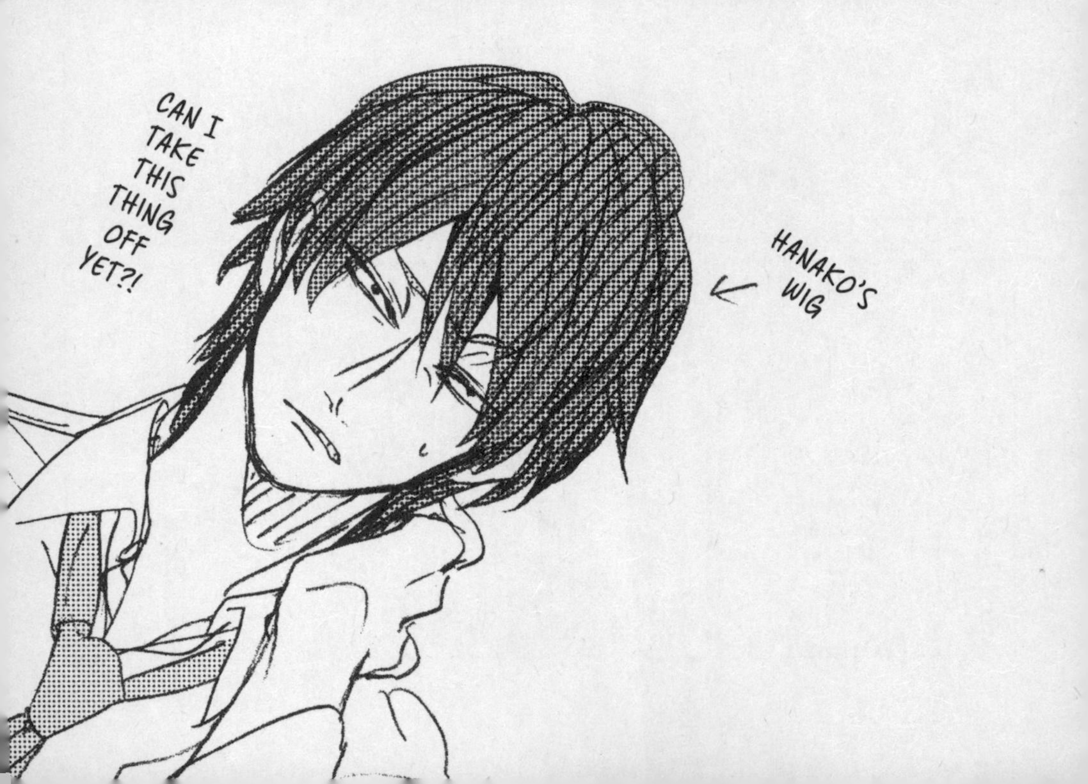
CAN I TAKE THIS THING OFF YET?!
HANAKO'S WIG

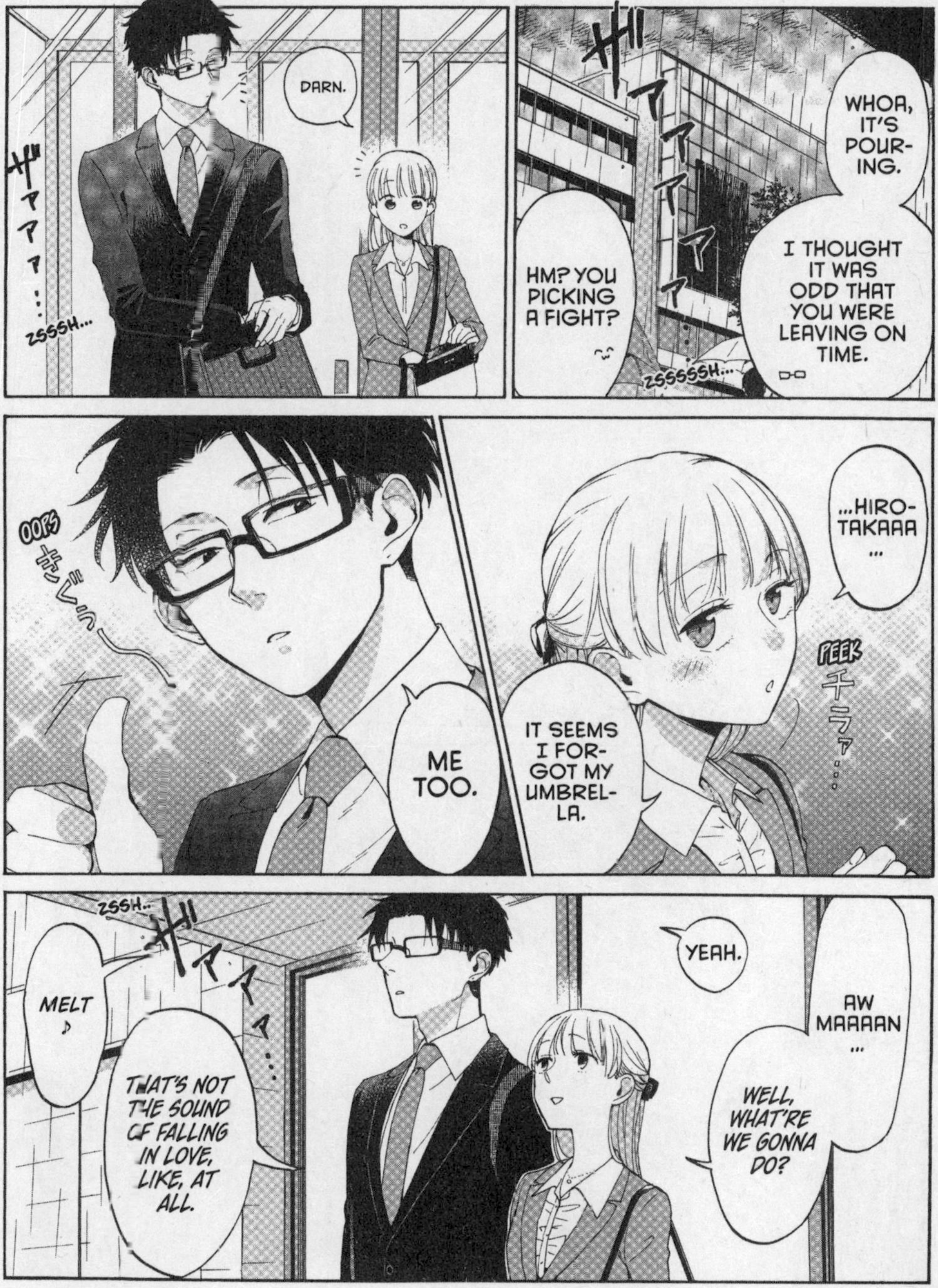
WHOA, IT'S POURING.
I THOUGHT IT WAS ODD THAT YOU WERE LEAVING ON TIME.
HM? YOU PICKING A FIGHT?
ZSSSSSH...
DARN.
ZSSSH...
...HIRO-TAKAAA...
PEEK
IT SEEMS I FOR-GOT MY UMBREL-LA.
ME TOO.
OOPS
AW MAAAAN...
WELL, WHAT'RE WE GONNA DO?
YEAH.
ZSSH..
MELT ♪
THAT'S NOT THE SOUND OF FALLING IN LOVE, LIKE, AT ALL.

(A Futile situation)

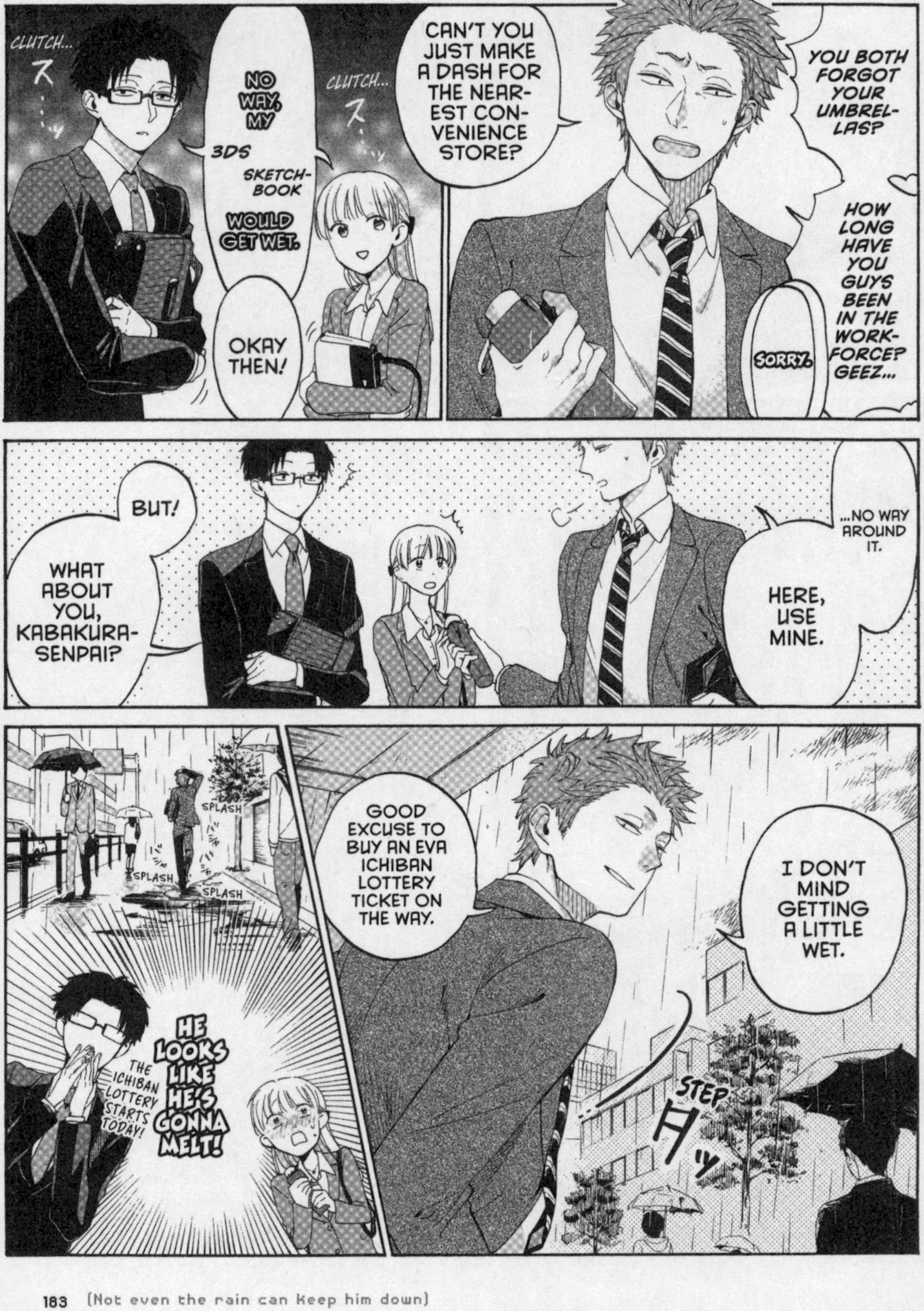
YOU BOTH FORGOT YOUR UMBRELLAS?
HOW LONG HAVE YOU GUYS BEEN IN THE WORKFORCE? GEEZ...
SORRY.
CAN'T YOU JUST MAKE A DASH FOR THE NEAREST CONVENIENCE STORE?
NO WAY, MY 3DS SKETCHBOOK WOULD GET WET.
CLUTCH... ス
OKAY THEN!
CLUTCH... ス
...NO WAY AROUND IT.
HERE, USE MINE.
BUT!
WHAT ABOUT YOU, KABAKURA-SENPAI?
I DON'T MIND GETTING A LITTLE WET.
GOOD EXCUSE TO BUY AN EVA ICHIBAN LOTTERY TICKET ON THE WAY.
STEP
SPLASH
SPLASH
SPLASH
HE LOOKS LIKE HE'S GONNA MELT!
THE ICHIBAN LOTTERY STARTS TODAY!

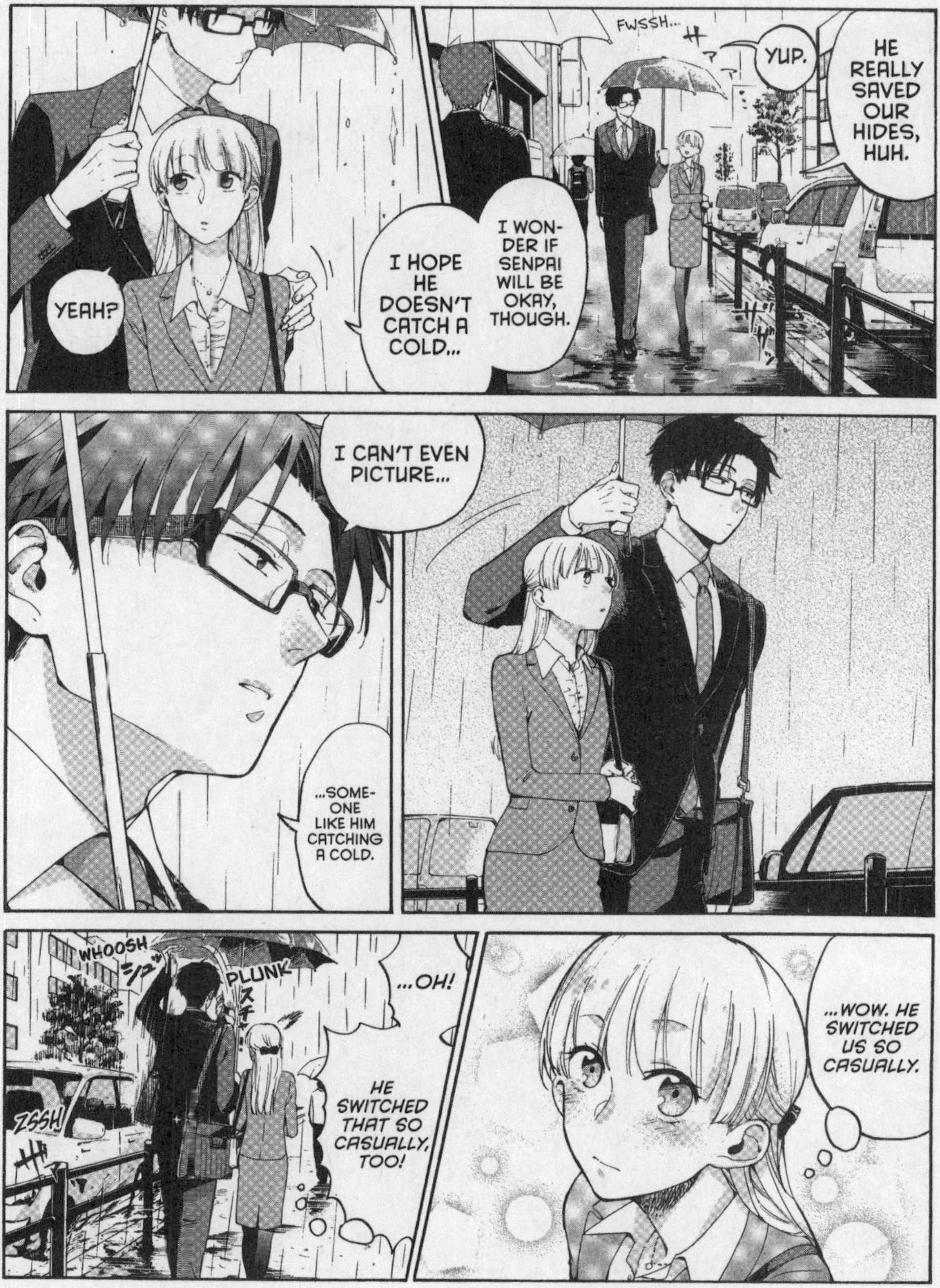
HE REALLY SAVED OUR HIDES, HUH.
YUP.
FWSSH...
I WONDER IF SENPAI WILL BE OKAY, THOUGH.
I HOPE HE DOESN'T CATCH A COLD...
YEAH?
I CAN'T EVEN PICTURE...
...SOME-ONE LIKE HIM CATCHING A COLD.
...WOW. HE SWITCHED US SO CASUALLY.
...OH!
WHOOSH
PLUNK
HE SWITCHED THAT SO CASUALLY, TOO!
ZSSH!

(He doesn't like getting wet)

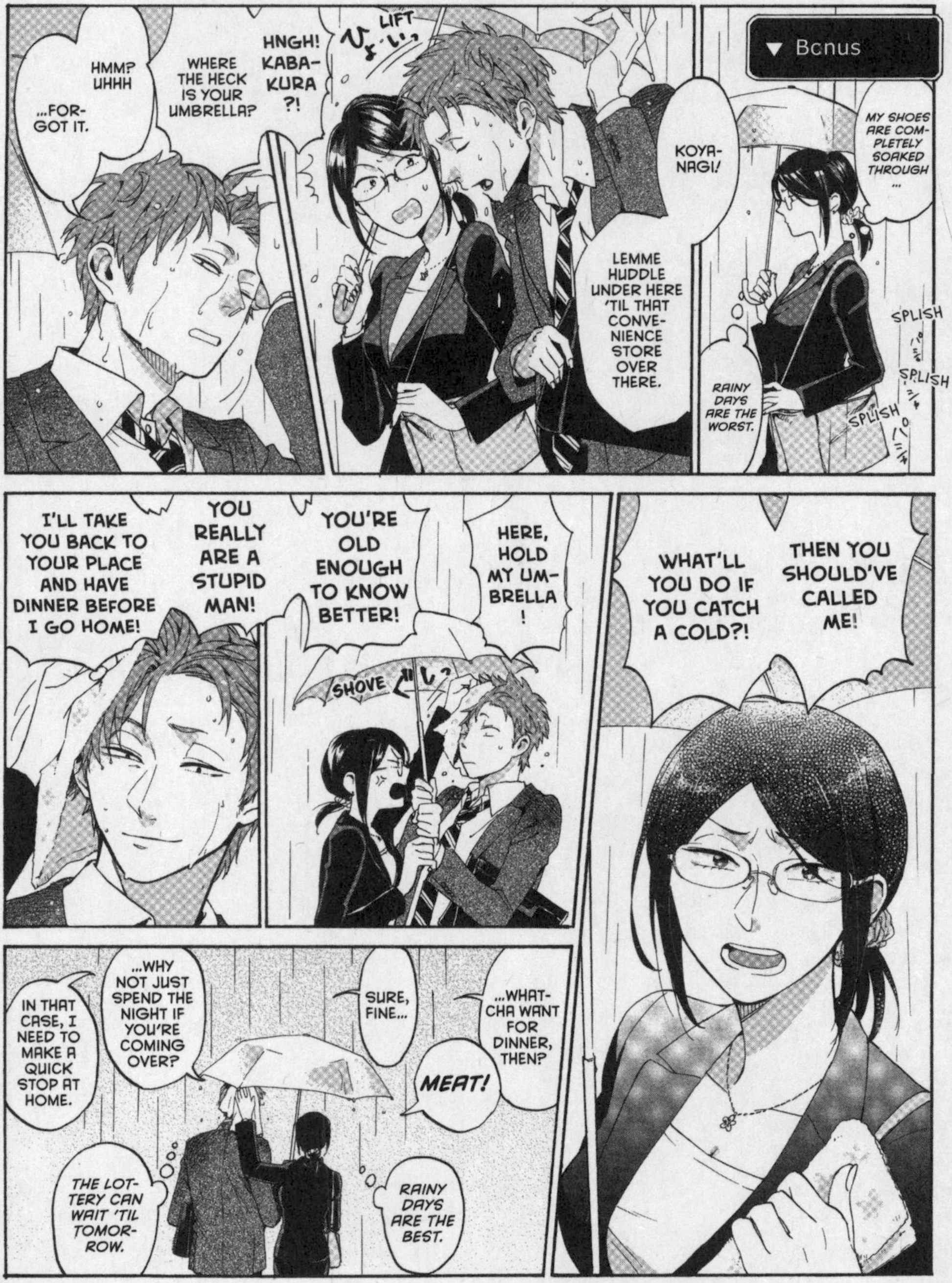
▼ Bonus
MY SHOES ARE COMPLETELY SOAKED THROUGH ...
RAINY DAYS ARE THE WORST.
SPLISH
SPLISH
SPLISH
KOYA-NAGI!
LEMME HUDDLE UNDER HERE 'TIL THAT CONVENIENCE STORE OVER THERE.
HNGH! KABA-KURA ?!
LIFT
WHERE THE HECK IS YOUR UMBRELLA?
HMM? UHHH
...FOR-GOT IT.
THEN YOU SHOULD'VE CALLED ME!
WHAT'LL YOU DO IF YOU CATCH A COLD?!
HERE, HOLD MY UM-BRELLA !
YOU'RE OLD ENOUGH TO KNOW BETTER!
SHOVE
YOU REALLY ARE A STUPID MAN!
I'LL TAKE YOU BACK TO YOUR PLACE AND HAVE DINNER BEFORE I GO HOME!
...WHAT-CHA WANT FOR DINNER, THEN?
MEAT!
SURE, FINE...
...WHY NOT JUST SPEND THE NIGHT IF YOU'RE COMING OVER?
IN THAT CASE, I NEED TO MAKE A QUICK STOP AT HOME.
RAINY DAYS ARE THE BEST.
THE LOT-TERY CAN WAIT 'TIL TOMOR-ROW.

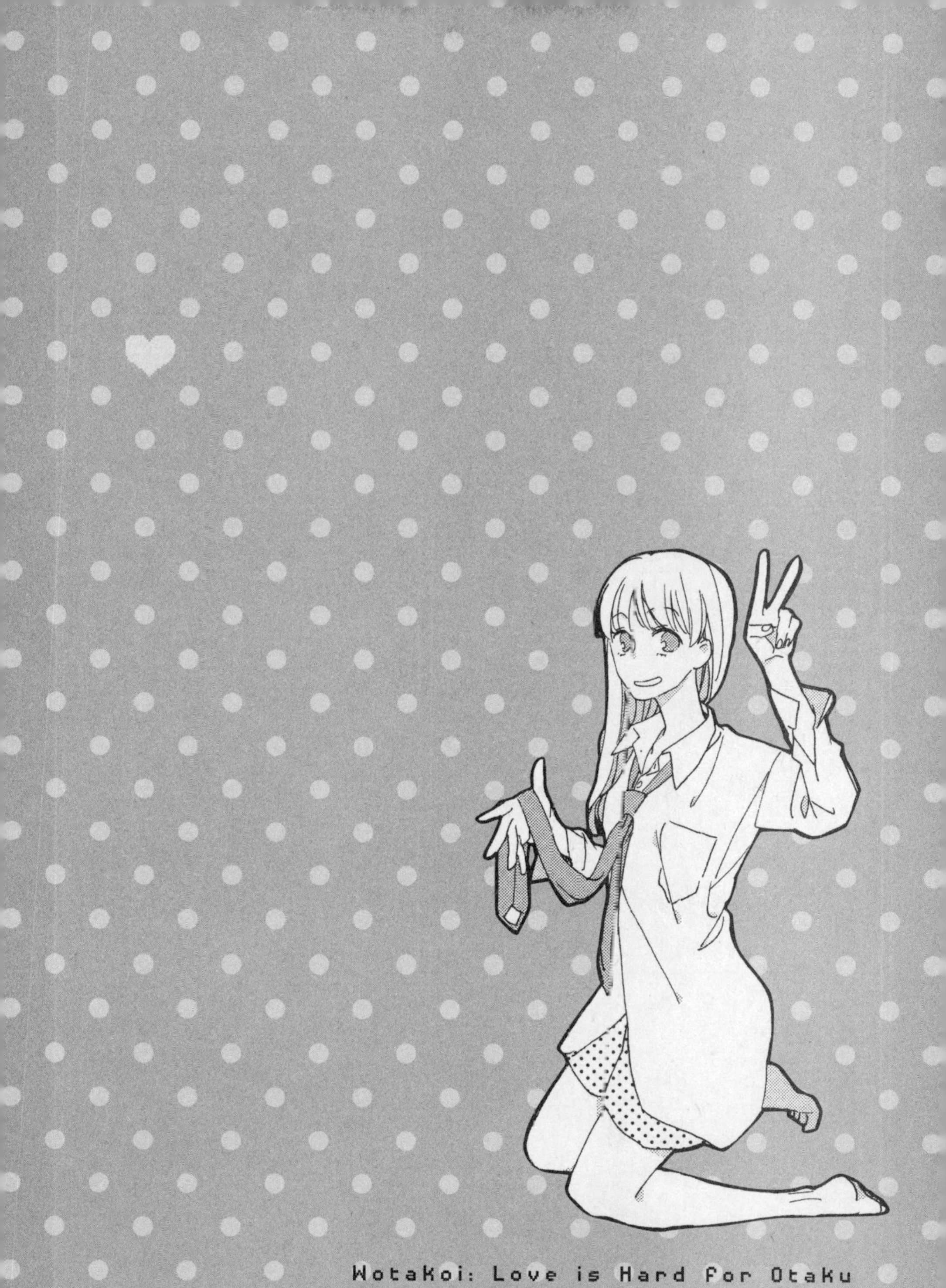

WotaKoi: Love is Hard for Otaku

Episode....9

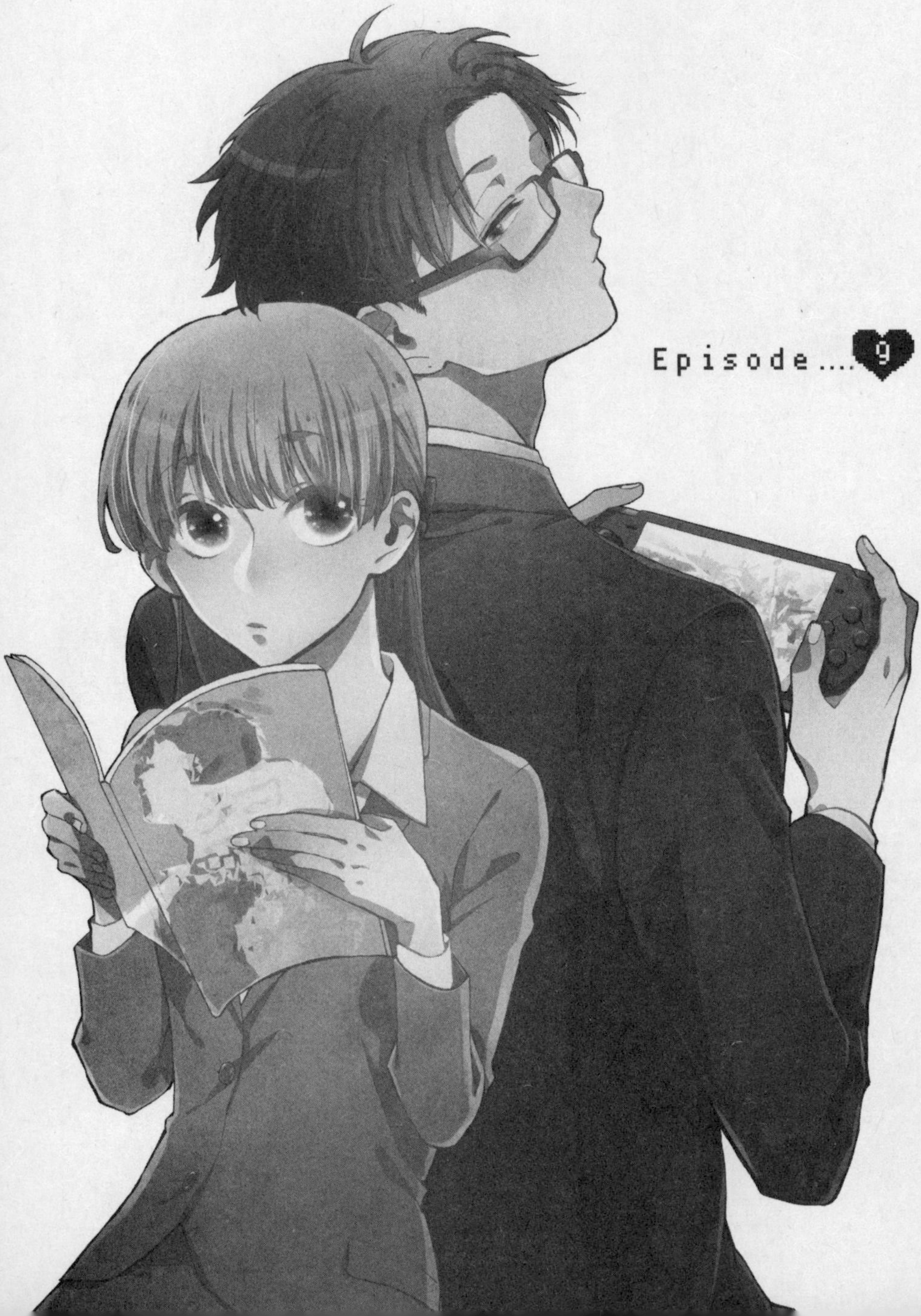

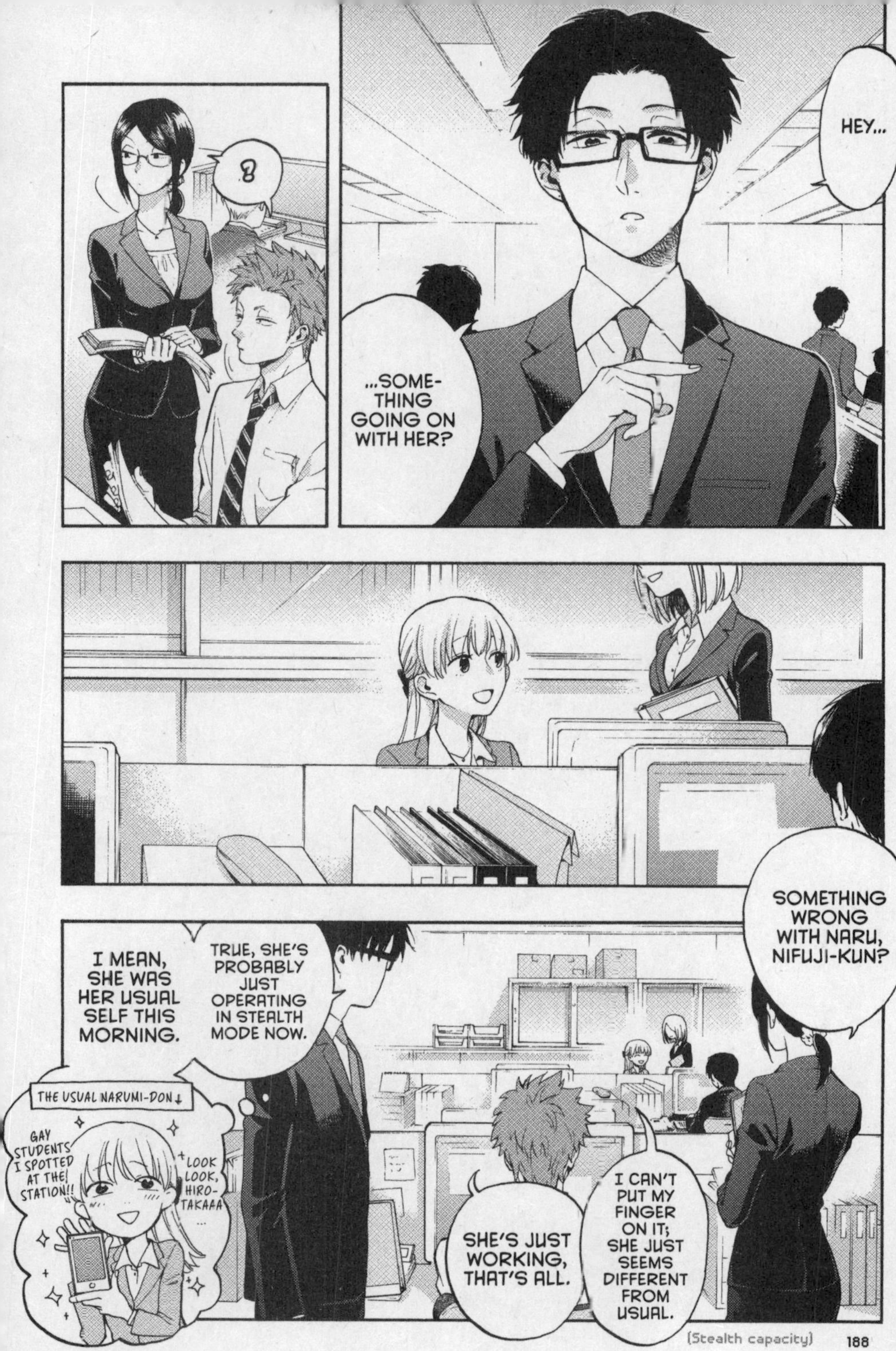
HEY...
...SOME-THING GOING ON WITH HER?
?
SOMETHING WRONG WITH NARU, NIFUJI-KUN?
I CAN'T PUT MY FINGER ON IT; SHE JUST SEEMS DIFFERENT FROM USUAL.
SHE'S JUST WORKING, THAT'S ALL.
TRUE, SHE'S PROBABLY JUST OPERATING IN STEALTH MODE NOW.
I MEAN, SHE WAS HER USUAL SELF THIS MORNING.
THE USUAL NARUMI-DON↓
LOOK LOOK, HIRO-TAKAAA...
GAY STUDENTS I SPOTTED AT THE STATION!!

(Stealth capacity)

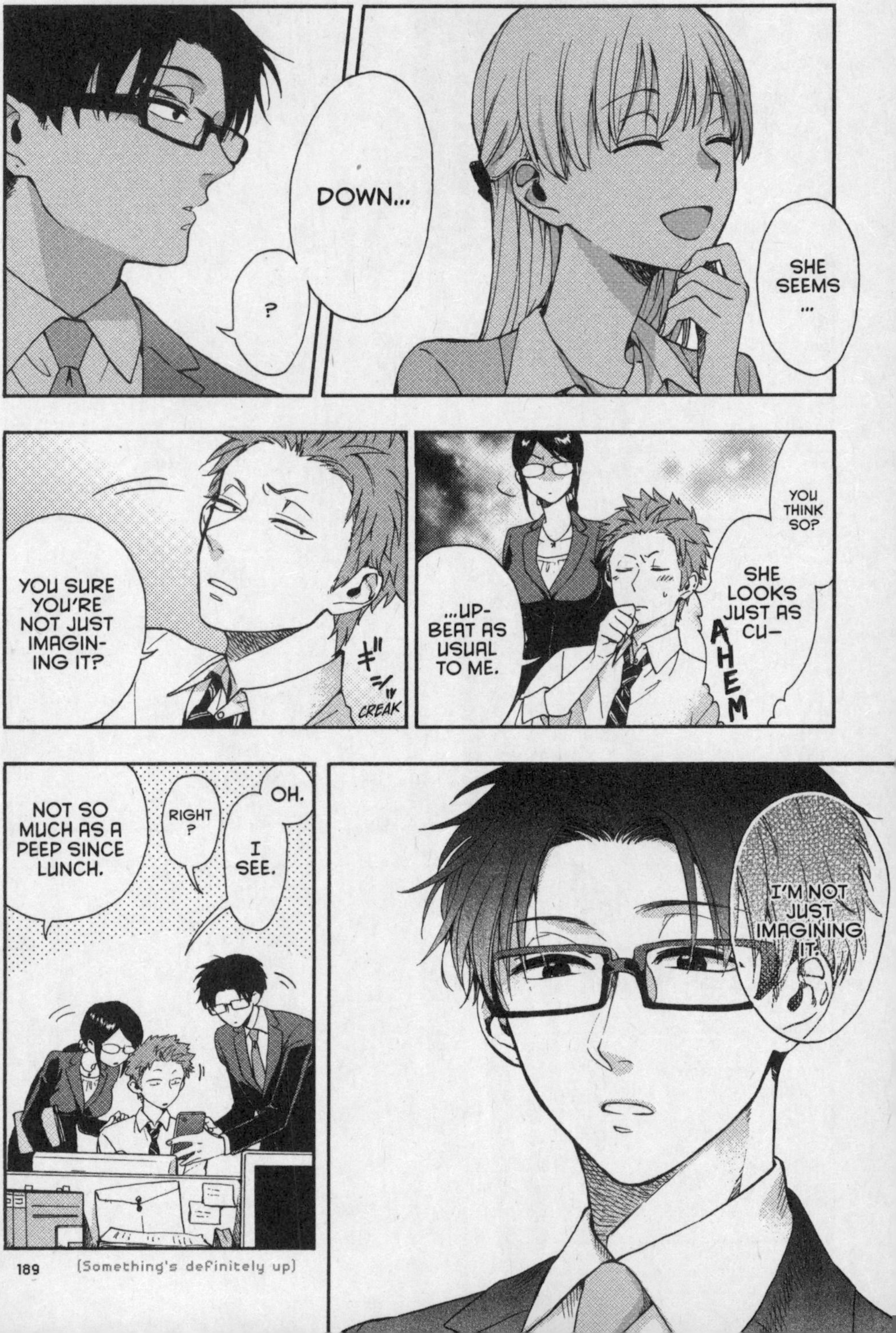

SHE SEEMS ...
DOWN...
?
YOU THINK SO?
SHE LOOKS JUST AS CU-
AHEM
...UP-BEAT AS USUAL TO ME.
YOU SURE YOU'RE NOT JUST IMAGINING IT?
ギ
CREAK
I'M NOT JUST IMAGINING IT.
OH.
I SEE.
RIGHT?
NOT SO MUCH AS A PEEP SINCE LUNCH.

 (Something's definitely up)

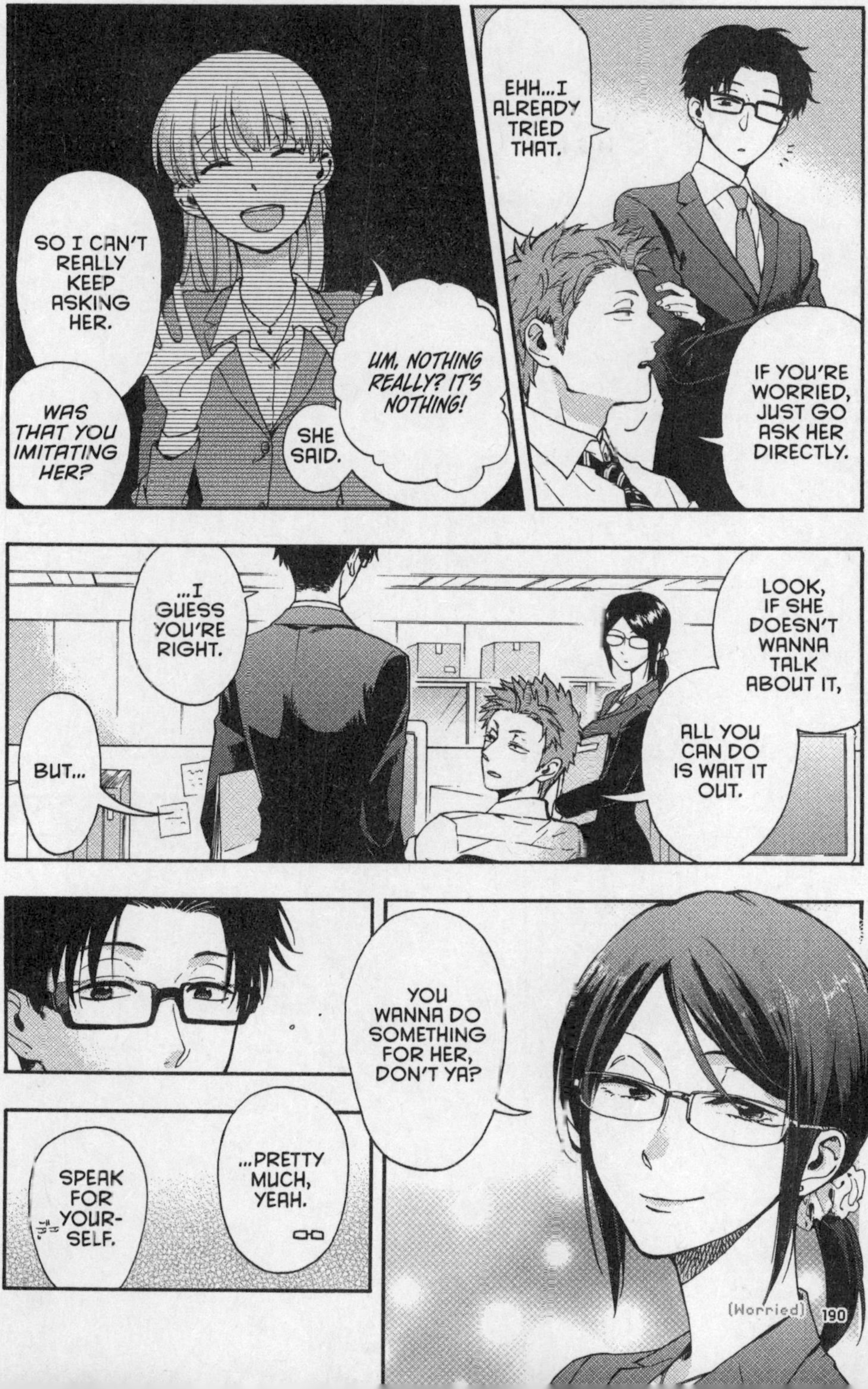
IF YOU'RE WORRIED, JUST GO ASK HER DIRECTLY.
EHH...I ALREADY TRIED THAT.
UM, NOTHING REALLY? IT'S NOTHING!
SHE SAID.
SO I CAN'T REALLY KEEP ASKING HER.
WAS THAT YOU IMITATING HER?
LOOK, IF SHE DOESN'T WANNA TALK ABOUT IT,
ALL YOU CAN DO IS WAIT IT OUT.
...I GUESS YOU'RE RIGHT.
BUT...
YOU WANNA DO SOMETHING FOR HER, DON'T YA?
...PRETTY MUCH, YEAH.
SPEAK FOR YOUR-SELF.
(Worried)

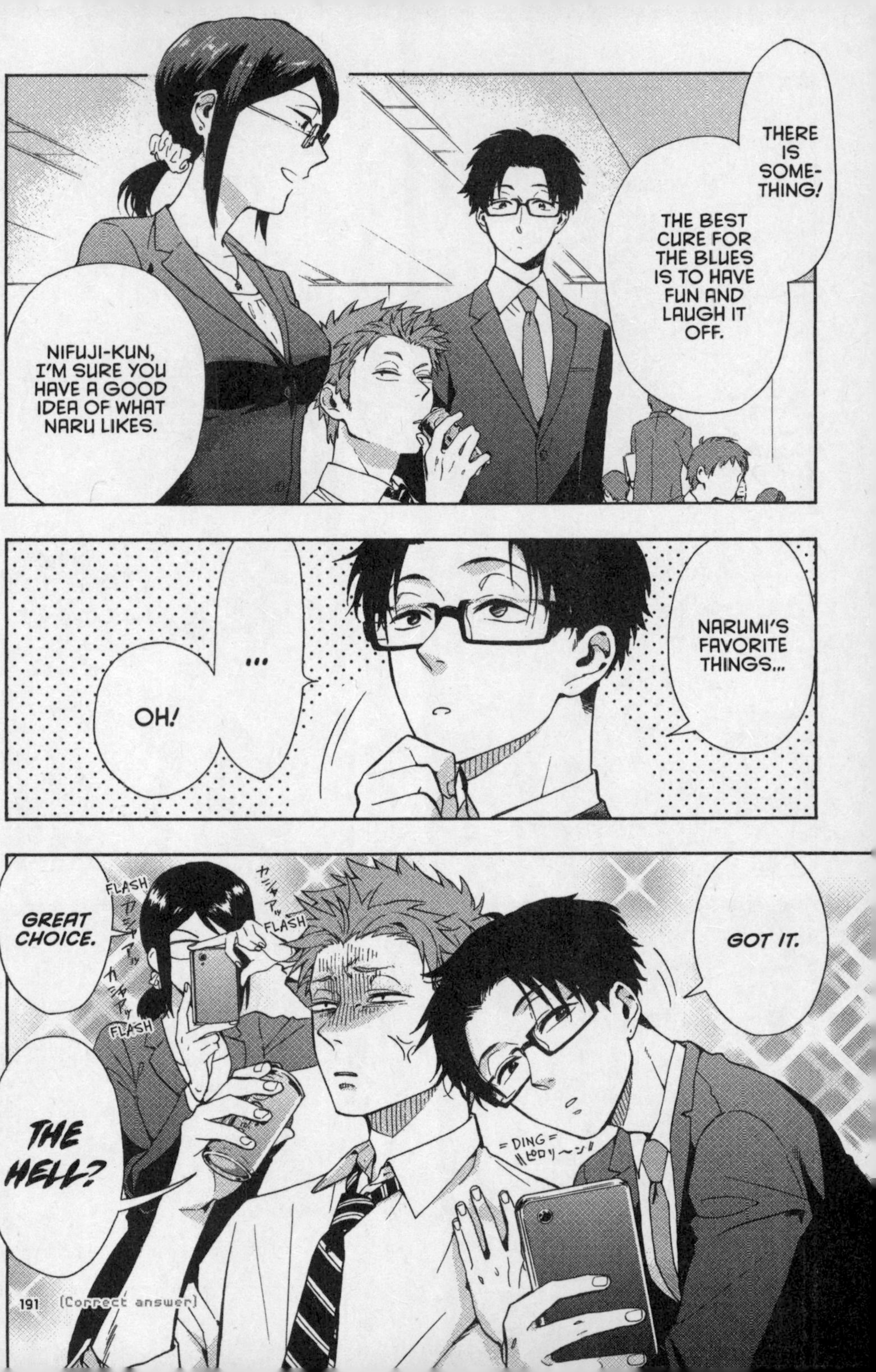
THERE IS SOME-THING!
THE BEST CURE FOR THE BLUES IS TO HAVE FUN AND LAUGH IT OFF.
NIFUJI-KUN, I'M SURE YOU HAVE A GOOD IDEA OF WHAT NARU LIKES.
NARUMI'S FAVORITE THINGS...
...
OH!
GOT IT.
GREAT CHOICE.
FLASH
FLASH
FLASH
=DING=
THE HELL?
(Correct answer)

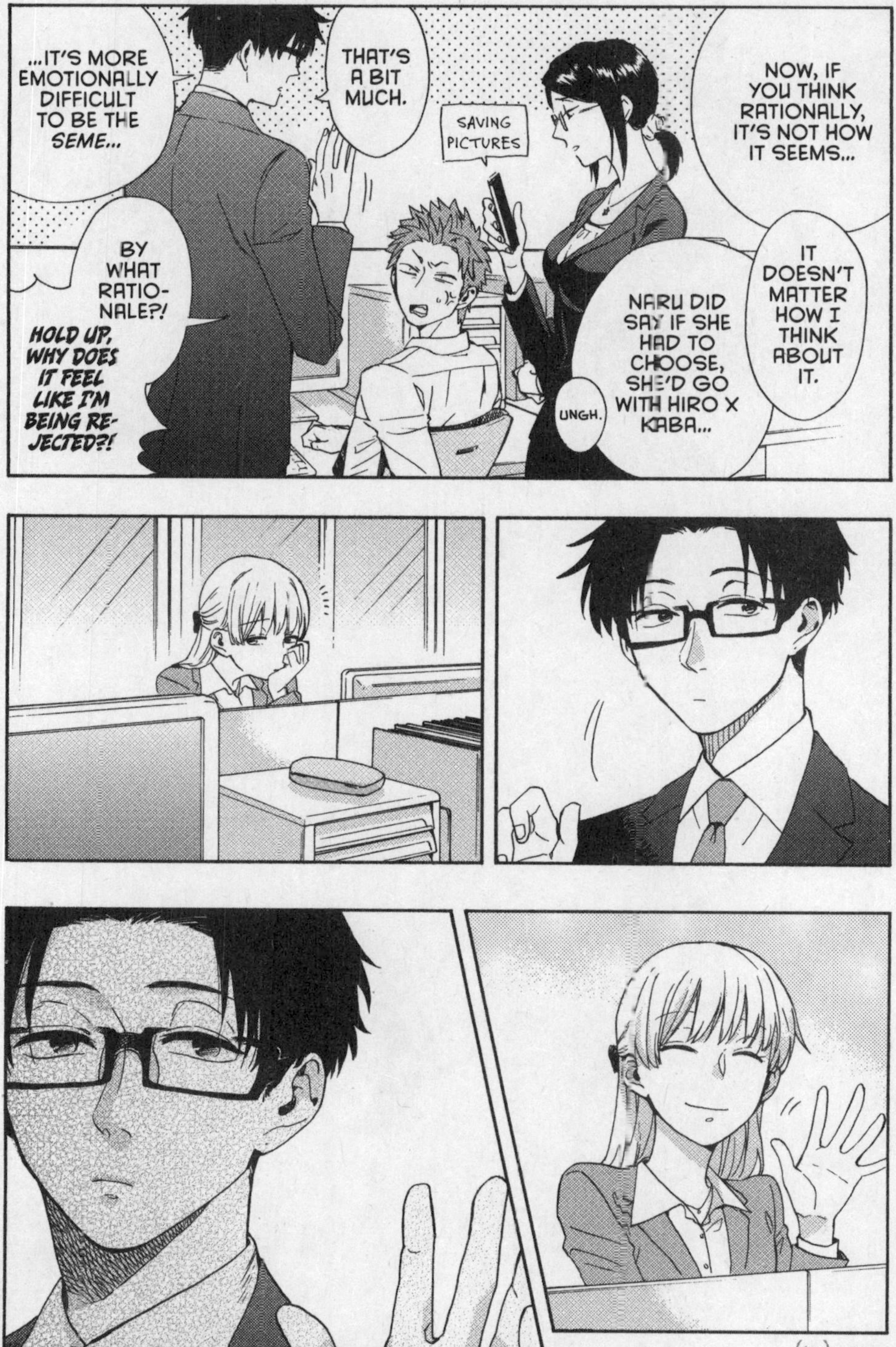
NOW, IF YOU THINK RATIONALLY, IT'S NOT HOW IT SEEMS...
IT DOESN'T MATTER HOW I THINK ABOUT IT.
NARU DID SAY IF SHE HAD TO CHOOSE, SHE'D GO WITH HIRO X KABA...
UNGH.
SAVING PICTURES
THAT'S A BIT MUCH.
...IT'S MORE EMOTIONALLY DIFFICULT TO BE THE SEME...
BY WHAT RATIONALE?!
HOLD UP, WHY DOES IT FEEL LIKE I'M BEING REJECTED?!

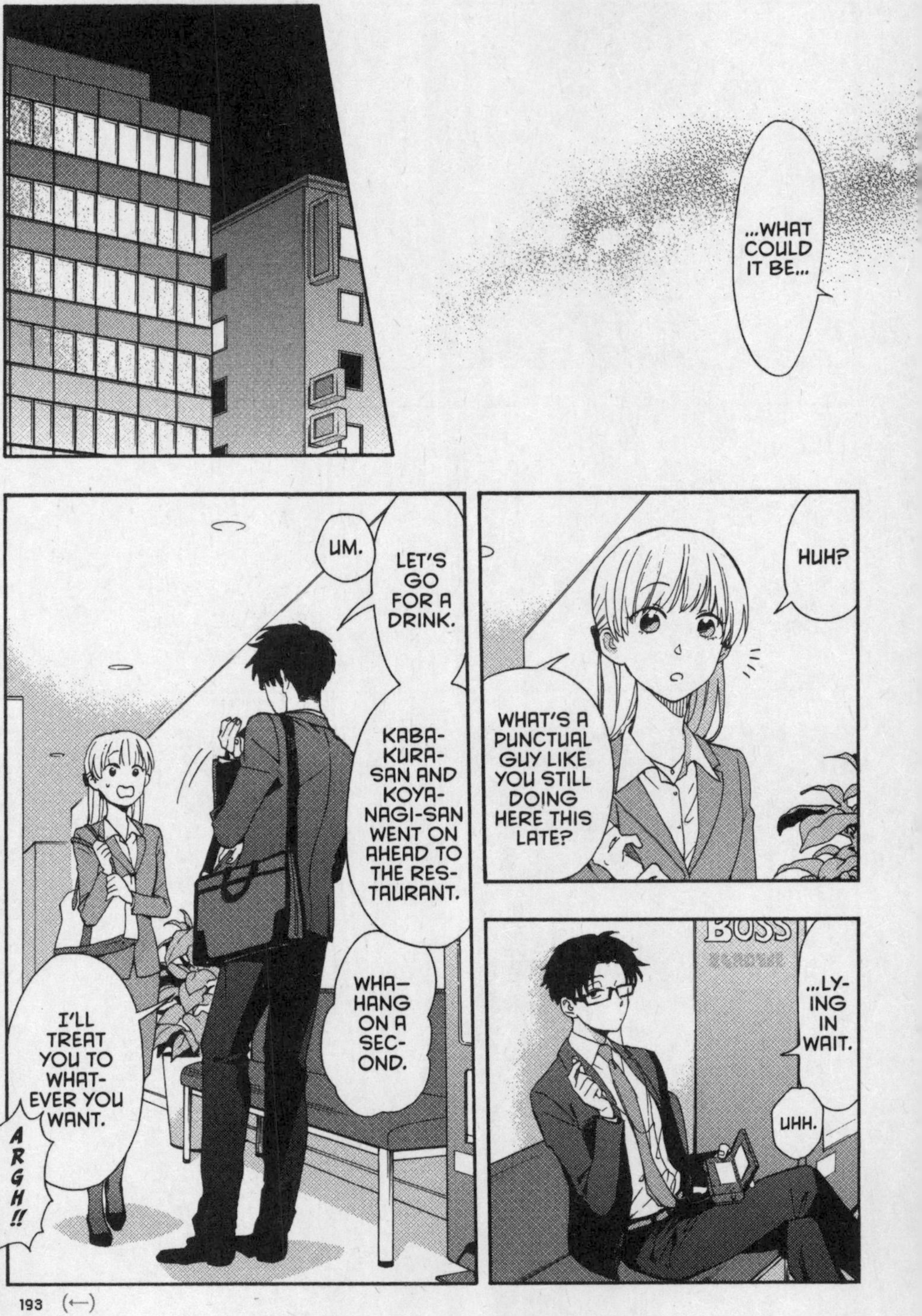
...WHAT COULD IT BE...
HUH?
WHAT'S A PUNCTUAL GUY LIKE YOU STILL DOING HERE THIS LATE?
...LYING IN WAIT.
UHH.
UM.
LET'S GO FOR A DRINK.
KABAKURA-SAN AND KOYANAGI-SAN WENT ON AHEAD TO THE RESTAURANT.
WHA— HANG ON A SECOND.
I'LL TREAT YOU TO WHATEVER YOU WANT.
ARGH!!

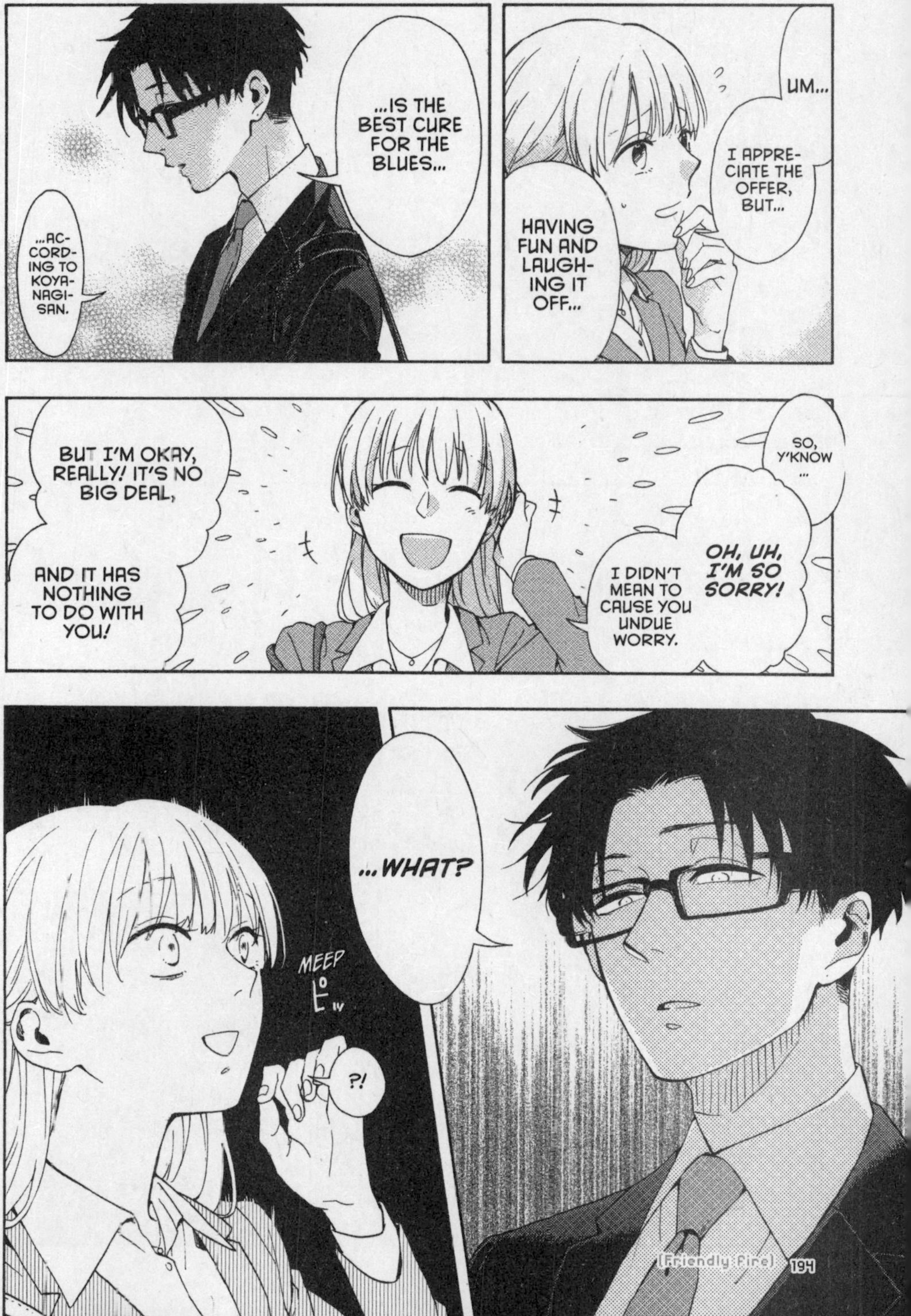
UM...
I APPRECIATE THE OFFER, BUT...
HAVING FUN AND LAUGHING IT OFF...
...IS THE BEST CURE FOR THE BLUES...
...ACCORDING TO KOYANAGI-SAN.
SO, Y'KNOW ...
OH, UH, I'M SO SORRY!
I DIDN'T MEAN TO CAUSE YOU UNDUE WORRY.
BUT I'M OKAY, REALLY! IT'S NO BIG DEAL,
AND IT HAS NOTHING TO DO WITH YOU!
...WHAT?
MEEP
?!

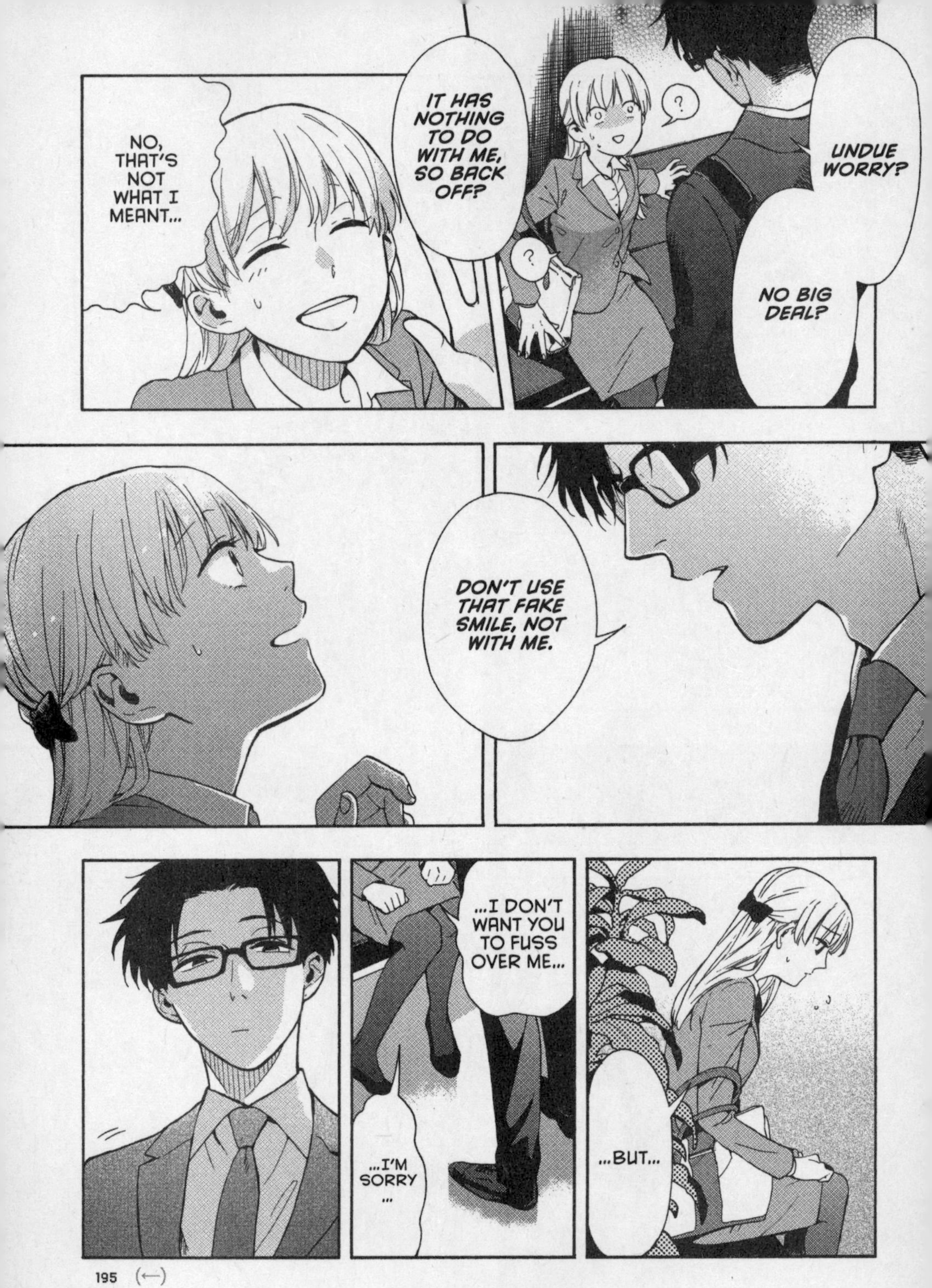
UNDUE WORRY?
NO BIG DEAL?
IT HAS NOTHING TO DO WITH ME, SO BACK OFF?
?
?
NO, THAT'S NOT WHAT I MEANT...
DON'T USE THAT FAKE SMILE, NOT WITH ME.
...BUT...
...I DON'T WANT YOU TO FUSS OVER ME...
...I'M SORRY ...

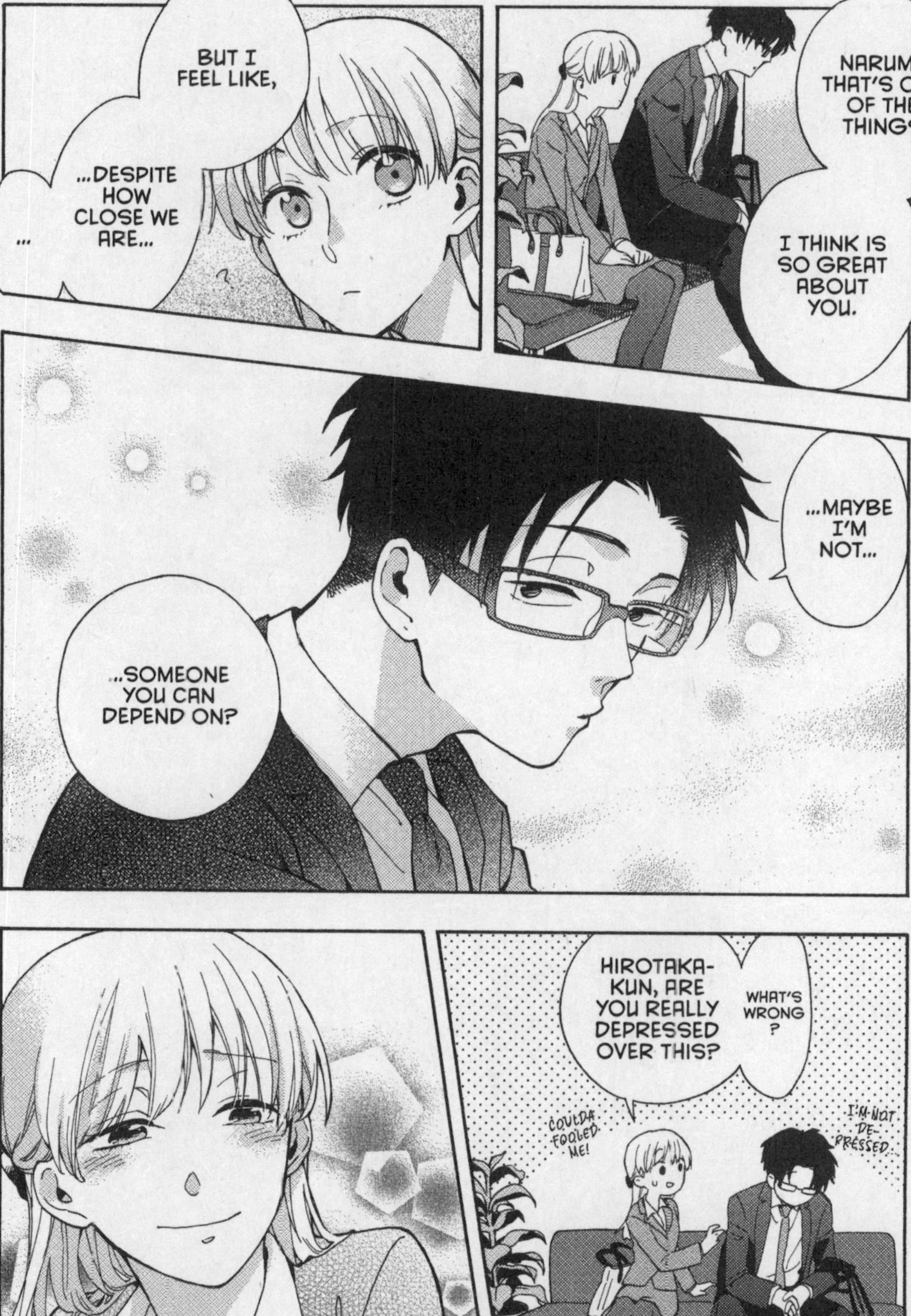
NARUMI, THAT'S ONE OF THE THINGS
I THINK IS SO GREAT ABOUT YOU.
BUT I FEEL LIKE,
...DESPITE HOW CLOSE WE ARE...
...
...MAYBE I'M NOT...
...SOMEONE YOU CAN DEPEND ON?
HIROTAKA-KUN, ARE YOU REALLY DEPRESSED OVER THIS?
WHAT'S WRONG?
I'M NOT DEPRESSED.
COULDA FOOLED ME!

(But I'm unreliable)

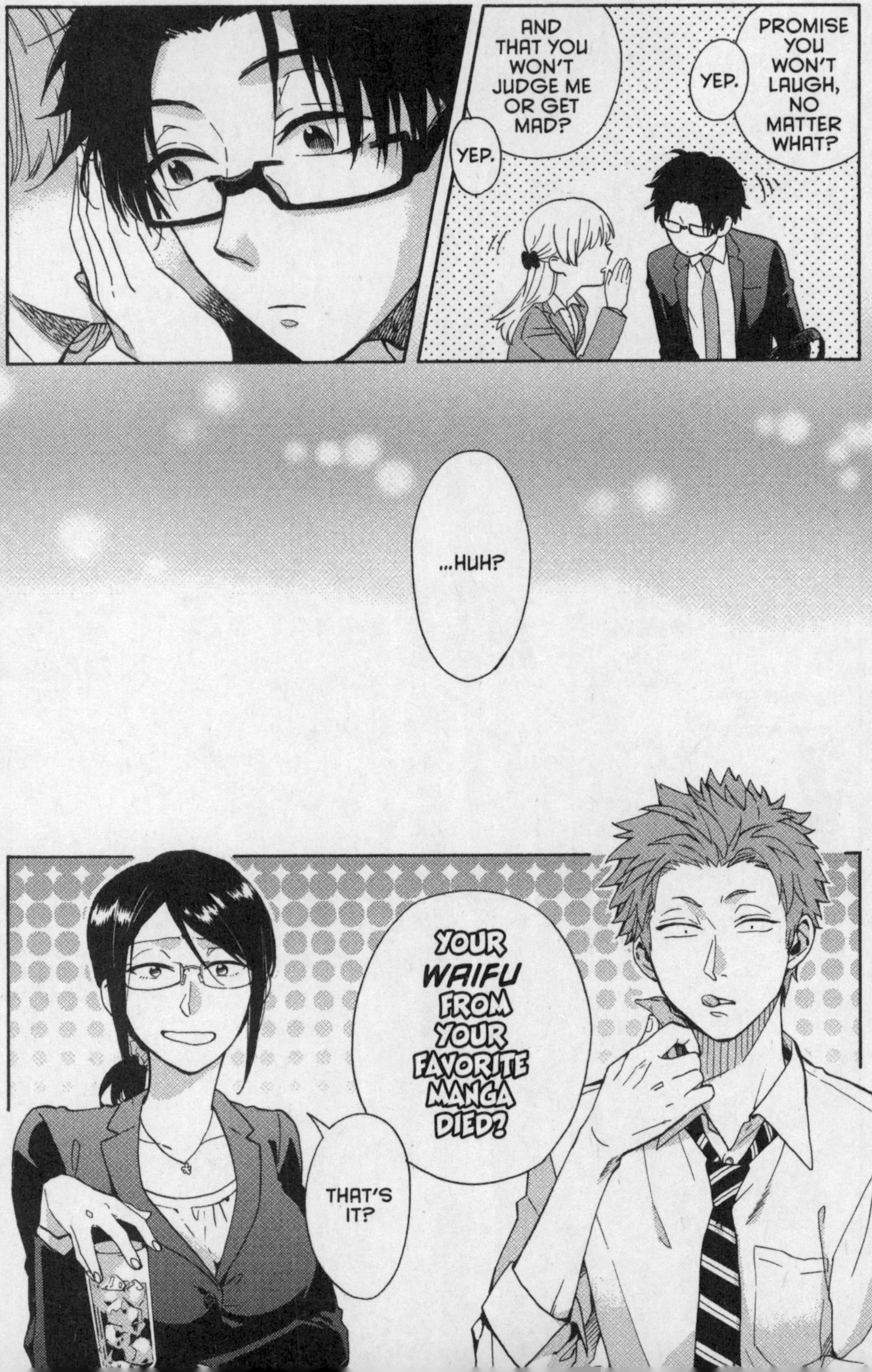
PROMISE YOU WON'T LAUGH, NO MATTER WHAT?
YEP.
AND THAT YOU WON'T JUDGE ME OR GET MAD?
YEP.
...HUH?
YOUR *WAIFU* FROM YOUR FAVORITE MANGA DIED?
THAT'S IT?

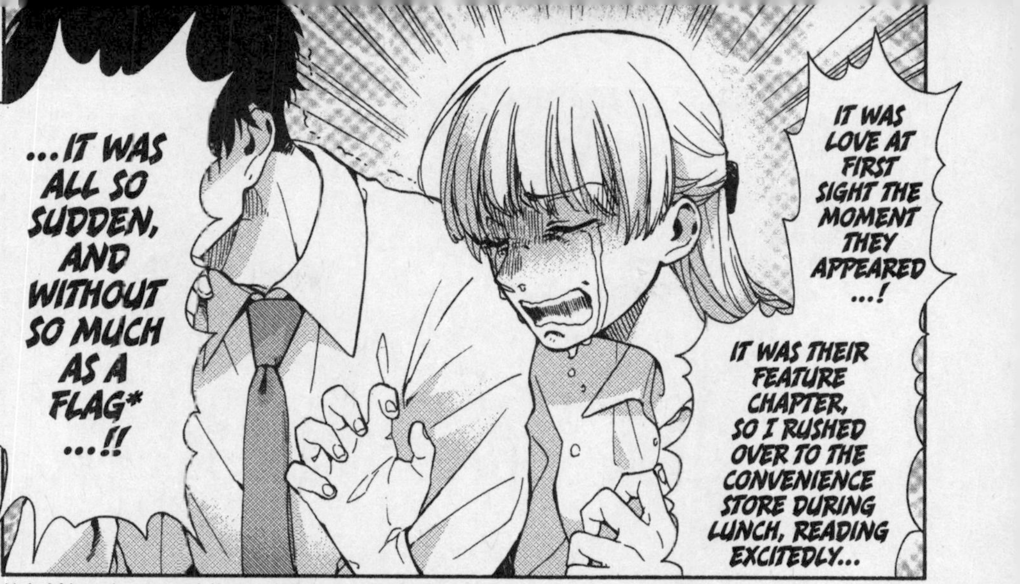
IT WAS LOVE AT FIRST SIGHT THE MOMENT THEY APPEARED ...!
IT WAS THEIR FEATURE CHAPTER, SO I RUSHED OVER TO THE CONVENIENCE STORE DURING LUNCH, READING EXCITEDLY...
...IT WAS ALL SO SUDDEN, AND WITHOUT SO MUCH AS A FLAG* ...!!

*A clue left in an anime, manga, and video games hinting at a character's future status (death, survival, love, etc.).

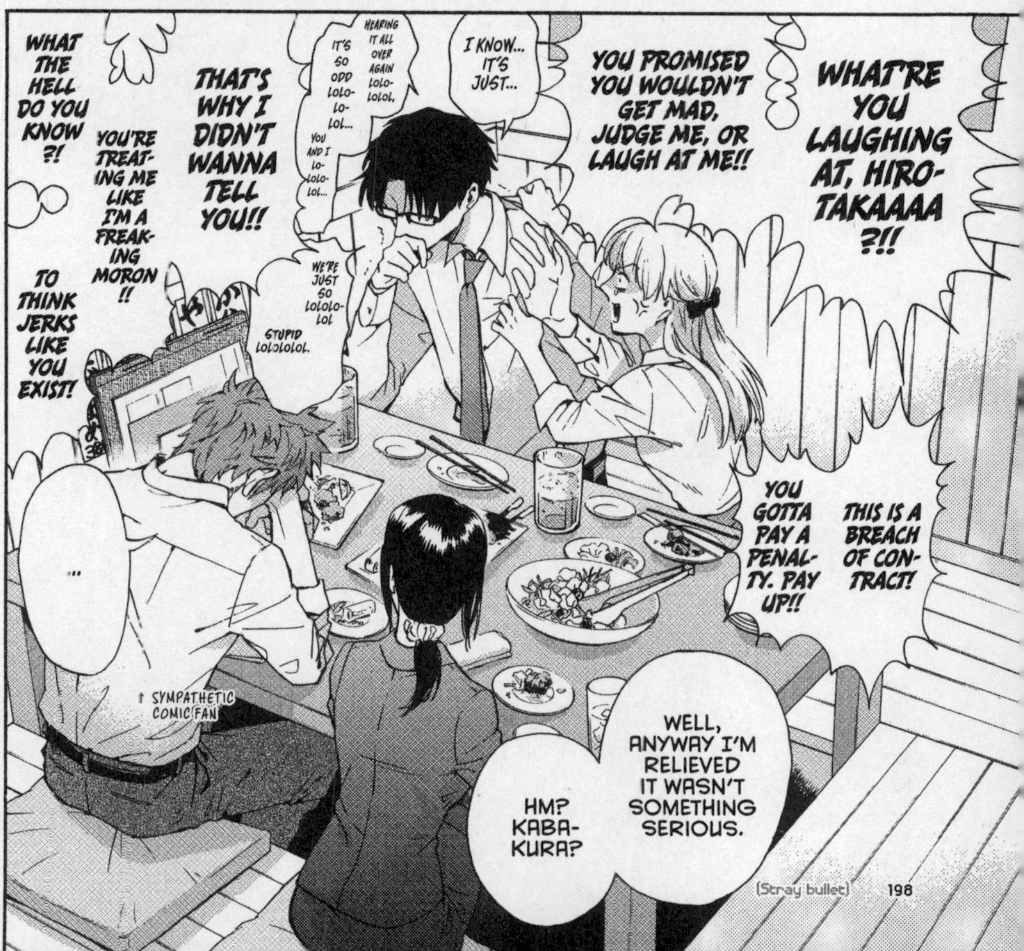
WHAT'RE YOU LAUGHING AT, HIRO-TAKAAAA ?!!
YOU PROMISED YOU WOULDN'T GET MAD, JUDGE ME, OR LAUGH AT ME!!
I KNOW... IT'S JUST...
HEARING IT ALL OVER AGAIN LOLO-LOLOL.
IT'S SO ODD LOLO-LO-LOL...
YOU AND I LO-LOLO-LOL...
THAT'S WHY I DIDN'T WANNA TELL YOU!!
WHAT THE HELL DO YOU KNOW ?!
YOU'RE TREAT-ING ME LIKE I'M A FREAK-ING MORON !!
TO THINK JERKS LIKE YOU EXIST!
WE'RE JUST SO LOLOLO-LOL
STUPID LOLOLOLOL.
THIS IS A BREACH OF CON-TRACT!
YOU GOTTA PAY A PENAL-TY. PAY UP!!
...
↑ SYMPATHETIC COMIC FAN
WELL, ANYWAY I'M RELIEVED IT WASN'T SOMETHING SERIOUS.
HM? KABA-KURA?
(Stray bullet)

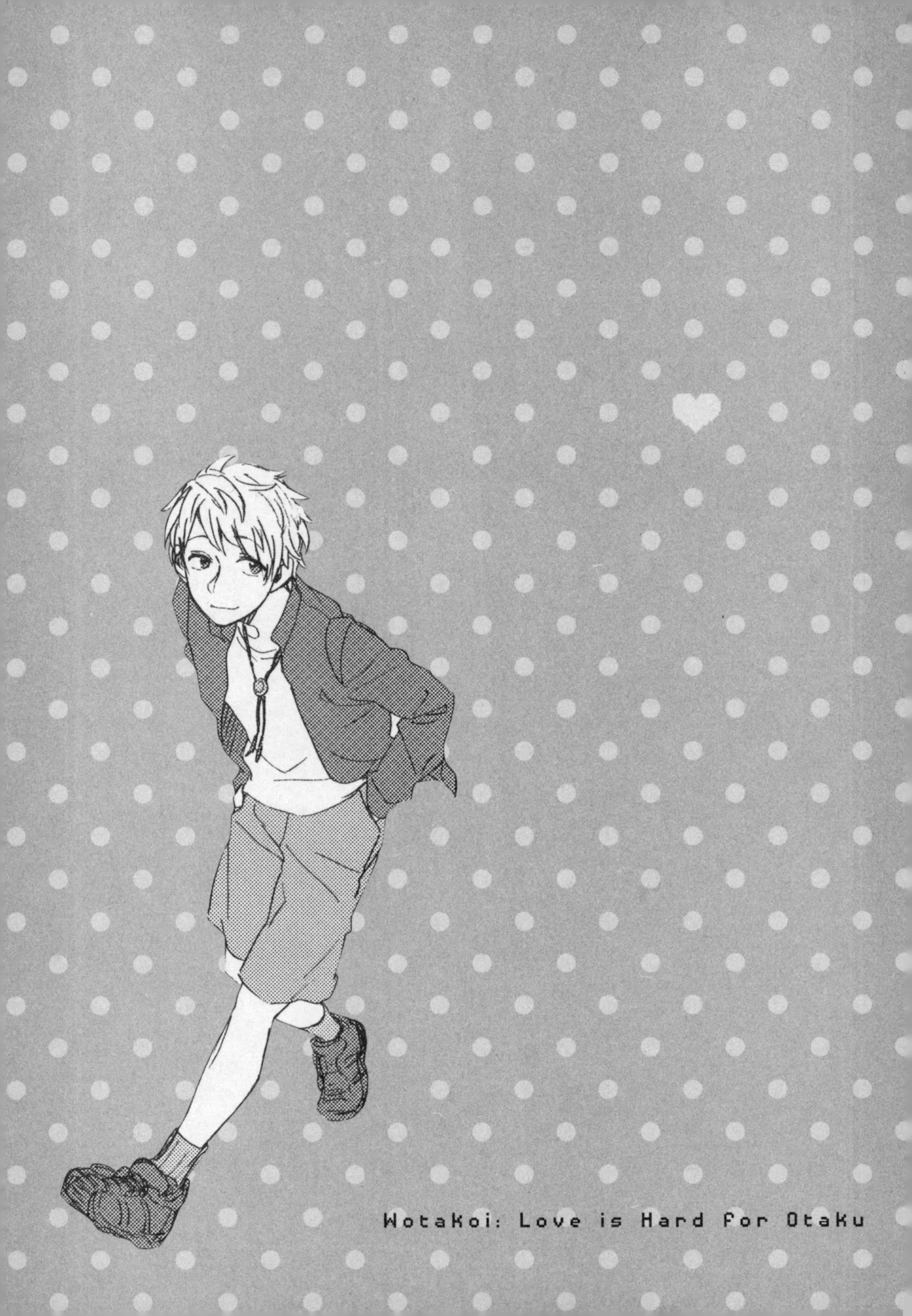
Wotakoi: Love is Hard for Otaku

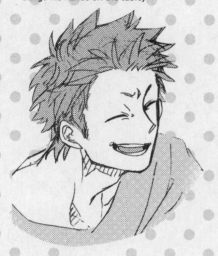

▶ Comparison of Smiles

▼ The type to show her teeth when she smiles (her smile seems a little discreet)

▼ The type to smile with his mouth open (he also laughs loudly and bangs his hands on the table)

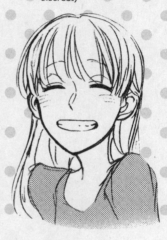

▼ The type whose smile depends on the recipient (he suddenly returns to his deadpan expression)

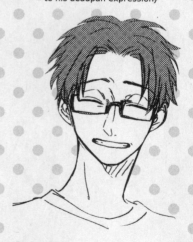

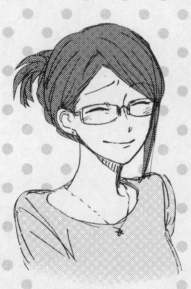

▼ The type who sneers rather than smiles (often referred to as "laughing snottily")

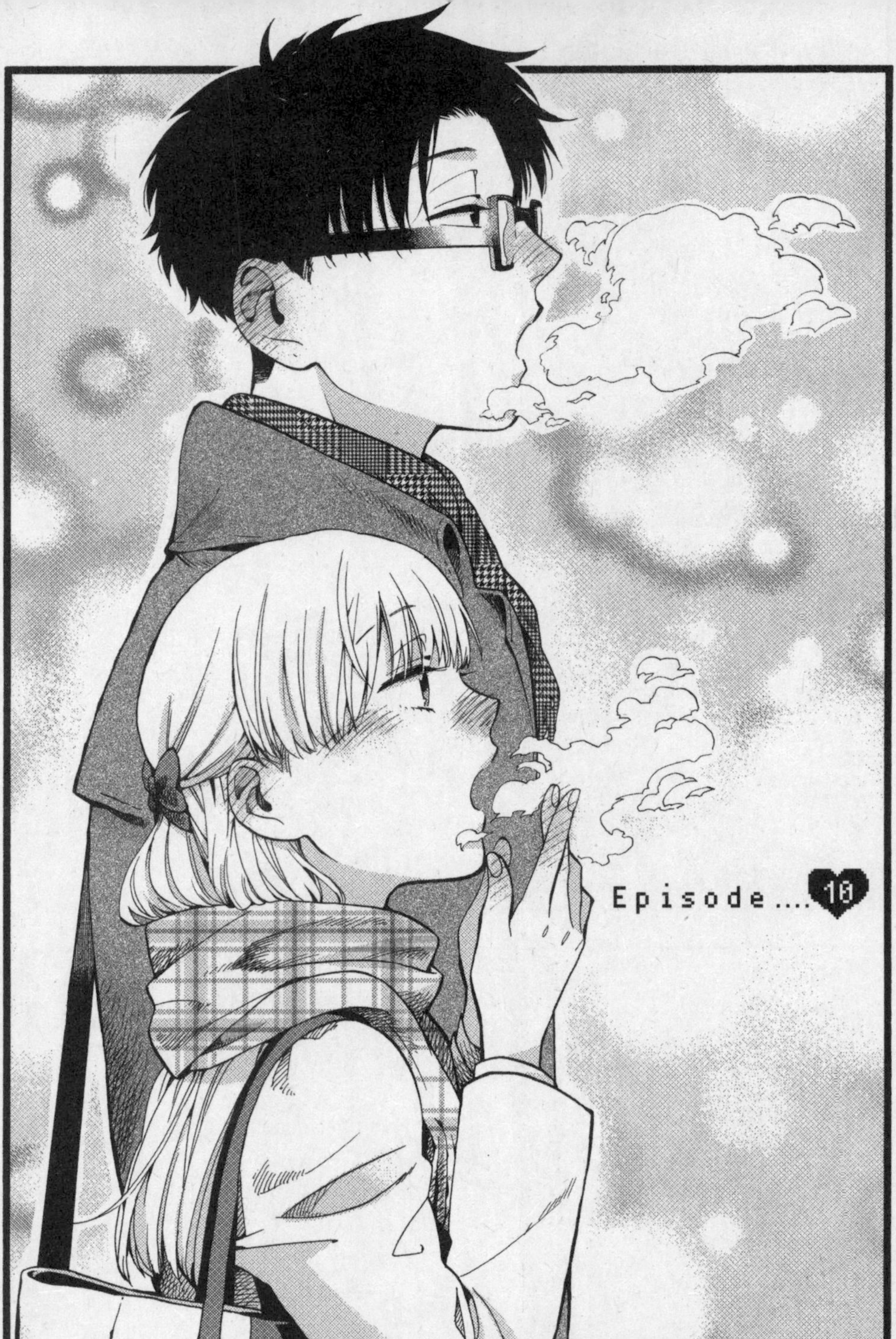
Episode.... 10

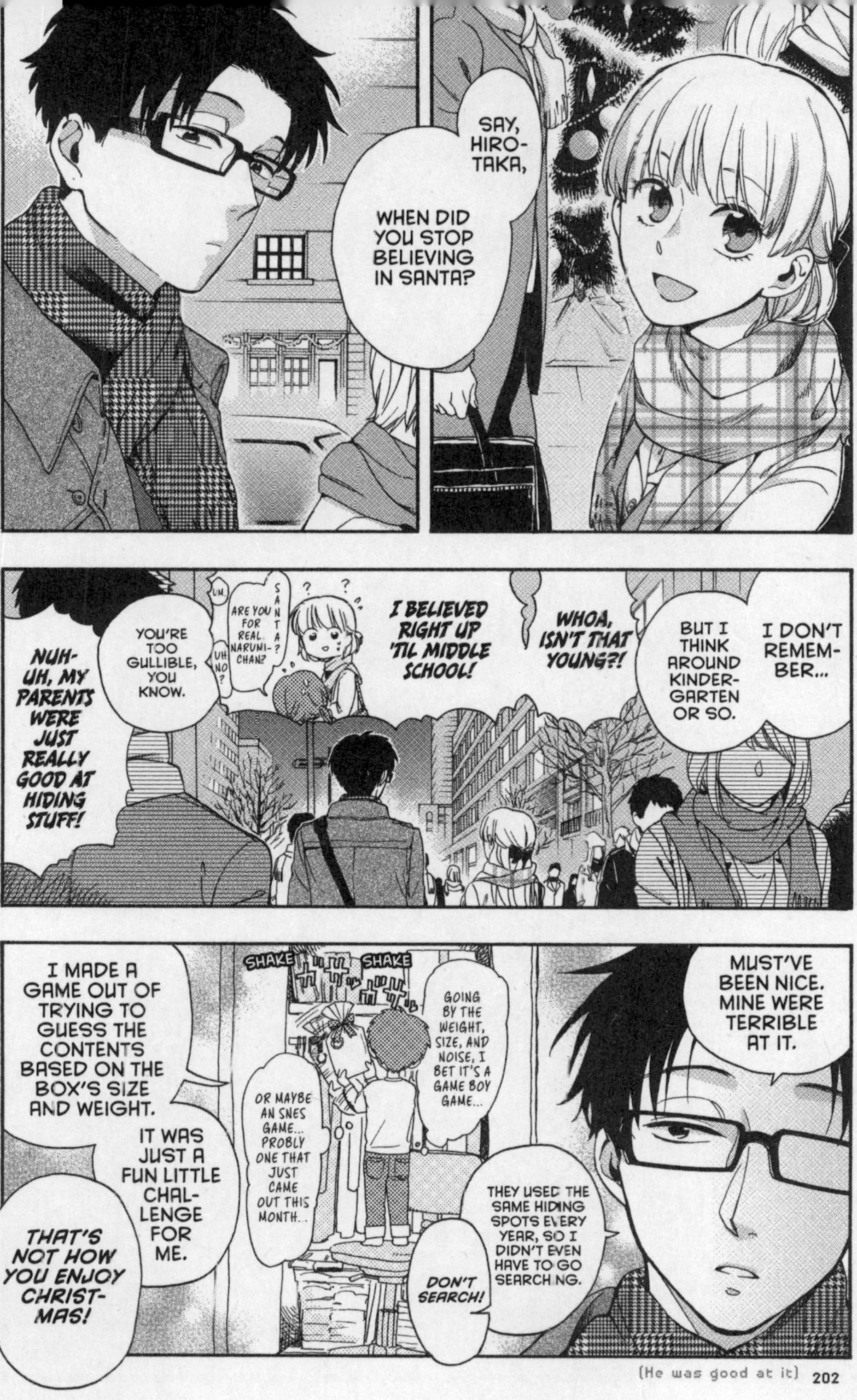
SAY, HIRO-TAKA,
WHEN DID YOU STOP BELIEVING IN SANTA?
I DON'T REMEMBER...
BUT I THINK AROUND KINDERGARTEN OR SO.
WHOA, ISN'T THAT YOUNG?!
I BELIEVED RIGHT UP 'TIL MIDDLE SCHOOL!
SANTA?
ARE YOU FOR REAL, NARUMI-CHAN?
UM,
UH NO?
YOU'RE TOO GULLIBLE, YOU KNOW.
NUH-UH, MY PARENTS WERE JUST REALLY GOOD AT HIDING STUFF!
MUST'VE BEEN NICE. MINE WERE TERRIBLE AT IT.
THEY USED THE SAME HIDING SPOTS EVERY YEAR, SO I DIDN'T EVEN HAVE TO GO SEARCHING.
DON'T SEARCH!
SHAKE
SHAKE
GOING BY THE WEIGHT, SIZE, AND NOISE, I BET IT'S A GAME BOY GAME...
OR MAYBE AN SNES GAME... PROBLY ONE THAT JUST CAME OUT THIS MONTH...
I MADE A GAME OUT OF TRYING TO GUESS THE CONTENTS BASED ON THE BOX'S SIZE AND WEIGHT.
IT WAS JUST A FUN LITTLE CHALLENGE FOR ME.
THAT'S NOT HOW YOU ENJOY CHRISTMAS!

(He was good at it)

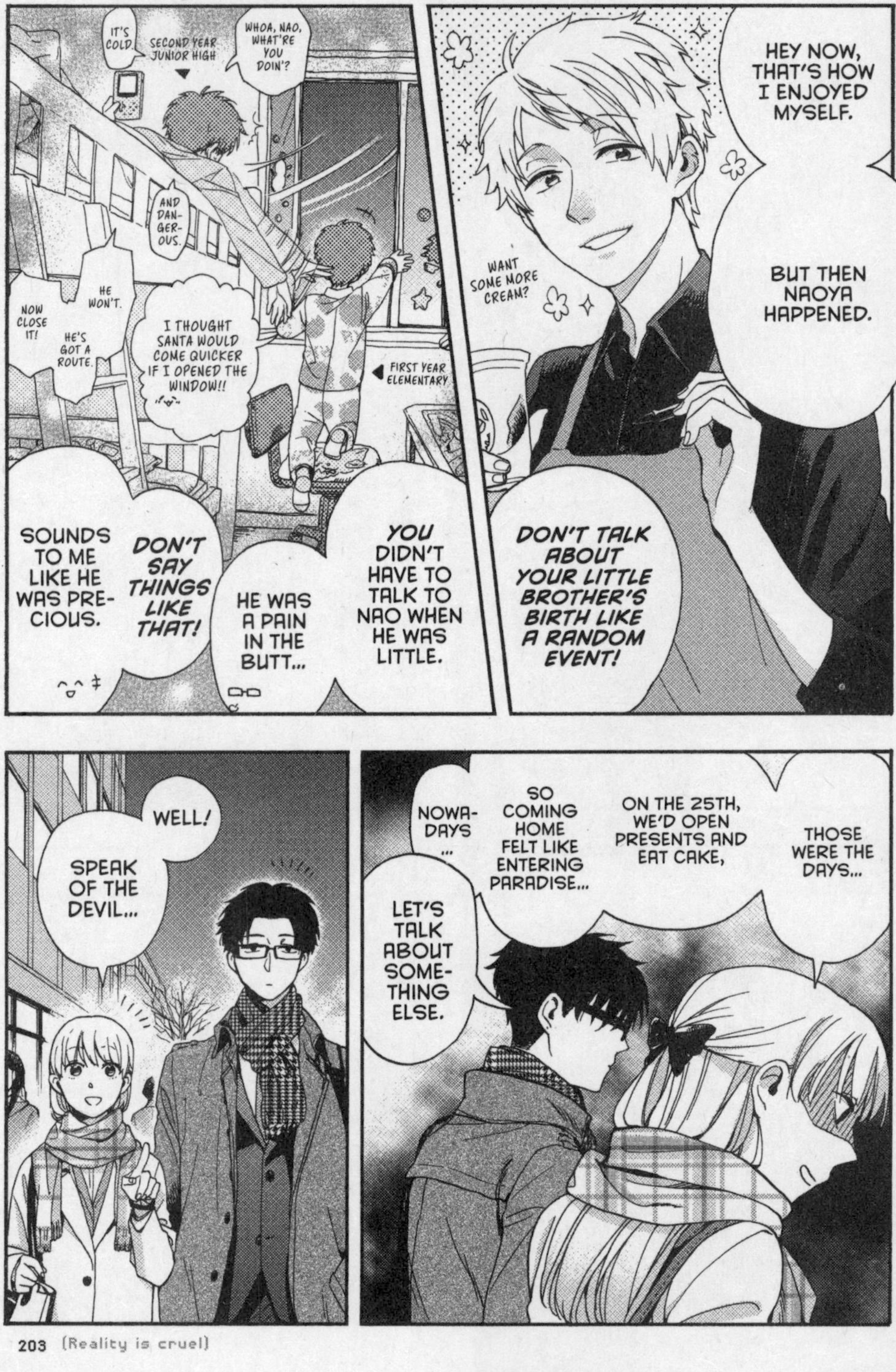
HEY NOW, THAT'S HOW I ENJOYED MYSELF.
BUT THEN NAOYA HAPPENED.
WANT SOME MORE CREAM?
DON'T TALK ABOUT YOUR LITTLE BROTHER'S BIRTH LIKE A RANDOM EVENT!
WHOA, NAO, WHAT'RE YOU DOIN'?
SECOND YEAR JUNIOR HIGH
IT'S COLD.
AND DAN-GER-OUS.
FIRST YEAR ELEMENTARY
I THOUGHT SANTA WOULD COME QUICKER IF I OPENED THE WINDOW!!
HE WON'T.
HE'S GOT A ROUTE.
NOW CLOSE IT!
YOU DIDN'T HAVE TO TALK TO NAO WHEN HE WAS LITTLE.
HE WAS A PAIN IN THE BUTT...
DON'T SAY THINGS LIKE THAT!
SOUNDS TO ME LIKE HE WAS PRE-CIOUS.
THOSE WERE THE DAYS...
ON THE 25TH, WE'D OPEN PRESENTS AND EAT CAKE,
SO COMING HOME FELT LIKE ENTERING PARADISE...
NOWA-DAYS ...
LET'S TALK ABOUT SOME-THING ELSE.
WELL!
SPEAK OF THE DEVIL...

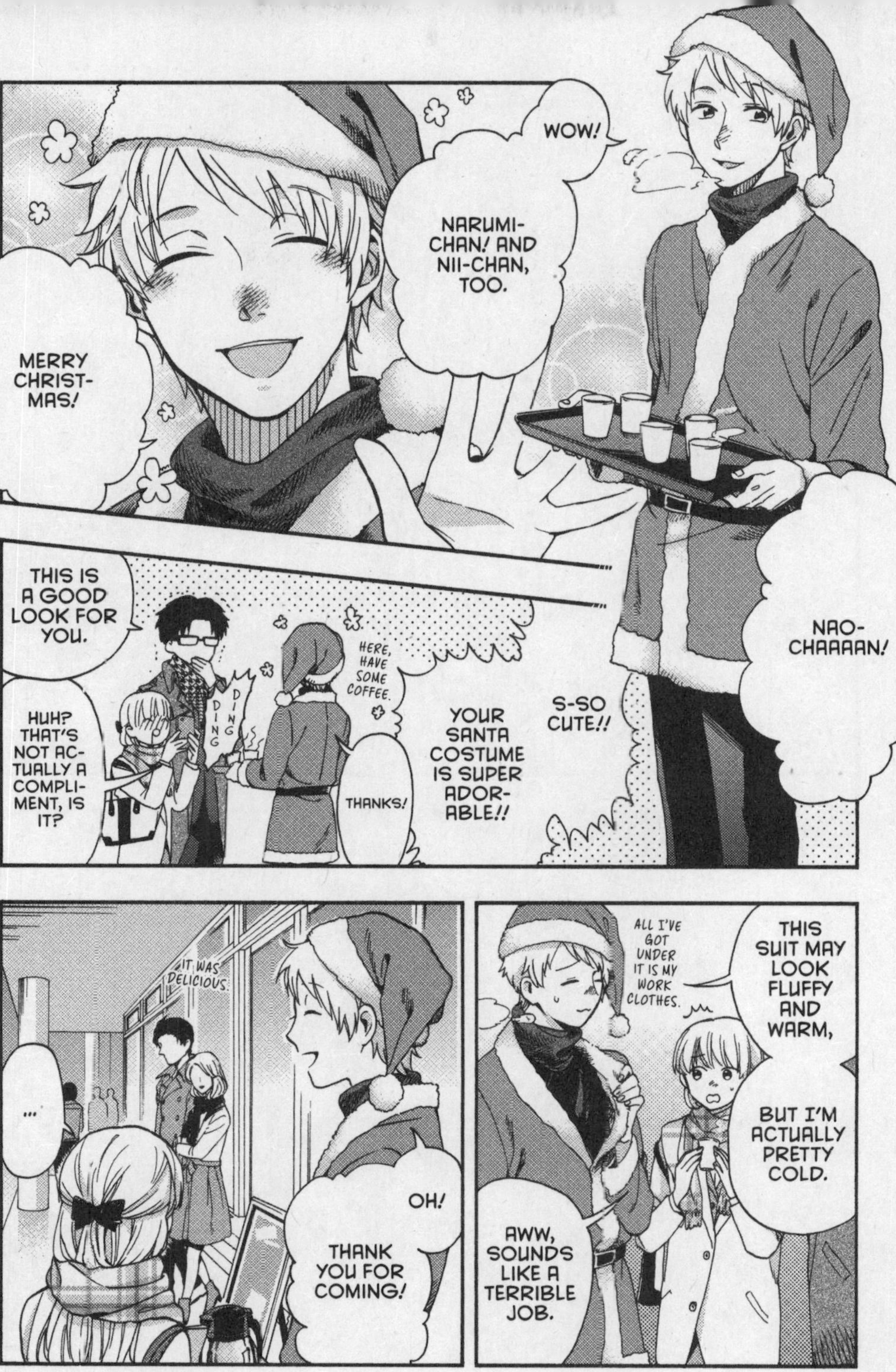
WOW!
NARUMI-CHAN! AND NII-CHAN, TOO.
MERRY CHRIST-MAS!
NAO-CHAAAAN!
S-SO CUTE!!
YOUR SANTA COSTUME IS SUPER ADORABLE!!
THANKS!
HERE, HAVE SOME COFFEE.
DING DING
THIS IS A GOOD LOOK FOR YOU.
HUH? THAT'S NOT ACTUALLY A COMPLIMENT, IS IT?
THIS SUIT MAY LOOK FLUFFY AND WARM,
ALL I'VE GOT UNDER IT IS MY WORK CLOTHES.
BUT I'M ACTUALLY PRETTY COLD.
AWW, SOUNDS LIKE A TERRIBLE JOB.
IT WAS DELICIOUS.
OH!
THANK YOU FOR COMING!
...

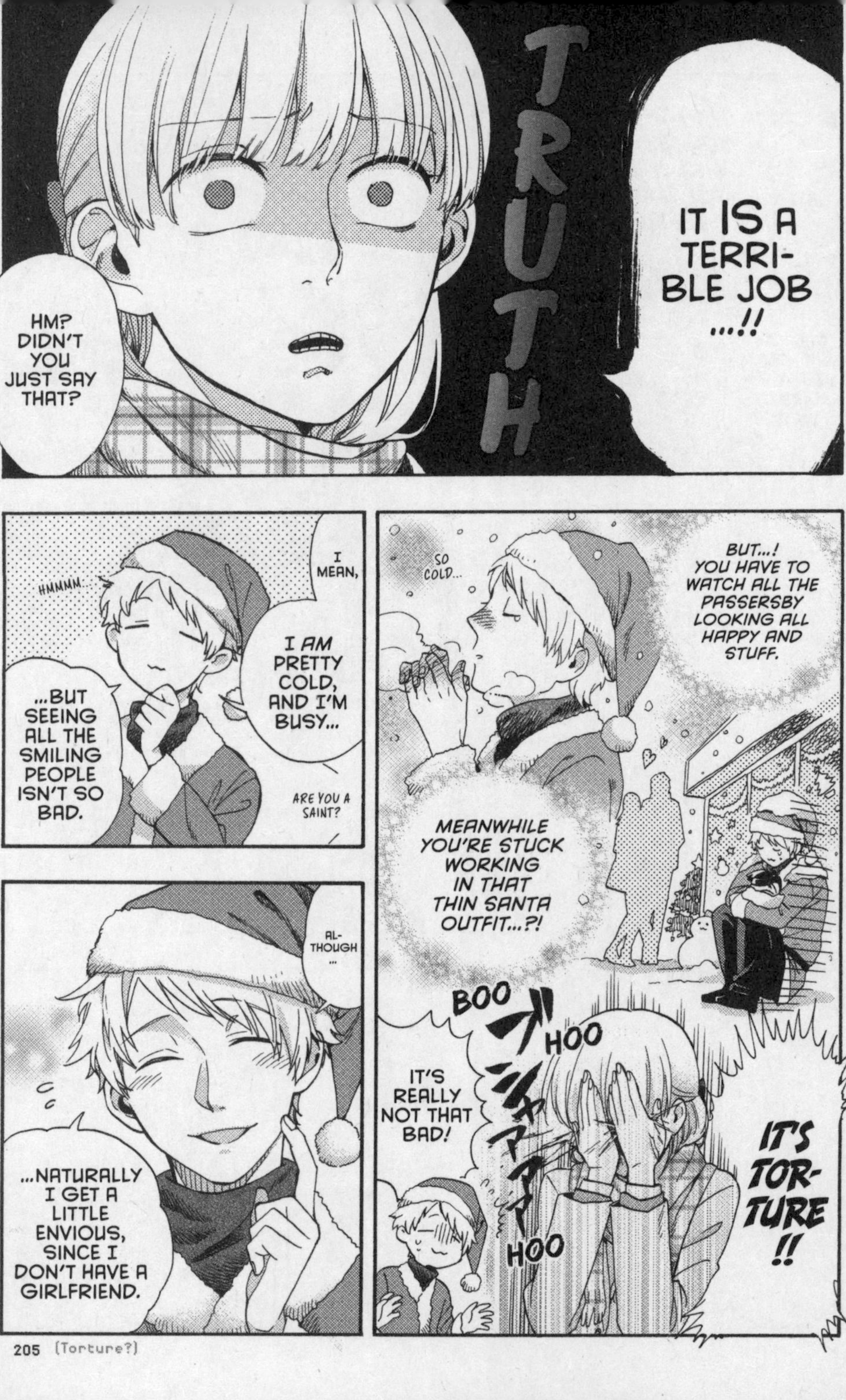
IT IS A TERRIBLE-BLE JOB ...!!
TRUTH
HM? DIDN'T YOU JUST SAY THAT?
BUT...! YOU HAVE TO WATCH ALL THE PASSERSBY LOOKING ALL HAPPY AND STUFF.
SO COLD...
MEANWHILE YOU'RE STUCK WORKING IN THAT THIN SANTA OUTFIT...?!
BOO HOO
ブシャアア
IT'S TORTURE!!
IT'S REALLY NOT THAT BAD!
HOO
I MEAN,
HMMMM.
I AM PRETTY COLD, AND I'M BUSY...
...BUT SEEING ALL THE SMILING PEOPLE ISN'T SO BAD.
ARE YOU A SAINT?
ALTHOUGH ...
...NATURALLY I GET A LITTLE ENVIOUS, SINCE I DON'T HAVE A GIRLFRIEND.

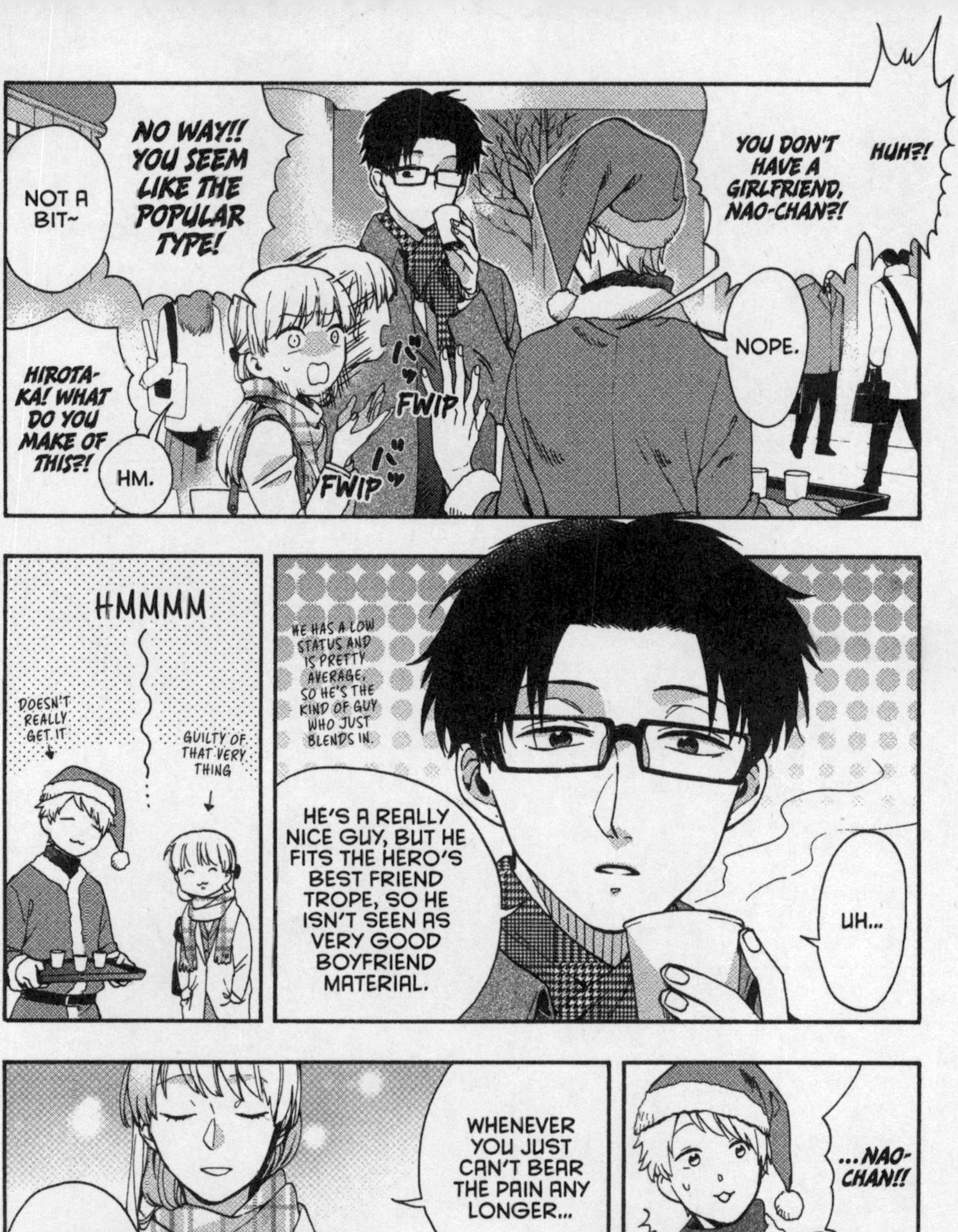
HUH?!
YOU DON'T HAVE A GIRLFRIEND, NAO-CHAN?!
NOPE.
NO WAY!! YOU SEEM LIKE THE POPULAR TYPE!
NOT A BIT~
FWIP
FWIP
HIROTAKA! WHAT DO YOU MAKE OF THIS?!
HM.
UH...
HE HAS A LOW STATUS AND IS PRETTY AVERAGE, SO HE'S THE KIND OF GUY WHO JUST BLENDS IN.
HE'S A REALLY NICE GUY, BUT HE FITS THE HERO'S BEST FRIEND TROPE, SO HE ISN'T SEEN AS VERY GOOD BOYFRIEND MATERIAL.
HMMMM
GUILTY OF THAT VERY THING
DOESN'T REALLY GET IT
...NAO-CHAN!!
YES?
TURN
WHENEVER YOU JUST CAN'T BEAR THE PAIN ANY LONGER...
SST...
REMEMBER THESE WORDS...

(Say it with me)

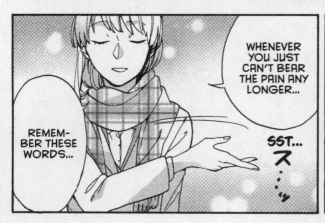

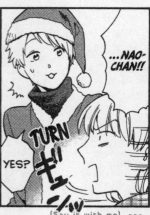

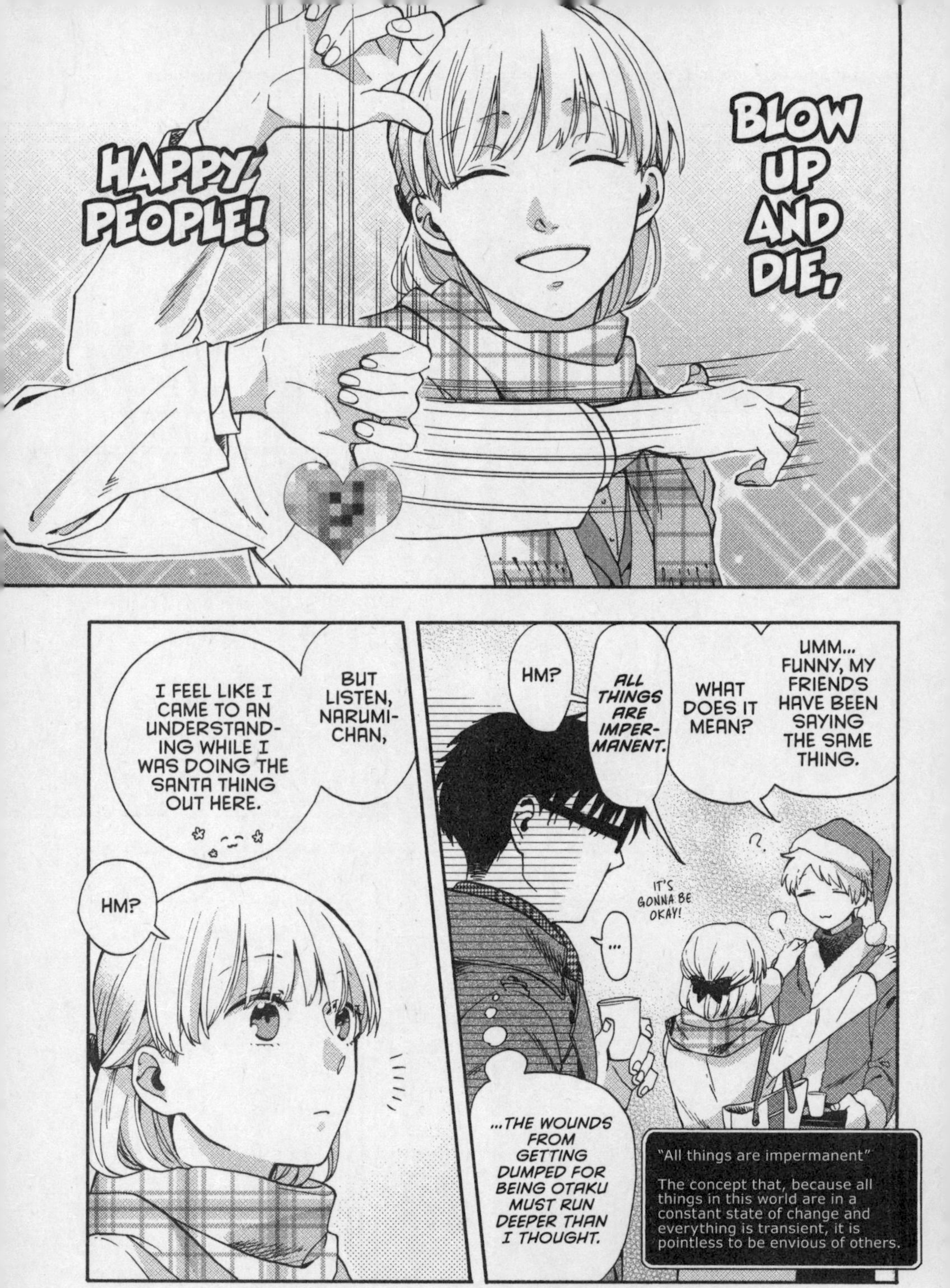
BLOW UP AND DIE,
HAPPY PEOPLE!
UMM... FUNNY, MY FRIENDS HAVE BEEN SAYING THE SAME THING.
WHAT DOES IT MEAN?
ALL THINGS ARE IMPERMANENT.
HM?
IT'S GONNA BE OKAY!
...
...THE WOUNDS FROM GETTING DUMPED FOR BEING OTAKU MUST RUN DEEPER THAN I THOUGHT.
"All things are impermanent"
The concept that, because all things in this world are in a constant state of change and everything is transient, it is pointless to be envious of others.
BUT LISTEN, NARUMI-CHAN,
I FEEL LIKE I CAME TO AN UNDERSTANDING WHILE I WAS DOING THE SANTA THING OUT HERE.
HM?

 (It's the hand sign for happiness)

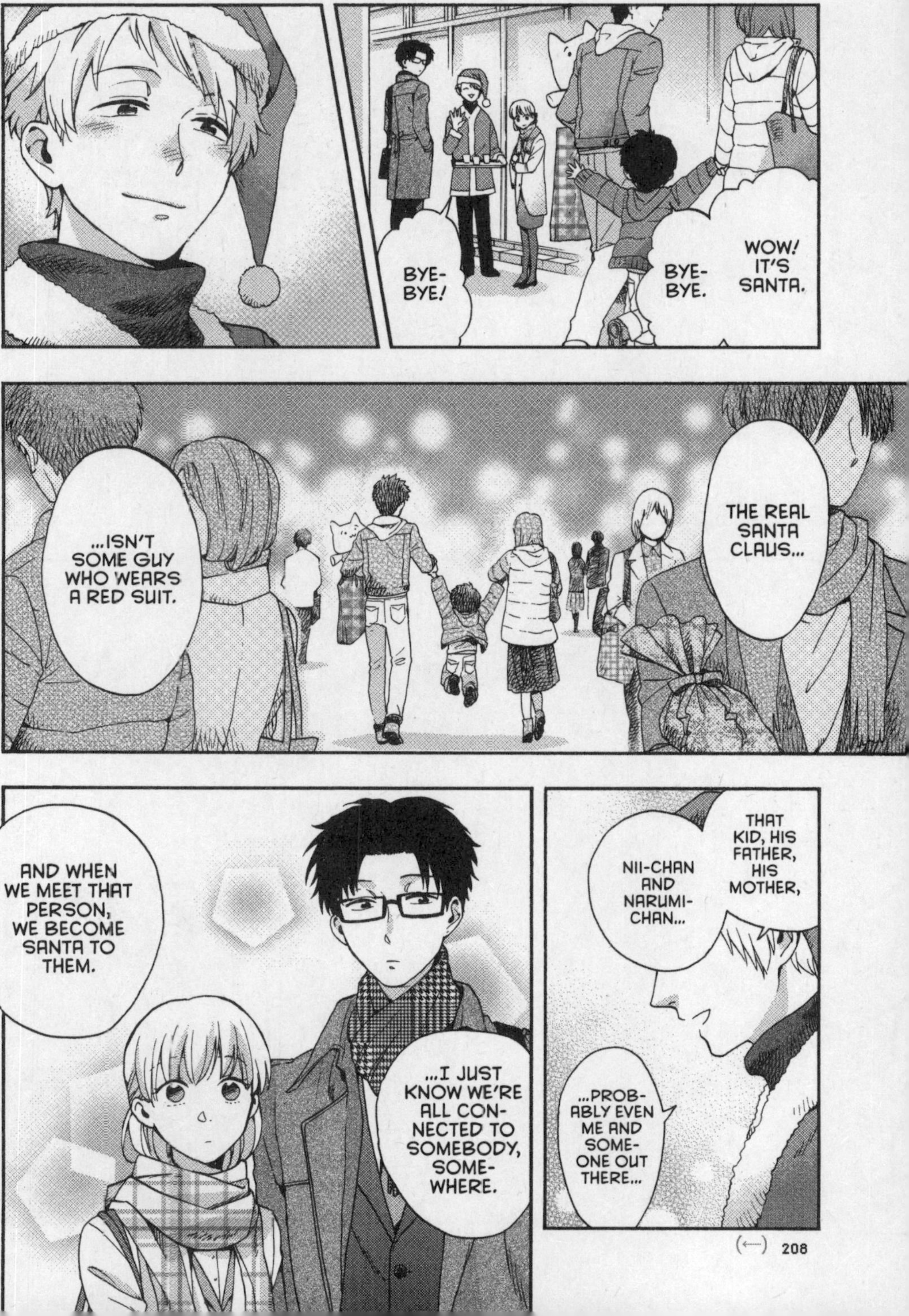
WOW! IT'S SANTA.
BYE-BYE.
BYE-BYE!
THE REAL SANTA CLAUS...
...ISN'T SOME GUY WHO WEARS A RED SUIT.
THAT KID, HIS FATHER, HIS MOTHER,
NII-CHAN AND NARUMI-CHAN...
...PROBABLY EVEN ME AND SOMEONE OUT THERE...
...I JUST KNOW WE'RE ALL CONNECTED TO SOMEBODY, SOMEWHERE.
AND WHEN WE MEET THAT PERSON, WE BECOME SANTA TO THEM.

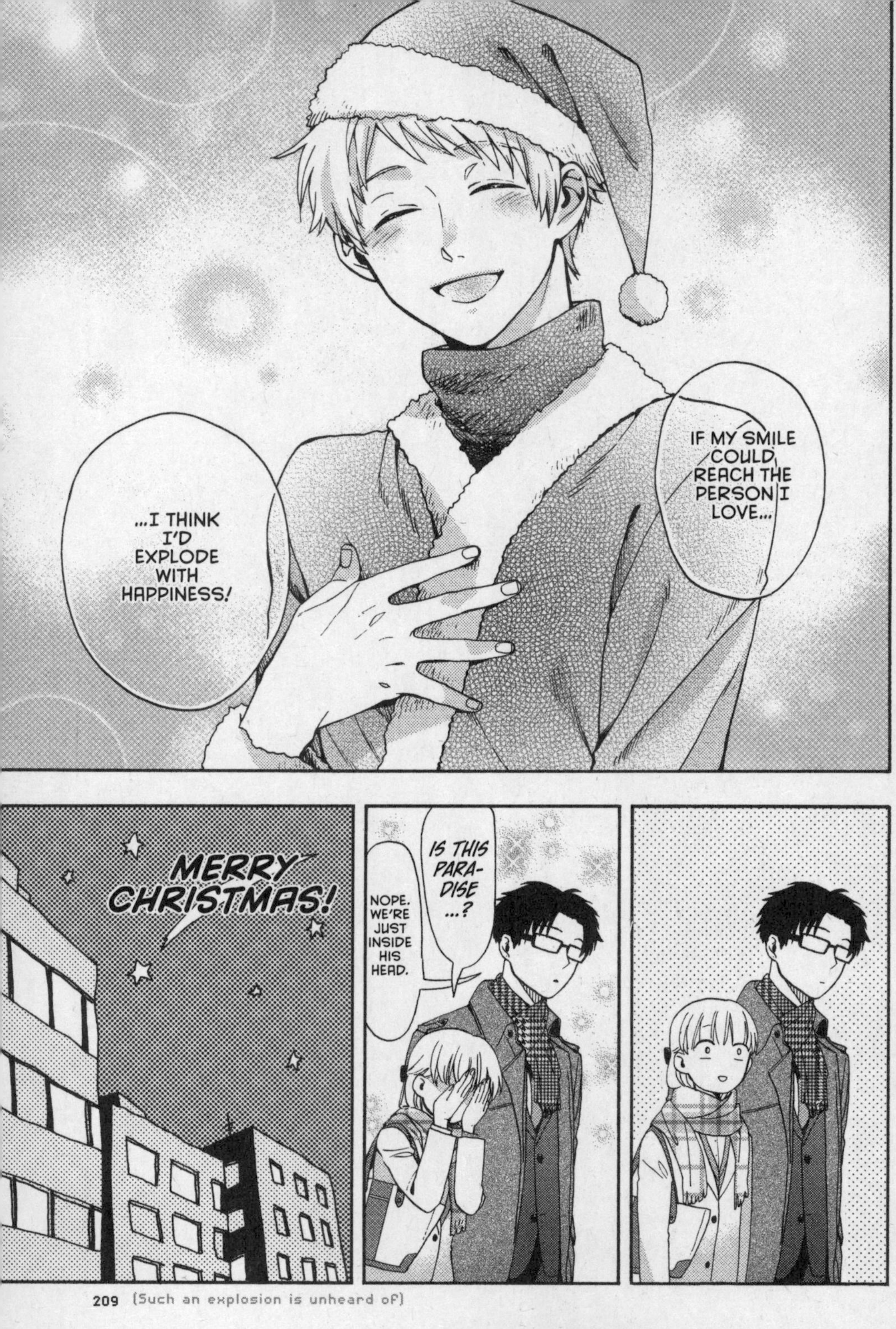
IF MY SMILE COULD REACH THE PERSON I LOVE...
...I THINK I'D EXPLODE WITH HAPPINESS!
IS THIS PARA-DISE ...?
NOPE. WE'RE JUST INSIDE HIS HEAD.
MERRY CHRISTMAS!

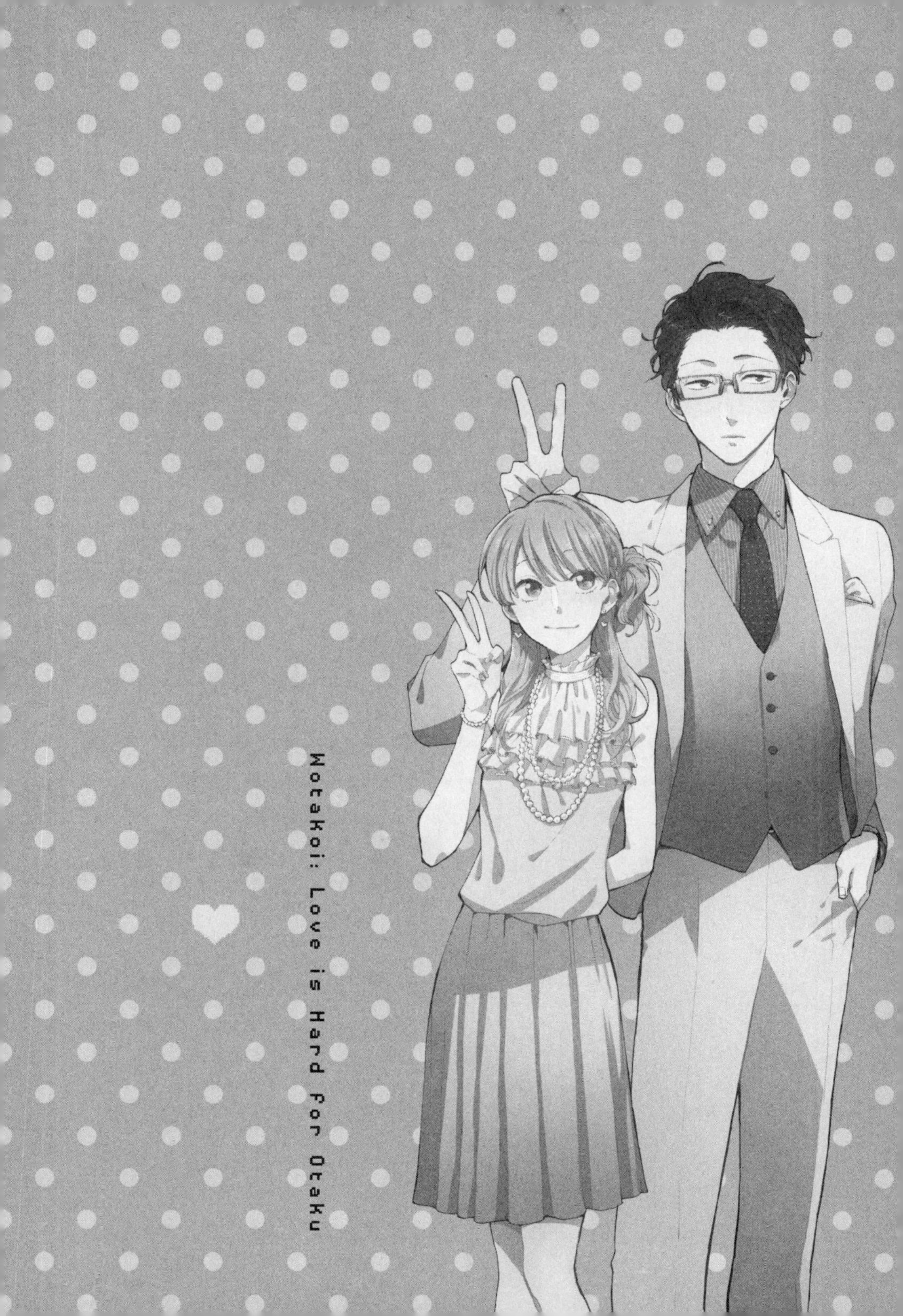
Wotakoi: Love is Hard for Otaku

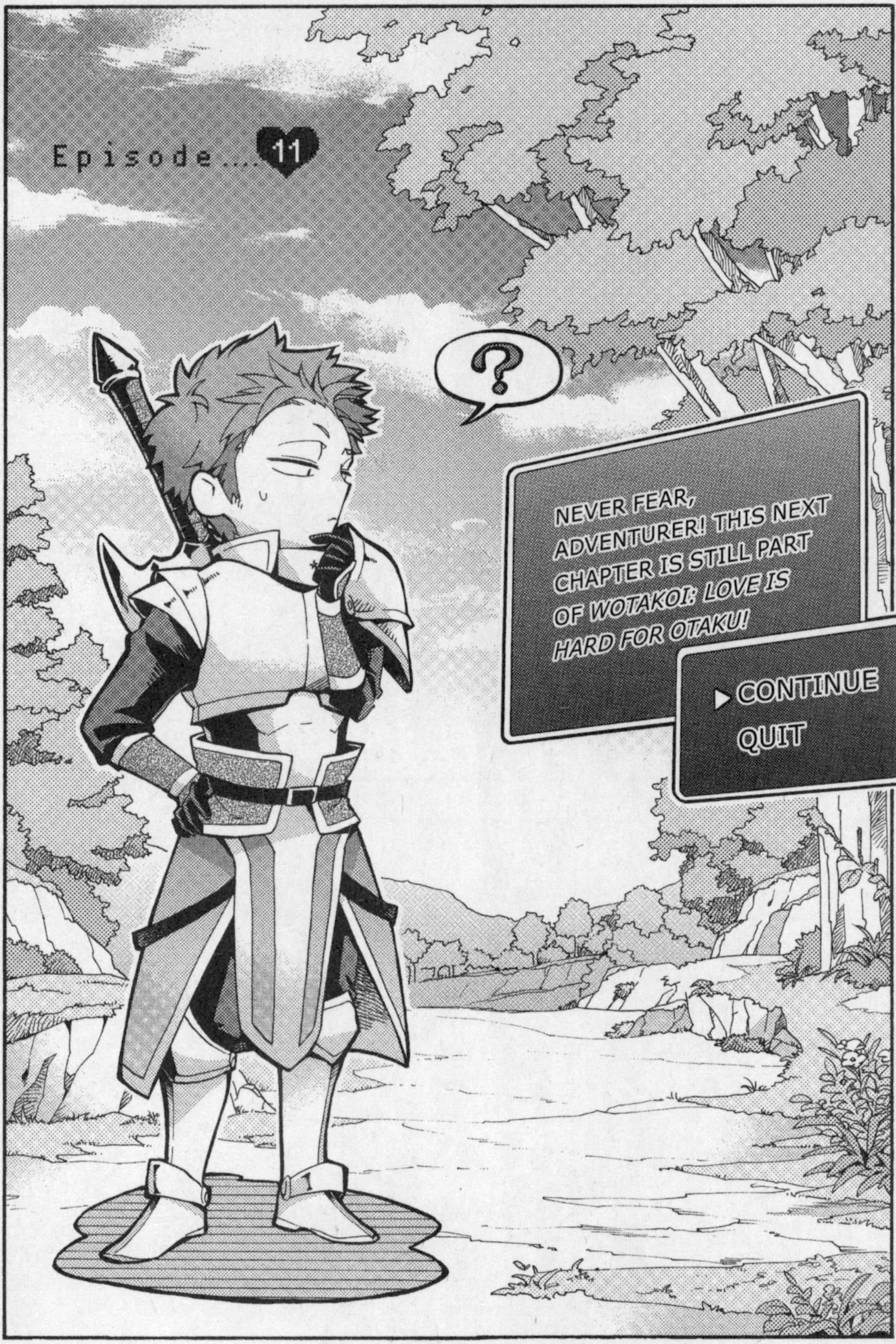
Episode.....11
?
NEVER FEAR, ADVENTURER! THIS NEXT CHAPTER IS STILL PART OF WOTAKOI: LOVE IS HARD FOR OTAKU!
▶CONTINUE
QUIT

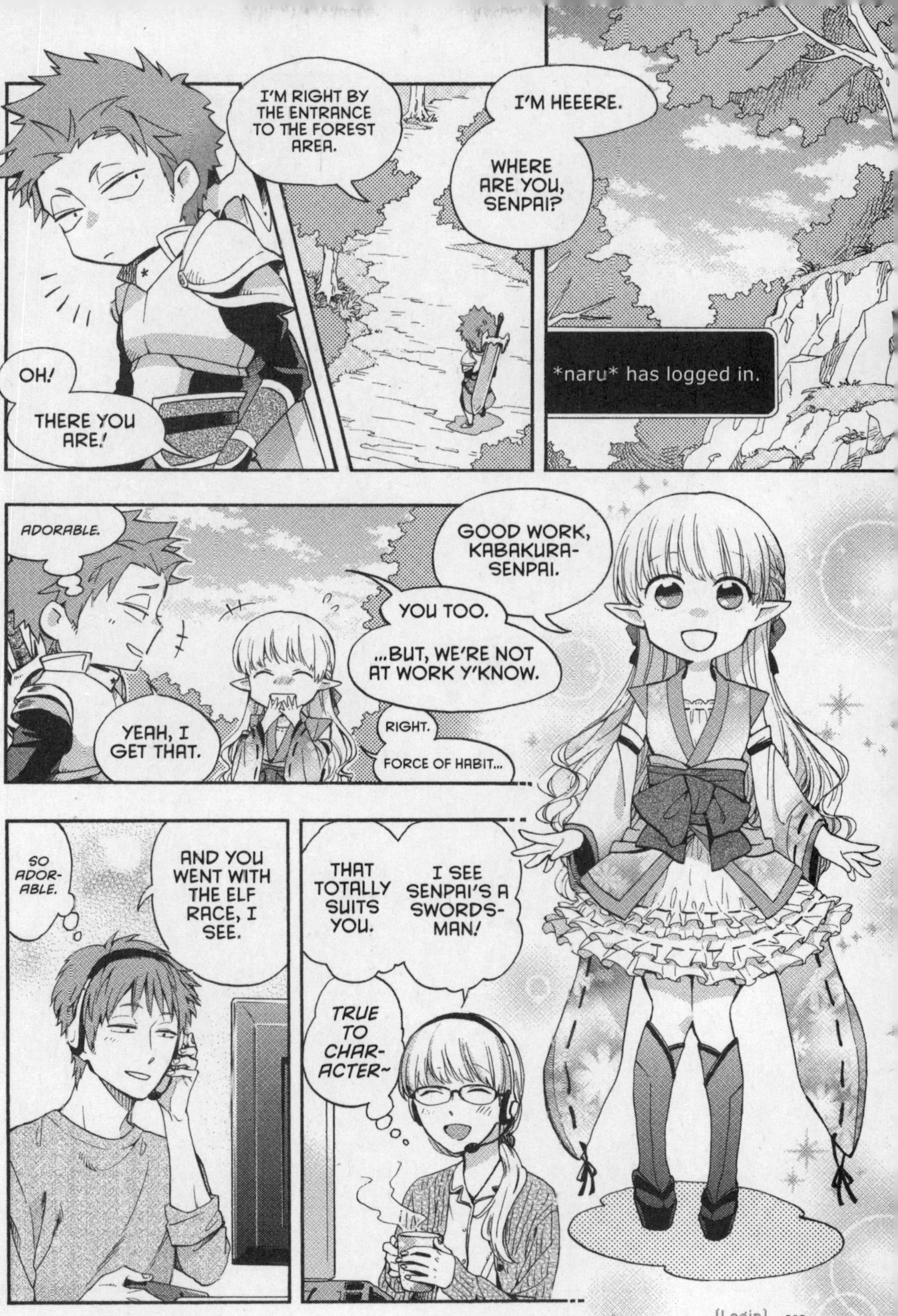
naru has logged in.
I'M HEEERE.
WHERE ARE YOU, SENPAI?
I'M RIGHT BY THE ENTRANCE TO THE FOREST AREA.
OH!
THERE YOU ARE!
GOOD WORK, KABAKURA-SENPAI.
YOU TOO.
...BUT, WE'RE NOT AT WORK Y'KNOW.
ADORABLE.
RIGHT.
FORCE OF HABIT...
YEAH, I GET THAT.
I SEE SENPAI'S A SWORDS-MAN!
THAT TOTALLY SUITS YOU.
TRUE TO CHAR-ACTER~
AND YOU WENT WITH THE ELF RACE, I SEE.
SO ADOR-ABLE.

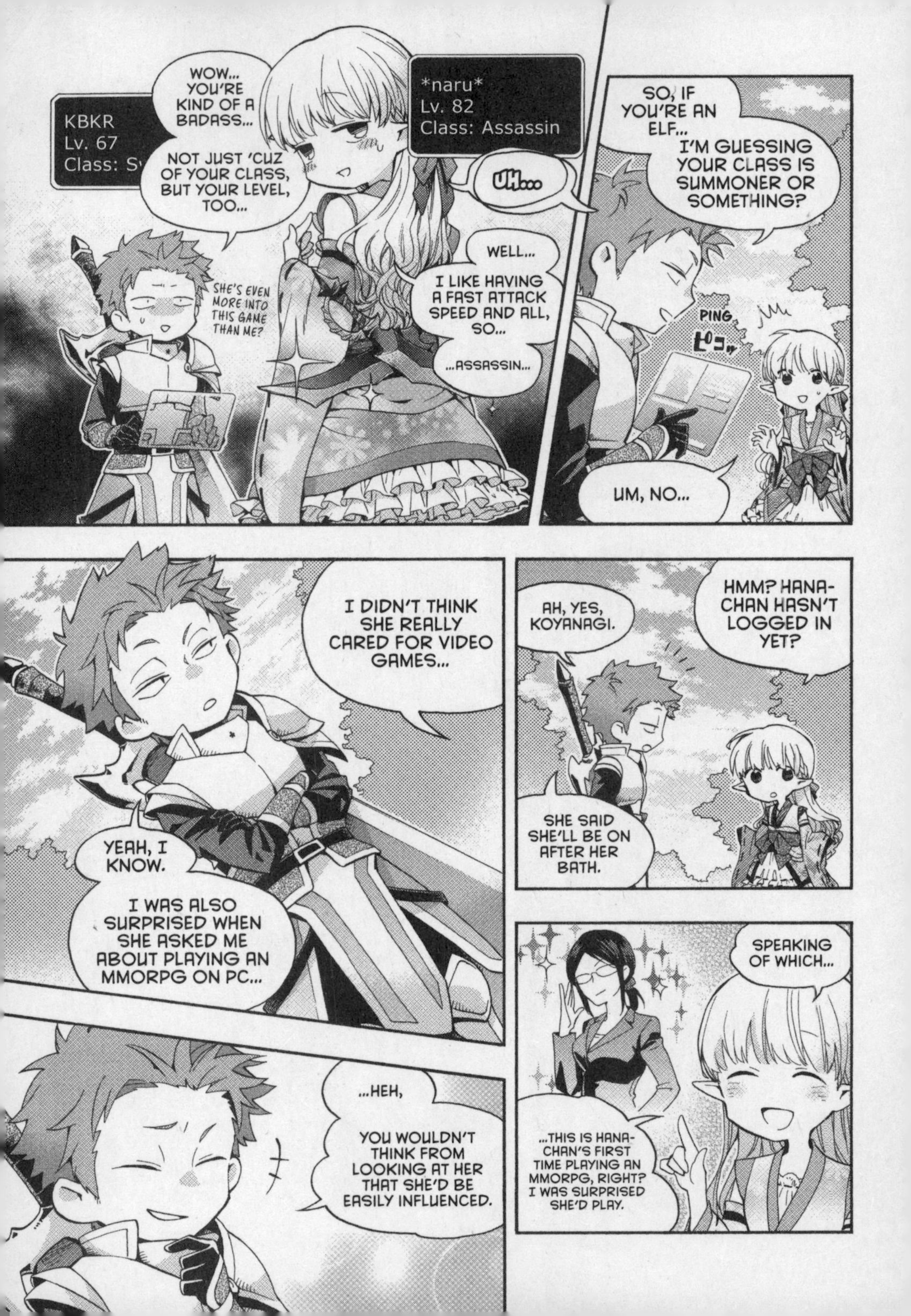
SO, IF YOU'RE AN ELF...
I'M GUESSING YOUR CLASS IS SUMMONER OR SOMETHING?
PING
UM, NO...
naru
Lv. 82
Class: Assassin
WOW... YOU'RE KIND OF A BADASS...
KBKR
Lv. 67
Class: S
NOT JUST 'CUZ OF YOUR CLASS, BUT YOUR LEVEL, TOO...
UH...
WELL...
I LIKE HAVING A FAST ATTACK SPEED AND ALL, SO...
...ASSASSIN...
SHE'S EVEN MORE INTO THIS GAME THAN ME?
HMM? HANA-CHAN HASN'T LOGGED IN YET?
AH, YES, KOYANAGI.
SHE SAID SHE'LL BE ON AFTER HER BATH.
SPEAKING OF WHICH...
...THIS IS HANA-CHAN'S FIRST TIME PLAYING AN MMORPG, RIGHT? I WAS SURPRISED SHE'D PLAY.
I DIDN'T THINK SHE REALLY CARED FOR VIDEO GAMES...
YEAH, I KNOW.
I WAS ALSO SURPRISED WHEN SHE ASKED ME ABOUT PLAYING AN MMORPG ON PC...
...HEH,
YOU WOULDN'T THINK FROM LOOKING AT HER THAT SHE'D BE EASILY INFLUENCED.

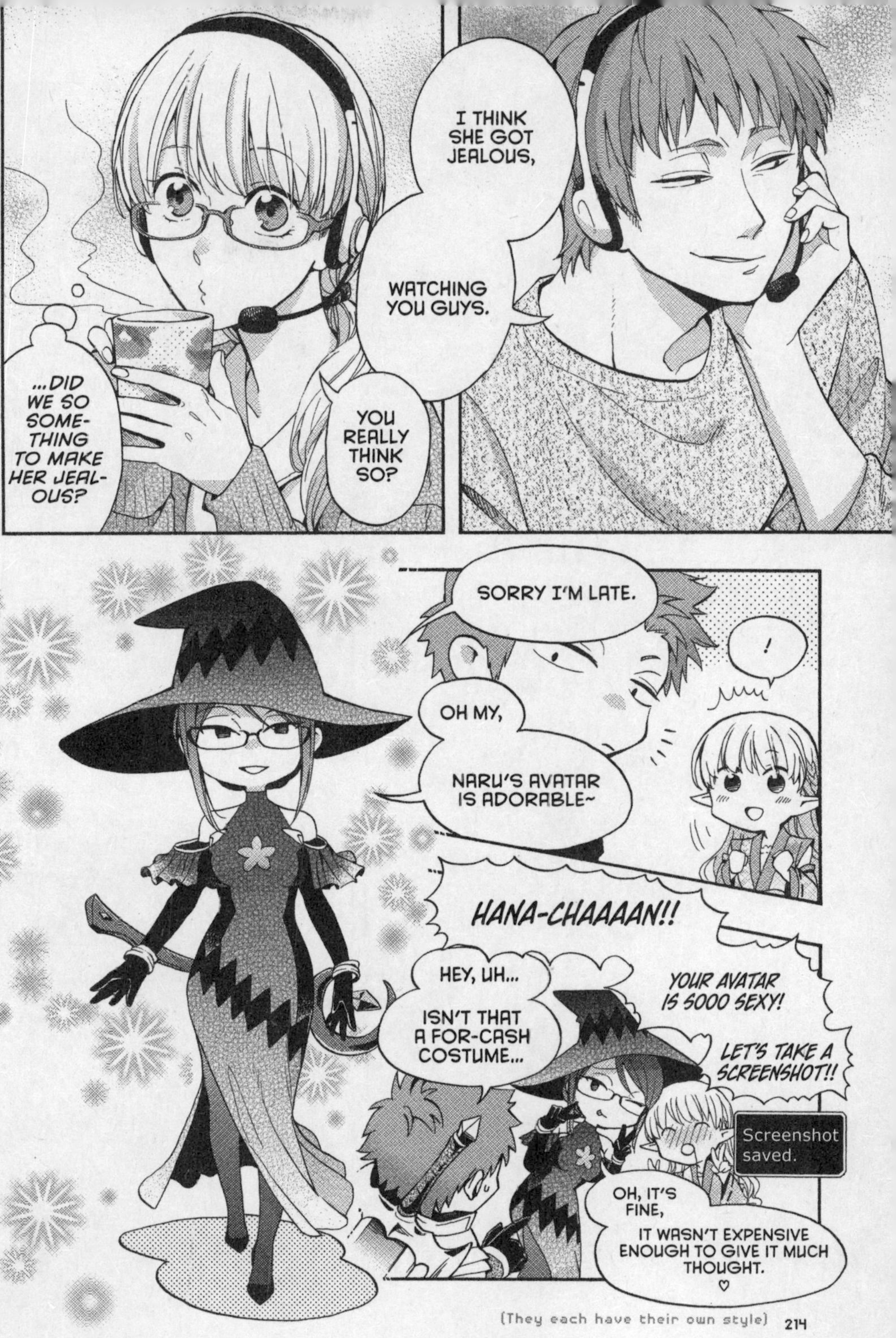
I THINK SHE GOT JEALOUS,
WATCHING YOU GUYS.
YOU REALLY THINK SO?
...DID WE SO SOMETHING TO MAKE HER JEALOUS?
SORRY I'M LATE.
!
OH MY,
NARU'S AVATAR IS ADORABLE~
HANA-CHAAAAN!!
YOUR AVATAR IS SOOO SEXY!
LET'S TAKE A SCREENSHOT!!
HEY, UH...
ISN'T THAT A FOR-CASH COSTUME...
Screenshot saved.
OH, IT'S FINE,
IT WASN'T EXPENSIVE ENOUGH TO GIVE IT MUCH THOUGHT. ♡

(They each have their own style)

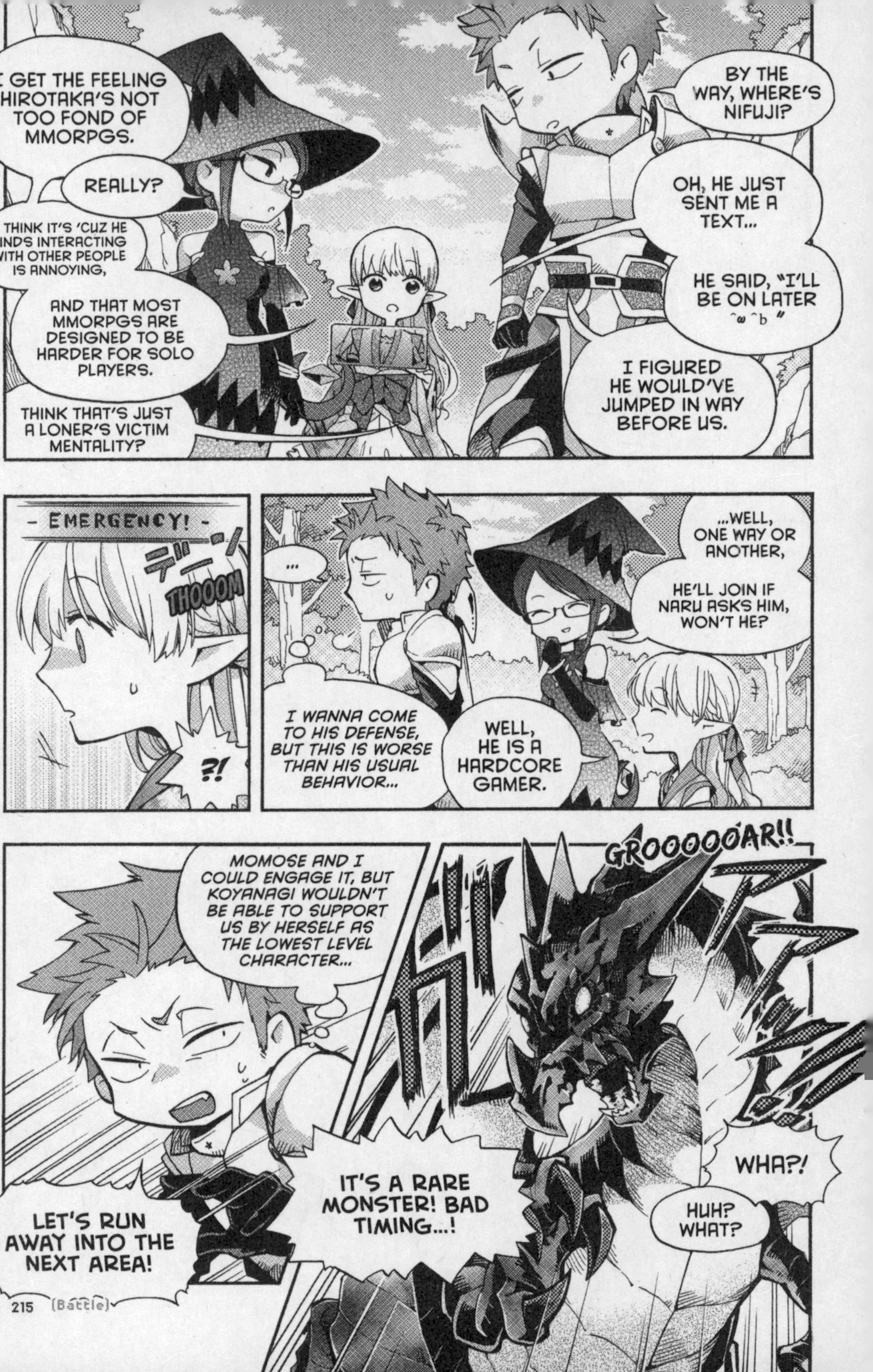
BY THE WAY, WHERE'S NIFUJI?
OH, HE JUST SENT ME A TEXT...
HE SAID, "I'LL BE ON LATER ^ω^b"
I FIGURED HE WOULD'VE JUMPED IN WAY BEFORE US.
I GET THE FEELING HIROTAKA'S NOT TOO FOND OF MMORPGS.
REALLY?
I THINK IT'S 'CUZ HE FINDS INTERACTING WITH OTHER PEOPLE IS ANNOYING,
AND THAT MOST MMORPGS ARE DESIGNED TO BE HARDER FOR SOLO PLAYERS.
THINK THAT'S JUST A LONER'S VICTIM MENTALITY?
...WELL, ONE WAY OR ANOTHER,
HE'LL JOIN IF NARU ASKS HIM, WON'T HE?
...
WELL, HE IS A HARDCORE GAMER.
I WANNA COME TO HIS DEFENSE, BUT THIS IS WORSE THAN HIS USUAL BEHAVIOR...
- EMERGENCY! -
デーン
THOOOM
?!
GROOOOOOAR!!
WHA?!
HUH? WHAT?
IT'S A RARE MONSTER! BAD TIMING...!
MOMOSE AND I COULD ENGAGE IT, BUT KOYANAGI WOULDN'T BE ABLE TO SUPPORT US BY HERSELF AS THE LOWEST LEVEL CHARACTER...
LET'S RUN AWAY INTO THE NEXT AREA!

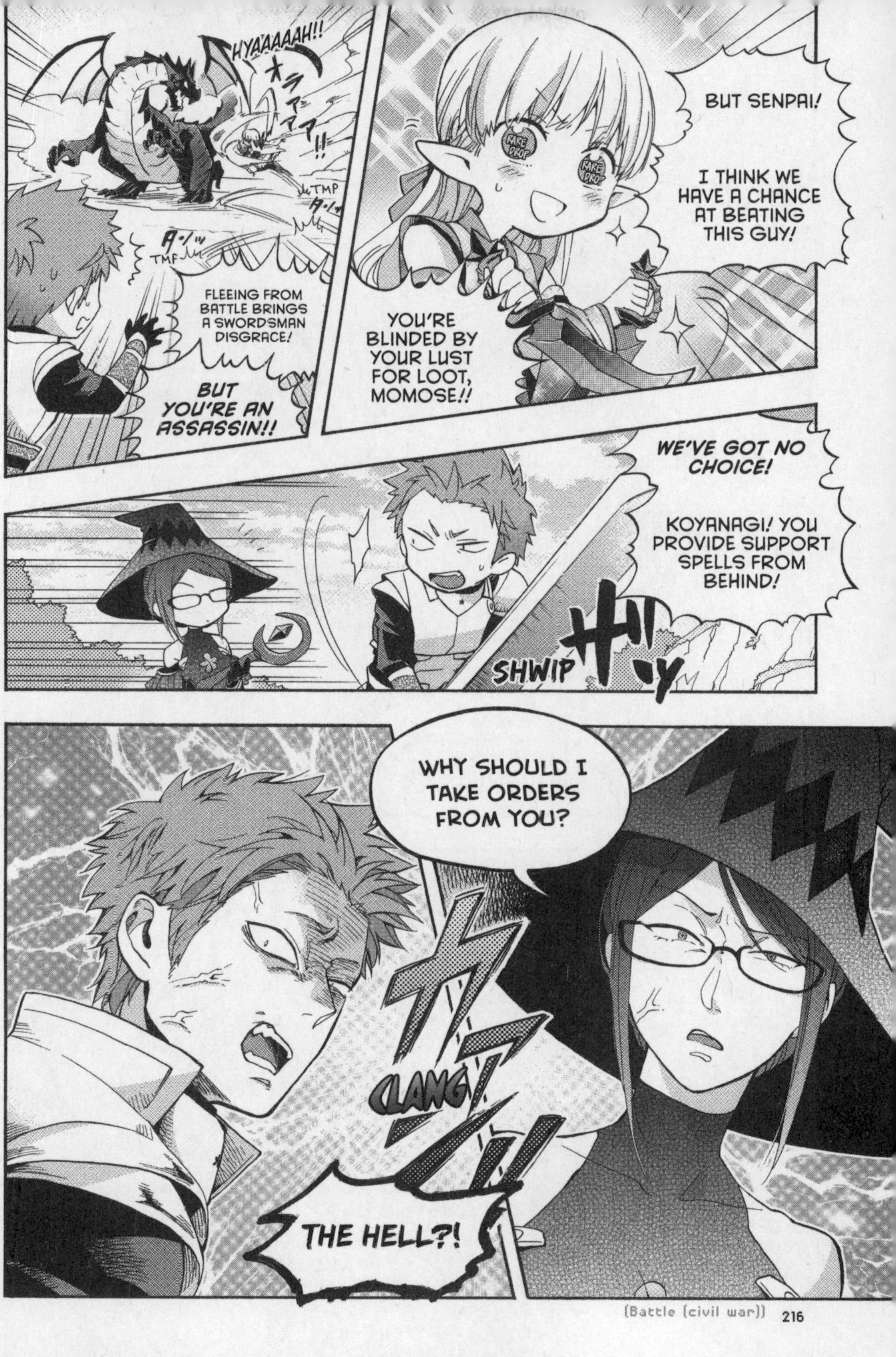
BUT SENPAI!
RARE DROP
RARE DROP
I THINK WE HAVE A CHANCE AT BEATING THIS GUY!
YOU'RE BLINDED BY YOUR LUST FOR LOOT, MOMOSE!!
HYAAAAAH!!
TMP
TMF
FLEEING FROM BATTLE BRINGS A SWORDSMAN DISGRACE!
BUT YOU'RE AN ASSASSIN!!
WE'VE GOT NO CHOICE!
KOYANAGI! YOU PROVIDE SUPPORT SPELLS FROM BEHIND!
SHWIP
WHY SHOULD I TAKE ORDERS FROM YOU?
CLANG
THE HELL?!

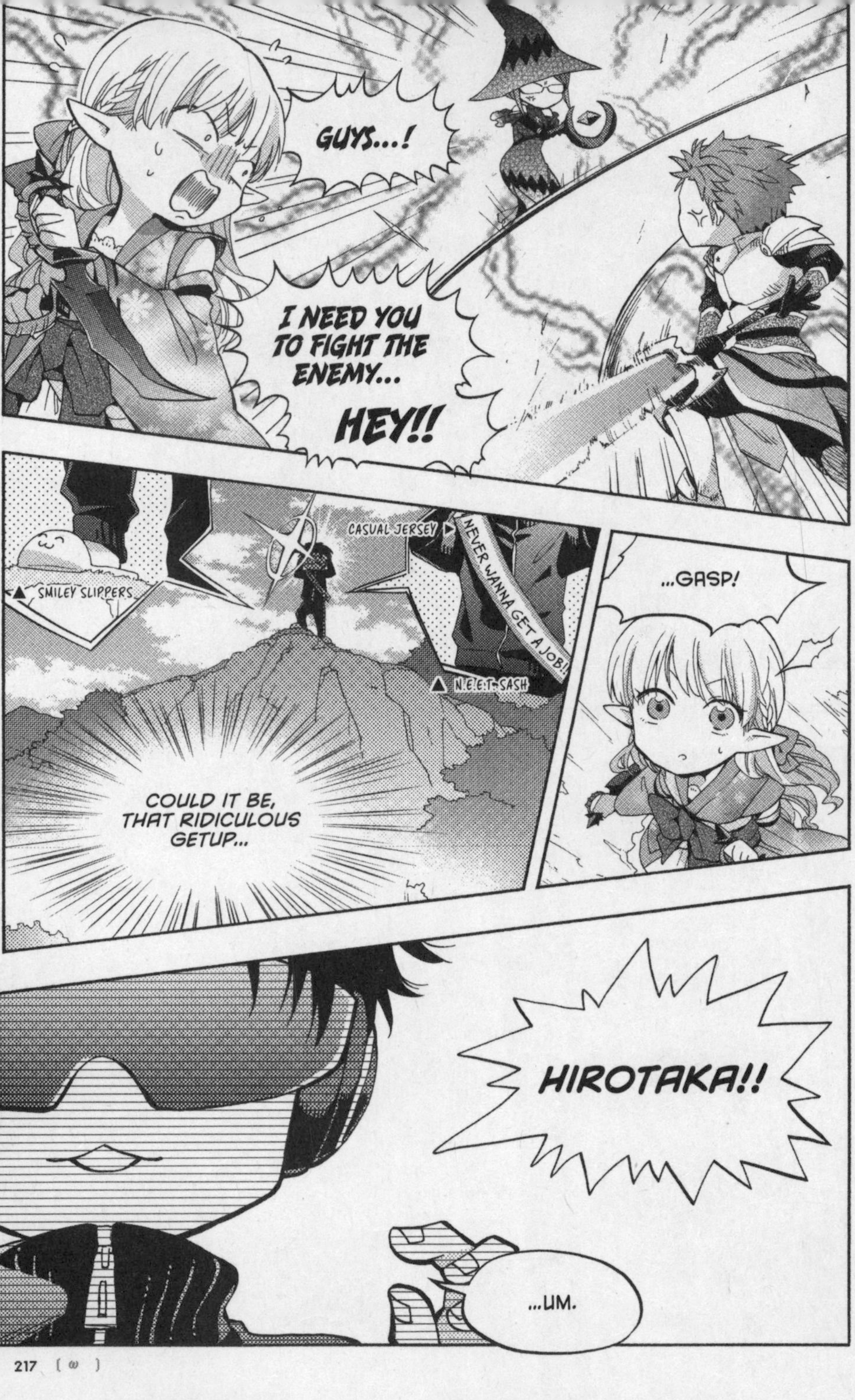
GUYS...!
I NEED YOU TO FIGHT THE ENEMY...
HEY!!
...GASP!
CASUAL JERSEY ▶
NEVER WANNA GET A JOB!!
▲ N.E.E.T. SASH
▲ SMILEY SLIPPERS
COULD IT BE, THAT RIDICULOUS GETUP...
HIROTAKA!!
...UM.

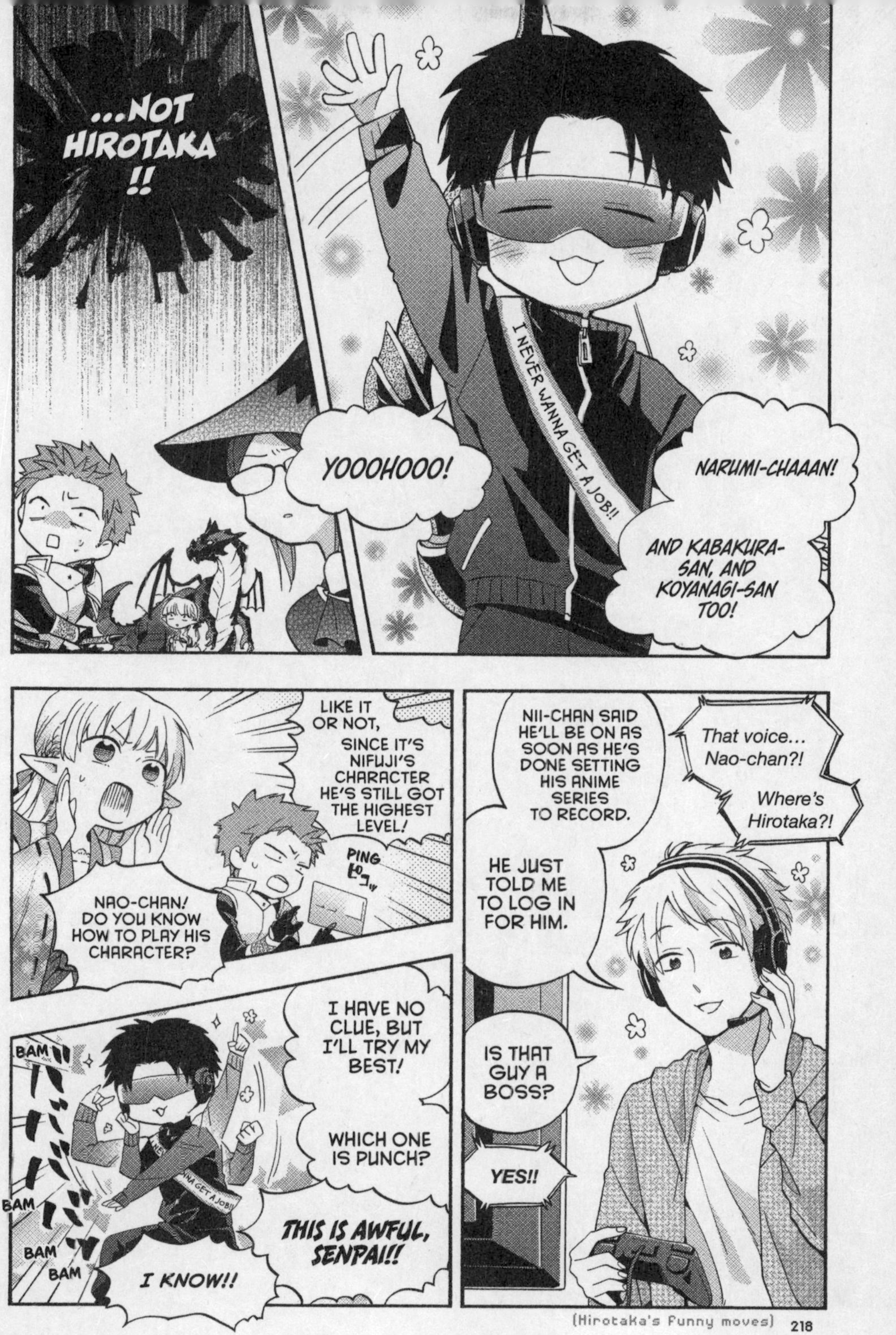

NARUMI-CHAAAN!
AND KABAKURA-SAN, AND KOYANAGI-SAN TOO!
I NEVER WANNA GET A JOB!!
YOOOHOOO!
...NOT HIROTAKA!!
That voice... Nao-chan?!
Where's Hirotaka?!
NII-CHAN SAID HE'LL BE ON AS SOON AS HE'S DONE SETTING HIS ANIME SERIES TO RECORD.
HE JUST TOLD ME TO LOG IN FOR HIM.
IS THAT GUY A BOSS?
YES!!
LIKE IT OR NOT, SINCE IT'S NIFUJI'S CHARACTER HE'S STILL GOT THE HIGHEST LEVEL!
PING
NAO-CHAN! DO YOU KNOW HOW TO PLAY HIS CHARACTER?
I HAVE NO CLUE, BUT I'LL TRY MY BEST!
WHICH ONE IS PUNCH?
BAM
BAM
BAM
BAM
THIS IS AWFUL, SENPAI!!
I KNOW!!

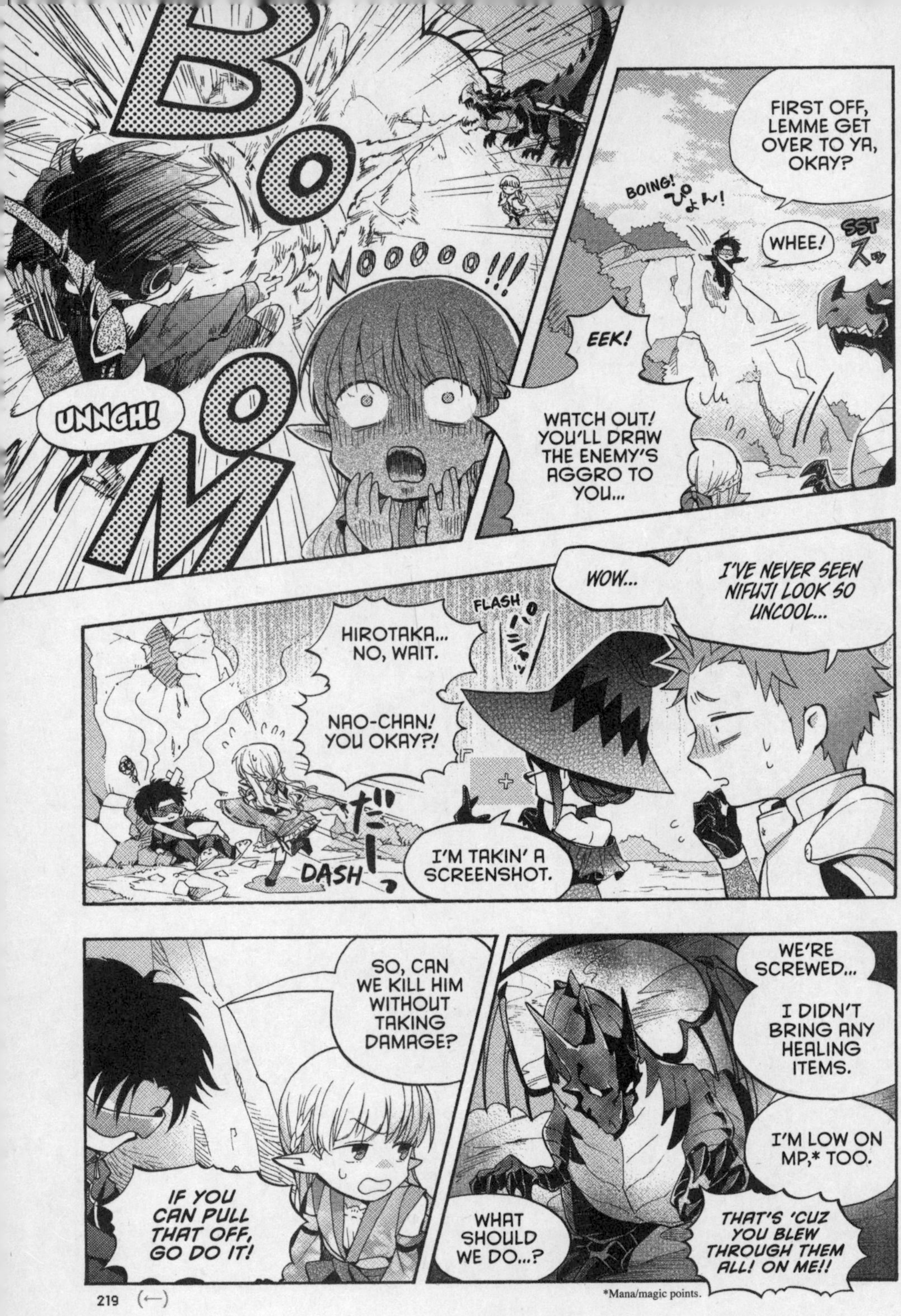
FIRST OFF, LEMME GET OVER TO YA, OKAY?
BOING! ぴょん!
WHEE!
SST スッ
EEK!
WATCH OUT! YOU'LL DRAW THE ENEMY'S AGGRO TO YOU...
BOOOM
NOOOOOO!!!
UNNGH!
WOW...
I'VE NEVER SEEN NIFUJI LOOK SO UNCOOL...
FLASH パシャッ
HIROTAKA... NO, WAIT.
NAO-CHAN! YOU OKAY?!
I'M TAKIN' A SCREENSHOT.
DASH だーっ
WE'RE SCREWED...
I DIDN'T BRING ANY HEALING ITEMS.
I'M LOW ON MP,* TOO.
THAT'S 'CUZ YOU BLEW THROUGH THEM ALL! ON ME!!
WHAT SHOULD WE DO...?
SO, CAN WE KILL HIM WITHOUT TAKING DAMAGE?
IF YOU CAN PULL THAT OFF, GO DO IT!

*Mana/magic points.

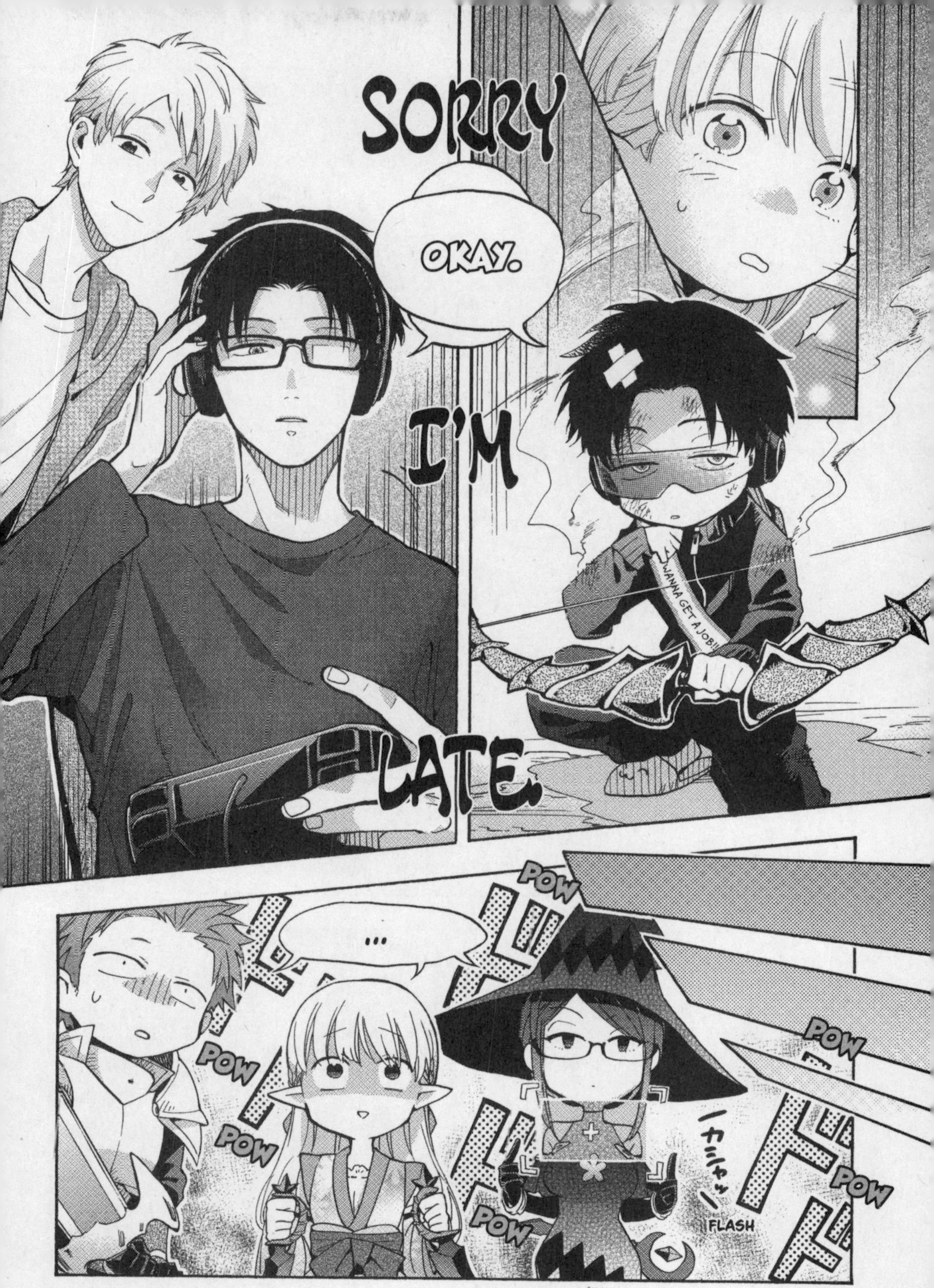
WANNA GET A JOB!!
OKAY.
SORRY
I'M
LATE.
POW
...
POW
カシャッ
FLASH
POW
POW
POW
POW

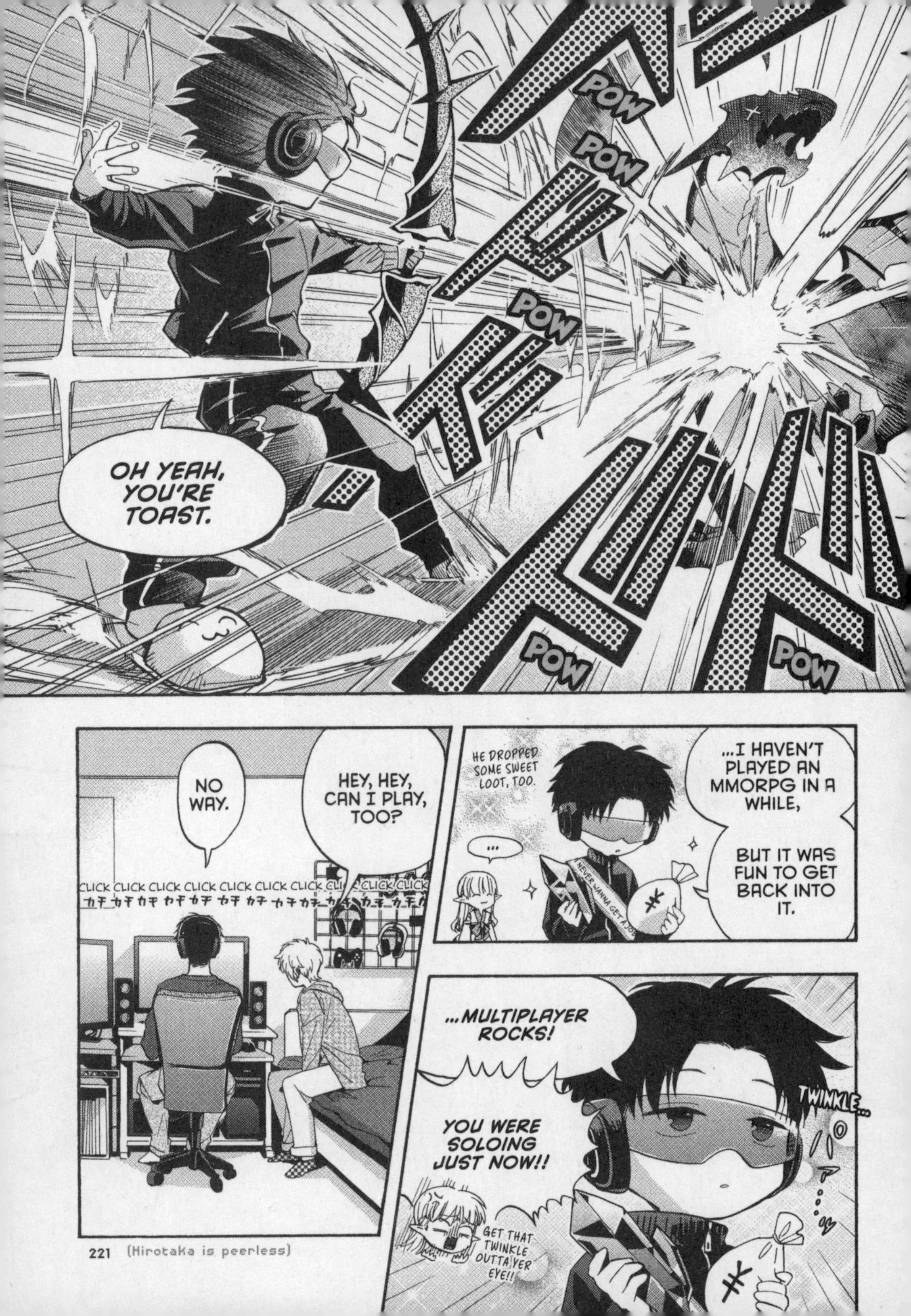
POW
POW
POW
OH YEAH, YOU'RE TOAST.
POW
POW
...I HAVEN'T PLAYED AN MMORPG IN A WHILE,
BUT IT WAS FUN TO GET BACK INTO IT.
HE DROPPED SOME SWEET LOOT, TOO.
...
NEVER WANNA GET A JOB
...MULTIPLAYER ROCKS!
TWINKLE...
YOU WERE SOLOING JUST NOW!!
GET THAT TWINKLE OUTTA YER EYE!!
HEY, HEY, CAN I PLAY, TOO?
NO WAY.
CLICK CLICK CLICK CLICK CLICK CLICK CLICK CLICK CLICK CLICK

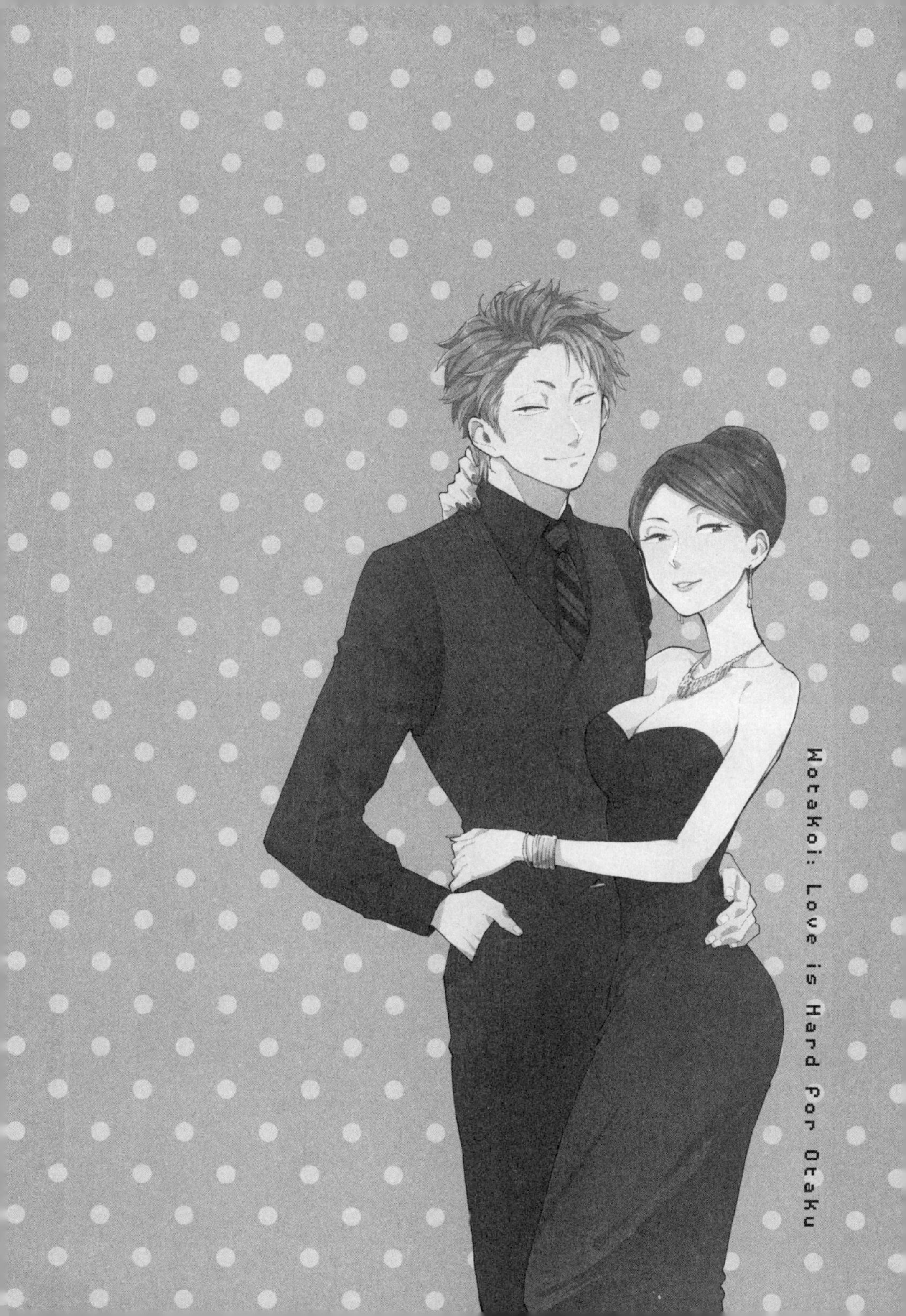
Wotakoi: Love is Hard for Otaku

Episode.... 12

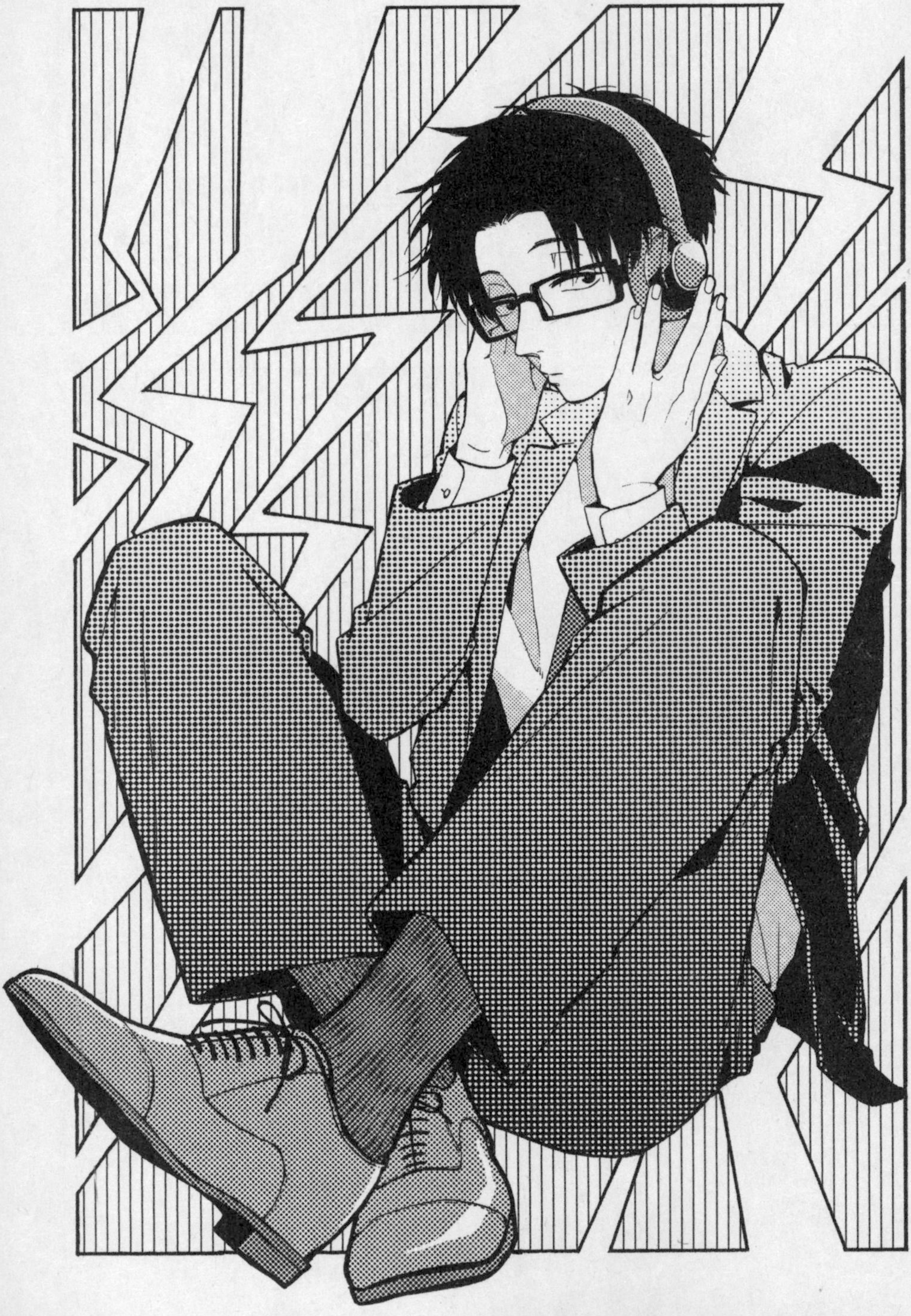

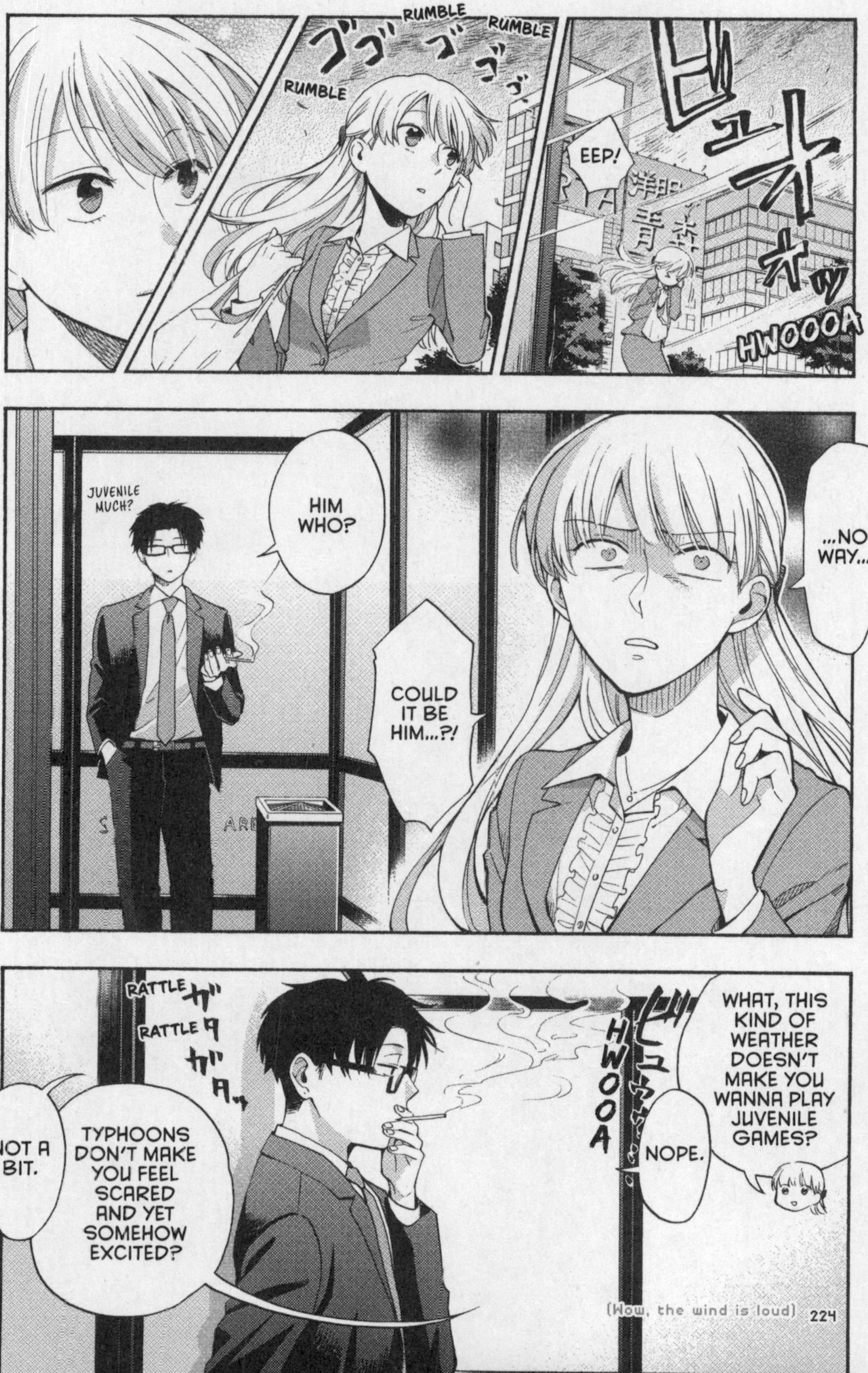
EEP!
ビュオオッ
HWOOOA
RUMBLE
RUMBLE
ゴゴゴゴ
RUMBLE
...NO WAY...
COULD IT BE HIM...?!
HIM WHO?
JUVENILE MUCH?
WHAT, THIS KIND OF WEATHER DOESN'T MAKE YOU WANNA PLAY JUVENILE GAMES?
NOPE.
HWOOOA
TYPHOONS DON'T MAKE YOU FEEL SCARED AND YET SOMEHOW EXCITED?
NOT A BIT.
RATTLE
RATTLE
(Wow, the wind is loud)

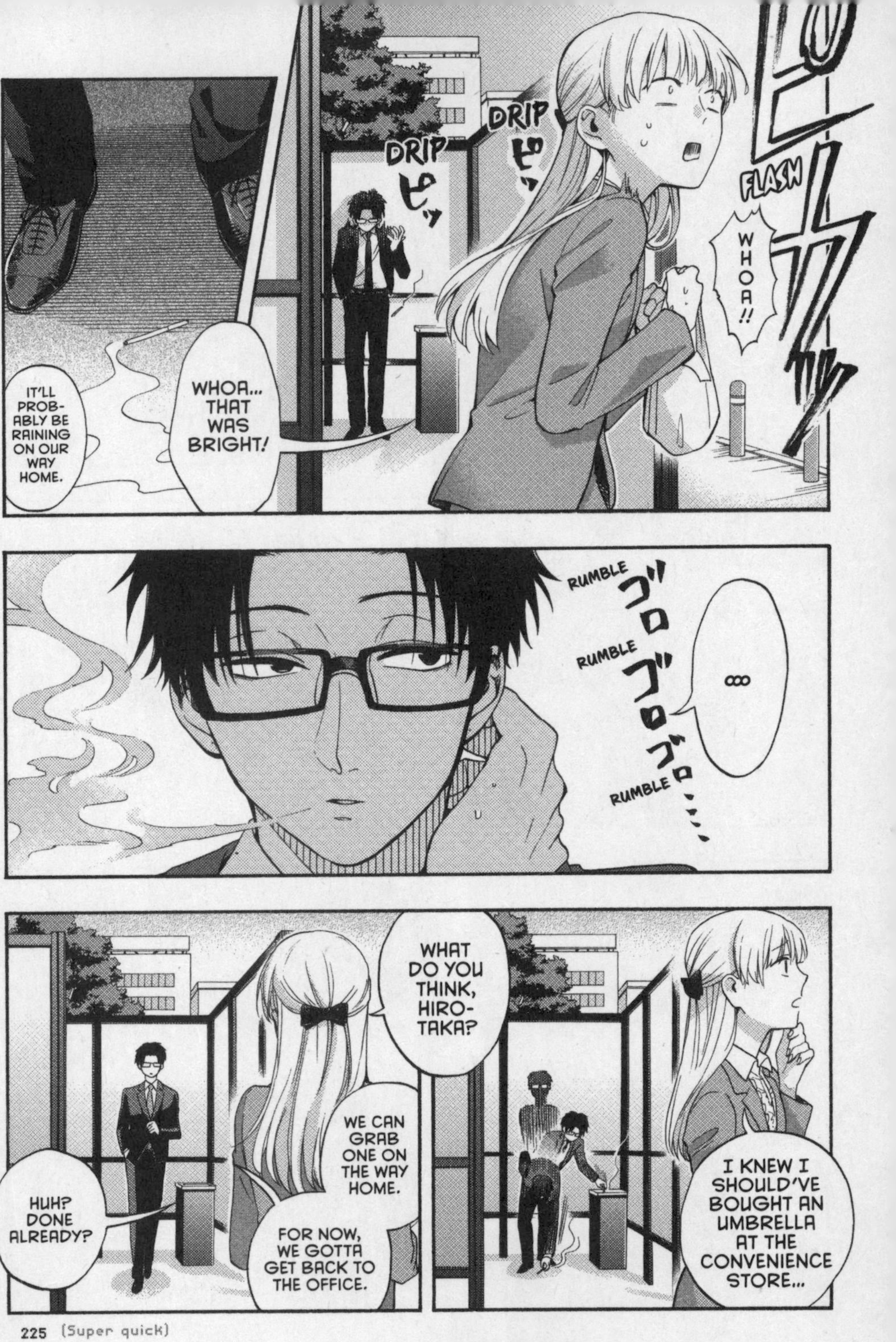
FLASH
WHOA!!
DRIP ピッ
DRIP ピッ
WHOA... THAT WAS BRIGHT!
IT'LL PROBABLY BE RAINING ON OUR WAY HOME.
RUMBLE ゴロ
RUMBLE ゴロ
RUMBLE ゴロ...
...
I KNEW I SHOULD'VE BOUGHT AN UMBRELLA AT THE CONVENIENCE STORE...
WHAT DO YOU THINK, HIRO-TAKA?
WE CAN GRAB ONE ON THE WAY HOME.
FOR NOW, WE GOTTA GET BACK TO THE OFFICE.
HUH? DONE ALREADY?

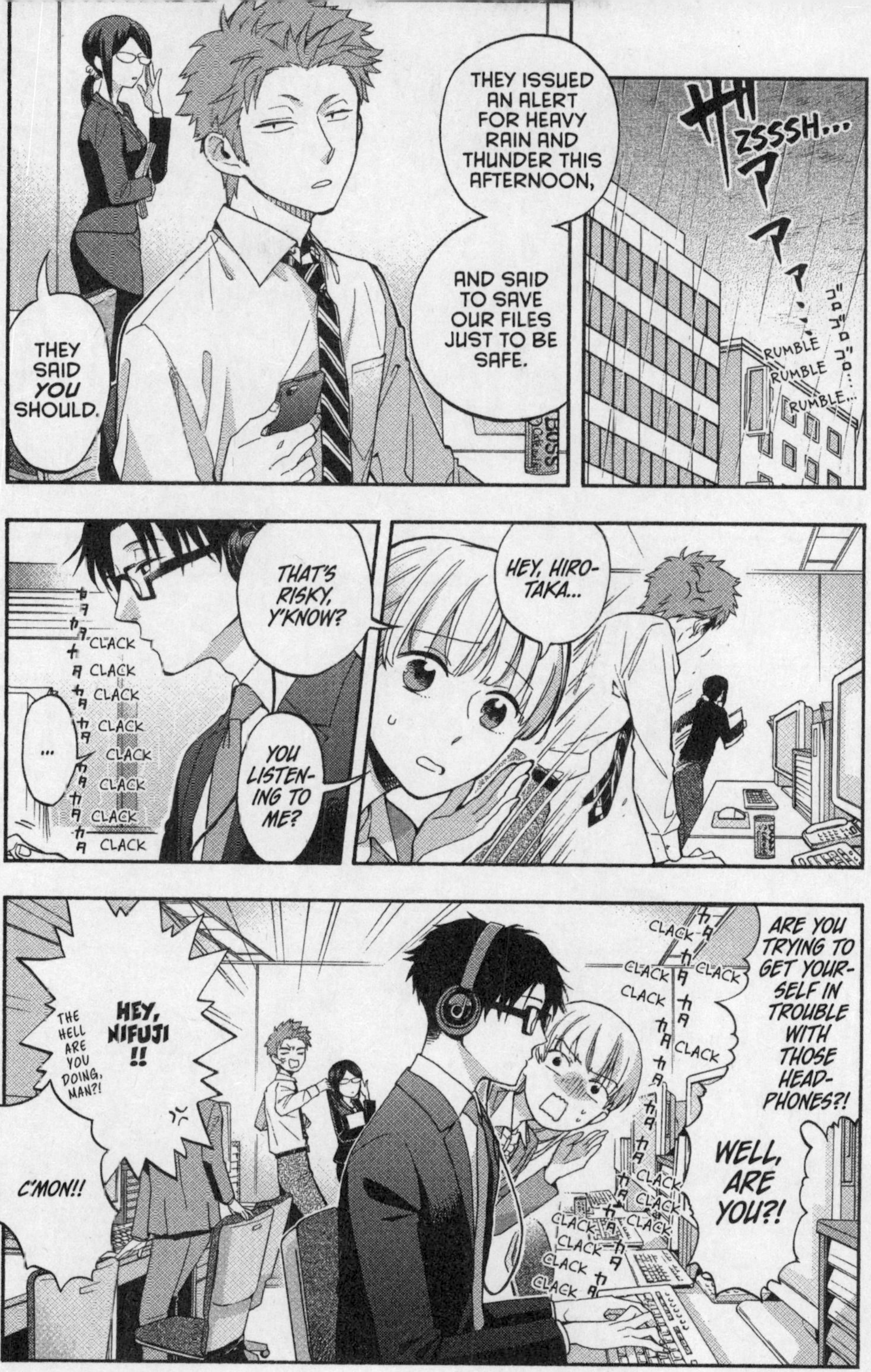
ZSSSH...
RUMBLE
RUMBLE
RUMBLE...
THEY ISSUED AN ALERT FOR HEAVY RAIN AND THUNDER THIS AFTERNOON,
AND SAID TO SAVE OUR FILES JUST TO BE SAFE.
THEY SAID YOU SHOULD.
HEY, HIRO-TAKA...
THAT'S RISKY, Y'KNOW?
YOU LISTEN-ING TO ME?
CLACK CLACK CLACK CLACK CLACK CLACK CLACK CLACK
...
ARE YOU TRYING TO GET YOUR-SELF IN TROUBLE WITH THOSE HEAD-PHONES?!
WELL, ARE YOU?!
CLACK CLACK CLACK CLACK CLACK CLACK CLACK CLACK CLACK CLACK CLACK
HEY, NIFUJI!!
THE HELL ARE YOU DOING, MAN?!
C'MON!!

(Don't try this at home, kids)

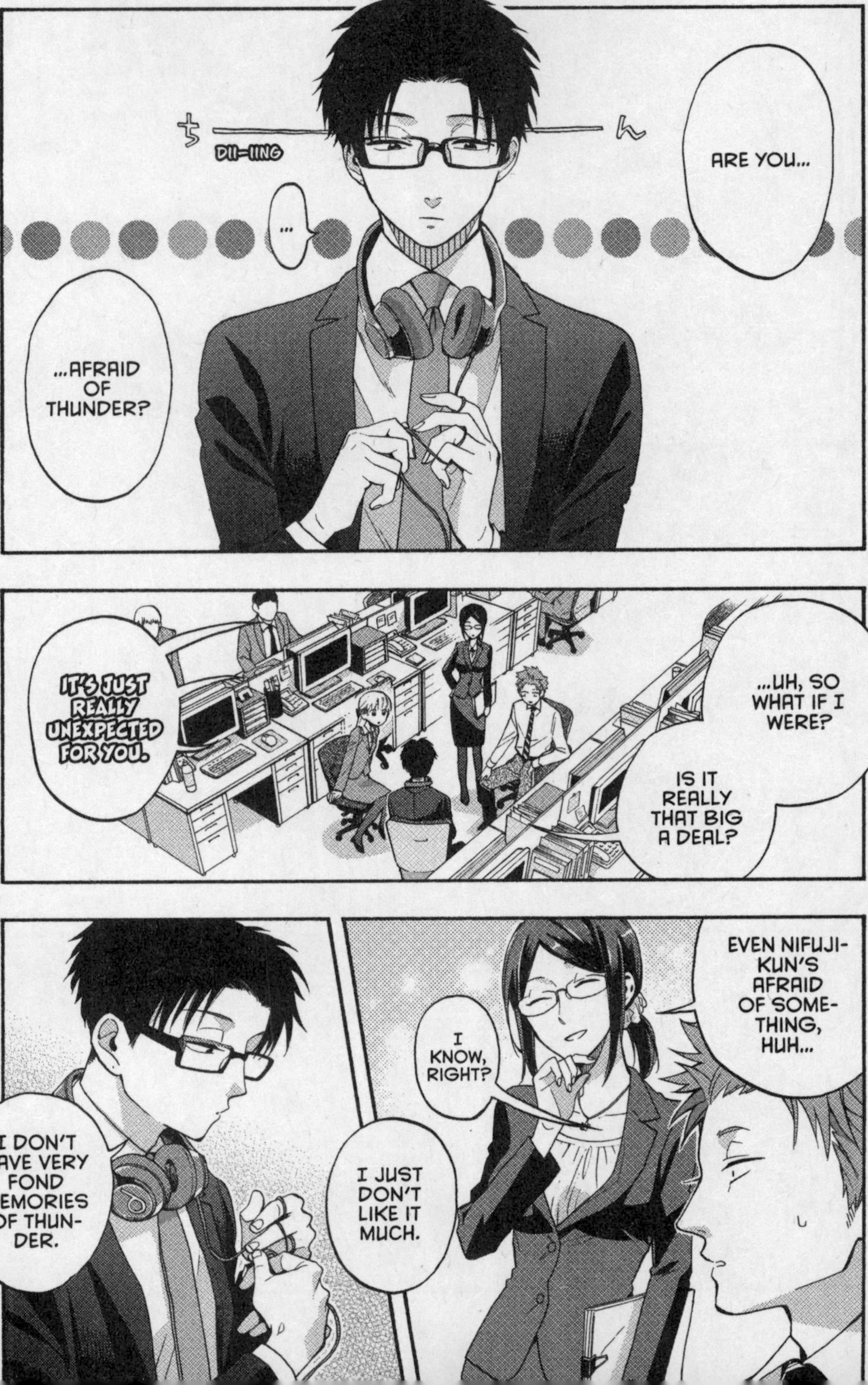
ARE YOU...
ち——ん
DII-IING
...
...AFRAID OF THUNDER?
...UH, SO WHAT IF I WERE?
IS IT REALLY THAT BIG A DEAL?
IT'S JUST REALLY UNEXPECTED FOR YOU.
EVEN NIFUJI-KUN'S AFRAID OF SOME-THING, HUH...
I KNOW, RIGHT?
I JUST DON'T LIKE IT MUCH.
I DON'T HAVE VERY FOND MEMORIES OF THUN-DER.

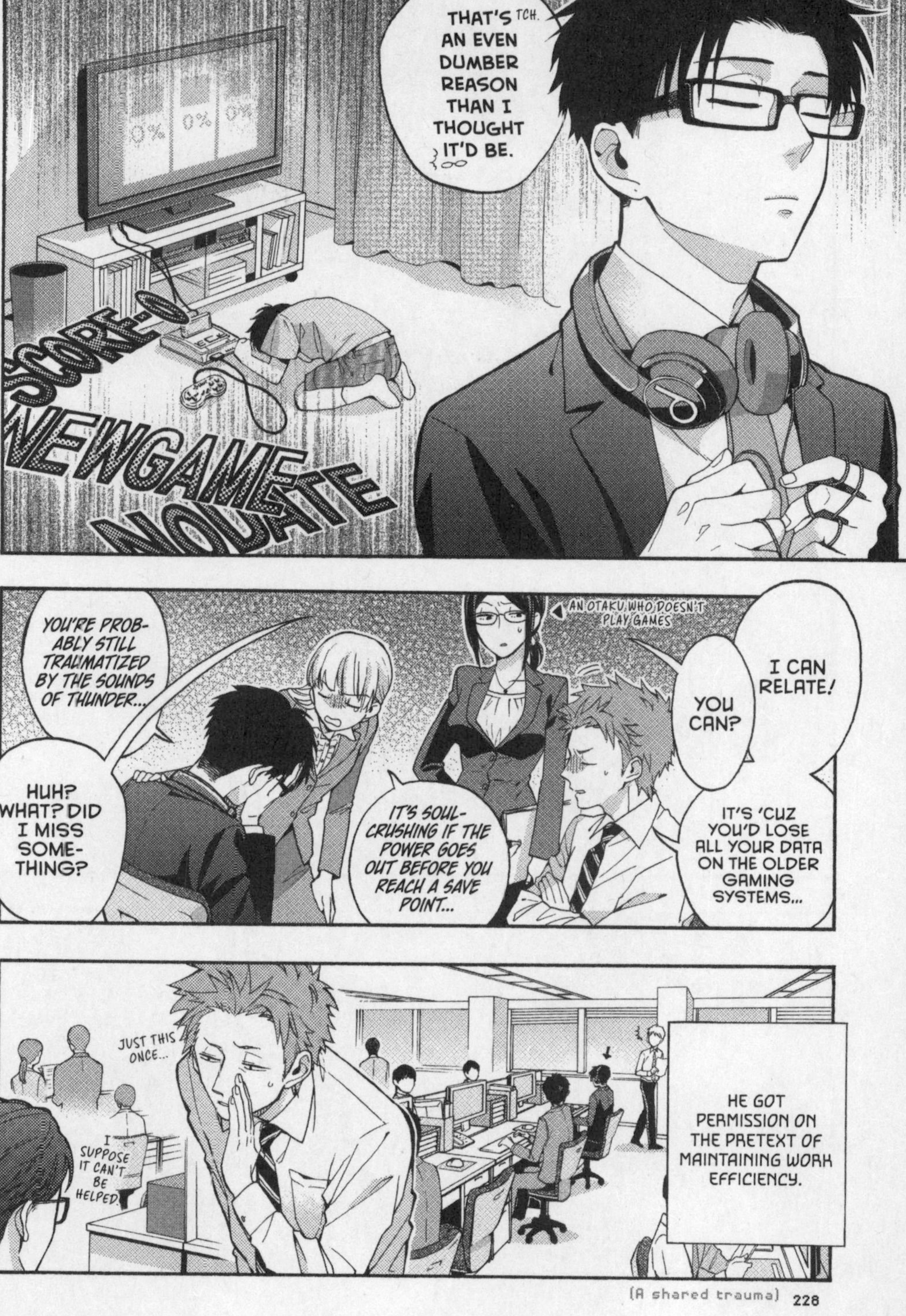
THAT'S AN EVEN DUMBER REASON THAN I THOUGHT IT'D BE.
TCH.
SCORE-0
NEWGAME
I CAN RELATE!
YOU CAN?
IT'S 'CUZ YOU'D LOSE ALL YOUR DATA ON THE OLDER GAMING SYSTEMS...
AN OTAKU WHO DOESN'T PLAY GAMES
YOU'RE PROB-ABLY STILL TRAUMATIZED BY THE SOUNDS OF THUNDER...
IT'S SOUL-CRUSHING IF THE POWER GOES OUT BEFORE YOU REACH A SAVE POINT...
HUH? WHAT? DID I MISS SOME-THING?
HE GOT PERMISSION ON THE PRETEXT OF MAINTAINING WORK EFFICIENCY.
JUST THIS ONCE...
I SUPPOSE IT CAN'T BE HELPED.

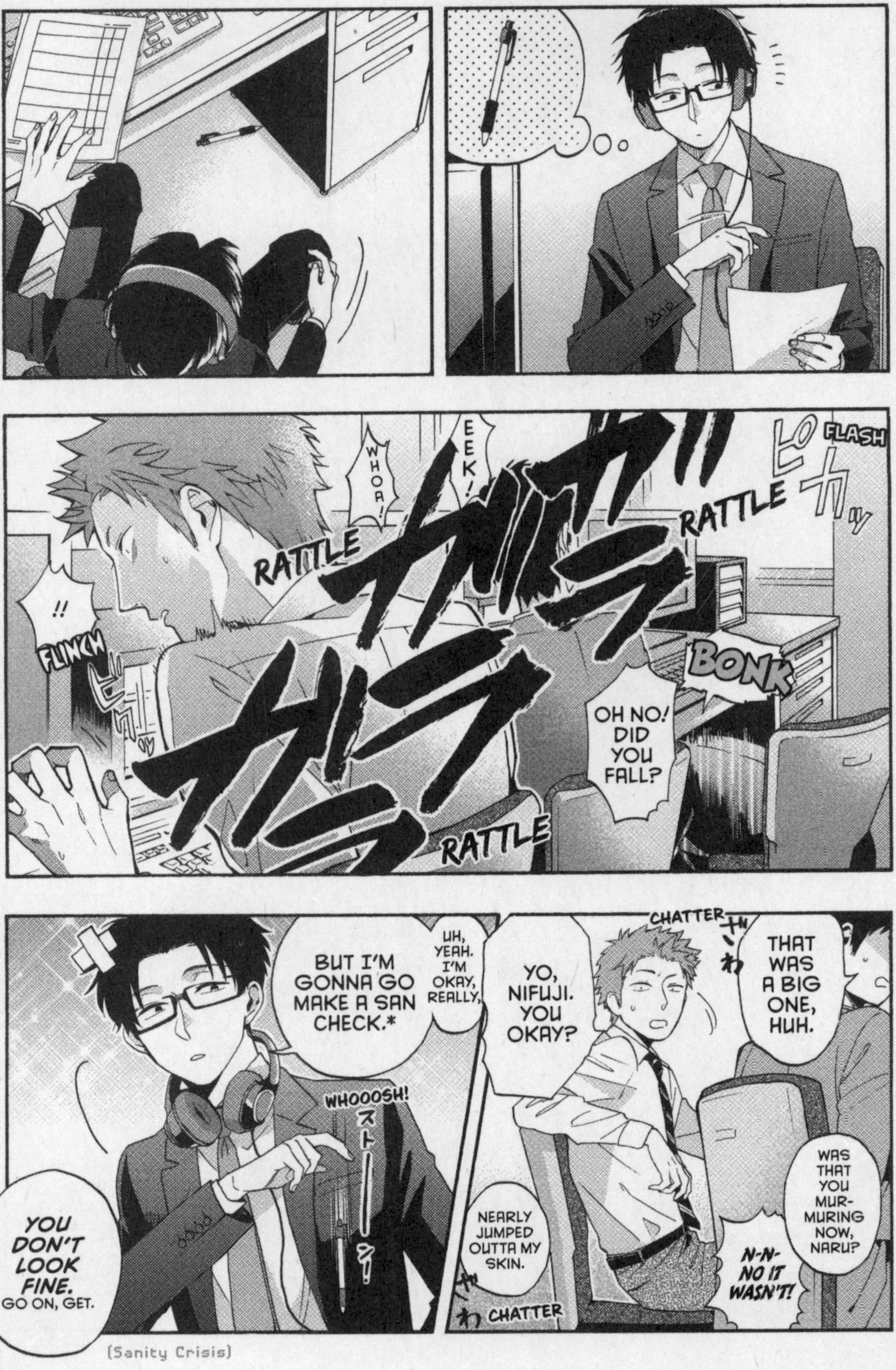
FLASH
RATTLE
EEK!
WHOA!
RATTLE
!!
FLINCH
BONK
OH NO! DID YOU FALL?
RATTLE
CHATTER
THAT WAS A BIG ONE, HUH.
YO, NIFUJI. YOU OKAY?
WAS THAT YOU MUR-MURING NOW, NARU?
N-N-NO IT WASN'T!
NEARLY JUMPED OUTTA MY SKIN.
CHATTER
UH, YEAH. I'M OKAY, REALLY,
BUT I'M GONNA GO MAKE A SAN CHECK.*
WHOOOSH!
YOU DON'T LOOK FINE. GO ON, GET.

*Short for sanity check; a term from gaming, especially tabletop gaming.

(Sanity Crisis)

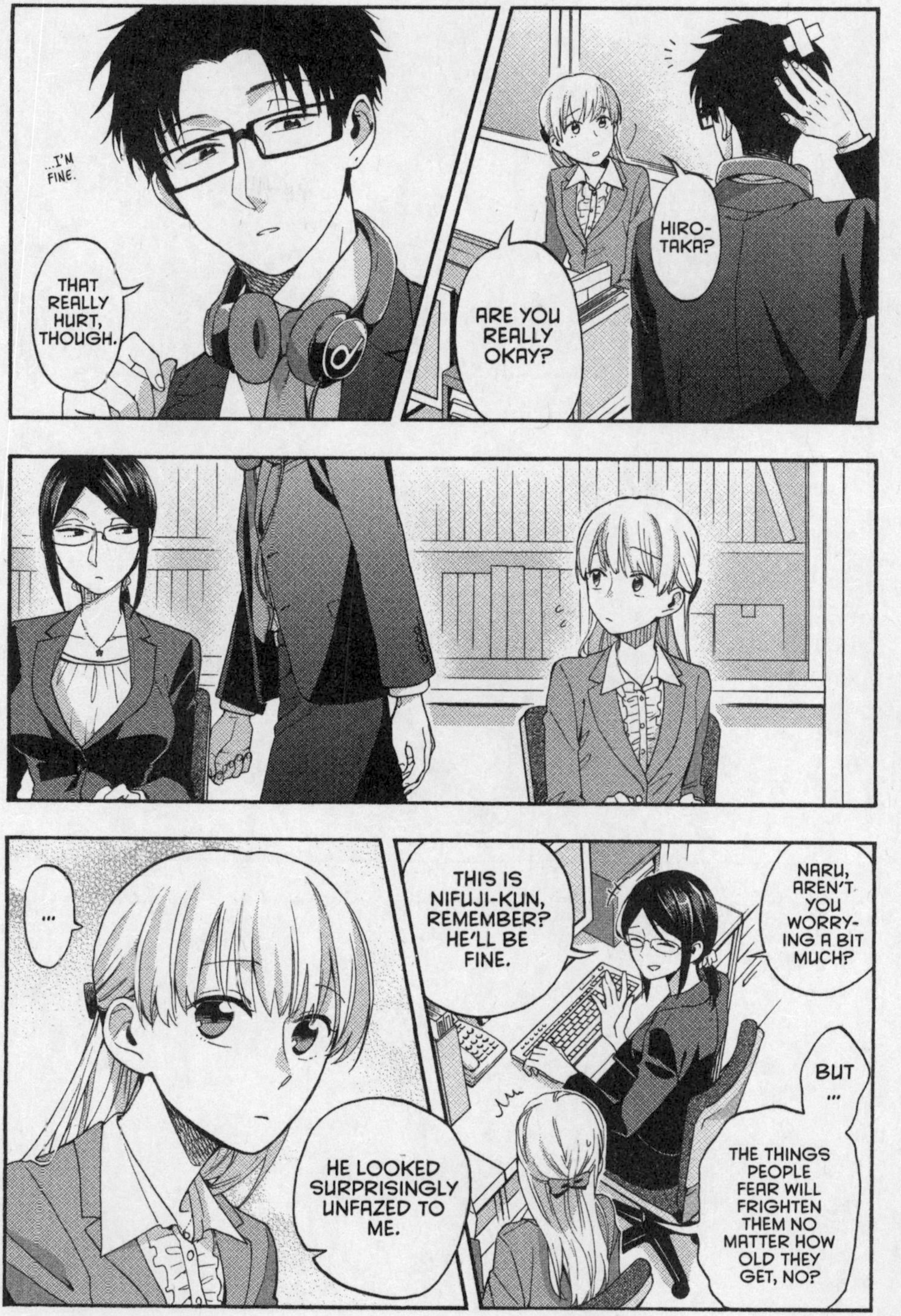
HIRO-TAKA?
ARE YOU REALLY OKAY?
...I'M FINE.
THAT REALLY HURT, THOUGH.
NARU, AREN'T YOU WORRY-ING A BIT MUCH?
THIS IS NIFUJI-KUN, REMEMBER? HE'LL BE FINE.
BUT ...
THE THINGS PEOPLE FEAR WILL FRIGHTEN THEM NO MATTER HOW OLD THEY GET, NO?
...
HE LOOKED SURPRISINGLY UNFAZED TO ME.

(Is he fine?)

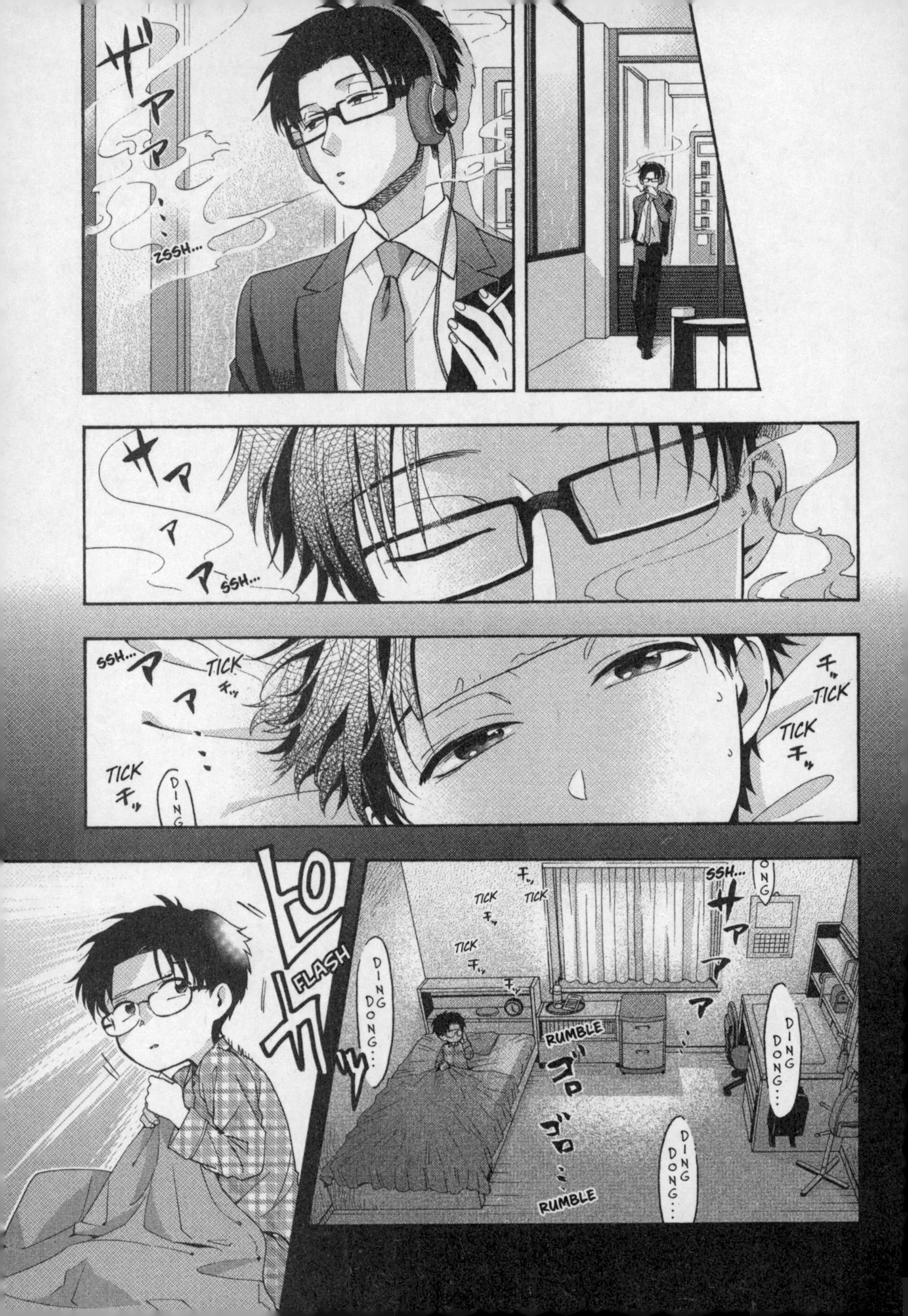

ザァァ…
ZSSH...
ザァァ
SSH...
チッ
TICK
TICK
チッ
SSH...
ァァ…
TICK
チッ
TICK
チッ
DING
SSH...
ザァァ…
DONG
チッ
TICK
TICK
チッ
TICK
チッ
チッ
DING DONG...
DING DONG...
RUMBLE
ゴロゴロ…
RUMBLE
DING DONG...
ビクッ
FLASH

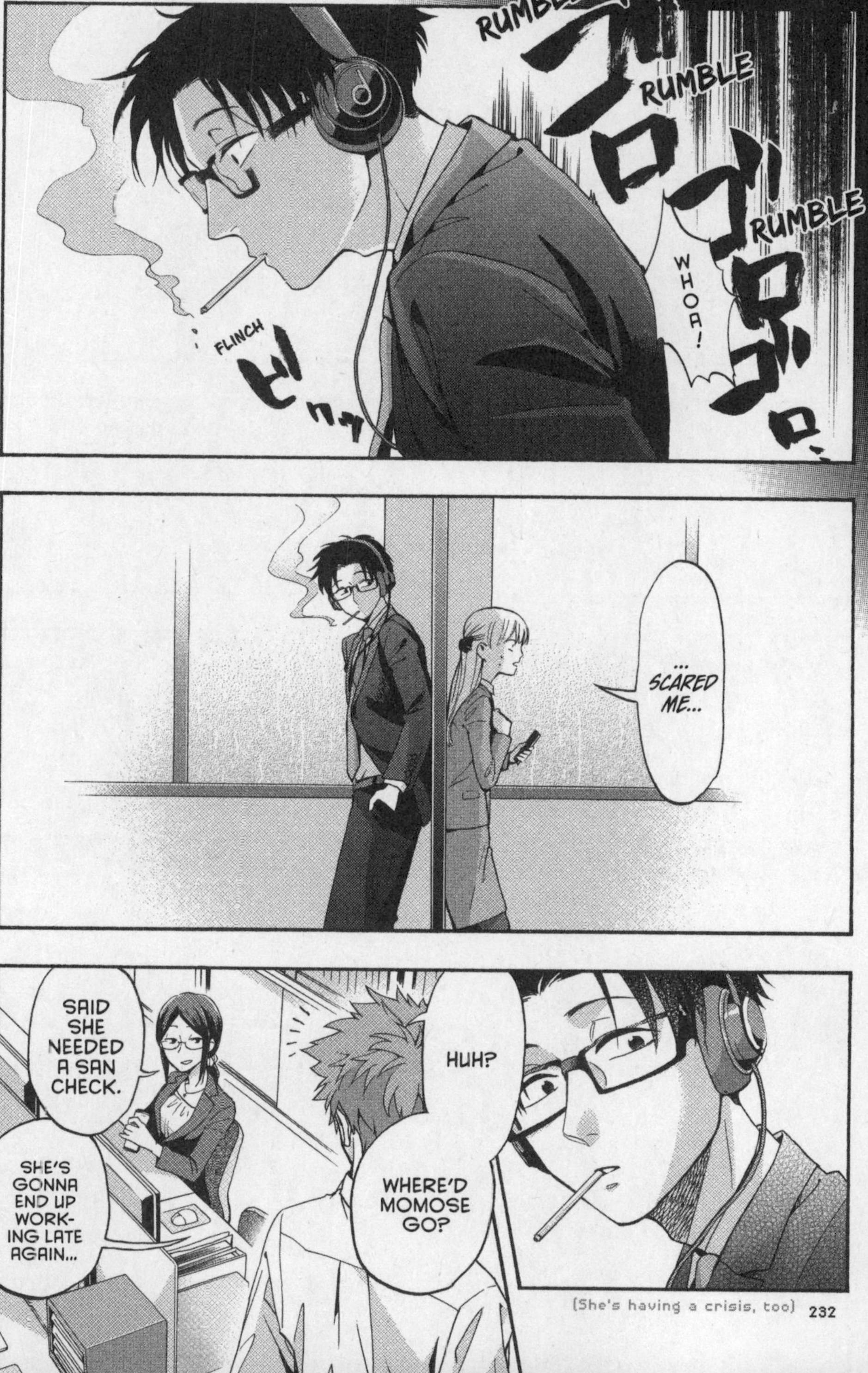
RUMBLE
RUMBLE
RUMBLE
WHOA!
FLINCH
...SCARED ME...
HUH?
WHERE'D MOMOSE GO?
SAID SHE NEEDED A SAN CHECK.
SHE'S GONNA END UP WORKING LATE AGAIN...

(She's having a crisis, too)

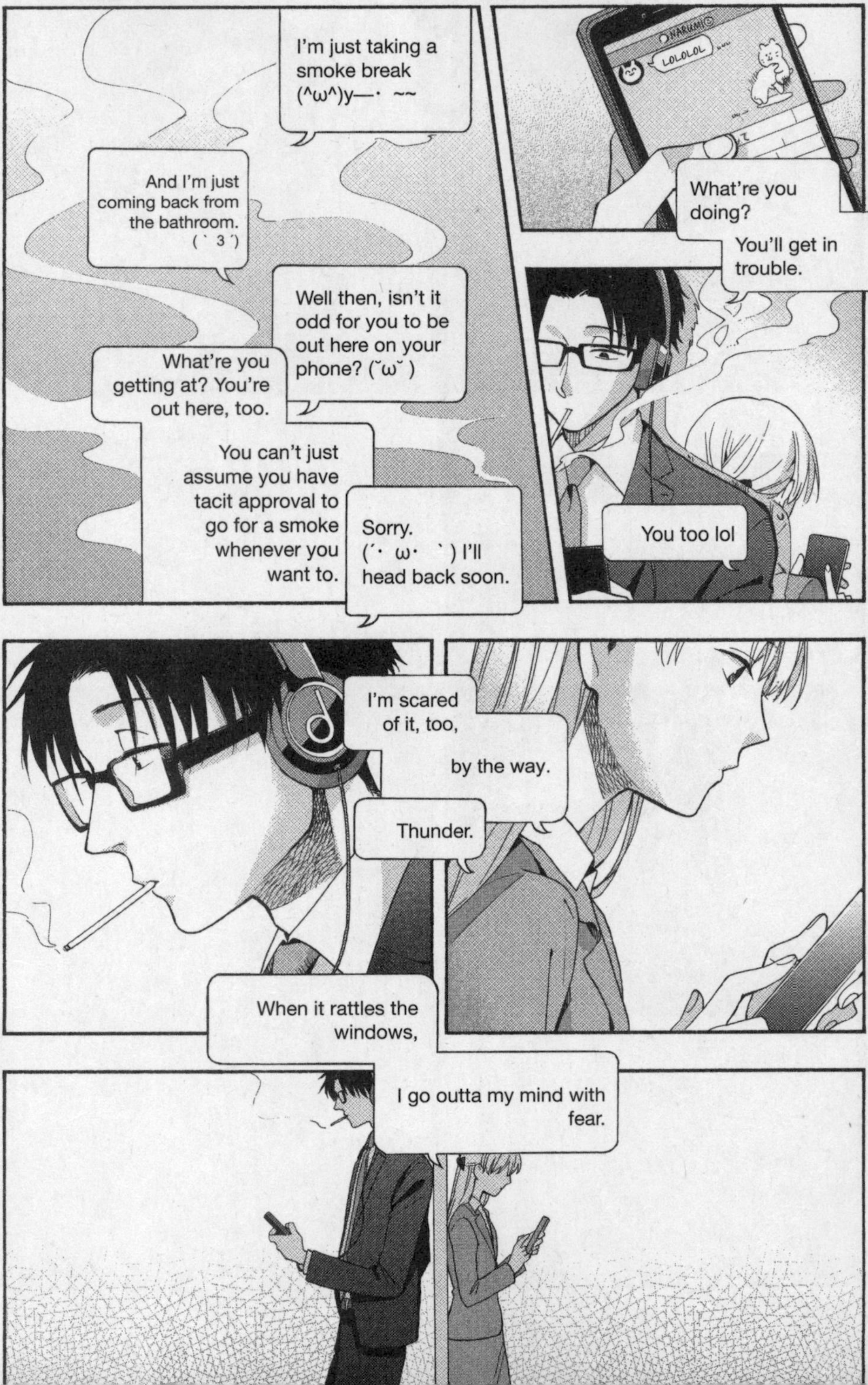
NARUMI
LOLOLOL
What're you doing?
You'll get in trouble.
You too lol
I'm just taking a smoke break (^ω^)y—・ ~~
And I'm just coming back from the bathroom. (｀3´)
Well then, isn't it odd for you to be out here on your phone? (˘ω˘)
What're you getting at? You're out here, too.
You can't just assume you have tacit approval to go for a smoke whenever you want to.
Sorry. (´・ω・｀) I'll head back soon.
I'm scared of it, too,
by the way.
Thunder.
When it rattles the windows,
I go outta my mind with fear.

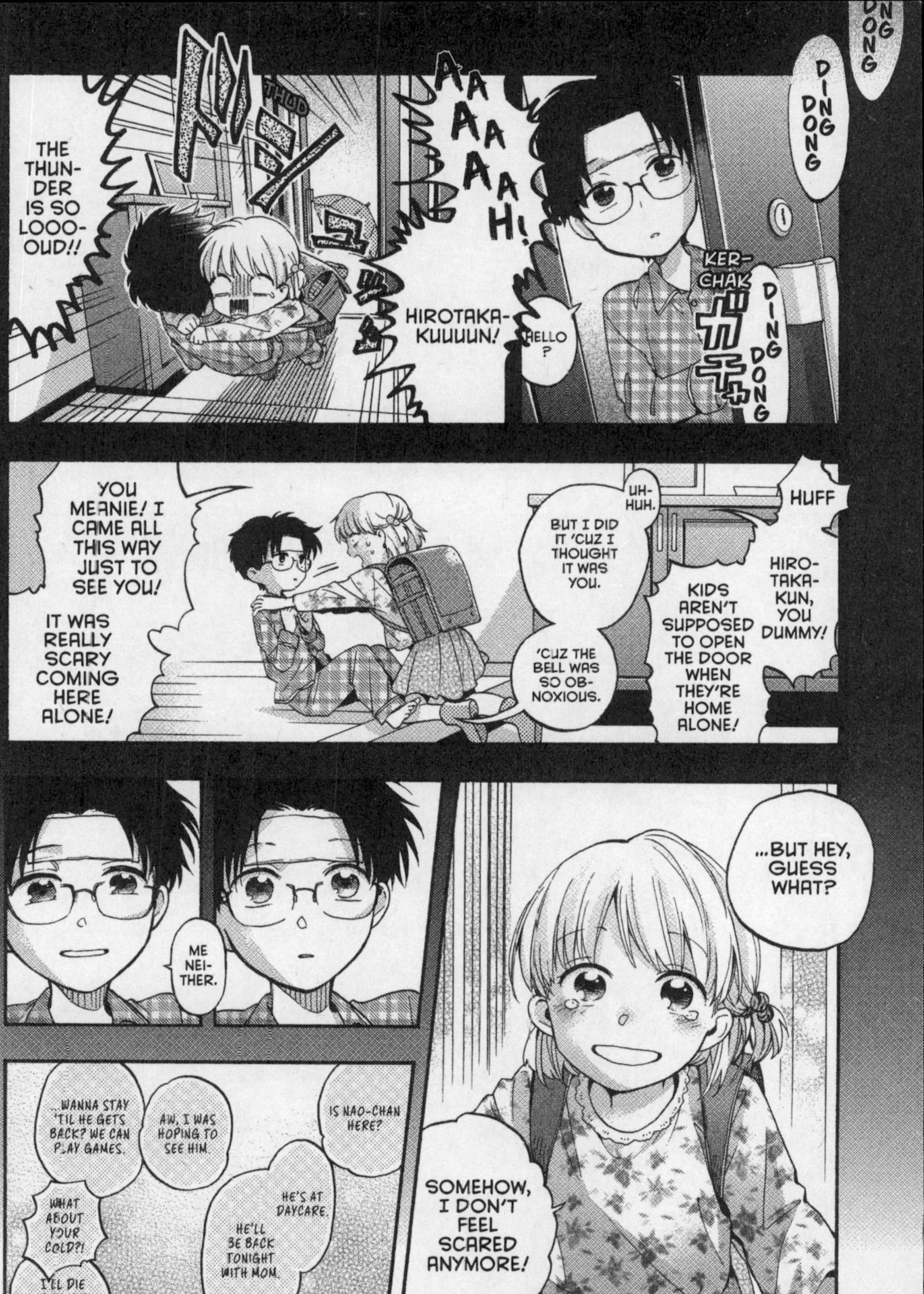
DING DONG
DING DONG
KER-CHAK
DING DONG
HELLO?
AAAAAH!
HIROTAKA-KUUUUN!
THUD
THE THUNDER IS SO LOOOOUD!!
HUFF
HIRO-TAKA-KUN, YOU DUMMY!
KIDS AREN'T SUPPOSED TO OPEN THE DOOR WHEN THEY'RE HOME ALONE!
UH-HUH.
BUT I DID IT 'CUZ I THOUGHT IT WAS YOU.
'CUZ THE BELL WAS SO OB-NOXIOUS.
YOU MEANIE! I CAME ALL THIS WAY JUST TO SEE YOU!
IT WAS REALLY SCARY COMING HERE ALONE!
...BUT HEY, GUESS WHAT?
SOMEHOW, I DON'T FEEL SCARED ANYMORE!
ME NEITHER.
IS NAO-CHAN HERE?
HE'S AT DAYCARE.
HE'LL BE BACK TONIGHT WITH MOM.
AW, I WAS HOPING TO SEE HIM.
..WANNA STAY 'TIL HE GETS BACK? WE CAN PLAY GAMES.
WHAT ABOUT YOUR COLD?!
I'LL DIE WITHOUT GAMES.

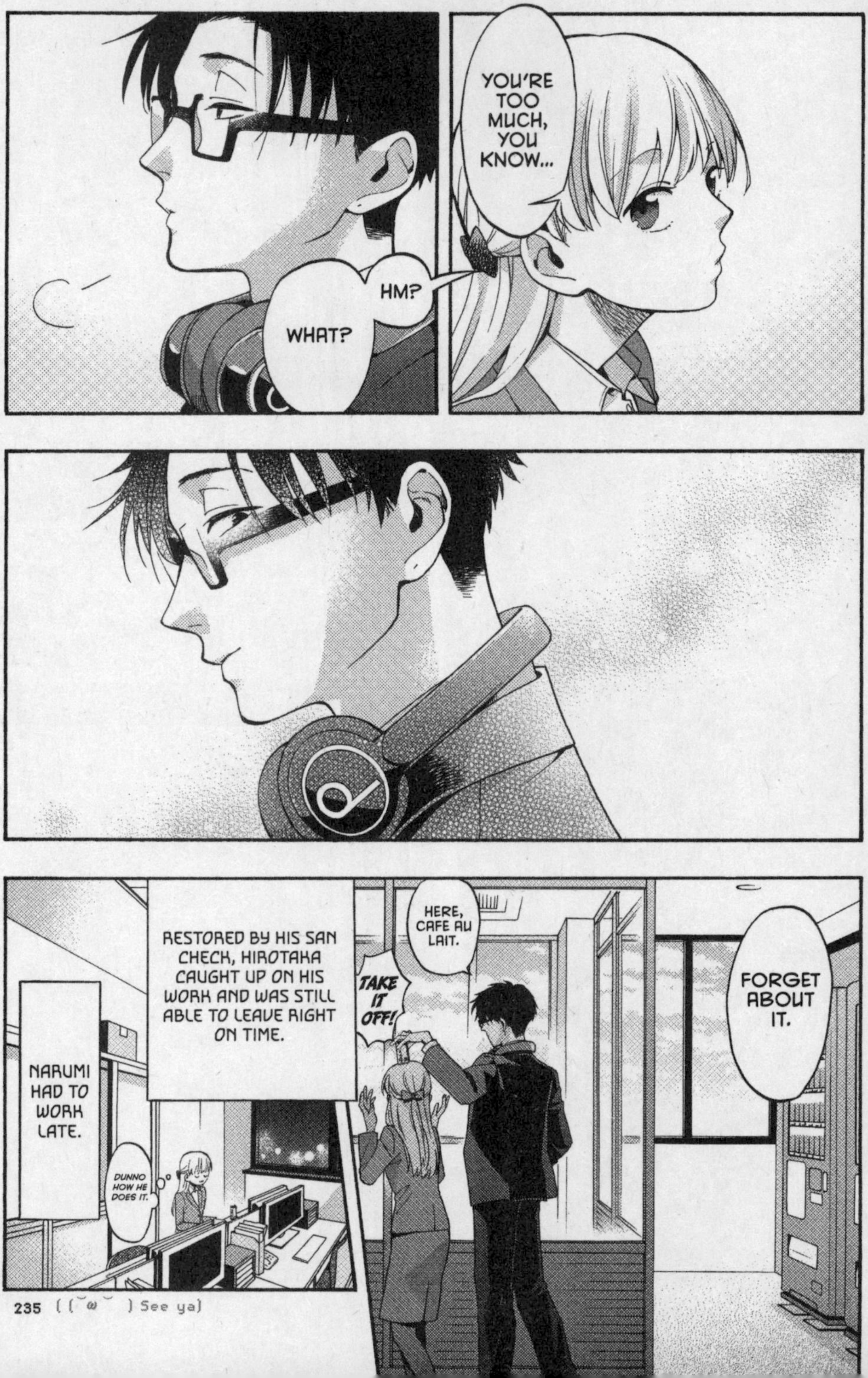
YOU'RE TOO MUCH, YOU KNOW...
HM?
WHAT?
FORGET ABOUT IT.
HERE, CAFE AU LAIT.
TAKE IT OFF!
RESTORED BY HIS SAN CHECK, HIROTAKA CAUGHT UP ON HIS WORK AND WAS STILL ABLE TO LEAVE RIGHT ON TIME.
NARUMI HAD TO WORK LATE.
DUNNO HOW HE DOES IT.

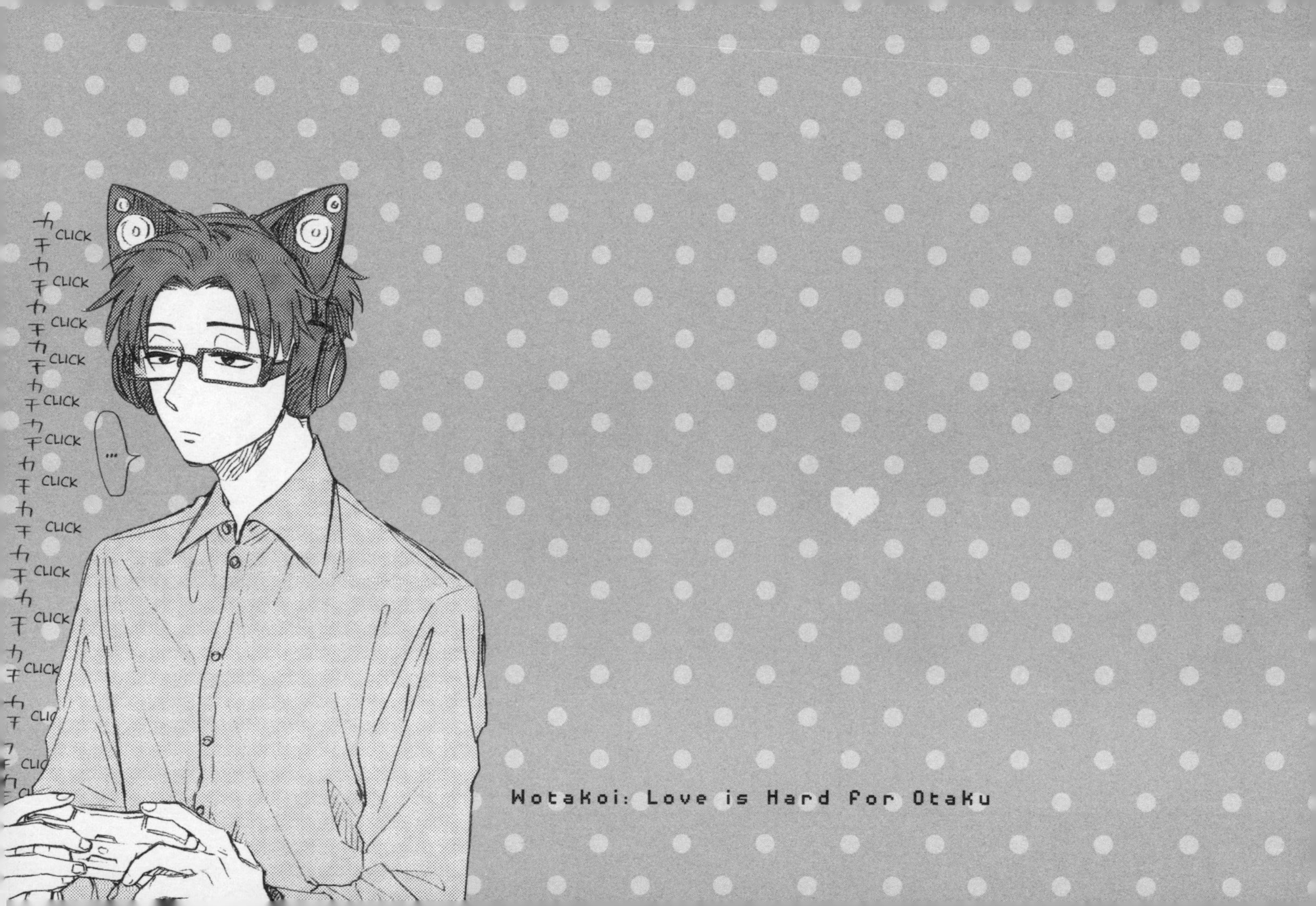
…
カチ CLICK
カチ CLICK
カチ CLICK
カチ CLICK
カチ CLICK
カチ CLICK
カチ CLICK
カチ CLICK
カチ CLICK
カチ CLICK
Wotakoi: Love is Hard for Otaku

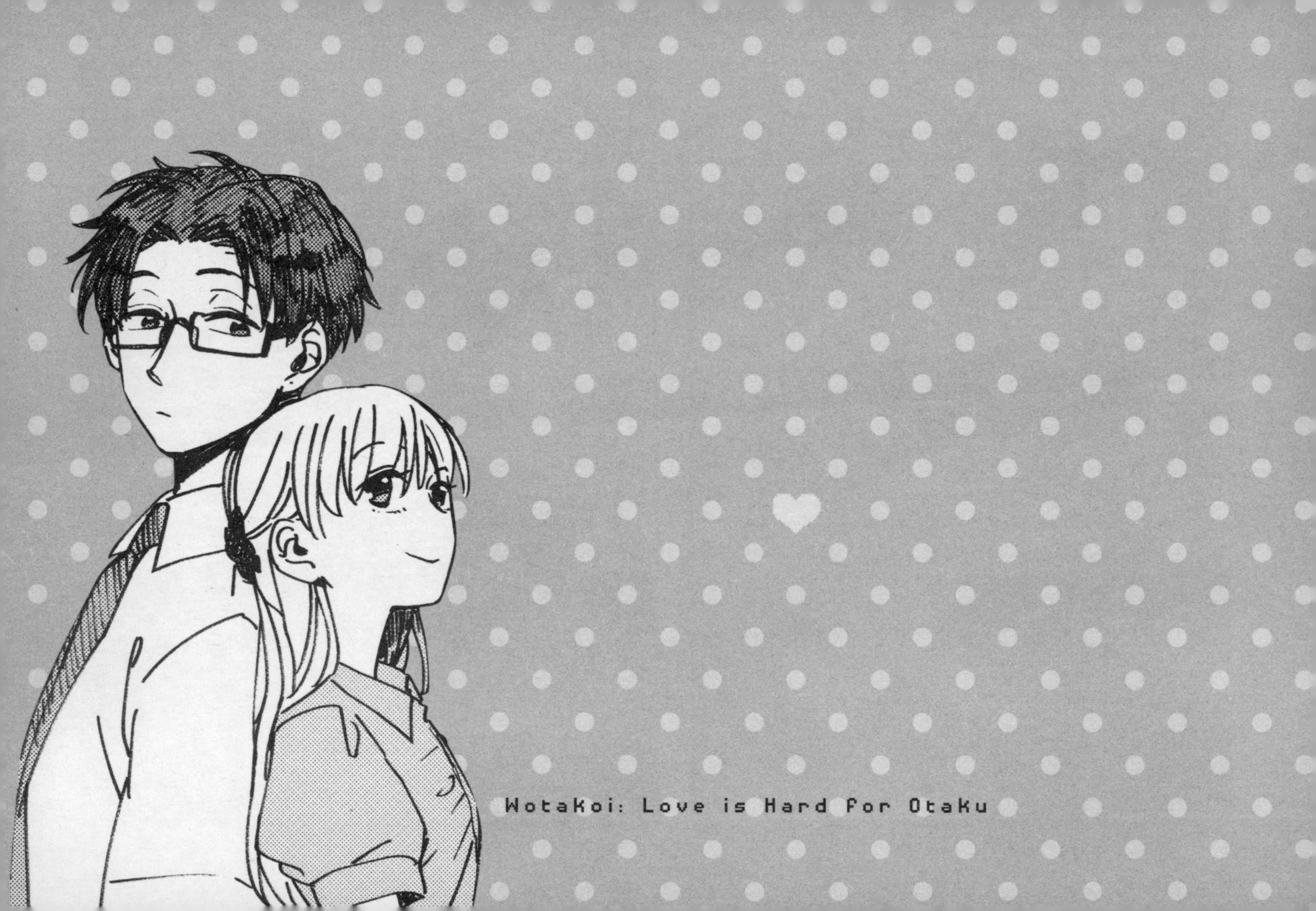
WotaKoi: Love is Hard for OtaKu

Not Cool

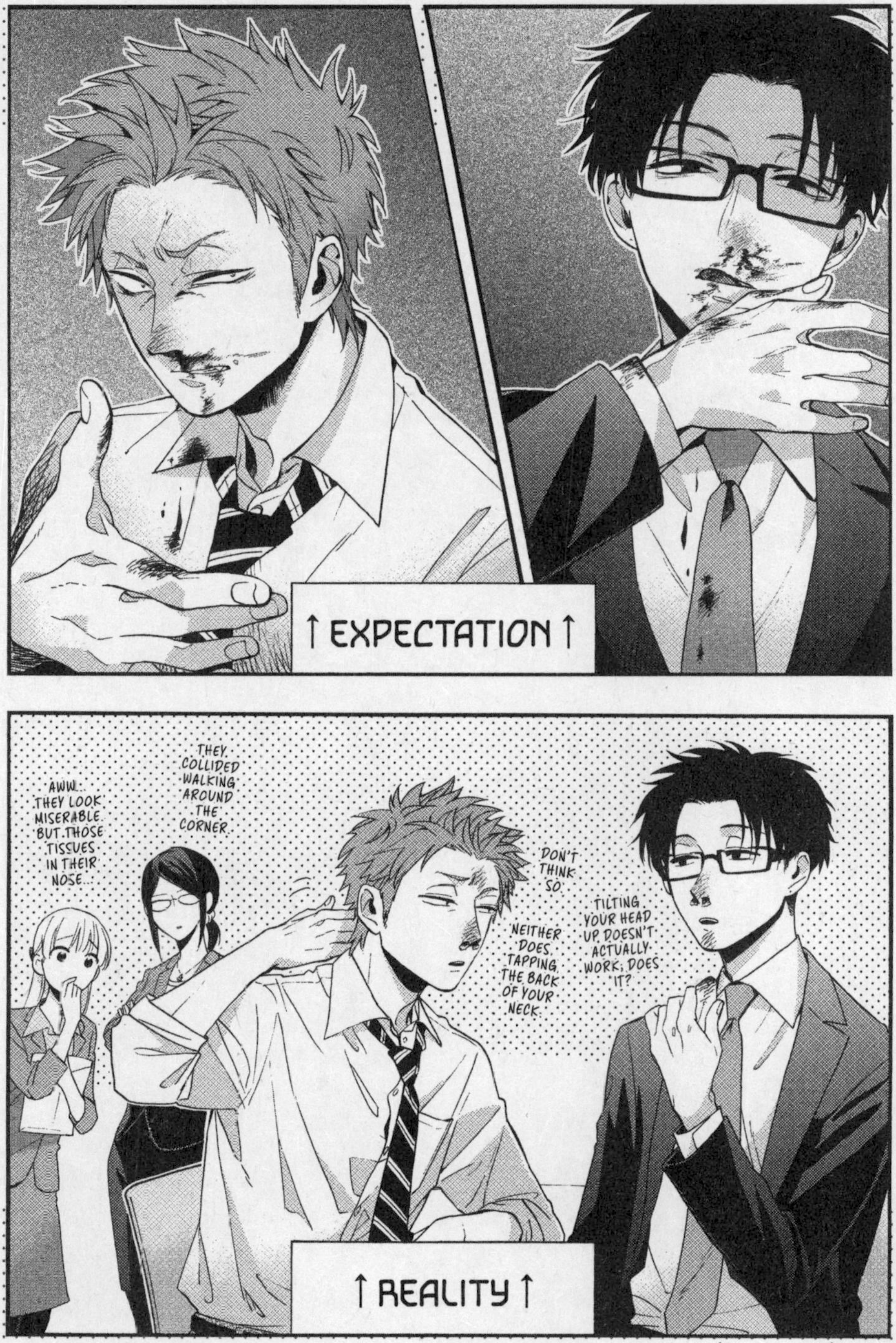
↑ EXPECTATION ↑
TILTING YOUR HEAD UP DOESN'T ACTUALLY WORK, DOES IT?
DON'T THINK SO.
NEITHER DOES TAPPING THE BACK OF YOUR NECK.
THEY COLLIDED WALKING AROUND THE CORNER.
AWW... THEY LOOK MISERABLE. BUT THOSE TISSUES IN THEIR NOSE...
↑ REALITY ↑

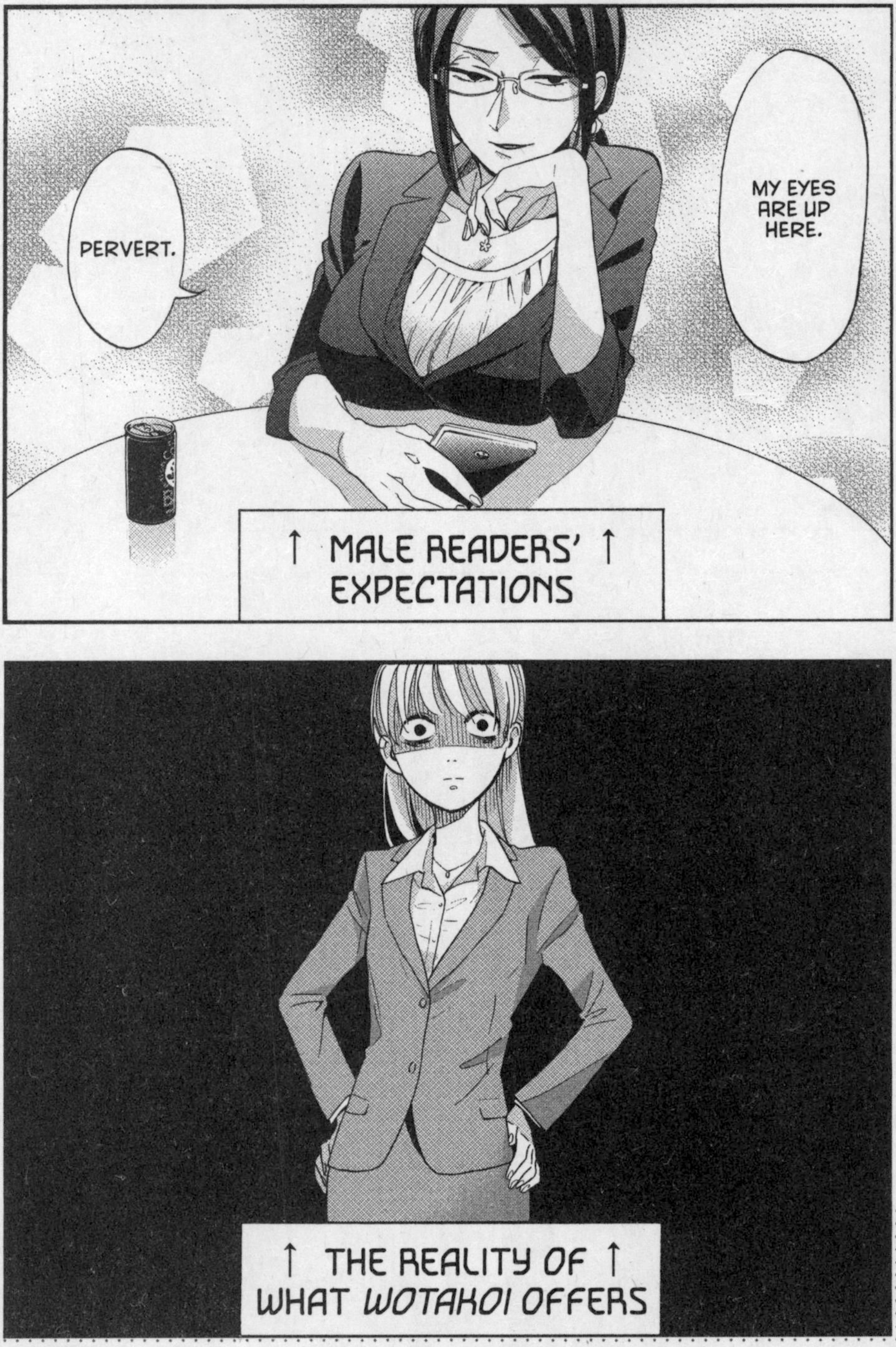
MY EYES ARE UP HERE.
PERVERT.
↑ MALE READERS' ↑ EXPECTATIONS
↑ THE REALITY OF ↑ WHAT *WOTAKOI* OFFERS

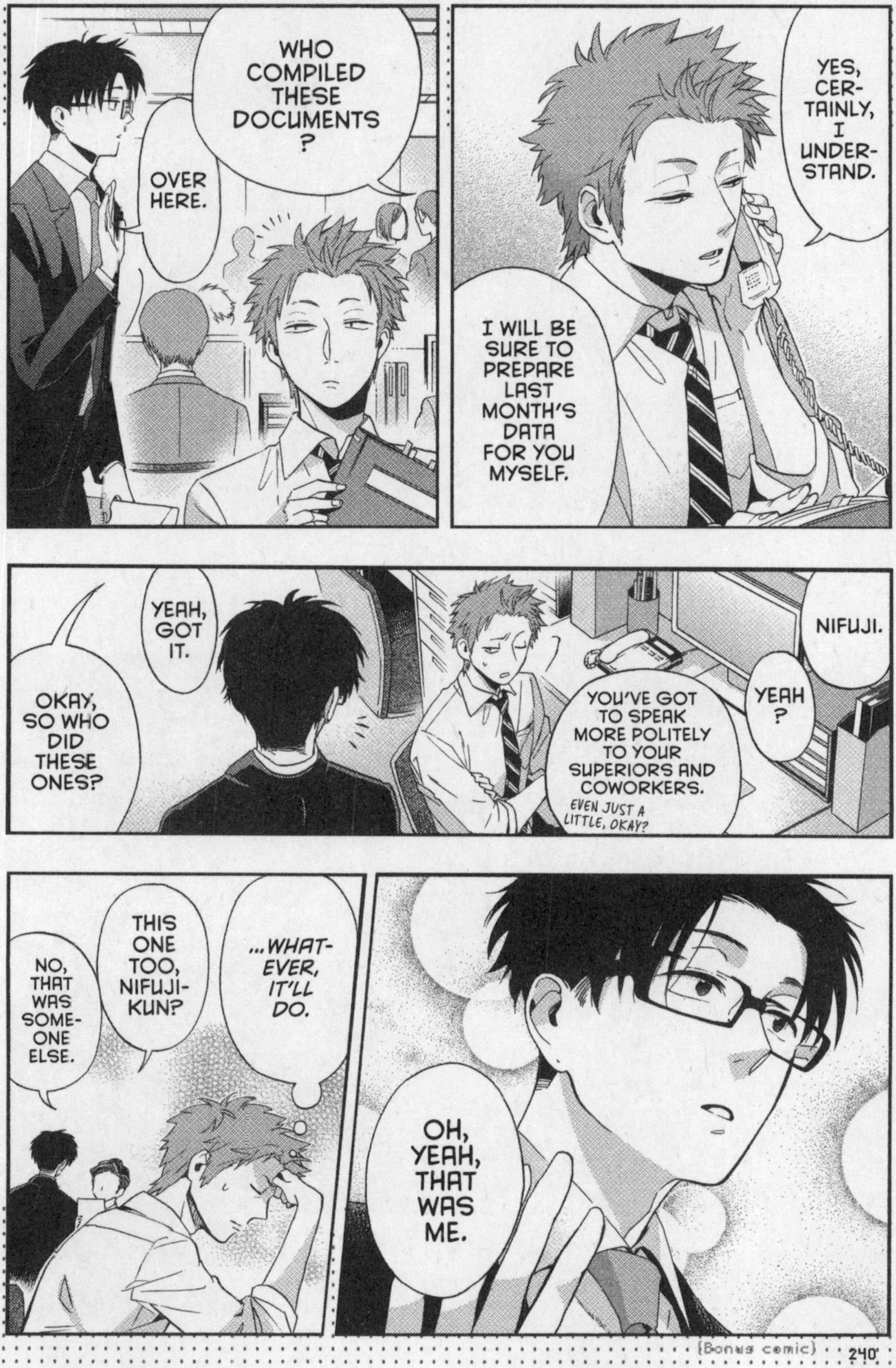
YES, CERTAINLY, I UNDERSTAND.
I WILL BE SURE TO PREPARE LAST MONTH'S DATA FOR YOU MYSELF.
WHO COMPILED THESE DOCUMENTS?
OVER HERE.
NIFUJI.
YEAH?
YOU'VE GOT TO SPEAK MORE POLITELY TO YOUR SUPERIORS AND COWORKERS.
EVEN JUST A LITTLE, OKAY?
YEAH, GOT IT.
OKAY, SO WHO DID THESE ONES?
OH, YEAH, THAT WAS ME.
...WHATEVER, IT'LL DO.
THIS ONE TOO, NIFUJI-KUN?
NO, THAT WAS SOMEONE ELSE.

Nothing Changes

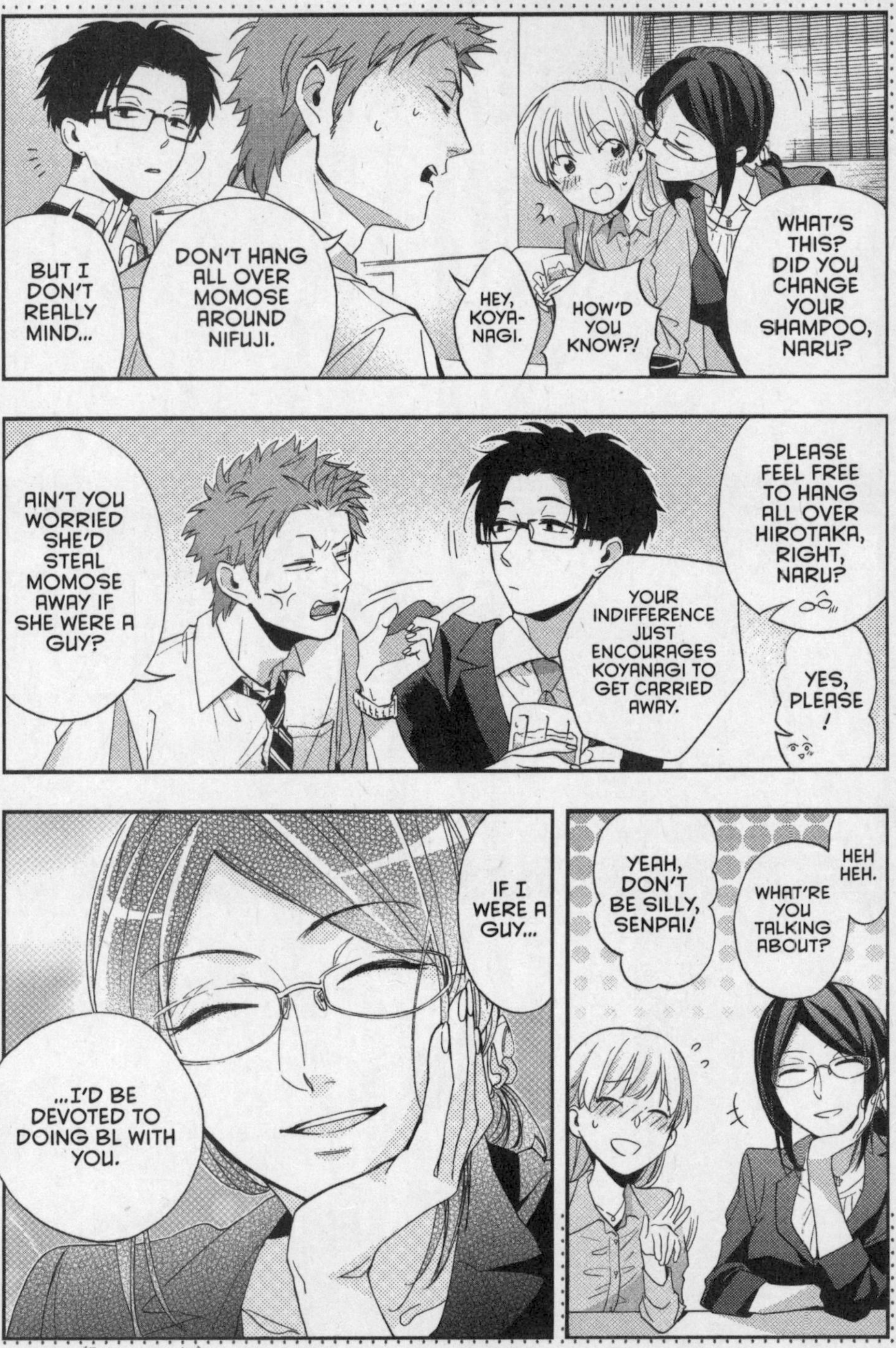
WHAT'S THIS? DID YOU CHANGE YOUR SHAMPOO, NARU?
HOW'D YOU KNOW?!
HEY, KOYA-NAGI.
DON'T HANG ALL OVER MOMOSE AROUND NIFUJI.
BUT I DON'T REALLY MIND...
PLEASE FEEL FREE TO HANG ALL OVER HIROTAKA, RIGHT, NARU?
YES, PLEASE!
YOUR INDIFFERENCE JUST ENCOURAGES KOYANAGI TO GET CARRIED AWAY.
AIN'T YOU WORRIED SHE'D STEAL MOMOSE AWAY IF SHE WERE A GUY?
HEH HEH.
WHAT'RE YOU TALKING ABOUT?
YEAH, DON'T BE SILLY, SENPAI!
IF I WERE A GUY...
...I'D BE DEVOTED TO DOING BL WITH YOU.

Heartbreak (1)

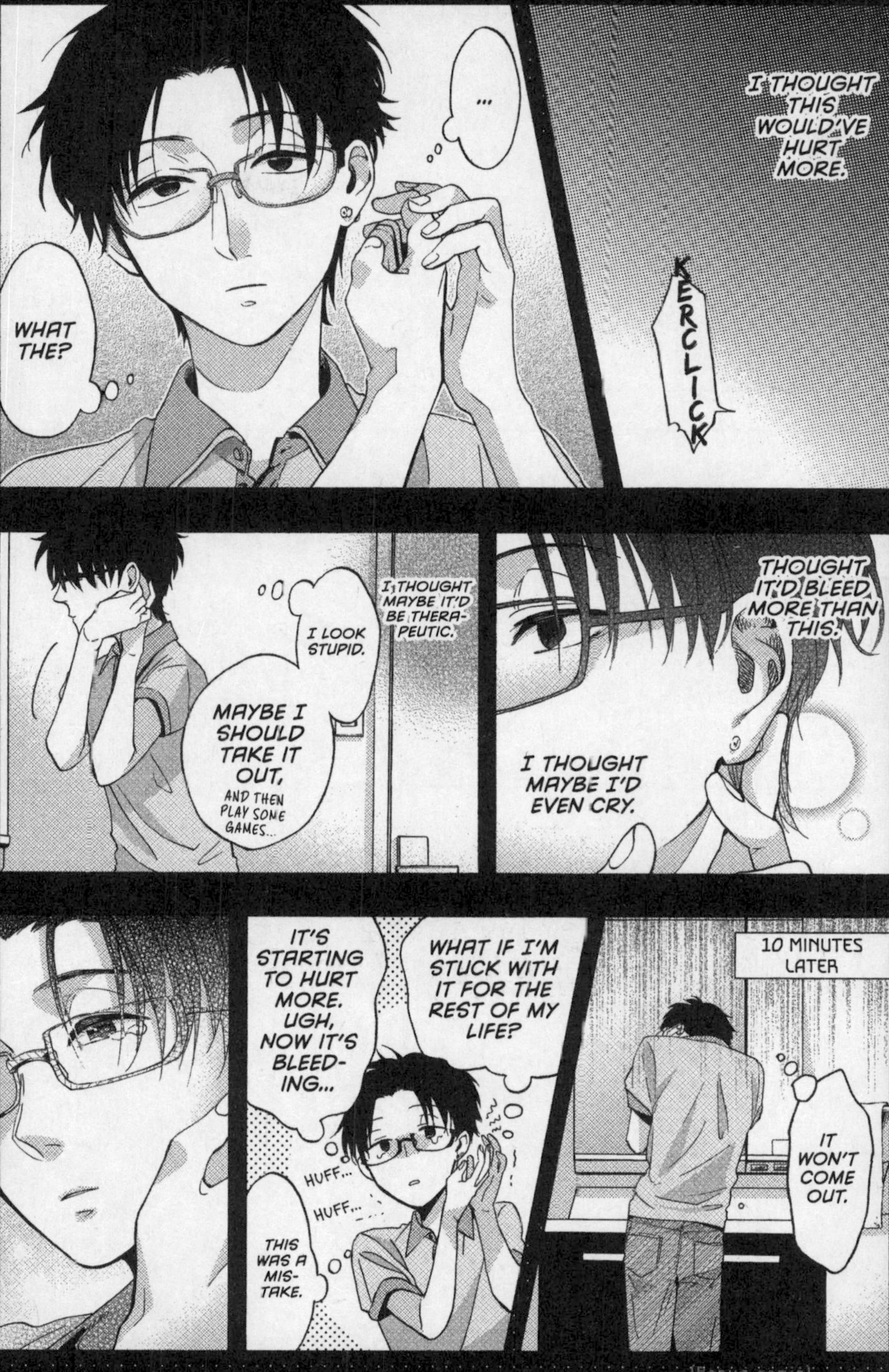
I THOUGHT THIS WOULD'VE HURT MORE.
KERCLICK
...
WHAT THE?
THOUGHT IT'D BLEED MORE THAN THIS.
I THOUGHT MAYBE I'D EVEN CRY.
I THOUGHT MAYBE IT'D BE THERA-PEUTIC.
I LOOK STUPID.
MAYBE I SHOULD TAKE IT OUT, AND THEN PLAY SOME GAMES...
10 MINUTES LATER
IT WON'T COME OUT.
WHAT IF I'M STUCK WITH IT FOR THE REST OF MY LIFE?
IT'S STARTING TO HURT MORE. UGH, NOW IT'S BLEED-ING...
HUFF...
HUFF...
THIS WAS A MIS-TAKE.

Heartbreak (2)

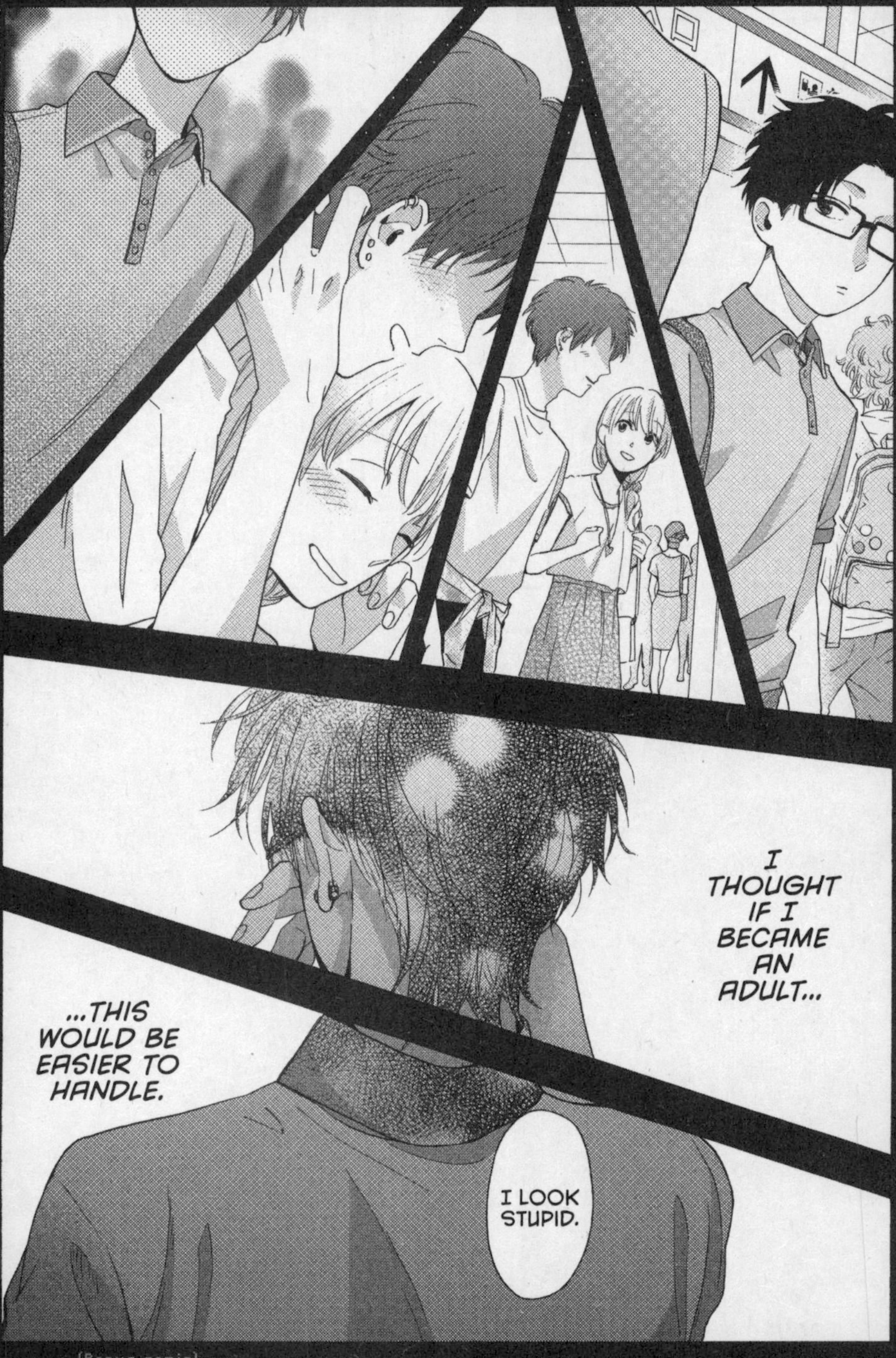
I THOUGHT IF I BECAME AN ADULT...
...THIS WOULD BE EASIER TO HANDLE.
I LOOK STUPID.

The Type Who Tries in Secret

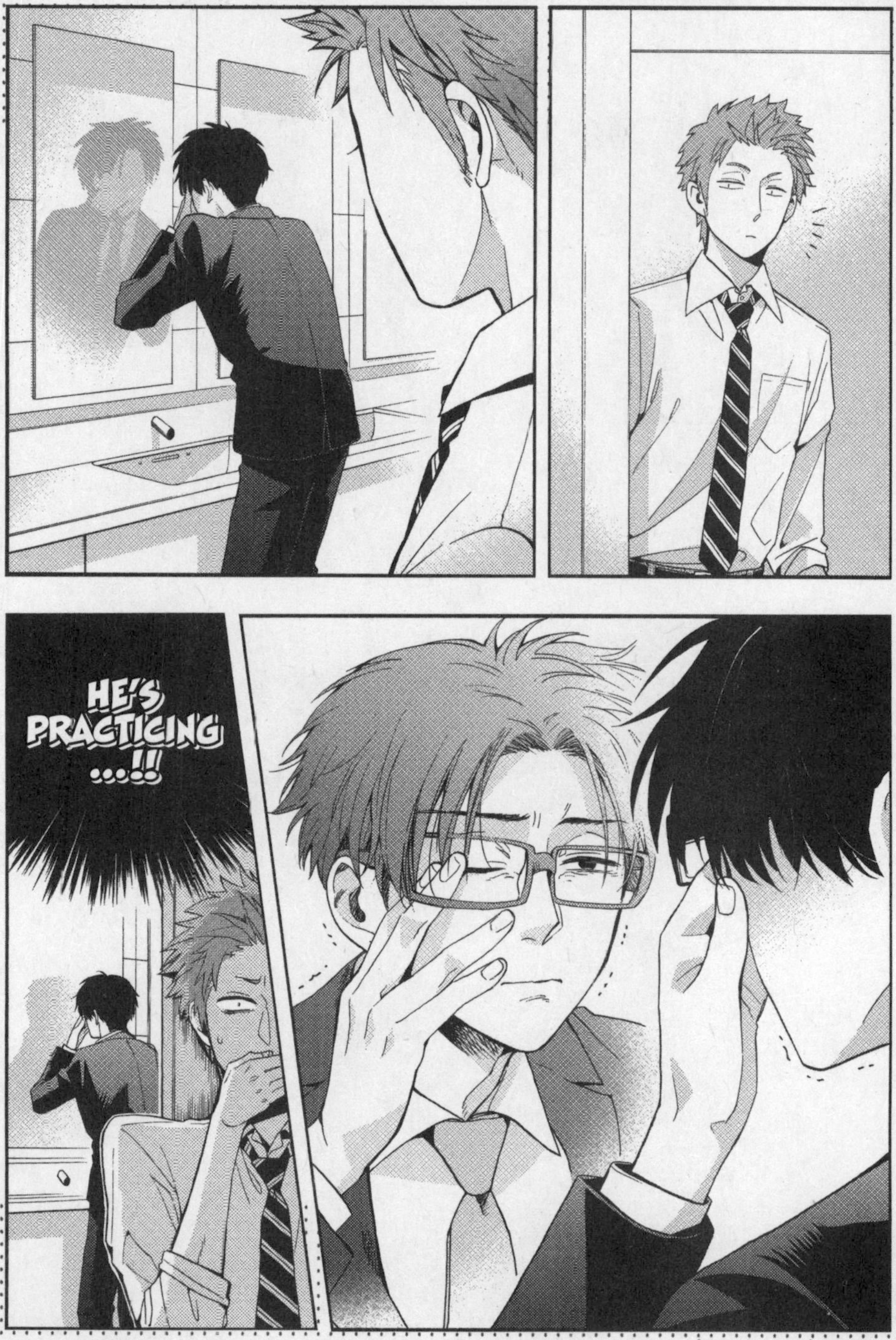
HE'S PRACTICING ...!!

Self-Respect

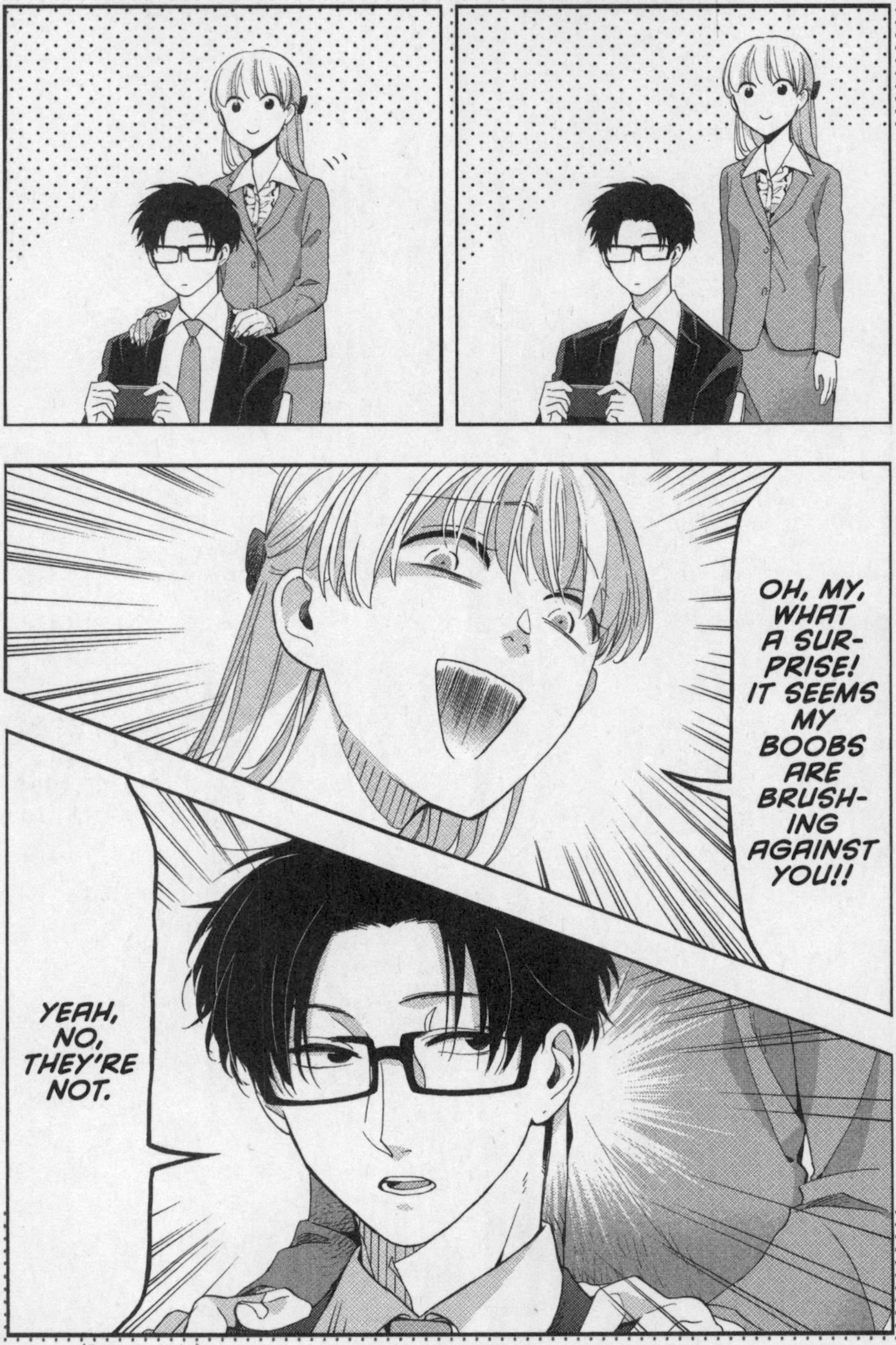

OH, MY, WHAT A SUR-PRISE! IT SEEMS MY BOOBS ARE BRUSH-ING AGAINST YOU!!
YEAH, NO, THEY'RE NOT.

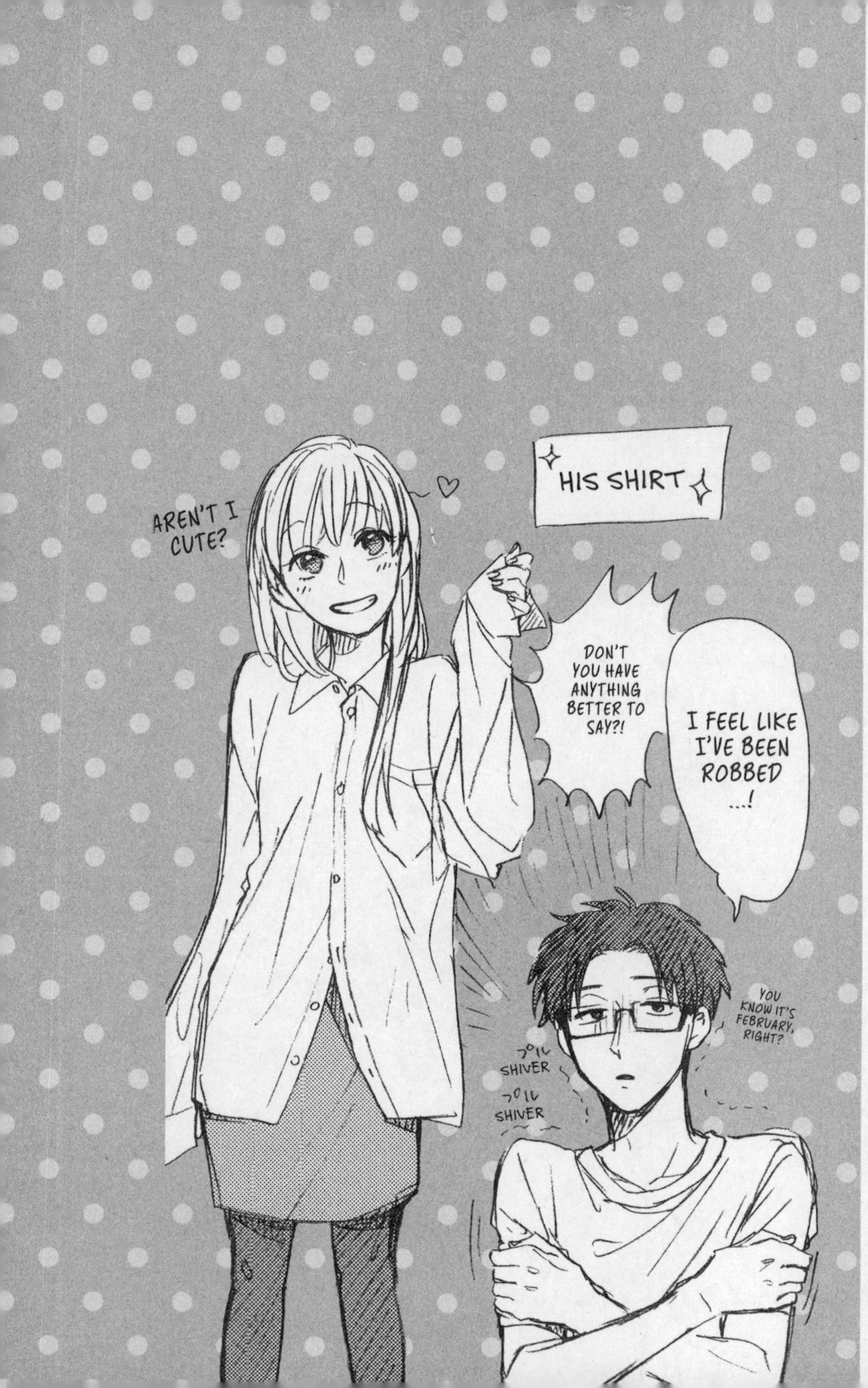
HIS SHIRT
AREN'T I CUTE?
I FEEL LIKE I'VE BEEN ROBBED ...!
DON'T YOU HAVE ANYTHING BETTER TO SAY?!
YOU KNOW IT'S FEBRUARY, RIGHT?
ブル SHIVER
ブル SHIVER

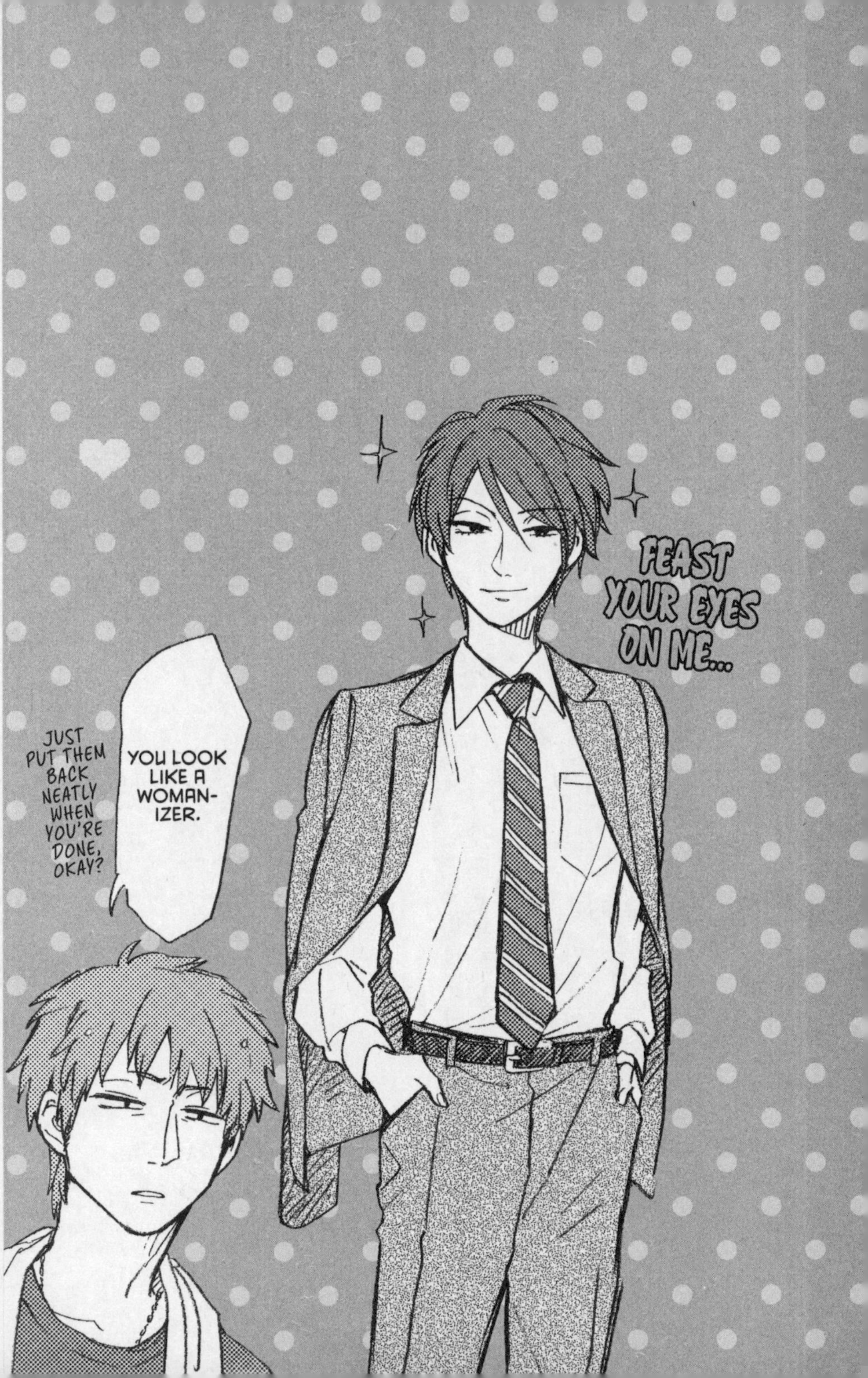
FEAST YOUR EYES ON ME...
YOU LOOK LIKE A WOMAN-IZER.
JUST PUT THEM BACK NEATLY WHEN YOU'RE DONE, OKAY?

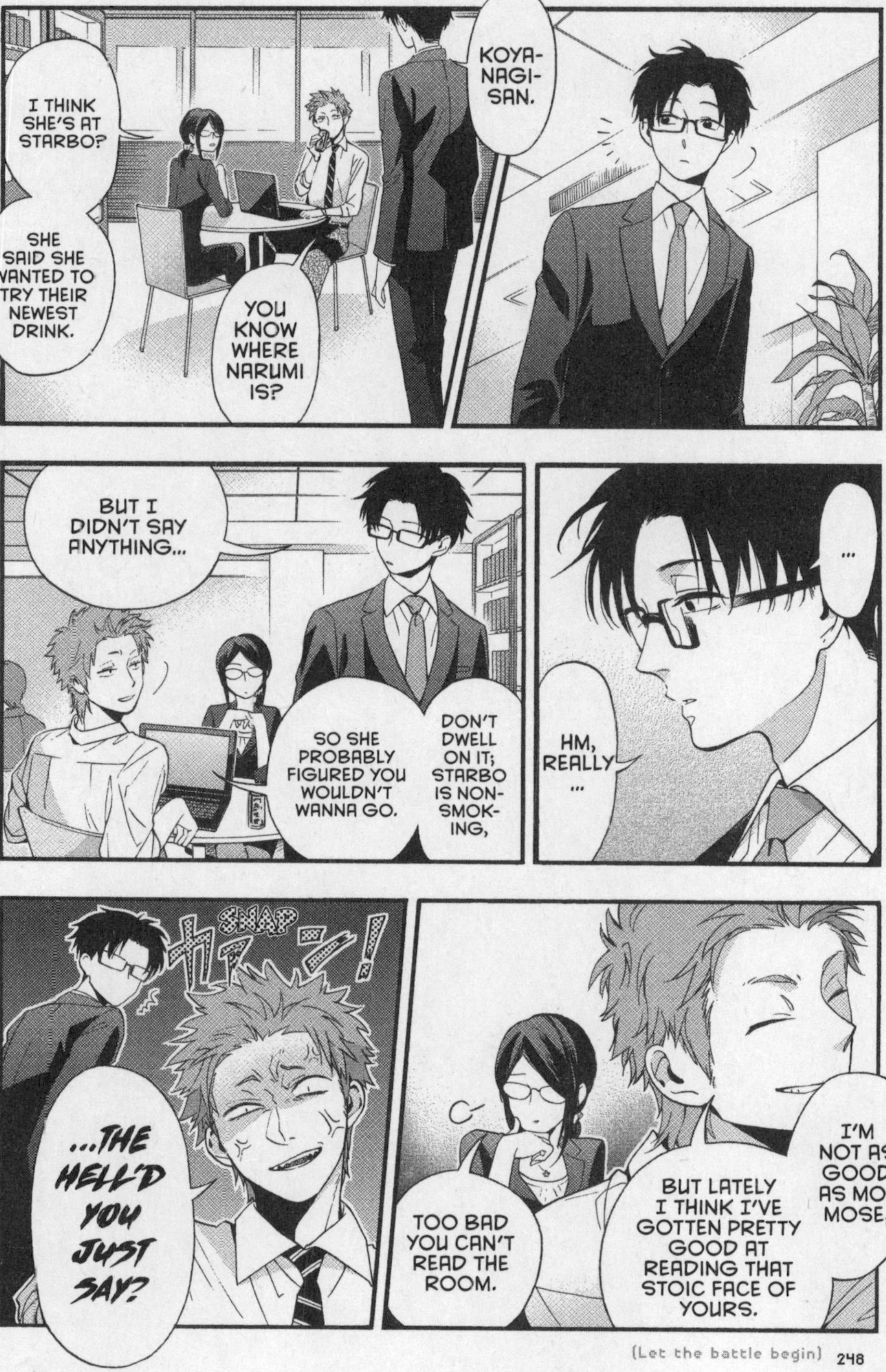
KOYA-NAGI-SAN.
YOU KNOW WHERE NARUMI IS?
I THINK SHE'S AT STARBO?
SHE SAID SHE WANTED TO TRY THEIR NEWEST DRINK.
...
HM, REALLY...
DON'T DWELL ON IT; STARBO IS NON-SMOK-ING,
SO SHE PROBABLY FIGURED YOU WOULDN'T WANNA GO.
BUT I DIDN'T SAY ANYTHING...
I'M NOT AS GOOD AS MO-MOSE,
BUT LATELY I THINK I'VE GOTTEN PRETTY GOOD AT READING THAT STOIC FACE OF YOURS.
TOO BAD YOU CAN'T READ THE ROOM.
SNAP
...THE HELL'D YOU JUST SAY?

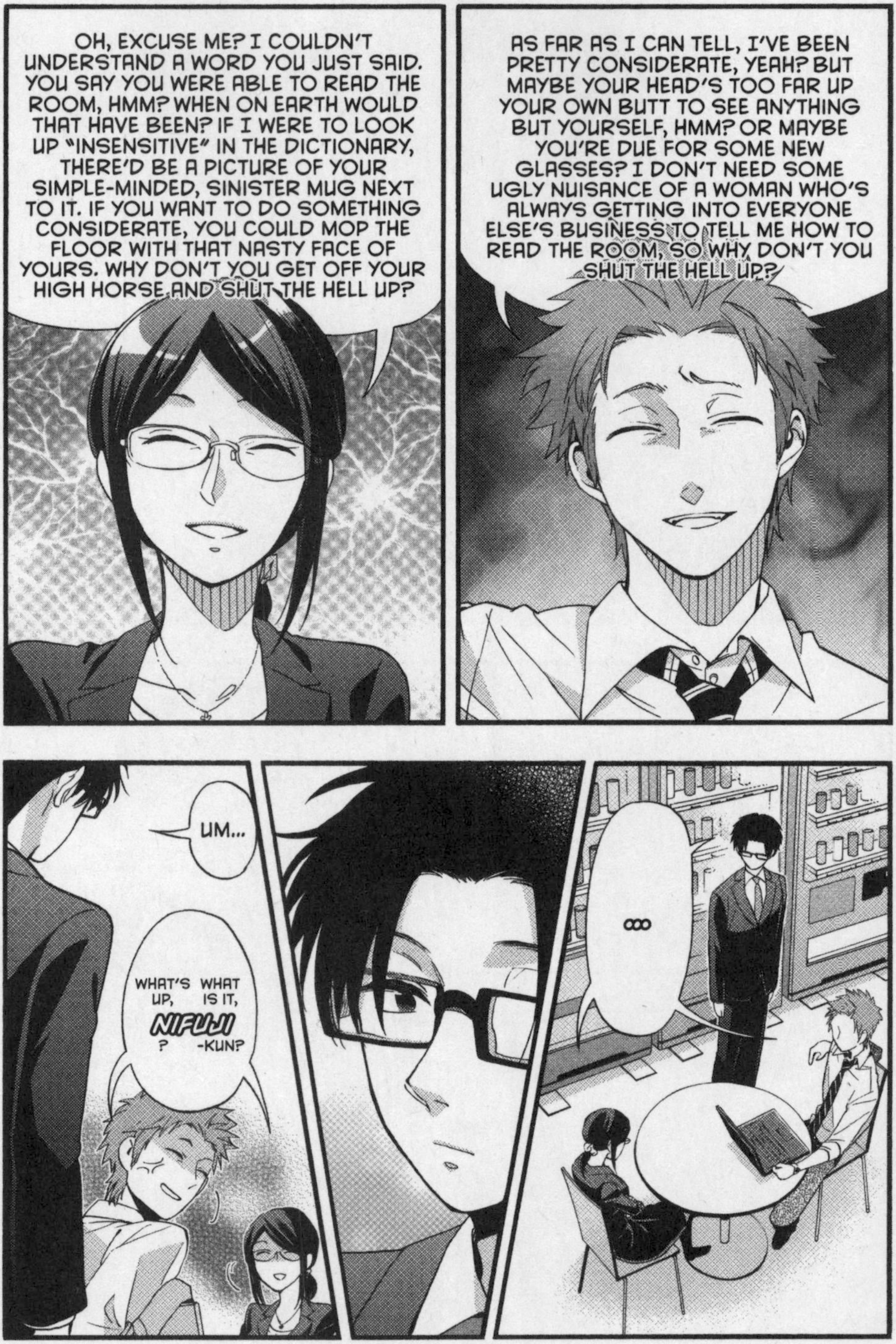
AS FAR AS I CAN TELL, I'VE BEEN PRETTY CONSIDERATE, YEAH? BUT MAYBE YOUR HEAD'S TOO FAR UP YOUR OWN BUTT TO SEE ANYTHING BUT YOURSELF, HMM? OR MAYBE YOU'RE DUE FOR SOME NEW GLASSES? I DON'T NEED SOME UGLY NUISANCE OF A WOMAN WHO'S ALWAYS GETTING INTO EVERYONE ELSE'S BUSINESS TO TELL ME HOW TO READ THE ROOM, SO WHY DON'T YOU SHUT THE HELL UP?
OH, EXCUSE ME? I COULDN'T UNDERSTAND A WORD YOU JUST SAID. YOU SAY YOU WERE ABLE TO READ THE ROOM, HMM? WHEN ON EARTH WOULD THAT HAVE BEEN? IF I WERE TO LOOK UP "INSENSITIVE" IN THE DICTIONARY, THERE'D BE A PICTURE OF YOUR SIMPLE-MINDED, SINISTER MUG NEXT TO IT. IF YOU WANT TO DO SOMETHING CONSIDERATE, YOU COULD MOP THE FLOOR WITH THAT NASTY FACE OF YOURS. WHY DON'T YOU GET OFF YOUR HIGH HORSE AND SHUT THE HELL UP?
...
UM...
WHAT IS IT, NIFUJI-KUN?
WHAT'S UP, NIFUJI?

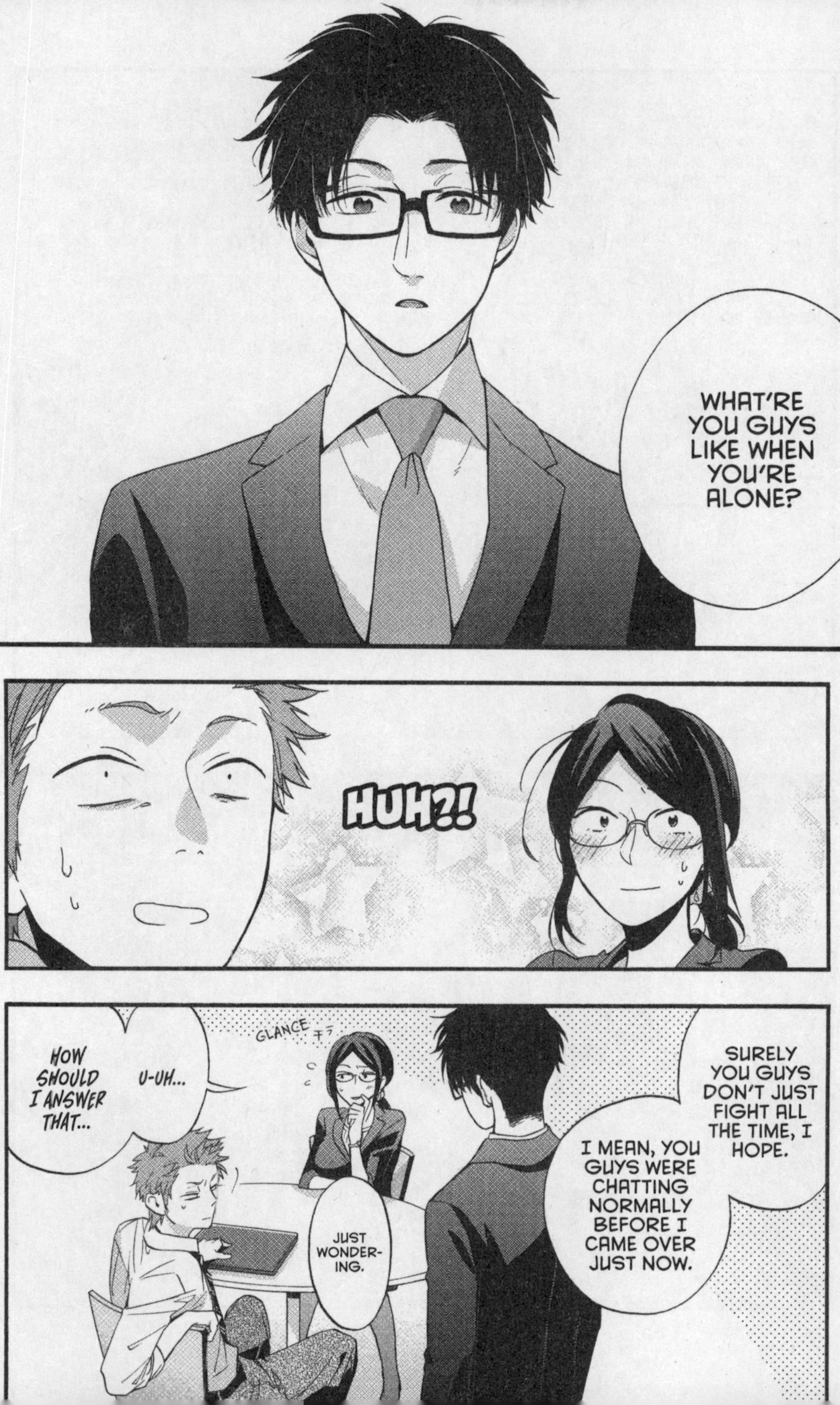
WHAT'RE YOU GUYS LIKE WHEN YOU'RE ALONE?
HUH?!
SURELY YOU GUYS DON'T JUST FIGHT ALL THE TIME, I HOPE.
I MEAN, YOU GUYS WERE CHATTING NORMALLY BEFORE I CAME OVER JUST NOW.
JUST WONDERING.
GLANCE
U-UH...
HOW SHOULD I ANSWER THAT...

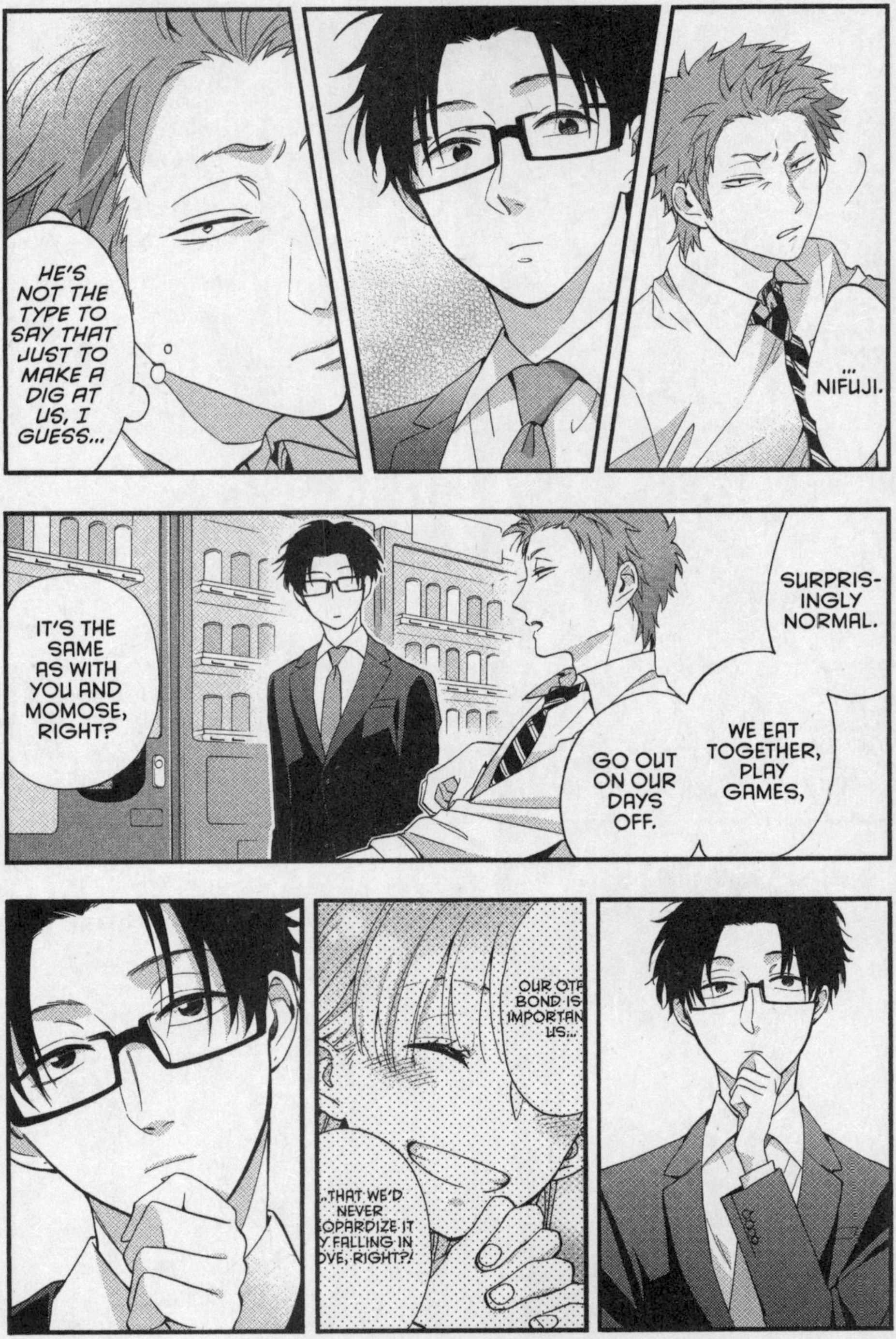
... NIFUJI.
HE'S NOT THE TYPE TO SAY THAT JUST TO MAKE A DIG AT US, I GUESS...
SURPRIS-INGLY NORMAL.
WE EAT TOGETHER, PLAY GAMES,
GO OUT ON OUR DAYS OFF.
IT'S THE SAME AS WITH YOU AND MOMOSE, RIGHT?
OUR OTA BOND IS IMPORTAN US...
...THAT WE'D NEVER OPARDIZE IT Y FALLING IN OVE, RIGHT?!

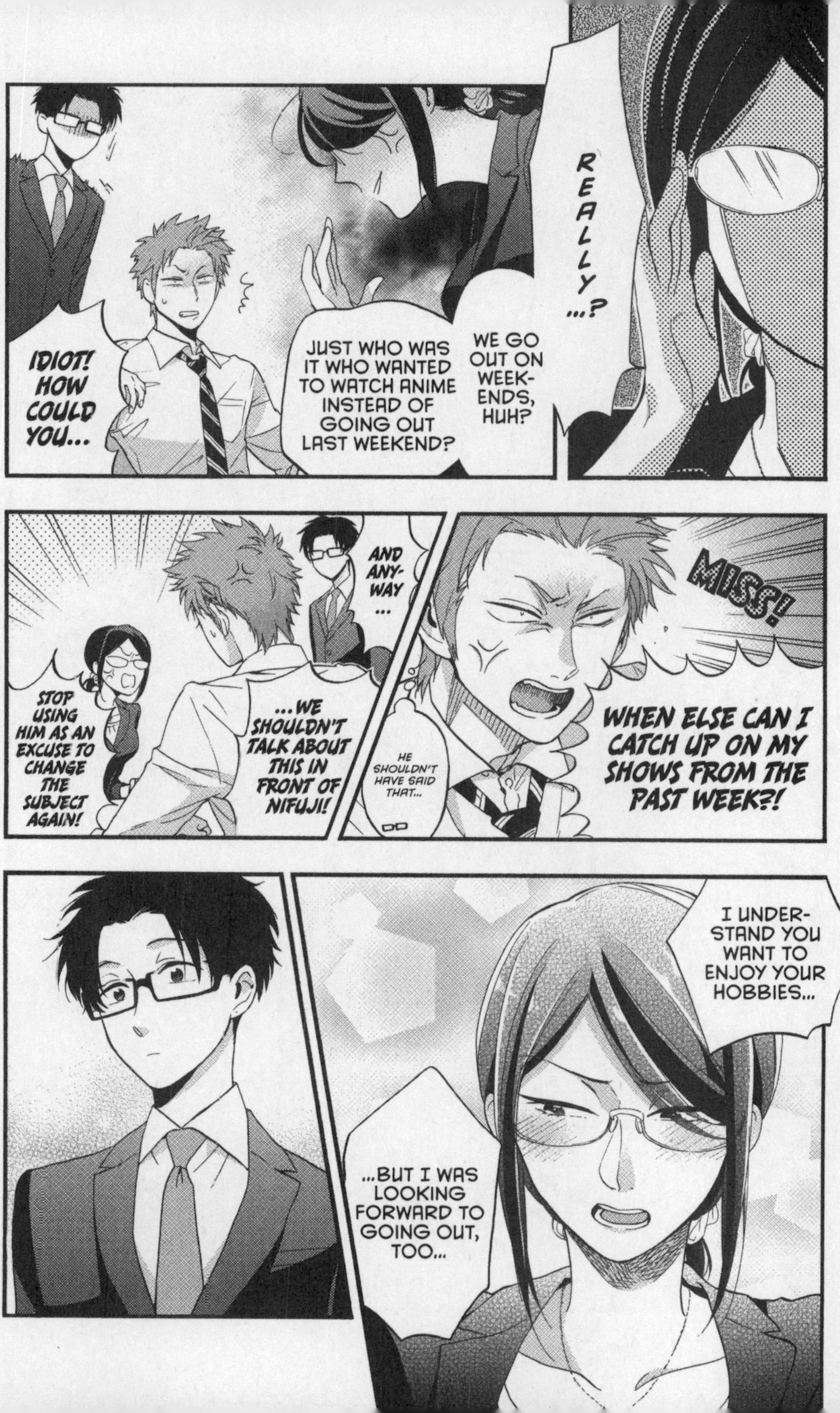
REALLY...?
WE GO OUT ON WEEKENDS, HUH?
JUST WHO WAS IT WHO WANTED TO WATCH ANIME INSTEAD OF GOING OUT LAST WEEKEND?
IDIOT! HOW COULD YOU...
MISS!
WHEN ELSE CAN I CATCH UP ON MY SHOWS FROM THE PAST WEEK?!
HE SHOULDN'T HAVE SAID THAT...
AND ANYWAY...
...WE SHOULDN'T TALK ABOUT THIS IN FRONT OF NIFUJI!
STOP USING HIM AS AN EXCUSE TO CHANGE THE SUBJECT AGAIN!
I UNDERSTAND YOU WANT TO ENJOY YOUR HOBBIES...
...BUT I WAS LOOKING FORWARD TO GOING OUT, TOO...

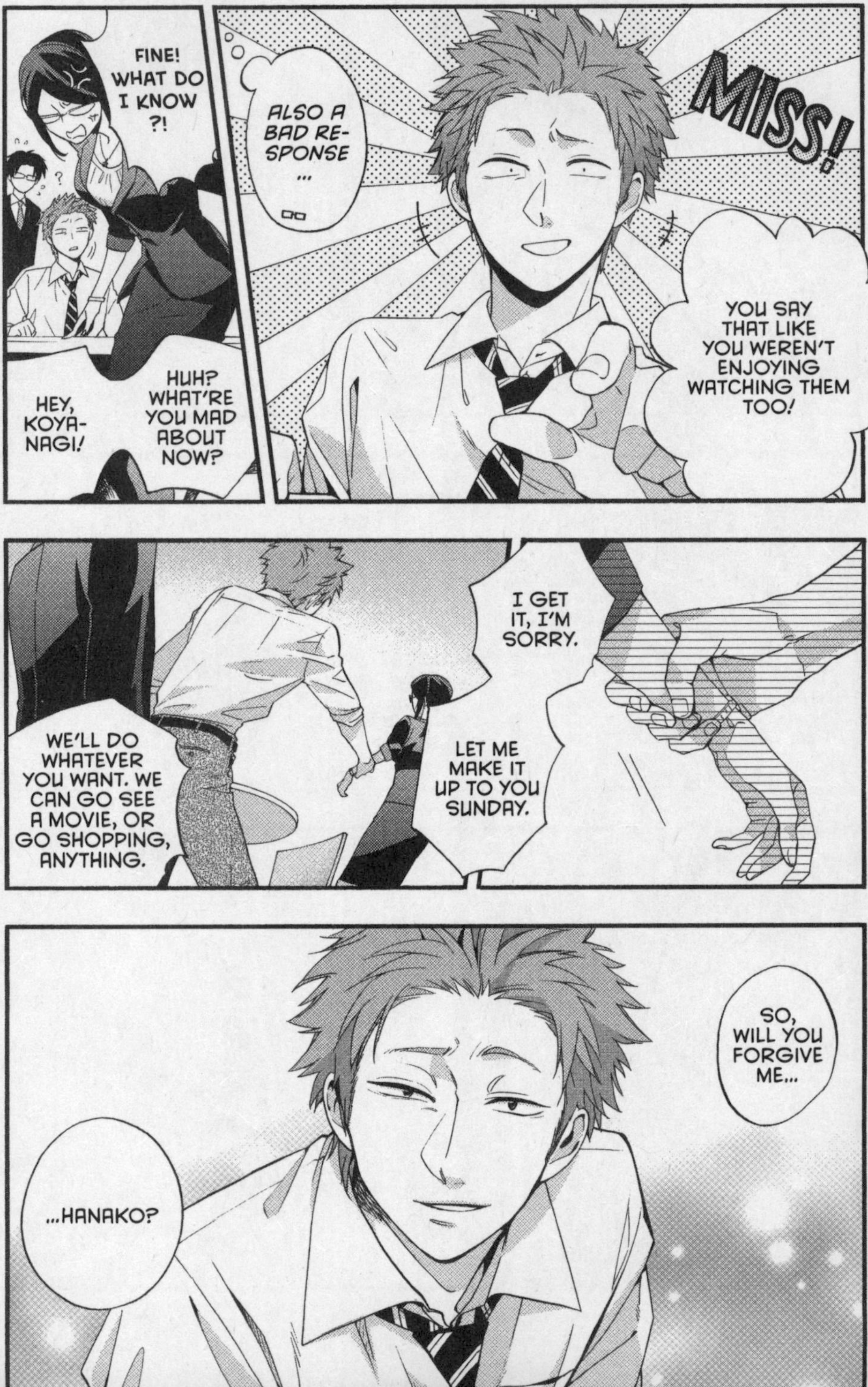
MISS!
YOU SAY THAT LIKE YOU WEREN'T ENJOYING WATCHING THEM TOO!
ALSO A BAD RE-SPONSE ...
FINE! WHAT DO I KNOW ?!
HUH? WHAT'RE YOU MAD ABOUT NOW?
HEY, KOYA-NAGI!
I GET IT, I'M SORRY.
LET ME MAKE IT UP TO YOU SUNDAY.
WE'LL DO WHATEVER YOU WANT. WE CAN GO SEE A MOVIE, OR GO SHOPPING, ANYTHING.
SO, WILL YOU FORGIVE ME...
...HANAKO?

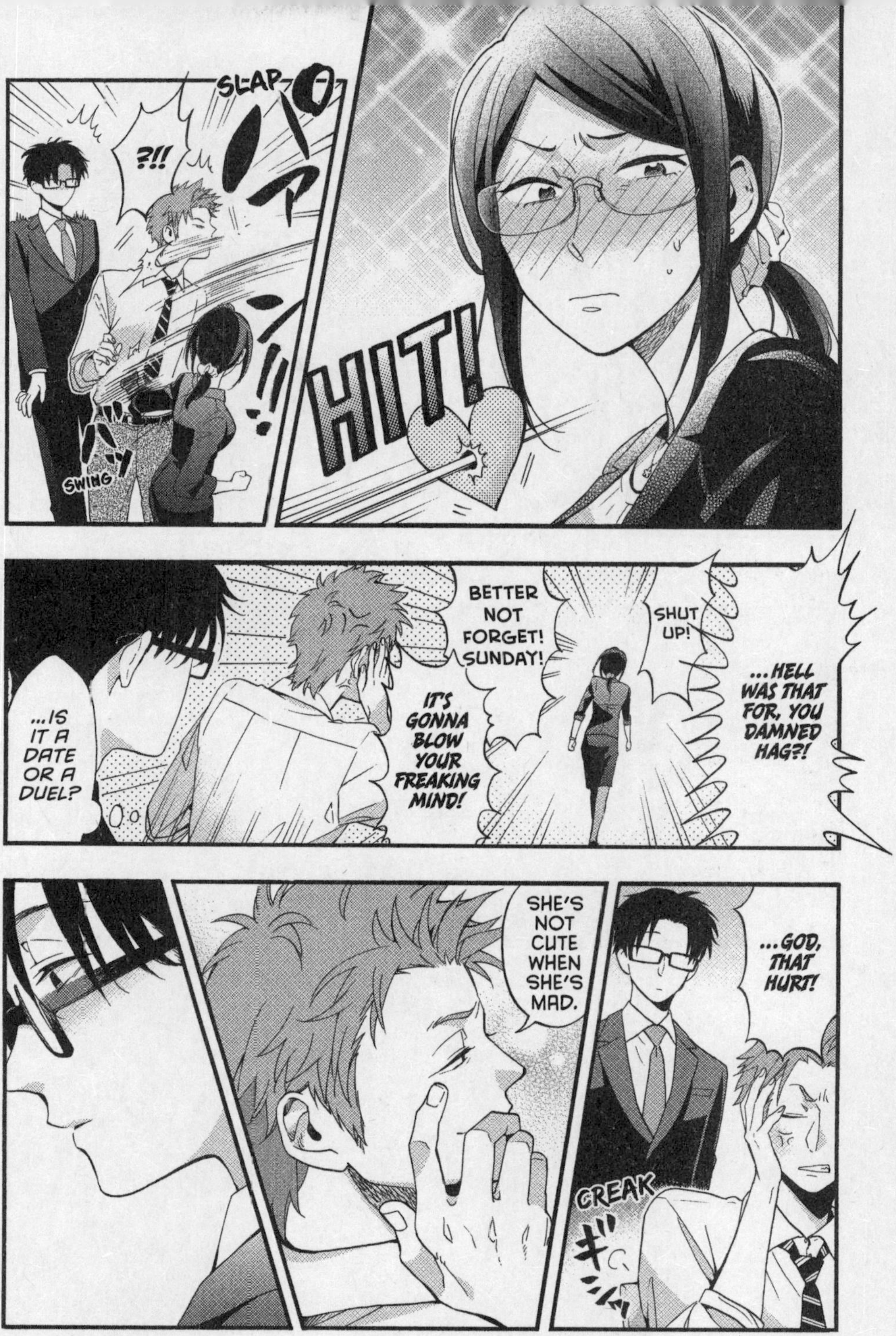
HIT!
SLAP
?!!
SWING
...HELL WAS THAT FOR, YOU DAMNED HAG?!
SHUT UP!
BETTER NOT FORGET! SUNDAY!
IT'S GONNA BLOW YOUR FREAKING MIND!
...IS IT A DATE OR A DUEL?
...GOD, THAT HURT!
CREAK
SHE'S NOT CUTE WHEN SHE'S MAD.

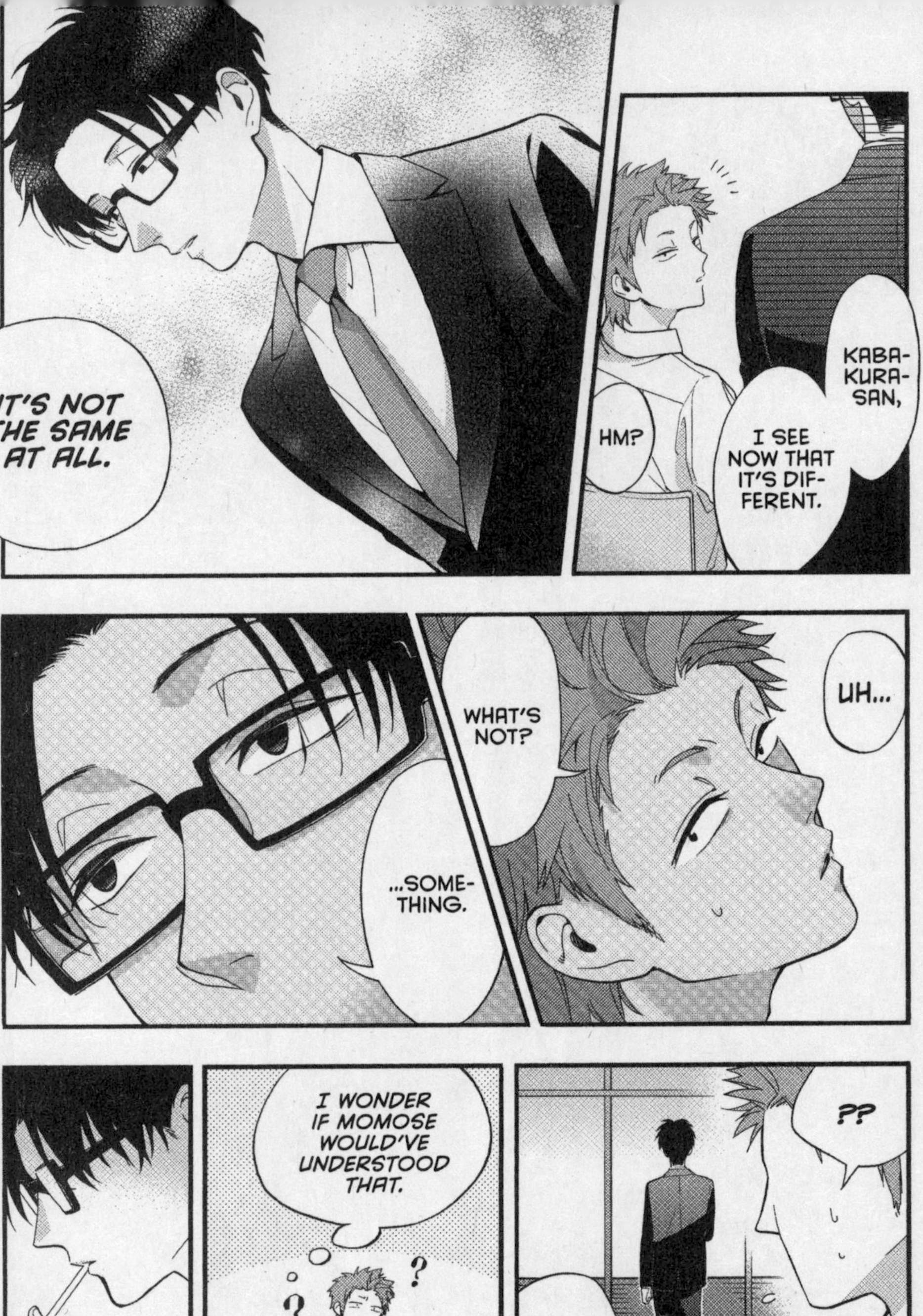
KABA-KURA-SAN,
I SEE NOW THAT IT'S DIF-FERENT.
HM?
IT'S NOT THE SAME AT ALL.
UH...
WHAT'S NOT?
...SOME-THING.
??
YO, NIFUJI?
I WONDER IF MOMOSE WOULD'VE UNDERSTOOD THAT.
? ?

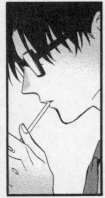

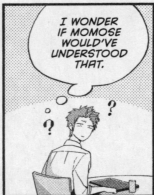

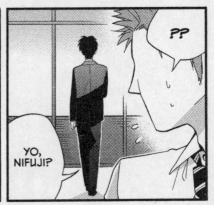

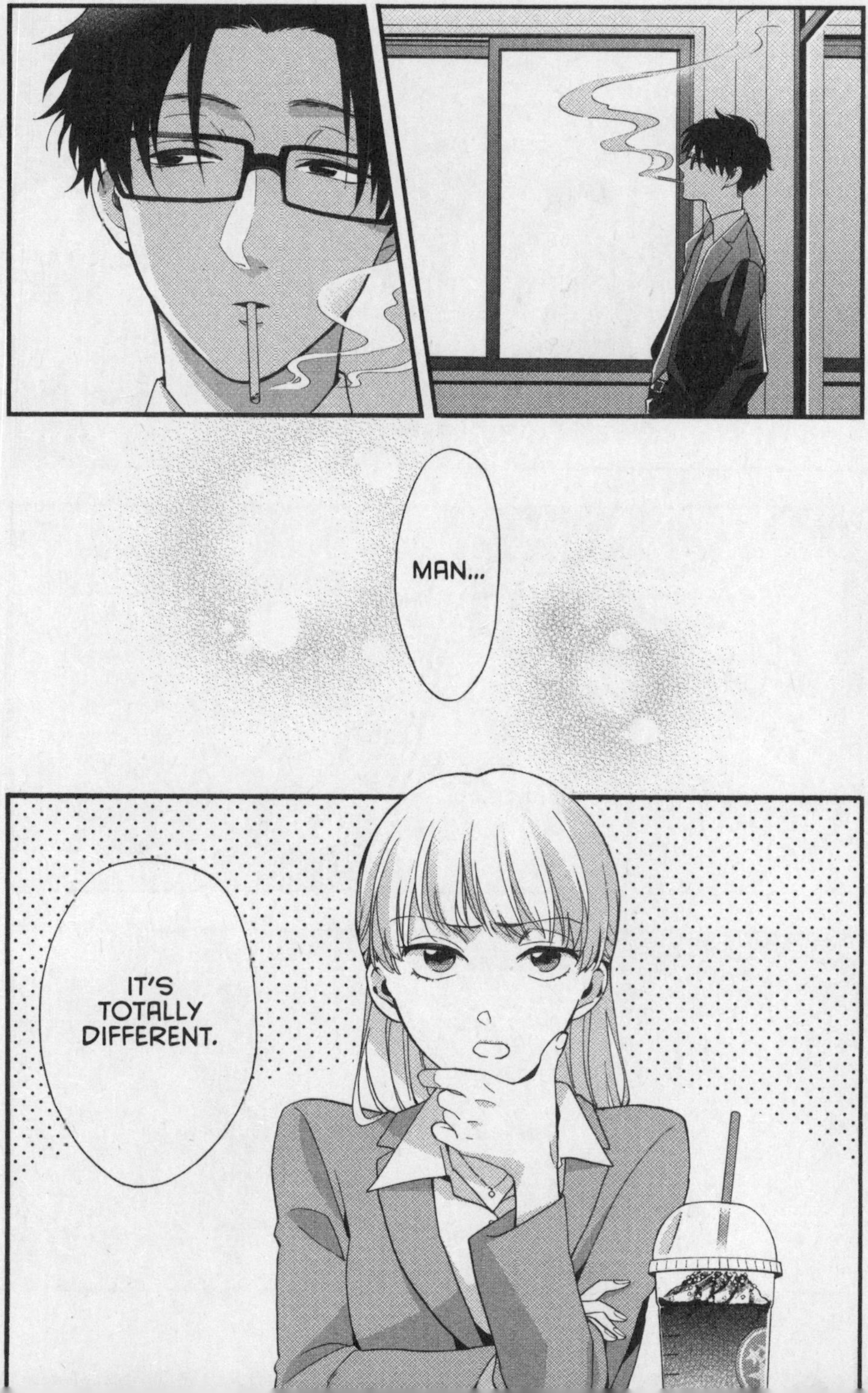
MAN...
IT'S TOTALLY DIFFERENT.

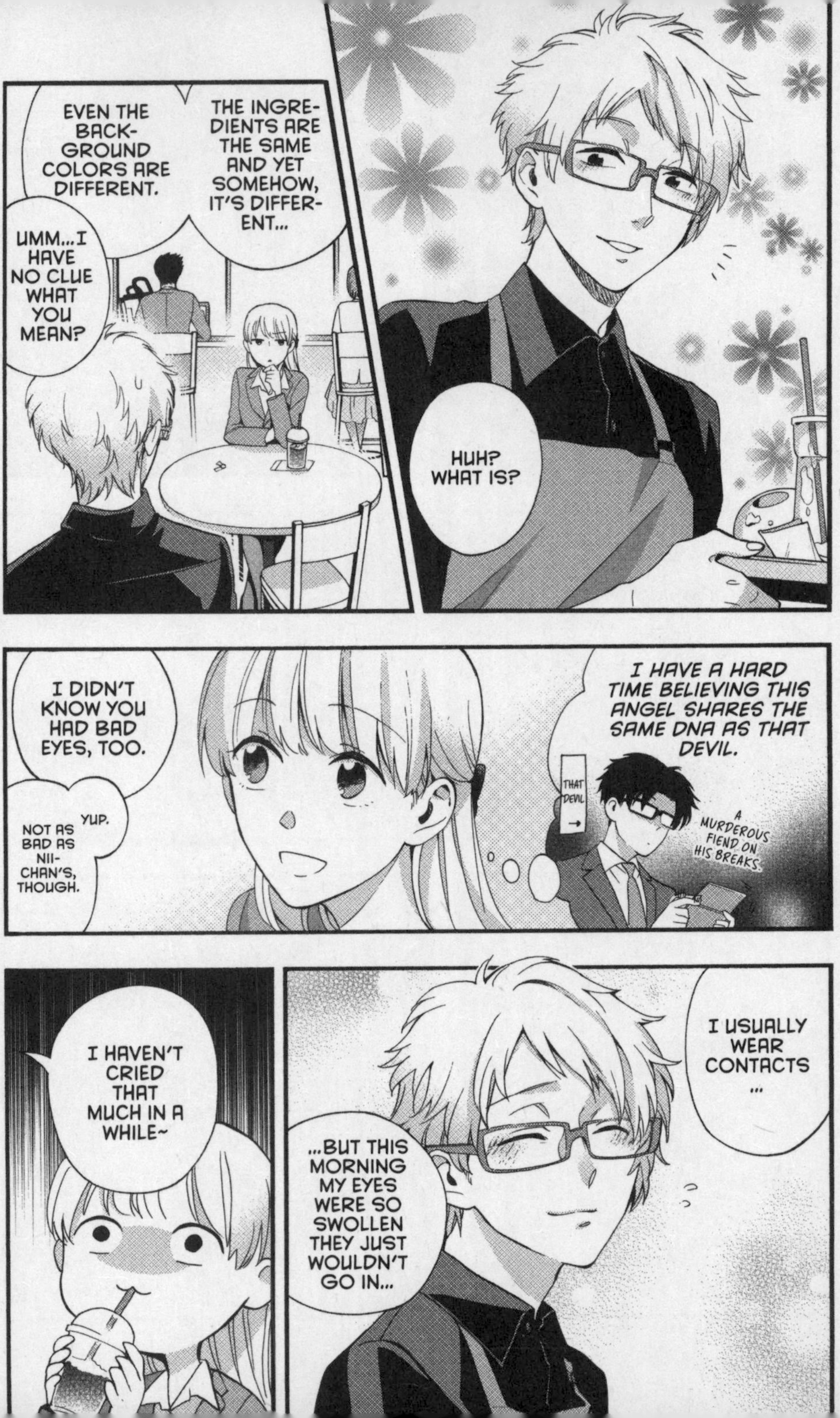
HUH? WHAT IS?
THE INGREDIENTS ARE THE SAME AND YET SOMEHOW, IT'S DIFFERENT...
EVEN THE BACKGROUND COLORS ARE DIFFERENT.
UMM...I HAVE NO CLUE WHAT YOU MEAN?
I HAVE A HARD TIME BELIEVING THIS ANGEL SHARES THE SAME DNA AS THAT DEVIL.
THAT DEVIL →
A MURDEROUS FIEND ON HIS BREAKS.
I DIDN'T KNOW YOU HAD BAD EYES, TOO.
YUP.
NOT AS BAD AS NII-CHAN'S, THOUGH.
I USUALLY WEAR CONTACTS...
...BUT THIS MORNING MY EYES WERE SO SWOLLEN THEY JUST WOULDN'T GO IN...
I HAVEN'T CRIED THAT MUCH IN A WHILE~

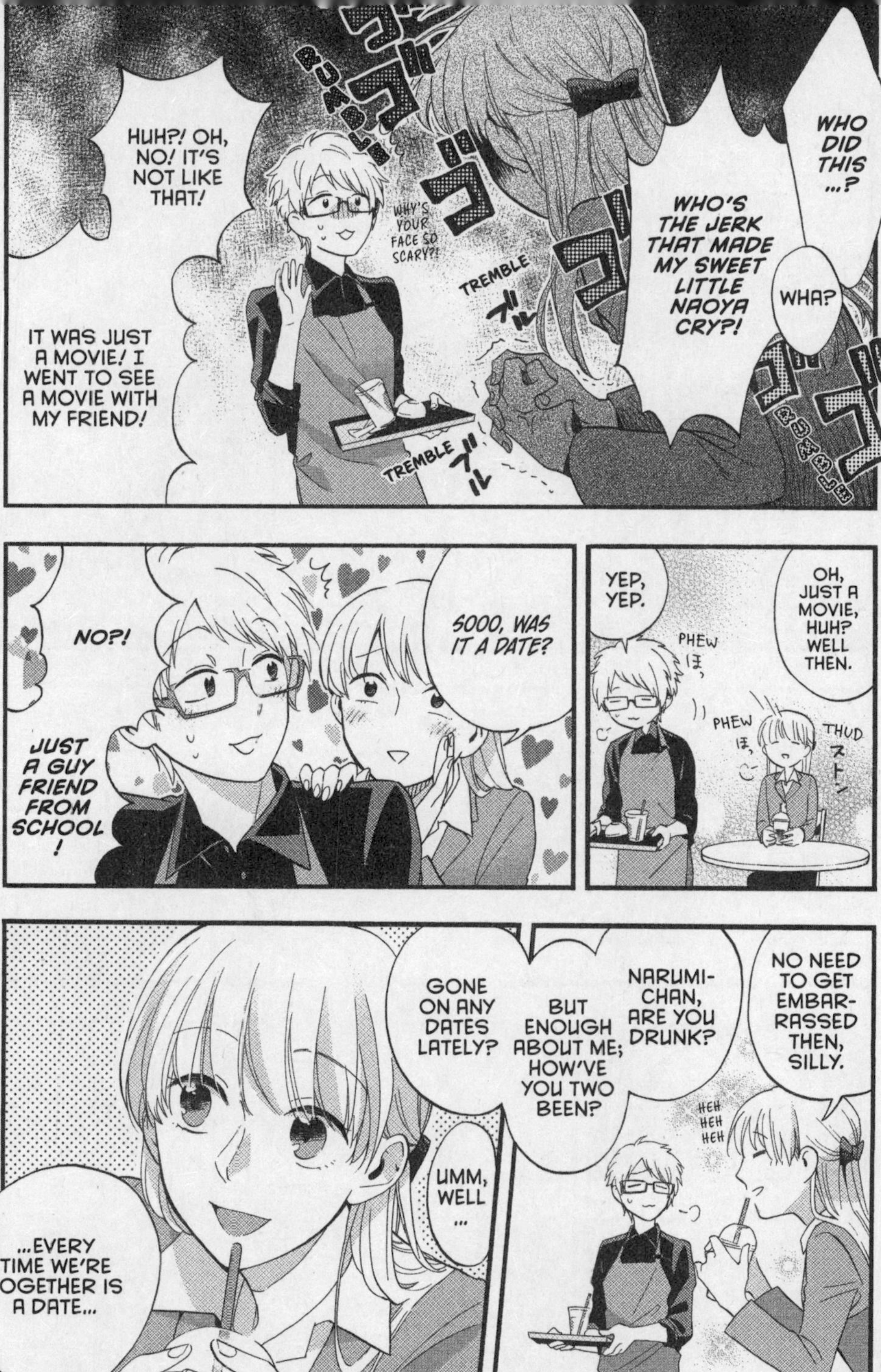
WHO DID THIS ...?
WHO'S THE JERK THAT MADE MY SWEET LITTLE NAOYA CRY?!
WHA?
RUMBLE
TREMBLE
TREMBLE
HUH?! OH, NO! IT'S NOT LIKE THAT!
WHY'S YOUR FACE SO SCARY?!
IT WAS JUST A MOVIE! I WENT TO SEE A MOVIE WITH MY FRIEND!
OH, JUST A MOVIE, HUH? WELL THEN.
THUD
PHEW
YEP, YEP.
PHEW
SOOO, WAS IT A DATE?
NO?!
JUST A GUY FRIEND FROM SCHOOL!
NO NEED TO GET EMBARRASSED THEN, SILLY.
HEH HEH HEH
NARUMI-CHAN, ARE YOU DRUNK?
BUT ENOUGH ABOUT ME; HOW'VE YOU TWO BEEN?
GONE ON ANY DATES LATELY?
UMM, WELL ...
...EVERY TIME WE'RE TOGETHER IS A DATE...

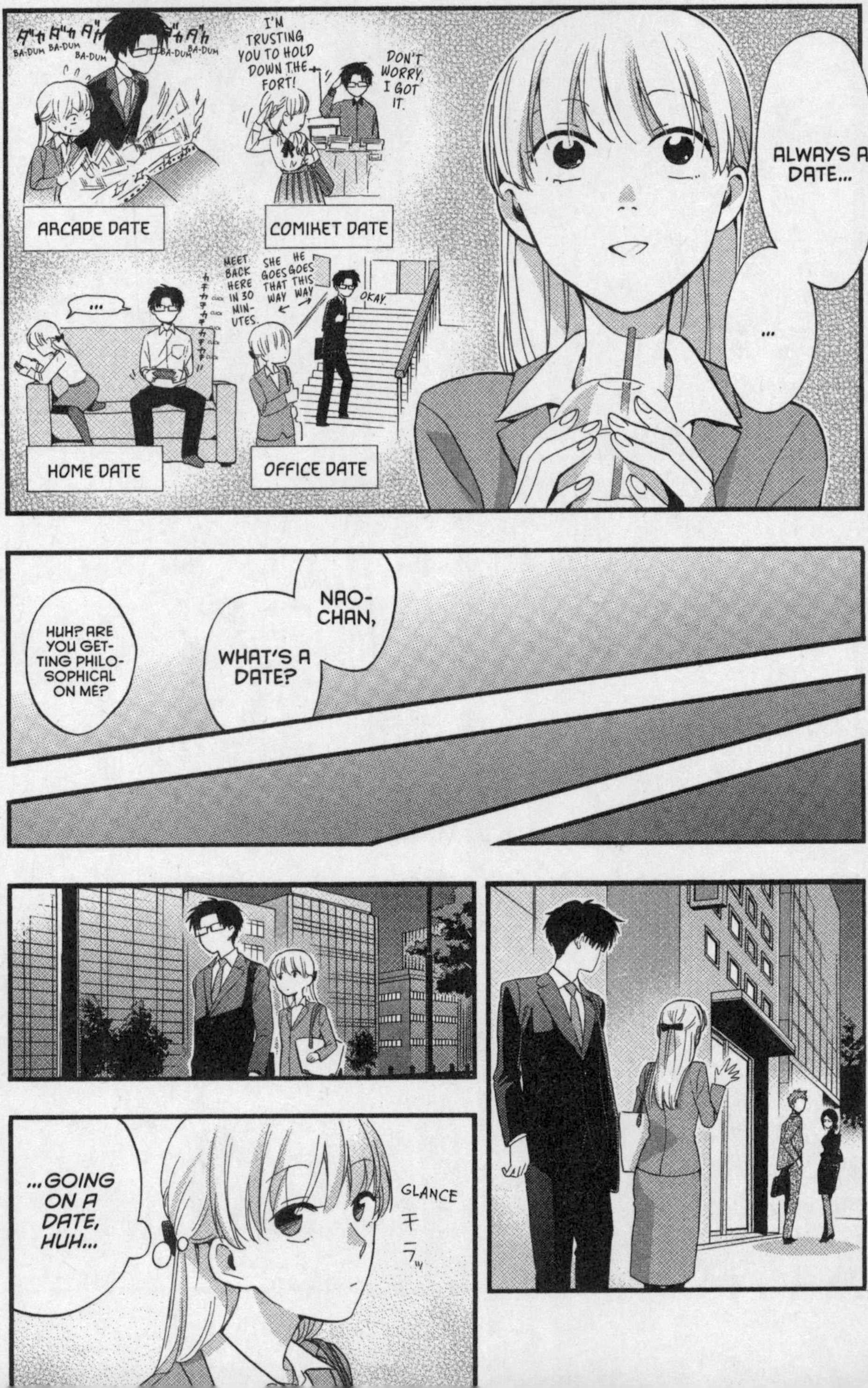
ALWAYS A DATE...
...
I'M TRUSTING YOU TO HOLD DOWN THE FORT!
DON'T WORRY, I GOT IT.
COMIKET DATE
BA-DUM BA-DUM BA-DUM BA-DUM BA-DUM
ARCADE DATE
OKAY.
HE GOES THIS WAY
SHE GOES THAT WAY
MEET BACK HERE IN 30 MINUTES.
OFFICE DATE
CLICK
...
HOME DATE
NAO-CHAN, WHAT'S A DATE?
HUH? ARE YOU GETTING PHILOSOPHICAL ON ME?
GLANCE
...GOING ON A DATE, HUH...

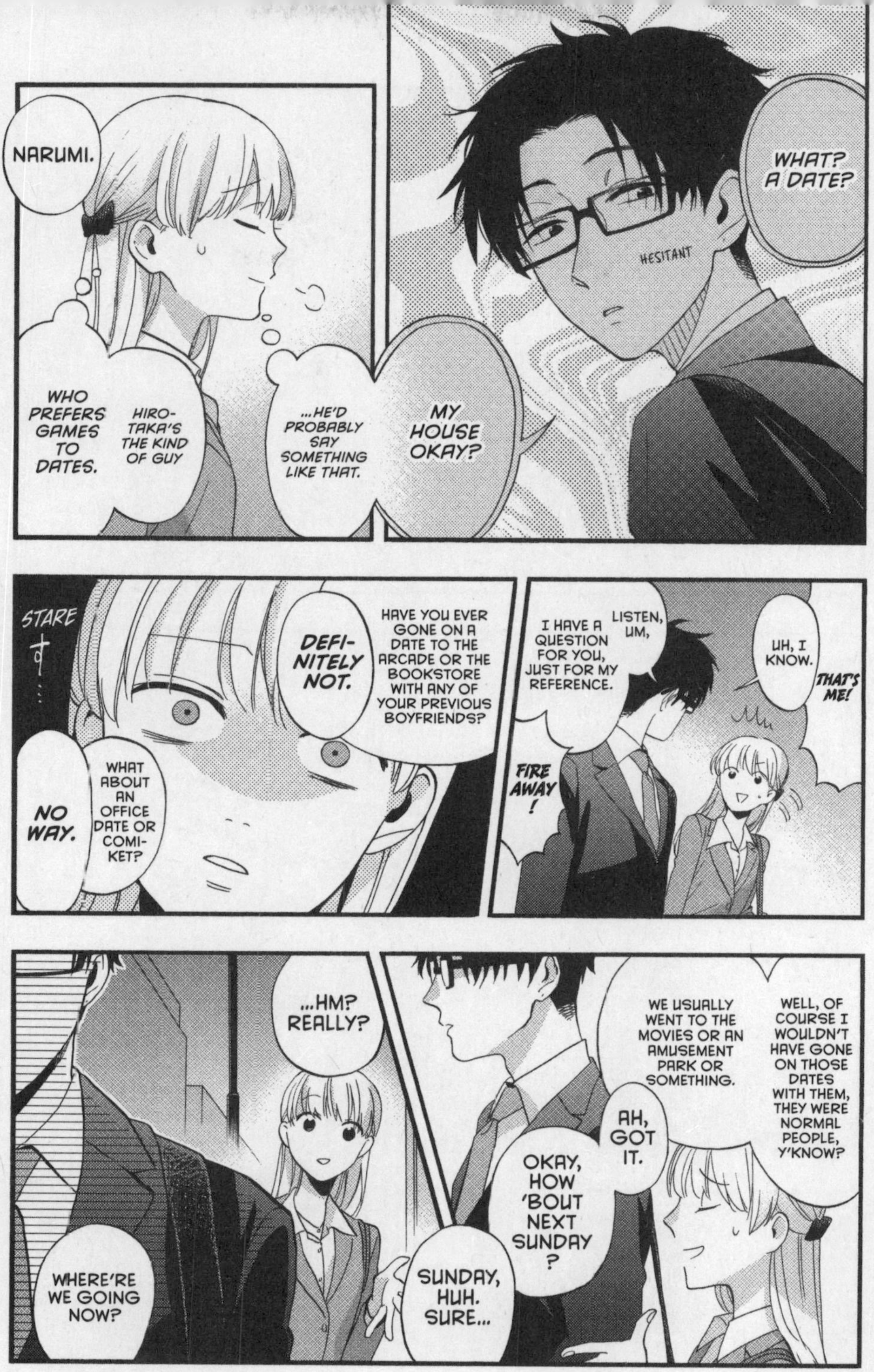
WHAT? A DATE?
HESITANT
MY HOUSE OKAY?
...HE'D PROBABLY SAY SOMETHING LIKE THAT.
HIRO-TAKA'S THE KIND OF GUY
WHO PREFERS GAMES TO DATES.
NARUMI.
UH, I KNOW.
THAT'S ME!
LISTEN, UM,
I HAVE A QUESTION FOR YOU, JUST FOR MY REFERENCE.
FIRE AWAY!
HAVE YOU EVER GONE ON A DATE TO THE ARCADE OR THE BOOKSTORE WITH ANY OF YOUR PREVIOUS BOYFRIENDS?
DEFI-NITELY NOT.
STARE
す…
WHAT ABOUT AN OFFICE DATE OR COMI-KET?
NO WAY.
WELL, OF COURSE I WOULDN'T HAVE GONE ON THOSE DATES WITH THEM, THEY WERE NORMAL PEOPLE, Y'KNOW?
WE USUALLY WENT TO THE MOVIES OR AN AMUSEMENT PARK OR SOMETHING.
AH, GOT IT.
OKAY, HOW 'BOUT NEXT SUNDAY?
SUNDAY, HUH. SURE...
...HM? REALLY?
WHERE'RE WE GOING NOW?

(Silly question)

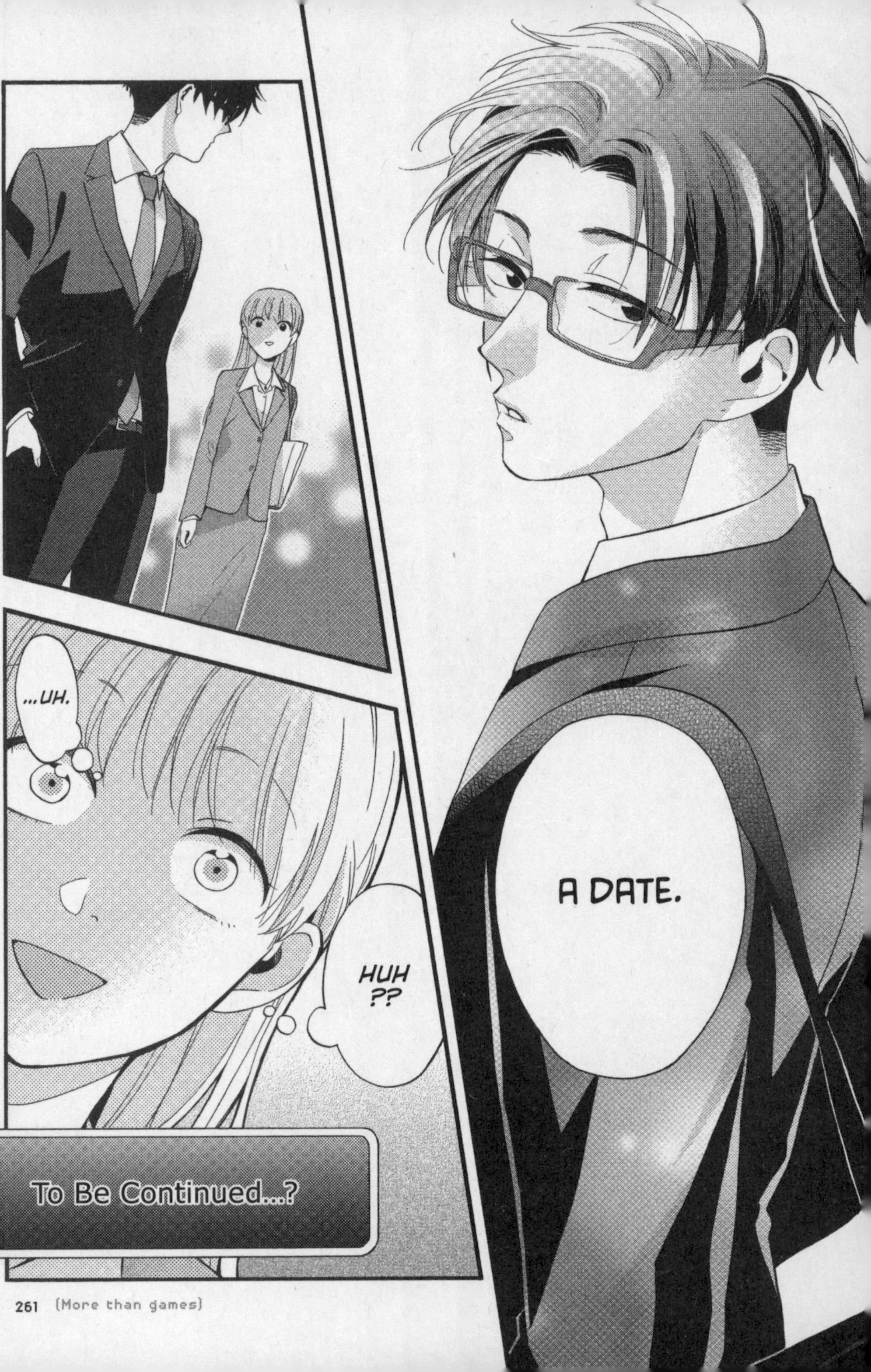
A DATE.
...UH.
HUH ??
To Be Continued...?

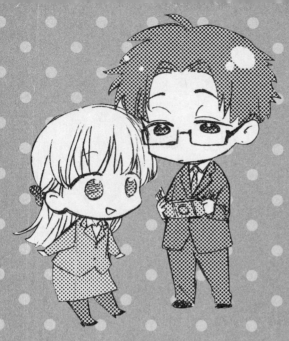

Wotakoi: Love is Hard for Otaku

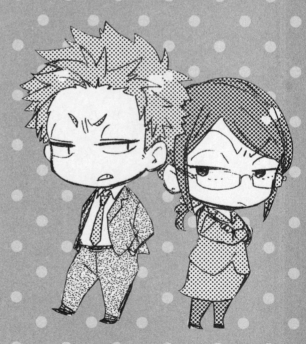

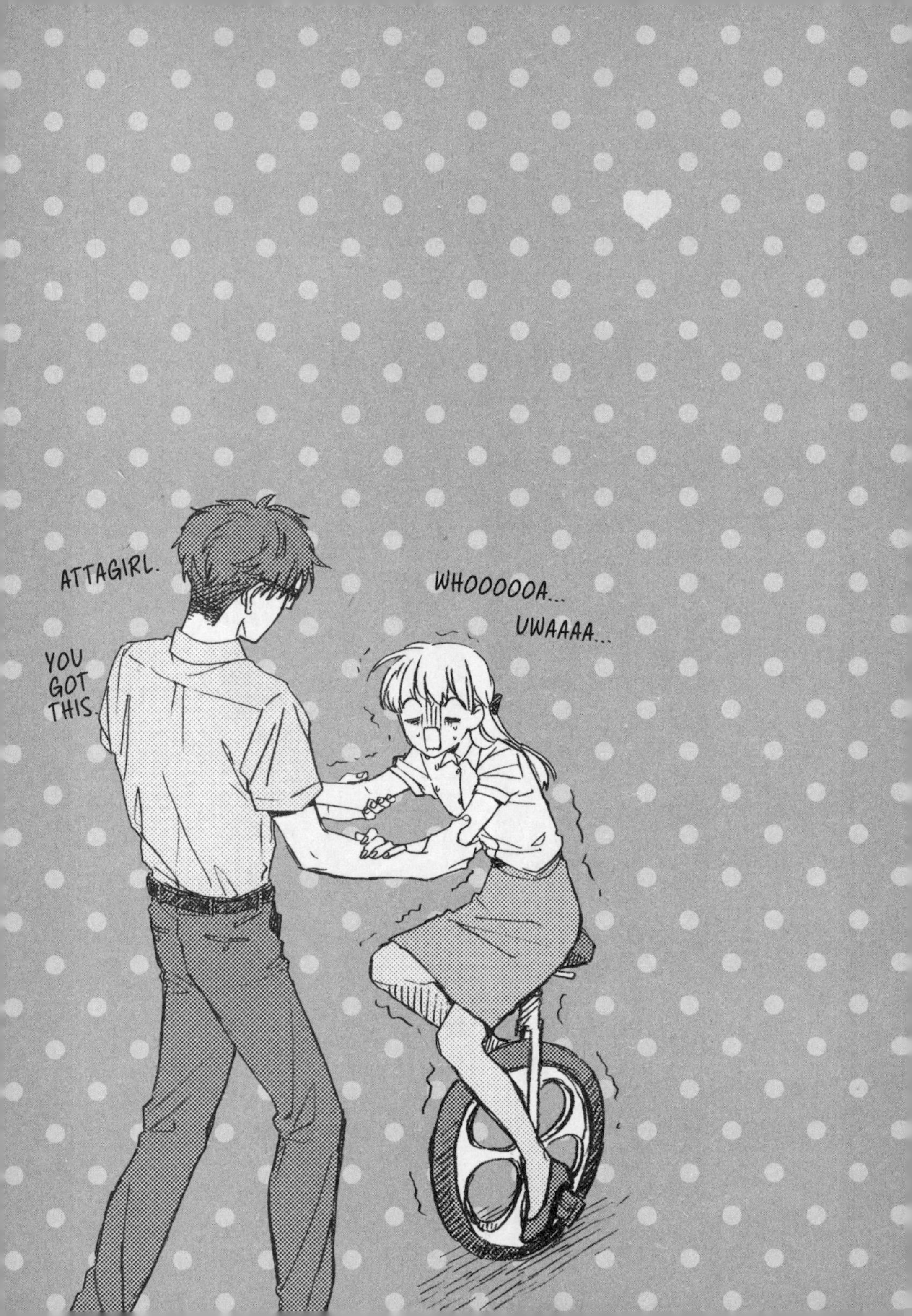
WHOOOOOA...
UWAAAA...
ATTAGIRL.
YOU GOT THIS.

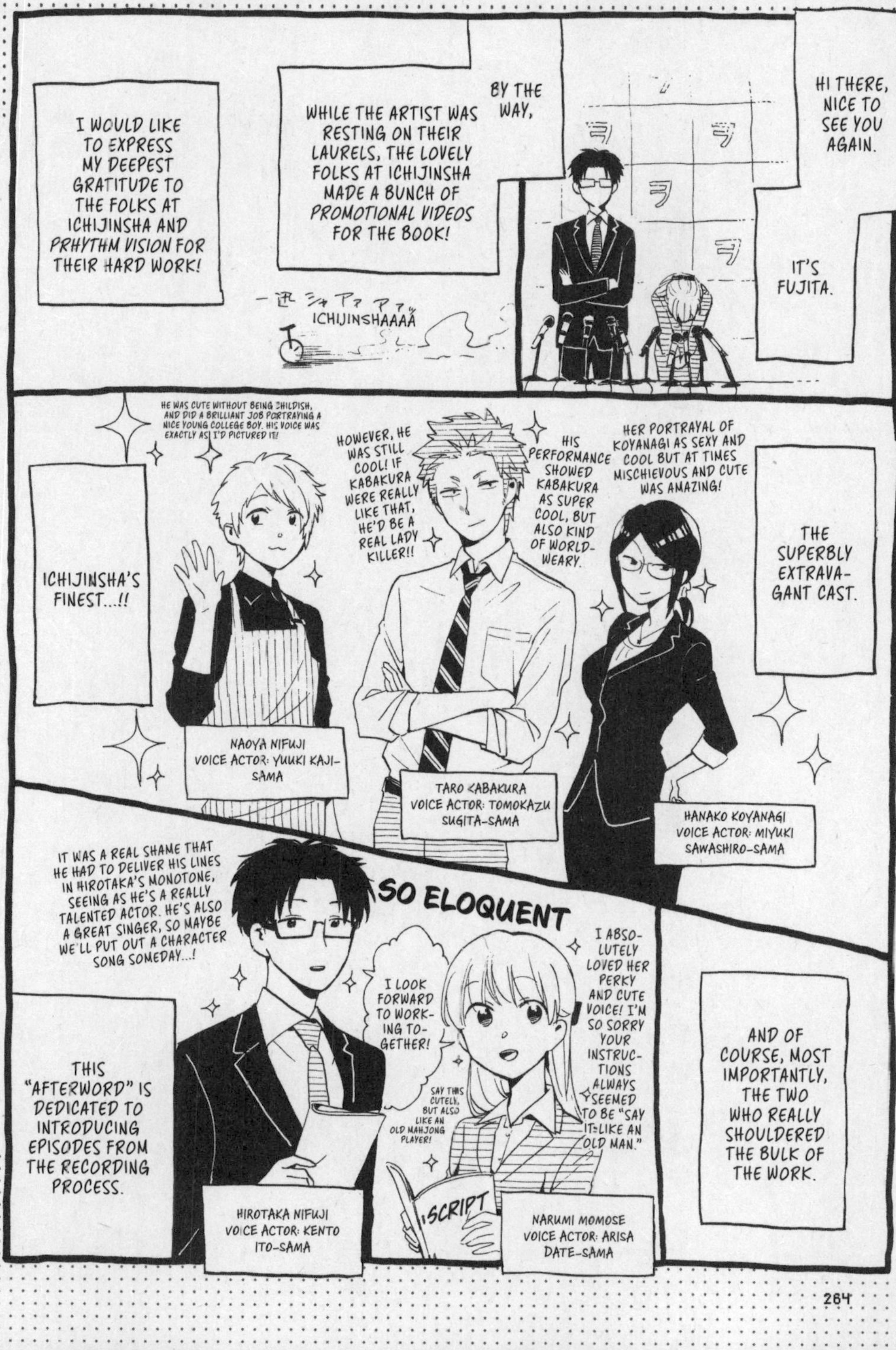
HI THERE, NICE TO SEE YOU AGAIN.
IT'S FUJITA.
BY THE WAY,
WHILE THE ARTIST WAS RESTING ON THEIR LAURELS, THE LOVELY FOLKS AT ICHIJINSHA MADE A BUNCH OF PROMOTIONAL VIDEOS FOR THE BOOK!
I WOULD LIKE TO EXPRESS MY DEEPEST GRATITUDE TO THE FOLKS AT ICHIJINSHA AND PRHYTHM VISION FOR THEIR HARD WORK!
一迅シャァァァッ
ICHIJINSHAAAA
THE SUPERBLY EXTRAVAGANT CAST.
HER PORTRAYAL OF KOYANAGI AS SEXY AND COOL BUT AT TIMES MISCHIEVOUS AND CUTE WAS AMAZING!
HANAKO KOYANAGI VOICE ACTOR: MIYUKI SAWASHIRO-SAMA
HIS PERFORMANCE SHOWED KABAKURA AS SUPER COOL, BUT ALSO KIND OF WORLD-WEARY.
HOWEVER, HE WAS STILL COOL! IF KABAKURA WERE REALLY LIKE THAT, HE'D BE A REAL LADY KILLER!!
TARO KABAKURA VOICE ACTOR: TOMOKAZU SUGITA-SAMA
HE WAS CUTE WITHOUT BEING CHILDISH, AND DID A BRILLIANT JOB PORTRAYING A NICE YOUNG COLLEGE BOY. HIS VOICE WAS EXACTLY AS I'D PICTURED IT!
NAOYA NIFUJI VOICE ACTOR: YUUKI KAJI-SAMA
ICHIJINSHA'S FINEST...!!
AND OF COURSE, MOST IMPORTANTLY, THE TWO WHO REALLY SHOULDERED THE BULK OF THE WORK.
I ABSOLUTELY LOVED HER PERKY AND CUTE VOICE! I'M SO SORRY YOUR INSTRUCTIONS ALWAYS SEEMED TO BE "SAY IT LIKE AN OLD MAN."
SAY THIS CUTELY, BUT ALSO LIKE AN OLD MAHJONG PLAYER!
NARUMI MOMOSE VOICE ACTOR: ARISA DATE-SAMA
SCRIPT
I LOOK FORWARD TO WORKING TOGETHER!
SO ELOQUENT
IT WAS A REAL SHAME THAT HE HAD TO DELIVER HIS LINES IN HIROTAKA'S MONOTONE, SEEING AS HE'S A REALLY TALENTED ACTOR. HE'S ALSO A GREAT SINGER, SO MAYBE WE'LL PUT OUT A CHARACTER SONG SOMEDAY...!
HIROTAKA NIFUJI VOICE ACTOR: KENTO ITO-SAMA
THIS "AFTERWORD" IS DEDICATED TO INTRODUCING EPISODES FROM THE RECORDING PROCESS.

Background: Wo.

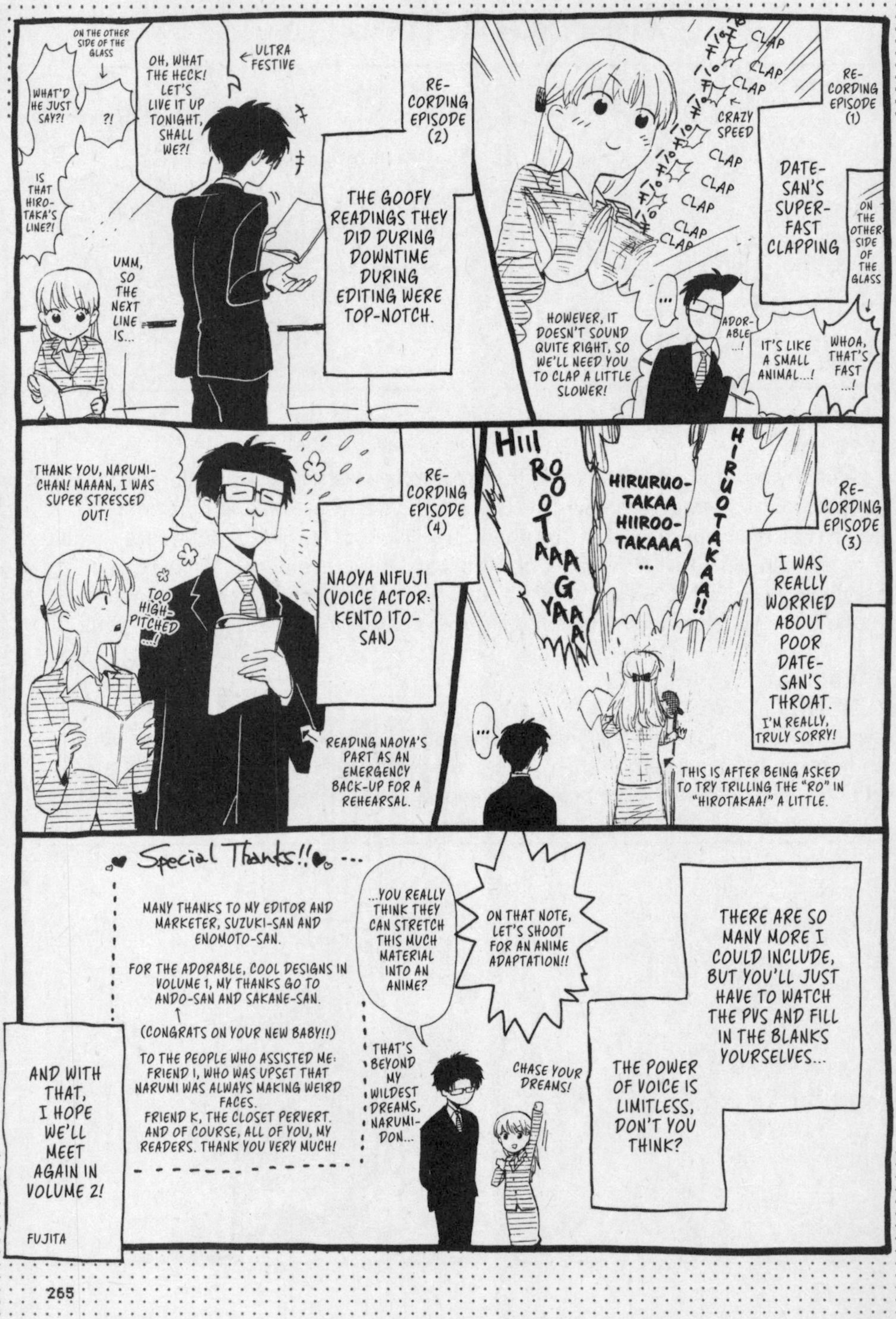

RE-CORDING EPISODE (1)
DATE-SAN'S SUPER-FAST CLAPPING
ON THE OTHER SIDE OF THE GLASS
CLAP CLAP CLAP
CRAZY SPEED
CLAP CLAP CLAP CLAP CLAP
WHOA, THAT'S FAST ...!
IT'S LIKE A SMALL ANIMAL...!
ADOR-ABLE ...!
HOWEVER, IT DOESN'T SOUND QUITE RIGHT, SO WE'LL NEED YOU TO CLAP A LITTLE SLOWER!
...
RE-CORDING EPISODE (2)
THE GOOFY READINGS THEY DID DURING DOWNTIME DURING EDITING WERE TOP-NOTCH.
ULTRA FESTIVE
OH, WHAT THE HECK! LET'S LIVE IT UP TONIGHT, SHALL WE?!
ON THE OTHER SIDE OF THE GLASS
?!
WHAT'D HE JUST SAY?!
IS THAT HIRO-TAKA'S LINE?!
UMM, SO THE NEXT LINE IS...
RE-CORDING EPISODE (3)
I WAS REALLY WORRIED ABOUT POOR DATE-SAN'S THROAT.
I'M REALLY, TRULY SORRY!
HIRUOTAKAA!!
HIRURUO-TAKAA HIIROO-TAKAAA...
HIIIROOOTAAAGYAAAA
...
THIS IS AFTER BEING ASKED TO TRY TRILLING THE "RO" IN "HIROTAKAA!" A LITTLE.
RE-CORDING EPISODE (4)
NAOYA NIFUJI (VOICE ACTOR: KENTO ITO-SAN)
THANK YOU, NARUMI-CHAN! MAAAN, I WAS SUPER STRESSED OUT!
TOO HIGH-PITCHED ...!
READING NAOYA'S PART AS AN EMERGENCY BACK-UP FOR A REHEARSAL.
THERE ARE SO MANY MORE I COULD INCLUDE, BUT YOU'LL JUST HAVE TO WATCH THE PVS AND FILL IN THE BLANKS YOURSELVES...
THE POWER OF VOICE IS LIMITLESS, DON'T YOU THINK?
ON THAT NOTE, LET'S SHOOT FOR AN ANIME ADAPTATION!!
...YOU REALLY THINK THEY CAN STRETCH THIS MUCH MATERIAL INTO AN ANIME?
CHASE YOUR DREAMS!
THAT'S BEYOND MY WILDEST DREAMS, NARUMI-DON...
Special Thanks!! ...
MANY THANKS TO MY EDITOR AND MARKETER, SUZUKI-SAN AND ENOMOTO-SAN.
FOR THE ADORABLE, COOL DESIGNS IN VOLUME 1, MY THANKS GO TO ANDO-SAN AND SAKANE-SAN.
(CONGRATS ON YOUR NEW BABY!!)
TO THE PEOPLE WHO ASSISTED ME: FRIEND I, WHO WAS UPSET THAT NARUMI WAS ALWAYS MAKING WEIRD FACES.
FRIEND K, THE CLOSET PERVERT.
AND OF COURSE, ALL OF YOU, MY READERS. THANK YOU VERY MUCH!
AND WITH THAT, I HOPE WE'LL MEET AGAIN IN VOLUME 2!
FUJITA

TRANSLATION NOTES

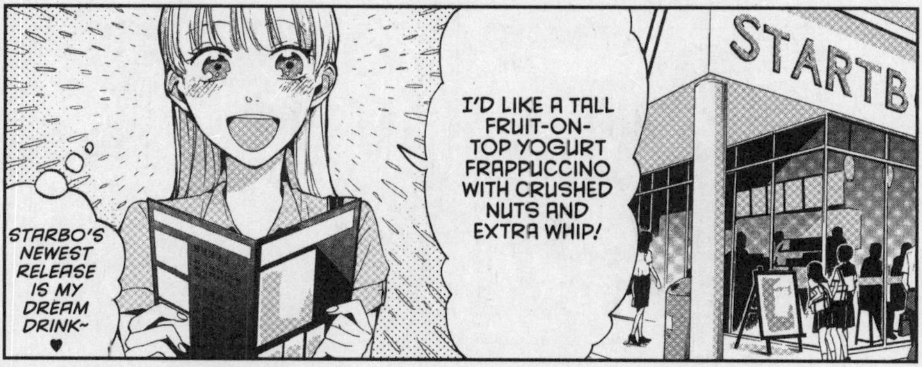

I'D LIKE A TALL FRUIT-ON-TOP YOGURT FRAPPUCCINO WITH CRUSHED NUTS AND EXTRA WHIP!
STARBO'S NEWEST RELEASE IS MY DREAM DRINK~ ♥
STARTB

▲STARBO/STARTBOX,
PAGE 148

A pseudonym the artist has given to refer to Starbucks (frequently abbreviated in Japanese to *Staba*) indirectly. This is a common contraction and portmanteau pattern in Japan whereby they take the first syllable or two of the first part of the term and combine it with the start of the second half. Often used for borrowed foreign words, but not always. Other notable examples include "Smartphone → *smaho*," "Pocket Monsters → Pokémon," "Tokyo Daigaku (College) → *Todai*," etc.

▼RARE CAT,
PAGE 151

A limited-edition cat from the smartphone app Neko Atsume, in which players put items out in their yard in the hopes of attracting different cats to visit. Rare cats only have a chance to appear when special items are put out, and are, as the name suggests, much more difficult to collect.

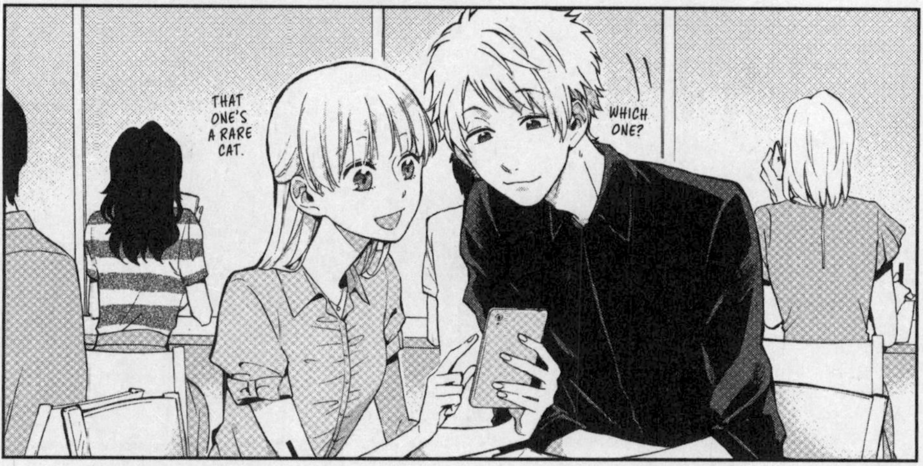

WHICH ONE?
THAT ONE'S A RARE CAT.

NII-CHAN, PAGE 155

Nii-chan is an affectionate way to refer to one's older brother, a contraction of the more formal onii-san.

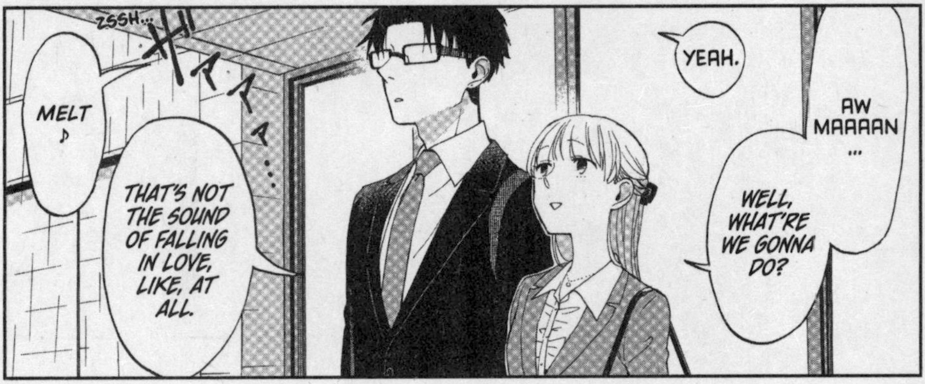
AW MAAAAN ...
WELL, WHAT'RE WE GONNA DO?
YEAH.
ZSSH...
MELT ♪
THAT'S NOT THE SOUND OF FALLING IN LOVE, LIKE, AT ALL.

▲MELT,
PAGE 182

Hirotaka is singing to the tune of "Melt" by vocaloid Miku Hatsune. The song is about a girl sharing an umbrella with a boy she likes on a rainy day.

▼SEME/UKE,
PAGE 192

In yaoi and BL anime and manga, characters fall into two groups: *seme* and *uke*. The *seme* is the partner who is on top during intercourse and tends to be more dominant/aggressive, taller, and older. Conversely, the *uke* is the partner who is on the bottom and is usually more submissive, affectionate, smaller, and younger than the *seme*. These terms were adapted from martial arts terms: *seme* comes from the verb "to attack" and *uke* comes from the verb "to receive."

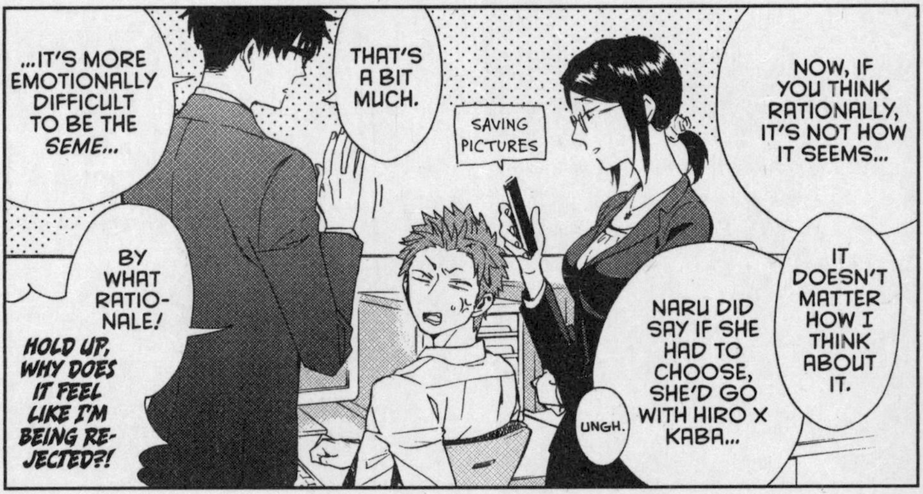
NOW, IF YOU THINK RATIONALLY, IT'S NOT HOW IT SEEMS...
IT DOESN'T MATTER HOW I THINK ABOUT IT.
NARU DID SAY IF SHE HAD TO CHOOSE, SHE'D GO WITH HIRO X KABA...
UNGH.
SAVING PICTURES
THAT'S A BIT MUCH.
...IT'S MORE EMOTIONALLY DIFFICULT TO BE THE *SEME*...
BY WHAT RATIONALE!
HOLD UP, WHY DOES IT FEEL LIKE I'M BEING REJECTED?!

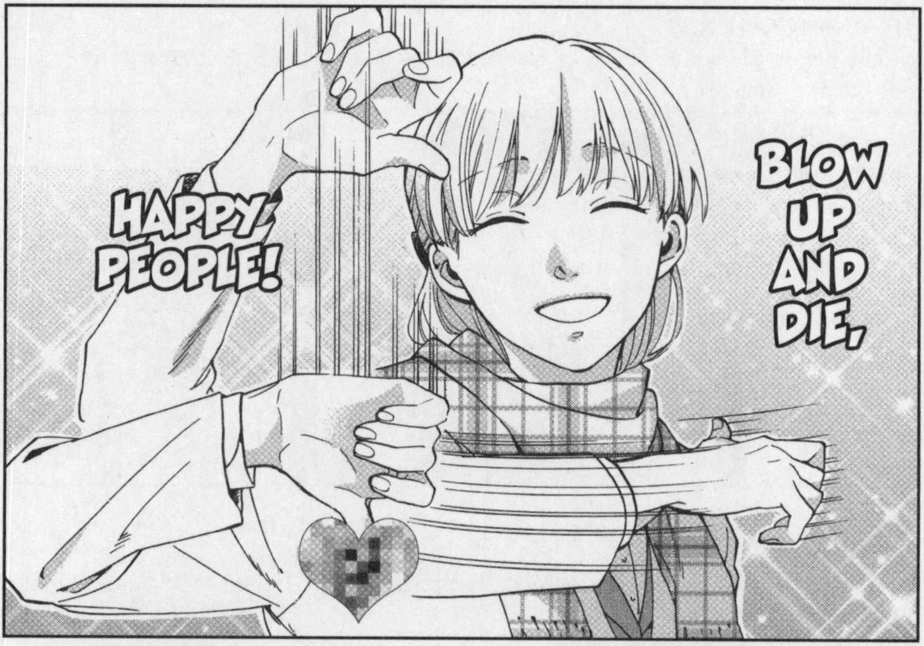
BLOW UP AND DIE,
HAPPY PEOPLE!

▲BLOW UP AND DIE, HAPPY PEOPLE, PAGE 207

A song with the same title from vocaloid artist Miku Hatsune, and a popular internet meme. "Happy people" comes from the term *riajuu*, which refers to people who primarily live their lives off the net and are happy with their real-life lives, as opposed to the "unhappy" otaku.

▶MMORPG, PAGE 213

MMORPG stands for Massively Multiplayer Online Role-Playing Game, and is often referred to as an MMO for short. These games involve friends and strangers coming together to play missions and events in real time, and are meant to offer a collaborative experience.

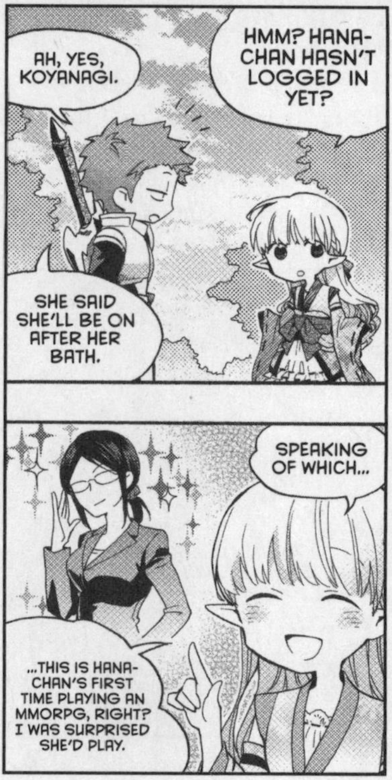
HMM? HANA-CHAN HASN'T LOGGED IN YET?
AH, YES, KOYANAGI.
SHE SAID SHE'LL BE ON AFTER HER BATH.
SPEAKING OF WHICH...
...THIS IS HANA-CHAN'S FIRST TIME PLAYING AN MMORPG, RIGHT? I WAS SURPRISED SHE'D PLAY.

▼N.E.E.T., PAGE 217

Stands for "Not in Education, Employment, or Training," and refers to a demographic of young adults from their late teens to mid-30s who do not have a job, are not in college, live at home but do not help with housework, and are generally not engaged in any activities to better themselves. A large majority of Japanese society perceives these youths as being lazy people who don't want to work, while a smaller number of people see them as youths who choose to reject society's rigid definition of adulthood.

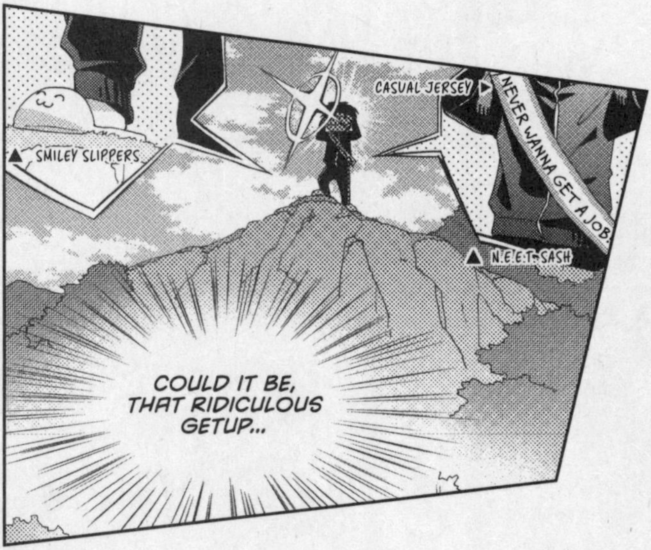
CASUAL JERSEY
NEVER WANNA GET A JOB
SMILEY SLIPPERS
N.E.E.T. SASH
COULD IT BE, THAT RIDICULOUS GETUP...

▼HEADPHONES, PAGE 226

Japanese office environments are traditionally structured in more of an open floor plan, without cubicles. Wearing headphones is usually not permitted, as it's seen as rude.

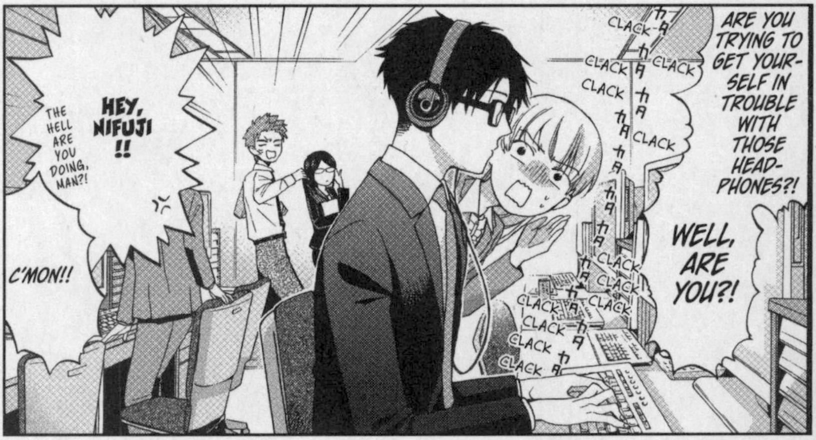
ARE YOU TRYING TO GET YOURSELF IN TROUBLE WITH THOSE HEADPHONES?!
WELL, ARE YOU?!
CLACK CLACK CLACK CLACK CLACK
CLACK CLACK CLACK CLACK CLACK CLACK CLACK
HEY, NIFUJI!!
THE HELL ARE YOU DOING, MAN?!
C'MON!!

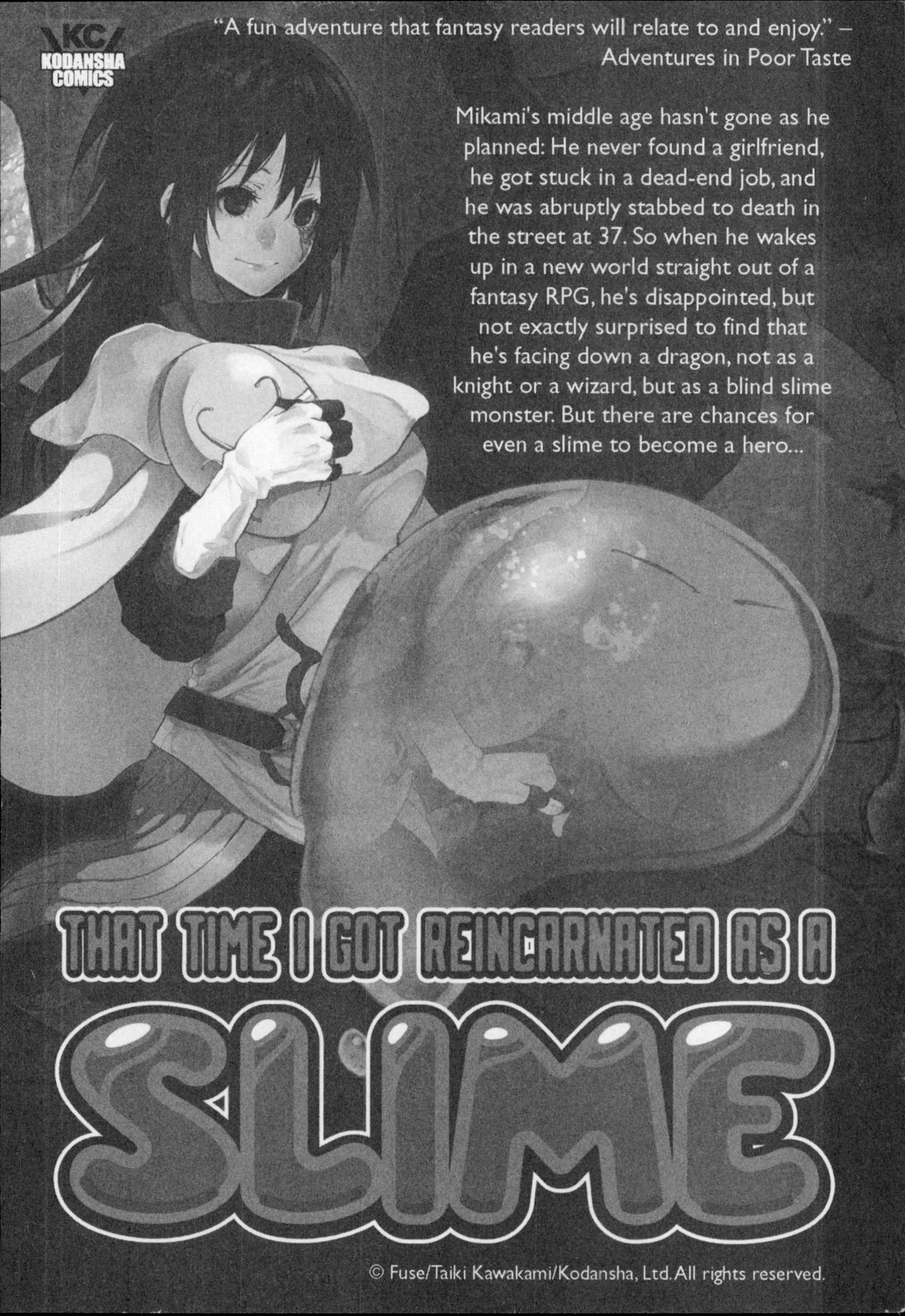

"A fun adventure that fantasy readers will relate to and enjoy." –
Adventures in Poor Taste

Mikami's middle age hasn't gone as he planned: He never found a girlfriend, he got stuck in a dead-end job, and he was abruptly stabbed to death in the street at 37. So when he wakes up in a new world straight out of a fantasy RPG, he's disappointed, but not exactly surprised to find that he's facing down a dragon, not as a knight or a wizard, but as a blind slime monster. But there are chances for even a slime to become a hero...

THAT TIME I GOT REINCARNATED AS A SLIME

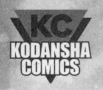

KC
KODANSHA
COMICS

Japan's most powerful spirit medium delves into the ghost world's greatest mysteries!

Story by Kyo Shirodaira, famed author of mystery fiction and creator of *Spiral*, *Blast of Tempest*, and *The Record of a Fallen Vampire*.

Both touched by spirits called yôkai, Kotoko and Kurô have gained unique superhuman powers. But to gain her powers Kotoko has given up an eye and a leg, and Kurô's personal life is in shambles. So when Kotoko suggests they team up to deal with renegades from the spirit world, Kurô doesn't have many other choices, but Kotoko might just have a few ulterior motives...

IN/SPECTRE

STORY BY KYO SHIRODAIRA
ART BY CHASHIBA KATASE

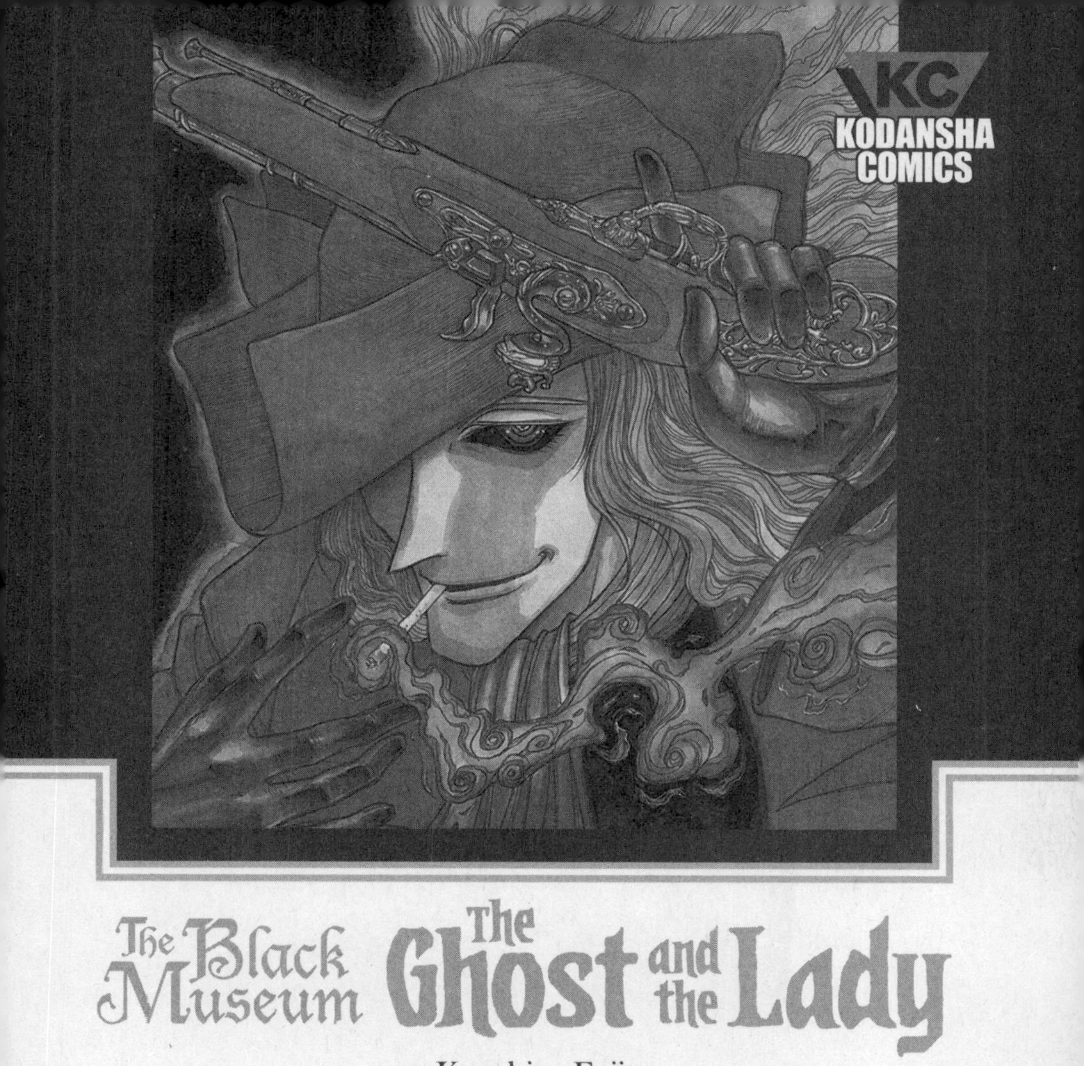
KC
KODANSHA COMICS

The Black Museum The Ghost and the Lady

By Kazuhiro Fujita

Deep in Scotland Yard in London sits an evidence room dedicated to the greatest mysteries of British history. In this "Black Museum" sits a misshapen hunk of lead–two bullets fused together–the key to a wartime encounter between Florence Nightingale, the mother of modern nursing, and a supernatural Man in Grey. This story is unknown to most scholars of history, but a special guest of the museum will tell the tale of The Ghost and the Lady...

Praise for Kazuhiro Fujita's *Ushio and Tora*

"A charming revival that combines a classic look with modern depth and pacing... **Essential viewing both for curmudgeons and new fans alike.**" — Anime News Network

"**GREAT!** The first episode of Ushio and Tora captures the essence of '90s anime." — IGN

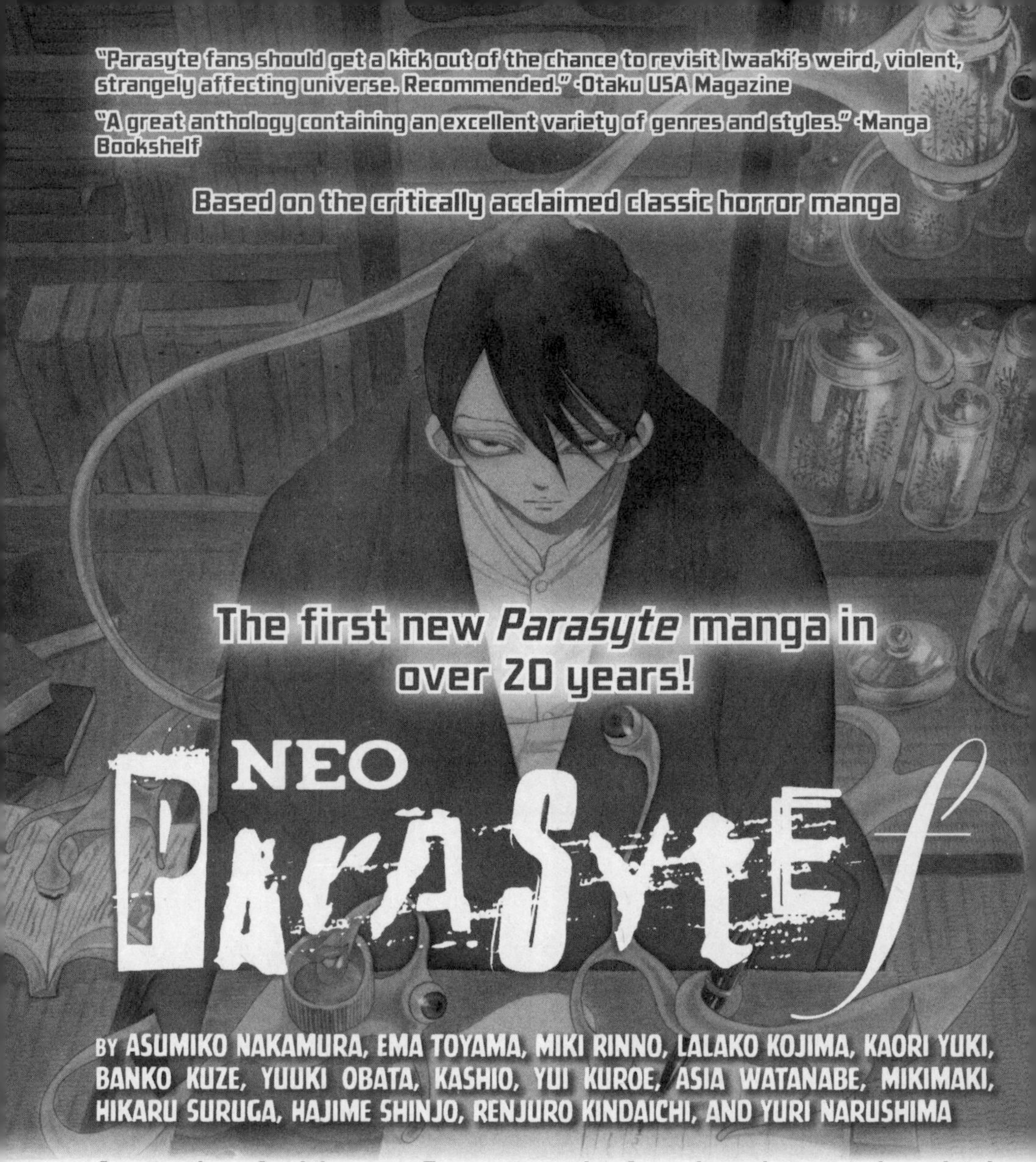

Based on the critically acclaimed classic horror manga

The first new *Parasyte* manga in over 20 years!

NEO ParaSyte f

BY ASUMIKO NAKAMURA, EMA TOYAMA, MIKI RINNO, LALAKO KOJIMA, KAORI YUKI, BANKO KUZE, YUUKI OBATA, KASHIO, YUI KUROE, ASIA WATANABE, MIKIMAKI, HIKARU SURUGA, HAJIME SHINJO, RENJURO KINDAICHI, AND YURI NARUSHIMA

A collection of chilling new *Parasyte* stories from Japan's top shojo artists!

Parasites: shape-shifting aliens whose only purpose is to assimilate with and consume the human race... but do these monsters have a different side? A parasite becomes a prince to save his romance-obsessed female host from a dangerous stalker. Another hosts a cooking show, in which the real monsters are revealed. These and 13 more stories, from some of the greatest shojo manga artists alive today, together make up a chilling, funny, and entertaining tribute to one of manga's horror classics!

KC KODANSHA COMICS

A Kodansha Comics Trade Paperback Original.

Wotakoi: Love is Hard for Otaku volume 1 copyright © 2015, 2016 Fujita
English translation copyright © 2018 Fujita

Published in the United States by Kodansha Comics, an imprint of Kodansha USA Publishing, LLC, New York.

Publication rights for this English edition arranged through Kodansha Ltd., Tokyo.

First published in Japan in 2015, 2016 by Ichijinsha Inc., Tokyo. as *Wotaku ni koi ha muzukashi* volumes 1 & 2

ISBN 978-1-63236-704-4

Printed in the United States of America.

www.kodanshacomics.com

9th Printing

Translation: Jessica Sheaves
Lettering: AndWorld Design
Editing: Lauren Scanlan
Kodansha Comics edition cover design: Phil Balsman